Christianity and Ecology

**Harvard University Center for the
Study of World Religions Publications**

General Editor: Lawrence E. Sullivan
Senior Editor: Kathryn Dodgson
Associate Editor: Eric Edstam

Religions of the World and Ecology

Series Editors: Mary Evelyn Tucker and John Grim

Cambridge, Massachusetts

Christianity and Ecology

Seeking the Well-Being of Earth and Humans

edited by

DIETER T. HESSEL

and

ROSEMARY RADFORD RUETHER

distributed by
Harvard University Press
for the
Harvard University Center for the
Study of World Religions

Grateful acknowledgment is made for permission to reprint the following:

Revised versions of Larry Rasmussen, "Global Eco-Justice: The Church's Mission in Urban Society," and Rosemary Radford Ruether, "Conclusion: Eco-Justice at the Center of the Church's Mission," published in *Mission Studies: Journal of the International Association for Mission Studies* 16, no. 1 (1999).

Library of Congress Cataloging-in-Publication Data

Christianity and ecology : seeking the well-being of earth and humans / edited by Dieter T. Hessel and Rosemary Radford Ruether.
     p. cm. — (Religions of the world and ecology)
  Includes bibliographical references and index.
  ISBN 0-945454-19-8 (hard cover : alk. paper)
  ISBN 0-945454-20-1 (pbk. : alk. paper)
  1. Human ecology—Religious aspects—Christianity. I. Hessel, Dieter T.
II. Ruether, Rosemary Radford. III. Series.
BT695.5 .C49 2000
261.8'362—dc21   99-044576

Acknowledgments

The series of conferences on religions of the world and ecology took place from 1996 through 1998, with supervision at the Harvard University Center for the Study of World Religions by Don Kunkel and Malgorzata Radziszewska-Hedderick and with the assistance of Janey Bosch, Naomi Wilshire, and Lilli Leggio. Narges Moshiri, also at the Center, was indispensable in helping to arrange the first two conferences. A series of volumes developing the themes explored at the conferences is being published by the Center and distributed by Harvard University Press under the editorial direction of Kathryn Dodgson and with the skilled assistance of Eric Edstam.

These efforts have been generously supported by major funding from the V. Kann Rasmussen Foundation. The conference organizers appreciate also the support of the following institutions and individuals: Aga Khan Trust for Culture, Association of Shinto Shrines, Nathan Cummings Foundation, Dharam Hinduja Indic Research Center at Columbia University, Germeshausen Foundation, Harvard Buddhist Studies Forum, Harvard Divinity School Center for the Study of Values in Public Life, Jain Academic Foundation of North America, Laurance Rockefeller, Sacharuna Foundation, Theological Education to Meet the Environmental Challenge, and Winslow Foundation. The conferences were originally made possible by the Center for Respect of Life and Environment of the Humane Society of the United States, which continues to be a principal cosponsor. Bucknell University, also a cosponsor, has provided support in the form of leave time from teaching for conference coordinators Mary Evelyn Tucker and John

Grim as well as the invaluable administrative assistance of Stephanie Snyder. Her thoughtful attention to critical details is legendary. President William Adams of Bucknell University and Vice-President for Academic Affairs Daniel Little have also granted travel funds for faculty and students to attend the conferences. Grateful acknowledgment is here made for the advice from key area specialists in shaping each conference and in editing the published volumes. Their generosity in time and talent has been indispensable at every step of the project. Finally, throughout this process, the support, advice, and encouragement from Martin S. Kaplan has been invaluable.

Contents

Preface

LAWRENCE E. SULLIVAN

Religion distinguishes the human species from all others, just as human presence on earth distinguishes the ecology of our planet from other places in the known universe. Religious life and the earth's ecology are inextricably linked, organically related.

Human belief and practice mark the earth. One can hardly think of a natural system that has not been considerably altered, for better or worse, by human culture. "Nor is this the work of the industrial centuries," observes Simon Schama. "It is coeval with the entirety of our social existence. And it is this irreversibly modified world, from the polar caps to the equatorial forests, that is all the nature we have" (*Landscape and Memory* [New York: Vintage Books, 1996], 7). In Schama's examination even landscapes that appear to be most free of human culture turn out, on closer inspection, to be its product.

Human beliefs about the nature of ecology are the distinctive contribution of our species to the ecology itself. Religious beliefs—especially those concerning the nature of powers that create and animate—become an effective part of ecological systems. They attract the power of will and channel the forces of labor toward purposive transformations. Religious rituals model relations with material life and transmit habits of practice and attitudes of mind to succeeding generations.

This is not simply to say that religious thoughts occasionally touch the world and leave traces that accumulate over time. The matter is the other way around. From the point of view of environmental studies, religious worldviews propel communities into the world with fundamental predispositions toward it because such religious world-views are primordial, all-encompassing, and unique. They are *primordial* because they probe behind secondary appearances and stray thoughts to rivet human attention on realities of the first order: life at its source, creativity in its fullest manifestation, death and destruction at their origin, renewal and salvation in their germ. The revelation of first things is compelling and moves communities to take creative action. Primordial ideas are prime movers.

Religious worldviews are *all-encompassing* because they fully absorb the natural world within them. They provide human beings both a view of the whole and at the same time a penetrating image of their own ironic position as the beings in the cosmos who possess the capacity for symbolic thought: the part that contains the whole—or at least a picture of the whole—within itself. As all-encompassing, therefore, religious ideas do not just contend with other ideas as equals; they frame the mind-set within which all sorts of ideas commingle in a cosmology. For this reason, their role in ecology must be better understood.

Religious worldviews are *unique* because they draw the world of nature into a wholly other kind of universe, one that appears only in the religious imagination. From the point of view of environmental studies, the risk of such religious views, on the one hand, is of disinterest in or disregard for the natural world. On the other hand, only in the religious world can nature be compared and contrasted to other kinds of being—the supernatural world or forms of power not always fully manifest in nature. Only then can nature be revealed as distinctive, set in a new light startlingly different from its own. That is to say, only religious perspectives enable human beings to evaluate the world of nature in terms distinct from all else. In this same step toward intelligibility, the natural world is evaluated in terms consonant with human beings' own distinctive (religious and imaginative) nature in the world, thus grounding a self-conscious relationship and a role with limits and responsibilities.

In the struggle to sustain the earth's environment as viable for future generations, environmental studies has thus far left the role of religion unprobed. This contrasts starkly with the emphasis given, for example, the role of science and technology in threatening or sustaining the ecology. Ignorance of religion prevents environmental studies from achieving its goals, however, for though science and technology share many important features of human culture with religion, they leave unexplored essential wellsprings of human motivation and concern that shape the world as we know it. No understanding of the environment is adequate without a grasp of the religious life that constitutes the human societies which saturate the natural environment.

A great deal of what we know about the religions of the world is new knowledge. As is the case for geology and astronomy, so too for religious studies: many new discoveries about the nature and function of religion are, in fact, clearer understandings of events and processes that began to unfold long ago. Much of what we are learning now about the religions of the world was previously not known outside of a circle of adepts. From the ancient history of traditions and from the ongoing creativity of the world's contemporary religions we are opening a treasury of motives, disciplines, and awarenesses.

A geology of the religious spirit of humankind can well serve our need to relate fruitfully to the earth and its myriad life-forms. Changing our habits of consumption and patterns of distribution, reevaluating modes of production, and reestablishing a strong sense of solidarity with the matrix of material life—these achievements will arrive along with spiritual modulations that unveil attractive new images of well-being and prosperity, respecting the limits of life in a sustainable world while revering life at its sources. Remarkable religious views are presented in this series—from the nature mysticism of Bashō in Japan or Saint Francis in Italy to the ecstatic physiologies and embryologies of shamanic healers, Taoist meditators, and Vedic practitioners; from indigenous people's ritual responses to projects funded by the World Bank, to religiously grounded criticisms of hazardous waste sites, deforestation, and environmental racism.

The power to modify the world is both frightening and fascinating and has been subjected to reflection, particularly religious reflection, from time immemorial to the present day. We will understand ecology better when we understand the religions that form the rich soil of memory and practice, belief and relationships where life on earth is rooted. Knowledge of these views will help us reappraise our ways and reorient ourselves toward the sources and resources of life.

This volume is one in a series that addresses the critical gap in our contemporary understanding of religion and ecology. The series results from research conducted at the Harvard University Center for the Study of World Religions over a three-year period. I wish especially to acknowledge President Neil L. Rudenstine of Harvard University for his leadership in instituting the environmental initiative at Harvard and thank him for his warm encouragement and characteristic support of our program. Mary Evelyn Tucker and John Grim of Bucknell University coordinated the research, involving the direct participation of some six hundred scholars, religious leaders, and environmental specialists brought to Harvard from around the world during the period of research and inquiry. Professors Tucker and Grim have brought great vision and energy to this enormous project, as has their team of conference convenors. The commitment and advice of Martin S. Kaplan of Hale and Dorr have been of great value. Our goals have been achieved for this research and publication program because of the extraordinary dedication and talents of Center for the Study of World Religions staff members Don Kunkel, Malgorzata Radziszewska-Hedderick, Kathryn Dodgson, Janey Bosch, Naomi Wilshire, Lilli Leggio, and Eric Edstam and with the unstinting help of Stephanie Snyder of Bucknell. To these individuals, and to all the sponsors and participants whose efforts made this series possible, go deepest thanks and appreciation.

Series Foreword

MARY EVELYN TUCKER and JOHN GRIM

The Nature of the Environmental Crisis

Ours is a period when the human community is in search of new and sustaining relationships to the earth amidst an environmental crisis that threatens the very existence of all life-forms on the planet. While the particular causes and solutions of this crisis are being debated by scientists, economists, and policymakers, the facts of widespread destruction are causing alarm in many quarters. Indeed, from some perspectives the future of human life itself appears threatened. As Daniel Maguire has succinctly observed, "If current trends continue, we will not."[1] Thomas Berry, the former director of the Riverdale Center for Religious Research, has also raised the stark question, "Is the human a viable species on an endangered planet?"

From resource depletion and species extinction to pollution overload and toxic surplus, the planet is struggling against unprecedented assaults. This is aggravated by population explosion, industrial growth, technological manipulation, and military proliferation heretofore unknown by the human community. From many accounts the basic elements which sustain life—sufficient water, clean air, and arable land—are at risk. The challenges are formidable and well documented. The solutions, however, are more elusive and complex. Clearly, this crisis has economic, political, and social dimensions which require more detailed analysis than we can provide here. Suffice it to say, however, as did the *Global 2000 Report:* ". . .once such global environmental problems are in motion they are difficult to reverse. In fact few if any of the problems addressed in the *Global 2000*

Report are amenable to quick technological or policy fixes; rather, they are inextricably mixed with the world's most perplexing social and economic problems."[2]

Peter Raven, the director of the Missouri Botanical Garden, wrote in a paper titled "We Are Killing Our World" with a similar sense of urgency regarding the magnitude of the environmental crisis: "The world that provides our evolutionary and ecological context is in serious trouble, trouble of a kind that demands our urgent attention. By formulating adequate plans for dealing with these large-scale problems, we will be laying the foundation for peace and prosperity in the future; by ignoring them, drifting passively while attending to what may seem more urgent, personal priorities, we are courting disaster."

Rethinking Worldviews and Ethics

For many people an environmental crisis of this complexity and scope is not only the result of certain economic, political, and social factors. It is also a moral and spiritual crisis which, in order to be addressed, will require broader philosophical and religious understandings of ourselves as creatures of nature, embedded in life cycles and dependent on ecosystems. Religions, thus, need to be reexamined in light of the current environmental crisis. This is because religions help to shape our attitudes toward nature in both conscious and unconscious ways. Religions provide basic interpretive stories of who we are, what nature is, where we have come from, and where we are going. This comprises a worldview of a society. Religions also suggest how we should treat other humans and how we should relate to nature. These values make up the ethical orientation of a society. Religions thus generate worldviews and ethics which underlie fundamental attitudes and values of different cultures and societies. As the historian Lynn White observed, "What people do about their ecology depends on what they think about themselves in relation to things around them. Human ecology is deeply conditioned by beliefs about our nature and destiny—that is, by religion."[3]

In trying to reorient ourselves in relation to the earth, it has become apparent that we have lost our appreciation for the intricate nature of matter and materiality. Our feeling of alienation in the modern period has extended beyond the human community and its patterns of material exchanges to our interaction with nature itself. Especially in technologically sophisticated urban societies, we have become removed from the recognition of our dependence on nature. We no longer know who we are as earthlings; we no longer see the earth as sacred.

Thomas Berry suggests that we have become autistic in our interactions with the natural world. In other words, we are unable to value the life and beauty of nature because we are locked in our own egocentric perspectives and shortsighted needs. He suggests that we need a new cosmology, cultural coding, and motivating energy to overcome this deprivation.[4] He observes that the magnitude of destructive industrial processes is so great that we must initiate a radical rethinking of the myth of progress and of humanity's role in the evolutionary process. Indeed, he speaks of evolution as a new story of the universe, namely, as a vast cosmological perspective that will resituate human meaning and direction in the context of four and a half billion years of earth history.[5]

For Berry and for many others an important component of the current environmental crisis is spiritual and ethical. It is here that the religions of the world may have a role to play in cooperation with other individuals, institutions, and initiatives that have been engaged with environmental issues for a considerable period of time. Despite their lateness in addressing the crisis, religions are beginning to respond in remarkably creative ways. They are not only rethinking their theologies but are also reorienting their sustainable practices and long-term environmental commitments. In so doing, the very nature of religion and of ethics is being challenged and changed. This is true because the reexamination of other worldviews created by religious beliefs and practices may be critical to our recovery of sufficiently comprehensive cosmologies, broad conceptual frameworks, and effective environmental ethics for the twenty-first century.

While in the past none of the religions of the world have had to face an environmental crisis such as we are now confronting, they remain key instruments in shaping attitudes toward nature. The unintended consequences of the modern industrial drive for unlimited economic growth and resource development have led us to an impasse regarding the survival of many life-forms and appropriate management of varied ecosystems. The religious traditions may indeed be critical in helping to reimagine the viable conditions and long-range strategies for fostering mutually enhancing human-earth relations.[6] Indeed, as E. N. Anderson has documented with impressive detail, "All traditional societies that have succeeded in managing resources well, over time, have done it in part through religious or ritual representation of resource management."[7]

It is in this context that a series of conferences and publications exploring the various religions of the world and their relation to ecology was initiated by the Center for the Study of World Religions at Harvard. Coordinated by Mary Evelyn Tucker and John Grim, the conferences involved some six hundred scholars, graduate students, religious leaders, and environmental activists over a period of three years. The collaborative nature of the project is intentional. Such collaboration maximizes the opportunity for dialogical reflection on this issue of enormous complexity and accentuates the diversity of local manifestations of ecologically sustainable alternatives.

This series is intended to serve as initial explorations of the emerging field of religion and ecology while pointing toward areas for further research. We are not unaware of the difficulties of engaging in such a task, yet we have been encouraged by the enthusiastic response to the conferences within the academic community, by the larger interest they have generated beyond academia, and by the probing examinations gathered in the volumes. We trust that this series and these volumes will be useful not only for scholars of religion but also for those shaping seminary education and institutional religious practices, as well as for those involved in public policy on environmental issues.

We see such conferences and publications as expanding the growing dialogue regarding the role of the world's religions as moral forces in stemming the environmental crisis. While, clearly, there are major methodological issues involved in utilizing traditional philosophical and religious ideas for contemporary concerns, there are also compelling reasons to support such efforts, however modest they may be. The world's religions in all their complexity and variety remain one of the principal resources for symbolic ideas, spiritual inspiration, and ethical principles. Indeed, despite their limitations, historically they have provided comprehensive cosmologies for interpretive direction, moral foundations for social cohesion, spiritual guidance for cultural expression, and ritual celebrations for meaningful life. In our search for more comprehensive ecological worldviews and more effective environmental ethics, it is inevitable that we will draw from the symbolic and conceptual resources of the religious traditions of the world. The effort to do this is not without precedent or problems, some of which will be signaled below. With this volume and with this series we hope the field of reflection and discussion regarding religion and ecology will begin to broaden, deepen, and complexify.

Qualifications and Goals

The Problems and Promise of Religions

These volumes, then, are built on the premise that the religions of the world may be instrumental in addressing the moral dilemmas created by the environmental crisis. At the same time we recognize the limitations of such efforts on the part of religions. We also acknowledge that the complexity of the problem requires interlocking approaches from such fields as science, economics, politics, health, and public policy. As the human community struggles to formulate different attitudes toward nature and to articulate broader conceptions of ethics embracing species and ecosystems, religions may thus be a necessary, though only contributing, part of this multidisciplinary approach.

It is becoming increasingly evident that abundant scientific knowledge of the crisis is available and numerous political and economic statements have been formulated. Yet we seem to lack the political, economic, and scientific leadership to make necessary changes. Moreover, what is still lacking is the religious commitment, moral imagination, and ethical engagement to transform the environmental crisis from an issue on paper to one of effective policy, from rhetoric in print to realism in action. Why, nearly fifty years after Fairfield Osborne's warning in *Our Plundered Planet* and more than thirty years since Rachel Carson's *Silent Spring,* are we still wondering, is it too late?[8]

It is important to ask where the religions have been on these issues and why they themselves have been so late in their involvement. Have issues of personal salvation superseded all others? Have divine-human relations been primary? Have anthropocentric ethics been all-consuming? Has the material world of nature been devalued by religion? Does the search for otherworldly rewards override commitment to this world? Did the religions simply surrender their natural theologies and concerns with exploring purpose in nature to positivistic scientific cosmologies? In beginning to address these questions, we still have not exhausted all the reasons for religions' lack of attention to the environmental crisis. The reasons may not be readily apparent, but clearly they require further exploration and explanation.

In discussing the involvement of religions in this issue, it is also appropriate to acknowledge the dark side of religion in both its institutional expressions and dogmatic forms. In addition to their oversight with regard to the environment, religions have been the source of enormous manipulation of power in fostering wars, in ignoring racial and social injustice, and in promoting unequal gender relations, to name only a few abuses. One does not want to underplay this shadow side or to claim too much for religions' potential for ethical persuasiveness. The problems are too vast and complex for unqualified optimism. Yet there is a growing consensus that religions may now have a significant role to play, just as in the past they have sustained individuals and cultures in the face of internal and external threats.

A final caveat is the inevitable gap that arises between theories and practices in religions. As has been noted, even societies with religious traditions which appear sympathetic to the environment have in the past often misused resources. While it is clear that religions may have some disjunction between the ideal and the real, this should not lessen our endeavor to identify resources from within the world's religions for a more ecologically sound cosmology and environmentally supportive ethics. This disjunction of theory and practice is present within all philosophies and religions and is frequently the source of disillusionment, skepticism, and cynicism. A more realistic observation might be made, however, that this disjunction should not automatically invalidate the complex worldviews and rich cosmologies embedded in traditional religions. Rather, it is our task to explore these conceptual resources so as to broaden and expand our own perspectives in challenging and fruitful ways.

In summary, we recognize that religions have elements which are both prophetic and transformative as well as conservative and constraining. These elements are continually in tension, a condition which creates the great variety of thought and interpretation within religious traditions. To recognize these various tensions and limits, however, is not to lessen the urgency of the overall goals of this project. Rather, it is to circumscribe our efforts with healthy skepticism, cautious optimism, and modest ambitions. It is to suggest that this is a beginning in a new field of study which will affect both religion and ecology. On the one hand, this process of reflection will inevitably change how religions conceive of their own roles, missions, and identities, for such reflections demand a new sense of the sacred as not divorced from the earth itself. On the other hand, environmental studies can recognize that religions have helped to shape attitudes toward nature. Thus, as religions themselves evolve they may be indispensable in fostering a more expansive appreciation for the complexity and beauty of the natural world. At the same time as religions foster awe and reverence for nature, they may provide the transforming energies for ethical practices to protect endangered ecosystems, threatened species, and diminishing resources.

Methodological Concerns

It is important to acknowledge that there are, inevitably, challenging methodological issues involved in such a project as we are undertaking in this emerging field of religion and ecology.[9] Some of the key interpretive challenges we face in this project concern issues of time, place, space, and positionality. With regard to time, it is necessary to recognize the vast historical complexity of each religious tradition, which cannot be easily condensed in these conferences or volumes. With respect to place, we need to signal the diverse cultural contexts in which these religions have developed. With regard to space, we recognize the varied frameworks of institutions and traditions in which these religions unfold. Finally, with respect to positionality, we acknowledge our own historical situatedness at the end of the twentieth century with distinctive contemporary concerns.

Not only is each religious tradition historically complex and culturally diverse, but its beliefs, scriptures, and institutions have themselves been subject to vast commentaries and revisions over time. Thus, we recognize the radical diversity that exists within and among religious traditions which cannot be encompassed in any single volume. We acknowledge also that distortions may arise as we examine earlier historical traditions in light of contemporary issues.

Nonetheless, the environmental ethics philosopher J. Baird Callicott has suggested that scholars and others "mine the conceptual resources" of the religious traditions as a means of creating a more inclusive global environmental ethics.[10] As Callicott himself notes, however, the notion of "mining" is problematic, for it conjures up images of exploitation which may cause apprehension among certain religious communities, especially those of indigenous peoples. Moreover, we cannot simply expect to borrow or adopt ideas and place them from one tradition directly into another. Even efforts to formulate global environmental ethics need to be sensitive to cultural particularity and diversity. We do not aim at creating a simple bricolage or bland fusion of perspectives. Rather, these conferences and volumes are an attempt to display before us a multiperspectival cross section of the symbolic richness regarding attitudes toward nature within the religions of the world. To do so will help to reveal certain commonalities among traditions, as well as limitations within traditions, as they begin to converge around this challenge presented by the environmental crisis.

We need to identify our concerns, then, as embedded in the constraints of our own perspectival limits at the same time as we seek common ground. In describing various attitudes toward nature historically, we are aiming at *critical understanding* of the complexity, contexts, and frameworks in which these religions articulate such views. In addition, we are striving for *empathetic appreciation* for the traditions without idealizing their ecological potential or ignoring their environmental oversights. Finally, we are aiming at the *creative revisioning* of mutually enhancing human-earth relations. This revisioning may be assisted by highlighting the multiperspectival attitudes toward nature which these traditions disclose. The prismatic effect of examining such attitudes and relationships may provide some necessary clarification and symbolic resources for reimagining our own situation and shared concerns at the end of the twentieth century. It will also be sharpened by identifying the multilayered symbol systems in world religions which have traditionally oriented humans in establishing relational resonances between the microcosm of the self and the macrocosm of the social and natural orders. In short, religious traditions may help to supply both creative resources of symbols, rituals, and texts as well as inspiring visions for reimagining ourselves as part of, not apart from, the natural world.

Aims

The methodological issues outlined above were implied in the overall goals of the conferences, which were described as follows:

1. To identify and evaluate the *distinctive ecological attitudes,* values, and practices of diverse religious traditions, making clear their links to intellectual, political, and other resources associated with these distinctive traditions.

2. To describe and analyze the *commonalities* that exist within and among religious traditions with respect to ecology.

3. To identify the *minimum common ground* on which to base constructive understanding, motivating discussion, and concerted action in diverse locations across the globe; and to highlight the specific religious resources that comprise such fertile ecological ground: within scripture, ritual, myth, symbol, cosmology, sacrament, and so on.

4. To articulate in clear and moving terms *a desirable mode of human presence with the earth;* in short, to highlight means of respecting and valuing nature, to note what has already been actualized, and to indicate how best to achieve what is desirable beyond these examples.

5. To outline the most significant areas, with regard to religion and ecology, in need of *further study;* to enumerate questions of highest priority within those areas and propose possible approaches to use in addressing them.

In this series, then, we do not intend to obliterate difference or ignore diversity. The aim is to celebrate plurality by raising to conscious awareness multiple perspectives regarding nature and human-earth relations as articulated in the religions of the world. The spectrum of cosmologies, myths, symbols, and rituals within the religious traditions will be instructive in resituating us within the rhythms and limits of nature.

We are not looking for a unified worldview or a single global ethic. We are, however, deeply sympathetic with the efforts toward formulating a global ethic made by individuals, such as the theologian Hans Küng or the environmental philosopher J. Baird Callicott, and groups, such as Global Education Associates and United Religions. A minimum content of environmental ethics needs to be seriously considered. We are, then, keenly interested in the contribution this series might make to discussions of environmental policy in national and international arenas. Important intersections may be made with work in the field of development ethics.[11] In addition, the findings of the conferences have bearing on the ethical formulation of the Earth Charter that is to be presented to the United Nations for adoption within the next few years. Thus, we are seeking both the grounds for common concern and the constructive conceptual basis for rethinking our current situation of estrangement from the earth. In so doing we will be able to reconceive a means of creating the basis not just for sustainable development, but also for sustainable life on the planet.

As scientist Brian Swimme has suggested, we are currently making macrophase changes to the life systems of the planet with microphase wisdom. Clearly, we need to expand and deepen the wisdom base for human intervention with nature and other humans. This is particularly true as issues of genetic alteration of natural processes are already available and in use. If religions have traditionally concentrated on divine-human and human-human relations, the challenge is that they now explore more fully divine-human-earth relations. Without such further exploration, adequate environmental ethics may not emerge in a comprehensive context.

Resources: Environmental Ethics Found in the World's Religions

For many people, when challenges such as the environmental crisis are raised in relation to religion in the contemporary world, there frequently arises a sense of loss or a nostalgia for earlier, seemingly less complicated eras when the constant questioning of religious beliefs and practices was not so apparent. This is, no doubt, something of a reified reading of history. There is, however, a decidedly anxious tone to the questioning and soul-searching that appears to haunt many contemporary religious groups as they seek to find their particular role in the midst of rapid technological change and dominant secular values.

One of the greatest challenges, however, to contemporary religions remains how to respond to the environmental crisis, which many believe has been perpetuated because of the enormous inroads made by unrestrained materialism, secularization, and industrialization in contemporary societies, especially those societies arising in or influenced by the modern West. Indeed, some suggest that the very division of religion from secular life may be a major cause of the crisis.

Others, such as the medieval historian Lynn White, have cited religion's negative role in the crisis. White has suggested that the emphasis in Judaism and Christianity on the transcendence of God above nature and the dominion of humans over nature has led to a devaluing of the natural world and a subsequent destruction of its resources for utilitarian ends.[12] While the particulars of this argument have been vehemently debated, it is increasingly clear that the environmental crisis and its perpetuation due to industrialization, secularization, and ethical indifference present a serious challenge to the world's religions. This is especially true because many of these religions have traditionally been concerned with the path of personal salvation, which frequently emphasized otherworldly goals and rejected this world as corrupting. Thus, as we have noted, how to adapt religious teachings to this task of revaluing nature so as to prevent its destruction marks a significant new phase in religious thought. Indeed, as Thomas Berry has so aptly pointed out, what is necessary is a comprehensive reevaluation of human-earth relations if the human is to continue as a viable species on an increasingly degraded planet. This will require, in addition to major economic and political changes, examining worldviews and ethics among the world's religions that differ from those that have captured the imagination of contemporary industrialized societies which regard nature primarily as a commodity to be utilized. It should be noted that when we are searching for effective resources for formulating environmental ethics, each of the religious traditions have both positive and negative features.

For the most part, the worldviews associated with the Western Abrahamic traditions of Judaism, Christianity, and Islam have created a dominantly human-focused morality. Because these worldviews are largely anthropocentric, nature is viewed as being of secondary importance. This is reinforced by a strong sense of the transcendence of God above nature. On the other hand, there are rich resources for rethinking views of nature in the covenantal tradition of the Hebrew Bible, in sacramental theology, in incarnational Christology, and in the vice-regency (*khalifa Allah*) concept of the Qur'an. The covenantal tradition draws on the legal agreements of biblical thought which are extended to all of creation. Sacramental theology in Christianity underscores the sacred dimension of material reality, especially for ritual purposes.[13] Incarnational Christology proposes that because God became flesh in the person of Christ, the entire natural order can be viewed as sacred. The concept of humans as vice-regents of Allah on earth suggests that humans have particular privileges, responsibilities, and obligations to creation.[14]

In Hinduism, although there is a significant emphasis on performing one's *dharma,* or duty, in the world, there is also a strong pull toward *mokṣa,* or liberation, from the world of suffering, or *saṃsāra.* To heal this kind of suffering and alienation through spiritual discipline and meditation, one turns away from the world (*prakṛti*) to a timeless world of spirit (*puruṣa*). Yet at the same time there are numerous traditions in Hinduism which affirm particular rivers, mountains, or forests as sacred. Moreover, in the concept of *līlā,* the creative play of the gods, Hindu theology engages the world as a creative manifestation of the divine. This same tension between withdrawal from the world and affirmation of it is present in Buddhism. Certain Theravāda schools of Buddhism emphasize withdrawing in meditation from the transient world of suffering (*saṃsāra*) to seek release in *nirvāṇa.* On the other hand, later Mahāyāna schools of Buddhism, such as Hua-yen, underscore the remarkable interconnection of reality in such images as the jeweled net of Indra, where each jewel reflects all the others in the universe. Likewise, the Zen gardens in East Asia express the fullness of the Buddha-nature (*tathāgatagarbha*) in the natural world. In recent years, socially engaged Buddhism has been active in protecting the environment in both Asia and the United States.

The East Asian traditions of Confucianism and Taoism remain, in certain ways, some of the most life-affirming in the spectrum of world religions.[15] The seamless interconnection between the divine, human, and natural worlds that characterizes these traditions has been described as an anthropocosmic worldview.[16] There is no emphasis on radical transcendence as there is in the Western traditions. Rather, there is a cosmology of a continuity of creation stressing the dynamic movements of nature through the seasons and the agricultural cycles. This organic cosmology is grounded in the philosophy of *ch'i* (material force), which provides a basis for appreciating the profound interconnection of matter and spirit. To be in harmony with nature and with other humans while being attentive to the movements of the *Tao* (Way) is the aim of personal cultivation in both Confucianism and Taoism. It should be noted, however, that this positive worldview has not prevented environmental degradation (such as deforestation) in parts of East Asia in both the premodern and modern period.

In a similar vein, indigenous peoples, while having ecological cosmologies have, in some instances, caused damage to local environments through such practices as slash-and-burn agriculture. Nonetheless, most indigenous peoples have environmental ethics embedded in their worldviews. This is evident in the complex reciprocal obligations surrounding life-taking and resource-gathering which mark a community's relations with the local bioregion. The religious views at the basis of indigenous lifeways involve respect for the sources of food, clothing, and shelter that nature provides. Gratitude to the creator and to the spiritual forces in creation is at the heart of most indigenous traditions. The ritual calendars of many indigenous peoples are carefully coordinated with seasonal events such as the sound of returning birds, the blooming of certain plants, the movements of the sun, and the changes of the moon.

The difficulty at present is that for the most part we have developed in the world's religions certain ethical prohibitions regarding homicide and restraints concerning genocide and suicide, but none for biocide or geocide. We are clearly in need of exploring such comprehensive cosmological perspectives and communitarian environmental ethics as the most compelling context for motivating change regarding the destruction of the natural world.

Responses of Religions to the Environmental Crisis

How to chart possible paths toward mutually enhancing human-earth relations remains, thus, one of the greatest challenges to the world's religions. It is with some encouragement, however, that we note the growing calls for the world's religions to participate in these efforts toward a more sustainable planetary future. There have been various appeals from environmental groups and from scientists and parliamentarians for religious leaders to respond to the environmental crisis. For example, in 1990 the Joint Appeal in Religion and Science was released highlighting the urgency of collaboration around the issue of the destruction of the environment. In 1992 the Union of Concerned Scientists issued the statement "Warning to Humanity," signed by over 1,000 scientists from 70 countries, including 105 Nobel laureates, regarding the gravity of the environmental crisis. They specifically cited the need for a new ethic toward the earth.

Numerous national and international conferences have also been held on this subject and collaborative efforts have been established. Environmental groups such as World Wildlife Fund have sponsored interreligious meetings such as the one in Assisi in 1986. The Center for Respect of Life and Environment of the Humane Society of the United States has also held a series of conferences in Assisi on Spirituality and Sustainability and has helped to organize one at the World Bank. The United Nations Environmental Programme in North America has established an Environmental Sabbath, each year distributing thousands of packets of materials for use in congregations throughout North America. Similarly, the National Religious Partnership on the Environment at the Cathedral of St. John the Divine in New York City has promoted dialogue, distributed materials, and created a remarkable alliance of the various Jewish and Christian denominations in the United States around the issue of the environment. The Parliament of World Religions held in 1993 in Chicago and attended by some 8,000 people from all over the globe issued a statement of Global Ethics of Cooperation of Religions on Human and Environmental Issues. International meetings on the environment have been organized. One example of these, the Global Forum of Spiritual and Parliamentary Leaders held in Oxford in 1988, Moscow in 1990, Rio in 1992, and Kyoto in 1993, included world religious leaders, such as the Dalai Lama, and diplomats and heads of state, such as Mikhail Gorbachev. Indeed, Gorbachev hosted the Moscow conference and attended the Kyoto conference to set up a Green Cross International for environmental emergencies.

Since the United Nations Conference on Environment and Development (the Earth Summit) held in Rio in 1992, there have been concerted efforts intended to lead toward the adoption of an *Earth Charter* by the year 2000. This *Earth Charter* initiative is under way with the leadership of the Earth Council and Green Cross International, with support from the government of the Netherlands. Maurice Strong, Mikhail Gorbachev, Steven Rockefeller, and other members of the Earth Charter Project have been instrumental in this process. At the March 1997 Rio + 5 Conference a benchmark draft of the *Earth Charter* was issued. The time is thus propitious for further investigation of the potential contributions of particular religions toward mitigating the environmental crisis, especially by developing more comprehensive environmental ethics for the earth community.

Expanding the Dialogue of Religion and Ecology

More than two decades ago Thomas Berry anticipated such an exploration when he called for "creating a new consciousness of the multiform religious traditions of humankind" as a means toward renewal of the human spirit in addressing the urgent problems of contemporary society.[17] Tu Weiming has written of the need to go "Beyond the Enlightenment Mentality" in exploring the spiritual resources of the global community to meet the challenge of the ecological crisis.[18] While this exploration has also been the intention of both the conferences and these volumes, other significant efforts have preceded our current endeavor.[19] Our discussion here highlights only the last decade.

In 1986 Eugene Hargrove edited a volume titled *Religion and Environmental Crisis.*[20] In 1991 Charlene Spretnak explored this topic in her book *States of Grace: The Recovery of Meaning in the Post-Modern Age.*[21] Her subtitle states her constructivist project clearly: "Reclaiming the Core Teachings and Practices of the Great Wisdom Traditions for the Well-Being of the Earth Community." In 1992 Steven Rockefeller and John Elder edited a book based on a conference at Middlebury College titled *Spirit and Nature: Why the Environment Is a Religious Issue.*[22] In the same year Peter Marshall published *Nature's Web: Rethinking Our Place on Earth,*[23] drawing on the resources of the world's traditions. An edited volume titled *Worldviews and Ecology,* compiled in 1993, contains articles reflecting on views of nature from the world's religions and from contemporary philosophies, such as process thought and deep ecology.[24] In this same vein, in 1994 J. Baird Callicott published *Earth's Insights,* which examines the intellectual resources of the world's religions for a more comprehensive global environmental ethics.[25] This expands on his 1989 volumes, *Nature in Asian Traditions of Thought* and *In Defense of the Land Ethic.*[26] In 1995 David Kinsley issued a book titled *Ecology and Religion: Ecological Spirituality in a Cross-Cultural Perspective,*[27] which draws on traditional religions and contemporary movements, such as deep ecology and ecospirituality. Seyyed Hossein Nasr wrote his comprehensive study *Religion and the Order of Nature* in 1996.[28] Several volumes of religious responses to a particular topic or theme have also been published. For example, J. Ronald Engel and Joan Gibb Engel compiled a monograph in 1990 titled *Ethics of Environment and Development: Global Challenge, International Response*[29] and in 1995 Harold Coward edited the volume *Population, Consumption and the Environment: Religious and Secular Responses*.[30] Roger Gottlieb edited a useful source book, *This Sacred Earth: Religion, Nature, Environment*.[31] Single volumes on the world's religions and ecology were published by the Worldwide Fund for Nature.[32]

The series Religions of the World and Ecology is thus intended to expand the discussion already under way in certain circles and to invite further collaboration on a topic of common concern—the fate of the earth as a religious responsibility. To broaden and deepen the reflective basis for mutual collaboration was an underlying aim of the conferences themselves. While some might see this as a diversion from pressing scientific or policy issues, it was with a sense of humility and yet conviction that we entered into the arena of reflection and debate on this issue. In the field of the study of world religions, we have seen this as a timely challenge for scholars of religion to respond as engaged intellectuals with deepening creative reflection. We hope that these volumes will be simply a beginning of further study of conceptual and symbolic resources, methodological concerns, and practical directions for meeting this environmental crisis.

Notes

1. He goes on to say, "And that is qualitatively and epochally true. If religion does not speak to [this], it is an obsolete distraction." Daniel Maguire, *The Moral Core of Judaism and Christianity: Reclaiming the Revolution* (Philadelphia: Fortress Press, 1993), 13.

2. Gerald Barney, *Global 2000 Report to the President of the United States* (Washington, D.C.: Supt. of Docs. U.S. Government Printing Office, 1980–1981), 40.

3. Lynn White, Jr., "The Historical Roots of Our Ecologic Crisis," *Science* 155 (March 1967):1204.

4. Thomas Berry, *The Dream of the Earth* (San Francisco: Sierra Club Books, 1988).

5. Brian Swimme and Thomas Berry, *The Universe Story* (San Francisco: Harper San Francisco, 1992).

6. At the same time we recognize the limits to such a project, especially because ideas and action, theory and practice do not always occur in conjunction.

7. E. N. Anderson, Ecologies of the Heart: Emotion, Belief, and the Environment (New York and Oxford: Oxford University Press, 1996), 166. He qualifies this statement by saying, "The key point is not religion per se, but the use of emotionally powerful symbols to sell particular moral codes and management systems" (166). He notes, however, in various case studies how ecological wisdom is embedded in myths, symbols, and cosmologies of traditional societies.

8. *Is It Too Late?* is also the title of a book by John Cobb, first published in 1972 by Bruce and reissued in 1995 by Environmental Ethics Books.

9. Because we cannot identify here all of the methodological issues that need to be addressed, we invite further discussion by other engaged scholars.

10. See J. Baird Callicott, *Earth's Insights: A Survey of Ecological Ethics from the Mediterranean Basin to the Australian Outback* (Berkeley: University of California Press, 1994).

11. See, for example, The Quality of Life, ed. Martha C. Nussbaum and Amartya Sen, WIDER Studies in Development Economics (Oxford: Oxford University Press, 1993).

12. White, "The Historical Roots of Our Ecologic Crisis," 1203–7.

13. Process theology, creation-centered spirituality, and ecotheology have done much to promote these kinds of holistic perspectives within Christianity.

14. These are resources already being explored by theologians and biblical scholars.

15. While this is true theoretically, it should be noted that, like all ideologies, these traditions have at times been used for purposes of political power and social control. Moreover, they have not been able to prevent certain kinds of environmental destruction, such as deforestation in China.

16. The term "anthropocosmic" has been used by Tu Weiming in *Centrality and Commonality* (Albany: State University of New York Press, 1989).

17. Thomas Berry, "Religious Studies and the Global Human Community," unpublished manuscript.

18. Tu Weiming, "Beyond the Enlightenment Mentality," in *Worldviews and Ecology,* ed. Mary Evelyn Tucker and John Grim (Lewisburg, Pa.: Bucknell University Press, 1993; reissued, Maryknoll, N.Y.: Orbis Books, 1994).

19. This history has been described more fully by Roderick Nash in his chapter entitled "The Greening of Religion," in The Rights of Nature: A History of Environmental Ethics (Madison: University of Wisconsin Press, 1989).

20. *Religion and Environmental Crisis,* ed. Eugene Hargrove (Athens: University of Georgia Press, 1986).

21. Charlene Spretnak, *States of Grace: The Recovery of Meaning in the Post-Modern Age* (San Francisco: Harper San Francisco, 1991).

22. *Spirit and Nature: Why the Environment Is a Religious Issue,* ed. Steven Rockefeller and John Elder (Boston: Beacon Press, 1992).

23. Peter Marshall, *Nature's Web: Rethinking Our Place on Earth* (Armonk, N.Y.: M. E. Sharpe, 1992).

24. *Worldviews and Ecology,* ed. Mary Evelyn Tucker and John Grim (Lewisburg, Pa.: Bucknell University Press, 1993; reissued, Maryknoll, N.Y.: Orbis Books, 1994).

25. Callicott, *Earth's Insights.*

26. Both are State University of New York Press publications.

27. David Kinsley, *Ecology and Religion: Ecological Spirituality in a Cross-Cultural Perspective* (Englewood Cliffs, N.J.: Prentice Hall, 1995).

28. Seyyed Hossein Nasr, *Religion and the Order of Nature* (Oxford: Oxford University Press, 1996).

29. *Ethics of Environment and Development: Global Challenge, International Response,* ed. J. Ronald Engel and Joan Gibb Engel (Tucson: University of Arizona Press, 1990).

30. *Population, Consumption, and the Environment: Religious and Secular Responses,* ed. Harold Coward (Albany: State University of New York Press, 1995).

31. This Sacred Earth: Religion, Nature, Environment, ed. Roger S. Gottlieb (New York and London: Routledge, 1996).

32. These include volumes on Hinduism, Buddhism, Judaism, Christianity, and Islam.

Introduction: Current Thought on Christianity and Ecology

DIETER T. HESSEL and
ROSEMARY RADFORD RUETHER

Increasing numbers of Christian theologians and ethicists are responding to the environmental challenge as the world gets hotter, stormier, more unequal, crowded, violent, and less biodiverse. Their response to a pervasive ecological and social crisis comes none too soon, since this crisis will deepen in coming decades and will reach maximum stage at next century's midpoint. Exponential growth curves in resource depletion, production, pollution, population, migration, gene manipulation, and species extinction will reach a point where they either crash disastrously or moderate and stabilize sustainably. The most probable scenario is a combination of overshoot and collapse and a wise change of course, mixing the clashing realities of deep suffering and hopeful living.

What will Christian ecotheology and ethics contribute to the struggle to secure the well-being of the earth community in these freighted times? This collaborative book underscores a pivotal human obligation, in every place and pursuit, to express respect and show care for Earth as God's creation and life's home, while seeking justice for biodiverse otherkind as well as humankind. Toward that end, eighty leading Christian scholars, together with concerned observers, gathered at the American Academy of Arts and Sciences in Cambridge, Massachusetts, 16–19 April 1998, for a conference on Christianity and ecology organized by the Harvard University Center for the Study of World Religions. Papers presented and discussed there, and published here, show the impressive range of work being done to reexamine and rediscover elements of scripture and tradition and to refocus and re-present Christian theology and ethics in ecologically alert terms.

Because Christianity's multiple traditions take competing and cooperative forms, and convey emphases that can be constricting or liberating, the authors of these essays were asked to do three things: 1) to explore problemmatic themes that contribute to ecological neglect or abuse and/or suppressed elements in the traditions that can make a positive contribution to ecological-social healing; 2) to discuss new emphases needed in Christian theology or ethics; and 3) to identify praxis implications for church and society. They were also enjoined *not* simply to review past developments, but to offer constructive insights, building on the last one-third century of ecumenical Christian thought about the ecological crisis.[1] Their contributions to this volume should acquaint a much wider audience to the fact and progress of significant ecotheological and ethical reflection—a development of religious thought that is not yet widely understood and appreciated, even in the churches or among Christian scholars. This volume, by featuring many key scholars grappling with this subject matter, offers a unique, comprehensive discussion of the responsive role of Christian faith.

Ecotheology first surfaced noticeably in North America through the Faith-Man-Nature Group convened by Philip Joranson in 1963 with support from the National Council of Churches.[2] That initiative was stimulated by pioneering thinkers, such as Joseph Sittler, whose 1961 speech to the World Council of Churches called for earthy Christology and greater emphasis on cosmic redemption. The turn toward environmental theology was also influenced by the prophetic nature writing of Rachael Carson, *Silent Spring* (1962), and by the movement toward participatory environmentalism, which received early expression in the Port Huron Statement (also 1962) of Students for a Democratic Society.

In retrospect, we can see that a few Christian thinkers anticipated, and then a larger number joined, Lynn T. White, Jr., and other environmental philosophers to grapple with the disastrous assumptions underlying modern philosophical and religious thought. The development of ecological reflection by Christian theologians since the 1960s parallels the critique that has come from philosophers and scientists about the problematic of the modern era at the close of the millennium. But theologians and religious ethicists are in the best position to evaluate the negative and positive contributions of the biblical and Christian traditions to this crisis. These scholars recognize that the ecological challenge confronts biblical exegesis and Christian theology across the conservative-liberal spectrum, on an even deeper level than was discerned in liberation, Black, and feminist critiques of recent decades.

Emphases of Christian Ecotheology and Ethics

First, Christian theology has rediscovered that all of the earth community is valuable to God, who continues to create, sustain, and redeem the whole. God, understood in wholistic, organic terms, relates directly to and cares for the well-being of everykind, not just humankind. Otherkind exist to enjoy being in their own right, not only to function as companions or helpers of humankind.

Christian faith and ethics are being reoriented by the knowledge that the cosmos (and this planet) bodies forth the power, wisdom, and love of God. Christianity in the modern period almost lost interest in the revelatory power of the natural world and reinforced the tendency to set humanity over against nature in a manipulative, polluting way of life. Contemporary cosmology rediscovers the universe and Earth's nature to be a dynamic relational system—in Thomas Berry's term, a "communion of subjects" with whom humans are to live fittingly.

Second, adequate ecotheology explores the complex relation between cosmology, spirituality, and morality. It is necessary to rethink Christian cosmology, God's relation to the world, and the vocation of humanity, with ecological seriousness from "the ground." Cosmologies built on Greek philosophical dualism must be deeply recast in the light of both the new "universe story" and a recognition of the way the older cosmologies were themselves rationalizations and justifications of human domination over otherkind.

The ecological challenge brings new dimensions to theological revisioning that received little attention across the modern theological spectrum. Now, all who do theology must reconsider how to speak more meaningfully of theological symbols, such as God, creation, soul/body, Christ, sin, evil, salvation, and eschatology, in a world facing deep environmental challenge.

Third, deep Christian thinking on this subject is shaped not only by ecological awareness, but also by a melding of sacramental sensibility and covenantal commitment,[3] both of which are required for sustainable community. The goal is *not* to supplant sociocultural critique with ecological motifs. Sound Christian environmental thought and practice builds on the reenvisioning of theology by social justice movements and it deepens them by placing them in the context of ecological crisis. The result is not ecology versus justice, but theologies and ethics of "eco-justice," including specific foci, such as theologies of ecofeminism and of environmental racism that explore the link between ecological integrity and social justice.

Fourth, in eco-justice theology, the plight of the earth and of people, particularly the most abused, are seen together. Eco-justice theology and ethics are the focus of several recent publications.[4] In this spiritually grounded moral perspective, all beings on earth make up one household (*oikos*), which benefits from an economy (*oikonomia*) that takes ecological and social stewardship (*oikonomos*) seriously. Eco-justice provides a dynamic framework for thought and action that fosters ecological integrity with social-economic justice. It emerges through constructive human responses that serve environmental health and social equity together.

Christian thought of this kind challenges both religious beliefs and rituals that are preoccupied only with human salvation and expressions of grassroots environmentalism that are indifferent to socio-economic justice. The basic norms of eco-justice ethics include:

- solidarity with other people and creatures—companions, victims, and allies—in the earth community, reflecting a deep respect for creation;
- ecological sustainability—environmentally fitting habits of living and working that enable life to flourish, utilizing ecologically and socially appropriate technology;
- sufficiency as a standard of organized sharing, requiring basic floors and definite ceilings for equitable, or "fair," consumption; and
- socially just participation in decisions about how to obtain sustenance and to manage community life for the good in common and the good of the commons.

These norms illumine a biblically informed imperative to pursue in reinforcing ways what is both ecologically fitting and socially just. Solidarity comprehends the full dimensions of the earth community and of interhuman obligation. Sustainability gives high visibility to ecological integrity and wise behavior throughout the resource-use cycle. The third and fourth norms express the requirement of distributive and participatory justice in a world that has reached or is exceeding resource, pollution, and population limits.[5]

Anticipating an Ecological Reformation

The essays in this volume announce that an ecological reformation, or eco-justice reorientation, of Christian theology and ethics is now prominently on the ecumenical agenda. The need for ecological reformation arises from fundamental failures of Christian and other religious traditions: to adapt to the limiting conditions of life; to recognize intricate and interdependent relationships involving humankind with the rest of nature; and to respond with benevolence and justice to "the theological and biological fact of human kinship with all other creatures."[6] Ecologically reformed Christian theology will reinterpret basic doctrinal themes in ways that integrate ecological insight and value and reconceive Christian ethics to effectively encompass human relationships with other beings in the biosphere. Ecologically attuned faith and ethics should utilize knowledge gained from contemporary biophysical sciences and foster eco-justice praxis concerned with reducing consumption and adopting habits of sustainability, while encouraging the positive responsibility of government to protect the commons, preserve biodiversity, advance human environmental rights, limit population-consumption growth, curtail polluting technologies, and distribute the costs equitably.

An ecological reformation of religion and ethics intersects, rather than competes with, struggles for racial and gender justice. With enlightened awareness of both nature's rights and human rights, Christianity must recycle some inherited categories that are socially and ecologically dysfunctional. For example, it is time for Christians to discard the pattern of colonial thinking and gender hierarchy that the church built into its doctrine of creation and that defined the popular map of social relations (for more, see Rosemary Radford Ruether, "Ecofeminism: The Challenge to Theology," in this volume).

A reformation for the sake of eco-justice rereads scripture as a basis for critiqueing theological tradition and reviving the right relatedness of faith. Reinterpretation of scripture and critique of tradition has resulted in "an ecumenical consensus that has moved decisively beyond the views which secularized nature as an object for domination and justified careless and destructive 'subduing' of the earth."[7] In theology transformed by ecological awareness, the paradigm of mastery over the earth is replaced by a new model of healthy human-earth interrelationship that has biblical resonance.

An ecological reformation redefines faithfulness—that is, the human vocation—within common life, including politics, where ecology and justice flourish together, or not at all. The focus is on right relatedness, earthy virtues, and action for the earth community. The objective is to specify human obligations, or our shared vocation in every place and pursuit, to express respect and care for Earth as God's creation and everykind's home.

A reformation for the sake of eco-justice also produces fresh ecclesial self-understanding of the church's role in ecumenical Earth. A church committed to eco-justice ministry will foster liturgical reform responsive to what God is doing as Creator, Christ, and Spirit.

But at this late date, despite the engagement of environmentally active members, most of the churches remain quite slow to meet the environmental challenge. The exciting prospect of Christianity's ecosocial transformation contrasts sharply with the reality of sluggish ecclesial life and rigid theologizing. A majority of Christian communions and theologians on every continent still think and act with old pictures of the world and of humanity's place therein, rather than refocusing on the worldview, liturgy, and praxis of eco-justice. Yet, there are signs that significant elements of this world religion are converting to the service of the earth community. The essays in this volume emphasize constructive resources of Christian theology and ethics to guide movement in that direction.

Here we confront an important issue: Is the religious defect regarding the environment within Christian faith itself or in particular expressions of church life and thought? Most ecotheologians and the majority of the contributors to this volume focus on the latter. They, and we, refuse to condemn Christianity per se as anti-earth, or simply to overthrow its symbol structure. But we agree that some (often dominant) expressions of this world religion are toxic or are at least complicit in earth destruction. So, following the logic of ecological science that something in the environment is degraded wherever species of plants and animals are threatened, theologians reflecting on the environmental challenge discern that some forms of religious thought, ritual, and practice are unhealthy and threatening to the earth community.

Christian theology played a key role in ecological and cultural malformation by giving impetus to the modern, rational, scientific conquest of nature. Now it can contribute to achieving a sustainable human-earth relationship by utilizing the relationality paradigm of contemporary physics and ecology and connecting it effectively with the eco-justice sensibility of biblical thought. Toward that end, this volume presents leading-edge essays and respondent commentaries on Christianity and ecology (using "ecology" to refer to natural and cultural systems facing pressure from resource extraction, polluting technologies, urban development, population growth, unbridled consumerism, and political-economic domination).

Topics Discussed

The contributions to this volume show how to recast Christian beliefs and ethics in terms of their combined ecological and social significance. They construe the subject broadly and often reflect interdisciplinary awareness in exploring eco-justice theology ethics, biblical exegesis, and praxis. The essays are grouped in five parts:

- Creator, Christ, and Spirit in Ecological Perspective
- Vision, Vocation, and Virtues for the Earth Community
- The Universal and Particular in Ethics and Spirituality
- Toward Global Security and Sustainability
- Christian Praxis for Ecology and Justice

In the lead essay of part one, Elizabeth Johnson discusses cosmological dimensions of a living faith that is reexamining the doctrinal tradition and rediscovering creation. She explores why both Catholicism and Protestantism in the modern period lost interest in the natural world and set humanity over against nature in a "violently ruinous" way of life. Both the challenge of modern science to traditional

cosmology and the renewed Augustinianism of the Reformation
served to focus Catholic and Protestant theologies on an anthropocentric individualism no longer connected with a vision of cosmic community. Johnson then highlights the positive leads offered by contemporary cosmology for rediscovering nature as a dynamic relational
system inclusive of the human species. And she points to some new
challenges to the religious symbols and Christian praxis.

Her respondent, Gordon Kaufman, pushes the critique further. He
sees the fundamental anthropocentric model of God in the biblical
tradition—a volitional agent acting in history—as a major impedi-
ment to an integration of theology and ecology. To address this
problem, Kaufman calls for a new nonanthropological model of the
Divine perceived as the "serendipitous creativity" of the universe.

This section's second lead essay, by Sallie McFague, proposes that
Christianity is actually well supplied with christological perspectives,
in the prophetic, sacramental, and wisdom traditions, as well as eschatological, process, and liberation theologies, that can be extended to
address ecological issues. McFague outlines the features of an ecological Christology that views "God with us" in full sacramental and
prophetic dimensions. She draws out the praxis that eco-Christology
implies, illustrating it in terms of the costly responses needed from
Christians to meet climate change.

Kwok Pui-lan affirms this but notes that social and cultural
location diversifies the ways Christians interpret scripture and find
eco-justice insights therein. Asian Christians, like herself, have not
suffered the split between humanity and nature in the same way as
Christians in the West. Asian Christians are also suspicious of the
imperialist uses of themes such as the "cosmic Christ."

Mark Wallace presents an earth-centered model of the Spirit, or
nature-based pneumatology, as the power of life-giving breath (*rūah*)
continually working to transform and renew all life-forms. He
recovers earth-centered biblical images of the Spirit as "a healing and
subversive *life-form*—as water, light, dove, mother, fire, breath, and
wind." Wallace finds that nature enfleshes God's trinitarian love and
draws out the implications for cruciform living in a sinful, suffering
world, especially "the killing fields of urban America." Wallace also
suggests that a theological vision of the Spirit incarnate in suffering
nature also renews in cosmic terms the issues of how one can speak of
God suffering and dying.

Eleanor Rae affirms Wallace's emphasis on the immanent Spirit in nature but questions the usefulness of emphasizing the suffering Christ and salvation history. Rae draws attention to Wisdom Woman as a crucially important biblical image of the Spirit and to the process theology concept of a consequent God as a powerful response to creation's suffering.

John Chryssavgis complements Wallace's model by providing a Greek Orthodox perspective on the Spirit and on the sacredness of creation. He proposes that, in the world of the icon, heaven and earth, spirit and body, interpenetrate, restoring communion between God and the natural world. In the icon God is incarnate in matter, and matter becomes a vehicle of the Spirit. He also suggests other themes of the Orthodox traditions, such as apophatic (mystical, aesthetic) theology, which can be useful for ecological reflection.

Rosemary Radford Ruether concludes this group of essays by showing the historical development of the worldview dividing mind and body, God and nature, that underlies theologies of domination. She then sketches an ecofeminist reconstruction of Christian belief about the self, soul/body relations, finitude, evil, redemption, God, Christ, and revelation. Heather Eaton responds to Ruether by emphasizing the seriousness of the flight from finitude and mortality and critiquing the justifications of domination in Christian theology. Eaton outlines the steps toward a deep transformation of theology needed to become woman- and nature-friendly.

Part two opens with an essay by the noted "geologian" and cultural historian Thomas Berry calling for an appropriate human response to the new universe story. Berry reviews the historical origins of deep-rooted human alienation from the earth and Christian estrangement from the universe. But he also points to positive leads in Christian thought for rapport between humans and the rest of the natural community. Our "great work" is to support a new pattern of human presence on the planet.

Louke van Wensveen engages in a dialogue between the "dirty virtues" of nature conservation and the virtue tradition of Thomistic ethics to show both the usefulness and the limitations of this tradition for an ecological ethic. She suggests going beyond the limits of the Thomistic worldview by doing as he did rather than according to what he said in his time—that is, by integrating the new worldview of the science of our time. Steven Bouma-Prediger affirms van

Wensveen's direction and seeks to show the usefulness of biblical stories in providing key themes for an ecological virtue ethic.

Early challenges to the Christian tradition by thinkers such as Lynn White saw the Bible, and particularly the theme of "dominion," as a major cause of ecological crisis today. Biblical exegetes have responded to this challenge by exploring both alternative ways of reading such themes as "dominion" and alternative traditions within the Bible itself to shape an ecologically positive vision of the relation of God, humanity, and nature. By such exegetical quests they cut away the overlay of modern anthropocentric interpretation, exposing how much scripture has to offer as a guiding resource for life with the rest of nature.

Theodore Hiebert engages in this kind of evaluation of the creation stories of Genesis. He shows that the tradition of dominion in Genesis 1 cannot just be explained away as a benign concept of "stewardship." Rather, it reveals the worldview and social location of its priestly authors who saw the human relation to God in the light of their own view of themselves as unique representatives of divine sovereignty, set apart from and over the rest of nature. But this is not the only perspective on the God/human/nature relation in Genesis. The quest for a more ecological anthropology should consult the Genesis 2–3 tradition where humanity and the rest of nature are all seen as sharing a common substance as "earth creatures," made from the same soil and all sharing the Creator's vivifying breath. This tradition reflects the worldview of the farmers of Israel and is more conducive to an ecological solidarity of humans with the rest of creation.

The concluding book of the New Testament, Revelation, offers particular challenges to an ecological theology with its apocalyptic vision of God's destruction and re-creation of nature. Theologian Catherine Keller views as ecologically problemmatic the vision of salvation in this book in which "there will be no more sea." She sees this theme as reflecting a deep negativity in aspects of theological tradition toward the "watery deep" as the symbol of chaos, often associated with the female body, that is to be abolished in order to "save" the world. By contrast, she suggests that a nature-friendly theology must come to terms with chaos and integrate it into our worldview, rather than seek to abolish it. Mary Ann Hinsdale appreciates Keller's method as "truly ecological in its attempt to reuse, recycle, . . . and renew the text/tradition" while opening up to resonant contemporary art, music, and ritual. She finds it to be a model of fully ecosystemic theology, rooted in human experience of the "depths" of the sea, that would nurture appropriate Christian practices.

Barbara Rossing takes a sharply different view than does Keller of Revelation's possibilities for ecological theology. She sees hostility to the "sea" and the quest to abolish it as a sociopolitical, not an ontological, symbol. The sea represents the trade economy of imperial Rome, and its abolition is a part of creating a restored human environment rooted in a restored nature. By abolishing the imperialism of Babylon (Rome), with its vast system of injustice to humans and exploitation of nature, a renewed world where God dwells in our midst is envisioned, empowering us to struggle for eco-justice in society.

Part three reexamines some basic tasks of Christian ethics to meet the environmental challenge. James Nash and Cristina Traina explore an ecologically sensitized and reformed natural law approach that can challenge and overcome the strongly anthropocentric views of nature and hierarchical moral teachings dominant in church tradition. After a careful critique of that tradition, Nash recommends following nature in the sense of "ecosystemic compatibility," or fittingness that accommodates biological limits and cycles to assure sustainability. Traina's response complements Nash's discussion by emphasizing natural law's theological character, concerned with "fulfilling temporal ends in a way that advances or coheres with transcendent ends." We use our reason and creativity to shape ourselves and our surroundings for the common good within physical limits and social possibilities, as well as "within the transcendent bounds of our ultimate telos." Our responsibility is to understand the places of humans and other entities with the global ecosystem and then to fit into its directionality and order.

Daniel Cowdin focuses on the moral status of otherkind in Christian ethics. His essay is informed by recent environmental philosophy and surveys the theological state of the question. He notes that the life and sentience approaches to the moral status of otherkind fit more easily into the Christian narrative than does a land ethic. But, following Aldo Leopold in extending moral obligation to the land, human activity should enhance, not jeopardize, ecosystemic integrity, stability, and beauty, while also caring for individual organism and creatures, informed by the promise of "new creation."

Zoologist Calvin DeWitt concentrates on such biblical texts as

Job 40:15–24, celebrating Behemoth (the hippopotamus), in God's second speech from the whirlwind. What at first was seen merely as a target for arrow, bullet, or harpoon, is so marvelous and beautiful and fit to its habitat that only its Maker has "author-ity" to extinguish its life or its kind. Otherkind are the handiwork of the Lord. Respectful people behold them thankfully and "con-serve" them in their habitats.

Other chapters in part three highlight the aesthetic dimensions of ecotheology. Douglas Burton-Christie, following the lead of Amos Wilder, discusses "creative theopoetics" to revitalize Christian theology—especially its understanding of the Word Incarnate—by revisiting its own most profound mythic and poetic resources and paying attention to the insights of contemporary nature writing. Peter Lee engages in a dialogue between Christian and Chinese traditions on the ideas of goodness, beauty, and holiness, showing the complementarity of the two traditions on these themes. Heup Young Kim affirms Lee's efforts to synthesize Christian and Asian traditions, but he finds the mystical and sacramental traditions of Christianity more helpful than the rationalist forms of Protestantism that Lee has employed for this purpose. Kim also calls for a more critical look at the imperial and paternalist aspects of the Chinese tradition and the need to integrate social justice with cosmic harmony.

Paul Knitter leads us toward deep ecumenicity, which is concerned with finding common ground on a common earth: "The more deeply religious persons become ecologically attuned, the more effectively they will become ecumenically connected." We have an ethical challenge to elaborate a way of acting in the world for the good of earth community. Religions provide the foundation by envisioning the sacred, fostering ethical reflection, and engendering political responsibility.

Several essays in part four focus on meeting urgent environmental problems with Christian ethical discipline. Ian Barbour explores the contributions of science in understanding human environmental impacts and fostering awareness of ecological interdependence. Scientific insights converge with religious thought in affirming respect for all forms of life and in expressing the need to become stewards of life's continuity. We are called to respect the evolutionary wisdom and divine activity embodied in the natural world, to be accountable to the common good and future generations, and to foster a communal and less resource-consumptive vision of the good life.

Daniel Maguire declares the world religions are in default for failing to address the realities of the population-consumption explosion. He critiques the influence of religious natalism, environmental racism, and sacralized marketism on the attitudes and behavior of affluent Christians in particular. Susan Power Bratton and James Martin-Schramm point the way toward constructive response in the church's ministry and in social policy.

David Hallman surveys the role played by the ecumenical movement in grappling with human-induced climate change—a fundamental problem of justice and ethics precipitated by the rich industrialized nations, with disproportionate consequences on poor developing countries and future generations. William French and Preston Williams concentrate on public policies for sustainability. French examines some of the forces driving the global growth agenda and emphasizes the stake that Christian communities have in promoting ecological sustainability. In the policy arena, he urges the promotion of green (or carbon) taxes to help restrain unsustainable patterns of resource and energy use, habitat destruction, species extinction, and population growth.

Patterns of religious thought and ritual function to provide a binding sense of what on Earth is sacred and the role of humans therein. If that is what concerns religion, then we find ourselves in the throes of a life-and-death struggle between historic world religions that fostered "oikonomia" and an ultramodern religion of "economism," as John Cobb labels it,[8] that depletes the world's natural "resources" for profit and fosters "consumption" for happiness at the expense of sustainable communities and biodiverse ecosystems. The church must become more engaged with protecting natural places and building community while resisting false worship of a universal, "free" market system driven by globalized capitalist investment.

What pattern of ecclesial and social praxis is needed to meet the environmental challenge? The final group of essays, part five, focuses on the churches' role in eco-justice ministry and citizenship. Larry Rasmussen opens this section with an important overview of the church's eco-justice mission in an increasingly urbanized society. That mission, in his words, is to address the social and ecological questions together for the sake of comprehensive sustainability in a time of economic "globalization," in which nature, knowledge, and culture —all life's human and nonhuman communities—are being recast.

Praxis for ecology and justice involves participation in earth stewardship, for example, through Zimbabwaen tree planting by earthkeeping churches in Southern Africa, described by Marthinus Daneel. Martin Robra's response emphasizes that the earthkeeping ministry of African Independent Churches exemplifies the cultural adaptability of Christian symbols. It also challenges the way Christians in the North have accommodated to the culture of domination. The Zimbabwean example enjoins churches everywhere to develop "practical consciousness" that results in a life-style of ecology and justice.

Praxis involves environmental justice organizing in North American communities, as Vernice Miller-Travis illustrates in her narrative account. Praxis also requires more focused religious leadership, the subject of the chapter by William Somplatsky-Jarman, Walter Grazer, and Stan LeQuire, who describe the work being done among and by Christians in the United States through the National Religious Partnership for the Environment.

Patricia Mische reminds us that eco-justice praxis is instilled through a communal ethos and habits of earthkeeping at local and bioregional levels. Praxis also involves reform of liturgy and spiritual practice; and it includes nonpartisan political advocacy, as exemplified by civil society organizations, such as Global Education Associates.

Part five is followed by Rosemary Radford Ruether's concluding essay on the centrality of eco-justice in authentic Christian witness. For Ruether, this is not a new or marginal emphasis for Christian life and thought; rather, it is central to a full understanding of the church's mission as witness to and participant in God's redemption of creation.

This volume on Christianity and ecology appears roughly a one-third century after Christians began to rethink biblical exegesis, theology, and ethics for planetary well-being. It illustrates much of the major work being done by Christian scholars to meet the environmental challenge. We trust that the creative spiritual and moral insights in these essays will encourage readers and churches to strengthen and deepen an emerging, vital consensus that the gospel calls Christians to be engaged, with others of good will, in a healing struggle for the well-being of everykind and of diverse communities under increasing ecosocial stress.

Notes

1. For well-documented critical surveys, see the overview essay and annotations of Peter W. Bakken, Joan Gibb Engel, and J. Ronald Engel, *Ecology, Justice, and Christian Faith: A Critical Guide to the Literature* (Westport, Conn.: Greenwood Press, 1995); and chapters on state-of-the-art scholarship in *Theology for Earth Community: A Field Guide,* ed. Dieter T. Hessel (Maryknoll, N.Y.: Orbis Books, 1996).

2. Early Christian scholarly work by the Faith-Man-Nature Group, exemplifying "The Greening of Religion," is described in Roderick F. Nash, *The Rights of Nature: A History of Environmental Ethics* (Madison: University of Wisconsin Press, 1989), chap. 4. For an ecologically aware history of Christian doctrine, see H. Paul Santmire, *The Travail of Nature: The Ambiguous Ecological Promise of Christian Theology* (Philadelphia: Fortress Press, 1985). An overview of North American ecumenical Christian environmental response since the 1960s is provided by Dieter T. Hessel, "Where Were/Are the U.S. Churches in the Environmental Movement?" in *Theology for Earth Community: A Field Guide* (Maryknoll, N.Y.: Orbis Books, 1996), chap. 16.

3. Rosemary Radford Ruether, who introduced this distinction in *Gaia and God: An Ecofeminist Theology of Earth Healing* (San Francisco: HarperSanFrancisco, 1992), discusses it further in the conclusion to this present volume.

4. See, e.g., *After Nature's Revolt: Eco-Justice and Theology,* ed. Dieter T. Hessel (Minneapolis: Fortress Press, 1992); *Good News for Animals? Christian Approaches to Animal Well-Being,* ed. Charles Pinches and Jay B. McDaniel (Maryknoll, N.Y.: Orbis Books, 1993); "Concern for Creation: Voices on the Theology of Creation," ed. Viggo Mortensen, *Tro and Tanke* (Lutheran World Federation) 5 (1995); *"And God Saw That It Was Good": Catholic Theology and the Environment,* ed. Drew Christiansen and Walter Grazer (Washington, D.C.: United States Catholic Conference, 1996); "Eco-Justice and the Environment," ed. Jerome A. Stone, *American Journal of Theology and Philosophy* 18, no. 1 (January 1997); and Stephen Bede Scharper, *Redeeming the Time: A Political Theology of the Environment* (New York: Continuum, 1997).

5. For a discussion of these eco-justice norms, see Dieter Hessel, "Ecumenical Ethics for Earth Community," *Theology and Public Policy* 8, no. 1-2 (summer/winter 1996): 17–29.

6. James A. Nash, "Toward the Ecological Reformation of Christianity," *Interpretation* 50, no. 1 (January 1996).

7. See Wesley Granberg-Michaelson, "Creation in Ecumenical Theology," in *Ecotheology: Voices from South and North,* ed. David G. Hallman (Geneva: WCC Publications; Maryknoll, N.Y.: Orbis Books, 1994), 103.

8. See Herman E. Daly and John B. Cobb, Jr., *For the Common Good: Redirecting the Economy toward Community, the Environment, and a Sustainable Future,* 2d ed. (Boston: Beacon Press, 1994).

I. Creator, Christ, and Spirit in Ecological Perspective

Losing and Finding Creation
in the Christian Tradition

ELIZABETH A. JOHNSON

Introduction

The image of our home planet from space, widely reproduced as a marvelous photo of a blue marble swirled around with white clouds, evokes a profound sense of the earth as a community of life. Astronauts who have seen this view in reality speak of its transforming power. Saudi Arabian astronaut Sultan bin Salman al-Saud, part of an international crew, recollected: "The first day we all pointed to our own countries. The third day we were pointing to our continents. By the fifth day, we were all aware of *only* one Earth."[1]

On the brink of the third millennium, a new consciousness of the earth is taking hold among persons around the globe, an understanding shaped by a unique dialectic: new knowledge of the earth's intricate workings discovered and popularized by contemporary science, in tension with the realization of how human predation is currently spoiling the natural world. On the one hand, perception of the vast age, size, and complexity of the universe, awareness of the cosmic processes that have shaped and continue to create it, appreciation of the workings of matter at the atomic and quantum levels, realization of the astonishing complexity of biological evolution up to and including the human species, and understanding the interconnectedness of all life—all of this knowledge gives rise to the sense that the world is a wonder. On the other hand, cognizance that human practices of unbridled reproduction, overconsumption, exploitative use of resources, and efflorescing pollution are rapidly depleting the life-supporting planetary systems of land, sea, and air while leading hosts of other species to extreme distress or extinction—this realization engenders a contrasting experience whereby the treasure of nature is known to be under mortal threat. Wonder at the world in the face of wasting the world: for a growing number of religious persons today, this experience provides a new entry into ancient forms of contemplation along with a call to fresh ethical acts of prophetic witness and repair of the world.[2]

In this context of Earth's distress and human awakening to our critical responsibility, it can prove instructive to trace how the theme of the natural world, called "creation" when it is viewed in relation to God, got lost in Christian reflection. It is with deliberation that I say "got lost," because for the last five hundred years the religious value of the earth has not been a subject of theology, preaching, or religious education. Should today's Christian scholars consult their own experiences, they will most likely remember that the natural world was largely ignored as a subject in their religious formation and education, whether catechetical or scholarly. This silence has been true, until very recently, of both Catholic and Protestant branches of Western Christianity.

Looking back over the whole two thousand years of Christian tradition, however, leads to a surprise, namely, that such amnesia about the cosmic world has not always been the case. In fact, for three-quarters of this history, creation was actively present as an intrinsic part of theological reflection. This is not to say that thought about creation led our ancestors to a highly developed ecological consciousness such as is needed today. Present wonder and protest at wasting the world reflect a genuinely new moment in history; our scientific knowledge, technology, and means of imaging and communication are genuinely different. But such theology kept alive the sense that creation had a certain religious value and was deserving of a modicum of respect when subject to human action.

After a background look at creation's long presence in the Christian tradition, in all of its power and ambivalence, this essay tracks discrete reasons why the natural world became overlooked, problems that still operate as roadblocks to genuine conversion of mind and heart to the earth. It then identifies movements that are finding the natural world again and charts challenges to thought and action arising from nature's current rediscovery.

The First Fifteen Hundred Years of Christianity

We begin by noting that in the scriptures of the Jewish tradition, from which Christianity took its early orientation, the natural world is pervasively and comfortably present.[3] Not only is it depicted as God's good creation and covenant partner, but it shares in the blessings of the human covenant as well as in judgment when that covenant is broken. In the deuteronomic tradition, the practice of sabbath, when even the animals rest, and of Jubilee, when the land is refreshed by lying fallow, give concrete expression to ways in which the world is an intrinsic part of the community's religious life before God. In the prophetic tradition, both land and people flourish or are ravaged together: "The vine languishes, the merry-hearted sigh . . . the gladness of the earth is banished" (Isa. 24:7), which implies that fruitful fields, serious merrymaking, and general *shalom* are all of a piece. In the psalms, the world praises God: meadows sing with gladness; the stars shout out for joy. Conversely, the earth can groan and mourn, lament, and cry out to God for mercy. The wisdom writings portray Holy Wisdom pervading the world with her holy spirit, knowing the changes of the seasons, the movements of animals, the healing properties of herbs, and renewing all things with her life-giving energy. While not in itself a matter for explicit meta-reflection, the earth, it is clear, is the Lord's with all its fullness (Ps. 24:1); the whole earth is filled with God's glory (Isa. 6:3); and it would be unthinkable to divorce the natural world from what is religiously important.

The Christian scriptures, while focused on life in Christ, bear rich themes that are implicitly earth-affirming: incarnation, where the Word becomes flesh and so enters into the living matter of this world; resurrection of the body, signifying an eternal worth to the flesh; eucharistic sharing, in which bread and wine made from grain and grape usher the assembled people into communion with the Divine; and hope, that the future will bring on a cosmic scale the gracious redemption that has already occurred in Christ, the firstborn of all creation.

A certain ambivalence pervades this positive assessment, especially in view of the dominion texts of Genesis, Psalm 8, and elsewhere, along with the otherworldly or antiworld impulse of some Pauline and Johannine texts. These were to do much mischief as they were received by later centuries marked by dualistic constructions of reality. On balance, however, the Jewish and Christian scriptures honor the religious value of the earth, and they are open to such an interpretation today. They teach that the creating and redeeming God loves and takes delight in the natural world, which correspondingly enjoys an integrity that is not dependent on human decision.

In varying degrees, early Christian and medieval theologians took this view of things for granted.[4] They reasoned that since there is only one God, and since this God created all that exists, then everything is encompassed in the scope of theology's interest. Hence, theology deals with humanity and the natural world as creation in relation to God. God-world-humanity: these form a metaphysical trinity. Take one away and understanding of the other two becomes incomplete. Consequently, theologians brought the natural world into their theology on a consistent basis, interpreting it as God's good creation, a revealing pathway to the knowledge of God, and a partner in human salvation. One fascinating metaphor frequently used was that of nature as a book of revelation. It was common for Augustine, for example, to preach that God has put two books at our disposal, the book of sacred scripture and the book of nature. If we learn to read the book of nature aright, we will hear God's true word and be led to knowledge about God's wisdom, power, and love.

Appreciation of the natural world in Christian thought reached its zenith in the twelfth and thirteenth centuries. Inspired by the translation of ancient Greek scientific works along with works by Jewish and Muslim scholars, medieval theologians applied themselves to constructing an all-embracing view of the world, writing innumerable treatises on the universe, on the world, on the picture of the world, on the philosophy of the world, on the nature of things. Their endeavor to interpret the whole world in the light of Christian faith gave vitality to their work and inspired impressive systems in which cosmology, anthropology, and theology of God formed a harmonious unity. Three examples:

In her *summa* of Christian doctrine, *Scivias,* Hildegard of Bingen sees the whole universe imbued with the love of Christ, the sun of justice, who shines with "the brilliance of burning charity of such great glory that every creature is illumined by the brightness of this light."[5] In the midst of this marvelous vision stand human beings, "made in a wondrous way with great glory from the dust of the earth and so intertwined with the strengths of the rest of creation that we can never be separated from them."[6]

Bonaventure instructs the soul journeying toward God to see the universe as a wonderful work of art in which one recognizes traces of its Maker: "Whoever is not enlightened by the splendor of created things is blind; whoever is not aroused by the sound of their voice is deaf; whoever does not praise God for all these creatures is mute; and whoever after so much evidence does not recognize the First Principle is an idiot" (*stultus est*).[7]

Aquinas believes that theologians ought quite consciously to study nature and include a consideration of its way in their work. His own writing is pervaded with a cosmic sense as well as instructive analogies from the natural world, everything from urine to fire. Indeed, the whole cosmos itself is an astonishing image of God:

> God brought things into being in order that the divine goodness might be communicated to creatures and be represented by them. And because the divine goodness could not be adequately represented by one creature alone, God produced many and diverse creatures, that what was wanting in one in the representation of divine goodness might be supplied by another. For goodness, which in God is simple and uniform, in creatures is manifest and divided. Thus the whole universe together participates in divine goodness more perfectly and represents it better than any single creature whatever.[8]

Early Christian and medieval theologies brought God, humanity, and the world into an ordered harmony. Lest we get nostalgic, it must be remembered that these systems of thought were pervaded with a hierarchical dualism that was indigenous to the Aristotelian and Neo-platonic categories they employed. Spirit was clearly delineated from matter and assigned a higher value, as were the associated realities of male vis-à-vis female and humanity vis-à-vis the nonhuman world. Creation was arranged in a hierarchy of being with the human person, that is, the elite male human person, endowed with a rational soul at the apex. Given the oppressive relations of domination and sub-ordination in such a model, this is not a pattern that can serve our quest for right relationship with the earth community today. However, the very fact that the world *was* included in an ordered harmony with humanity before God is noteworthy. So too is the fact that time and again creation slipped the bonds of hierarchical dualism and power-fully shaped religious consciousness, as can be seen even today in the art and architecture, liturgy and poetry of these centuries.

Strange as it may seem in light of this fifteen-hundred-year-old heritage, after the Reformation neither Catholic nor Protestant theology continued to include the earth as a subject of interest. Instead, they focused on God and the human self, leaving the natural world to the side. They did so for different reasons, but the effect was equally deadly.

Losing Creation

In principle, there was no intellectual pressure for Catholic theology in the post-Reformation and Enlightenment periods to ignore the natural world. Scholasticism's notion of general revelation through nature and natural law, its positive assessment of human nature even after the Fall, and its sacramental principle that sees the world as a vehicle for the Divine would conspire to keep the traditional three pillars of theology intact. However, the advance of modernity saw creation slip from view as a subject for vigorous and creative reflection. Why this should have been the case has not been sufficiently studied.

One key factor that can be cited is political: namely, the seventeenth-century censure of Galileo, whose investigation of the heavens challenged the medieval picture of the universe as geocentric, static, and perfectly, hierarchically ordered. On the occasion of Galileo's rehabilitation in 1992, Pope John Paul II, commenting on what had gone wrong, noted that at the heart of the conflict was the fact that, to church leaders, "geocentrism seemed to be part of scriptural teaching itself." To have avoided the conflict, "it would have been necessary all at once to overcome ingrained habits of thought and to devise a way of teaching capable of enlightening the people of God."[9] But this most of them were unable to do. Hence, church leadership used its considerable power to try to stamp out new insight.

Being punished rather than rewarded for a certain work has a way of dampening enthusiasm. Under pressure of repeated ecclesiastical censure, Galileo's not being the only case, Catholic theologians for the most part began to ignore the questions arising from a heliocentric and then evolutionary worldview. Theology became estranged from ongoing discoveries about the universe in the secular, and thus freer, disciplines. Even as the medieval world picture disintegrated and was no longer available as a cosmological framework for Christian doctrine, the spirit of the medieval synthesis lingered like a ghost in the nineteenth-century neoscholastic manuals. The world picture may have been untenable, but at least the texts implied that there was a natural world there, worthy of consideration before God. However, the deductive, overrationalistic theology of the manuals in service of an increasingly juridical church prevented any serious engagement with the world being newly conceived by contemporary science. And the efforts of a thinker such as Teilhard de Chardin to connect the evolutionary earth with religious doctrine were met, once again, with ecclesiastical condemnation and silencing.[10]

The Second Vatican Council marked a turning point in this saga of Catholic theology, directing thought with new openness toward dialogue with the modern world and with ecumenical and interreligious partners. Far from putting Catholic thought in touch with Christian theology that had kept pace with scientific advance, however, the first contacts with Protestantism but heightened absorption with anthropology. For under pressure of the Reformation's great *sola*s—Christ alone, faith alone, grace alone, scripture alone—Protestant thought had taken an intensely anthropocentric turn. To the anxious question, "How can I find a gracious God," revelation discloses a merciful God bent over our sinfulness and justifying us in Christ. Individual human consciousness thus becomes *the* place of encounter with God, who consoles terrified consciences with the promise of mercy in Christ. The center of gravity shifts to the human subject.

Early Reformation thought continued to reflect a somewhat positive assessment of creation. Calvin, for example, wrote that God has inscribed divine glory in the works of creation so clearly and strikingly that "withersoever you turn your eyes, there is not an atom of the world in which you cannot behold some brilliant sparks at least of his glory," although, due to sin, we need the scriptures as spectacles to see this fully.[11] However, the trajectory of Protestant theology shows increasing repudiation of anything remotely smacking of Catholic natural theology and its association with works' righteousness. Human nature in its fallenness is depraved; nature as a whole can only refer to fallen creation, which is empty of God's presence and in need of God's sovereign act of salvation given only in Christ. Theology's vision thus stays focused on humanity where the all-important saving action of God takes place.

In addition to this internal logic, Protestant theology was also more open to developments in society at large, and thus imbibed antinature views characteristic of the developing human disciplines of science, philosophy, and history. The growth of early modern science was impelled by the idea that it was the supreme human vocation to establish the power of the human race itself over the rest of nature. Betraying the subliminal antifemale bias accompanying this idea, Francis Bacon opined that the investigator must learn to wrest new knowledge from nature's womb; his technology must seize her by the hair of the head and mold her into something new; he must penetrate her mysteries and subdue her. The earth thus becomes merely useful matter to be probed and harnessed, a submissive object at the disposal of the ruling human subject, "man." This attitude is summed up in his infamous phrase about scientific techniques that are designed to lead to man "Nature with all of her children to bind her to your service and make her your slave."[12] In philosophy, the Cartesian notion of the self and then the Kantian turn to the subject likewise divorced the knowing human person from nature, relating them as active subject to external, passive object. The modern construal of history further strengthened this split. Understood as actual events in linear time, this idea was pressed into service in Protestant biblical interpretation to yield the religious assessment of history as the locus of God's mighty, saving acts. By contrast, nature was seen as the realm of cyclic time where pagan deities reigned. Nature thus became not only a stage on which the drama of salvation history is played out; it even became a symbol of what human beings are rescued *from*.

Shaped by forces both internal and external to its own founding insights, the resulting attitude that sets nature over against humanity and renders the former religiously and morally mute has had real staying power in twentieth-century Protestant theologies.[13] Existentialist theology from Kierkegaard to Bultmann, for example, located the truly human in the realm of freedom to decide, to fashion one's own world, to make meaning. This freedom was explicitly contrasted with a deterministic, even mechanistic view of nature. Nature and freedom were on different, unrelated planes, the former simply the backdrop for the drama of the latter. Not only existentialism but also neoorthodoxy, liberalism, political theology, most liberation theologies in their early stages, virtually all fundamentalism, and what may be called typical "seminary theology"[14] assume nature to be little more than a platform, a resource, an external habitat on which the truly important story of the human person is played out. With the outstanding exception of American process thought, creation, for all practical purposes, disappeared as a partner and subject of theology.

Roadblocks

Today, people in both Protestant and Catholic traditions are increasingly aware that their losing creation has been a contributing factor to a social way of life that is violently ruinous to life and cannot be sustained: "the stark sign of our times is a planet in peril at our hands."[15] Efforts to find the world again as a living community worthy of value are afoot on many fronts. Institutional enterprises are making a contribution. Most noteworthy here is the World Council of Churches' linkage of justice and peace with the integrity of creation, and the historic Canberra Assembly with its theme "Come, Holy Spirit, Renew the Whole Creation!" Catholic papal and episcopal pastoral messages also serve to raise consciousness, evoking the traditional sacramental principle to reinstate the value of the earth and human responsibility toward it.[16]

In addition to the words and deeds of institutional churches, popular religious task forces, commissions, and action groups translate care for the earth into practical action "on the ground." In this effort, scholars in religious studies have also been active, and indeed bear a particular responsibility insofar as ecologically broadening a narrow, human-centered vision of religious faith and ethical action has the potential to change the commonplace thinking and practice of large communities of citizens of this world. Thus, it is heartening to note that, in addition to process theologians, many other practitioners of the craft of theology and ethics have begun to incorporate the natural world as part or even the center of their work.[17] This effort is immeasurably strengthened by liberation and feminist theologies that underscore the links that exist between exploitation of the earth and injustice among human beings themselves. Attending to these voices prevents retrieval of the cosmos from being tagged as simply the concern of a first world, male, academic elite. These are all hopeful developments. Agreement is growing that, for the sake of the world and its future, we need to get the Christian tradition back onto the track from which it fell off five hundred years ago.

Yet, there are deeply embedded roadblocks to finding creation again, commensurate with the reasons Catholic and Protestant thought lost it in the first place. For the Catholic tradition, the authoritarian structure of power in the church itself ensures an official vested interest in maintaining the traditional view of the world ordered according to a hierarchy of being. This prevents thought from going the distance needed to reconceive the profound kinship of the human race with the rest of nature not as a pyramid of increasing privilege but as a circular, global community of life. One example: in a series of very fine statements, John Paul II's 1990 World Day of Peace communiqué emphasizes that no peaceful society can afford to neglect the integrity of creation; that social justice is an essential ingredient in protecting the earth's well-being; and that the ecological crisis is a profound moral problem. However, while speaking of the need to "keep ever alive a sense of 'fraternity' with all those good and beautiful things which Almighty God has created," the pope's message concludes by positing "our serious obligation to respect and watch over them with care, in light of that greater and higher fraternity that exists within the human family."[18] The social location of these and other such teachings within a hierarchical system held to be set up according to the unchanging design of divine will creates an inability to imagine another kind of godly order structured according to genuine interdependence and mutuality.

For the Protestant tradition, intense suspicion of "fallen" nature, both human and the world as a whole, continues to sway currents of thought, however implicitly, like a drowned continent. *Finitum non est capax infiniti*—the finite is not capable of bearing the infinite: only the Word can save. When this suspicion about the goodness of the world is coupled with concentration on the sinful human subject in need of divine mercy, it sets up a powerful roadblock to bringing the earth permanently into view as a subject of religious interest. In various ways, nearly all philosophy and theology prominent in the Protestant West bless the divorce of nature from history. Contemporary efforts to think otherwise have to contend with a perspective that is deeply rooted in the stance of the whole Reforming tradition.

Challenges of Finding Creation

When religious reflection today opens its door to the natural world, it is met with a wondrous array of insights. Medieval cosmology, which saw the world as geocentric, unchanging, and hierarchically ordered, is gone. But gone too is the Enlightenment prejudice that held a deterministic and mechanistic view of nature inimical in many ways to religious values. Instead, contemporary science is discovering a natural world that is surprisingly dynamic, organic, self-organizing, indeterminate, chancy, boundless, and open to the unknown. There are still many gaps and uncertainties, but enormous discoveries are being made in our day.[19]

The world is almost unimaginably *old*. About 15 billion years ago a single numinous speck exploded in an outpouring of matter and energy, shaping a universe that is still expanding. Roughly five billion years ago, one of those giant, aging stars died in a great supernova explosion that cooked simpler atoms into heavier metals such as iron, spewing this debris into the cosmos. Some of this cloud of dust and gas reignited to become our sun, a second-generation star. Some of it coalesced in chunks too small to catch fire, forming the planets of our solar system, including Earth. Only much later, in the last few million years, did the human race begin to exist.

The world is almost incomprehensibly *large*. From 50 to 100 billion galaxies, each comprised of 100 billion stars, and no one knows how many moons and planets, all of this visible and audible matter is only a fraction of the matter in the universe. In this huge universe the earth is a small planet orbiting a medium-sized star toward the edge of one spiral galaxy.

The world is almost mind-numbingly *dynamic*. Out of the big bang the stars; out of the stardust the earth; out of the molecules of the earth, single-celled living creatures; out of the evolutionary life and death of these creatures, an advancing tide of life, fragile but unstoppable: single-celled plankton, jelly fish, creatures that live in shells, amphibians, insects, flowers, birds, reptiles, mammals, among whom emerged human beings with a consciousness and freedom that concentrate the self-transcendence of matter itself. We are the cantors of the universe.

The world is unfathomably *organic*. Everything is connected with everything else; nothing conceivable is isolated. In the words of the scientist and theologian Arthur Peacocke, "Every atom of iron in our blood would not be there had it not been produced in some galactic explosion billions of years ago and eventually condensed to form the iron in the crust of the earth from which we have emerged."[20] Humans share with all other living creatures on our planet the same common ancestry. Bacteria, pine trees, sparrows, horses, the great gray whales—we are all genetic kin in the great community of life.

These and other discoveries of contemporary science coalesce into a picture of the world that calls out for new interpretations, both of traditional religious symbols and of moral teachings, especially as classical dualisms and hierarchical orderings can no longer be seriously maintained.

Challenge to religious symbols: Intellectually, a host of questions arise that prod theology to rethink the basic symbols of Christian discourse. What wisdom about the world can be found in biblical and classical Christian authors, and the writings or oral legacy of the world's other religious traditions? In such an old, vast, dynamic, and organic world, how and for what reasons does one come to belief in God? Indeed, how is the incomprehensible mystery of God to be conceived, imaged, and preached? What does the book of nature teach in our day about the Creator of this magnificence, who continues to work creatively within its open and unpredictable systems? How to interpret the irreversible entrance of God into precisely *this* world through the incarnation of divine Wisdom and the transformation of *this* flesh in the resurrection of Jesus Christ? How to understand that the love revealed in Jesus' healings and feedings and poured out on the cross is deeply connected with the "Love that moves the sun and other stars,"[21] so that Dante's vision is no pious lyricism but a theological truth? How to interpret the Spirit of the baptismal font as none other than the very Giver of life to all the creatures of the rain forest?

Whence evil in such a self-organizing universe, and how does sin gain a foothold? How to extend understandings of sin and grace not only from the person to social structures but from the human to ecological dimensions as well? How to preach salvation as healing and rescue for the whole world rather than as an acosmic relation to God? How to let go of contempt for matter, the body and its sexuality, change and mortality and revalue them as a blessed part of the cosmic whole? How to interpret human beings as primarily "earthlings" rather than tourists or aliens whose true home is elsewhere?[22] How to redesign the hierarchy of being into a circle of the community of life, so that we can grasp the uniqueness of being human as itself an expression of nature and affirm our profound, interdependent kinship with the rest of nature? How to conceive of the church, its mission and structures, in an evolving universe? How to recognize the sacraments as symbols of divine graciousness in a universe which is itself the primordial revelation and sacrament? How to hope for the eschatological redemption of the whole universe, even now groaning, in such a way that it unleashes critical and creative energies for care of the earth even now? Bringing the natural world into Christian symbolic discourse shifts the axis of all theological questions, setting an intellectual agenda for years to come.

Challenge to praxis: Ethically, too, a host of insights arise that shed a new light on what is right and what is wrong to do. If the earth is indeed creation, a sacrament of the glory of God with its own intrinsic value, then, for those of the Christian persuasion, ongoing destruction of Earth bears the marks of deep sinfulness. Through greed, self-interest, ignorance, and injustice, human beings are bringing violent disfigurement and death to this living, evolving planet that God created as "very good" (Gen. 1:31). Ecocide, biocide, geocide—these new terms attempt to name the killing of ecosystems and species that are meant to radiate the glory of God but, instead, end up broken or extinct. One of the "books" that teaches about the ultimate Giver of life is being ruined: as matter for religious concern, this has the character of a moral imperative.

In light of this devastation, grace brings about a genuine conversion of mind and heart back *to* the earth, with repentance for the violence done. Granting intrinsic and not just instrumental value to the natural world paves the way for extension of moral consideration, the demands of justice and love, from the human neighbor to "other-kind"[23] and the earth itself. If nature be the new poor, then justice and compassion are called into play. Solidarity with victims, options for the poor, and action on behalf of justice widen out to embrace life systems and other species to ensure vibrant communion in life for all.

For a genuinely sustainable outcome, the angle of vision of marginalized people plays a particularly decisive role. Economic poverty coincides with ecological poverty, for, as liberation theologies have argued, the poor suffer disproportionately from environmental destruction.[24] Examples redound. In third world countries the onset of economic development for corporate profit brings deforestation, soil erosion, and polluted waters, which in turn lead to the disruption of local cycles of nature and the sustenance economies on which most poor people depend. Sheer human misery results. Plantation farming of commodity crops for export not only destroys biodiversity, but also creates wealth for a few from the backbreaking labor of a whole class of poor people. Correlatively, lack of land reform pushes dispossessed rural peoples to the edges of cultivated land. In order to stay alive they practice slash-and-burn agriculture, in the process destroying pristine habitat, killing rare animals, and displacing indigenous peoples. To give a North American example, companies in the United States export work to factories across the Mexican border (*maquiladoras*) that cheaply employ thousands of young, rural women to make high-quality consumer goods for export, while they themselves live in unhealthy squalor in an environment spoiled by toxic waste.

In a global perspective, all these conditions result from an international economic system driven by profit that preys endlessly on nature's resources and seeks cheap labor to turn these resources into consumer products. The beneficiaries are the wealthy classes and nations, who consume a disproportionate amount of the earth's resources. The gap between rich and poor divides these wealthy countries. The economically well-off can choose to live amid acres of green while poor people, mostly people of color, are housed near factories, refineries, or waste-processing plants that heavily pollute the environment; birth defects, general ill health, and disease result.

In sum, social injustice has an ecological face. Ravaging of people and ravaging of the land go hand in hand. To be truly effective, therefore, moral teaching must include commitment to ecological wholeness within the wider struggle for a more just social order. The aim is to establish and protect healthy ecosystems where all living creatures can flourish.

Exploitation of the earth also coincides with the subordination of women within the global system of patriarchy. Because women are the life-givers to every human child, female symbolism for nature pervades human cultures. The earth is seen as the mother who brings forth all life. But feminist thought has analyzed a negative use of this connection between women and nature in human cultures. In classical Greek and Christian thought, women and nature are largely identified with principles of matter, potency, and passionate bodiliness while men are associated with spirit, act, and rationality. Consequently, women and nature are assigned mainly instrumental value in this world and are excluded from direct contact with God imaged in analogy with transcendent male consciousness beyond the realm of coming to be and passing away. As Rosemary Radford Ruether pointed out decades ago, women, whose bodies mediate physical existence to humanity, thus become the oldest symbol of the connection between social domination and the domination of nature.[25]

Even in modern culture the mentality that sees nature as something to be dominated continues to draw on the imagery and attitudes of men's domination of women. We speak of the rape of the earth, revealing the extent to which exploitation of nature is identified with violent sexual conquest of women, and of virgin forest, as yet untouched by man but awaiting his exploration and use. These and other linguistic metaphors link male hierarchy over women and nature, with both intended for his service, while man, in his nobility and superiority, has a duty to control and a right to use them both.

Women of color and third world women are deepening this analysis. Womanist theologian Delores Williams makes a telling connection between the violation of nature and the practice of breeding black women under slavery, both defilements leading to exhaustion of the body and depletion of the spirit.[26] Asian theologian Aruna Gnanadason describes the Chipko movement to protect local stands of trees in India and the Green Belt movement for reforestation in Kenya, both led largely by women. She shows how women are affirming the worth of their own bodily selves in the process.[27] On every continent today, women's growing bodily, psychological, and spiritual self-confidence is a powerful factor that flows against the tide of ecological collapse, even while it meets mighty opposition in the process. In sum, sexism, too, has an ecological face. The devastating consequences of ravaging the earth cannot be fully addressed until the patriarchal system is faced as a whole. To be truly effective, therefore, conversion to the earth needs to cut through the knot of misogynist prejudice and shift from the worldview of patriarchal hierarchy to a holistic worldview of relationships in mutual community.

Conclusion

For roughly fifteen centuries, our ancient and medieval ancestors intuitively held the natural world in some form of close relationship with humanity and God in their doctrinal and moral reflection. Then, for a variety of reasons, theology became intensely anthropocentric. Now, under pressure of the earth's intense distress, we are the generation poised to find the earth again in a wholly new ecological framework and rethink it as an integral part of the Christian tradition's vision and concern. Whatever our subdisciplines, we must develop religious thought and ethical action having a tangible and comprehensive ecological dimension. I am not suggesting that all we need is a renewed theology of creation, although that is indeed required. But the reality and well-being of the actual world needs to become the context, the overarching vision, within which all topics are approached, as well as a substantive partner in theological interpretation and a subject of ethical action.

There is hard work ahead. We need to appreciate all over again that the whole universe is a sacrament, vivified by the energy of the Creator Spirit present in all creation as its very animation. The Spirit effects the redemption of both languishing vines and broken-hearted merrymakers: that is, the Spirit's presence is for *all* species. We need to realize that the destruction of this vibrant, complex natural world is tantamount to sacrilege. And we need to fathom that the human species is embedded as an intrinsic, interdependent part of the magnificence of this universe, not as lords of the manor but kin in the community of life, charged with being sisters and brothers, friends and lovers, mothers and fathers, priests and prophets, cocreators and children of the earth that is God's good creation.

Recovering the cosmocentric power of the fuller Christian tradition puts us in line with our ancient and medieval forebears and fosters the intellectual and moral integrity of our discipline. Not doing so makes our scholarly reflection increasingly irrelevant and, worse, irresponsible to the future of this planet. On the brink of the third millennium, losing creation again is not an option. The quest to find creation, this generation's great intellectual religious adventure, is a matter of life or death.

Notes

1. Cited in Michael Dowd, *Earthspirit: A Handbook for Nurturing an Ecological Christianity* (Mystic, Conn.: Twenty-Third Publications, 1991), 95.

2. See Catherine Keller, "Women against Wasting the World: Notes on Eschatology and Ecology," in *Reweaving the World: The Emergence of Ecofeminism*, ed. Irene Diamond and Gloria Feman Orenstein (San Francisco: Sierra Club Books, 1990), 249.

3. For overviews of biblical evidence, see Richard Clifford, "The Bible and the Environment," in *Preserving the Creation: Environmental Theology and Ethics,* ed. Kevin W. Irwin and Edward D. Pellegrino (Washington, D.C.: Georgetown University Press, 1994), 1–26; and Vitor Westhelle, "Creation Motifs in Search for a Vital Space: A Latin American Perspective," in *Lift Every Voice: Constructing Christian Theologies from the Underside,* ed. Susan Brooks Thistlethwaite and Mary Potter Engel (New York: Harper and Row, 1990), 128–40.

4. For a review of patristic and medieval centuries, see N. Max Wildiers, *The Theologian and His Universe: Theology and Cosmology from the Middle Ages to the Present,* trans. Paul Dunphy (New York: Seabury Press, 1982), chaps. 1–3.

5. Hildegard of Bingen, *Scivias*, trans. Columba Hart and Jane Bishop (New York: Paulist Press, 1990), 94.

6. Ibid., 98; adapted for inclusivity.

7. Bonaventure, *The Mind's Journey to God,* trans. Lawrence S. Cunningham (Chicago: Franciscan Herald Press, 1979), chap. 1, no. 15.

8. Thomas Aquinas *Summa Theologiae* (New York: Benziger Bros., 1947) 1.47.1.

9. John Paul II, "Lessons of the Galileo Case," *Origins* 22, no. 22 (1 November 1992): 369–73; see Wildiers, *The Theologian and His Universe,* 130–48.

10. Pierre Teilhard de Chardin, *The Phenomenon of Man* (New York: Harper, 1959); *The Divine Milieu* (New York: Harper, 1960); *Hymn of the Universe* (New York: Harper and Row, 1965); see Wildiers, *The Theologian and His Universe,* 188–212.

11. John Calvin, *Institutes of the Christian Religion*, trans. John Allen (Philadelphia: Presbyterian Board of Christian Education, 1936), 1.5.64. Similar sentiments can be found in Martin Luther's *Lectures on Genesis, Chapters 1–5, being Luther's Works,* vol. 1, ed. Jaroslav Pelikan (Saint Louis: Concordia Pub., 1958); in the writings a century later of the Anglican divines; and of John Wesley in the century after that.

12. Francis Bacon, *The Masculine Birth of Time,* cited in Carolyn Merchant, *The Death of Nature: Women, Ecology, and the Scientific Revolution* (San Francisco: Harper and Row, 1980), 170; see Wildiers, *The Theologian and His Universe,* 148–53, 165–83.

13. See the analysis in Catherine Keller, "The Lost Fragrance: Protestantism and the Nature of What Matters," *Journal of the American Academy of Religion* 65, no. 2 (1997): 355–70; and Larry L. Rasmussen, *Earth Community, Earth Ethics* (Maryknoll, N.Y.: Orbis Books, 1996), 188–92.

14. I am indebted to John B. Cobb for this point.

15. World Council of Churches, *Signs of the Spirit: Official Report, Seventh Assembly, Canberra, Australia, 7–20 February 1991,* ed. Michael Kinnamon (Geneva: WCC Publications; Grand Rapids, Mich.: Eerdmans, 1991), 55.

16. John Paul II, "Peace with All Creation," *Origins* 19, no. 28 (14 December 1989): 465–68.

17. I note pioneering work in the field, such as John B. Cobb, *God and the World* (Philadelphia: Westminster Press, 1969); Rosemary Radford Ruether, *New Woman, New Earth* (New York: Seabury Press, 1975); and Thomas Berry, *The Dream of the Earth: Sexist Ideologies and Human Liberation* (San Francisco: Sierra Club Books, 1988); as well as works by contributing scholars, such as John Haught, *The Cosmic Adventure: Science, Religion, and the Quest for Purpose* (New York: Paulist Press, 1984), and *The Promise of Nature: Ecology and Cosmic Purpose* (New York: Paulist Press, 1993); Gordon Kaufman, *Theology for a Nuclear Age* (Philadelphia: Westminster Press, 1985); Jürgen Moltmann, *God in Creation: A New Theology of Creation and the Spirit of God* (San Francisco: Harper and Row, 1985); Sean McDonagh, *To Care for the Earth: A Call to a New Theology* (Santa Fe: Bear and Company, 1987); *Liberating Life: Contemporary Approaches to Ecological Theology,* ed. Charles Birch, William Eakin, and Jay B. McDaniel (Maryknoll, N.Y.: Orbis Books, 1990); James A. Nash, *Loving Nature: Ecological Integrity and Christian Responsibility* (Nashville: Abingdon Press, 1991); and Sallie McFague, *The Body of God: An Ecological Theology* (Minneapolis: Fortress Press, 1993).

18. John Paul II, "Peace with All Creation," 468.

19. Several key works that deal with scientific concepts in relation to theology are: Ian Barbour, *Religion in an Age of Science,* 2 vols. (San Francisco: Harper and Row, 1990–91); Arthur Peacocke, *Theology for a Scientific Age: Being and Becoming—Natural, Divine, and Human* (Minneapolis: Fortress Press, 1993); John Polkinghorne, *One World: The Interaction of Science and Theology* (Princeton: Princeton University Press, 1986); and the series edited by Robert J. Russell et al., *Physics, Philosophy, and Theology: A Common Quest for Understanding* (1988), *Quantum Cosmology and the Laws of Nature: Scientific Perspectives on Divine Action* (1993), etc. (Rome: Vatican Observatory Press; Berkeley: Center for Theology and the Natural Sciences).

20. Arthur Peacocke, "Theology and Science Today," in *Cosmos as Creation: Theology and Science in Consonance,* ed. Ted Peters (Nashville: Abingdon Press, 1989), 32.

21. Dante, *The Divine Comedy,* canto 33, line 14; trans. Dorothy Sayers and Barbara Reynolds (Harmondsworth, England: Penguin Books, 1962).

22. The term is Sallie McFague's; *The Body of God,* 110 and passim.

23. See Rasmussen, *Earth Community, Earth Ethics,* xii and passim.

24. E.g., *Ecotheology: Voices from South and North,* ed. David Hallman (Geneva: WCC Publications; Maryknoll, N.Y.: Orbis Books, 1994); and *Ecology and Poverty: Cry of the Earth, Cry of the Poor,* ed. Leonardo Boff and Virgil Elizondo (Maryknoll, N.Y.: Orbis Books, 1995).

25. Rosemary Radford Ruether, *New Woman, New Earth*; see also her *Gaia and God: An Ecofeminist Theology of Earth Healing* (San Francisco: HarperSanFrancisco, 1992); *Ecofeminism and the Sacred,* ed. Carol J. Adams (New York:

Continuum, 1993); and *Readings in Ecology and Feminist Theology,* ed. Mary Heather MacKinnon and Moni McIntyre (Kansas City: Sheed and Ward, 1995).

26. Delores Williams, "Sin, Nature, and Black Women's Bodies," in Adams, *Ecofeminism and the Sacred*, 24–29; see also Shamara Shantu Riley, "Ecology Is a Sistah's Issue Too," in MacKinnon and McIntyre, *Readings in Ecology and Feminist Theology,* 214–29.

27. Aruna Gnanadason, "Towards a Feminist Eco-Theology for India," in *A Reader in Feminist Theology,* ed. Prasanna Kumari (Madras, India: Gurukul Lutheran Theological College and Research Institute, 1993), 95–105.

Response to Elizabeth A. Johnson

GORDON D. KAUFMAN

Elizabeth Johnson has given us a very fine introduction to some of the problems with which today's rapidly growing ecological consciousness confronts Christian believers and theologians. In many respects our inherited Christian understandings of the human place in the natural order—especially as these have developed for the last several hundred years—have encouraged and supported human attempts thoroughly to dominate the rest of creation in the interests of our own human-centered purposes and desires. Through the development of the modern sciences, however, our knowledge of the cosmos as a whole, and of planet Earth and the many forms of life that have come to inhabit it, has increased enormously; and we can now see that our attempts to dominate the earth have brought about serious imbalances in the earth's ecological system, leading to extinction of countless species of life and threatening our own continuing existence. It is necessary now, therefore (she argues), that Christians move to transform certain of our faith-understandings, attitudes, and behaviors, so that we can live and work in ways much more supportive of the ecological web that has given birth to us and continues to sustain us, along with the many other forms of life. This clear call by Elizabeth Johnson for Christian repentance and for a transformation of many still-present Christian attitudes, ideas, and behaviors is surely the right place to begin an examination of Christianity and ecology.

There are many points in Johnson's essay that would be worth repeating and underlining, but I will confine myself to mentioning just three. First, she reminds us that Christian theological neglect of, even disdain for, the natural order is a largely modern phenomenon—that in the biblical materials and in the first fifteen hundred years of Christian history the natural world roundabout, understood as God's good creation, was much glorified and rejoiced in—and that there are, therefore, important resources in the Christian tradition for encouraging and developing ecologically appropriate attitudes and practices. Second, she points out, rightly, that in the last generation or so it has become apparent to many Christian believers and theologians that any continuing religious disparagement of the natural order in Christian beliefs and practices must be replaced by ecologically sensitive attitudes, understandings, and behaviors. There are now a good many Christian movements directed toward accomplishing this transformation. Third, she insists that the growing Christian attention to ecological issues does not in any way imply that traditional Christian moral concerns about such evils as poverty and disease, gross injustice, and other forms of human misery may be in any respect lessened.

The overall impression given by Johnson's discussion, it seems to me, is that although much in Christian thinking and practice in the modern era needs to be changed, there are in fact adequate resources in Christian traditions—especially if we move back far enough in history—to address the problems posed by our modern ecological consciousness. That is an important and (for Christians) an encouraging claim. In my view, however, there are some deeper problems that she has not taken up. I would like now to call attention to one such problem.

I want to suggest that the very ideas of God, and of humanity's relation to God, as these have been worked out over the millennia of Christian history, in fact tend to blur or even conceal our *embeddedness* in the natural order as we today have come to conceive it. The great religious struggle between Israel and Canaan was over the metaphysical importance of *natural power and process,* on the one hand, and *personal moral will,* on the other. When Yahweh won that struggle, it meant that the object of ultimate loyalty and devotion for humans in Judaism, Christianity, and Islam would be conceived largely in terms of a model rooted in our *moral and personal* experience, not in our sense of dependence upon and interconnection with the orders and processes of nature. For in these religious traditions it has been the symbol "God"—not "nature"—that has functioned as the ultimate point of reference in terms of which all human life, indeed all reality, is to be understood.

The model in terms of which this symbol, from the biblical texts on, has been constructed is basically anthropomorphic: God has been thought of as essentially an agent, an actor, one who is *doing things*. (This imagery and rhetoric is continued throughout Johnson's essay, though she clearly wants to downplay its impact and speaks even of a "cosmocentric" dimension of Christian faith.) Human existence, then, is to be oriented most fundamentally on this transworldly reality God, not on anything in the world, or indeed on the world as a whole—that is, not on the natural order. For us to orient ourselves and our lives on anything other than God would be idolatry—a turning away from the very source and ground of humanity's being and life, and a direct violation of God's will.

When, then, as in modernity/postmodernity, the context and ground of human life is increasingly thought of in evolutionary and ecological terms, *nature* becomes a direct rival of God for human attention and devotion. Thinking of the ultimate reality with which we humans have to do in largely *ecological* terms, that is, in terms of the interconnectedness and interdependent powers and processes of nature—instead of in such more traditionally religious terms as, for example, our "heavenly father" whose children we are, or the "Lord" of the universe whose loyal subjects we seek to be—leads to sharply different understandings of who or what we humans are and how we ought to live. It is really not, then, all that "strange," as Johnson suggests it is, that "after the Reformation neither Catholic nor Protestant theology continued to include the earth as a subject of interest" or that neither "had kept pace with scientific advance." A tension between modern science and Christian theology was implicit from the beginning. In these theological traditions the central symbol intended to focus all our human devotion and service, worship and reflection— God—was constructed largely in terms of a model drawn not from the natural order roundabout but rather from such distinctly *human* activities and experiences as choosing, setting purposes, willing, thinking, creating, speaking, making covenants, and the like. To the extent that modern science has persuaded us to take our experience of natural powers and processes as of central importance in orienting our lives and projects, we have been led inevitably to think of the world in which we live, and our human place within it, quite differently from what we had been taught by our principal Western religious traditions.

A great deal more could be said about this intrinsic tension between the symbol "God"—so largely constituted, as it has been, by essentially anthropomorphic images and ideas—and the concept of nature, understood today in basically ecological and evolutionary terms. But I hope my brief remarks have at least made it clear that there is a distinct and important problem here with which Christian faith and theology need to come to terms. It is not that there is no way to reconcile Christian ideas and faith with modern ecological thinking. To accomplish this, however (in my view), the basic *anthropomorphism* of most of our received concepts and images of God—a remaining vestige of the deeply rooted *anthropocentrism* of our Jewish, Christian, and Moslem traditions—needs to be deconstructed, so that God can be reimagined and reconceived in ways that will facilitate more directly our becoming oriented *religiously* in terms appropriate to today's ecological understandings of the human interconnectedness with the orders of nature.

As some of you are aware, I have suggested the idea of *serendipitous creativity* as a basic metaphor for thinking of God, in place of the personalistic and agential language so prominent in our traditions. I use the conception of "creativity" here—rather than the traditional idea of "God the creator"—because it presents the coming into being of the new, the novel, as an ongoing process or activity in the world, and does not call forth an image of a kind of "cosmic person" standing somehow beyond the world and working out "his" (I use the word advisedly) purposes in it. In my view, if we wish to continue using the word "God" today, we would do well to understand it as referring to this mysterious awe-inspiring creativity manifest in the evolutionary development of the cosmos and of life. In such activities as worship or prayer, of course, when we directly address the creativity at work in the world in adoration, hope, or thanksgiving—or on other occasions when we want to identify ourselves clearly with the long personalistic tradition from which our modern understandings of God emerged—we may find it helpful to employ personal metaphors. But we should not regard this sort of rhetoric, however appropriate and meaningful on such occasions, as adequately characterizing the reality we are addressing.

There is not space, and this is not the place, to elaborate this notion of serendipitous creativity and its implications. I will simply say in conclusion that understanding the ultimate reality with which we have to do—God—as the creative activity manifest throughout the universe will help orient us more effectively, in our ecologically ordered world, than the anthropomorphicly conceived divine person that has been the focus of so much Christian faith and thinking. According to this perspective, we humans today are being drawn beyond our present condition and order of life by creative impulses manifest in our historical context, within its setting in nature—creative impulses suggesting decisions and movements now required of us.

If we respond, in appropriately creative ways, to the historical and ecological forces impinging upon us on all sides, there is a possibility—though no certainty—that a niche for humankind, better fitted to the wider ecological order on Earth than our present niche, may be brought into being. However, if we fail to so respond, it seems likely that we humans may not survive much longer. Are we willing to commit ourselves to live and act in accord with the imperatives laid upon us by the ecological and historical situation in which we find ourselves, in the hope that our actions will be supported and enhanced by cosmic, serendipitously creative events?

A hope of this sort, grounded on the mystery of creativity manifest in the universe—though carrying much less assurance and specificity than our traditional anthropocentric expectations of the coming of God's kingdom—can help motivate us men and women to devote our lives to bringing about the more humane and ecologically rightly ordered world to which we all aspire. In my view it is this kind of hope, and faith, and commitment to which the evolutionary and historical trajectory that has brought us into being—an expression of the awe-inspiring creativity in the world, God—now calls us. In this way we can find again in fresh images those dimensions, of what Elizabeth Johnson called the "lost" meaning of "creation in the Christian tradition," that are most appropriate for faith in our time and our world.

An Ecological Christology: Does Christianity Have It?

SALLIE MCFAGUE

Ecological Christologies

Thirty years ago when Lynn White, in a now-famous essay, accused Christianity of being ecologically bankrupt, he revealed an ignorance of theological history.[1] To be sure, for the last few centuries Christianity's celebrated "turn to the self" has meant a neglect of nature and, as liberation theologians have pointed out, millions of oppressed human beings as well. But it was not always so. From the earliest days of Christianity, the cosmological context was a major interpretive category along with the psychological and the political.[2]

The renewal of creation, the salvation of the individual, and the liberation of the people were all seen as necessary components of the work of God in Christ. The cosmological context—the assertion that the Redeemer is the Creator—is deeply rooted in Hebrew faith and surfaces in John's incarnational Christology, Paul's cosmic Christ, Irenaeus's notion of Christ recapitulating all of creation, as well as in sacramental motifs in Augustine and Thomas. Christianity is not entirely anthropocentric, although it was substantially so from the Enlightenment until recently and therein lies the justification for White's indictment.

Since Christology is the heart of Christianity, we must ask whether Christology can be ecological. This question cannot be answered simply by citing Christianity's cosmological roots. What creation meant in the first or third or twelfth century cannot serve as an answer to the question, how can Christians act responsibly toward nature in the twenty-first century?

Jesus' enigmatic question to Peter, "Who do you say that I am?" must be answered differently in every age. Is there an ecological answer? This is not a frivolous question; in fact, it is one of the central questions that recent theologians have tried to answer, and it is one that cannot be avoided. To be a Christian is to deal with Jesus; Jesus is, for Christians, Emmanuel, God with us. Hence, current issues of oppression needing God's saving grace provide the contexts for christological interpretation. In our time ecology is one such important context. Christologies written since White's essay appeared thirty years ago acknowledge this context and reveal a wealth of ecological potential.

A typology of some of these Christologies includes the following motifs: prophetic, wisdom, sacramental, eschatological, process, and liberation. While a theologian's Christology might embrace several motifs, a typology can only lift up the ecological assets and limitations of each. Thus, like all typologies, it will be artificial, but it can at least suggest the rich ecological potential of contemporary Christologies.

Prophetic or covenantal Christologies focus on Jesus' ministry to the oppressed—his inheritance of Hebraic concerns with justice, evident in his parables overturning conventional hierarchies, in his healings to the suffering, and in his practice of eating with outcasts. Jesus is paradigmatic of a way of life that ends on the cross, since the rights of the oppressed will usually be opposed by the powerful. For the disciples who practice this way, life will be cruciform, characterized by justice for the oppressed and limitations on the oppressor.

This Christology is easily extended to nature: nature is the "new poor"; nature deserves justice; other life-forms have rights that must be acknowledged; human beings are in a covenantal relationship with God to protect nature even as they should care for other human beings.[3] The ecological value of prophetic Christologies is the insistence that Jesus' message of justice is relevant to nature: other life-forms are not means to our ends, but like human subjects, have intrinsic worth and should be considered as deserving ethical consideration. Prophetic Christologies provide a firm base for extending *rights* to other life-forms, countering the supposition that sentimental attachment to nature is sufficient. A limitation of this position is its possible deformation toward individualism; for example, emphasis on the rights of particular animals rather than focus on the well-being of an entire ecosystem.

Wisdom Christologies understand Jesus as the embodiment of *Sophia,* God's creative and ordering energy in both the human and natural worlds.[4] Untying Jesus from the Logos tradition, which feminists see as both patriarchal and anthropocentric, and attaching him to the Hebraic Wisdom trajectory allows his work to include nature. As Elizabeth Johnson writes, "As the embodiment of *Sophia* who is fashioner of all that exists, Jesus' redeeming care extends to the flourishing of all creatures and the whole earth itself."[5] A form of incarnationalism, Wisdom Christologies understand the Divine in Jesus (and in his followers) in a natural, everyday way—wherever justice, care, and respect for others, including nature, occur—rather than focusing on "once-for-all sacred deeds in history."[6] The ecological value of this Christology is its turn to the earth, a turn that contemporary Christians profoundly need. The rich textual resources of the Hebrew scriptures for reinterpreting Jesus' work and person in Wisdom rather than Logos imagery has ecological potential for both liturgy and ethics. The considerable assets of this tradition in supporting everyday life point to a limitation: it says little about the cross, a feature of Christology which many of us would rather avoid; but dealing with it, I believe, is integral to Christian faith.

Sacramental Christologies are characterized by divine immanentalism, the incarnation of God in Jesus (and often in the world at large).[7] Whether the form of divine incarnation is the Logos, Wisdom, or the Spirit, the direction of these Christologies is toward immanentalism, overcoming the traditional emphasis in Christianity on divine transcendence—often God-world dualism. These Christologies can see Jesus as the explicit expression of what is implicit everywhere: divine presence. As Gerard Manley Hopkins expresses the sacramental perspective, "The world is charged with the grandeur of God."[8] While a narrow incarnational Christology—Jesus alone as embodying divine presence—is anthropocentric, a wider incarnational interpretation is very hospitable to ecological concerns: God is in nature as well as in Jesus. And all of nature, human beings included, is knit together organically. This wider view was the basis for the oldest Christian affirmation of nature, seen preeminently in Augustine and his love of "light and melody and fragrance and food and embrace" as ways to God.[9]

Incarnationalism affirms the flesh, the body, and hence, by implication, nature. But as we are all well aware, Christianity's extraordinary verbal affirmation of the body—bread and wine as the body and
blood of Christ, the resurrection of the body, the church as the body of
Christ—has not resulted in appreciation for bodies (especially the
female body) or, until recently, great concern for starving, tortured, or
raped human bodies. And it certainly has not resulted in a love of
nature. Hence, while sacramental Christologies find God in nature,
do they respect nature itself? Do they pay attention to the other or do
they use it, however subtly, as a way to God?

The three other types of Christology—eschatological, process, and
liberation—can be dealt with more briefly, for in significant ways
they overlap with prophetic, Wisdom, and sacramental Christologies.
However, each of them offers one or more significant notes for an
ecological Christology.

Eschatological Christologies, such as those of Jürgen Moltmann
and Catherine Keller, underscore renewal and hope: God's Spirit
working in Christ re-creates, transforms, the entire universe toward
reconciliation and peace. As the firstborn of the new creation, the
resurrected Christ symbolizes the power of life over death. Nothing,
no scrap of creation, will be excluded from this new life: "the body of
Christ is the whole cosmos."[10] Eschatological Christologies speak to
one of the most difficult issues in ecological praxis: despair. The slow
unraveling of the earth's living networks permits human beings to be
in a state of denial concerning the seriousness of the deterioration.
Those who wake up to reality often experience hopelessness: Can
anything be done? The eschatological images of a resurrected
creation speak to this despair.

Process Christologies also provide ecological motifs; specifically,
those of nature's intrinsic worth and its interrelationship and interdependence.[11] Similar in some respects to sacramental Christologies
in their stress on organic unity, process Christologies differentiate the
subjects in this unified body more adequately. Process ontology, in
which everything, from an atom to God, is both subject and object,
understands the intrinsic worth of all beings, including those in the
natural world. The process view of the one and the many, of unity and
differentiation, is close to the ecological view: unity is characterized
by radical individuation in networks of profound interrelationship

and interdependence. Process thinking offers a contemporary way to speak of the subjecthood or intrinsic worth of *all* life-forms.

Finally, a word about the contributions to an ecological Christology from the very broad and diverse category called liberation theologies.[12] To a signficant degree, most liberation Christologies fall under the prophetic type, focusing as they do on Jesus' ministry to the oppressed and his death as a consequence of this solidarity. Initially, most liberation Christologies were not cosmological; in fact, they were militantly political, concerned with the liberation of oppressed people and often only of people with a particular oppression. But increasingly, liberation theologies have recognized the intrinsic connections between human oppression and nature's oppression.

Leonardo Boff speaks of social ecology as "the study [of] social systems in interaction with ecosystems," acknowledging the way human well-being and nature's well-being are mutually dependent.[13] Or, Chung Hyun Kyung invokes the Spirit through the spirits of all the oppressed, from the murdered "spirit of the Amazon rainforest" to the spirits of exploited women and indigenous peoples, victims of the Holocaust and of Hiroshima, as well as Hagar, Jephthah's daughter, Malcolm X, Oscar Romero, and all other life-forms, human and non-human, that, like "the Liberator, our brother Jesus," have been tortured and killed for greed and through hate.[14] Thus, recent liberation theologies make an essential contribution to an ecological Christology: the intrinsic connection between all forms of oppression, and especially between that of poor people and degraded nature.

From our brief overview of recent Christologies, we can appreciate the ecological potential they offer. Specifically, the following points emerge as needed dimensions of an ecological Christology: the insistence on justice to the oppressed, including nature, and the realization that solidarity with the oppressed will result in cruciform living for the affluent; the need to turn to the earth, respecting it and caring for it in local, ordinary, mundane ways; the recognition that God is with us, embodied not only in Jesus of Nazareth but in all of nature, thus uniting all creation and sanctifying bodily life; the promise of a renewed creation through the hope of the resurrection, a promise that includes the entire cosmos and speaks to our ecological despair; the appreciation of the intrinsic worth of all life-forms, not just of human beings; and, finally, acknowledgment that human salvation or well-being and nature's health are intrinsically connected.

An Ecological Christology: Prophetic and Sacramental Praxis

Can these various motifs be united into an ecological Christology? I am sure there are many ways they might be; I will attempt just one. Needless to say, my attempt will be from my own context as a white, North American, middle-class feminist. Its limitations and partiality will be obvious.

Before turning to this Christology, we need to ask about the urgency of answering the christological question from an ecological perspective. Edward Schillebeeckx helps us with this issue when he suggests that the way to pose the christological question today is not "Who do you say that I am?" but "How have you been committed to the reign of God?"[15] Most contemporary Christians do not know what it means to be committed to the reign of God when it comes to nature. Nature has not been a central Christian concern for several hundred years. In order to have a Christian praxis toward nature—a nature-oriented commitment to the reign of God—we will need to look at Jesus, at Christology, but also at contemporary knowledges about nature. If Christian nature praxis is the goal of the christological question, then we need guidance from both Christology and ecological science. The rest of this essay will be concerned with these matters: we will see how Christology might guide our praxis and we will then turn to "a hole in the center," our lack of acquaintance with how nature works.

My attempt at an ecological Christology can be summarized by the phrase "God with us." I will try to unpack this phrase in several stages of increasing detail. An ecological Christology means that *God* is with us—we are dealing with the power and love of the universe; it means that God is *with* us—on our side, desiring justice and health and fulfillment for us; it means that God is with *us*—all of us, all people and all other life-forms, but especially those who do not have justice, health, or fulfillment. This ecological Christology would then be very "high" and very "low": it will acknowledge that in Jesus we see the presence of God, and that God's presence is embodied, paradigmatically, in a mere human being. However, such a Christology, centered as it is on God's presence with all of us, is not Jesusolatry: Jesus is the finger pointing to the moon.

An ecological Christology summarized by the phrase "God with us" focuses on the ministry of Jesus of Nazareth for the *content* of our praxis toward nature and on the incarnation and resurrection for its *range* and *promise*. What is a Christian nature praxis? How inclusive is it? Can we practice it without despair?

Prophetic Christology

The first question is answered in the prophetic ministry of Jesus and his death on a cross. While there is little in Jesus' teachings about nature (and it is futile to rummage about with fig trees and hens, trying to make Jesus into a nature-lover), his ministry to the oppressed can be extended to nature. His parables, which overturn conventional human hierarchies, should include the hierarchy of humans over nature; his healing stories can be extended to the deteriorating ecosystems of our planet; his practice of eating with outcasts is pertinent to the extinction of species and loss of habitats due to human over-development and consumption.

Who are the oppressed to whom Jesus' message of hope and renewal is preached? The answer has changed over the centuries. The circle has widened to include among the poor those suffering because of their gender, race, sexual orientation, or physical and mental challenges. The inclusion of nature as the "new poor" may seem sentimental or even ludicrous from an anthropocentric perspective, but it does not seem so from either a theocentric or a cosmocentric point of view. If the Redeemer is the Creator, then surely God cares also for the other 99 percent of creation, not just for the 1 percent (actually, less than 1 percent) that humans constitute.

Hence, I am suggesting that all the language about justice, rights, care, and concern that Christians believe the human neighbor, especially the oppressed neighbor, deserves should be extended to the natural world. What this will mean in practice is complex, varied, and costly, just as love for the needy neighbor is. But the *principle* that Jesus' ministry is focused on God's oppressed creatures must, in our day, include the deteriorating planet.

To say that Jesus' ministry to the oppressed should be extended to nature suggests a similar extension of the Great Commandments. We are told to love God and neighbor as "subjects," as valuable in and for themselves, as ends rather than means, but we are given no instructions concerning nature. Should we not extend that model—the

model of loving others as having intrinsic worth and hence deserving
of justice and care—to the natural world?

Jesus' ministry to the oppressed resulted in his death on a cross.
Solidarity with the oppressed is likely to end this way, as many of his
loyal disciples over the centuries have discovered. This suggests a
theology of the cross: reality has a cruciform shape. Jesus did not
invent the idea that from death comes new life. We see it in nature; for
instance, in the "nurse" logs on the ground in old-growth forests
which, in their decaying state, provide warmth and nutrients for new
saplings. Some must give that others might live. Raising the cruciform shape of reality as the central principle for human living is
Jesus' contribution.

But it is not easy to live this way, especially for the well-to-do.
Cruciform living has particular relevance to today's affluent Christians, whether of the first or third worlds, in regard to their praxis
toward nature. Our consumer culture defines the "abundant life" as
one in which "natural resources" are sacrificed for human profit and
pleasure and "human resources" are the employees who will work for
the lowest wages. Both nature and poor people are means to the end
of consumerism. The World Council of Churches in several of its recent publications has stated that it is crucial to redefine the abundant
life in terms that recognize the limits of our planet, that encourage
sustainable communities, that embrace a philosophy of "enough-
ness."[16] For affluent Christians this should mean a different understanding of abundance, one which embraces the contradiction of the
cross: giving up one's life to find it, limitation and diminishment,
sharing and giving—indeed, sacrifice. This sacrifice is summed up in
Charles Birch's pithy statement: "The rich must live more simply that
the poor may simply live."[17]

Sacramental Christology

"God with us" also suggests the range and promise of divine concern.
In the discussion of prophetic Christology we considered what it
meant ecologically to say God with us; now we consider the inclusivity of justice for and care of nature, as well as the possibility of
such inclusion. In sacramental Christology we move from the anthropological to the metaphysical: from the human Jesus and his distinc-

tive ministry and death to issues of divine scope and power. This metaphysical move is necessary because Christology is not just about a prophet, even a unique prophet, but about *God*. This move avoids Jesusolatry and anti-Judaism. It means salvation is not just for me or for humans, but for all of creation; it gives hope for the well-being of all. In other words, sacramental Christology underscores that it is God who we are dealing with (and who is dealing with us) and that this God cares for the entire creation. And since God is with us, we need not despair of the outcome. We are, then, concerned here with the incarnation and the resurrection, with the embodiment of God in creation as well as the hope of a new creation.

The incarnation is a crucial feature of an ecological Christology for two reasons: inclusion and embodiment. By bringing God into the realm of the body, of matter, nature is included within the divine reach. This inclusion, however, is possible only if incarnation is understood in a broad, not a narrow, fashion; that is, if Jesus as the incarnate Logos, Wisdom, or Spirit of God is paradigmatic of what is evident everywhere else as well.[18] In other words, nature, not just Jesus, is the sacrament of God; the entire creation is *imago Dei,* as Thomas Aquinas suggests when he claims that the whole panorama of creation is needed to reflect the divine glory.[19] The scope of God's power and love is cosmological. It must include every scrap of creation: atoms and newts, black holes and elephants, giant redwoods and dinosaurs. Otherwise, God would not be God. The logic of divinity pushes to the limits; a God of history is a lesser God than the God of nature, since human history is embraced within nature. Christianity has expressed this inclusivity with the phrase "the cosmic Christ."

In addition to inclusivity, incarnational Christology underscores embodiment. The tradition has expressed this in John's phrase "the Word became flesh." But often, Logos Christologies are narrow, validating only Jesus' flesh. Recent Spirit and Wisdom Christologies widen the range: both can include other life-forms—the Spirit of God can dwell in spirits other than human ones, and Wisdom makes her home in creation.[20] Incarnational Christology valorizes matter; moreover, it focuses the justice and care of the prophetic dimension of Christology on physical needs and well-being.

Incarnational Christology means that salvation is neither solely human nor spiritual. It must be for the entire creation, and it must address what makes different creatures and ecosystems flourish.

Incarnational Christology says that God wants all of nature, human beings and all other entities, to enjoy well-being in body and spirit. Incarnational Christology, then, expands the ministry and death of Jesus, the model for Christians of "God with us," to envelop the entire universe. The metaphysical dimension of Christology is its big bang, exploding that gram of matter to the limits of the universe.

Sacramental Christology adds one more crucial note to an ecological Christology: hope. There are few contemporary issues that engender more despair than ecological deterioration: climate change, the extinction of species and habitats, clear-cutting of old-growth forests, the pollution of streams and lakes—the problems are overwhelming, seemingly infinite, and deeply saddening. To be sure, many people deny that there is ecological decay because they fear the costly personal and commercial changes that are necessary to reverse it. But others, even those who feel ready to live in a cruciform way so that other people and creatures can survive, feel despair over the immensity and complexity of environmental issues. Needless to say, the resurrection will not solve our ecological crisis; it will not tell us what to do with regard to either small or large problems.

But it can give us hope. Whatever else the resurrection might mean, it certainly symbolizes the triumph of life over death. As Dante knew a long time ago when he wrote *The Divine Comedy,* Christianity is not a tragic vision. The resurrection claims, as a woman in labor knows, that new life is hard. It is usually preceded by diminishment and pain; it sometimes involves death. But it is a sign of hope. Christians see the resurrection of Christ as the first day of the new creation. His resurrection is emblematic of the power of God on the side of life and its fulfillment. We are not alone as we struggle for the planet's well-being: God is on our side.

In summary, an ecological Christology, characterized by the prophetic and the sacramental, claims that "God is with us." This Christology looks Godward through Jesus: Jesus is the model for Christians of what "God with us" means. God is with us in Jesus' particular ministry of justice and care as well as in his death, which gives us a pattern for cruciform living. God is also with us through inclusive divine embodiment, valorizing physical well-being as well as divine victory over the powers of death and despair. Both of these dimensions—the prophetic and the sacramental—are necessary in an ecological Christology. The one tells us how to live with nature; the other informs us that all of nature and nature's renewal is within divine love and power.[21] Together, they suggest an ecological Christology summarized by "God with us." The focus of this Christology is not on Jesus except as the lens through whom we see God. Hope for our world lies not only in what Jesus tells us to do, but also, and more deeply, in Christian belief that God is with us as we attempt to do it.

A Hole in the Center: Is Christology Enough?

For the past several hundred years, Christians have not had a practice of loving nature; we have not practiced justice toward nature, nor cared for it. We have lacked a well-informed, respectful, unsentimental concern for nature similar to that which we have tried to develop toward other human beings. There is a hole in the center of Christianity's environmental ethic, and it is not a theological or christological hole. It is a hole created by centuries of indifference, ignorance, and destruction of nature. Christians need to become reacquainted with nature at all levels: local, regional, planetary. We need to learn about the natural world by taking care of houseplants; working to create city parks; fighting environmental racism; and informing ourselves about climate change, soil degradation, deforestation, and sustainability.

The task now is to embody in praxis the ecological Christologies that have been developing over the last several decades. Further refining Christology is less critical than putting Christology into practice. The problem is not that we need to know more Christology; rather, we need to know more about nature and how to live out these Christologies in relation to nature.

The benchmark draft of the Earth Charter, which is presently being hammered out as nature's "civil rights," makes this point repeatedly in its list of principles: Respect Earth and all life; Care for Earth, protecting and restoring it; Live sustainably; Share equitably between rich and poor, and so on.[22] In order to follow these principles, we must know what helps different life-forms flourish, how the health of human beings and nature's health are interrelated, what sustainability involves in different bioregions, how economics interfaces with ecology, what limits and reductions are required of wealthy individuals and nations so that poorer ones can have a fair share. In other words,

Christians need to become "ecologically literate" in order to embody an ecological Christology appropriately and justly.

Ecological literacy means learning how our planet works. "Ecology," or words about the *oikos,* the house called Earth, is the study of how living things are related to one another and to their environment. This study results in some "house rules," a few of which are so essential that they ought to be stuck on everyone's refrigerator.

The first and most essential rule is "There is no free lunch," or, more eloquently, the second law of thermodynamics. This law says that whenever anything changes (moves, heats up, cools down), it uses energy and this energy dissipates in quality, though the quantity remains the same. For instance, when wood is burned to cook meals or heat homes, it dissipates into the atmosphere as carbon dioxide. This gas is a less usable form of energy than wood; it cannot be recycled; and in order for human beings to have the benefit of this energy, something must pay for it—in this case, trees.

The implications of the second law are self-evident: in order for the elites of the world to have the abundant life, consumer-style, which depends on burning vast amounts of fossil fuels, nature must pay, and it pays dearly. As one commentator puts it, "The device by which an organism maintains itself at a fairly high level of orderliness really consists in continually sucking orderliness from its environment."[23] If that "organism" is over five billion human beings, most of whom yearn for a high-energy-use life-style, the house rule becomes alarmingly important: No free lunch.

Nature is not the only one that pays; the poor also do. Since energy resources on the planet are limited, those with power will be able to steer a disproportionate percentage of the resources their own way. Thus, nature and the poor will tend to suffer at similar rates. If we want a barometer of how nature and the poor are faring on our planet, we should look at the representative human being of the twenty-first century: a poor, third world woman of color who lives at the juncture of human poverty and nature's poverty, often reduced to gathering the few remaining sticks of wood to cook her family's meal. The elites of the world mask both ecological and social injustice, for they (we) have the power to suck large amounts of energy out of nature as well as deprive poorer human beings of their fair share of energy.

The second law of thermodynamics, then, is an illustration of one necessary bit of knowledge Christians need in order to put an ecological Christology into practice. It tells us that we live on a planet with finite energy sources; if we use these finite resources in non-sustainable ways, we will destroy nature as well as deal unjustly with other human beings. The second law raises ecological, economic, and justice issues: Who benefits? Who pays?

These issues can be illustrated using the example of climate change—a hot topic in every sense of the word. Ecological and economic knowledge, the consumer life-style, corporate profits, the degradation of nature, injustice to poor people: all come together in this complex, highly contentious, and potentially devastating problem. In order to respond justly and with care to the changing climate, and to understand the full reality of the problem, Christians need to study the 1995 Report of the Intergovernmental Panel on Climate Change. In the report, twenty-five hundred of the world's top weather experts state that human influence on the world's warming trend is now discernible, that temperatures will rise significantly over the next century, and that the effects, especially on third world and low-lying countries, will be devastating.[24]

Big business and others who do not want to control rampant consumerism question the report, claiming that "some scientists" disagree. Yet, the IPCC report was passed by the twenty-five hundred scientists with no dissenting or minority report. And, the findings of the IPCC are based on greater scientific certitude than were the Montreal Protocols, which the world's nations adopted in order to reduce ozone depletion. While scientific predictions of a matter as complex as weather can never be absolute, the "precautionary principle" advises us, as it did with the ozone issue, to act now. Climate change challenges the fossil fuel industry, as well as America's love affair with the car. Hence, denial and resistance are high.

The climate change case calls Christology into immediate practice. For affluent Christians, it demands a different view of the abundant life, one that includes cruciform living, the practice of restraint, diminishment, the death of unlimited desire, and control of ecological selfishness.[25] Ecological Christology defines sin as the refusal to share the necessities of life with others, both other humans and other life-forms. Sin is insatiable greed, wanting to have it all. Acting justly toward nature and other human beings demands sacrifices from Christian elites. Sustainable living involves acceptance of finite limits, such as how we drive our cars, emissions controls, and carbon taxes on industry. It includes "free trade," the policies of the World Bank, and stock market investments, as they affect the natural world and poor people. When we see where Christology, economics, and ecology intersect on an issue such as climate change, the need for different practices at personal, professional, national, and global levels becomes apparent.

The incarnate Christ joins the prophetic Jesus in underscoring this point. The God who is with *all* of creation, especially the poor, has a word of judgment about climate change, unlike President Clinton's painless policy, which will "create a wealth of new opportunities for entrepreneurs. . . ."[26] As an editorial in the *New York Times* summed it up, "innovation, incentives and the free market can get the job done without serious economic turmoil."[27] An incarnational Christology takes a dimmer view: too little and too late for a country with 5 percent of the world's population, 22 percent of its wealth, and 25 percent of its emissions. The impact on other people, especially third world populations, and on nature itself is not considered by Clinton's statement or the *Times*'s editorial. An incarnational Christology announces divine concern as planet-wide and judges harshly those who have contributed most to its present deterioration. Christians need to respond from a christological position that will indeed be painful to practice.

Finally, Christology also provides a word of hope in dismal times. Christians believe not only in the prophetic and incarnate God, but also in divine renewal, in the possibility of a new creation. Belief in the resurrection helps Christians overcome denial and despair on an issue such as climate change. Denial comes not only from ecological selfishness, but also from ignorance over what to do and feelings of hopelessness about results. Becoming ecologically literate overcomes ignorance, but not despair. How can we keep from burning out on an issue such as climate change, when the government, Wall Street, and consumer-oriented citizens want to do as little as possible?

Ezekiel's valley of the dry bones, one of scriptures's most haunting and lovely resurrection texts, makes a suggestion. When God leads Ezekiel to the valley and asks him, "Mortal, can these bones live?" Ezekiel answers (with, one imagines, a bit of despair), "O Lord God, you know." God then undertakes a second creation story, forming sinews, flesh, and skin onto dry bones, bringing life out of death, but God does not do it alone, as in the first creation story. Now God has two helpers: a human being and nature. Ezekiel is the mediator of God's word, told by God to prophesy to the bones, which he does and they come together, bone to bone, forming a whole being. The body, however, is still dead—there is no breath in it. So God calls on a second helper, nature, the "four winds," to supply the breath. Then the new beings become alive and stand up. The power of life can override the reality of death with the help of God's partners, human beings and nature itself. The passage says that with God all things are possible, even the reconstitution of dry bones.

In my mind's eye I see huge mounds of elephant bones, remnants of the ivory trade; the spindly remains of an old-growth forest after a clear-cutting; and the visible skeleton of a starving child. Can they also live? Those who trust in the God of creation and re-creation, the God of the resurrection, answer, Yes—even these dry bones can live. But, remembering the cruciform reality of Christian life, we must add, only if we, as partners of God, turn from ecological selfishness and live a *different* abundant life.

Notes

1. Lynn White, Jr., "The Historical Roots of Our Ecologic Crisis," *Science* 155 (10 March 1967): 1203–7.

2. For a brief treatment of these categories, see George S. Hendry, *Theology of Nature* (Philadelphia: Westminster Press, 1980), chap. 1.

3. Christologies with prophetic motifs include those of Rosemary Radford Ruether, H. Paul Santmire, James A. Nash, and Larry L. Rasmussen.

4. Outstanding work on Wisdom Christologies has been done by Elisabeth Schüssler Fiorenza and Elizabeth A. Johnson.

5. Elizabeth A. Johnson, "Wisdom Was Made Flesh and Pitched Her Tent among Us," in *Reconstructing the Christ Symbol,* ed. Mary Anne Stevens (New York: Paulist Press, 1993), 113.

6. Ibid., 97.

7. The wide range of sacramental Christologies includes the disparate ones of Pierre Teilhard de Chardin, Karl Rahner, Matthew Fox, Carter Heyward, Brian Swimme and Thomas Berry, and Eastern Orthodoxy.

8. *A Gerard Manley Hopkins Reader,* ed. John Hick (New York: Oxford University Press, 1953), 13.

9. Augustine, *The Confessions of St. Augustine,* bks. 1–10, trans. F. J. Sheed (New York: Sheed and Ward, 1942), 10.6.

10. Jürgen Moltmann, *The Way of Jesus Christ: Christology in Messianic Dimensions,* trans. Margaret Kohl (San Francisco: HarperCollins, 1990), 275. Elsewhere he writes: "Christology can only arrive at its completion at all in a cosmic Christology" (278).

11. Among others, see the Christologies of John Cobb, Jr., Rita Nakashima Brock, Jay McDaniel, and Charles Birch.

12. Even a partial listing of ecologically significant liberation Christologies is not possible. I will simply mention a few theologians whose work in this regard I have found helpful: Leonardo Boff, Dorothee Soelle, Chung Hyun Kyung, Delores Williams, Gustav Gutierrez, Ada Maria Isasi-Diaz, Mercy Amba Oduyoye.

13. Leonardo Boff, *Ecology and Liberation: A New Paradigm,* trans. John Cumming (Maryknoll, N.Y.: Orbis Books, 1995), 26.

14. Chung Hyun Kyung, "Welcome the Spirit; Hear Her Cries: The Holy Spirit, Creation, and the Culture of Life," *Christianity and Crisis* 51 (15 July 1991): 223.

15. As quoted by Elizabeth A. Johnson, *Consider Jesus: Waves of Renewal in Christology* (New York: Crossroad Press, 1991), 62.

16. See, for instance, *Sustainable Growth: A Contradiction in Terms?* (Geneva: Visser 't Hooft Endowment Fund, 1993).

17. In his address to the World Council of Churches' fifth assembly (Nairobi 1975), "Creation, Technology, and Human Survival," reprinted in *Ecumenical Review* 28 (January 1976): 70.

18. Sarah Coakley gives six definitions of incarnation; her first two definitions suggest incarnation as I am using the term. The first definition says that it is characteristic of God to reveal the divine self to humanity; the second definition, that in Jesus God takes a special initiative for the sake of humankind (*Christ without*

Absolutes: A Study of the Christology of Ernst Troeltsch [Oxford: Clarendon Press, 1988], 104). I would, however, modify Coakley's object of divine incarnation from humanity to include as well the natural world.

19. "But creatures cannot attain to any perfect likeness of God so long as they are confined to one species of creatures; because, since the cause exceeds the effect in a composite and manifold way. . . . Multiplicity, therefore, and variety, was needful in the creation, to the end that the perfect likeness of God might be found in things according to their measure" (as quoted in Arthur O. Lovejoy, *The Great Chain of Being: A Study of the History of an Idea* [Cambridge, Mass.: Harvard University Press, 1936], 76).

20. As Moltmann says, "Logos Christology is originally Wisdom Christology and is as such cosmic Christology" (*The Way of Jesus,* 282). For Spirit, see chap. 5 of my book, *The Body of God: An Ecological Theology* (Minneapolis: Fortress Press, 1993).

21. The prophetic and the sacramental as critical to environmental ethics are mentioned in different ways by both Rosemary Radford Ruether and Elizabeth A. Johnson. Ruether's treatment occurs as "The Covenantal Tradition" and "The Sacramental Tradition" in *Gaia and God: An Ecofeminist Theology of Earth Healing* (San Francisco: HarperSanFrancisco, 1992). Johnson compares covenantal and sacramental ecological ethics to orthodox Christologies in *Consider Jesus,* 70: the ascending, historical, salvation history, from below (covenantal) and the descending, metaphysical, incarnational, from above (sacramental).

22. "The Earth Charter: Benchmark Draft," *Earth Ethics* 8 (winter/spring 1997): 1–3. These principles carry through into Benchmark Draft II of the Earth Charter, April 1999.

23. As quoted in Ian Barbour, *Issues in Science and Religion* (Englewood Cliffs, N.J.: Prentice-Hall, 1966), 319.

24. IPCC, Second Assessment Report of the Intergovernmental Panel on Climate Change, Geneva, 1995.

25. For more information on climate change and a Christian analysis of it, see the new booklet from the World Council of Churches, "Climate Change and the Quest for Sustainable Societies" (Geneva: WCC, 1988). Fax: +41-22 791 0361; E-Mail: mpt@wcc-coe.org.

26. *New York Times,* 23 October 1997, sec. A14.

27. Ibid., sec. A20.

Response to Sallie McFague

KWOK PUI-LAN

I am very honored to have been invited to respond to Sallie McFague's paper on ecological Christology. In her distinguished career, she has contributed much to our understanding of the nature of religious language, the different models of God, and the constructive task of theology. Her books and articles on ecological theology have opened new avenues to help us address the ecological crises that are threatening to destroy the earth.

Sallie McFague points out in her paper that one's conceptualization of an ecological Christology is influenced by one's social location. She describes her context as that of a white, North American, middle-class feminist. Coming from a Chinese background, with practicing Buddhists, Taoists, and Christians in my extended family, my background is very different from hers. McFague observes that nature has not been a central Christian concern in the West for several hundred years. In the Asian religious traditions, nature is a major theme, and to live in harmony with nature has been the vision and ideal for philosophers, artists, and intellectuals, as well as for ordinary folks, for millennia. McFague's essay does not take into consideration the contributions of other religious resources of humankind. Coming from a multireligious and multiscriptural context, I would have to engage in deeper dialogue with friends and relatives who belong to other faith traditions. Sallie McFague's audiences are likely to be middle-class Christians in the postindustrial world. In the Asian contexts, there are many people, living in the preindustrial world, having to struggle daily to obtain safe water, food, and fuel. In the rapidly developing Pacific Rim, many countries have found that jumping on the bandwagon of the global capitalist market system has brought disasters to their natural environment. The burning of forests in Indonesia and the resulting smog in Southeast Asia in 1997 are just recent examples.

Although we come from divergent contexts, I would like to affirm two central and important thrusts McFague makes in her essay. First, she argues for a democratization of Christology. Instead of locating the presence of the Divine—God with us—in a historical figure, Jesus, alone, McFague urges us to think about God as immanent everywhere. "Nature, not just Jesus, is the sacrament of God," she says. Second, she challenges Christians living in the more affluent societies to practice cruciform living. She points out that United States has only 5 percent of the world's population but 22 percent of its wealth and 25 percent of its emissions.

To further our conversation I would like to focus my comments on the central part of her essay in which she articulates her own thoughts on prophetic and sacramental Christology. I was surprised that she began her discussion on prophetic Christology with the following remarks: "While there is little in Jesus' teachings about nature (and it is futile to rummage about with fig trees and hens, trying to make Jesus into a nature lover), his ministry to the oppressed can be extended to nature. His parables, which overturn conventional human hierarchies, should include the hierarchy of humans over nature." My reading of the New Testament and especially the Gospels is quite the opposite. Jesus himself uses nature in his parables and teachings a lot, and Paul speaks about the groaning and moaning of creation. Furthermore, coming from an East Asian cultural background, I do not think these natural images are just rhetorical devices or embellishments of Jesus' teaching because I think they are an inseparable part of his message.

I agree that we should not make Jesus into a nature lover, modeled after current New Age gurus. But if we take into consideration Jesus' peasant background and his status as a member of the colonized peoples in the Roman Empire, a different reading of the Gospels becomes possible. For example, in the Syro-Phoenician woman's story (Mark 7:24–30; Matt. 15:21–28), we have the perplexing saying of Jesus: "Let the children be fed first, for it is not fair to take children's food and throw it to the dogs." According to Gerd Theissen, Jesus' harsh remarks might have been based on the exploitation of the poor peasants in the rural territory by the urban class. The Syro-Phoenician woman was a Hellenized Phoenician who belonged to the Greek-speaking upper class. Jesus was a Galilean prophet belonging to Tyre.

Another example can be taken from Jesus' teaching in the synagogue at the beginning of his mission (Luke 4:16–19). Citing Isaiah, he describes his mission as preaching good news to the poor, recovering sight to the blind, as well as proclaiming the acceptable year of the Lord. This is based on the tradition described in Isaiah 49 that on the day of salvation, God will set free the prisoners and restore the land. Salvation of the land is an integral part of God's preferential option for the poor. From these examples, I do not see the need to extend Jesus' concern for the oppressed to the "new poor," that is, nature. This stills sounds like we take care of human beings first and then reach out to nature. For me, eco-justice is at the heart of Jesus' teaching from the beginning. In other words, social ecology cannot be separated from natural ecology.

While I applaud McFague's lifting up of the prophetic dimension of Christology, I am also concerned about one aspect of the teachings of the prophets. In the Hebrew tradition, the prophets admonished the rich for exploiting the poor. They also adamantly condemned other religious traditions of the Ancient Near East, some of which emphasized the natural circle and living closed to nature. C. S. Song, an Asian theologian from Taiwan, has warned that the prophets' negative attitudes toward other religions and cultures should not be overlooked. He has said that the prophets' failure to appreciate the so-called idols as symbols with religious meanings and their exclusive attitude toward other religions have contributed to Christianity's hostility toward people of other faiths. Today, we are living increasingly in a pluralistic society, whether in Asia or in the United States. A reassessment of the prophetic teachings is in order.

As one from a culture that speaks of the Tao as all embracing and self-generating, I share McFague's commitment to speak of Christology in a more sacramental and wholistic way. She points out three important motifs in her understanding of a sacramental Christology: inclusion, embodiment, and hope. I would like briefly to contrast these motifs with the Chinese visions of nature as discussed by Tu Weiming of Harvard University. Tu says the Chinese believe in the continuity of being. The organismic and spontaneously self-generating life process exhibits three basic motifs: continuity, wholeness, and dynamism. Continuity points to the interdependent chain of being, wholeness speaks of all-embracing, and dynamism evokes change, openness, and transformation. I would like to see a little more discussion of the interdependence and transformational aspects in McFague's discussion of sacramental Christology.

Sallie McFague observes that Christianity has expressed the inclusive understanding of incarnation with the phrase, "the cosmic Christ." This is a very controversial image in the Asian setting. On the one hand, some Asian theologians have used this image to speak about the immanence of God in all things. On the other, some have painfully reminded us that the image had grown in significance during the time when Christianity became intertwined with the power of the Roman state. The notion was used to sanction the political power of the emperors in the Roman Empire. Later on, the claim that Christ is the universal savior contributed to the ideology of colonization of peoples and land.

Toward the end of her paper McFague raises the important question, "Is Christology enough?" She says: "The problem is not that we need to know more Christology; rather, we need to know more about nature and how to live out these Christologies in relation to nature." I would certainly agree with her that our theological deliberations about Christ will not save the planet without an accompanying concrete praxis. Here, I differ from her slightly about how to articulate our hope. She says Christianity offers us hope because of the belief that God is with us. The resurrection symbolizes the triumph of life over death. For me, hope cannot be grounded solely in the belief that God is with us; it must also be grounded in the witness and testimony of human beings struggling against life-threatening forces.

At the Earth Summit in Rio de Janeiro in 1992, I had the privilege of listening to Rigoberto Menchu and other third world and indigenous peoples testifying to their long struggle to protect their land and forests. Poor women in many parts of the third world are putting food on the table for their families. They are gatherers and planters, vital agents in the water cycle and food chain. Our hope lies in their unceasing yearning for a better future and in the solidarity expressed by many people of different faiths who are helping to create a livable habitat for ourselves and our children. Indeed, without putting our ideas into practice, no discussion of Christology will ever be enough.

The Wounded Spirit as the Basis for
Hope in an Age of Radical Ecology

MARK I. WALLACE

I enter a swamp as a sacred place,—a *sanctum sanctorum*.[1]

In the beginning [the Spirit] hovers like a great mother bird
over her egg, to hatch the living order of the world out of
primordial chaos (Gen. 1:2).[2]

At the dawn of a new millennium I believe we are witnessing a profound sea change in the spiritual sensibilities of our culture. Many people now sense that we live in the "age of the Spirit," a time in which late-twentieth-century culture is undergoing a fundamental shift in its religious sensibilities. The medieval mystic Joachim of Fiore prophesied that humankind has lived through the periods of the Father and the Son and has now entered the age of the Spirit.[3] Karl Barth mused at the end of his life that the Holy Spirit might well be the best point of departure for a theology that is right for the present situation.[4] The theorist Ihab Hassan locates the topic of the "Holy Spirit" along with such themes as "play," "desire," and "immanence" as distinctly postmodern emphases that challenge an earlier modernist paradigm.[5] Practitioners of nature-based religion, from native peoples to modern neopagans, claim that a reverence for the Spirit in all life-forms, from people and animals to trees and watersheds, is the most promising response to the threat of global ecological collapse at the end of the second millennium.[6] There appears to be an emerging sentiment that the topic of pneumatology is the right focus for an ecumenical theology that speaks to the spiritual hopes and desires of our age.

And yet amidst this renewed religious longing for the Spirit is a deeply felt theological and cultural pessimism. The origins of this malaise are many, but I am convinced that one of the root causes of our corporate anxiety—if not the chief cause—is a profound disquiet about the prospects for future generations on this planet. Few observers of the contemporary situation doubt that we face today an ecological crisis of unimaginable proportions. Whether through slow and steady environmental degradation or the sudden exchange of nuclear weapons, the specter of ecocide haunts all human and non-human life that shares the resources of our planet home. Many of us have become numb to the various dimensions of the crisis: acid rain, ozone depletion, global warming, food-chain pesticides, soil erosion, mass consumption of nonrenewable fossil fuels, agricultural runoff, radioactive wastes, overpopulation, deforestation and desertification, carbon emissions, and loss of habitat.[7] In our time nature has been commodified and domesticated into a piece of real estate; it has become one more consumer item to be bought and sold in order to maximize profits. Once a source of terror and awe, nature no longer functions as wild and sacred space for the eruption of the sublime or the manifestation of transcendence. We have exchanged the power and mystery of the earth for the invisible hand of the marketplace and we are all the poorer for it.

These two phenomena—the yearning for the Spirit in religious life and the cultural anxiety over the environmental crisis—have led many theologians to a profound awareness of the deep interrelationship between God and the earth.[8] Could it be, then, that the most compelling response to the threat of ecocide lies in a recovery of the Holy Spirit, as God's power of life-giving breath (*rūah*), who indwells and sustains all life-forms?[9] In this essay my thesis is that hope for a renewed earth is best founded on belief in the Spirit as the divine force within the cosmos who continually works to sustain all forms of life. The Nicene (Constantinopolitan) Creed named the Spirit as "the Lord, the Giver of Life." The purpose of this paper is to contemporize this ancient appellation by reenvisioning the Holy Spirit as God's invigorating presence within the global society of all living beings.

This life-centered model of the Spirit expands the understanding of the Spirit beyond its *intratrinitarian* role (traditionally expressed as the bond of unity between the Father and the Son) to include the Spirit's *biocentric* role as the power of healing and renewal within all creation.

Ecological Pneumatology

My methodological approach here is rhetorical and exegetical. I do not attempt to prove the reality of the Spirit but rather to perform a hermeneutical retrieval of certain biblical tropes of the Spirit in a manner that is self-reflexively aware of my own commitments and passions. In this vein I seek to recover a variety of earth-centered images of the Spirit in the Bible for the purpose of addressing the environmental crisis we currently face, especially the urban environmental crisis. In conversation with current work in theology and environmental studies I offer a very particular theology of the Spirit that uses imaginative-symbolic discourses as well as argumentative-propositional analyses.

I believe the Spirit is best understood not as a metaphysical entity but as a healing life-force which engenders human flourishing as well as the welfare of the planet. I label this approach "ecological pneumatology" in order to distinguish it from metaphysically based notions of the Spirit characteristic of normative Western thought. I want this distinction to relocate understandings of the Spirit outside the philosophical question of being and squarely within a nature-based desire for the integrity and health of all life-forms—human and non-human. This model understands the Spirit not as divine intellect or the principle of consciousness but as a healing and subversive *life-form*—as water, light, dove, mother, fire, breath, and wind—on the basis of different biblical figurations of the Spirit in nature. Philosophers of consciousness (for example, G. W. F. Hegel) have bequeathed to contemporary theology a metaphysically burdened idea of the Spirit that has little purchase on the role of the Spirit in creation as the power of unity between all natural kinds. The wager of this paper is that a rhetorical understanding of the Spirit (beyond the categories of being) can provide resources for confronting the environmental violence that marks our time.

My plea for a postmetaphysical "green" pneumatology stems from a desire to preserve the complete freedom of God as Spirit apart from the limitations imposed on the concept of God by metaphysics. In the history of metaphysics (which includes such otherwise disparate thinkers as Aristotle, Hegel, and Wolfhart Pannenberg) God is understood as the supreme Being who is the source of unity among all other beings. In this model the otherness of God (including the otherness of God as Spirit) is colonized by a reductive philosophical analysis of God as a reality within, or coterminous with, Being itself. But in order to preserve divine freedom and novelty, I suggest that God as Spirit is not by any metaphysical necessity the Being of beings; rather, the Spirit, in free and indeterminate decision, desires to be the life-giving breath who animates and maintains the whole natural order. In this vein God as Spirit is best understood not as the Being of beings but, paradoxically, as *beyond* Being and still radically *immanent* to all beings within the natural order. Dialectically understood, therefore, God as Spirit should be figured as both *wholly other* to creation and *wholly enfleshed* within creation as the green love who nurtures and sustains all living things. The move away from defining God according to Being and toward imagining God as life-source is not an exchange of one metaphysical absolute ("Being") for another ("Life" or "Nature"). Rather, this move attempts to open up conceptual space for reenvisioning the freedom of God as Spirit to "blow where the Spirit wills" and not be determined by the question of Being within the domain of speculative philosophy.[10]

The idea of the Spirit has only existed in the borderlands of Western culture and the academy since Hegel's masterful but flawed attempts to subsume all philosophical inquiry under this rubric. Recent studies of the nature of Spirit (or spirit) have reawakened Hegel's concern, but both conventional usage of and residual philosophical prejudice against spirit language have prevented an overturning of the traditional biases.[11] "In Western theology and philosophy the very concept of 'spirit' has for the most part been fraught with difficulties, conveying something vapid and dualistic, implying a separation of and a hierarchy between the mental and the physical, the soul and the body, the human and the natural, the male and the female, the holy and the profane."[12] Discourse about spirit remains saddled with ethereal and pejorative connotations, conjuring images of ghosts, phantoms, and other incorporeal forces; of vaporous clouds and gaseous substances; of whatever is airy, immaterial, invisible, nonsubstantial, bloodless, bodiless, passionless, and unearthly.

A nature-based pneumatology challenges these conventional assumptions by figuring the Spirit as a living, embodied being who works for healthy communities within our shared planet home. An ecological pneumatology that is right for the current crisis will recapture the disorienting freedom of the Spirit as a wild and insurgent natural force in the healing of human persons' violence toward nature and one another. As the divine wind in Genesis, the dove in the Gospels, or the tongues of flame in Acts, the Spirit reveals herself in the biblical literatures as a life-form who labors to create, sustain, and renew humans and otherkind in solidarity with one another. An earth-based understanding of the Spirit will not domesticate the Spirit by locating her activity simply alongside nature; rather, nature itself in all its variety will be construed as the primary mode of being for the Spirit's work in the world. Now the earth's waters and winds and birds and fires will not be regarded only as *symbols* of the Spirit but rather as sharing in her very *being* as the Spirit is enfleshed and embodied through natural organisms and processes.

Here let me make some stylistic comments about writing the Spirit. Throughout this essay I capitalize "Spirit" in order to distinguish the divine personality (Holy Spirit or Spirit of the Lord) from other similar spirit-term significations (spirit of the times, public spirit, and so forth). Nevertheless, I suggest that the realities of Spirit and spirit should often be viewed as active on the same continuum, as when, for example, the Spirit of God empowers the embattled spirit of an urban community to resist the forces of ecocidal oppression (see note 24 below).[13] I also use the female pronoun for the Spirit in order rhetorically to realize aspects of the transgressive freedom that the Spirit promises, including the freedom to complicate and confuse her/his/its gender. This complication is not original to me: grammatically speaking, the term for Spirit in Hebrew is feminine (*rūah*), neuter in Greek (*pneuma*), and masculine in Latin (*spiritus*) and its derivative Romance languages.[14] Finally, I refer to divine, human, and non-human realities simultaneously as "life-forms" or "natural beings" in order to signal the value of construing all entities as interdependent members of a common biotic community.

The Green Face of God

In historic Christian thought, the work of the Holy Spirit has always been understood in terms of communion, mutuality, and the overcoming of divisions. The early Latin Fathers conceived of the Spirit in the bosom of the Trinity as the divine power that unites the Father and the Son in a bond of mutual love. Basil of Caesarea wrote that the Holy Spirit is the agent of inseparable union within the Trinity. The Spirit labors alongside the Creator and the Redeemer as the Perfector who strengthens and completes the divine work of salvation in the world.[15] Similarly, Augustine analyzed the role of the Spirit in terms of the *vinculum caritatis* or the *vinculum Trinitatis,* the communion that binds the other two members of the Godhead together in dynamic unity.[16] The Spirit enables the mutual indwelling of each divine person in the other. Moreover, as the bond of peace and love universal, the Spirit is not only the power of relation between the other members of the Trinity but also between God and the whole creation.

Later medieval iconographers make a similar point but in a pictorial medium. The doctrine of the Spirit as the *vinculum caritatis* is graphically set forth in the trinitarian miniatures of the medieval *Rothschild Canticles,* in which the Spirit is pictured as a giant encircling "dove" whose wings enfold the Father and Son and whose large talons and tail provide points of intersection for all three figures. In the *Canticles* the Spirit is represented less like the domesticated birds or pigeons of traditional church art and more like the wild raptors of the mountain wildernesses. The Spirit-Bird in the *Canticles* spins and twirls the other two members of the Godhead into amorous and novel combinations and permutations. As the *Canticles* progress, each life-form within the Trinity loses its separate identity in a blur of erotic passion and movement and color. As the Trinity twists and turns into surprising recombinations, the human Father and Son smile and twirl and dance around the aviary Spirit, symbolizing the union of each figure in the sacred bird—as well as the union of all life-forms in a common biotic order.[17] The Spirit-Bird of the *Canticles* insures the interrelationship of each divine person in a ludic celebration of perichoretic harmony.[18] As the Spirit exists perichoretically within the Godhead to foster communion between the divine persons, my proposal is that the Spirit also performs the role of the *vinculum caritatis* within nature in order to promote the well-being and fecundity of creation.

A vision of the Spirit as the *vinculum caritatis* elucidates the distinctive temporality of each member of the Godhead. The trinitarian actions of each divine person are embedded in particular temporal structures—present, past, and imperfect—that mediate God's passionate concern for the integrity of the earth and its biotic communities. In the Bible and church tradition, the first person of the Trinity is represented in the present tense as the God who actively nurtures and supports all members of the biosphere. The second member of the Godhead, the Son of God, is definitively figured in the aorist tense as having acted once-and-for-all to redeem the cosmic order from its bondage to sorrow through the death and resurrection of Jesus. Acting in the registry of the imperfect tense, the third member of the Trinity is portrayed as moving on the earth and sustaining all living things in solidarity with one another. Each member of the Trinity acts in its own time: the God who *loves* is the God who *loved* us to the point of death even as this selfsame God continually *is loving* toward us in the maintenance of the biosphere's health and vitality. God is the God of love whose love for all forms of life is both manifested in the cross and actively performed on a daily, ongoing basis as the Spirit invigorates the biota that constitute our common web of life.

From the perspective of biocentric trinitarian theology, nature is the enfleshment of God's sustaining love. As Trinity, God bodies forth divine compassion for all life-forms in the rhythms of the natural order. The divine Trinity's boundless passion for the integrity of all living things is revealed in God's preservation of the life-web that is our common biological inheritance. God as Trinity is set forth in the Father/Mother God's creation of the biosphere, the Son's reconciliation of all beings to himself, and the Spirit's gift of life to every member of the created order who relies on her beneficence for daily sustenance. As creator, God is manifested in the ebb and flow of the seasons whose plantings and harvests are a constant reminder of Earth's original blessings. As redeemer, God is revealed in the complex interactions of organisms and the earth in mutual sustenance— an economy of interdependence best symbolized by Jesus' reconciling work of the cross. And as sustainer, God shows Godself through breathing the breath of life into all members of the life-web, a living testimony to the Divine's compassion for all things.

God's presence in the living Christ through the Spirit's maintenance of the ecosphere is the basis for the greening of trinitarian

theology. The then and there incarnation of God in Jesus is recapitulated in the here and now embodiment of the Spirit in the world
which hearkens back to the originary Mother God's birthing of order
out of chaos. This trinitarian enfleshment of God in nature represents
a tripartite movement. The first move to an embodied doctrine of God
is signaled by the inaugural hymn of Genesis where the Creator Spirit
(*rūah*) breathes the world into existence and thereby enfleshes itself
in the creation and maintenance of the natural order. The embodiment
of the divine life in Jesus—an earth creature like Adam who is
fashioned from the soil—is the second move toward a nature-
centered model of the Godhead. And the perichoretic union of Jesus
in the Spirit—figured in the biblical tropes of water, dove, fire, and
wind—represents the third move toward a biophilic notion of God. It
is the move to embodiment—the procession of Godself into the biotic
realm that sustains all life—that is the basis for unity within the Godhead. In perichoresis, God as Trinity subsists in interpersonal unity
through incarnating Godself in all things that swim, creep, crawl, run,
fly, and grow upon the earth.

The understanding of the Spirit as a life-form intrinsically related
to nature emphasizes a generally neglected model of the Spirit in the
history of Western theology. In theory, the Spirit has always been defined as both the Spirit *of God* and the Spirit *of creation*. As the Spirit
of God, the Spirit is both the power of reciprocity between the first
two persons of the Trinity and also the interior power of redemption
within human beings. As the Spirit of creation, the Spirit has been
defined as the breath of God who indwells and sustains the cosmos. In
practice, however, the Spirit has been almost exclusively understood
as the Spirit of God; the stress has fallen on its roles as the source of
consubstantiality within the Godhead and the divine agent of human
salvation. The result is that the biocentric role of the Spirit as the
power of life-giving breath within creation, of nonhumans as well as
humans, has been consistently downplayed.[19]

This long-standing de-emphasis on the Spirit's ecological identity
is remarkable given the abundance of imagery about the Spirit drawn
from the natural world within the Bible. Indeed, the body of
symbolism that is arguably most central to the scriptural portraiture
of the Spirit is suffused with nature imagery. Consider the following
tropes for the Spirit within the Bible: the *vivifying breath* that animates all living things (Gen. 1:2, Ps. 104:29–30), the *healing wind*

that brings power and salvation to those it indwells (Judg. 6:34, John 3:6, Acts 2:1–4), the *living water* that quickens and refreshes all who drink from its eternal springs (John 4:14, 7:37–38), the *purgative fire* that alternately judges evildoers and ignites the prophetic mission of the early church (Acts 2:1–4, Matt. 3:11–12), and the *divine dove,* with an olive branch in its mouth, that brings peace and renewal to a broken and divided world (Gen. 8:11, Matt. 3:16, John 1:32).[20] These nature-based descriptions of the Spirit are the basis of my attempt to shift the theological focus back to the Spirit as the Spirit of creation. Such a focus neither denigrates nor ignores the normative understanding of the Spirit's other roles as the power of relationship between the Father and Son or as the agent of human sanctification within the history of salvation. Rather, this emphasis on the Spirit's cosmic identity as the divine breath who interanimates all other life-forms readdresses our attention to the Spirit's work in *all* realms of life—which includes, but is not limited to, the inner life of God and salvation history. Part of the burden of this essay, then, is to shift the weight of theological emphasis away from understanding the Spirit either *theocentrically* or *anthropocentrically* toward an explicitly *biocentric* model of the Spirit in nature.

The Wounded Spirit

To reconceive the Spirit as the enfleshment of God's sustaining power in the biosphere is to emphasize the coinherence of the Spirit and the natural world. Whether manifesting herself as a living, breathing organism like a dove, or an inanimate life-form, such as wind or fire, the Spirit indwells nature as its interanimating force in order to lead all creation into a peaceable relationship with itself. Spirit and Earth internally condition and permeate one another; both modes of being coinhere through and with one another without collapsing into un-differentiated sameness or equivalence. The reciprocal indwelling of Spirit and Earth is neither an absorption of the one into the other nor a confusion of the two. By the same token, this mutual indwelling is not an outward and transitory connection between the two realities but rather an internal and abiding union of the two in a common life together. Insofar as the Spirit abides in and with all living things, Spirit and Earth are *inseparable* and yet at the same time *distinguishable*. Spirit and Earth are internally indivisible because both modes of being are living realities with the common goal of sustaining other life-forms. But Spirit and Earth also possess their own distinctive identities insofar as the Spirit is the unseen power who vivifies and sustains all living things while the earth is the visible agent of the life that pulsates throughout creation.

Under the control of this dialectic, the earth is the body of the Spirit. Metaphorically speaking, God as Spirit corporealizes Godself through her interanimation of the biosphere. In breathing life into humankind and otherkind a fundamental transformation within Godself occurs: God is fully incarnated in the green fuse that drives all forms of life to their natural fruition in a carnival of praise to the Creator Spirit. As once God became human in the body of Jesus, so God continually enfleshes Godself in the embodied reality of life on Earth. Quintessentially, both Spirit and Earth are life-givers: the Spirit ensouls the earth with the quickening breath of divine life and the earth enfleshes the Spirit as it offers spiritual and physical sustenance to all living things. The Spirit inhabits the earth as its invisible and life-giving breath (*rūah*), and the earth (*gaia*) manifests the Spirit as its body, showing forth the Spirit's presence within that maintains all life-forms.[21]

This proposal for an ecological pneumatology of internal relatedness presents an extraordinary challenge to the traditional Aristotelian and early Christian doctrine of God as an unchangeable and self-subsistent being fundamentally unaffected by the creation God has spun into existence. One intriguing but troubling implication of ecological pneumatology, therefore, is that it places the divine life at risk in a manner that an extrinsic doctrine of the Spirit vis-à-vis the earth does not. The theological problem is that if Spirit and Earth mutually indwell one another, then it appears that God as Spirit is vulnerable to serious loss and trauma insofar as the earth is abused and despoiled.

In an earth-centered model of the Spirit, God is a thoroughgoing incarnational reality who decides in freedom, and not by any internal necessity, to indwell all things. But in making this decision the Spirit places herself at risk by virtue of her coinherence with a continually degraded biosphere. God, then, is so internally related to the universe that the specter of ecocide raises the risk of deicide: to wreak environmental havoc on the earth is to run the risk that we will do irreparable harm to the Love and Mystery we call God. The wager of this model is that while God and world are not identical to one another, their basic unity and common destiny raises the possibility that ongoing assaults against the earth's biotic communities may eventually result in permanent injury to the divine life itself.

Jürgen Moltmann's *The Crucified God* (and the wealth of similar books it spawned on the topic of divine suffering) argues that God in Jesus suffers the godforsaken death of the cross.[22] While the cross does not signify the "death of God," it does enact the death of Jesus as a terrifying event of loss and suffering within the inner life of God-self. The cross is not an instance of God dying but an event in Godself where the divine life takes into itself the death of the godless son of God crucified for the sins of the world. In the cross God now becomes radically discontinuous with Godself by taking up the crucified one.

> [W]hat happened on the cross was an event between God and God. It was a deep division in God himself, insofar as God abandoned God and contradicted himself, and at the same time a unity in God, insofar as God was at one with God and corresponded to himself. In that case one would have to put the formula in a paradoxical way: God died the death of the godless on the cross and yet did not die. God is dead and yet is not dead.[23]

In the cross God splits Godself by incorporating the godless death of Jesus into the inner life of the Godhead. In this rift caused by Jesus' death, God now undergoes a permanent and fundamental change by becoming a willing victim of death itself.

As Jesus' death on the cross brought death and loss into Godself, so the Spirit's suffering from persistent environmental trauma engenders chronic agony in the Godhead. From the perspective of ecological pneumatology, Moltmann's "crucified God" has a double valence: death enters the inner life of God through the cross of Jesus even as the prospect of ecological mass death enters the life of God through the Spirit's communion with a despoiled planet. We see, then, that the Spirit is Christ-like or cruciform because she suffers the same violent fate as did Jesus—but now a suffering not confined to the onetime event of the cross insofar as the Spirit experiences daily the continual degradation of the earth and its inhabitants. This trauma deeply grieves the Spirit who pleads with God's people to nurture and protect the fragile bioregions we all share. Paul writes that human arrogance causes the whole creation to groan in agony as it waits for deliverance. As the creation sighs in pain, the Spirit likewise groans on our behalf in sounds too deep for words—interceding so that God's love for all creation will be consummated (Rom. 8:18–39). In the midst of the current crisis the created order groans under the weight of humankind's habitual ecoviolence, and the Spirit in turn intensely beseeches us to care for our planetary heritage. God as Spirit agonizes over the squalor we have caused and implores us through her abiding earthly presence to stop the violence before it is too late.

As the God who knows death through the cross of Jesus is the crucified God, so also the Spirit who enfleshes divine presence in nature is the wounded Spirit. Jesus' body as God's enfleshed presence was inscribed with the marks of human sin; so also the earth body of the Spirit is lacerated by continued assaults upon our planet home. Consider the sad parallels between the crucified Jesus and the cruciform Spirit. The lash marks of human sin cut into the body of the crucified God are now even more graphically displayed across the expanse of the whole planet, as the body of the wounded Spirit bears the incisions of continual abuse. As God suffered on a tree by taking onto Godself humankind's sin, so God continually suffers the agony of death and loss by bringing into Godself the environmental squalor that humankind has wrought.

The Spirit in the Killing Fields of Urban America

In an ecocidal age, I have proposed that we reenvision the Spirit as the cruciform Spirit who bears in herself the deep wounds caused by our sins against the earth community. Could it be, then, that an adequate basis for hope in a restored earth lies in a recovery of the Holy Spirit as God's power of life-giving breath (*rūah*) who indwells and sustains all life-forms? Perhaps. But a Spirit-centered and earth-centered basis for such a theological hope is difficult to sustain on a planet scarred by savage violence. Such hope is difficult to sustain when one's bioregion is under daily assault by ravenous demonic forces that labor to destroy hope through the politics of despair. Such is the case in the bioregion where I live, in close proximity to the city of Chester, Pennsylvania, near my home and the college where I teach.

I remember well my first visit, a couple of years ago, to the west end of the city of Chester. I knew Chester, a postindustrial city just outside Philadelphia, at the time as an urban area notorious for its chronic environmental problems, and I had traveled there to see firsthand the nature of its difficulties. The first thing I noticed upon arriving in Chester was the smell: waves of noxious fumes enveloped me like the stench of rotting meat. Next I felt the bone-jarring rumble of giant eighteen-wheel trash trucks, dozens of trucks from all over the mid-Atlantic and eastern seaboard, bearing down on the residential streets where I was walking with tons of trash—trash which I knew contained everything from toxic chemicals and contaminated soil to sewage sludge and body parts. Then I remember looking to the horizon and seeing the destination of these terrible truck convoys: a line of giant chemical and waste processing plants belching putrid smoke—like Blake's dark Satanic mills—tightly interspersed among the homes and churches and businesses of Chester residents. I was then and remain now overwhelmed by the bald injustice of siting these plants in a residential area. Since the time of this visit I have asked myself what is the role of an earth-centered faith in the Spirit—in short, what is the role of green spirituality—in resisting and combatting the injustice done to the people, and the wider biosphere, of Chester.

Many local economies in urban and rural America today are dependent upon the production and management of toxic wastes. In economically distressed communities the promise of a stabilized tax base, improved infrastructure, and jobs for underemployed residents is almost impossible to resist. The waste management industry offers an immediate quick-fix to chronic poverty and instability in declining cities and neighborhoods that can no longer attract government and private investment. The price for allowing the storage and treatment of biohazardous materials in one's community may be long-term environmental problems. But people in the grip of poverty and joblessness have few options when their very survival, materially speaking, is contingent upon the construction of a trash incinerator or chemical dump in their neighborhood.

Corporate investors know a good thing when they see it. Waste management facilities cannot be sited where politically empowered middle- and upper-class residents will fight through the courts the establishment of such facilities. Close proximity to hazardous industries immediately depresses property values in residential areas where virtually no one wants to risk endangering his or her physical and economic well-being by allowing such a liability to be built in their own backyard. And in those rare instances where such facilities have come on line in high-income areas, the residents have the means and mobility to "'vote with their feet' and move away from a high risk place of residence."[24]

Chester is an impoverished, predominantly African American community in an almost all-white suburb, Delaware County. Its median family income is 45 percent lower than the rest of Delaware County; its poverty rate is 25 percent, more than three times the rate in the rest of Delaware County; and its unemployment rate is 30 percent. Chester has the highest infant mortality rate and the highest percentage of low-weight births in the state.[25] In the light of its alarmingly bad public health, Chester would appear to be the last place to build a constellation of hazardous facilities. Nevertheless, three waste and treatment plants recently have been built on a square-mile site surrounded by homes and parks in a low-income neighborhood in Chester. The facilities include the American Ref-Fuel trash-to-steam incinerator, the Delcora sewage-treatment plant, and the Thermal Pure Systems medical-waste autoclave. A fourth waste processing plant devoted to treating PCB-contaminated soil has recently received a construction permit. The clustering of waste industries only a few yards from a large residential area has made worse the high rate of asthma and other respiratory and health problems in Chester; it has brought about an infestation of rodents, the impact of five hundred trucks a day at all hours into the neighborhood, soot and dust covering even the insides of people's homes, and waves of noxious odors that have made life unbearable.[26] In a landmark health study of the environmental degradation of Chester, the EPA found that lead poisoning is a significant health problem for the majority of Chester children; that toxic air emissions have raised the specter of cancer to two and one half times greater than the average risk for area residents; and that the fish in Chester waters are hopelessly contaminated with PCBs from current and previous industrial abuses.[27]

The EPA study has made public what many Chester residents have long known: the unequal dumping of municipal wastes in Chester has permanently undermined the health and well-being of its population. Chester is a stunning example of environmental racism. One hundred percent of all municipal solid waste in Delaware County is burned at the incinerator; 90 percent of all sewage is treated at the Delcora plant; and close to one hundred tons of hospital waste per day from a half-dozen nearby states is sterilized at the Thermal Pure plant.[28] As Jerome Balter, a Philadelphia environmental lawyer puts it, "When Delaware County passes an act that says all of the waste has to come to the city of Chester, that *is* environmental racism."[29] Or, as Peter Kostmayer, former congressman and head of the EPA's mid-Atlantic region, says, high levels of pollution in Chester would "not have happened if this were Bryn Mawr, Haverford or Swarthmore [nearby well-to-do white suburbs]. I think we have to face the fact that the reason this happened is because this city is largely—though not all—African American, and a large number of its residents are people of low income."[30] Chester has become a "local sacrifice zone" where the disproportionate pollution from its waste-industrial complex is tolerated because of the promise of economic revitalization.[31] But the promise of dozens of jobs and major funds for the immediate areas around the existing toxics industries have never materialized. Indeed, of the $20 million the incinerator pays to local governments in taxes, only $2 million goes to Chester while $18 million goes to Delaware County.[32]

Chester is Delaware County's sacrifice zone. The surrounding middle-class, white neighborhoods would never allow for the systematic overexposure of their citizens to such a toxics complex. The health and economic impact of siting even one of the facilities now housed in Chester would likely be regarded as too high a risk. But to build a whole cluster of such complexes in nearby Chester is another matter. Nevertheless, many in Chester have tried to fight this exercise in environmental apartheid. The Chester Residents Concerned for Quality Living, led by community activist (or, as she prefers, "reactivist") Zulene Mayfield, has used nonviolent resistance tactics—mass protests, monitoring of emissions levels, protracted court actions, and so forth—to block the expansion of the complex. In opposition to the granting of a permit for operation for the fourth waste facility to be built in the area, the soil remediation plant, the former mayor of Chester, Barbara Bohannan-Sheppard, concluded her remarks at a public hearing with the following:

> Chester should not and will not serve as a dumping ground. A dumping
> ground for what no other borough, no other township, or no other city

will accept. Yes, Chester needs the taxes, Chester needs the jobs. But, Chester also needs to improve its image and not be a killing field.[33]

Hope is not lost in Chester. There is a growing awareness of the injustice being done to low-income, often minority communities that have suffered from the unequal distribution of environmental hazards in their neighborhoods. President Clinton in 1995 signed an executive order mandating all federal agencies to ensure the equitable location of polluting industries across race and economic lines.[34] And in 1998 the Third Circuit Court of Appeals in Philadelphia ruled that the Chester residents' organization has the legal right to file a class action lawsuit against the Department of Environmental Protection charging that the DEP violated their civil rights by clustering a series of waste-processing facilities in their neighborhood.[35]

What role, if any, can green spirituality play in the struggle against environmental racism in areas such as Chester, Pennsylvania? What is the place of the wounded Spirit, the green face of God, in the struggle for environmental equity in neighborhoods that bear a dispropor-tionate and unfair burden for society's pollution? In response, it should first be noted that few people see it in their interests to express solidarity with disadvantaged communities that have suffered the brunt of unequal distribution of environmental risks. Many people have become inured to the gradual environmental degradation of their home and work environments and most likely consider the develop-ment of occasional toxic "sacrifice zones" and "killing fields" to be a tragic but necessary result of modern technological life and its attendant creature comforts. If everyone has the right to pursue his or her own material self-interests, and if some persons are better able to do this than others due in part to their family or national origin, socio-economic class, and so forth, then it follows that some disadvantaged groups will be marginalized in the human struggle for increased wealth, security, and power. A spirituality centered on the wounded Spirit challenges this self-centered assumption by affirming instead that all persons are fundamentally equal and that everyone has the right to family stability and meaningful work in a healthy environment, regardless of one's racial, cultural, economic, or sexual identity. Green spirituality affirms the common interdependence of all persons with each other—indeed, of all species with each other— as we all struggle to protect the integrity of the life-web that holds together our planet home.[36] Insofar as the Spirit breathes into and sustains life for all members of the web, green religion testifies to the bond of unity that unites all God's children together on a sacred earth. As the participants of the First National People of Color Environmental Leadership Summit put it: "Environmental justice affirms the sacredness of Mother Earth, ecological unity and the interdependence of all species, and the right to be free from ecological destruction."[37] Thus, earth-centered religion values the interconnections between all members of the biosphere in contradistinction to the egoistic ideal of maximizing self-interest.

Conclusion

I have suggested that we refer to the Spirit in our time as the "wounded Spirit" or "cruciform Spirit" who, like Christ, takes into herself the burden of human sin and the deep ecological damage this sin has wrought in the biosphere. But, as Christ's wounds become the eucharistic blood that nourishes the believer, so also does the Spirit's agony over damage to the earth become a source of hope for communities facing seemingly hopeless environmental destitution. The message of the cross is that senseless death is not foreign to God because it is through the cross that God lives in solidarity with all who suffer. Now the promise of new life that flows from the suffering God hanging from a tree is recapitulated in the ministry of the wounded Spirit whose solidarity with a broken world is a token of divine forbearance and love.

Hope, then, for a restored earth in our time is theologically rooted in the belief in the Spirit's benevolent cohabitation with all of the damaged and forgotten members of the biosphere—human and nonhuman alike. The Spirit's abiding presence in a world wracked by human greed is a constant reminder that God desires the welfare of all members of the life-web. No population of life-forms is beyond the ken of divine love, no matter how serious, even permanent, the ecological damage is to these biotic communities.

One of the many ironies of Christian faith is the belief that out of death comes life, from loss and suffering comes the possibility of hope and renewal. This irony is symbolized in the Creator's emptying of herself in creation so that all beings may enjoy fullness of life. It is represented in Jesus' crucifixion where the spilling of his life blood becomes the opportunity for all persons to experience the fullness of new life in him. Finally, it is manifest in the Spirit's kenotic coinherence with the earth, enduring our ecological violence so that we can be offered, again and again, the chance to change our habits and reenter the sorority of the earth and her Creator. Our rapacious habits daily wound the Earth Spirit who breathes life into all things; and daily the Earth Spirit intercedes for us and protects us by allowing us to remain richly alive in spite of our deadly behavior.

The Spirit in and through the body of the earth groans in travail over our addictions to ecoviolence. But in her wounds we have life because it is in the wounded Spirit that we see God's abundant love poured out on our behalf. In her wounds we see that God does not remain aloof from creation—apathetic, unmoved, uncaring. Rather, God enfleshes herself in all of the processes and life-forms that constitute life as we know it. We continue unabated in our ravaging of the earth body of the one who has given herself for us so that we might live. But the cruciform Spirit still has not withdrawn her sustaining presence from the planet—a reminder to us that God is a lover of all things bodily and earthly. Thereby, we are called to a renewed passion for nurturing and protecting the biosphere that is our common inheritance and common home.

Notes

1. Henry David Thoreau, "Walking," in *The Norton Book of Nature Writing,* ed. Robert Finch and John Elder (New York: W. W. Norton and Company, 1990), 183.

2. Elizabeth A. Johnson, *She Who Is: The Mystery of God in Feminist Theological Discourse* (New York: Crossroad Press, 1992), 134.

3. See the analysis of Joachim's tripartite theology of history in George H. Tavard, "Apostolic Life and Church Reform," in *Christian Spirituality: High Middle Ages and Reformation,* ed. Jill Raitt (New York: Crossroad Press, 1987), 1–11.

4. See Eberhard Busch, *Karl Barth: His Life from Letters and Autobiographical Texts,* trans. John Bowden (Philadelphia: Fortress Press, 1976), 494.

5. Ihab Hassan, quoted in David Harvey, *The Condition of Postmodernity* (Oxford: Blackwell, 1990), 42–45.

6. See Margot Adler, *Drawing Down the Moon: Witches, Druids, Goddess-Worshippers, and Other Pagans in America Today,* rev. ed. (Boston: Beacon Press, 1986).

7. See Bill McKibben, *The End of Nature* (New York: Random House, 1989), and Jeremy Rifkin, *Biosphere Politics: A Cultural Odyssey from the Middle Ages to the New Age* (San Francisco: HarperSanFrancisco, 1991), 71–91.

8. The dual topics of Spirit and Earth were the focus of the seventh assembly of the World Council of Churches in Canberra, Australia, February 1991, entitled "Come Holy Spirit, Renew the Whole Creation."

9. In her earlier work Sallie McFague argued that the model of God as Spirit is not retrievable in an ecological age, criticizing traditional descriptions of the Spirit as ethereal and vacant. But in her recent writing McFague performs the very retrieval of pneumatology she had earlier claimed to be impossible: a revisioning of God as Spirit in order to thematize the immanent and dynamic presence of the divine life within all creation. See *The Body of God: An Ecological Theology* (Minneapolis: Fortress Press, 1993), 141–50. For an appreciation and critique of McFague's ecotheology, see my *Fragments of the Spirit: Nature, Violence, and the Renewal of Creation* (New York: Continuum, 1996), 139–44. Some of the material in this section of my essay is borrowed from *Fragments of the Spirit.*

10. On the history of the problematic relation between metaphysics and pneumatology, see Alan M. Olson, *Hegel and the Spirit: Philosophy as Pneumatology* (Princeton: Princeton University Press, 1992), 3–35, 107–62. For a defense of a countermetaphysical model of God, see Jean-Luc Marion, *God without Being: Hors-Texte,* trans. Thomas A. Carlson (Chicago: University of Chicago Press, 1991).

11. A number of recent texts have initiated recoveries of discourse about "spirit," "the Spirit," or "the spiritual" in a variety of genres. In theology, see José Comblin, *The Holy Spirit and Liberation,* trans. Paul Burns (Maryknoll, N.Y.: Orbis Books, 1989); Peter C. Hodgson, *Winds of the Spirit: A Constructive Christian Theology* (Louisville: Westminster/John Knox Press, 1994); Chung Hyun Kyung, "Welcome the Spirit; Hear Her Cries: The Holy Spirit, Creation, and the Culture of Life," *Christianity and Crisis* 51 (15 July 1991): 220–23; Elizabeth A. Johnson, *She Who Is: The Mystery of God in Feminist Theological Discourse* (New York: Crossroad

Press, 1992); Jürgen Moltmann, *God in Creation: A New Theology of Creation and the Spirit of God,* trans. Margaret Kohl (San Francisco: Harper and Row, 1985); idem, *The Spirit of Life: A Universal Affirmation,* trans. Margaret Kohl (Minneapolis: Fortress Press, 1992); idem, *The Source of Life: The Holy Spirit and the Theology of Life,* trans. Margaret Kohl (Minneapolis: Fortress Press, 1997); and Michael Welker, *God the Spirit,* trans. John F. Hoffmeyer (Minneapolis: Fortress Press, 1994). In philosophy, see Jacques Derrida, *Of Spirit: Heidegger and the Question,* trans. Geoffrey Bennington and Rachel Bowlby (Chicago: University of Chicago Press, 1989); idem, *Specters of Marx: The State of the Debt, the Work of Mourning, and the New International,* trans. Peggy Kamuf (New York: Routledge, 1994); and Steven G. Smith, *The Concept of the Spiritual: An Essay in First Philosophy* (Philadelphia: Temple University Press, 1988). And in cultural studies, see Joel Kovel, *History and Spirit: An Inquiry into the Philosophy of Liberation* (Boston: Beacon Press, 1991).

12. Hodgson, *Winds of the Spirit,* 276.

13. The problem of effacing the difference between Spirit and spirit in favor of S/spirit is apparent in an otherwise excellent postmodern pneumatology by Mark McClain Taylor, "Tracking Spirit: Theology as Cultural Critique in America," in *Changing Conversations: Religious Reflection and Cultural Analysis,* ed. Dwight N. Hopkins and Sheila Greeve Davaney (New York: Routledge, 1996), 123–44.

14. On the history of woman-identified language for the Spirit, see Gary Steven Kinkel, *Our Dear Mother the Spirit: An Investigation of Count Zinzendorf's Theology and Praxis* (Lanham, Md.: University Press of America, 1990), and Johnson, *She Who Is,* 128–31.

15. Basil of Caesarea *De Spiritu Sancto* bk. 16.

16. Augustine *De Trinitate* bk. 15.

17. For reproductions and commentary, see Jeffrey F. Hamburger, *The Rothschild Canticles: Art and Mysticism in Flanders and the Rhineland Circa 1300* (New Haven: Yale University Press, 1990), 118–42. I am grateful to Ellen Ross for directing my attention to this volume.

18. *Perichoresis* is the doctrine that teaches the coinherence of the members of the Trinity in each other. For a fuller discussion of this term and its relevance to contemporary theology, see Catherine Mowry LaCugna, *God for Us: The Trinity and Christian Life (*San Francisco: HarperSanFrancisco, 1991), 270–78.

19. There are notable exceptions to this general orientation (for example, Chung Hyun Kyung, Johnson, Moltmann, Welker), but most other contemporary theologies of the Holy Spirit generally deemphasize, or ignore altogether, the model of the Spirit as God's power of ecological renewal and healing within the cosmos. This shortcoming applies to a number of otherwise invaluable books in pneumatology, including Yves M. J. Congar, *I Believe in the Holy Spirit,* trans. Geoffrey Chapman, 3 vols. (New York: Seabury Press, 1983); Alasdair I. C. Heron, *The Holy Spirit: The Holy Spirit in the Bible, the History of Christian Thought, and Recent Theology* (Philadelphia: Westminster Press, 1983); G. W. H. Lampe, *God as Spirit* (Oxford: Clarendon Press, 1977); and John V. Taylor, *The Go-Between God: The Holy Spirit and the Christian Mission* (London: SCM Press, 1972). As well, the writings on the Spirit in the important systematic theologies of authors such as Barth, Rahner, and Tillich reflect a similar lacuna, though this oversight is understandable given the

general lack of cultural awareness of the ecocrisis at the time these authors were writing. (This anachronistic qualification applies to some of the other writers listed above as well.)

20. My basic source for a life-centered portrait of the Spirit is the Bible. In *Fragments of the Spirit* I note, however, that since the Bible is in travail over its depictions of the Spirit—the Spirit is alternately portrayed as healing and life-giving, on the one hand, and as capricious and judgmental, on the other—a biblically informed pneumatology must guard against an overly positive and one-sided view of the Spirit's ministry of renewal and reconciliation. Throughout the scriptures the Spirit is generally figured as empowering persons and communities to live in solidarity with the poor and oppressed. But this is not the whole story when it comes to the Spirit in the Bible. In Judges, for example, the Spirit is presented as a vengeful power who inspires Israel's wars against its aggressors (*pace* Welker, *God the Spirit,* 56 passim). And in Acts the Spirit is similarly portrayed as a terrifying judge who condemns to death two renegade disciples, Ananias and Sapphira, for their lying and disobedience. A well-rounded understanding of the Spirit for our time must account for the Spirit's Janus-faced role as both healing and exacerbating the plight of victims within the stories of the Bible. Unfortunately, however, the virtual absence of discussion about this double-edged portrait of the Holy Spirit in the current literature is symptomatic, I fear, of a studied ignorance concerning the "dark side" of the Spirit within contemporary theology.

21. See Jürgen Moltmann's *The Spirit of Life,* 274–89, and his model of the Spirit as the *vita vivificans* who sustains all creation, and James E. Lovelock's *Gaia: A New Look at Life on Earth* (Oxford: Oxford University Press, 1979) in defense of the model of the earth as a single living organism which supports all life-forms within a common ecosystem. Regarding the problems with Moltmann's nature theology, see my "The Wild Bird Who Heals: Recovering the Spirit in Nature," *Theology Today* 50 (1993): 13–28.

22. See, among others, Edward Farley, *Divine Empathy: A Theology of God* (Minneapolis: Fortress Press, 1996), Joseph Halloran, *The Descent of God: Divine Suffering in History and Theology* (Minneapolis: Fortress Press, 1992), and Grace Jantzen, *God's World, God's Body* (Philadelphia: Westminster Press, 1984).

23. Jürgen Moltmann, *The Crucified God,* trans. R. A. Wilson and John Bowden (New York: Harper and Row, 1974), 244.

24. Bob Edwards, "With Liberty and Environmental Justice for All: The Emergence and Challenge of Grassroots Environmentalism in the United States," in *Ecological Resistance Movements: The Global Emergence of Radical and Popular Environmentalism,* ed. Bron Raymond Taylor (Albany: State University of New York Press, 1995), 37. On the challenge of urban environmentalism also see Robert Gottlieb, *Forcing the Spring: The Transformation of the American Environmental Movement* (Washington, D.C.: Island Press, 1993), and Carolyn Merchant, *Radical Ecology: The Search for a Livable World* (New York: Routledge, 1992).

25. I have drawn this information from "Chester Decides It's Tired of Being a Wasteland," *Philadelphia Inquirer,* 26 July 1994; and Chester Residents Concerned for Quality Living, "Environmental Justice Fact Sheet" and "Pollution and Industry in Chester's 'West End,'" pamphlets. I am grateful to former Swarthmore College

students Laird Hedlund and Ryan Peterson for making available to me their expertise and research concerning the Chester waste facilities.

26. Maryanne Voller, "Everyone Has Got to Breathe," *Audubon,* March-April 1995.

27. Editorial, "Chester a Proving Ground," *Delaware County Daily Times,* 8 December 1994, and "EPA Cites Lead in City Kids, Bad Fish," *Delaware County Daily Times,* 2 December 1994.

28. Voller, "Everyone Has Got to Breathe," and Chester Residents Concerned for Quality Living, "Environmental Justice Fact Sheet."

29. "Chester's Environmental Crisis," *Delaware County Times,* 1 August 1995.

30. Howard Goodman, "Politically Incorrect," *Philadelphia Inquirer Magazine,* 11 February 1996.

31. The phrase belongs to Carolyn Merchant, *Radical Ecology,* 163.

32. Chester Residents Concerned for Quality Living, "Pollution and Industry in Chester's 'West End.'"

33. Barbara Bohannan-Sheppard, "Remarks" (Department of Environmental Resources Public Hearing, 17 February 1994, transcript).

34. Bill Clinton, Executive Order Number 12898, February 1995; cf. Gretchen Leslie and Colleen Casper, "Environmental Equity: An Issue for the 90s?" *Environmental Insight,* 1995.

35. "Minority Areas Gain in Suit on Waste Sites," *Philadelphia Inquirer,* 1 January 1998.

36. For further development on this point see my "Environmental Justice, Neo-preservationism, and Sustainable Spirituality," in *The Ecological Community: Environmental Challenges for Philosophy, Politics, and Morality,* ed. Roger S. Gottlieb (New York: Routledge, 1997), 292–310.

37. The First National People of Color Environmental Leadership Summit, "Principles of Environmental Justice," in *This Sacred Earth: Religion, Nature, Environment,* ed. Roger S. Gottlieb (New York: Routledge, 1996), 634.

Response to Mark I. Wallace:
Another View of the Spirit's Work

$\mathbf{M}$**ark Wallace** brings us firmly into the presence of the Holy
Spirit as the Immanent Spirit of Creation, as the One who is incarnated in Nature. And I thank him for giving us such a graphic description of what happens when she is not honored. My response to his
paper will emphasize: first, the critical need to add Wisdom Woman
to the images of the Holy Spirit as breath, wind, water, fire, and dove
that Wallace presented; and second, a suggestion that process
theology's understanding of the consequent nature of the Holy Spirit
offers a powerful response to the suffering of the earth and all of its
creatures.

I.

In the Hebrew scriptures, we find that, as regards their actions, the
Spirit and Wisdom are equated. We also find Wisdom imaged as the
Feminine Divine.[1] The idea of the Wisdom literature as creation theology is not a recent development but dates back at least to 1964 when
Walther Zimmerli identified Wisdom as being within the framework
of a theology of creation.[2] For example, in the book of Ecclesiastes,
the Deity presented is preeminently a creator deity. All that is created
is beautiful and/or appropriate to its time.[3] "The sages did not analyze
nature in the subject-object manner that is ours. Ps. 104 and the
saying in Prov. 30 show this. All things, especially all living things,

were appreciated for simply existing, for being alive."[4] There was no dualistic view of creation. Rather, all had intrinsic worth and nothing was an object to be valued merely because it was useful. There was no sacred versus profane; all was permeated with the divine presence. This would lead me to say, in the present environmental crisis, a wisdom spirituality is to be found in such things as the food I purchase and eat and the way I treat my yard by refraining from the use of poisons. Likewise, the biblical sages, through the illustration of daily experiences, were able to draw people into the mystery that was the divinity. According to Roland Murphy, they "penetrated into the divine mystery in a manner that even the prophets never equaled."[5]

Gerhard von Rad also discerned a holistic vision in the Wisdom literature. He contends that Israel "did not differentiate between a 'life wisdom' that pertained to the social orders and a 'nature wisdom' because she was unable to objectify these spheres in the form of such abstractions."[6] For von Rad, the continuity of the Wisdom literature is based on seeing Wisdom as self-revelatory. In other words, the Wisdom writers had "unwavering certainty that creation herself will reveal her truth to the man who becomes involved with her and trusts her, because this is what she continually does."[7] Thus, it may truly be said that Wisdom is a way of understanding divine revelation.[8] While the more usual way to understand divine revelation has been as salvation history, I would suggest that divine revelation as seen in creation is more appropriate for today. One obvious reason is that it is the story of all humankind. This story is critically needed today if we are all to act together to save the earth from ecological disaster.

The Wisdom literature does not separate the world from the Creator. Rather, the two are held in tension—the all-pervasive causality of the Divine (for both good and evil) and the autonomy of creation, as seen, for example, in the ants, locusts, lizards, and badgers who teach wisdom (Prov. 30:24–28). Creation is understood as the revelation of the Creator (Wis. of Sol. 13:1). To see the world is to see the Creator. Wisdom literature displays little interest in the world's origins; rather, it is interested in the world as the place of divine activity. This is the world that humans learn from and react to—the surface of the earth on which Lady Wisdom plays (Prov. 8:31).[9] In Job, the first biblical book in which personified Wisdom appears, the Divinity reveals itself in creation in such a way that Job is transformed (Job 38–39). Job responds to this revelation: "I had heard of you by word of mouth, but now my eye has seen you" (Job 42:5).

The book of Job presents a nonanthropomorphic understanding of creation. God points out to Job that rain falls where human beings do not live (38:26–27); that the Divinity is the one who hunts for the lion (38:39–40); that, as exemplified in the ostrich, creation's design includes that which the human does not value (39:13–17). Rather than vanquishing the "monsters," as occurs in traditional cosmogonies, God admires them in splendid poetry. Placing Job at the periphery, God celebrates creation for its own worth, a testament to his power and grace.[10]

The language of wisdom that creation speaks is peculiar (Ps. 19), steady, nonverbal, and heard (Ps. 19:2).[11] It is the language of the sages and the language of the nonhuman. The four small creatures—the ants, the badgers, the locusts, the lizards—are referred to as being exceedingly wise; they are so called because of their behavior (Prov. 30:24–28). Job also cites beasts and birds, reptiles and fish as the teachers of the human (Job 23:7–8). In Sirach 39:12–35, the goodness of all the works of creation is extended to the "inanimate" world. Here, the theme is the goodness of all the works of the Divinity. This theme is illustrated through the motif of *kairos,* or right time. Even fire and hail, famine and disease are seen as having their proper time. Sirach 42:15–43:33 is a hymn in praise of creation where all obey, even hail, rain, and lightning. The hymn reaches its high point as it cites the Divinity as the source and sustenance of all that is: "He is the all" (43:27). Further, the compassion of the Divinity is extended to all living beings; this contrasts to the human who has compassion only for the neighbor (18:13).[12]

The language of the Wisdom literature is also the language of experience. This is a pertinent source today for ecofeminists who are developing an experiential ethics. In the Wisdom literature is found, not lofty abstract principles, but the human experience, including human experience of the Divine. The human is always both wholly in the world and in relation to Divinity. The Wisdom literature exhorts us to learn everything we can and to use it in our daily living. Yet, no matter what we know, there is always the element of mystery in the end result. This is an acknowledgment of human limitations. One must always remain open for the completely new experience.[13] Von Rad summarizes this meaning and power of wisdom in the following way:

There is the fact that the truth about the world and man can never become the object of our theoretical knowledge; that reliable knowledge
can be achieved only through a relationship of trust with things; that it
is the highest wisdom to abstain from the attempt to control wisdom in
abstract terms; that it is much wiser to let things retain their constantly
puzzling nature and that means to allow them to become themselves
active and, by what they have to say, to set man to rights.[14]

In the Wisdom literature, we find a language which encompasses
both good and evil (for example, in Job and Ecclesiastes). Ours is an
age in which the reality of evil has appeared in massive proportions—
on both the structural and the personal levels. Facing this reality, we
seem to have even less insight than ages past on how to conceive of a
Divinity who we call good and yet who "allows" such evil to occur.
We might begin a contemporary theodicy by looking at the Wisdom
literature and acknowledging its insight that all—both things we call
good and things we call evil—are somehow the work of the Divinity.
If nothing else, this might enable us to rethink the idea of our own
deaths. The earth and all we know is here only because of the death of
stars. In the same manner, might not our own deaths be seen, not so
much as an evil, but as the opportunity for new lives for others? Perhaps Plato's insight in the *Timaeus,* that the creator was not omnipotent but only doing the best that could be done, may be valid after all.
This insight does not downplay human responsibility for evil; nor
does it negate the power of the One who paints purple and pink sun-
sets that fill the sky.

Finally, the language of Wisdom is the language found in the
public places where the people are gathered: in the streets, the plazas,
by the city gates (Prov. 1:20–21). Commenting on this passage,
Bernhard Lang observes that "the basic reason is that Wisdom must
demonstrate Her usefulness in the arena of public life."[15] It is more
necessary today, when the systems of air, water, and soil, which have
made life possible on the earth, face destruction, that the voice of
Wisdom once again be heard in the public places.

II.

On the issue of the suffering of the earth and its creatures, I find the
analogy to the suffering Christ to be problematic. In part, this is an

issue of time, as the agony of Christ was a matter of hours, while parts of the earth and its creatures have suffered for millennia. I propose that a more powerful analogy for the suffering of the Divinity is found in what process theology calls the consequent nature of the Divine, that is, the Holy Spirit.

Alfred North Whitehead was himself articulate about suffering in the world. He expressed the problem succinctly when he said:

> The ultimate evil in the temporal world is deeper than any specific evil. It lies in the fact that the past fades, that time is a "perpetual perishing."[16]

Thus, for Whitehead:

> The task of Theology is to show how the World is founded on something beyond mere transient fact, and how it issues in something beyond the perishing of occasions. The temporal World is the stage of finite accomplishment. We ask of Theology to express that element in perishing lives which is undying by reason of its expression of perfections proper to our finite natures. In this way we shall understand how life includes a mode of satisfaction deeper than joy or sorrow.[17]

The disciples of Whitehead deal theologically with the question of ultimate evil by saying that in the consequent nature of the Divinity, equated with the Holy Spirit, the accomplishments and failings of each human person live forever and are forever available to succeeding generations.

The consequent nature of Divinity may be described as the reaction of creativity with the world through the reception of the world's objective immortality.[18] In contrast to the primordial nature, which is conceptual, the consequent nature is formed by taking up into Divinity the physical experience of the world. While it may be said that the world is brought to completion by the conceptual nature of the Divine, analogously it may also be said that the Divine is brought to completion by the physical nature of the world. Whitehead characterizes the primordial nature as free, complete, eternal, yet actually deficient and unconscious, while characterizing the consequent nature as determined, incomplete, consequent, everlasting, fully actual, and conscious.[19] So it may be said that the Holy Spirit is actually formed by taking up into the Godhead the physical experience of the world.

For his concept of the direct immanence of the Divinity in the world, Whitehead claimed to be relying on the Alexandrian and Antiochian theologians. When confronted with the problem of the nature of God, these theologians accounted for the unity and the multiplicity of God in terms of the mutual immanence of the Divinity. Likewise, when confronted with the problem of the nature and person of Jesus Christ, they expressed their understanding of him as being one person in whom the direct immanence of God was present. Further, Whitehead sees these theologians as deciding to express doctrinally their understanding of the direct immanence of God in the world in a general sense, in addition to the particular sense in which it is present in Christ. This direct immanence of God in the world generally was expressed in terms of the third person of the Trinity, the Holy Spirit.[20] This Whitehead contrasts with Plato's metaphysics, which emphasizes secondary images rather than direct presence.

John B. Cobb, Jr., and David Ray Griffin are among the followers of Whitehead who equate the consequent nature with the Spirit but go on to make the further identification with the Feminine.[21] However, this identification between the Holy Spirit and the feminine must not be too facile, for besides exhibiting those traits that are usually regarded as feminine, the Spirit is also "profoundly active and directive as an agent and ruling principle in the Church."[22] Cobb, in *Christ in a Pluralistic Age,* offers feminine and other images for our consideration as we ponder the person of the Holy Spirit. As the Feminine, the Spirit is identified with receptivity, empathy, suffering, redemption, and preservation. It is this feminine aspect of the Divine which is inclusive, final, and fully actual.

The Spirit may be said to be related to the Father as my feelings are related to myself. As transcendent, she may be seen as the resurrection of the dead or as the Kingdom of Heaven. As immanent, she is the one who makes the journey toward the eschaton possible in time. For Cobb, these images are not to be considered final but are to be looked at in terms of our tradition and valued for their helpfulness in our imaging of the Divine. If they should prove useless, they are to be cast aside.[23] In our imaging of the Divine, we are ever now, and always will be, in process.

Process theologians, including Norman Pittenger, Daniel Day Williams, and G. Palmer Pardington, III, have addressed the question of the relationship between the Holy Spirit and the world. They see both a cosmic and a relational role for the Holy Spirit. In the cosmos, the Spirit operates as love, a theme also found in the pneumatology of Paul's letter to the Romans. This theme of the Spirit as love is picked up by Augustine who, while agreeing with the Johannine saying that God is love expressed in all three persons of the Trinity, nevertheless applies love to the Holy Spirit in a special way.[24] Thomas Aquinas uses Augustine's pneumatology, and that of Gregory the Great, and teaches that the very name of the Holy Spirit is Love.[25] And, in our own times, Pittenger points out that in Christian hymnody, the Spirit is frequently referred to as the Spirit of love.[26] This is echoed in Paul in regard to the cosmic role of the Holy Spirit (Rom. 8:22–23), a theme also taken up by the Greek fathers, St. Augustine, and the twelfth-century theological school of Chartres.[27]

Thus, while process theologians may be said to be situated firmly within the tradition, both in their understanding of the cosmic role of the Spirit and in their understanding of the Spirit as love, their contribution to contemporary theology lies in the meaning that this action of the Spirit imparts to the cosmos and the particular character they predicate to love. For the process theologian, the cosmos itself participates creatively, along with the Holy Spirit, in the evolutionary process. And because of this active participation, the cosmos itself embodies such elements as value, purpose, experience, freedom, and relationship. In regard to the Spirit as love, process theology would see not only a creative, active aspect to that love but also a passive aspect which may be characterized, Daniel Day Williams suggests, as the willingness to suffer and to be formed by the other.[28] This love, which is the Holy Spirit, specifically manifests itself in those situations which call for eco-justice, thus moving toward a much needed coming together of the concepts of love and justice.

In concrete terms, what are some of the implications of this intimate relationship between the Holy Spirit and the world—both the world of nature and the world of people? If, in fact, the cosmos is the proper home of the Spirit, then there is no element of the world about which the Christian is allowed to show lack of concern. Thus, process theology appears to be summoning the Christian community to the development of a theology of the environment.[29] This theology would be based on the sound religious principle of the Holy Spirit as the immanence of the Holy One within that environment. In addition, if it is a religious fact that the Spirit is present in any situation where love is manifested, the Christian is called to deeper relationship and dialogue with persons of goodwill both in religions other than Christianity and in atheistic ideologies. Conversely, if love is the criterion for the Spirit's presence, then the Christian must ask herself or himself the meaning of church situations which are characterized by an absence of love.

Notes

1. Eleanor Rae and Bernice Marie-Daly, *Created in Her Image: Models of the Feminine Divine* (New York: Crossroad Press, 1990), 9–28.

2. Walther Zimmerli, "The Place and Limit of the Wisdom in the Framework of the Old Testament Theology," *Scottish Journal of Theology* 17 (1964): 148.

3. Roland E. Murphy, *The Tree of Life: An Exploration of Biblical Wisdom Literature* (New York: Doubleday, 1990), 57–59.

4. Ibid., 125.

5. Ibid.

6. Gerhard von Rad, *Wisdom in Israel* (Nashville: Abingdon Press, 1972), 71.

7. Ibid., 317.

8. Murphy, *The Tree of Life,* 126. Israel's ability to see creation as divine revelation may be based on its understanding of history as not only "the recollection of times past, but also the analysis of daily experience in which the variable and the incalculable often appear" (113).

9. Murphy, *The Tree of Life,* 118–20.

10. Richard J. Clifford, *Creation Accounts in the Ancient Near East and in the Bible* (Washington, D.C.: Catholic Biblical Association, 1994), 193–97.

11. Roland E. Murphy, "Wisdom and Creation," *Journal of Biblical Literature* 104, no. 1 (1985): 6. A personal experience that fulfills these criteria occurred during a Lenten meditation on death. While I planned to meditate on my own personal death, what I experienced instead was the raging of the earth's molten core, a rage provoked by what we humans are doing to the earth. I seemed to be being asked how I could place significance on my own death when all around me creation is in the process of being ravaged and destroyed.

12. Murphy, *The Tree of Life,* 71–72.

13. Von Rad, *Wisdom in Israel,* 88–106.

14. Ibid., 318.

15. Bernhard Lang, *Wisdom and the Book of Proverbs: A Hebrew Goddess Redefined* (New York: Pilgrim Press, 1986), 31.

16. Alfred North Whitehead, *Process and Reality: An Essay in Cosmology,* corrected ed. (New York: Free Press, 1978), 340.

17. Alfred North Whitehead, *Adventures of Ideas* (New York: Free Press, 1967), 172.

18. Whitehead, *Process and Reality,* 31–32.

19. Ibid., 347.

20. Athanasius seems to be the source for Whitehead's inspiration on the immanence of the Divine. And Athanasius is generally credited with developing the theology of the Holy Spirit that became the doctrine of the church. Athanasius expresses a strong sense of the Holy Spirit as the immanence of God when he informs Serapion, in referring to Eph. 4:6, that if you make the Spirit a creature, you have in fact destroyed the doctrine of the immanence of God.

21. John B. Cobb, Jr., and David Ray Griffin, *Process Theology: An Introductory Exposition* (Philadelphia: Westminster Press, 1976), 135.

22. Ibid.

23. John B. Cobb, Jr., *Christ in a Pluralistic Age* (Philadelphia: Westminster Press, 1975), 261–64.

24. Augustine *De Trinitate* 6.5.7.

25. Thomas Aquinas *Summa Theologica*

26. Norman Pittenger, *The Holy Spirit* (Philadelphia: United Church Press, 1974), 13.

27. Ewert Cousins, "Teilhard and the Theology of the Spirit," *Cross Currents* 19, no. 4 (winter 1969): 167–71.

28. Daniel Day Williams, *The Spirit and the Forms of Love* (New York: Harper and Row, 1968), 135–41.

29. See, e.g., Charles Birch and John B. Cobb, Jr., *The Liberation of Life: From the Cell to the Community* (Cambridge: Cambridge University Press, 1981). This book represents the joint effort of a biologist and a process theologian to develop an ethical system that encompasses the whole of creation.

The World of the Icon and Creation: An Orthodox Perspective on Ecology and Pneumatology

JOHN CHRYSSAVGIS

Theology and Mystery

Any discussion of the beauty or sacredness of the world, at least from an Orthodox perspective, necessarily involves an exploration into the theology and mystery of the icon, that is to say, into the doctrine behind and the vision beyond icons. For the world of the icon not only presupposes a way of thinking and demands a way of living, but it also offers new insights into our worldview, new perceptions of the world around us, and something of the eternal in everything we see. Our generation is characterized by behavior that results from an autism with regard to the natural cosmos: a certain lack of awareness, or recognition, causes us to use, even waste, the beauty of the world. And so we are locked inside the confines of our own concerns, with no access to the outside world. We have disestablished a continuity between ourselves and the outside, with no possibility for intimate communion and mutual enhancement. The world of the icon restores this relationship by reminding us what is outside and beyond, what ultimately gives value and vitality.

The iconographer aspires to achieve the inner vision of the world, an image of the world as intended by God. The "iconic" world, however, is not an unreal world; rather, it is the real world which is called to ingress upon, and to spill over into, this world. Orthodox iconography seeks to discover and then to disclose the reality of the experience of the heavenly kingdom in this world. In fact, the icon articulates with theological conviction the faith in this kingdom and its activity in the earthly realm. Unfortunately, we have desacralized, or denaturalized, this world by disconnecting it from "heaven." The icon reverses perspective as we know it and does away with the "objective" distance between this world and the next. There is no double order in creation. There is no sharp line of demarcation between "material" and "spiritual." The icon constitutes the epiphany of God in the world and the existence of the world in the presence of God. It is neither idealism nor idolatry. Like the unborn child in the womb of its mother, the icon presents to us the visible seeds of the divinity in the world. Its art and beauty represent God's art and beauty in the creation. The icon speaks in this world, yet in the language of the age to come.

The icon is an integral part of Orthodox spirituality, a central aspect of the celebration of creation. Like the Incarnation and the Creation, the icon is meant to be the piercing of space and time, that is, matter is met by God's eternal nature. The entire church building—with its architecture, frescoes, and mosaics—accomplishes through space and matter what the liturgy does through time and praise: the anticipation of the heavenly kingdom and the participation of the divine presence. The seeming contradiction of an inaccessible God and a crucified Christ constitutes the ultimate measure of God's measureless love for the world. For it is God's freedom that makes God's limitless love so powerful that it breaks all barriers and all limitations. The God who created out of love, who was incarnated out of love, now saturates the whole world with divine energies.

The icon reveals all the tensions, conflicts, and contradictions through which one is called to transparency; every fall is inscribed on it. But there is ultimately resurrection through communion, for to encounter Christ in the icon is to encounter an image beyond suffering, solitude, and hell, an image that will never die. Therefore, the basis of the icon is christological, allowing the wholly inaccessible to be shared entirely. With the event of the Incarnation, as with the epiphany of the icon, the cycle of the nonrepresentation of the Old Testament God (cf. Exod. 20:4–5 and John 1:18) is completed.

"God became human that humanity might be deified," wrote the Christian fathers.[1] The saints are those who emanate the light of deified humanity, while icons indicate the participation of humanity and the entire created world in divine life and light. As a result, faces of saints in icons are always frontal, "all eyes" (Bessarion), transparent, susceptive of divine energy.[2] I see someone also means I am seen, and therefore I am in communion.

Creator and Creation

Since the doctrine of the divine Incarnation is at the heart of iconography, what is being represented is God's affirmation and assumption of the world. In color and on wood, the icon proclaims "God was made flesh" (John 1:14). In his work entitled *On Divine Images,* John of Damascus, the eighth-century champion of icons, claims, "I do not adore creation in place of the creator, but I worship the One who became a creature."[3] And since it is through matter that "God has worked out our salvation,"[4] there is an appropriate honor due to material things. I would argue that it is this sense of the salvific power of matter that we have lost today and which we need to rediscover. As John of Damascus writes: "Because of the Incarnation, I salute all remaining matter with reverence."

In the Western High Middle Ages, the "image of God" in the human person was identified with rational nature, deemed superior to the rest of creation. Such an individualistic view of humanity has contributed greatly to the rise of our ecological problems. In the Greek fathers' view, however, the "image of God" in humanity lay in its specific value of freedom. The human person must be associated with, and not dissociated from, the created world, for it is through the human person that the created world must be transformed and offered to God. And so the world is freed from its natural limitations and becomes a bearer of life. In the words of Metropolitan John (Zizioulas) of Pergamon:

> We believe that in doing this "in Christ" we, like Christ, act as priests of creation. When we receive these elements back, after having referred them to God, we believe that because of this reference to God we can take them back and consume them no longer as death but as life. Creation acquires for us in this way a sacredness which is not inherent in its nature but "acquired" in and through Man's free exercise of his *imago Dei,* i.e. his personhood. This distinguishes our attitude from all forms of paganism, and attaches to the human being an awesome responsibility for the survival of God's creation.[5]

This view of the priestly or parapriestly character of the human person was in earlier times acknowledged by Leontius of Cyprus (seventh century):

> Through heaven and earth and sea, through wood and stone, through relics and Church buildings and the Cross, through angels and people, through all creation visible and invisible, I offer veneration and honor to the Creator and Master and Maker of all things, and to him alone. For the creation does not venerate the Maker directly and by itself, but it is through me that the heavens declare the glory of God, through me the moon worships God, through me the stars glorify him, through me the waters and showers of rain, the dew and all creation, venerate God and give him glory.[6]

Thus, an entire anthropology and cosmology are given artistic shape and utterance in the icon. This is why the two main events for Orthodox iconography are the Incarnation and the Transfiguration. The first reforms what was "originally" deformed through sin and grants to the world the possibility of sanctification. The second realizes the consequences of divinization and grants to the world a foretaste even now of the beauty and light of the last times. We are, in this world, placed at a point of intersection between the present age and the future age, uniting the two as one. In his perceptive book, *The Sacred in Life and Art,* Philip Sherrard claims that the art of the icon presents holy personages

> ready to convert the beholder from his restricted and limited point of view to the full view of their spiritual vision. For the art of the icon is ultimately so to transform the person who moves towards it that he no longer opposes the worlds of eternity and time, of spirit and matter, of the Divine and the human, but sees them united in one Reality, in that ageless image-bearing light in which all things live, move, and have their being.[7]

The Light That Knows No Evening

The light of an icon is an uncreated, sanctifying light, a light that is not of this world and knows no evening. Perspective is abolished, history is telescoped, and proportion is altered. The icon bears witness to a "different way of life."[8] This life and light are shed from the Risen body of Christ and reveal the joy of the Resurrection.

The value of the icon is not pedagogical or aesthetic, but mystical or "sacramental." It surpasses any opposition between this world and the next, uniting the two in an act of communion. It also transcends any opposition between figurative or nonfigurative art and appears instead as transfigurative. The icon presupposes and even proposes another means of communication, beyond the conceptual, written, or spoken word. It is the articulation of what cannot be expressed in theology.

"In the Image and Likeness of God"

The human person, too, is an icon. Created in the image of God, humanity is also a living image of the created universe. The church fathers see humanity as existing on two levels simultaneously—on the level of the spiritual and on the level of material creation. The human person is characterized by paradoxical dualities: humanity is limited yet free, animal yet personal, individual yet social, created yet creative. To attempt escaping this fundamental tension within humanity would be to undermine the Christian doctrine of humanity created "in the image and likeness of God" (Gen. 1:26) and as the image of Jesus Christ who is at once human and divine. A human being, says Gregory the Theologian (fourth century), is like "another universe,"[9] standing at the center of creation, midway between strength and frailty, greatness and lowliness. Humanity is the meeting point of all the created order. The idea of the human person as a bridge, a point of contact and union, is developed as early as the seventh century by the lay monk Maximus Confessor.[10] As an image of the world, the human person constitutes a microcosm. Another monastic writer, Nilus of Ancyra (fifth century), makes this point very clearly:

> You are a world within a world. . . . Look within yourself and there you will see the entire world.[11]

The world in its entirety forms part of the liturgy of heaven. Or, as we have already seen, the world constitutes a cosmic liturgy. God is praised by the trees and the birds, glorified by the stars and the moon (see Ps. 18:2), worshiped by the sea and the sand. There is a dimension of art, music, and beauty in the world. And the very existence of material creation constitutes a revelation of God (Eph. 4:6), awaiting its liberation through the children of God (Rom. 8:19). The world, then, becomes the clearest, albeit the most silent and inconspicuous, sermon declaring the word of God, a sign of the kingdom of heaven, the bridal chamber (Ps. 18), where God can touch the work of creation in the most intimate manner.

When Orthodox Christians enter a church, they bow down before the altar, reverence the holy icons, bow to the minister, and lower their heads at certain points of the liturgy. After receiving the Sacrament of the Eucharist, however, they depart bowing to none, for their conviction is that the life of the world and the heart of the Church are at that moment seeded and seated deeply inside their own heart. When one is initiated into the mystery of the Resurrection and transformed by the light of the Transfiguration, then one understands the purpose for which God has created all things.[12] The world is rendered as a gift—a gift received from, and returned to, God. The climax of the Orthodox Liturgy is found in the words: "Your own from your own we offer to you, in all and through all."

Someone who sees the whole world as an icon experiences from this world the realities of the future and final resurrection. That person has already entered the life of resurrection and eternity. John Climacus, the abbot at St. Catherine's Monastery on Mt. Sinai, was convinced that, in the very beauty and beyond the shattered image of this world:

> such a person always perceives everything in the light of the Creator God, and has therefore acquired immortality before the ultimate resurrection.[13]

There is a sense in which this person is indicating and anticipating here and now the transfiguration of the world. The result is a prefiguration of the restored image of the world, a configuration in this world of uncreated and created elements.

The Icon as Communion

When the Russian monk St. Andrei Rublev (ca. 1360–1430) painted his masterpiece *The Holy Trinity*—which depicts the Old Testament narrative of the three angels who visited Abraham and Sarah (Gen.

18:1–33), sometimes also known as "the hospitality of Abraham"—he was in fact representing the open communion of the triune Godhead, a love that is showered upon the face of the earth and in the hearts of people. The Rublev icon is an image of what the Trinity is: a celebration and communication of life. This is why there is an empty or open place at the table of communion. The three persons of the Trinity are seated on three of the four sides of the rectangular table, allowing for, or rather inviting, the world to communion. Indeed, the very contours of their bodies create and reproduce in macro-image the communion chalice about which these angels are seated.[14] The potential sacredness of the world is more than a mere possibility; it is a vocation.

The Image of Christ

There is no thing, no place, no time, and no person that escapes, or is excluded from, the comprehensive love of Christ (John 1:9). For Christ is God's categorical affirmation and assumption of the whole world. And there is, as a result, no condition, no tragedy, no experience outside the embrace of Christ. To be an imitator of Christ is to be assimilated to him. One can then walk on Earth as Christ and in the authority of Christ: "For it is not I who lives but Christ lives in me" (Gal. 2:20).

The Christ dimension is also suggested in Orthodox icons of the enthroned Jesus, particularly in the truly magnificent mosaic of the late thirteenth century which still survives in the Constantinopolitan monastery of Chora (later known as the Kariye Cami). The icon of Christ over the door to the nave is entitled "The land [χώρα] of the living." The same notion of the resurrection of the dead or newness of life is envisaged in our personal spiritual life through the dynamic stage of for-give-ness (συγ-χώρη-σις), which implies a death to self and "allowing room for others," making space (χώρα) for the rest of the world, giving up of the self, and opening up in communion and acts of giving and givenness. Nothing and no one is excluded. Symeon the New Theologian poetically describes this cohabitation, or co-indwelling, of Christ in the world:

> You make of all Your home and dwelling-place; You become a home to all, and we dwell in You.[15]

Everything therefore assumes a Christ dimension; everything is in some way sacramental. All depends on the receptiveness and openness of our hearts. By the same token, everything is rendered unique, inasmuch as it has its particular place and meaning. Nothing is secular or profane; nothing is pagan or foreign.[16] Indeed, if God were not visibly present in the material creation, then we could not properly worship him as invisible. Were God not tangibly accessible in the very earthliness of this world, then he would not be the loving, albeit transcendent author of the universe. This is surely the implication of the basis of the Christian faith, namely, that "the Word assumed [or became] flesh" (John 1:16), which we all too often, in a reductionist manner, take to mean "became human." Yet, the early Christian writers categorically stated that "what God did not assume, God did not heal."[17] What God did not reach out and touch, did not come down and sanctify, cannot possibly be related to or loved by God. And unless Christ may be discovered "in the least of his brethren" (Matt. 25:40) and in the least particle of matter, then he is too distant to matter. There is a wonderful saying attributed to Jesus, which expresses the reality of his presence everywhere:

> Lift up the stone, and there you will find me; cleave the wood, and I am there.[18]

Matter is not merely an object for our possession and exploitation. The earth has not only economic but also moral and sacramental value. For "the earth and all its fullness" (Ps. 23:1) is a bearer of God, a place of encounter with Christ, the very center of our salvation. In the words of Leonardo Boff:

> All things are sacraments when viewed in God's perspective and light. The word, human beings, and things are signs and symbols of the transcendent.[19]

Theology in Color

The theological statement made by the icon is, therefore, threefold:

1. that the world was created good, and therefore needs to be loved;

2. that at the Incarnation, Christ assumed a human body, thereby affirming the intrinsic value of the whole created world; and
3. that salvation embraces all of created matter, as well as human body and soul.

The entire world is an icon. The whole of creation constitutes an icon painted before all ages, an image eternally engraved by the unique iconographer of the Word of God, namely, the Holy Spirit. This image is never totally destroyed, never fully effaced. Our aim is simply to reveal this image in the heart and to reflect it in the world. Yet, the image itself, the icon, is indelible, for the world has been forever "sealed with the gift of the Holy Spirit."[20] In our age, green is perhaps most fittingly the color of the Holy Spirit, recalling as it does Greek patristic thought[21] and indicating the renewal of life itself and the revival of all things.

Pneumatology and Ecology

This brings me to emphasize the close connection of pneumatology and ecology. Nature speaks a truth scarcely heard among theologians: the world relates in very tangible terms the spiritual connection between the uncreated and the creation.

Just as the Spirit is the "air" that the whole world breathes, so too the earth is the "ground" which we all share. Were God not present in the density of a city, or in the beauty of a forest, or in the sand of a desert, then God would not be present in heaven either. So if, indeed, there exists today a vision that is able to transcend—perhaps transform—all national and denominational tensions, it may well be that of our environment understood as sacrament of the Spirit. The breath of the Spirit brings out the sacramentality of nature and bestows on it the fragrance of resurrection.

Eastern theological thought has been concerned with the metahistorical or the spiritual dimensions of this world seen in the light of the kingdom of heaven and the liturgical nature of time. Facts and figures are considered in terms of the Holy Spirit; power is understood from the perspective of the Sacrament of the Eucharist; the world around is appreciated in relation to the heavens above. The understanding is that eschatology is not an apocalyptic teaching, the last chapter of the New Testament, or perhaps an unnecessary chapter of a Christian manual of doctrine. Rather, it is the teaching about the "last-ness" and "lasting-ness" of all things.

Ascetic Theology

A second characteristic of Orthodox spirituality is the ascetic tradition. The discipline of ascesis is the necessary and critical corrective for the excess of our consumption. We have learned all too well and only too painfully that the ecological crisis both presupposes and builds upon the economic injustice in the world. Ascesis is a reality of the spiritual life because it is the reassurance of our difficult and painful struggle to relate our theology to the world, our justice and our economy to the poor.

Ascesis is not primarily an achievement, but an attitude of attendance to and expectation of the Spirit. Hence, once again, the liturgical aspect of ascesis is a continual invocation (epiclesis) of the Paraclete. As one Orthodox theologian puts it: "we are called not just to do something, but simply to stand there." Ascesis is not another or a better way of acting; it is, in fact, a way of inaction, of stillness, of vigilance. We are called to remember that the present ecological crisis is a result precisely of our action—of considerable human effort and success to "change" or "better" the world—and not only of our greed or covetousness. The primary cause of our devastation and destruction is the relentless pursuit of what many people consider a good or desirable thing—namely, the modern, industrial-technological model of development. Yet, this "developmental" ideology has not created a sustainable world for everyone; it has encouraged exploitation and an unsustainable world.

Ascesis means allowing room for the Spirit, for an action beyond our action. It means "leaving space" (lit., "for-give-ness" or *syn-chore-sis*). The patristic term *peri-chore-sis* has the same root etymologically as *syn-choresis*: *synchoresis* includes the aspect of reconciliation, while *perichoresis* includes the dimension of joy and celebration toward nature for the sake of future generations. When we reduce the spiritual or religious life to ourselves (to *our* concerns, to *our* needs, and to *our* interests), then we forget the calling of the Church to implore God—always and everywhere—for the salvation of the whole polluted cosmos, to the least of our brothers and sisters, and to the last speck of dust in the universe.

It is always alarming to see how easily the term "spirituality" is used without reference to the Spirit which is the giver of all gifts. The Greek patristic tradition does not even have an equivalent term for spirituality, preferring rather to speak about the action of the Holy Spirit in the world. It is not always clear in contemporary theological writings if the Spirit is anything more than just certain abstract nouns—love, justice, peace, or perhaps green peace—with capital letters. The Spirit, of course, "blows where it wills" (John 3:8), as Christ confided to one of his friends on a rooftop. We only know of the Spirit what we may experience on a rooftop on a hot summer's day with a cool breeze blowing: we know that we are touched, that we are refreshed, and that our clothes move a little. The Spirit is only known in contact and in communion with our environment.

The distinction between the "Spirit of God" and the "Spirit of Creation" was one that early Christian ascetics experienced in their very bodies, in their intense struggle to maintain the interdependence of body and soul. The Spirit is indeed the "giver of life" and of all forms of life. It penetrates and permeates the world and cannot be conceived apart from this world. Yet, if the Spirit and the earth are *conformed,* or confused, then the Church is no longer called to *transform* the world; then the Spirit itself ceases to be something that is promised, and becomes something that is compromised. This is why the patristic tradition underlined that the divine Spirit is at once known and unknown, both seen and unseen, revealed and veiled alike. Such is the conviction of Symeon the New Theologian and of Gregory Palamas. Such is the depth of the distinction between divine essence and divine energy. In his treatise *On Divine Names,* Dionysius the Areopagite describes the divinity as *en-cosmic,* as *peri-cosmic,* and as *hyper-cosmic.*[22]

Apophatic Theology

This brings me to a third characteristic of Orthodox theology, the close connection between theology and poetry, between "ascetics" and "aesthetics." Often, our theology does not have sufficient poetry. There has undoubtedly occurred an unfortunate shift in emphasis: from God to man, from body to soul, from theological symbolism to mathematical analysis. Yet, in the tradition of the Orthodox, certainly the greatest and most acclaimed of theologians were also poets: John the Divine, Gregory of Nazianzus, and Symeon the New Theologian. There is always much more to be said than can ever be expressed. This is why the emphasis in the East is on the apophatic dimension of all theological talk and thought. I believe that this apophatic dimension is wonderfully, indeed "naturally," fostered in creation. The breadth and beauty of this earth is a reflection of the boundlessness and splendor of divine grace; and our respect toward the environment results in a parallel allowance for the surprising abyss of God. Our admiration for creation reflects our adoration of the absolute, a vocation to the beyond, an invitation to transfiguration.

Apophasis is an element of *askesis;* the silence of poetry is a form of surrender to the living God; it is like dying to the flesh in order to live fully in the Spirit. Silence and death go hand in hand; to be utterly silent can feel like death. Silence and ascesis issue in resurrection and new life through the Spirit.

Conclusion

If, indeed, there is a Spirit of God, and it is the very Spirit of Creation; if this world is the Body of God, the actual flesh of the divine Word; if, in fact, the Spirit of God reveals the Image of God in creation, beyond the brokenness and shatteredness of this world; then there is a sense in which this earth is not merely a reflection,[23] but even a perfection of heaven. Just as we are incomplete without the rest of the animal and the material creation, so, too, the kingdom of God remains incomplete without the world around us.

Notes

1. See Athanasius *On the Divine Incarnation* 54.

2. Bessarion, saying 11, in *Sayings of the Desert Fathers,* trans. Benedicta Ward (London: A. R. Mowbray, 1975), 35. Reference to "all eyes" is also found in Barsanuphius *Letters* 120 and 241.

3. John of Damascus *On Divine Images* 1.4.

4. Ibid., 16.

5. "Preserving God's Creation," *King's Theological Review* (London) 13, no. 1 (1990): 5. See also the first two parts of this illuminating article in vol. 12, no. 1-2 (1989): 1–5 and 41–45. These articles have, with additional material and editorial changes, appeared in a book published in Greek, entitled *The Creation as Eucharist* (Athens: Akritas, 1992).

6. See *Apologetic Sermon 3 . . . on the Holy Icons* (Migne *PG* 93.1604ab).

7. Philip Sherrard, *The Sacred in Life and Art* (Ipswich, England: Golgonooza Press, 1990), 84.

8. From the Resurrection Canon chanted at Easter Matins.

9. Gregory the Theologian *Homily* 38.11 (Migne *PG* 36.321–24).

10. Maximus Confessor *De Ambiguis* 91. See also his *Mystagogia* 7 (Migne *PG* 91.672).

11. Nilus of Ancyra *Epistles* 2.119 (Migne *PG* 79:252b). See also Origen *Homily on Leviticus* 5.2 (Migne *PG* 12.448–50). See also D. S. Wallace-Hadrill, *The Greek Patristic View of Nature* (Manchester: Manchester University Press, 1968), especially 66–79.

12. See Maximus Confessor *Gnostic Chapters* 1.66 (Migne *PG* 90.1108ab). On the priestly character of humanity, see Kallistos Ware, "The Value of the Material Creation," *Sobornost* (London) 6, no. 3 (1971): 154–65.

13. John Climacus *The Ladder of Divine Ascent, Step 4,* 58 (Migne *PG* 88.892d–893a).

14. For a detailed description of selected icons, including that by Rublev of the Trinity, see Paul Evdokimov, *The Art of the Icon: A Theology of Beauty,* trans. Fr. Steven Bigham (Redondo Beach, Calif.: Oakwood Publications, 1990). About the icon of Rublev, Pavel Florensky once exclaimed: "there is Rublev's *Trinity,* therefore there is God." See V. V. Bychkov, *The Aesthetic Face of Being* (Crestwood, N.Y.: St. Vladimir's Seminary Press, 1993), 42.

15. Symeon the New Theologian *Hymn* 15.132–33. As with the concept of "sophia," so also the notion of "chora" may equally be applied to the Virgin Mary (cf. the Akathistos Hymn, Stasis 1: She "contained [*choresasa*] the One who contains [*chorei*] the universe"). On the relationship between liturgy, iconography, and creation, see the articles in *Orthodoxy and Ecology: Resource Book* (Bialystok: Syndesmos, 1996), 72–81.

16. See Leonardo Boff, *Sacraments of Life—Life of Sacraments* (Washington, D.C.: Pastoral Press, 1987), 49–51.

17. Gregory Nazianzus *Letter 101 to Cleidonius* (Migne *PG* 37.181c).

18. In Joachim Jeremias, *Unknown Sayings of Jesus,* trans. Reginald H. Fuller (London: SPCK, 1957), 95.

19. Boff, *Sacraments,* 38. Pierre Teilhard de Chardin wrote in similar fashion echoing Maximus Confessor's image of the "cosmic liturgy." See Teilhard, *Mass on the World,* in *Hymn of the Universe,* trans. G. Vann (New York: Harper and Row, 1972), 16: "Once again the fire has penetrated the earth . . . the flame has lit up the whole world from within."

20. From the Service of the Sacrament of Baptism in the Orthodox Church.

21. See Dionysius the Areopagite *Celestial Hierarchy* 15.7 (Migne *PG* 3.336bc).

22. Dionysius the Areopagite *On Divine Names* 1.6 (Migne *PG* 3.596) and 13.1–2 (Migne *PG* 3.977); translation mine. For the works of Dionysius, see *Pseudo-Dionysius: The Complete Works,* trans. Colm Luibheid, The Classics of Western Spirituality (New York: Paulist Press, 1987).

23. This is a significant point of divergence between Christian theology and Platonist philosophy. The Hellenistic conception of the created world as a "mirror," or "image," of the eternal realm is a privilege as well as a problem in terms of the value and sacredness of creation. Perhaps this is also the reason for the "ambivalence" of the patristic texts themselves, which will sometimes underline the creation of this world by a loving God, while at other times undermine the intimate connection between the Creator and the creation. The result is an apparent paradox between a "monarchical" theology and its consequential "dualistic" anthropology and cosmology to which Sallie McFague and others rightly react.

Ecofeminism:
The Challenge to Theology

ROSEMARY RADFORD RUETHER

It is the contention of this paper that ecofeminism poses a profound challenge to classical Christian theology and, indeed, to all the classical religions shaped by the worldview of patriarchy. Here I am focusing on Christianity, with its roots in the worldviews of the ancient Near East and Greco-Roman worlds. Let me start with a brief definition of ecofeminism. Ecofeminism, or ecological feminism, examines the interconnections between the domination of women and the domination of nature. It aims at strategies and worldviews to liberate or heal these interconnected dominations through a better understanding of their etiology and enforcement.

There are two levels on which this relation between sexism and ecological exploitation can be made: on the cultural-symbolic level and on the socioeconomic level. My assumption is that the first is an ideological superstructure that reflects and ratifies the second. That is, social patterns developed, deeply rooted in the distortion of gender relations with the rise of patriarchal slavocracies in the ancient Near East, that subjugated women as a gender group. The system of domination of women itself was rooted in a larger patriarchal hierarchical system of priestly and warrior-king control over land, animals, and slaves as property, which monopolized wealth, power, and knowledge.

As this system of domination was shaped socially, ideological tools were constructed to ratify it as a reflection of the "nature of things" and the "will of God/the gods." Law codes were developed to define these relations of power of dominant men over women, slaves, animals, and land as property.[1] These law codes are described as handed down to an inspired lawgiver by God/the gods. Creation stories were spun out to depict this hierarchical social order as itself a reflection of the cosmic order.

In the ancient Near East and classical Athens several creation stories were constructed to ratify this design of society. In the Babylonian creation story, which goes back to the third millennium B.C.E., the story of cosmogony is told as a theogony of the gods that culminates in an intergenerational conflict between the old earth mother, Tiamat, and her great-grandson Marduk. A mother-dominated old world of primal energies is set against a new world order of city-states championed by Marduk.[2]

Marduk is seen as conquering chaos and creating the cosmos by conquering the primal mother, treading her body underfoot and splitting it in half, using one half to fashion the starry firmament above and the other half the earth below. Her subordinate male consort is then slain, and from his blood, mixed with the earth, are fashioned human beings to be the slaves of the gods so the gods can be at leisure. The elemental mother is turned into "matter" which can then be used to shape a hierarchical cosmos. The creation of humans as slaves to the gods within this cosmos defines the primary social relation as that of masters over slaves.

In both the Hebrew and the Greek creation stories this primal battle against the mother, that suggested an earlier, alternative world, is concealed. These stories begin with the presupposition of patriarchal dualism as the foundational nature of things. For the Greek philosophical story, told by Plato, the primal dualism of mind divided from matter was the first state of things. On the one side stood Mind, containing the archetypal ideas; on the other side, unformed matter, the receptacle, or "nurse," of things to be. Between the two stood disembodied male agency as the divine architect or Creator, who shapes matter into a cosmos by fashioning it after the intellectual blueprint of the divine ideas.[3]

The Creator shapes a circular and hierarchically ordered cosmos, with the fixed stars and the realm of the gods at the outer edge, the earth at the bottom, and the planetary spheres ranged in between. He then fashions the world soul to set this cosmos in motion. Taking the residue of the world soul, he cuts this into individual souls and places them in the stars. There they have a preincarnational vision of the eternal ideas. Then they are encased in bodies, fashioned by the planetary gods, and put on the earth.

The task of the soul is to control the passions that arise from the body and to cultivate the intellect. If the soul succeeds in this task, it will doff the body at death and return to its native star, there to live "a blessed and congenial existence." But if it fails to control the body, it will enter a cycle of reincarnation, entering the bodies of lower beings, women, lower social classes, and animals.[4] The fall into an animal is terminal for the soul, but from lower forms of humans, women, and lower classes, the soul can rise through successive incarnations into the highest state, the elite Greek male, and be liberated into disembodied bliss.

Although Christianity would shed the ideas of the preexistence and reincarnation of the soul,[5] it followed key presuppositions of Plato's cosmology, reading the Genesis story through the lens of the *Timaeus*. It continued the presuppositions that the soul is an ontological substance separable from the body, living in an alienated state on Earth, whose true home lies in Heaven. It attempted to combine the Platonic eschatology of the soul's return to the stars with the radically different Hebrew eschatology of the resurrected body on a millennial earth by imagining a "spiritual body" stripped of its mortal components that would clothe the soul in its final heavenly state.[6]

Like Plato, Christianity imaged the soul in relation to the body as male controlling power over female-identified body and passions that are to be controlled. Although Christianity concedes that women also possess a redeemable soul in God's image, the classical Christian theological tradition sees this soul as nongendered. A genderless soul that can be redeemed through baptism into Christ is distinguished from women as female who are seen as inherently closer to the sin-prone bodily tendencies.

This lower nature demands that women be subordinated and kept under control by men, but it also means that women are prone to insubordination and subversion of male rational control. It is through this female tendency that the male was seduced into sin in the beginning and paradise was lost, ushering humanity into a fallen world.

In this story of original paradise, sin and fall Christianity drew on a very different cosmology and earth story from the Hebrews. The Genesis story posits a patriarchal God who shapes an original chaotic matter into cosmos through his word-command during a six-day work week, culminating in sabbatical rest. The human, created male and female on the sixth day and given the command to rule over the earth and its plants and animals, is not created as a slave, but as a royal servant, or administrator, of the earth as representative of God, or "in God's image."[7]

There is no explicit mandate for the domination of some humans over others, as male over female or master over slave, in the Hebrew story. This fact allowed the Genesis story to be used as a potent basis for an egalitarian view of all humans as equal in God's image in later Christian movements that sought to dismantle slavery and sexism. But this later Christian usage of Genesis 1 overlooks what was implicit in the Hebrew story, and explicit in Hebrew law and exegesis. Adam is a generic human who is assumed to be embodied by the male patriarchal class which represents dependent humans, women, slaves, and children and rules over God's creation.[8]

Moreover, in Genesis 2–3, as if to make the gender assumptions explicit, the male is identified with the original male human being, out of which the female is created by the male God and handed over to the male to be his wife-servant. Contrary to modern feminist apologetics, this is not an egalitarian relation, but one in which the male is the normative human and the female a derivative auxiliary.[9] This derivative female is then described as initiating disobedience to God's command, thus causing the pair to be thrown out of paradise to live an oppressive existence. His punishment is hard labor by the sweat of his brow, while hers is painful childbearing and subjugation to her husband.

Although the present fallen world is sunk in sin, Hebrew thought looks forward to a future time when paradise will be restored. When humans (Israel's patriarchal class) turn and obey God, God will restore them to an idyllic world where there will be no violence between man and man, alienation between man and nature will be overcome, harmonic relations will reign on a peaceful and prosperous earth. Originally, this Hebrew hope for a future paradise was earth- and mortality-bound. It assumed that redeemed humans would live a long, healthy, but mortal life on a peaceful and bountiful but mortal earth.[10]

Later contact with Persian eschatology and Platonism would re-shape Hebrew futurism into apocalyptic scenarios in which the dead of past generations rise, are judged by a messianic king and the whole earth transformed into immortal conditions. It is this apocalyptic eschatology that is received by the Christian movement and fused with elements of Platonic cosmology to create the classic Christian story of creation, fall, and redemption.

Since Christianity dropped the ideas of the soul's preexistence and reincarnation, it also lost the explanation for women's inferiority based on the view that women are born through the failure of souls in past male incarnations to control their bodily passions. Some early Christian movements suggested a subversive liberation in Christ from all relations of subjugation—women to men, slaves to masters, subjugated to ruling nations. The original equality prior to sexual differentiation was seen as restored, drawing on the Galatians text, "In Christ there is no more male and female, Jew and Greek, slave and free."[11]

As Christianity was institutionalized in the patriarchal family and political order, however, it moved quickly to suppress these radical interpretations of redemption in Christ. Although equal access to heavenly redemption was conceded to women, this future hope was not allowed to subvert patriarchal relations on Earth in the newly forming Christian church and society. This was already expressed in the post-Pauline dicta in 1 Timothy, which declared that women were created second and sinned first and therefore are to keep silence and to have no authority over men in the Christian community.[12]

Augustine, in his late-fourth- and early-fifth-century commentaries on Genesis, would shape the theological rationale for women's subordination that would be followed by the dominant line of Christian theologians through the Reformation. For Augustine, woman, although given a nongendered soul by the Creator that enables her to be redeemed, was created in her female nature to be subordinate to the male in the sexual-social roles of wife and childbearer. For Augustine, femaleness itself represents the inferior bodily nature, while the male represents the intellect which is to rule over both his body and hers. He is the collective Adam made in God's image, while woman as woman does not possess the image of God in herself but images the subordinate body. She is "in the image of God" only when taken together with the male, "who is her head."[13]

Moreover, for Augustine, due to her inferior and more sin-prone nature, Eve initiated disobedience to God. The male, by assenting to her prompting, conceded to his lower self. Only thus does the whole human fall into sin.[14] Although humans as a whole are punished by a loss of original immortality that was the gift of union with God and have lost the free will that allowed them to choose God over their sinful self-will, women are punished for their special fault by coercive subjugation.[15]

For Augustine, woman was created subordinate but is now in a state of forced subjugation, to punish her for her original insubordination and to keep her in her place. Redemption does not liberate her from this subordination. Rather, through voluntary acceptance of it, she makes herself obedient to God and a fit subject of heavenly bliss. Then, finally, there will be no hierarchy of male over female, but all the blessed will live in gloriously spiritualized bodies freed from sin and death.

These patriarchal patterns that fused Hebrew and Greek thought reigned in Christian cosmology, anthropology, Christology, and soteriology until modern times, being taken up and renewed by the mainline Reformers, Luther and Calvin. In the sixteenth and seventeenth centuries a few maverick feminist humanists and the Quakers challenged the doctrine of male domination as the order of nature and punishment due women for their priority in sin. They returned to suppressed early Christian themes of radical egalitarianism and argued that all humans were made equal in the original creation.[16]

For these thinkers the domination over women, as well as other forms of domination, such as slavery, came about through sin; not women's sin, but the sin of dominant males who distorted the original harmony by usurping power over others. Christ came to overcome all such dominations and to restore the equality of women and men, but male church leaders have distorted the gospel into new rationales for sexism. Redemption means not just a promise of spiritual equality in heaven, but a socal struggle to overcome unjust domination of men over women, masters over slaves, here on Earth.

This theology of original and redeemed equality over against patriarchal slavocracy was picked up and developed by abolitionist feminists of the nineteenth century, such as the Grimké sisters and Lucretia Mott. In the pithy words of Sarah Grimké, writing in 1837, "All I ask of my brethen is, that they take their feet from off our necks and permit us to stand upright on the ground which God designed us to occupy."[17] Sarah Grimké had no doubt that woman's ground is one of an autonomous human being created as man's peer and equal partner, not his subordinate.

This anthropology of original and restored equality was rediscovered by modern feminist theology and has been the basis for a critique of patriarchal anthropology in recent decades. But the nineteenth-century feminists did not question an anthropocentric worldview in which man and woman together were created to dominate and rule over the nonhuman creation. It is only with the deepening of feminist theology in ecofeminism that there has been a questioning of patriarchal cosmology and a recognition of the need to grapple with the whole structure of the Christian story, and not just with gender relations in its anthropology.

When I speak about the challenge of ecofeminism to theology, it is in the context of a radicalization that takes place as ecological consciousness is incorporated into feminist theology. One then realizes the need to question and reconstruct the cosmological framework out of which the Christian worldview grew from its ancient roots in the Hebrew and Greek worlds. A full treatment of the implications of these deeper questions is still very much in process. One awaits a full presentation of what an ecofeminist theology would look like. Here, I will only attempt a few suggestions about how the self, sin and redemption, God, cosmology, and eschatology are being rethought by ecofeminist theology.

I begin with a view of the self in ecofeminist theology as the starting point for a challenge to the Platonic construct of soul and body which still reigns officially in Christian thought, although with failing conviction. The basic assumption of ecofeminist theology (although seldom clearly articulated) is that the dualism of soul and body must be rejected, as well as the assumptions of the priority and controlling role of male-identified mind over female-identified body. This anthropology is at the heart of the distortion in Western thought of our relation to ourselves, as well as to our fellow earth creatures and the cosmos as a whole.

Humans are latecomers to the planet. The plants and animals existed billions of years before us. We are descendents of the long evolution of increasingly complex life-forms on Earth. Our consciousness does not set us radically apart from the rest of the life-forms on Earth; rather, there is a continuity of matter-energy dynamics on different levels of organization, moving from inorganic energy to life, then to awareness of life, and then to self-reflecting consciousness in organisms with progressively more complex brains. We were not created to dominate and rule the earth, for it governed itself well and better for millions of years when we did not exist or existed as nondominant mammals.

Only in very recent earth history, in the last few thousand years, has *Homo sapiens* emerged as an increasingly dominant species, using its special gifts for thinking and organizing to control and exploit the majority of humans and the nonhuman earth community. Stewardship is not a primal command, but an ex post facto effort of dominant males to correct overabuse and become better managers of what they have presumed to be their patrimony, namely, ownership of the rest of the world.

We need to recognize that our self-reflective consciousness is not a separable ontological substance but our experience of our own interiority, which is integral to our brain-body and dies with it. We are finite moments of self-conscious life which arose from the earth and return to it at death. Our consciousness did not fall from a heaven outside the earth and will not escape outside of it into an eternal life. Our destiny and calling is of and for this earth, our only and true home. Immortality lies not in the preservation of our individual consciousness as a separate substance but in the miracle and mystery of endlessly recycled matter-energy out of which we arose and into which we return. A better translation of the Ash Wednesday proclamation is: "we are earth; to earth we shall return."

This means we need to use our special capacities for thought, not to imagine ourselves as ruling over others, superior to them, and as escaping our common mortality, but rather to celebrate the wonder of the whole cosmic process and to be the place where this cosmic process comes to celebrative consciousness. We also need to use our capacities to contemplate and understand these processes so that we may harmonize our lives with the life of the whole earth community. This demands a spirituality and ethic of mutual limitation and of reciprocal life-giving nurture, the very opposite of the spirituality of separation and domination.

This ecological consciousness of self calls for a very different understanding of the nature of evil and its remedies. We need to give up the presuppositions of an original paradise, when there was no evil, and a future paradise, when evil and death are overcome. Rather, we need to look more closely at the etiology of our particular distortion of our relation to one another and to the earth through myths of separation and domination. Here, I find myself particularly instructed by Brazilian ecofeminist theologian Ivone Gebara.

In Gebara's view, evil, in the sense of finitude and tragedy, has always been with us and with all life-forms on Earth, and this will always be so. The primal sin is not a disobedience that caused us to fall into a mortality to which we were not originally subjected. Rather, the primal sin lies in the effort to escape from mortality, finitude, and vulnerability. The desire to escape from mortality may have long been a part of human fear of death, but it took organized, pernicious forms with the rise of powerful males who sought to monopolize power over other humans, land, and animals. For them the ultimate power over others was to rise superior to death itself, to organize their power to assure themselves of an invulnerability to that finitude that is the common lot of earth creatures.[18]

This very effort to secure man's own invulnerability from want and death impelled an endless process of seeking to amass power at the expense of the rest of humans and the earth. These dominant men, seeking ultimate salvation from vulnerability, constructed systems of abuse and exploitation of other humans and the earth to achieve over-weening wealth and power. Women became the particular targets of this flight from vulnerability because they represented man's finite origins and the realities of earth-bound pain and limits. To rule over and to flee from woman, the body, and the earth was to seek to conquer and flee from one's own denied finitude.

For Gebara it is this impulse to dominate and exploit in order to conquer want, imagining oneself to have transcended finite limita-tions, that has created the system of distortion that heaps excessive want and untimely death on the majority of humans. This system of exploitation threatens to undo the processes that maintain the life cycle of all earth beings in relation to one another, crafted by the earth over billions of years. It is this system of domination and distortion which is sin, as distinct from tragedy and death, which are natural and inevitable.

This understanding of the etiology of sin and the fall into domination also dictates how Gebara understands salvation. Just as we must give up the original paradise where there was no tragedy or death, so we must give up the future paradise where tragedy and death are overcome.[19] We need to recognize that these myths of immortal and perfect beginnings and ends not only falsify our real possibilities but are themselves projections of the escape from vulnerability which is at the heart of sin.

The real salvation that is available to us is of much more modest dimensions and yet is, nevertheless, of world historic and global proportions. We need to dismantle the system of distortion that gives a privileged class overweening wealth and power at the expense of most humans and that is destroying the life-sustaining balances of the earth. In so doing, we will not expect a paradise free from tragedy and death but a community of mutual life-giving where we can hold one another in the celebrative as well as the tragic moments of our common life as earth creatures.

This more modest redemptive hope was summed up in the conclusion of the women's creed written by Robin Morgan for the Women's Conference in Beijing, China:[20]

> Bread. A clean sky. Active peace. A woman's voice singing somewhere. The army disbanded. The harvest abundant. The wound healed. The child wanted. The prisoner freed. The body's integrity honored. The lover returned. . . . Labor equal, fair and valued. No hand raised in any gesture but greeting. Secure interiors—of heart, home and land— so firm as to make secure borders irrelevant at last.

This is the vision of an ecological hope freed from false escapism and content to make common joys abundant and available to us all in the midst of those tragedies of limits, failures, and accidents that also should be equally shared, rather than heaped upon some in excess so a privileged few may imagine themselves immortal.

The dismantling of an escapist self and salvation history that is the root of human sin and *han*[21] (victimization of others and the pain of victimization) also demands a dismantling of the view of cosmology, God, and Christ that has sustained this distortion. Instead of modeling God after male ruling-class consciousness, outside of and ruling over nature as its controlling immortal projection, God in ecofeminist spirituality is the immanent source of life and the renewal of life that sustains the whole planetary and cosmic community. God is neither male nor anthropomorphic. God is the font from which the variety of particular beings "co-arise" in each generation, the matrix that sustains their life-giving interdependency with each other, and also the judging and renewing insurgency of life that enables us to overcome the distortions that threaten healthy relations.

This understanding of God is leading several ecofeminist theologians to reconstruct the understanding of the Trinity as the sustaining matrix of immanent relationality. Ivone Gebara sees the Trinity, not as a separate, self-enclosed relation of two divine males with each other, mediated by the Spirit, but as the symbolic expression of the basic dynamic of life itself as a process of vital interrelational creativity. Life as interrelational creativity exists on every level of reality. As cosmos it reveals itself as the whole process of cosmic unfolding and interrelation of planets and galaxies. As Earth it shows us the dynamic interrelational process of life unfolding in the biosphere.[22]

Each species ramifies into many differences, including human beings with their many races and cultures. We should celebrate this diversity of humanness and affirm our interrelation with each other in one community on Earth. Likewise, interpersonal society and the person herself exists as a creative dynamic of expanding plurality and new interrelationality, of unity and diversity in interaction. The trinitarian dynamic of life is both creational and salvational; it both creates new life and seeks to correct distorted relations and reestablish life-giving, loving relationality. The name of the Trinitarian God as sustaining, redeeming matrix of cosmic, planetary, social, and personal life is Sophia: Holy Wisdom.

In the context of this understanding of the ecological self, good and evil, and the Trinitarian God, what does it mean to speak of Jesus as Christ? Can we still affirm this one historical figure as the unique incarnation of God's creating Logos, even reinterpreted as Sophia? In what way is he both Sophia and Messiah?

Gebara questions the messianic myth of a heroic warrior who will deliver victims from oppression, punish the oppressors, and create an ideal earth freed from sin and want. She sees this myth as the counterpart, from the victims' perspective, of the desire to escape from finitude, but now coupled with the thirst for revenge upon those who have secured their own privilege at the expense of others. Messianic myths, as revenge scenarios of victims, reproduce, rather than break, the cycle of violence and create new victims and new victimizers.

Jesus, for Gebara, is a very different prophetic figure who sought to break through the cycle of violence. Taking the side of the victims, he also called those in power to repent and enter into a new community of mutual service. The dominant system could not tolerate his message and killed him to silence his countervision. But his followers also betrayed him by turning his call to a community of shared love into a new messianism, making him into the warrior imperial savior who would secure the Christian system of dominating power.[23]

Thus, to ask how Jesus is the Christ, one must overturn the messianic myth. Jesus stands instead as an antimessiah calling us to rediscover the community of equals that appears when the system of sin and *han,* of victimizers and victims, of rich and poor, is dismantled. We enter, then, not a community of immortal blessedness freed from finitude and limits, but a community of shared joys and sorrows as earth creatures, former Pharisees and prostitutes, the lame and the blind, women and men on the edges of the dominant system breaking bread together.

Likewise, if Jesus reveals God, the God he reveals is not the split-off, dominating Logos of immortalized male sovereignty but the Holy Wisdom of mutual self-giving and life-sustaining love. Jesus the Christ embodies the Holy Wisdom that creates and renews the creation, not as its exclusive and unique representative, but rather as a paradigm of her presence, one among many other sisters and brothers, to recall us to our true selves and relations and away from the madness of escapism and domination. These are the "temptations" from which we ask to be delivered, even as we pray for those conditions of daily bread and mutual forgiveness that recreate God's will done on Earth.

Gebara's understanding of the immanent Trinitarian God of life's dynamic relationality places revelation within our experience of nature. We read (and critique) our historical scriptures in the light of the book of nature. All life, from the evolution of the galaxies to the dynamics of the self, manifests the presence of God as sustaining Wisdom of creation. But this does not mean a blissful world of idyllic conditions. Nature reveals how life sustains its precarious balances by painful and tragic means. Lion and lamb do not lay down together but keep one another's population within sustainable limits by a bloody process of eating and being eaten.

We are tempted, in speaking of nature as revelatory, to see nature through a paradisal lens, ignoring its violent and tragic face. We imagine it as Eden only by removing ourselves from it and viewing it through the plate glass window of our momentary havens of invulnerability, purchased at the expense of many other humans. But a tornado can shatter this glass and sweep away this shelter at any moment.

Two revelatory commands come, from "nature" and from "history," that are not easy to reconcile. Some in Christian thought even saw them as revealing different gods opposed to one another. I call these two commands the call to sustainability and the call to preferential option for the poor. When I garden, I would be foolish to make a preferential option for the weak and the diseased. I need to root out the excess growth of many plants so that a few, the healthiest, can grow well. In like manner, as Jay McDaniel agonized, nature gives the pelican two eggs so that one will survive: if the first hatches well, the second will be pecked to death and thrown from the nest.[24] This cruelty is necessary for a sustainable population of pelicans or tomatoes. Sentimentality for the second pelican or the excess plants would be misplaced.

Likewise, humans need to limit their own species proliferation at the expense of the other species of Earth, as much as possible by decisions not to conceive rather than to abort. But to deny the need for birth limitation in the name of life is no favor to children. It means that thousands die each day of malnutrition soon after birth. To refuse to limit ourselves rationally means that these limits are imposed cruelly and violently.

A different call comes from our history of sin and *han,* arising as a protest against the distortion of relations between humans and with other creatures that results in overweening wealth for a few and impoverishment for the many. This pattern is not, contrary to social Darwinism, an expression of a natural ethic of the survival of the fittest, for nature does not favor the large carnivore, precariously perched at the top of the food chain, over all the creatures on which it depends, but seeks dynamic balance through a combination of mutual limits and cooperation. The scurrying insects that compost the forest are far more important to its well-being than the lion.

Preferential option for the poor seeks to correct the destructive option for the rich at the expense of the well-being of the whole community of life. The ethic of preferential option for the poor calls us to feed and nurture the child of the poor dying from malnutrition and unclean water and to rectify the conditions that are causing this untimely death, while the ethic of sustainability calls us to help the mother of this child limit her childbearing.

The two ethics often stand in tragic tension, but they should not be allowed to fall into irreconcilable dualism, with a war God of victory of the strong over the weak, on the one hand, and, on the other, a God of compassion for the weak distorted into a defense of fetuses against women. We need to seek a right balance between justice and sustainability. The challenge of ecological theology and ethics is to knit together, in the light of both earth knowledge and the crisis of human history, a vision of divine presence that underlies and sustains natural processes and struggles against the excesses of the powerful while reaching out to the victimized to create communities of mutual flourishing.

Notes

1. For these relations of patriarchal domination in Ancient Near Eastern and Greek law codes, see Rosemary Ruether, *Gaia and God: An Ecofeminist Theology of Earth Healing* (San Francisco: HarperSanFrancisco, 1992), 174–80.

2. See "The Creation Epic" in *Religions of the Ancient Near East: Sumero-Akkadian Religious Texts and Ugaritic Epics,* ed. Isaac Mendelsohn (New York: Liberal Arts Press, 1955), 17–46.

3. Plato *Timaeus* 49, from *The Dialogues of Plato,* trans. B. Jowett (New York: Random House, 1937), 2:29.

4. Plato *Timaeus* 42, ibid., 23. See also Plato's *Phaedrus,* where he adds the idea that the fallen soul will enter into various upper or lower class people depending on the extent of its fall into the passions; *Dialogues of Plato,* 2:248.

5. See Origen *On First Principles* 2.2.2 (New York: Harper and Row, 1966), 81–82: also Ruether, *Gaia and God,* 133.

6. Gregory Nyssa describes the risen body as stripping off all that has made it mortal; see his "On the Soul and the Resurrection," in *Nicene and Post-Nicene Fathers,* 2d ser. (New York: Parker, 1893), 5:464–65.

7. Gen. 1:26–27.

8. See Phyllis Bird, "'Male and Female He Created Them': Gen 1:27b in the Context of the Priestly Account of Creation," in *Image of God and Gender Models in Judaeo-Christian Tradition,* ed. Kari Borresen (Minneapolis: Fortress Press, 1995), 11–34.

9. See Phyllis Trible, "Depatriarchalizing in Biblical Interpretation," *Journal of the American Academy of Religion* 46, no. 1 (March 1973): 30–48.

10. See Rachel Zohar Dulin, "Old Age in the Hebrew Scriptures" (Ph.D. diss., Northwestern University, 1982).

11. Gal. 3:28. See Rosemary R. Ruether, *Women and Redemption: A Theological History* (Minneapolis: Fortress Press, 1998), chap. 1.

12. 1 Tim. 1:11–15. See Dennis R. MacDonald, *The Legend and the Apostle: The Battle for Paul in Story and Canon* (Philadelphia: Westminster Press, 1983).

13. Augustine *De Trinitate* 10.10.7. See Ruether, *Women and Redemption,* chap. 2.

14. Augustine *City of God* 14.11.

15. Augustine *On Genesis: Two Books on Genesis against the Manichees* 2.19; *The Fathers of the Church,* trans. Roland J. Teske, vol. 84 (Washington, D.C.: Catholic University of America Press, 1991). See Ruether, *Women and Redemption,* chap. 2.

16. Particularly the tract of Agrippa von Nettesheim (1509), *De Nobilitate et Praecellentia foeminei Sexus,* ed. Charles Béné (Geneva: Librairie Droz, 1990). See Ruether, *Women and Redemption,* chap. 4.

17. Sarah Grimké, "Letters on the Equality of the Sexes and the Condition of Women" (1837), in *Feminism: The Essential Historical Writings,* ed. Miriam Schneir (New York: Vintage, 1992), 38.

18. Ivone Gebara, *Teología a Ritmo de Mujer* (Madrid: San Pablo, 1995), 146–56. Ruether, *Women and Redemption,* chap. 8.

19. Gebara, *Teología a Ritmo de Mujer,* 146–56.

20. This women's creed, written by Robin Morgan for the United Nations Conference on Women in Beijing, China, in September 1995, was sent to me by Catherine Keller of Drew Theological Seminary in Madison, New Jersey.

21. The term *han* comes from Korean Minjung theology that discusses the experience of victimization. For a theology that interconnects the Western Christian emphasis on sin with the Minjung emphasis on *han,* see Andrew Sung Park, *The Wounded Heart of God: The Asian Concept of Han and the Christian Doctrine of Sin* (Nashville: Abingdon Press, 1993).

22. Ivone Gebara, "The Trinity and Human Experience," in Rosemary Radford Ruether, *Women Healing Earth: Third World Women on Ecology, Feminism, and Religion* (Maryknoll, N.Y.: Orbis Books, 1996), 13–23.

23. Gebara, *Teología a Ritmo de Mujer,* 146–56.

24. Jay B. McDaniel, *Of God and Pelicans: A Theology of Reverence for Life* (Louisville: Westminster/John Knox Press, 1989), 19–21.

Response to Rosemary Radford Ruether: Ecofeminism and Theology—Challenges, Confrontations, and Reconstructions

HEATHER EATON

The ecofeminist challenge to theology is profound and permeates all layers of theological reflection and praxis. As feminist theologies engage further with ecological concerns, and as ecofeminist analyses mature and become a dialogue partner with theology, we can begin to speak of ecofeminist theologies.[1] The extent of the ecofeminist challenge to and confrontation with classical theology is in the initial states of articulation, as evident in the works of Rosemary Radford Ruether.[2] My response explores elements of this articulation with reference to Ruether's "Ecofeminism: The Challenge to Theology," with a primary focus on the challenge to and confrontation with the foundations of classical theology. A second challenge is how to develop ecofeminist theology(ies) that are adequate and that will become a call to action to resist socioecological ruin.

Ecofeminism and Theology

Ecofeminist critiques of classical theology reveal a theological system rooted in a desire to flee the actual conditions of life—vulnerability, finitude, and mortality—and a theological structure based on a perceived need to dominate, exploit, and conquer in order to escape these conditions. Cornerstones of this theological system are the feminizing of the natural world, the naturalizing of women, and the domination of both in theoretical, historical, and cultural webs of entanglements. As Ruether points out, the cultural-symbolic level of the relationship between sexism and ecological exploitation is the ideological superstructure that reflects and sanctions the social, economic, and political order.

The ensuing distortions pervade and saturate classical theological discourses and are further imbedded in cultural ideologies and practices. Ecofeminist analyses reveal the engrained antiwomen and antinature stances and redefine elements which could assist theology in actively resisting the socioecological crises. Further, ecofeminist theologies hold in tension the relationship between religion and culture, ethics of nature and history, and theory and praxis and insist that we become conscious of the cultural effects of our theological reflections and systems. Ultimately, ecofeminist theologies, especially those emphasizing liberation, help to image a viable, although modest, theological and earthly future.

Those engaged in this revisioning process concur that ecofeminist theologies are fundamentally different from the hegemonic classical discourse in their method, attention to context, epistemological framework, and orientation toward liberatory praxis.[3] Much current work involves reinterpreting or expanding particular doctrines, symbols, and metaphors, such as the Trinity, to include the excluded, women, and the natural world. The immense task of challenging foundational presuppositions and reshaping the infrastructure of theology remains the substantive and more difficult work. It is increasingly necessary to be explicit about the depth of challenge that ecology and feminism together pose to theological discourses. There are core problems that cannot be underestimated. Although there are both continuities and discontinuities with classical methodologies and interpretations, there are some cherished notions that will need to be abandoned, even rejected.

Among the ecofeminist challenges Ruether presents to theology is that of Christology. Because Christology is dependent upon an image of God, the role of creation, sin and redemption, and anthropology, it cannot be divorced from the theological framework that sustains it. Therefore, it is the whole of theology that is being challenged. As Ruether says, there is a need to grapple with the whole structure of the Christian story. I would like to shed light on some central and perhaps controversial issues and foundational theological frameworks which lurk in the shadows of the ecofeminist challenge to theology. I will address, as an example, Ivone Gebara's christological reflections as described by Ruether.

At the basis of domination is a flight from life's proviso. The primal sin of escaping, the fall into domination, and the refusal to acknowledge the sufferings and limitations of life itself have created distortions at the level of foundational theological precepts. Given this interpretation, Gebara suggests that the christological messianic myth of a heroic warrior is inappropriate. It needs to be replaced with an understanding of Jesus as one who calls everyone to a radical community of equals. Jesus is an antimessiah; he is one who reveals the Wisdom of God. Jesus teaches and saves insofar as our salvation is found in returning to our embodied selves, away from escapism and domination, and embracing with joy and sorrow the genuine limitations, richness, and struggles of life in community and solidarity with all life. Jesus reveals a holy and creative paradigm of Wisdom. Jesus is a salvific figure, prophet, model, and paradigm; unique but not exclusive, one among many who "calls" the human community back to authenticity. Jesus continues to reveal many dimensions of life, including aspects of God, but the Christology is neither ascending nor descending. It is distinct in both theological method and substance.

This interpretation of an antimessiah Jesus is connected to Gebara's understanding of sin, redemption, revelation, Creation, anthropology, and the Divine, indeed the whole framework of theology. Her proposal leaves room for deep interreligious respect, supports liberation theologies, disputes otherworldly afterlife theologies, defies hierarchy, and confronts christofacism.[4] The challenge, even confrontation, to classical Christology and to the theological system that sustains it is evident; the distinctiveness and consequences are far-reaching.

I appreciate Ruether's and Gebara's proposals for a radically new way of doing theology, which is also emerging from others as ecological, feminist, and liberationist theologies coalesce.[5] Underlying these proposals is an (often) unarticulated need for a renewed comprehensive vision and framework that can provide a solid theological base. My response is to illustrate the foundational challenge that ecofeminism presents to theology by articulating some basic and interpretive frameworks which may support the efforts to resituate theology in ecological, feminist, and liberatory perspectives with a comprehensive foundation. I will present six frameworks, from least to most challenging, noting that each can be cradled in the next as the horizon of the frameworks expand. Many, if not all, of these are present implicitly in the example of Gebara's christological proposal.

Foundational Theological Frameworks for Ecofeminist Theologies

1. In strengthening Christian responses to the socioecological crises, the most accessible framework is that of sifting through the tradition and emphasizing those elements that could assist and validate attempts at cultural recovery. The retrieval of the insights of Hildegard of Bingen, the revival of Wisdom and Sophia, the restoration of the best of the medieval, organic synthesis of Thomas Aquinas, and the importance of concepts such as stewardship and covenant fall within this relatively innocuous framework for reappropriating Christianity for our era. This is both useful and least confrontational, as it involves internal shifts rather than foundational reconstruction. Although a generalization, the tradition is the predominant reference point.

2. A second framework is that of profound reinterpretations, such as Ruether proposes by envisioning the Trinity as a matrix of immanent relationships mirrored in a basic dynamic of life. This vital interrelational creativity exists on every level of reality—both creative and salvific. Such interpretations leave open the hermeneutical circle, allowing for imaginative, fluid meanings and correctives to enter into theological reflection. Although I appreciate such creative work, the detailed steps of the dance between the tradition and the contemporary era, and the specific twists and spins of selection, methodology, epistemological privileges, and preferential options are usually not displayed. This framework gives images their full potential and power, knowing that the contemporary crisis requires intense religious energy. The reference points are the contemporary context and elements of the tradition.

3. If, however, we were to situate our theological reflections within a broader framework of human anthropology examined through many lenses, we might be able to retrieve foundational insights about religious experiences, impulses, and moral imperatives. Such a framework would allow the great human history of sensitivity toward

the Sacred to be an interpretive reference for Christian reflections. Research from religious studies about the patterns of religious experiences and quests, the complex dialectic between religion and culture, and the ineffable dimension of reality that religions try to articulate, illuminate, and mediate is not customarily incorporated into theology. The Christian framework, in general, has been narrow and self-referent to the point that a return to the primary sentiment of the sacred dimension of the natural world is met with fears of pantheism or heresy. Yet such sentiments are foundational to most world religions and, until recently, to many cultures. Christians need to study general anthropology, cultural anthropology, and the cultural and historical backgrounds of many traditions in order to begin to grasp the profound nature of religious sensibilities, expressions, and the quest for the Sacred.[6]

4. To enlarge further the frameworks of interpretation, it is urgent that the Christian tradition not only engage in interreligious dialogue, but interpret itself in light of the worlds' religions within a tapestry of revelations.[7] We need to genuinely encounter other religious perspectives and allow ourselves and our theologies to be transformed by this process. The exclusive and semi-inclusive Christian attitudes continue to support a supremacy of Christianity, albeit differently.[8] The only viable option, it seems to me, is the emerging pluralist-correlational model for a theology of religions.[9] Although still in the initial stages of systemic articulation, this model and the proposed shift from Christocentrism to theocentrism, (a shift that many feminists and ecofeminists have advocated), is a way to preserve an/the essential meaning of Christianity. Yet it also releases the binds that prevent a genuine appreciation of other religious perceptions.

Further, with collective efforts, we can identify the transformative and prophetic insights of distinct traditions and affirm the particular values which will assist collaborative responses to the socio-ecological crises. This process, described by Mary Evelyn Tucker and John Grim as that of critical understanding, empathetic appreciation, and creative revisioning, is required to understand the multilayered symbol systems in world religions.[10] The central task, from an ecofeminist perspective, is to align religious efforts, and the spectrum of cosmologies, myths, symbols, rituals, values and ethical orientations, and self-understanding, within the rhythms and limits of the natural world.[11]

5. The fifth interpretive framework necessary for a comprehensive foundation for ecological-feminist theology is to situate the genesis and specific histories of each religion within the history of the earth. To consider earth history as a decisive framework is to perceive that the entire religious enterprise is an emerging process of human development within the evolutionary processes of the earth. Thomas Berry is a renowned advocate of this paradigm.[12] Although it is timely, indeed popular, to reiterate that "the earth is our home," the greater task is to allow our theological understanding to be transformed by this insight. To situate our religious traditions—the myriad names and faces of the sacred, the moral core and codes, and the magnificent rituals that mediate the sacred and make claims upon human actions—*within* the evolutionary processes of the earth prevents us from situating earth history within the boundaries of our religious traditions. This is a great challenge, as we are accustomed to our religious frameworks being the definitive references. The insights and teachings remain of ultimate value, although some religious interpretations and absolutes become relativized—decentered yet recentered—within a new understanding of the significance of our radical dependence on the earth and the evolutionary processes. We can begin to see the revelatory dimensions of the earth. This is a new religious moment, a threshold of religious consciousness in which we have creative and novel opportunities for religious awareness. It is a unique opportunity in human and earth history.

6. Finally, the grand narrative, the ultimate framework and point of reference, is cosmology or cosmogenesis, the story of the universe unfolding within human consciousness. For Thomas Berry, the universe is:

> the primary sacred community, the primary revelation of the Divine, the primary subject of incarnation, the primary unit of redemption, the primary referent in any discussion of reality or of value. Any human activity must be seen primarily as an activity of the universe and only secondarily an activity of the individual.[13]

To situate earth history within this immense epic and creative drama of the universe, of which we are an integral part, challenges the prevailing and dysfunctional cosmologies in which patriarchal religious traditions are immersed. Cosmology is that larger scheme of things, defined as a combination of natural science, philosophy, ethics, and religion—in short, a worldview. Cosmology reflects the cultural assumptions about the nature of the world.[14] Cosmologies, as cultural myths or narratives, deeply and elusively influence the formation of social order[15] and affect how human-earth relations are to be conducted.[16] Several ecofeminist theologians are engaged in recovering the significance of cosmology.[17] For example, Ruether continues to develop an ecofeminist theocosmology.[18] Reflection on cosmology is only beginning. Yet it can provide a new context for theology, a new mode of religious understanding, and a new theological agenda. According to Larry Rasmussen, nothing less than the cosmos itself, with its grandeur and adventure, is the proper horizon for our humanity.[19]

A comprehensive foundation comprised of these and other frameworks can assist the development of ecofeminist theologies and help to clarify the extent of the ecofeminist challenge to theology. They could avert the dangers of apologetic approaches or the subtle moves of "greening Christianity," which are appealing but do not address the root of the problem at the very level of theological foundations. These frameworks will help us rethink the foundations. The religious traditions developed in smaller and specific contexts and are thus unequipped to respond to the current context in their present form. Christianity needs to be situated within larger contexts of meaning and interpretation and can no longer be self-referent and exclusive.

In this light, Ruether's proposal of an ecological consciousness of self has ramifications beyond those apparent in her article. It is truly a new form of consciousness: of human awareness and moral exigence understood as emerging from an evolutionary process; of reactualizing Christian theology in view of the tapestry of religious revelations; of knowing the earth in its revelatory dimensions; and of relating to a dynamic cosmos, yet rooted in the myriad distinct contexts of communal life.

The same analyses can be applied to the Christology advanced by Gebara. The consequence is a relativizing of Christianity in light of the history of the universe and with respect to other religious expressions, and of Christology within Christianity. Christianity becomes one among many responses to humanity's search for meaning. (This is obviously the case but is just beginning to have a significant impact on theological method.) To advocate for such a radical shift in Christology would compel a change of theological paradigm. Insofar as theology hinges upon classical Christology, the revelatory dimension of the natural world will be an appendage. In Gebara's theocentric theology, the presence of God as sustaining wisdom and creativity is read through the evolution and dynamics of the universe and the earth. The revelatory word is in both nature and history— although these two ethics may stand in tragic tension. It is cosmology, and the revelatory dimension of the unfolding story of the universe in which the Christian story is situated, that is an adequate framework for an ecological theology. There are many efforts merging to develop such a perspective and to reimagine theology and religious meaning with these larger schema as basic references.

Ecofeminist Theologies and Praxis

The second challenge I would like to draw from Ruether's article is how to implement ecofeminist theological viewpoints. If ecofeminist theologies were to be essential in theological education, would that change into praxis? Feminist and ecofeminist theologies have something crucial to say about theological method, and about the distortions within and cultural consequences of theology. It is time to take these discourses seriously in the mainstream. If women, the poor and marginalized, and the natural world are invisible in our education, their destruction will be as well. We need sustained contemplation on the earth, on ecological and feminist theologies, and on the economic and political systems that generate socioecological ruin. As Daniel Maguire says, if we are not addressing these crises, religions are an obsolete distraction.[20] Worse still, they perpetuate and even indirectly condone the destruction.

Dorothee Soelle sends a clear warning in her distinctions between the neoconservative civic religion, helpless liberalism, and a theology of liberation. Only the latter, radical liberation theologies, are not in complicity with the systems of domination. Only liberation theologies can claim to be politically transformative and liberative, especially for those most oppressed. The limitation I see with Ruether's dismantling and remantling process is the move into transformative action. Given the acceleration of aggressive exploitation of most peoples and virtually all of the natural world, how can religious voices be relevant, reconstructive, and praxis-based? Within her text I see the challenge of holding together the retrieval of a cosmological dimension and reenchantment with the great Mystery of life as the basis of religious reflection, transforming theological methods and content, and resisting socioecological ruin at the material, economic, and political level. Further, we need to be explicit about our theological agenda and its purpose and frames of reference. If not, there is no evaluation of the transformative capacity.

Ruether reminds us that ecological, feminist, ethical theology must validate a vision of divine presence that both underlies and sustains natural processes and also struggles against the excesses of the powerful and reaches out to the victimized. I cannot think of a more urgent task in theology today. These two components, a comprehensive cosmology and praxis that consolidates the sociopolitical and ecological goals, need to unite.

There is no easy path to these transformations. In addition to the necessity of situating our theological reflection within comprehensive horizons that expand theological and intellectual frameworks, I have five modest and concrete suggestions that could advance ecofeminist liberation theologies. This first is a responsibility to teach radical liberation theologies. Liberal approaches have not proven themselves liberatory for many, and there is surely a need to counter the neoconservatives with strength and without fear. Middle ground is becoming extinct, along with the majority of species, and there is little time. Second, we need religious leadership that is committed to critical thinking, takes the concerns of the world seriously, and is active at political levels in moral advocacy and influencing public policy. Third, we need to become ecologically literate, learn about the tangled mechanisms of the socioecological crises, and aid in the deconstruction of cultural assumptions of what and who defines reality. Ecofeminist analyses are of exceptional benefit here. Fourth, we need to be active in our communities as organic intellectuals and integrate religious voices as one among the myriad others. Finally, there is a summons to be involved in interreligious dialogue on social and ecological issues and in the reinterpretations of all traditions in light of the ecological crisis and ecofeminist analyses.

Conclusion

Occurring in many societies is a profound quest for a sense of the sacred, and a thirst for meaning and relevance in this time of deep anxiety and destruction. Our traditions are depleted of remedies in their current forms and patterns, yet replete with insights, wisdom, and a genuine moral core that can assist in a reenchantment with the sacred and the natural world. We are at a decisive moment in earth and religious histories. Theology is in need of transubstantiation and renewed theological foundations and frameworks. As Rabbi Heschel remarked:

> Little does contemporary religion ask of man [sic]. It is ready to offer comfort; it has no courage to challenge. It is ready to offer edification; it has no courage to break idols, to shatter callousness. The trouble is that religion has become "religion"—institution, dogma, ritual. It is no longer an event. . . . However nothing counterfeit can endure forever.[22]

Ecofeminism is a religious event challenging contemporary theology.

Notes

1. See Heather Eaton, "Ecological-Feminist Theology: Contributions and Challenges," in *Theology for Earth Community: A Field Guide,* ed. Dieter T. Hessel (Maryknoll, N.Y.: Orbis Books, 1996), 77–92.

2. In addition to her many articles, see Rosemary Radford Ruether, *Gaia and God: An Ecofeminist Theology of Earth Healing* (San Francisco: HarperSanFrancisco, 1992). See also the overview and critique of ecofeminism in several religious traditions in Heather Eaton, "The Edge of the Sea: The Colonization of Ecofeminist Religious Perspectives," extended essay in *Critical Review of Books in Religion* 11 (1998): 57–82.

3. Anne Primavesi, *From Apocalypse to Genesis: Ecology, Feminism, and Christianity* (Minneapolis: Fortress Press, 1993).

4. Dorothee Soelle calls the rise of the Christian right a soft fascism, a highly seductive, new form of evangelization that supports militarism, racism, misogyny, and the abolishment of state-supported health and welfare. See "Christofacism," in Dorothee Soelle, *The Window of Vulnerability: A Political Spirituality,* trans. Linda M. Maloney (Minneapolis: Fortress Press, 1990), 133–40.

5. Chung Hyun Kyung, Aruna Gnanadason, Maria Pilar Aquino, and Dorothee Soelle are prominent voices developing this theology.

6. Thomas Berry states that to study the biblical, theological, and patristic traditions as the primary source of intelligibility of the Christian tradition allows for only a very narrow range of religious experience and insight. "The Catholic Church and the Religions of the World," *Riverdale Papers* 10 (1985): 5–6.

7. Ibid.

8. See Paul Knitter, *One Earth, Many Religions: Multifaith Dialogue and Global Responsibility* (Maryknoll, N.Y.: Orbis Books, 1995).

9. Ibid.

10. Mary Evelyn Tucker and John Grim, series foreword to *Christianity and Ecology,* xxii.

11. Ibid., xxiii.

12. Thomas Berry, *Dream of the Earth* (San Francisco: Sierra Club, 1988).

13. Berry, "The Catholic Church and the Religions of the World," 6.

14. Cosmology has developed an enlarged meaning that is more synonymous to worldview, inclusive of but not restricted to cosmogony. See *Worldviews and Ecology: Religion, Philosophy, and the Environment,* ed. Mary Evelyn Tucker and John Grim (Maryknoll, N.Y.: Orbis Books, 1994).

15. Carolyn Merchant, *The Death of Nature: Women, Ecology, and the Scientific Revolution* (San Francisco: Harper and Row, 1980).

16. Sally McFague, *The Body of God: An Ecological Theology* (Minneapolis: Fortress Press, 1993); Tucker and Grim, ed., *Worldviews and Ecology.*

17. See Heather Eaton, "Ecofeminism, Cosmology, and Spiritual Renewal," *Église et Théologie* 29 (1998): 115–28.

18. Ruether, *Gaia and God.*

19. Larry Rasmussen, "Ecocrisis and Theology's Quest," *Christianity and Crisis* 52 (16 March 1992): 86.

20. Daniel C. Maguire, *The Moral Core of Judaism and Christianity: Reclaiming the Revolution* (Minneapolis: Fortress Press, 1993), 13.

21. Soelle, *Window of Vulnerability,* 133–41.

22. Abraham Joshua Heschel, *I Asked For Wonder: A Spiritual Anthology,* ed. Samuel Dresner (New York: Crossroad Press, 1997), 39.

II. Vision, Vocation, and Virtues for the Earth Community

Christianity's Role in the Earth Project

THOMAS BERRY

The survival of the planet Earth in its integral reality is, it seems to me, the basic issue that confronts us here. In some fundamental sense the human project and the earth project are a single project. There is no way in which the human project can succeed if the earth project fails. That this is not understood by the guiding forces of the human community and the Christian community is, it seems to me, the challenge before us.

That the earth project is failing just now seems obvious both to ordinary observation and to more scientific understanding. In referring to the species extinction taking place in these times, Peter Raven of the Missouri Botanical Garden, Norman Myers of Cambridge University, and E. O. Wilson of Harvard University tell us that nothing at this order of magnitude has happened in the geobiological sequence of life on Earth since the beginning of the Cenozoic era, some 65 million years ago. Only recently the report has come from eight of the foremost nature organizations in the world concerning the status of plant species. This report indicates that one in every eight species throughout the world is imperiled. In the United States almost one in three is endangered. It is obvious, then, that the larger destiny not only of the human but even of more extensive life systems is being determined.

We need to grow accustomed to thinking in terms of the Cenozoic era, for this is the great lyric period in the sequence of life development on the planet. It is also the period when humans emerge into being. We are profoundly conditioned by the life-forms and the environmental surroundings that came into being at this time. Our inner world of genetic coding was shaped by these same forces that created the world about us. Our inner world is integral with this outer world. Our soul life is developed only in contact with these surrounding experiences. So integral is our inner world with the outer world that if this outer world is damaged, then the inner life of our souls is diminished proportionately. We are genetically coded for existence in that Cenozoic context in which the experiences narrated in the Book of Genesis and the other biblical books took place. When we extinguish the life-forms of this period in such a ruthless manner, we threaten the inner life of the human along with the other biosystems of the planet.

To preserve this sacred world of our origins from destruction, our great need is for a renewal of the entire Western religious-spiritual tradition in relation to the integral functioning of the biosystems of the planet Earth. We need to move from a spirituality of alienation from the natural world to a spirituality of intimacy with the natural world, from a spirituality of the Divine as revealed in verbal revelation to a spirituality of the Divine as revealed in the visible world about us, from a spirituality concerned with justice simply to humans to a spirituality concerned with justice to all those other components of the great earth community. The destiny of Christianity will be determined to a large extent by its capacity to fulfill these three commitments. My purpose here is to identify the present status of Christians in regard to these issues and to propose orientations that might assist in dealing with this situation.

As Christians we seem to have lost our intimacy with the natural world in three phases. The first phase occurred with the meeting of early Christian spirituality with Greek humanism to form the basis of an anthropocentrism that would in the course of the centuries so exalt the human as to lose the sense of the human as an integral component of the larger community of existence. Biblical revelation would overwhelm the revelation of the natural world; concern for the pathos of the human would leave little energy for concern for the nonhuman world; intensity of direct spiritual commitment to the Divine would weaken concern for the experience of the wonder and awesome qualities of the natural world. The world would eventually be experienced as a distraction from higher things. This did not happen at any given period. There were moments when a deep sense of the cosmic was incorporated into Christian spirituality. Yet there remained a deep sense of the human as existing in a world that was primarily for human use rather than for spiritual identity.

The second phase in the alienation of the human from the natural world came about when the Black Death occurred in Europe in the period from 1347 until 1349. This was a devastating period in Western civilization. One-third of Europe's population died during these years. We are told that the survivors did not mourn the dead; they felt that they would soon be dead themselves. The plague was especially severe in Florence where, in the summer of 1348, less than 45,000 persons survived out of the 90,000 who were there at the beginning of the year. In Sienna at this time, of a population of 40,000, only 15,000 persons survived.

The difficulty was that the people had no explanation for what was happening. They had no knowledge of germs. They could only conclude that the world had become wicked. God was punishing the world. The great need was for repentance, withdrawal from the world, and an increasing quest for redemption. A spirituality developed that was based on disengagement from worldly concerns. This spirituality of detachment found expression in the new devotional intensity directed toward the Savior personality. In Florence, at the Church of Santa Maria Novella, the Dominican preacher Jacopo Passavanti taught a severe doctrine of penance and discipline in relation to the natural world. He constantly presented frightening scenes of the torment to be inflicted on sinners. Bodily flagellation was recommended as appropriate penance for one's sins.

This was also the period of the Ars Moriendi, a kind of spiritual guide to assist and console the dying. Some forty manuscripts of this treatise still survive. In the late fourteenth and early fifteenth centuries the Dance of Death was invented. Added to all these events of this period were the morality plays that were composed and presented extensively throughout England. The theme of these plays was the strife of good and evil over the human soul. The fundamental principle articulated was that nothing is worthwhile that we cannot take with us when we die, basically our virtues. Everything else is a kind of vanity. The supreme morality play in England in the fifteenth century was Everyman, a play with a significant place in the origins of English drama. Art, too, was affected. For the first time there was an emphasis on Last Judgment scenes. Christ was sometimes depicted with upraised right hand condemning the wicked to hell. Hell became an artistic subject, with descriptions of decay and death and eternal misery.

The larger consequences of the Black Death can be seen in the spirituality of detachment from the world taught by Thomas à Kempis in the mid–fifteenth century. His book *The Imitation of Christ* became a classic of Christian spirituality throughout the five centuries from that time until the mid–twentieth century. Eventually, this teaching found expression in the theologians of the fifteenth century and later produced the Puritanism of the Protestant world and the Jansenism of the Catholic world.

This is the period when the Western soul established its radical alienation from the natural world. Instead of a delight in the natural world and a pervasive experience of the Divine in the beauty, wonder, and awesome qualities of the world about us, there developed a psychic-spiritual withdrawal from too intimate relations with the natural world. This attitude has continued until the present. A certain relief from this attitude occurred at the end of the eighteenth and the first half of the nineteenth century, when romanticism once again exalted the natural world as the presence of some higher numinous spirit. After this period came the reaction into realism leading eventually to the existentialism of the mid–twentieth century.

In the sixteenth and seventeenth centuries this religious alienation from the natural world left the scene open for the scientific perception of the world as mechanistic in its structure and as subject to whatever technological controls humans could invent to make the natural world increasingly useful to the human. In some sense it could be said that science and technology took over and exploited the planet because religious persons had abandoned it.

A third moment in our loss of intimacy with the natural world occurred at the end of the nineteenth century when we abandoned our role in an ever-renewing organic agricultural economy in favor of an industrial nonrenewing extractive economy. This was the decisive event that moved the entire scientific and technological might of the modern world into a merciless program of disruption of the organic functioning of the planet. At this time the planet lost its wonder and majesty, its grace and beauty, its life-giving qualities. The planet became an object of use. No remnant of its subjective qualities was permitted to remain. The engineers took over; the mechanical, electronic, chemical, and now the genetic engineers, all persons with the technical competence and the intellectual arrogance needed to assume that the planet would be better off under their control than under the primordial control of those forces that first brought the earth into being and guided its development down through the centuries.

Through these three phases of alienation from the planet, the profound spiritual aspect of Earth has been almost completely negated. The radiant presence of the Divine is no longer recognized. The saying of Saint Thomas, that "The Order of the Universe is the ultimate and noblest perfection in things," has lost its meaning. Any awareness of the spiritual communication made by the natural world to the human has been severely weakened. The universe has become a collection of objects, not a communion of subjects. Even the most sublime realities have become subject to economic exploitation. Planet Earth has become a commodity to be bought and sold, not a place where humans find both physical and spiritual nourishment.

The basic problem before us is how to recover a sense of a sacred universe. We cannot save ourselves without saving the world in which we live. There are not two worlds, the world of the human and a world of the other modes of being. There is a single world. We will live or die as this world lives or dies. We can say this both physically and spiritually. We will be spiritually nourished by this world or we will be starved for spiritual nourishment. No other revelatory experience can do for the human what the experience of the natural world does.

Yet, when we turn to understand the universe and our place in the universe, we find that we are doubly estranged from the universe. We are estranged from the universe of Genesis and also from the universe as we now know it through empirical observation and scientific insight. Spiritually, Christians are at home with the Genesis story. Yet, as regards understanding the universe, its emergence into being, the sequence of transformations through which it has passed, and the manner of its functioning, Genesis has nothing significant to communicate. At the same time the scientific story of the universe, such as we now know it, is communicated to us as material in its substance, mechanistic in its functioning, and random in its development. It is quite clear that the scientists cannot deal effectively with their own data. The fact that the human is integral with the emerging universe is sufficient evidence that the universe has a spiritual dimension from the beginning. For any downward reduction of the universe to its component parts must be completed by an upward reduction of the universe to see what these particles produce: the entire living world, even the human mode of being.

When we explain the universe as we now know it, in its originating moments and its long sequence of transformations, we are explaining the manner in which the Creator has brought the universe into being. Yet we must recognize that the universe is not a puppet appearance simply manipulated by some transcendent power. Such a creation would not satisfy the purposes of creations such as we know these to be. The created being would not have the independence needed to enter into an intimate divine-human relationship. Such a being could not freely offer divine praise.

For these reasons the Divine creates a phenomenal world with the capacity to create itself, for self-actualization. The wonderful thing about the universe is that it constitutes an absolute unity. The universe itself is self-referent in the phenomenal order since it has no larger frame of reference in the phenomenal world, while each component of the universe is universe-referent in its larger meaning. This universe, that we must now understand as our sacred universe, is the same universe as that presented to us in the Book of Genesis. It is, however, experienced through immediate empirical observation rather than simply through the inspired words of the narrator writing in a distant region, in ancient times, in a strange language. Through this observational process we have come to know the universe as an emergent process over an immense period of time. Once all this is seen within a religious-spiritual context, once it becomes clear that the universe itself has a spiritual dimension from the beginning, then we have the basis for a new sense of the universe in which all the biblical truths can be understood with a new depth of meaning.

Our difficulty is that we have been estranged from the universe over these past centuries. The prevalent feeling is that the Christian spiritual tradition does not really need to be concerned about the natural world. So long as we keep an intense belief in Jesus, so long as we develop our interior intimacy with the Divine, so long as we follow the Christian life discipline, so long as we carry out the spiritual and corporal works of mercy toward others, so long as we focus our lives on the Gospel; so long as we do all this, any concern about the universe or the planet Earth has no great urgency. It has no overwhelming relevance to the Christian life. If others take over the planet to exploit its resources, and even cause severe disruption in the life systems of the planet, then this is not of great personal or Christian concern.

To show the relevance of the larger world in the Christian tradition, we might note that apparently no divine communication could be given to humans until the cosmological setting had been established. Only when the Creation narrative had been presented in the Book of Genesis could the following sequence of events narrated in the scriptures be understood. In the Psalms also we find that the divine praise of all the universe constitutes the great cosmic liturgy. Saint John tells us that "God so loved the world (Kosmos) that he gave his only begotten son that the world might be redeemed by him." Saint Paul, in the Epistle to the Colossians, tells us that "in Christ all things hold together." Saint Thomas, the greatest of theologians in the medieval period, tells us that "The whole universe together participates in the divine goodness more perfectly and manifests it better than any single creature whatsoever."

These few observations concerning the basic Christian understanding of the universe establish quite clearly that the human community and the natural world are a single community with a single purpose: the exaltation and joy of existence, praise of the Divine, and participation in the great liturgy of the universe. Every single element in Christian belief and moral teaching, every aspect of our sacramental system, our patterns of worship, and our spirituality depend on the world about us. Indeed, the natural world is our primary revelation of the Divine.

Once we accept the universe as emergent reality, then what is said in Genesis, in the Psalms, in the writings of Saint John, in the Epistle to the Colossians, can be said of the universe as we now perceive it. This understanding expands rather than contracts our understanding of these scriptural and theological statements.

In this emergent process we can recognize the transformative moments as moments when the numinous presence in the phenomenal world manifests itself with special clarity. These moments include the moment of supernova collapse, or a second- or third-generation star that produced the ninety-some elements needed for the earth, for life and consciousness. These transformation events can be considered as cosmological moments of grace. Just as there are historical moments of grace and sacramental moments of grace, so too there are such cosmological moments. These are moments that deserve ritual commemoration, just as the moments in the annual solar cycle, the solstice and the spring equinox, are given ritual expression in the Nativity and in the Resurrection liturgy.

Finally, in reflecting on this essay, I would like to note that I have chosen to write on the historical basis of Christian alienation from concern over the destiny of the earth. I wish to indicate just how deep-rooted this alienation is within the Western psyche, even in the Christian soul. We are now so fixated on the industrial structures of our present situation that it is difficult to imagine just how a transition to a more integral relation of the human community with the earth can ever be achieved. Yet, the industrial world is itself reaching its own dissolution as the sources on which it depends begin to be exhausted. With the coming termination of petroleum resources a shock will be felt throughout the industrial world. The urgency of a new human relationship with the earth will manifest itself.

Christians have already begun their response to this situation with the critical understanding that is needed, as well as in the practical measures of bringing about a new, more viable situation. My own personal concern is that we see the issue in its full depth and that the solutions we offer be comprehensive enough and profound enough to support a new pattern of human presence on the planet. I call this our "great work." The Christian urgency is to save the beauty and wonder of a gracious world designed as a place suitable for the Divine indwelling, a place where the meeting of the Divine and the human would achieve some fullness of expression.

The Human Vocation: Origins and Transformations in Christian Traditions

THEODORE HIEBERT

The image that has determined most Christian thought about the human vocation in the world of nature is the image of dominion, drawn ultimately from the biblical story of creation in Genesis 1:

> So God created humankind in his image, in the image of God he created them, male and female he created them. God blessed them, and God said to them, "Be fruitful and multiply, and fill the earth and subdue it; and have dominion over the fish of the sea and over the birds of the air and over every living thing that moves upon the earth." (vv. 27–28; NRSV)

The powerful impact of this image is as apparent in the history of the church as it is in current Christian responses to the environmental crisis. This image is the point of reference for those who have attacked the Christian viewpoint as irresponsible in an ecological age as well as for most who have defended Christianity against these critics. Even in recent Christian theologies that wish to reposition God and humans within the universe, the biblical language of dominion often reemerges as if it were the foundation to which all Christian thought must ultimately return.

Christian traditions, however, contain richer and more complex perspectives on the human role in the natural world. An adequate understanding of the Christian view of the human vocation demands a consideration of the variety of perspectives in its traditions, an appreciation for the precise social contexts that gave rise to them, and an evaluation of their relative resourcefulness for constructing a viable view of the human vocation today. As a contribution to this task, I would like to examine two contrasting images of the human vocation in biblical thought, trace the transformations of these images in later Christian theology, and make some observations about the value of these images for understanding the role of the human race within nature today.

The Human as Priest: Genesis 1:1–2:4a

The concept of human dominion is often discussed with little attention to the historical context that gave rise to it. A knowledge of this context is crucial for assessing the appropriateness of its image of the human for modern ecological thought. Thus, I wish to begin this analysis of dominion by reviewing the evidence for the author who created this concept and by showing how this concept is related to the author's own particular social location.

Because of its formal liturgical style, its careful delineation of the orders of the cosmos, its concern with precise chronology, and especially because of its grounding of the sabbath in the orders of creation, scholars have long attributed the account of creation in Genesis 1 to a priest or a priestly community in ancient Israel. The priestly families of ancient Israel, as chief administrators of its religious shrines and institutions, held positions of authority and power in Israelite society. They were closely allied with the monarchy and played a primary role in the establishment and maintenance of the state (2 Sam. 8:15–17).[1] During the Persian period, when some believe the priestly traditions in Genesis reached their final form, the priesthood assumed both religious and political authority in Judah (Zech. 6:9–14).[2] Thus the priests, throughout Israel's history, were part of its ruling elite, legitimating its political leadership and performing the role of mediators between God and the people in Israelite worship.

The distinctive role played by the priests in the social world of ancient Israel is reflected in their conception of the role of the archetypal human in the world of creation as a whole. This is evident in the verbs by which the human role is defined and in the divine image given to humans alone. The verbs *rādâ,* "have dominion" (Gen. 1:26,

28), and *kābaš*, "subdue" (v. 28), mean to rule, to exercise power and authority. *Rādâ*, "have dominion," is used for the authority of the head of the house over household servants (Lev. 25:43, 46, 53), but more often it is employed for the rule of kings (1 Kings 5:4 [Eng: 1 Kings 4:24]; Ps. 72:8) and of their officials (1 Kings 5:30 [Eng: 1 Kings 5:16]), including the priests themselves (Jer. 5:31). When used of kings, *rādâ* is used primarily for rule over Israel's enemies (Ps. 110:2), and it occurs in descriptions of military conquest, where it is paired with such verbs as "destroy" (Num. 24:19) and "strike down" (Isa. 14:6). The verb clearly designates a potent authority. When used by the priestly writer in Genesis 1 for human rule over animals, *rādâ* may reflect more directly the priests' own authority in the ritual of animal sacrifice (Gen. 9:1–7; Lev. 8–9) and in the administration of laws regarding clean and unclean animals (Lev. 10–11).[3] It must also refer to the harnessing and herding of domestic animals (*bĕhēmâ,* Gen. 1:24–26) within Israel's subsistence agricultural economy.

The verb *kābaš*, "subdue" (Gen. 1:28), is even more forceful than *rādâ,* describing the actual act of subjugation, of forcing another into a subordinate position. It is used of military conquest, about which the same phrase used in Gen. 1:28 ("subdue the earth/land") can be employed to depict the destruction and occupation of conquered territory (Num. 32:22, 29). The verb "subdue" is also used of the king's forcing his people into slavery against God's wishes (Jer. 34:11, 16) and of rape (Esther 7:8; Neh. 5:5). The particular harshness of the term for the human-earth relationship in Genesis 1 may be best understood in the context of the particular harshness of subsistence agriculture in the Mediterranean highlands that provided the livelihood of the priests' constituency. Economic survival could thus be viewed, as does the priestly writer in Genesis 1, in adversarial terms as overpowering the intractable ground and subjugating the earth. The verbs that describe the human vocation in Genesis 1 thus grant humanity the same authority and power in creation that the priesthood exercized in ancient Israelite society.

The priestly view of dominion is amplified when humans are created in God's image (Gen. 1:26–27). No expression in Genesis 1 has been debated more forcefully by biblical scholars and theologians alike than the "image of God," in the attempt to discover what qualities the image of God bestows on the human race.[4] The clearest context for this expression in the biblical world is the royal ideology found in both Egypt and Mesopotamia, in which the king was regarded as the image or likeness of the deity. This resemblance between god and king was not primarily one of character or substance but one of function and position, so that it identified the king as the representative of the deity, with a divine mandate to rule.[5] Understood in this light, the expression "image of God" in Genesis 1 grants humans, not a unique essence, but a unique function within the created order: to exercise authority as God's representative in creation. Such a vocation reflects precisely the divine commission already described in which humans are assigned dominion in creation. And it directly parallels the priest's own role as the mediator of God's presence on the earth.

The priestly community responsible for Genesis 1 has thus created humanity in its own image. It is an image of humanity that can be seen elsewhere in the Hebrew scriptures, as in Psalm 8, in which humans are made a little lower than God, crowned with honor, and given dominion over the animal kingdom. On occasion, the entire community of Israel is viewed as assuming the priestly office (Exod. 19:6; Isa. 61:6). Viewed from this priestly perspective, the human vocation in Genesis 1 is one of impressive authority and control. It is based on a hierarchical view of nature and society in which the human being, like the priest, was assigned special status and power. It is a view of the human vocation—and this must be kept in mind in discussions of the legacy of this concept—reflecting the self-understanding and particular social location of the ancient Israelite priesthood.

The Human as Farmer: Genesis 2:4b–3:24

The human vocation is described in dramatically different terms in the Eden narrative of Genesis 2–3. Yet the long shadow cast by the priestly perspective over this following narrative and the efforts of later readers to harmonize the two accounts of creation have largely hidden this unique view of humanity from its heirs. For many years biblical scholars have regarded the Eden narrative as an independent account of creation, distinct in its origins and perspective from the priestly account that precedes it. It contains a different order of creation, has a particularly localized setting, and is composed in a different style, an important feature of which is the use of Israel's distinctive name for God: Yahweh (rendered "LORD" in most English translations). Hence, its unknown author has come to be known as the Yahwist. I wish to recover the Yahwist's image of the human vocation for our consideration by distinguishing it from the priestly image in Genesis 1 and by showing how this image itself reflects its own context: the life of the subsistence farmer in the Mediterranean highlands.

The view of the archetypal human as a farmer in the Eden narrative is illustrated in the first place by the creation of the first human being, not in the image of God, but out of arable soil. God makes the man/human being, *'ādām,*[6] out of topsoil, *'āpār,* from arable land, *'ādāmâ* (Gen. 2:7). Although *'ādāmâ* is usually translated by the more general word "ground," it is employed by the Yahwist more precisely for arable land, the soil cultivated in the growing of grains, vineyards, and orchards.[7] In recent years, interpreters have legitimately emphasized the fact that the very word for man/human being, *'ādām,* is related to the word for "ground," *'ādāmâ,* from which the first human was created. They have tried to capture this interrelationship with such translations as "earthling" from "earth" and "human" from "humus." Yet if the Yahwist's precise use of *'ādāmâ* for arable soil is taken seriously, a more accurate translation of *'ādām* from *'ādāmâ* would be "farmer" from "farmland."[8]

By being made from arable soil, the human being is not distinguished from other forms of life but identified with them. Plants (Gen. 2:9) and animals (2:19) are both produced by God out of the same arable soil from which the first human was made. In this regard, animals, too, share the agricultural identity of humans, as they are legitimate "helpers" on the farm, even if they are not sexually compatible partners (2:18–20). Receiving the breath of life (2:7) does not grant the first human being a soul or spiritual character different from the animals, since this breath is the physical breath of all animate life (cf. Gen. 7:22). The human being and animals alike are called "living beings" (*nepeš ḥayyâ;* 2:7, 19), an identity English translators have been unable to accept. The King James Version translated "living creature" for animals (2:19) and "living soul" for the human (2:7), while the New Revised Standard Version and the Jewish Publication Society use the subtler, but still theologically important, distinction between "living creature" (2:19) and "living being" (2:7) for this identical Hebrew phrase.

The understanding of the human vocation as farming is under-scored by the task God assigns the first human: to till, or cultivate, the garden's soil. This is the work God gives the human being inside the garden (Gen. 2:15) and the work God assigns the human being out-side the garden after his expulsion from Eden (3:17–19, 24). And it is the archetypal activity by which human life is defined at the very be-ginning of the Eden narrative. In the introductory clauses of the story of Eden (2:4b–5), the narrator speaks of the time before creation, not by describing nothingness, but by negating the most familiar realities of the audience's world: pastureland, grain in the fields, rain from God, and the human farmer ("there was no man ['*ādām*] to cultivate the arable soil ['*ădāmâ*]"; 2:5).

The verb employed by the Yahwist for cultivation is not *kābaš,* "subdue," used by the priestly writer in Genesis 1, but '*ābad,* "serve." In the Hebrew scriptures, '*ābad* is the customary term to express servitude, of slave to master (Gen. 12:6), of one people to another (Exod. 5:9), and of Israel's service to God in its life and worship (Exod. 4:23). This verb may have acquired a technical sense in the context of farming somewhat removed from its root meaning, just as the English "cultivation" does not necessarily call to mind its relation to "cult" and "culture." Yet its use for cultivation must stem from a sense of the vital power of the land over its creatures and of human submission to this power in the act of farming. This way of speaking of agriculture views the human as the servant, not the master, of the land. It emphasizes human dependence on, rather than dominion over, the earth.

Whoever we may imagine the Yahwist to be, the people's traditions that he has passed down in this narrative have created humanity in the image of the ordinary Israelite, the subsistence farmer of the biblical hill country.[9] This view of the human as a farmer in the Bible's second creation account represents a distinctly different understanding of the human vocation from the more familiar priestly view in Genesis 1. In fact, these two views of the human vocation in the natural world are almost inverse images of one another. The priestly writer views the human, created alone in God's image, as distinct from other forms of life, while the Yahwist views the human, made like the animals from the arable soil, as related to other forms of life. The priestly writer views the human as master of the earth, while the Yahwist views the human as its servant. For the priestly writer, the human vocation is one of dominion and supervision. For the Yahwist, the human vocation is one of dependence and service. Thus, at their origins, traditions of the human vocation within Christian thought are greatly varied. In addition to the familiar image of dominion that has been nearly equated with the Christian perspective stands a much more modest understanding of the human role in the world.

This modest view of the human reflected in the Yahwist's agrarian creation narrative is not an isolated point of view but a perspective shared by other biblical writers. In Psalm 104, an elaborate creation account sometimes compared to Genesis 1 in its overall structure, humans have no special status; rather, they participate in the cycles of day and night just as other animals do (vv. 19–23). When God takes back their breath, they return to the soil (v. 29). In the book of Job, God speaks about the powers of creation with the single apparent aim of teaching Job humility, or in Bill McKibben's words, "to rebut the notion that we are forever at the center of all affairs. The first meaning, I think, of God's speech to Job," McKibben continues, "is that we are a part of the whole order of creation—simply a part."[10]

Transformations in Early Christian Theology

From the beginning, Christian theologians understood these perspectives on the human vocation, not in their own terms, but in light of the theological currents of their day and by means of a harmonized reading of the two creation narratives. The result was the development of a theology of the human vocation in the formative centuries of the church that was based on the image of dominion in the first creation account (into which the second was subsumed) and amplified in terms of the Platonic idealism of the age.[11] In this Christian elaboration on the priestly perspective, the dominion of humanity and its distinctiveness from the rest of creation were both intensified.

An important early example of such a theology is that of Origen, who viewed reality as a hierarchical structure built upon a great chain of being. At the apex of the hierarchy is God, perfect spirit, and below God are angelic beings, then humans who are embodied spirits, and finally animals, plants, and the material elements.[12] This is a magnificent hierarchy that looks much like the priestly perspective in Genesis 1. What is new in it, however, is a metaphysical distinction between spirit and matter not made by the priests, according to which humans alone of all life share in the spiritual nature of the angelic beings and of God above. What was for the priests a specifically functional distinction between humans and other life, even in their understanding of the image of God, has become for Origen an ontological and substantive distinction, setting humans off from and above other life because of their unique spiritual character. In such a theology, humans are elevated higher and distinguished more clearly from other life than the priests could have imagined.

The two basic elements in Origen's thought regarding the position of humanity in the world, the hierarchy of being and the dualism of spirit and matter within its gradations, provided the fundamental framework for later Christian views of the human vocation. It is interesting to see how Augustine, for example, used the two accounts of creation to demonstrate the role of the human within a spirit-matter hierarchy, a kind of hierarchy unknown to the biblical priesthood:

> What we need to understand is how a man can be called, on the one hand, the image of God and, on the other, is dust and will return to dust. The former relates to the rational soul which God by his breathing or, better, by his inspiration communicated to man, meaning to the body of man; but the latter refers to the body such as God formed it from dust into the man to whom a soul was given. . . . The soul is not the entire man, but only his better part; nor is the body the entire man, but merely his inferior part. . . . [God] made man in his own image, for he created for him a soul endowed with reason and intelligence so that he might excel all the creatures of the earth, air, and sea which were not so gifted.[13]

In this perspective on the human vocation, Augustine harmonizes Genesis 1 and 2 within the framework of the priests' theology of dominion, and he regards that dominion as an expression of humanity's unique possession of a soul. Furthermore, Genesis 2 is drawn upon primarily to describe the inferior, material dimension of human existence.

The view of the human position in the world constructed by Origen and Augustine, based on the priestly perspective of Genesis 1 and amplified by a philosphical dualism that distinguished spirit from matter, has become Christianity's prevailing legacy. It was certainly the dominant view in the Middle Ages and fundamental in its basic outlines for the thought of Thomas Aquinas.[14] There does appear to have been an alternative tradition in Christian thought that held a more modest view of humanity and saw it sharing more deeply in the life of the nonhuman world. Yet representatives of this tradition— Benedictine and Irish monks and St. Francis, for example—still thought in terms of this basic legacy of human mastery, developing a more reserved form of it described by Paul Santmire as a "contemplative" or "cooperative mastery."[15]

This is too schematic a picture of the appropriation of the two biblical images of the human vocation from Genesis 1 and 2 in early Christian thought, but it does illustrate how quickly and powerfully the priestly view of humanity in Genesis 1 came to dominate Christian theology. Indeed, Emil Brunner could still claim in our own century, when speaking of the *imago Dei,* that "the whole Christian doctrine of man hangs upon the interpretation of this expression."[16] And Thomas Derr could speak of "*the* Judeo-Christian placement of man at the apex of creation as trustee for the rest of nature" (my emphasis), as if there were no other alternatives in Christian theology.[17] Such a survey, though brief, is also helpful in understanding more recent developments within Christian thought aimed at constructing a view of the human vocation viable in an age of environmental crisis.

Transformations in Contemporary Christian Theology

Contemporary Christian perspectives on the human vocation in an age of environmental crisis reflect first and foremost the continuing power of this historical tradition that has embraced the priestly view of humanity as normative for Christian thought. Most recent church statements and constructive theologies developed in response to the current ecological predicament take as their starting point the theology of dominion in Genesis 1. To be sure, they invest heavily in an interpretation of dominion that denies any self-serving, exploitative connotations to it, and they emphasize instead responsible, benevolent dimensions of biblical dominion.[18] As a description of such responsible dominion, the term "stewardship" has been coined, a term that has come to be regarded more than any other as a summation of the Christian view of the human vocation. Yet, behind these intepretations lies the assumption that Christians have in their traditions a single theological legacy, the priestly theology of human dominion founded in Genesis 1.

Several examples may illustrate this powerful trajectory in contemporary Christian thought. In the context of the development by the World Council of Churches of its statement entitled "Justice, Peace, and the Integrity of Creation," a consultation was held in 1987 by a group of Orthodox theologians representing twelve Eastern Orthodox and Oriental Orthodox churches, at the end of which a report, "Orthodox Perspectives on Creation," was issued and commended to the member churches for study, prayer, and action.[19] This report, rooted solidly in the priestly view of humanity in its early Christian form, affirms that

> humanity, created in God's image and likeness, transcends the material world because it participates in God spiritually and consciously, unlike the rest of creation. Humankind then stands on the boundary (*methorion*) between the material and spiritual worlds as a connecting link. . . . This means that we are called to exercise dominion over all creatures on earth (cf. Gen. 1:28), i.e. to be stewards (*oikonomoi*) of God's material world, caring for it, maintaining it in its integrity and perfecting it by opening it up to God through our own deification.[20]

This view of the human vocation, moreover, is linked closely with a corresponding Christology: "One of the Trinity, thus, became Incarnate, became man, revealing his Lordship over the whole of the creation, and showing humanity a Lordship in stewardship and service."[21] Stanley Harakas, who drafted this report, believes that it is only by assuming this role that humanity can save creation: "The 'integrity of creation' depends upon the kingly and priestly functioning of the microcosmic reality of humanity. . . . I believe that the lynchpin in understanding the full 'integrity of creation' is not to dethrone humanity from its kingly and priestly responsibility for such integrity, but to focus on it."[22]

This perspective on the human vocation may be illustrated as well by the theology of the protestant theologian Douglas John Hall, who, at the invitation of the National Council of Churches' Commission on Stewardship, wrote a study on human responsibility in nature, entitled *Imaging God: Dominion as Stewardship*.[23] Hall bases his reflections on the human vocation solidly on the priestly view of humanity in Genesis 1 and its counterpart, Psalm 8. But he wishes to move our understanding of this view away from its original hierarchic structure and the substantialistic ontology by which this structure was amplified in early Christianity. Hall interprets the *imago Dei* within the framework of an "ontology of communion," according to which the image of God bestows no special endowment but rather establishes a relationship in which the human is God's counterpart.[24] In this context, the human exercises dominion as "the representation of God within the sphere of creation. . . . The human creature is required to emulate God's own character and manner of rule; it is to image God within the creational realm."[25] Hall summarizes his viewpoint succinctly: "My thesis, stated in the most rudimentary manner, is that the vocation of the human being within creation is to image God, and that the imaging of God (*Dominus*) described in the tradition of Jerusalem would mean exercising the dominion of stewardship."[26]

This perspective has been popularized in any number of ways, one of the more significant of which may be the statement on environmental ethics, *Earth in the Balance: Ecology and the Human Spirit,*[27] written by Vice President Al Gore when he was a U.S. senator. He believes that the environmental crisis is at its heart a spiritual crisis, assumes that the single concept of the human vocation at the Christian's disposal is the concept of dominion and that the responsibility of the Christian is to understand and act upon its proper sense:

> In the Judeo-Christian tradition, the biblical concept of dominion is quite different from the concept of domination, and the difference is crucial. Specifically, followers of this tradition are charged with the duty of stewardship, because the same biblical passage that grants them "dominion" also requires them to "care for" the earth even as they "work" it.[28]

In his phrase, "the same biblical passage," Gore reflects the kind of harmonizing reading of Genesis 1 and 2 that has become typical in Christian thinking, since the term "dominion" comes from the priestly viewpoint in Genesis 1, while the terms "care for" and "work" (the Hebrew *'ābad,* "serve") come from the agrarian viewpoint in Genesis 2.

As these various theological statements show, the priestly image of dominion that prevailed in early Christian thought continues to exert wide influence in contemporary Christian reflection about the human vocation. At the same time, recent responses to the environmental crisis signal a revival of the perspective imbedded in the older agrarian image of the human found in Genesis 2, an image that has been eclipsed by, or subsumed under, the priestly image in most Christian thought. These new responses share two fundamental perspectives with the Yahwist's agrarian image of the human over against the priestly image. They emphasize the connectedness of the human with other life, a perspective more evident in the agrarian creation of humans together with all life from topsoil than in the priestly creation of humans alone in God's image. And they see the human as a member of an ecosystem rather than as its manager, a perspective more evident in the agararian image of the farmer tilling or serving (Hebrew, '*ābad*) the soil than in the priestly image of the human ruling creation. In some cases, these new responses reconnect themselves directly with this muted perspective in Christian tradition. In other cases, they share this perspective without recognizing these roots of it in their own religious history.

To illustrate the revival of this alternative view of the human vocation in recent Christian thought, let me begin with two "theologians" on the margins of the tradition, the naturalists John Muir and Aldo Leopold. John Muir was raised in a Scottish Presbyterian home and forced by his father to memorize all of the New Testament and most of the Old. Though he moved away from his strict Protestant upbringing, he appropriated its biblical heritage when he set about writing down his first thoughts on the human place in the world at age thirty, later collected in *A Thousand-Mile Walk to the Gulf.*[29] In his journal entries, Muir rejects the lofty view of the human that preachers in his youth had proclaimed: "The world we are told was made especially for man—a presumption not supported by all the facts. . . . Why should man value himself as more than a small part of the one great unit of creation?"[30] In place of this view, Muir proposes, not a more modest reading of the image of dominion, but another image entirely, the Yahwist's image of the human: "From the dust of the earth, from the common elementary fund, the Creator has made *Homo sapiens*. From the same material he has made every other creature, however noxious and insignificant to us. They are earth-born companions and our fellow mortals. . . . How narrow we selfish, conceited creatures are in our sympathies! How blind to the rights of all the rest of creation!"[31] In Muir's thought there is no reinterpretation of dominion, nor is there a harmonizing of Genesis 1 and 2 in order to qualifiy human dominion. Rather, there is a conscious judgment that the distinctive image of the human sharing an origin and destiny with other creatures in Genesis 2 more adequately describes the true role of humans within the natural world.

Aldo Leopold did not belong to an organized religion, though he did participate in a Bible study group at Yale. He was fascinated with the Old Testament and even wrote an article, "The Forestry of the Prophets": in these prophets he found a basic knowledge of conservation.[32] Leopold does not relate his thought directly to the two images of the human in Genesis 1 and 2 as does Muir. For Leopold the problematic biblical perspective is that of Abraham: "Conservation is getting nowhere because it is incompatible with our Abrahamic concept of land. We abuse land because we regard it as a commodity belonging to us."[33] But when he sets out to position the human properly in the world as part of his land ethic, he does so in language reminiscent of John Muir and of the Yahwist: "The land ethic simply enlarges the boundaries of the community to include soils, waters, plants, animals, or collectively: the land. . . . [It] changes the role of *Homo sapiens* from conqueror of the land to plain member and citizen of it. It implies respect for its fellow members, and also respect for the community as such."[34]

Two other "theologians" on the margins, the farmers Wendell Berry and Wes Jackson, have taken the contemporary American farmer seeking to construct a more sustainable agriculture as a point of departure for theology and practice. Their thought also revives the basic perspective of the ancient agricultural image of the human in Genesis 2. "The soil is the great connector of lives," writes Berry, "the source and destination of all. . . . Without proper care for it we can have no community, because without proper care of it we can have no life."[35] In such a world, the human is not a potentate above but a participant within a much larger system: "The Creation is bounteous and mysterious, and humanity is only a part of it—not its equal, much less its master. . . . The Creation provides a place for humans, but it is greater than humanity and within it even great men are small. Such humility is the consequence of an accurate insight, ecological in its bearing, not a pious deference to 'spiritual' value."[36] According to this perspective, the human vocation is not management but "alignment" with the larger cycles of energy and matter by which sustainable life is limited and upon which it depends.[37]

Such a viewpoint is echoed by Wes Jackson in his description of the philosophy that undergirds work at the Land Institute in Salina, Kansas: "Ecosystem principles represent the 'nature's wisdom' end of the spectrum of knowledge, and that's what we are thinking about and researching here at The Land. It is this end which has to dominate the 'human cleverness' end of the spectrum. None of us wants human cleverness to disappear. We just want to move it once and for all into a subordinate role."[38] In the opinion of both of these modern farmers, humans must subordinate their behavior to the natural processes on which the health of the land and species depends, much like the Yahwist's first farmer was commanded by God to till, "serve" (*'ābad*), the soil.

The interest in repositioning the human from the separate, dominant role of the priestly perspective to the more integrated, participatory role of the agrarian perspective is also evident in theologies of nature shaped in more traditional academic settings. A primary example is the thought of John Cobb, Jr., who has brought his process perspective into the discussions of ecological theology. In *For the Common Good: Redirecting the Economy toward Community, the Environment, and a Sustainable Future,* John Cobb and Herman Daly propose a theological framework for their new economic program based in a "biospheric vision." In their view, "the force of human transcendence is inherently disruptive" and demands a "substantial decrease in the human niche."[39] While this biospheric vision moves Daly and Cobb toward the perspective of the Yahwist, they connect their understanding of the human vocation with the priestly image of dominion, reinterpreted to temper its hierarchical character.[40] I do not wish to take lightly their careful rethinking of the priestly perspective within a modern setting but suggest that they have overlooked the significant ways in which their vision is deeply connected to the Yahwist view.

Rosemary Radford Ruether, who brings feminist liberation perspectives to ecological theology, is another example of a theologian who implicitly retrieves the alternative Yahwist view. Her work is dedicated to recovering the transformative legacy from Christian traditions and separating it from "the toxic waste of sacralized domination" in all of its forms.[41] "The urgent task of ecological culture," according to Ruether, "is to convert human consciousness to the earth, so that we can use our minds to understand the web of life and to live in that web of life as sustainers."[42] Though her discussion of the image of the human in biblical creation traditions centers on the priestly perspective that has become normative in Christian history, her constructive theology shares more deeply the images of integration and dependence grounded in the Yahwist's agrarian conception of the human.

Recreating the Human Vocation

This brief survey of Christian perspectives on the human vocation brings to light two aspects of the tradition that have particular importance as we refashion our image of the human role in the world today. The first aspect is that the images of the human vocation in Christian tradition arose originally out of concrete, ancient cultural contexts. These images reflected the self-understandings of particular social groups in biblical Israel. The image of human dominion and distinctiveness in Genesis 1 reflects the self-understanding of Israel's priesthood. It is based on priestly privilege and rule and on passion for distinctions in position and holiness among the creatures of the universe. In the same way, the image of human dependence on arable land and interrelationship with its creatures in Genesis 2 reflects the self-understanding of Israel's farmers, who occupied a narrow ecological niche in the highlands on the eastern shore of the Mediterranean Sea. Becoming reacquainted with the embeddedness of these images in specific historical, social, and ecological contexts shows us the limits inherent in them for contemporary application and may suggest new possibilities for their appropriation.

This survey also reminds us that Christian tradition is not monolithic. It contains different perspectives on the human vocation. This means that the discussion of the human vocation in Christian theology and ethics must shift from the question "How are we to understand human dominion in our situation?" to the question "How is the image of dominion to be weighed against other images in Christian traditions in light of our situation?" When we put this latter question to the two images of the human vocation analyzed above, we recognize first the power of both in ancient and modern cultures. Together they seem to capture the paradox of human existence. We today, as did the ancient editors of Genesis, may wish to preserve both. We recognize, as did Israel's priests, that humans possess unique powers to alter their environment. And we also recognize, as did Israel's farmers, that humans reside in a complex ecosystem they do not entirely understand and cannot ultimately control.

The priestly view of the human vocation carries into the twentieth century remarkably descriptive powers. The modern perception of the human as the culmination of the evolutionary process, the possessor of a unique self-consciousness, and the master of a vast new technological power to shape the environment seems to be but the contemporary expression of the ancient priestly view of the human as made in God's image to rule life and subdue the earth. To see this lofty human position as a sacred responsibility delegated by God appeals to many as an admirable model of the responsible exercise of power. Thus, the view of the human vocation that has dominated Christian traditions has gained a new currency under the concept of "stewardship" in contemporary thought.

At the same time, the ancient agrarian view of the human vocation, which has customarily been overlooked or subsumed under the priestly perspective, contains the roots of a perspective much closer to many modern ecological views of the human. First, it provides a more powerful image of the interrelationship of all of life than does the priestly perspective. By describing the common origin of plants, animals, and humans in the arable soil, the Yahwist identifies them all as part of a single reality dependent ultimately on the health and vitality of the land, the interconnected web of life. By contrast, the priestly passion for careful distinctions, by which humans alone are created in God's image, contains within it a segregating impetus in the spirit of which other dichotomies, unknown to the ancient priests, have been introduced into the tradition. The most powerful and perhaps most destructive of these, of course, is the spirit-matter dichotomy that quickly found a home in the priestly hierarchy and became virtually identified with it in Christian tradition.

Second, the ancient agrarian conception of the human vocation possesses a profound sense of human limits. By describing the archetypal human task as cultivating, or "serving," the soil, the Yahwist subordinates human behavior to the larger ecosystem upon which human survival depends. According to the Yahwist, the human vocation is not to manage the ecosystem of which humans are a part, but rather to align its activity to meet the demands and observe the limits imposed by this system upon all of its members. Humans must measure their activity by the health of the larger biotic community which they share. In an age of the relentless economic growth and rising consumerism, an image of the human vocation emphasizing limit and restraint may provide a more powerful challenge to the prevailing values of exploitation than an image of dominion and rule, no matter how benevolently that dominion is understood.

Finally, the agrarian image of the human vocation should be reconsidered today simply because it is agrarian, because it regards the human as a farmer. This may seem implausible and irrelevant in a highly industrialized, urban society such as the United States in which only 3 percent of the population are farmers. Yet, as Timothy Weiskel reminds us, "there is no such thing as a 'post-agricultural' society."[43] Wendell Berry makes the same point, with language indebted to the Yahwist: "No matter how urban our life, our bodies live by farming; we come from the earth and return to it, and so we live in agriculture as we live in the flesh."[44] The dangerous irony of an urban society is that it ignores the base of its own survival. "We now have more people using the land (that is, living from it) than ever before," observes Berry. "We are eating thoughtlessly, as no other entire society ever has been able to do."[45] Thus, the image of the human as a farmer is not an archaic, quaint, or marginal perspective. It is one with which modern urban society must reacquaint itself if it is to relearn its true location in the world and if it is to find a sustainable way of life within the world.

Notes

1. Frank Moore Cross, "The Priestly Houses of Early Israel," in *Canaanite Myth and Hebrew Epic* (Cambridge, Mass.: Harvard University Press, 1973), 195–215, esp. 211, 215; Robert B. Coote and David Robert Ord, *In the Beginning: Creation and the Priestly History* (Minneapolis: Fortress Press, 1991), 29–56.

2. J. Alberto Soggin, *A History of Ancient Israel: From the Beginnings to the Bar Kochba Revolt, A.D. 135* (Philadelphia: Westminster Press, 1984), 270–71; Gerhard von Rad, *Genesis* (Philadelphia: Westminster Press, 1972), 27–28.

3. Mary Douglas, *Purity and Danger: An Analysis of the Concepts of Pollution and Taboo* (London: Ark Paperbacks, 1985), 41–57; Howard Eilberg-Schwartz, "Creation and Classification in Judaism: From Priestly to Rabbinic Conceptions," *History of Religions* 26 (1986-87): 357–81; Coote and Ord, *In the Beginning,* 57–66.

4. Claus Westermann (*Genesis 1–11: A Commentary* [Minneapolis: Augsburg Publishing House, 1984], 147–60) provides a survey of the history of interpretation of the image of God in Genesis 1:26–27.

5. Phyllis A. Bird, "'Male and Female He Created Them': Gen 1:27b in the Context of the Priestly Account of Creation," *Harvard Theological Review* 74 (1981): 137–44; Nahum Sarna, *The JPS Torah Commentary: Genesis* (Philadelphia: Jewish Publication Society, 1989), 12; Westermann, *Genesis 1–11: A Commentary,* 151–54.

6. While there has been much recent debate whether the first person created in this account is male, sexually undifferentiated, or androgynous, I believe the best arguments support the view that this individual is at once male and representative of humanity; Theodore Hiebert, *The Yahwist's Landscape: Nature and Religion in Early Israel* (New York: Oxford University Press, 1996), 59–61. In my view, both the priestly and Yahwistic perspectives reflect the patriarchal structures of biblical society.

7. Ibid., 34–35.

8. The argument for the agricultural perspective of the Yahwist's narrative is worked out in detail in *The Yahwist's Landscape;* the creation narrative itself is analyzed on pp. 32–38, 51–62. This interpretation differs from that of Robert Coote and David Ord in *The Bible's First History* (Philadelphia: Fortress Press, 1989), who believe the Yahwist to be describing Israel's origins in terms of the pastoralist culture of the southern Bedouin.

9. Eden cannot be understood, as some ecological writers have, as a hunting and gathering stage of human evolution, as a preagricultural or pretechnological stage of civilization. For example, Herman E. Daly and John B. Cobb, Jr., *For the Common Good: Redirecting the Economy toward Community, the Environment, and a Sustainable Future* (Boston: Beacon Press, 1989), 387–91; J. Baird Callicott, "Genesis and John Muir," in *Covenant for a New Creation: Ethics, Religion, and Public Policy,* ed. Carol S. Robb and Carl J. Casebolt (Maryknoll, N.Y.: Orbis Books, 1991), 125; and Wes Jackson, *Altars of Unhewn Stone* (San Francisco: North Point Press, 1987), 6, 64.

10. Bill McKibben, *The Comforting Whirlwind: God, Job, and the Scale of Creation* (Grand Rapids, Mich.: Eerdmans, 1994), 37.

11. A helpful survey of the ecological implications of major Christian theologies in the history of the church is H. Paul Santmire's *The Travail of Nature: The Ambiguous Ecological Promise of Christian Theology* (Philadelphia: Fortress Press, 1985).

12. Ibid., 44–53.

13. Augustine *City of God* 13.24; 12.23.

14. Santmire, *The Travail of Nature,* 75–95.

15. Ibid., 78–80, 106–19.

16. Quoted in James Childs, *Christian Anthropology and Ethics* (Philadelphia: Fortress Press, 1978), 13.

17. Thomas Sieger Derr, "Religion's Responsibility for the Ecological Crisis: An Argument Run Amok," *Worldview* 18, no. 1 (January 1975): 43.

18. A helpful survey of the images of the human vocation in recent Christian thought can be found in Stephen Bede Scharper's *Redeeming the Time: A Political Theology of the Environment* (New York: Continuum, 1997).

19. Gennadios Limouris, *Justice, Peace, and the Integrity of Creation: Insights from Orthodoxy* (Geneva: WCC Publications, 1990), 1–15.

20. Ibid., 4.

21. Ibid., 5.

22. Ibid., 73, 75, 76.

23. Douglas John Hall, *Imaging God: Dominion as Stewardship* (Grand Rapids, Mich.: Eerdmans, 1986).

24. Douglas John Hall, *Professing the Faith: Christian Theology in a North American Context* (Minneapolis: Fortress Press, 1993), 210–21, 314–23. Cf. Claus Westermann's discussion (*Genesis 1–11: A Commentary,* 150–58) of a relational understanding of the image of God in biblical scholarship and later interpretation, especially that of Karl Barth.

25. Hall, *Professing the Faith,* 349, 350.

26. Hall, *Imaging God,* 60.

27. Al Gore, *Earth in the Balance: Ecology and the Human Spirit* (Boston: Houghton Mifflin Company, 1992).

28. Ibid., 243.

29. John Muir, *A Thousand-Mile Walk to the Gulf,* ed. William Frederick Badè (New York: Houghton Mifflin, 1916). J. Baird Callicott provides an excellent analysis of the impact of the image of the human in Genesis 2 on the thought of John Muir in "Genesis and John Muir," 107–40, though Callicott's analysis of Genesis 2 could be nuanced by some of the Hebrew data discussed at the beginning of this essay.

30. Muir, *A Thousand-Mile Walk,* 136–37; quoted in Callicott, "Genesis and John Muir," 114–15.

31. Muir, *A Thousand-Mile Walk,* 98–99, 139; quoted in Callicott, "Genesis and John Muir," 115.

32. Aldo Leopold, *The River of the Mother God and Other Essays,* ed. Susan L. Flader and J. Baird Callicott (Madison: University of Wisconsin Press, 1991), 71–77.

33. Aldo Leopold, *A Sand County Almanac* (New York: Oxford University Press, 1949), viii.

34. Ibid., 204.

35. Wendell Berry, *The Unsettling of America: Culture and Agriculture* (San Francisco: Sierra Club Books, 1977), 86, 94.

36. Ibid., 98.

37. Ibid., 87.

38. Wes Jackson is quoted here from correspondence to supporters of the Land Institute, dated 1 April 1994.

39. Daly and Cobb, *For the Common Good,* 389, 378.

40. Ibid., 387–91.

41. Rosemary Radford Ruether, *Gaia and God: An Ecofeminist Theology of Earth Healing* (San Francisco: HarperSanFrancisco, 1992), 3.

42. Ibid., 250.

43. Timothy C. Weiskel, "In Dust and Ashes: The Environmental Crisis in Religious Perspective," *Harvard Divinity Bulletin* 21, no. 3 (1992).

44. Berry, *The Unsettling of America,* 97.

45. Ibid., 38.

Christian Ecological Virtue Ethics:
Transforming a Tradition

LOUKE VAN WENSVEEN

Virtues play an important role in environmental circles. Participants in the "Christianity and Ecology" conference that led to this book variously stressed respect, care, compassion, humility, attention, and restraint. When we look beyond specifically Christian environmental circles, we find not necessarily the same configuration of virtues, but a similar proliferation.[1] This virtue praxis of environmentally committed people, Christians as well as non-Christians, strongly supports the insights of a handful of scholars, including Jay McDaniel, James Nash, Val Plumwood, and Mary Midgley,[2] who have for several years emphasized that in an age beset by environmental strains, virtues offer a promising path to lasting personal as well as social change.

What is more, virtues simply seem to emerge as part of our experience, often exactly where other moral concepts fail us. In the words of Mary Midgley:

> as we speak of things further and further out from ourselves, it gets steadily more suitable to speak in terms of awe, reverence, respect, wonder, or acceptance, and steadily less satisfactory to use a word like "value," whose original use is in describing everyday objects we might buy and possess.[3]

Thus, virtues are not just useful tools for transformation but part of a spontaneous and positive way of being that deserves its own consideration.

The question I address here is how this emerging virtue language compares with Christian virtue tradition. I ask the question because it clarifies the practical options before those of us who care to maintain links with our Christian heritage. If, at one end of the spectrum of possibilities, we find strong similarities with only superficial differences, then we can confidently pursue the option of simply retrofitting Christian virtue tradition for an ecological age. This would be an easy shortcut. If, however, at the other end of the spectrum, we find strong differences with only superficial similarities, then we should take a good look at existing ecological virtue language as a language of praxis that can guide a thorough transformation of Christian virtue tradition toward ecological attunement. (I am assuming here that we want to take ecological praxis seriously as a source for and expression of Christian ethics.) If we end up somewhere in the middle of the spectrum, we will have to find an appropriate medium between comfortable adaptation and radical change.

At this point it may well be objected that I am planning to compare two immensely complex, dynamic, and thus inherently elusive entities, or, to adapt a Barthian expression, two birds in flight. In fact, I will only attempt a relatively modest, but paradigmatic, comparison between the virtue language of ecological praxis, as I have described it in *Dirty Virtues*,[4] and the virtue theory of Thomas Aquinas as described in his *Summa Theologiae*, which continues to inspire one influential and fairly stable expression of Christian virtue ethics, the Aristotelian-Thomistic virtue tradition.[5]

A few words on context are in order here. The virtue theory of Thomas Aquinas has recently been of great interest to many Roman Catholic as well as Protestant ethicists.[6] In addition, some ecologically minded Roman Catholic interpreters have returned to Aquinas's larger work to develop what has been labeled "ecothomism."[7] Other ecotheologians, however, have portrayed major aspects of Aquinas's thought as antithetical to ecological ways of being in the world.[8] Given this diverse context of current interest in the thought of the "Angelic Doctor," the comparison I propose carries high stakes. Whichever the outcome, I stand to make both enemies and friends. However, I do not see myself as belonging to a particular camp. As a Dutch, nominally Protestant woman, employed at an American Jesuit university, I have over the years developed a cautious but deep respect for Aquinas's work. I focus on his theory here simply because it is the most comprehensive and richest Christian virtue theory I know,[9] and I intend to give it a fair reading.

Readers familiar with the broader history of ecotheology will recognize the process of comparison, as well as its loaded context. We have already gone through a similar process with the Bible and much systematic theology. In those areas we are now moving on to a more constructive "greening" phase. Christian virtue ethics lies a step behind in defining its relation to tradition in light of ecological awareness, but this step cannot be skipped. The choice between retrofitting and transforming tradition is not a foregone conclusion when both the tradition (Aquinas's theory) and the focus (virtue ethics) represent new frontiers in Christian ecotheology.

Aquinas and Ecological Virtue Ethics: A Comparison

In comparing the emerging ecological virtue ethic with Aquinas's theory, I concentrate on overarching themes that affect the meaning of individual virtues. However, I have also laced my discussion with examples of specific virtues, so that we can more easily test the argument against our own moral experiences as ecologically oriented interpreters. To help us see the new in light of the old, I have selected three themes that reflect the structure of Aquinas's theory: 1) Virtue and the Internal Natural Order; 2) Virtue and the External Natural Order; and 3) Virtue and the Supernatural Order.

Virtue and the Internal Natural Order

In the Aristotelian-Thomistic tradition, moral virtues are good qualities because they establish internal order, which orients persons toward God. Aquinas, following Augustine, argues that internal order marked human nature as originally created (*ST* 1.95.1), that this order was lost with the fall of humankind through Adam (*ST* 1.2.81.1; 1.2.82.3), and that it must now be regained through the combination of divine grace and human effort that characterizes the moral virtues (*ST* 1.2.63.2). The type of internal order Aquinas has in mind he calls the *order of nature*. It is an absolute order in which things are considered in themselves and prioritized according to the following criterion: "the more simple and the more abstract a thing is the nobler and higher it is in itself" (*ST* 1.82.3).[10]

By this criterion, but also in conformance with a long tradition, Aquinas rates the intellect as the highest part of the human soul, since its object consists of universal principles, whereas the rest of the soul focuses on particulars. Aquinas also believes that "the intellect is a faculty that is independent of an organ" (*ST* 1.85.6), which befits the immateriality of its object. As the highest part, the intellect must govern the other parts. Thus, when everything is in good order, reason is king, and the passions, which are tied up with bodily changes, behave like faithful subjects. Reason does not suppress the passions, however. Citing Aristotle, Aquinas observes that "*reason rules the irascible and concupiscible powers by a political command* such as that by which free men are ruled, who have in some respects a will of their own" (*ST* 1.2.56.4). This state of unforced order is key to personal happiness.

When I turn now to the praxis of ecological virtue ethics, two similarities stand out. For one thing, the cultivation of ecological virtues typically involves personal realignment guided by objectives. For example, ecological frugality is guided by the objective of letting others live. This is a rational process. Second, such personal realignment is perceived as part of a dynamic inner balance. Ecologically frugal people know how to balance their inclinations to use and consume material goods. The rational process maintains order.

When I pursue these similarities, however, deeper differences emerge. The pursuit of objectives that characterizes ecological virtues cannot be adequately described as a rule of reason in the conventional sense. When "embodied" or "carnal" knowing informs the process, which often happens, we look in vain for the traditional hallmark of reason: seeking and applying relevant "first principles" (cf. *ST* 1.79.8 and 12).[11]

Second, the balance maintained by this process cannot be adequately described as reason ranking a priori above emotions and inclinations. Insofar as ecological virtues involve inner harmony, such harmony is not a fixed order of any kind, let alone of reason only, but the experience of a cybernetic give-and-take between various dimensions that characterize us as persons.[12] Just as the pyramid image of nature has given way to the ecosystem, the pyramid image of personal flourishing has given way to the image of an internal self-adjusting circle. To return to my example, frugality has become a dance in which desire holds hands with such diverse partners as empathy, joy, fear, vision, prudence, intuition, and physical satisfaction. Because this internal circle is self-adjusting, like an ecosystem, no single element rules or even connects all the others.

The type of inner realignment involved in the cultivation of ecological virtues thus differs significantly from the rational ordering required by Aquinas's virtue theory. The differences, which involve core definitions and images, in fact strike me as more fundamental than the similarities, which involve only external form. Moreover, the differences are based on deliberate choices by real people, whereas the same cannot be said for the similarities. Many of the ecologically minded people who live out the model of a cybernetic process of inner realignment are at the same time aware of the alternative rationalistic model (although they may not have read Aquinas's theory), know it to be normative in the West, and deliberately reject it for lack of fit with their ecological worldviews. Thus, we are not just dealing with serendipitous differences, but rather with a targeted alternative.

Virtue and the External Natural Order

In the Aristotelian-Thomistic tradition, the internal rational order established by the moral virtues has as its main effect personal happiness. However, moral virtues also contribute to the harmony of creation as a whole. The virtue of justice, which ensures right relationships, plays a key role in ensuring this larger order. The other moral virtues contribute in a more general way.

Most of Aquinas's treatment of justice focuses on relationships between human beings. However, he does include "lower" nonhuman creation in his discussion. Justice between human beings and other physical creatures is governed by the general formula: "The imperfect is always for the sake of the perfect" (*ST* 2.2.64.1 and 2.2.66.1). Accordingly, although all nonhuman creatures on Earth are created and sustained by God, who remains their ultimate Sovereign, God has permanently ordained them for human use. Aquinas is not oblivious to the question whether certain uses, such as possession and killing, might be out of order. He concludes consistently that humans have full discretion in their use of lower creatures, as long as they remember God's original donorship (cf. *ST* 2.2.64.1 and 2.2.66.1).

When I now turn back to the praxis of ecological virtue ethics, I again see a similarity, at least with the dominion model that has a solid following in mainstream Christian circles.[13] According to this model, "human dominion from within a shared creation"[14] requires the virtue of eco-justice. Those who practice eco-justice give due consideration to all creatures and recognize their own ultimate accountability to the Creator.[15] Thus, dominion is something quite different from absolute and arbitrary domination.

When I further probe this similarity, however, again a deeper difference emerges. The virtue of eco-justice, also within the dominion model, puts concrete limits on human uses of nonhuman creation. We cannot, for example, mine the resources of the earth to the extent of even our reasonable needs. Eco-justice nowadays implies sacrifice. However, Aquinas's formula, "The imperfect is always for the sake of the perfect," cannot account for such sacrifice. Not surprisingly, therefore, none of Aquinas's examples of possible inappropriate uses of nonhuman beings leads to a limiting conclusion. In practical terms, when we follow Aquinas's logic, *any* use of nonhuman creation turns out to be a good use.[16] This we would not hear from the mouth of a modern proponent of eco-justice. The point in developing concepts of eco-justice is not just that we learn to include nonhuman creation in our moral vision—Aquinas already did that. The point is especially to provide specific guidelines and limits for our interactions with nonhuman creation.

Besides justice, all the other moral virtues also contribute to the harmony of the larger creation in Aquinas's theory. Again, though, his argument does not square very well with recent ecological insights. Aquinas holds that the mere existence of human beings contributes to the perfection of the universe (*ST* 1.65.2)—that is, provided they keep themselves in order through the virtues. This lucky macrocalibration is God's doing. Consequently, people need not actually think beyond the ordinary microlevel of their virtuous efforts.[17] Thus, someone arguing from within the Aristotelian-Thomistic tradition may well sum up the general relationship between the cultivation of virtues and the larger natural order as follows: I can be certain that my virtues benefit nonhuman creation, but I need not worry about the details.

By contrast, people who cultivate ecological virtues are likely to argue precisely the other way around: I worry about how, exactly, my virtues may benefit nonhuman creation, but I cannot be certain about the results. Recent research on ecosystem sustainability shows natural variation to be much greater and predictability much less than was initially assumed.[18] As a result, ecologically minded people are learning to expect the unexpected, to leave large margins for error, and to be constantly attuned to the changing features and needs of biological systems. I may care for a forest weakened by acid rain and hope that my caring will ultimately contribute to the well-being of that forest, but a little voice inside me never stops wondering: Does my caring really help?

Again, we must put the differences in a sociohistorical context in order to appreciate their full force. The confident beliefs that any use of nonhuman creation is a good use and that we can generally trust the macroeffects of the virtues we cultivate in our microworlds have become difficult to maintain in the face of mounting environmental problems. We cannot just point to vices like greed and arrogance as the causes behind the problems, for the road to destruction has also been paved by many good intentions, by things earnestly done in the name of justice and care. This has been hard to acknowledge, and the comfortable model of a stable and predictable natural harmony, one that still inspired the first ecological scientists,[19] is hard to give up. But insofar as the current praxis of cultivating ecological virtues shows constant questioning within a macroperspective, a choice has been made. Once again, we are not just dealing with a serendipitous difference, but with a considered alternative.

Virtue and the Supernatural Order

In the Aristotelian-Thomistic tradition, the personal happiness that can be achieved through the cultivation of the moral virtues is called natural happiness, which stands for an earthly satisfaction that, paradoxically, does not fully satisfy. By contrast, Aquinas also distinguishes supernatural happiness, which does fully satisfy but can only be attained imperfectly in this life. Supernatural happiness consists in the beatific vision of the Essence of a fully transcendent God (*ST* 1.2.3.8). People approach such bliss through a combination of divinely infused theological virtues (faith, hope, and charity), gifts of the Holy Spirit (which dispose them to receive the guidance of these virtues), and sacraments (*ST* 1.2.62.1; 1.2.68.1 and 2; 3.62.2).

Comparing Aquinas's notion of supernatural happiness with the praxis of ecological virtue ethics, I am struck by a similarity with the experiences of many environmentalists who live from a deep (albeit often unorthodox) religious sensibility. Through the cultivation of certain ecological virtues, we get closer to the Divine. When we open ourselves up to feel wonder at the vast power and hidden treasures of the ocean, when we quiet down and discover a sense of belonging in the presence of a mountain, when we focus our attention and are taken up in the daily habits of the squirrel who inhabits the backyard, the ordinary reveals itself as extraordinary—and we feel blessed, rejuvenated from beyond ourselves, complete, filled with love, sometimes exuberant.[20] Would we call this happiness "supernatural," though, and set apart the virtues of wonder, rootedness-in-a-place, and attention as specifically "theological" virtues? In the context of the experiences I have just described, Aquinas's terminology sounds off the mark.

The dissonance can be traced to the following reason: These experiences suggest a divine immanentism (though not necessarily a pantheism) that does not fit within Aquinas's natural/supernatural hierarchy. An ecological perspective brings out a spiritual dimension in the cultivation of ostensibly natural virtues and gives traditional theological virtues an unexpected earthy twist. For example, sensuousness can be a way to get in touch with the Divine, not so much by sending our focus "up" to the Maker and Ruler of all the amazing stuff we experience through our senses, but simply by putting us in touch with the stuff itself—with, as Sallie McFague has put it, the world as God's body.[21] Moreover, hope (one of Aquinas's three theological virtues [*ST* 2.2.17.5]) is an important virtue exactly insofar as it pertains to the future of *this* world. To conclude that, as such, hope cannot be called a theological virtue would be to deny that eschatological descriptions of a this-worldly liberation are theological descriptions. When we cultivate ecological virtues, we move across a physical-spiritual spectrum where both dimensions can be simultaneously present at all levels of cultivation and without a bifurcation of objectives into "worldly" and "otherworldly" aspects.

Once again we can deepen our appreciation of the difference by putting it in the context of recent Western developments. If the cultivation of ecological virtues like rootedness-in-a-place and sensuousness has become a religious experience for many Westerners, the unorthodoxy of such an experience in light of Christian teachings about divine transcendence does not usually elude them. For many, the newly found religious experience comes as a relief after years of feeling alienated from institutionalized Christianity. Others, who have stayed within the mainstream churches, find their faith surprisingly enriched by the heightened or even novel sense of divine immanence they discover in the process of cultivating ecological virtues. Some have had to pay for the discovery by being ostracized. These are no haphazard developments; they represent the emergence of a deliberately affirmed alternative.

Evaluation: Retrofit Spells Bad Fit

How does the virtue language that emerges from ecological praxis compare with Christian virtue tradition? By taking the virtue theory of Thomas Aquinas as an anchor, I have shown how superficial similarities, upon closer inspection, dissolve into rather significant differences. This means that the option of simply retrofitting the Aristotelian-Thomistic virtue tradition for ecological purposes becomes unrealistic. In fact, we would be seriously misguided if we were to pursue that option, for the points of difference involve those orthodox Christian tenets that have been linked with environmentally damaging attitudes. Let me give four examples.

First of all, the cybernetic alternative to the model of an internal rational order challenges the Thomistic *anthropology* that presents the human soul as a hierarchy of parts, with the reasoning part destined to be in charge (*ST* 1.77.4). If it is true that such an anthropology encourages the ecologically problematic views that humans are superior to other animals on account of exclusive rationality (cf. *ST* 1.96.2; 2.2.66.1 and 2.2.25.3), that men are superior to women on account of superior rationality (cf. *ST* 1.92.1 *ad* 2; but also 1.93.6 *ad* 2), that nonhuman animals are excluded from salvation on account of lack of rationality (cf. *ST* 2.2.25.3; 2.2.25.3 *ad* 2; and 1.75.3), and that nonhuman creation has only use value on account of lack of rationality,[22] then the challenge needs to be taken seriously.

Second, the cybernetic alternative to the model of an internal rational order also implies a challenge to the Thomistic theology of *justification* as the reestablishment of a lost internal rational order. Aquinas explains this view of justification as follows:

> Secondly, justice is so-called inasmuch as it implies a certain rectitude
> of order in the interior disposition of a man, in so far as what is highest
> in man is subject to God, and the inferior powers of the soul are subject
> to the superior, i.e., to the reason. . . . [J]ustification implies a trans-
> mutation from the state of injustice to the aforesaid state of justice.
> And it is thus that we are now speaking of the justification of the un-
> godly, according to the Apostle (Rom iv.5). . . . (*ST* 1.2.113.1)

If it is true that such a theology of justification encourages anthropocentrism by focusing attention primarily on the personal salvation
of culpable human beings, then the challenge needs to be taken
seriously.

Third, the open-ended alternative to the model of predictable natural harmony challenges the Thomistic theory of *divine providence* in
which a transcendent God guarantees a harmonious world as long as
human beings behave rationally (in the limited sense of the word). If
it is true that such a theory encourages overconfidence and neglect of
inculpable causes of disharmony (such as the atmospheric burden
caused simply by the methane gas produced by billions of human
bodies), then the challenge needs to be taken seriously.

Fourth, the immanentist alternative to the model of a supernatural
order challenges the *cosmology* underlying the Aristotelian-Thomistic virtue tradition, a cosmology in which God, as the primary agent,
operates in the created world without being part of its essence (*ST*
1.8.1–3, esp. 3 *ad* 1).[23] If it is true that such a cosmology encourages
the environmentally harmful attitude of otherworldliness, then the
challenge needs to be taken seriously.

With this final challenge, however, the very core of Aquinas's theology is affected. For Aquinas, God as the First Mover has to be un-
movable and immaterial (*ST* 1.3.1). While God is a continuous *cause*
behind and within creation, and as such "in all things by His essence"
(*ST* 1.8.3), creation itself, because it is changeable and material, can
never *contain* any part of the Divine Essence in its own essence or
accidents (*ST* 1.8.1–3). To insist that it can—when we discover the
ordinary *as* extraordinary, not just as *caused by* the extraordinary—is
to ask for another concept of God. There is no way around it: We
cannot just reheat Aquinas's *Summa Theologiae* and add a bit of
ecological flavoring. The flavoring will make the whole dish curdle.
Something different will have to be cooked up for a Christian ecological virtue ethic.

Transforming Tradition

Many of Aquinas's contemporaries saw the inclusion of Aristotelian teachings as a serious threat to Christian doctrine and practice. They were right: the ideas of Plato's pupil and critic did not mix well with the existing Platonic emphasis in theology, nor with its embodiment in monastic practices. Rather than deny the tensions, Aquinas faced them head-on and took a radical step. Instead of trying to feed Aristotle piecemeal into the existing theological system, which would have been a recipe for failure, he rebuilt the system from the bottom up, using Aristotle to provide much of its structure and content. In doing so, he also hastened the shift of emphasis from monastic to scholastic practices. Aquinas did not retrofit; he transformed his own tradition.

Today Aquinas's system itself has become tradition—revered by many, but also bewailed by others—and ecological praxis appears as a serious challenge. I propose that we follow the man Aquinas, rather than cling to the whole system of his thought, and engage in the creative task of transforming Christian virtue tradition from the bottom up, looking to ecological praxis to provide new structures and content. Some of Aquinas's insights can have a place in this venture, just as Aquinas did not altogether dismiss those who, like Augustine, Pseudo-Dionysius, and Gregory the Great, stood in the line of Plato. To transform a tradition means to transform what is handed on; the result does need to show a recognizable continuity with the past.

Similarly, the work of other theologians and philosophers who have shaped Christian virtue tradition can play a role in its ecological transformation.[24] We can also look beyond ready-made virtue theories to such key sources as the Bible, systematic theology, and the exemplary witness of individual Christians and Christian communities. This is exactly what James Nash and Steven Bouma-Prediger have begun to do.[25] As we look to traditional theological sources to inform the ecological transformation of Christian virtue tradition, however, we should use them with appropriate discretion, honesty, and respect for their own integrity.

The ecological transformation of Christian virtue tradition will be especially helped by bringing together the emerging praxis of people who cultivate ecological virtues with *ecological* interpretations of scripture and tradition,[26] as well as with *ecological* expressions of constructive theology and ethics.[27] For example, in environmental circles the virtue of humility tends to mean knowing your place in a dynamic web of earthly relations.[28] This image connects very well with a common idea in ecotheology, namely, that individual salvation belongs to a larger story of the liberation of all creation.[29] By combining ecological virtues with explicitly ecological theological reflection, we can expect a process of mutual enrichment and correction without the problems and cover-ups caused by strong differences. Virtue ethics may lag behind the rest of Christian theology in becoming ecologically transformed, but it may also benefit from the advances made in other areas of theology.

The ecological transformation of Christian virtue ethics will involve connecting ecological praxis and theological sources at the unique intersection of questions and concerns that has typically marked virtue theory. While some of these questions and concerns may themselves shift in the process, I want to give an indication of the kinds of topics that a Christian ecological virtue theory may well include (a deft observer will notice more than just an echo of Aquinas in this list):

1. Ecotheological concepts of virtue and vice;
2. How these concepts fit within larger ecotheological visions and narratives (for example, within Thomas Berry's "Story of the Universe");[30]
3. The significance of emotions, motives, understandings, inclinations, skills, bodily functions, and physical conditions for ecotheological virtues and vices (for example, the relationship of attraction to care);
4. How ecotheological virtues and vices relate to the evaluation of acts and states of affairs (for example, whether any destruction of divine creation can be called virtuous);
5. Criteria for genuine ecotheological virtues and vices (for example, consistency with the sustainability of ecosystems as a criterion for genuine virtue);
6. Different categories of ecotheological virtues and vices (for example, preservative virtues as virtues that preserve ecological ways of thinking—and thus also ecological systems);
7. Descriptions of specific ecotheological virtues and vices and their interrelationships;
8. Ecotheological cardinal virtues and deadly sins;

9. Ways of cultivating ecotheological virtues and overcoming vices (for example, how to sustain hope, and how to unlearn arrogance);
10. The role of the churches in the process of cultivation;
11. Connections between cultivating ecotheological virtues and social change toward sustainable communities.

This list is not meant to be definitive or exhaustive, but rather serves to give a concrete indication of the many tasks that can be expected in the construction of a Christian ecological virtue theory. Some of the work has already been done, mostly in the area of providing theologically informed descriptions of specific ecological virtues.[31] The bulk of this theoretical work still remains.

In the end, though, the ecological transformation of Christian virtue tradition is a very practical matter. Ideally, it involves millions of Christians learning to cultivate ecological virtues as a conscious and integrated part of their Christian identity, both personal and communal. This is already beginning to happen. We see it in church youth groups that clean up beaches as a way to heal creation, in homemakers who see recycling as a form of caring for God's creation, and in managers who learn to think about accountability in light of their stewardship of creation. Here we see the first fruits of a development with enormous potential for bringing about social change.

Notes

1. Louke van Wensveen, *Dirty Virtues* (Amherst, Mass.: Humanity Books, 1999).

2. Jay B. McDaniel, *Of God and Pelicans: A Theology of Reverence for Life* (Louisville: Westminster/John Knox Press, 1989), 73–74; James A. Nash, *Loving Nature: Ecological Integrity and Christian Responsibility* (Nashville: Abingdon Press, 1991), and "Toward the Revival and Reform of the Subversive Virtue: Frugality," in *The Annual of the Society of Christian Ethics* (Washington, D.C.: Georgetown University Press, 1995), 137–60; Val Plumwood, *Feminism and the Mastery of Nature* (New York: Routledge, 1993), 173; and Mary Midgley, "Sustainability and Moral Pluralism," *Ethics and the Environment* 1 (1996): 41–54. See also Thomas E. Hill, "Ideals of Human Excellence and Preserving Natural Environments," *Environmental Ethics* 5 (1983): 211–24; Geoffrey B. Frasz, "Environmental Virtue Ethics: A New Direction for Environmental Ethics," *Environmental Ethics* 15 (1993): 259–74; Jamie Ehegartner Schaefer, "Ethical Implications of Applying Aquinas's Notions of the Unity and Diversity of Creation to Human Functioning in Ecosystems" (Ph.D. diss., Marquette University, 1994); Deborah D. Blake, "Toward a Sustainable Ethic: Virtue and the Environment," in *"And God Saw That It Was Good": Catholic Theology and the Environment,* ed. Drew Christiansen and Walter Grazer (Washington, D.C.: United States Catholic Conference, 1996), 197–210; Michael S. Northcott, *The Environment and Christian Ethics* (Cambridge: Cambridge University Press, 1996); Bill Shaw, "A Virtue Ethics Approach to Aldo Leopold's Land Ethic," *Environmental Ethics* 19 (1997): 53–67; Steven Bouma-Prediger, "Creation Care and Character: The Nature and Necessity of the Ecological Virtues," *Perspectives on Science and Christian Faith* 50, no. 1 (March 1998): 6–21; and Laura Westra, *Living in Integrity: A Global Ethic to Restore a Fragmented Earth* (Lanham: Rowman and Littlefield, 1998).

3. Midgley,"Sustainability and Moral Pluralism," 50–51.

4. For a general overview of ecological virtue language, see Wensveen, *Dirty Virtues,* chapters 1 and 2. For a catalog of 189 virtues and 174 vices, see Appendix A.

5. Thomas Aquinas, *Summa Theologica,* trans. by the Fathers of the English Dominican Province (New York: Benziger Brothers, 1948).

6. See, for example, Stanley Hauerwas, *A Community of Character: Toward a Constructive Christian Social Ethic* (Notre Dame, Ind.: University of Notre Dame Press, 1981); Ralph McInerny, *Ethica Thomistica: The Moral Philosophy of Thomas Aquinas* (Washington, D.C.: Catholic University of America Press, 1982); Jean Porter, *The Recovery of Virtue: The Relevance of Aquinas for Christian Ethics* (Louisville: Westminster/John Knox Press, 1990); Lee H. Yearley, *Mencius and Aquinas: Theories of Virtue and Conceptions of Courage* (Albany: State University of New York Press, 1990); Paul J. Wadell, *The Primacy of Love: An Introduction to the Ethics of Thomas Aquinas* (New York: Paulist Press, 1992); Stephen J. Pope, *The Evolution of Altruism and the Ordering of Love* (Washington, D.C.: Georgetown University Press, 1994); Daniel Mark Nelson, *The Priority of Prudence: Virtue and Natural Law in Thomas Aquinas and the Implications for Modern Ethics* (University Park: Pennsylvania State University Press, 1992); and Bouma-Prediger, "Creation Care and Character."

7. For example, Schaefer,"Ethical Implications of Applying Aquinas's Notions"; and Pamela A. Smith, "Aquinas and Today's Environmental Ethics: An Exploration of How the Vision and the Virtue Ethic of 'Ecothomism' Might Inform a Viable Eco-Ethic" (Ph.D. diss., Duquesne University, 1995). Cf. also Matthew Fox, *Sheer Joy: Conversations with Thomas Aquinas on Creation Spirituality* (San Francisco: HarperSanFrancisco, 1992). Cf. also various essays in *"And God Saw That It Was Good": Catholic Theology and the Environment,* ed. Christiansen and Grazer. Note also the influence of Aquinas on Thomas Berry.

8. Grace Jantzen, *God's World, God's Body* (Philadelphia: Westminster Press, 1984); Jürgen Moltmann, *God in Creation: A New Theology of Creation and the Spirit of God* (London: SCM Press, 1985); and H. Paul Santmire, *The Travail of Nature: The Ambiguous Ecological Promise of Christian Theology* (Philadelphia: Fortress Press, 1985).

9. Also, Christian virtue tradition is heavily indebted to ancient Greek ideas. The apostle Paul, for example, adapted his influential catalogs of vices and virtues (e.g. 1 Cor. 6:9–10; Gal. 5:19–23) from commonly known Hellenistic Jewish lists (see Robin Scroggs, *The New Testament and Homosexuality: Contextual Background for Contemporary Debate* [Philadelphia: Fortress Press, 1983]). By focusing on the virtue theory of Thomas Aquinas, which builds on the theory of Aristotle, we can also deal with this Greek element.

10. Aquinas also recognizes a relative order, in which things are compared to each other in their actual states (*ST* 1.82.3), and an "order of generation and time," in which supporting conditions are recognized as more basic than what depends on them (*ST* 1.77.4; 1.82.4 *ad* 2). However, these alternative forms of ordering only function as sidelines in his theory.

11. On carnal knowing, see, for example, Margaret R. Miles, *Carnal Knowing: Female Nakedness and Religious Meaning in the Christian West* (Boston: Beacon Press, 1989), and Charlene Spretnak, *The Spiritual Dimension of Green Politics* (Santa Fe: Bear and Company, 1986). By contrast, Aristotle is very clear about the secondary status of perceptual knowledge based on an individual's sense experience vis-à-vis "universal judgement"; see Aristotle *Nicomachean Ethics* 7.3.

12. For an example of ecotheological anthropology, see Sallie McFague, *The Body of God: An Ecological Theology* (Minneapolis: Fortress Press, 1993), 99–129.

13. Dominion is typically interpreted as stewardship; see Douglas John Hall, *Imaging God: Dominion as Stewardship* (Grand Rapids, Mich.: Eerdmans, 1986). Many ecotheologians who promote stewardship in fact prefer not to use the term dominion.

14. I thank Christine Firer Hinze for this phrase.

15. For various interpretations of eco-justice, see *After Nature's Revolt: Eco-Justice and Theology,* ed. Dieter T. Hessel (Minneapolis: Fortress Press, 1992).

16. The key word here is "use," not to be confused with malificent or greedy "abuse," vices that Aquinas would not condone. Furthermore, Aquinas (following Augustine) contrasted use (*uti*) with enjoyment (*frui;* see *ST* 1.2.16.3). We can use creation, but not truly enjoy it other than as an expression of God's goodness (*ST* 1.2.11.3). By this principle, ironically, many of the joys reported by environmentalists—for example, the pleasures of hiking or birdwatching just for the joy of it—would be based on idolatrous self-deception.

The question does arise, however, whether the prospective of using up any part of creation (e.g., species extinction) presents a concrete limit within Aquinas's system. The following text suggests such a limit: "[B]ecause His goodness could not be adequately represented by one creature alone, He produced many and diverse creatures, that what was wanting to one in the representation of the divine goodness might be supplied by another" (*ST* 1.47.1). In order to complete the argument, one would have to establish the necessity for the continued demonstration of God's goodness through diversity, as well as the necessity of the full range of existing diversity (facing the objection, based on modern scientific data, that most species that have ever lived are already extinct). The limit of using up any part of creation would of course be a limit at the extreme; it would still leave open a vast range of destructive uses.

17. Jean Porter even argues that "though we recognize that our own existence, as individuals or as a species, is not the greatest created good, nonetheless, it is only right—that is, in accordance with the ordering of ourselves and all other things by God—for us to be concerned *first of all* with our own well-being, rather than with the good of the universe as a whole" (Porter, *The Recovery of Virtue,* 62; emphasis added).

18. Larry L. Rasmussen, *Earth Community, Earth Ethics* (Maryknoll, N.Y.: Orbis Books, 1996), 155.

19. Ibid., 161.

20. I consider wonder and rootedness-in-a-place "spontaneity virtues," because their cultivation involves the "effort of making no effort" required to let spontaneous inclinations come out as they are. I consider attention a "focus virtue," because its cultivation involves focusing—that is, enhancing and shaping—inclinations (e.g., concentration, curiosity, quietude).

21. McFague, *The Body of God.*

22. Cf. *ST* 2.2.64.1 *ad* 2: "Dumb animals and plants are devoid of the life of reason whereby to set themselves in motion; they are moved, as it were by another, by a kind of natural impulse, a sign of which is that they are naturally enslaved and accommodated to the uses of others." Also *ST* 2.2.25.3: "Nevertheless, we can love irrational creatures out of charity, if we regard them as the good things that we desire for others, in so far, to wit, as we wish for their preservation, to God's honor and man's use; thus too does God love them out of charity." The last text suggests that even God's consideration of "irrational creatures" is only instrumental, which undercuts the commonly made argument that nonhuman creatures have intrinsic value because God loves them.

23. As a result of God's creative activity, nonrational creatures represent a *trace* of the Trinity; rational creatures represent the *image* of the Trinity as well as a trace (*ST* 1.45.7; also 1.93.1, 2, and 6). A trace is simply an effect (like ashes are an effect of fire), whereas an image is a reflection. Neither should be confused with the original. In modern terms, these forms of likeness are best understood as analogies (cf. *ST* 1.4.3; 1.93.6).

24. The ecological potential of most Christian virtue theories still needs to be further explored. I think, for example, of the eighteenth-century theories of Joseph Butler and Jonathan Edwards and of the modern theories of Stanley Hauerwas, Gilbert Meilaender, James McClendon, Robert Adams, and Robert C. Roberts.

25. Nash, *Loving Nature,* and "Toward the Revival and Reform of the Subversive Virtue"; Bouma-Prediger, "Creation Care and Character."

26. E.g., Santmire, *The Travail of Nature*; Calvin B. DeWitt, *The Environment and the Christian: What Can We Learn from the New Testament?* (Grand Rapids, Mich.: Baker Book House, 1991); James Barr, *The Garden of Eden and the Hope of Immortality* (Minneapolis: Fortress Press, 1992); Rosemary Radford Ruether, *Gaia and God: An Ecofeminist Theology of Earth Healing* (San Francisco: HarperSanFrancisco, 1992); and Susan Power Bratton, *Christianity, Wilderness, and Wildlife: The Original Desert Solitaire* (Scranton, Pa.: University of Scranton Press, 1993).

27. E.g. John B. Cobb, Jr., *Is It Too Late? A Theology of Ecology* (Beverly Hills, Calif.: Bruce Publishing, 1972); Moltmann, *God in Creation;* McFague, *The Body of God;* Gordon Kaufman, *In Face of Mystery: A Constructive Theology* (Cambridge, Mass.: Harvard University Press, 1993); and James M. Gustafson, *A Sense of the Divine: The Natural Environment from a Theocentric Perspective* (Cleveland: Pilgrim Press, 1994).

28. See van Wensveen, *Dirty Virtues.*

29. On the accompanying eschatology, see, for example, Catherine Keller, "Talk about the Weather: The Greening of Eschatology," in *Ecofeminism and the Sacred,* ed. Carol J. Adams (New York: Continuum, 1993), 30–49; McFague, *The Body of God,* chap. 7; Wolfhart Pannenberg, *Toward a Theology of Nature* (Louisville: Westminster/John Knox Press, 1993); and John F. Haught, "Ecology and Eschatology," in *"And God Saw That It Was Good,"* ed. Christiansen and Grazer, 47–64.

30. Thomas Berry, *The Dream of the Earth* (San Francisco: Sierra Club Books, 1988), chap. 10. See also the later work: Brian Swimme and Thomas Berry, *The Universe Story* (San Francisco: HarperSanFrancisco, 1992).

31. E.g., Nash, *Loving Nature*, and "Toward the Revival and Reform of the Subversive Virtue"; Bouma-Prediger, "Creation Care and Character."

Response to Louke van Wensveen:
A Constructive Proposal

STEVEN BOUMA-PREDIGER

Humility, discernment, attentiveness, fortitude, restraint, wisdom, hope. These comprise merely a partial list of virtues mentioned at the gathering which occasioned this book. It should not be surprising to find these virtues discussed at a conference entitled "Christianity and Ecology," for the Christian scriptures and tradition are replete with stories about and references to the virtues. Explicit attention to the virtues, however, by Christians working in ecological ethics is surprisingly rare. Indeed, there are relatively few significant treatments of this important theme, despite the recent resurgence of interest in virtue theory in both theological ethics and moral philosophy.[1]

So I am delighted that this volume includes Louke van Wensveen's fine contribution to this topic and am pleased to offer my own constructive proposal. Like her, I view attention to the virtues—both the development of virtue theory and the cultivation of certain virtues—as "a promising path to lasting personal as well as social change." Indeed, I would go beyond van Wensveen's claim that the virtues are a "positive way of being that deserves its own consideration." While deontology and teleology have their legitimate place in any adequate moral framework, areteology—or, more exactly, the practical embodiment of ecological virtues in our everyday lives—is absolutely necessary if we are responsibly to fulfill our role as caretakers of creation.[2]

I would like to take one item from van Wensveen's suggestive list of topics that Christian ecological virtue theory should cover. I will offer some descriptions of specific ecological virtues and vices and their interrelationship (item 7 on her list) and in so doing illustrate a specific proposal to develop a Christian ecological virtue ethic. I concur that while the basic ingredients for a Christian ecological virtue ethic are already available from the praxis of ecologically committed people, many of us will want to make more explicit connections with our Christian heritage. Indeed, it is my experience that reconnecting Christians with their own story—the biblical story and the stories of the various Christian traditions—is one of the most powerful ways to foster longlasting care for creation.[3]

Before examining specific virtues, some understanding of virtue is required. Despite debates over how precisely to define virtue, all of us have some sense of what certain virtues are—like courage and patience and humility. We spot them in others, pray for them in our children, and seek to cultivate them in our own lives. For our purposes here, let me define virtue as Aristotle does.[4] Most simply, a virtue is a settled disposition to act excellently. It is a praiseworthy state of character, developed over time, which displays a kind of excellence— either of intellect or of character. A virtue, furthermore, is a mean between extremes. For example, courage is that excellence of character which disposes one to act, when fearful, in neither a rash nor a cowardly way. Patience is that habitual disposition which inclines one to act with calm forbearance, resisting both impulsiveness and indecision.

In addition, virtue is intimately connected to vision. Insofar as the virtues refer to a set of attributes which mark us as the particular people we are—that complex of traits formed by our past choices which we call character—the virtues shape our vision of the world. As Gilbert Meilaender reminds us, the virtues "influence how we describe the activities in which we engage, what we think we are doing and what we think is important about what we are doing."[5] And so too does fundamental life vision shape the virtues. In short, a virtue is a state of character—with the attendant desires, attitudes, and emotions —formed by choices and habits over time, which disposes us to act in certain excellent ways and shapes our vision of the world.

My method in what follows is this. First I examine the biblical story, since, as an evangelical Protestant, I view the Bible not only as one of the main places Christians go—along with tradition, reason, and experience—when seeking guidance on how to live, but as that source which takes precedence over all others. I explore certain texts which directly address matters ecological. I next identify particular theological themes which emerge from the biblical narrative. Not exactly full-fledged doctrines, these theological motifs nevertheless function like doctrines insofar as they, like doctrines, are portable stories.[6] That is, they attempt to summarize in one expression what the biblical text narrates. From these motifs I derive certain ethical principles and corresponding virtues or excellences. So from biblical story I move through theological motif and ethical principle to specific virtues and vices. In this way I have developed a schema of seven motifs and fourteen virtues (see the table). Let us look at some examples.

THE ECOLOGICAL VIRTUES

Biblical Story	Theological Motif	Ethical Principle	Virtue	Vice (deficiency)	Vice (excess)
Gen. 1 Ps. 104 Ps. 148	Creational integrity and dependence	Biodiversity	Respect Receptivity	Conceit Self-sufficiency	Reverence Addiction
Gen. 1 Exod. 16 Matt. 6:11	Creational finitude	Sufficiency	Self-restraint Frugality	Profligacy Greed	Austerity Stinginess
Gen. 2 Job 38–41 Ps. 8 Gen. 3	Human finitude and faultedness	Responsibility	Humility Honesty	Hubris Deception	Self-deprecation False honesty
Gen. 1 Deut. 22:6–7 Deut. 20:19–20 Gen. 6–9	Fruitfulness	Sustainability	Wisdom Hope	Foolishness Despair	——— Presumption
Gen. 2:1–3 Exod. 20:8–11 Lev. 25 Luke 4	Sabbath	Rejuvenation	Patience Serenity	Impetuousness Restlessness	Timidity Passivity
Gen. 2:15 Ps. 24 Ps. 95 Gen. 6–9	Earthkeeping	Beneficence	Benevolence Love	Malice Apathy	——— ———
Exod. 20:12–17 Amos 5 Mic. 6:8 Ps. 72 Matt. 5–7	Righteousness	Equity	Justice Courage	Injustice Cowardice	——— Rashness

Genesis 1 emphasizes, among other things, that creation is finite. Despite the manyness—many individual creatures, many kinds of creatures—there is no suggestion here that the panoply of God's creatures or the earth itself is unlimited. Creation has limits. Moreover, God's word to humans in verse 28 to be fruitful and multiply does not suggest, as some maintain, that the earth has an unlimited supply of "resources" for an ever-growing human population. It is often overlooked that this call by God to be fruitful and multiply is also given (in verse 22) to all living creatures. The sea monsters, the fish, and the birds—indeed, all living creatures—are given this command. The calling to reproduce is no special privilege unique to humans. Moreover, this imperative is actually not a command at all but a blessing by God on the swarms of living creatures brought forth by God's word. As Susan Power Bratton puts it, God's blessing "is not an ethical imperative, nor is it a way to please God by reaching to excess."[7] Rather, God's blessing conveys a reproductive power intended to contribute to the flourishing of all creatures on a finite planet. As Bratton concludes: "Human population growth has no mandate to damage or desecrate the cosmos."[8] Creation is finite and humans have no biblical license to act as if it is infinite.

This theme is present in other biblical texts. For example, after the Israelites escaped from Egypt, they wandered in the wilderness on the way to the promised land. As narrated in Exodus 16, God provided bread and meat—manna and quail—for them to eat, but only enough for one day at a time. The portions were sufficient for the day, but there was to be no excess. Their resources were not unlimited, lest they forget their dependence on the God who not only delivered them but continued to sustain them. Jesus calls to mind this experience in the wilderness when he teaches his followers what and how to pray. After three petitions concerning God's glory, he petitions God for human needs. He first prays "give us this day our daily bread" (Matt. 6:11). In other words, in the Lord's Prayer Jesus asks the provisioning God of the Exodus to give us the nourishment we need for today. As the Israelites received their daily bread, we also are to ask for and with gratitude receive food sufficient for the day. This text reiterates this theme of finitude and sufficiency. The Bible confirms what those most famous of photographs from space portray—that the blue-green sphere on which we live is finite.

These texts provide us with the theological motif of creational finitude. Creation is finite. There is only so much to go around. The only seemingly limitless physical resource is the energy from the sun, that divine provision fundamental to all life on Earth. All else is limited. From this theological motif comes the ethical principle of sufficiency. Put in the form of a moral maxim, it says: we should acknowledge the finitude of the earth and act so as to live within our means. More precisely, we have a prima facie duty to preserve non-renewable resources, to conserve scarce renewable resources, and to share both kinds of resources fairly. This duty applies to a wide range of things. We should, for example, conserve our fossil fuels like coal, oil, and natural gas, for once that solar savings account is depleted it will be a very long time before it is replenished.[9] So too we should preserve species, for that "resource," once gone, will never return.

Corresponding to the theological motif of creational finitude and the ethical principle of sufficiency, with its attendent duties, are the moral virtues of self-restraint and frugality. One of the cardinal virtues of the Greeks, self-restraint is moderation of inordinate desires. What is sought after is not the extinction of all desire, as if that were possible, but the control of desire. Disciplined desire is the goal. To use an old-fashioned word, the virtue here is temperance—habitual control of one's appetites or passions. The vice of deficiency that runs contrary to self-restraint is profligacy, or unrestrained desire. Profligate people are overly self-indulgent. They lack sufficient self-control. As Aristotle notes, "these people are called belly-gods, this implying that they fill their belly beyond what is right."[10] The vice of excess, in which there is too much self-control, is austerity. Overly self-controlled people mistake masochism for moderation. Austerity implies that the passions are inherently evil. Desire per se is dangerous.

Frugality is economy of use or efficient use, given the limits of the goods available. It is characterized not by a parsimonious wish to hold in or keep back, but rather by a desire to use sparingly that which God has provided in order to allow others to live and flourish. Thus, rightly understood, frugality represents a form of hospitality. And as its etymology suggests, to be frugal is to enjoy (*frui*) the proper use of the finite goods God has given us. The vice of deficiency which corresponds to frugality is greed—the disposition to acquire excessively, especially beyond one's need. Avarice is perhaps a more accurate term, for it denotes a craving to acquire that is blinded to the limits inherent in creation. Driven by cupidity, the greedy person lacks any sense of the finitude of the world. The vice of excess is stinginess, or thrift as an end in itself. Sparing to the point of being mean, the stingy person exhibits no generosity. Fearful of whether there will be enough, the penurious hold in and keep back. Economy for economy's sake is their motto. In the case of each vice, there is no enjoyment of that which God has provided.

Creation is finite. Thus, we have the moral obligation to preserve the resources God has provided and joyfully to live within our means. And so we must cultivate the virtues of self-restraint and frugality, thereby discouraging the vices of profligacy and greed while avoiding the vices of austerity and stinginess.

If creation is finite and we are creatures, then it follows that we are finite. It might seem that this rather obvious point needs no special attention. However, we have a penchant for forgetting this central feature of our existence. Indeed, we have a deep desire to avoid looking at our finitude, especially our temporal finitude or mortality, straight in the face.[11] To acknowledge the limited nature of our existence produces anxiety and raises the question of whether death is the end of one's life or whether there is One who is sufficiently able and willing to preserve our life beyond biological death and in whom we can rest in spite of our fear and anxiety. Not surprisingly the Bible speaks often of human finitude. For example, in Genesis 2 the narrative tells us that the human creature is formed out of the ground and made alive by God's life-giving breath (verse 7). We are earth creatures— *'ādām*—because we are clumps of earth—*'ădāmâ*—animated by the Spirit of God. Like all of God's creations we are finite.

The finitude of humanity is powerfully portrayed also in the book of Job. After numerous conversations between Job and his friends about Job's plight, chapters 38–41 narrate God's speech from a whirlwind. In the deluge of questions put by God, Job is forcibly reminded of his finitude. Job has not commanded the morning or entered the storehouses of the snow or provided prey for the ravens. He does not know when the mountain goats give birth or who let the wild asses go free. That the hawk soars and the eagle mounts up is not Job's doing. Job's power and knowledge are finite. He is a creature. Even Psalm 8, which speaks of humans as having been created a little lower than God and crowned with glory and honor, reminds us that humans are creatures and hence finite. We have a God-given dignity and calling, but we are nevertheless limited in our abilities.

But we are not just finite; we are faulted. Though often confused, these two are not the same. Finitude is a good feature of human existence. It is simply how God made us—a feature of our humanity to accept joyfully. Faultedness, however, is not God's intention. The brokenness we know in ourselves and all around us is something we acknowledge with regret and seek with God's grace to overcome. This feature of human existence is also powerfully depicted in the Genesis narrative. In chapter three we learn that Adam and Eve desired to transcend their creaturely finitude and to become, like God, omniscient. But in this attempt they fail to trust in God and thus become estranged from God. Their relationship with God is broken. In addition, they become estranged from each other: they scapegoat and attempt to pass the blame. They lose touch with their own true and best self: they hide and conceal their actions. And they are out of joint with the earth: working the earth becomes burdensome toil. In these four ways they, and we, are alienated. The Bible confirms what we know in our hearts: the world and our own lives are not the way they are supposed to be.[12]

In these and many other biblical texts we find the theological motif of human finitude and faultedness. As humans we are creatures, limited in power and knowledge as well as situated in space and time. We are 'ādām from the 'ādāmâ, humans from the *humus*. We are not God, though we are God's. Furthermore, we are faulted creatures, alienated from God, other humans, ourselves, and the earth. Though we are not God, we all too often think and act as if we are. From this theological motif comes the ethical principle of responsibility. Given the limited scope of our human knowledge and power and our stubborn unwillingness to admit such limitations, I propose the following moral maxim: we should act cautiously, in full acknowledgment of our limited ability to know the future consequences of our actions and with honest awareness of our penchant for self-aggrandizement and self-deception. To be more precise, we have a prima facie duty to survey all possible consequences before making decisions. In our care of creation we must be circumspect and exercise forethought.

The theological motif of human finitude and faultedness and the ethical principle of responsibility presuppose the moral virtues of humility and honesty. Humility is the proper estimation of one's abilities or capacities. It is the fitting acknowledgment that we humans

are earth creatures. Humility implies self-knowledge and unpreten-
tiousness. Aware of their weaknesses, humble people do not pretend
to be something other than what they are. The vice of deficiency is
hubris—exaggerated self-confidence or overweening pride. Here, as
for the Greeks, it means the failure to acknowledge one's own limits,
often resulting in tragic consequences. Overestimating their abilities,
prideful people are vain and boastful. The vice of excess is self-
deprecation. People who display this vice play down their abilities
and speak disparagingly of their legitimate achievements. They are
unable or refuse to assess their genuine strengths properly. Aristotle
speaks of those who disclaim or belittle their authentic accomplishments as mock modest.[13]

Honesty is the refusal to deceive—others, oneself, or God. Honest
people are without guile. They do not have a duplicitous bone in their
body. There is, rather, a singleness of intention, a straightforwardness
of conduct. Honesty brings with it a what-you-see-is-what-you-get
transparency and sincerity. There is no need to do business at night,
no need for cover-ups, slush funds, or secrets. The vice of deficiency
contrary to honesty is deception, or the culpable failure to be truthful.
Deception is willful fraud, represented in the lowest circles (eight and
nine) of Dante's *Inferno*. It is perversion of the truth for personal
gain. Deception is cunning misrepresentation, most often fueled by
envy and spite. The vice of excess is false honesty. Difficult to name
but understood by all, this vice has never known a secret that it did not
tell. Enamored by Kant's categorical imperative, persons who exhibit
this vice always tell "the truth," even if it means turning in Anne
Frank to the Nazi stormtroopers. They have no feeling for the
relational context of truth-telling, famously described by Dietrich
Bonhoeffer in his classic essay "What is Meant by 'Telling the
Truth'."[14] To the falsely honest, truth is truth and must be told, no
matter who the conversation partner or what the situation.

As humans we are both finite and faulted. Therefore, we have the
moral obligation to act responsibly and with forethought. And so we
must cultivate the virtues of humility and honesty while discouraging
the vices of hubris and self-deprecation, deception and false honesty.

On this issue of the ecological virtues enough has been said, I
hope, to illustrate my proposal for developing a constructive Christian ethic. The good work of earthkeeping is not possible without respect, receptivity, self-restraint, frugality, humility, honesty, wisdom,

hope, patience, serenity, benevolence, love, justice, and courage. But beyond the development of theory lies the concrete embodiment of these virtues in our everyday lives. For virtues are, as Aristotle reminds us, not only to be studied but to be put into practice: "Surely, as the saying goes, where there are things to be done the end is not to survey and recognize the various things, but rather to do them; with regard to virtue, then, it is not enough to know, but we must try to have and use it."[15] While clear and creative theorizing is important, the practice of theorizing is pointless unless it leads to a world filled and flourishing with shalom.[16]

Notes

1. See, e.g., Jay B. McDaniel, *Of God and Pelicans: A Theology of Reverence for Life* (Louisville: Westminster/John Knox Press, 1989), 73–74; James Nash, *Loving Nature: Ecological Integrity and Christian Responsibility* (Nashville: Abingdon Press, 1991), 63–67; Michael S. Northcott, *The Environment and Christian Ethics* (Cambridge: Cambridge University Press, 1996), 122–23.

2. This claim is developed in greater detail in Steven Bouma-Prediger, "Creation Care and Character: The Nature and Necessity of the Ecological Virtues," *Perspectives on Science and Christian Faith* 50, no. 1 (March 1998): 6–21.

3. Max Oelschlaeger makes a similar observation in *Caring for Creation: An Ecumenical Appeal to the Environmental Crisis* (New Haven: Yale University Press, 1994), e.g., on p. 236. Many books and articles point out the ecological riches of scripture and tradition, e.g., *The Environment and the Christian: What Does the New Testament Say about the Environment?* ed. Calvin B. DeWitt (Grand Rapids, Mich.: Baker Book House, 1991); H. Paul Santmire, *The Travail of Nature: The Ambiguous Ecological Promise of Christian Theology* (Philadelphia: Fortress Press, 1985); Susan Power Bratton, *Christianity, Wilderness, and Wildlife: The Original Desert Solitaire* (Scranton, Pa.: University of Scranton Press, 1993); Steven Bouma-Prediger, "Why Care for Creation? From Prudence to Piety," *Christian Scholar's Review* 27, no. 3 (spring 1998): 277–97.

4. The locus classicus is *Nicomachean Ethics,* book 2. A much more extensive inquiry into the nature of virtue and the virtues can be found in Bouma-Prediger, "Creation Care and Character."

5. Gilbert Meilaender, *The Theory and Practice of Virtue* (Notre Dame, Ind.: University of Notre Dame Press, 1984), 10–11.

6. This understanding of doctrine is developed in N. Thomas Wright, *The New Testament and the People of God* (Philadelphia: Fortress Press, 1992), chap. 5.

7. Susan Power Bratton, *Six Billion and More: Human Population Regulation and Christian Ethics* (Louisville: Westminster/John Knox Press, 1992), 43.

8. Ibid.

9. For a helpful analysis of this issue, see Loren Wilkinson et al., *Earthkeeping in the 90's* (Grand Rapids, Mich.: Eerdmans, 1991), chap. 4.

10. *Nicomachean Ethics* 1118b, 19.

11. For an insightful analysis of the human tendency to deny mortality and in so doing create and perpetuate evil, see Ernest Becker, *The Denial of Death* (New York: Macmillan, 1973), and *Escape from Evil* (New York: Macmillan, 1975).

12. Two recent books which illuminate the phenomenon of sin very clearly are Ted Peters, *Sin: Radical Evil in Soul and Society* (Grand Rapids, Mich.: Eerdmans, 1995), and Cornelius Plantinga, *Not the Way It's Supposed To Be: A Breviary of Sin* (Grand Rapids, Mich.: Eerdmans, 1995).

13. *Nicomachean Ethics* 1127a, 22.

14. Dietrich Bonhoeffer, *Ethics* (New York: Macmillan, 1955), 363ff.

15. *Nicomachean Ethics* 1179a35–1179b4.

16. This point is forcibly made by Nicholas Wolterstorff in chapter 8 of *Until Justice and Peace Embrace* (Grand Rapids, Mich.: Eerdmans, 1983). Many thanks to Louke van Wensveen and Christine Firer Hinze for helpful discussion of these issues.

No More Sea: The Lost
Chaos of the Eschaton

CATHERINE KELLER

> And the sea can shed shimmering scales indefinitely. Her
> depths peel off into innumerable thin, shining layers. And
> each one is the equal of the other as it catches a reflection
> and lets it go. As it preserves and blurs. As it captures the
> glinting play of light. . . . And with no end in sight.[1]

Luce Irigaray here confronts the masculine genius of a transcen-
dently dry order. Invoking the sea in both its material and metaphorical depths, her feminization of the deep, if not read as an essentialist
rhetoric, intimates the poetic possibilities of those waters where theology, ecology, and feminism overlap:

> Fluid and flaming as she is, are they not impatient to dry her up? To
> contain her in some enclosure where she finds her end. And thus be
> captive, stifled within the narrow limits of their perspectives. (48)

The question of the end brings us, more specifically, to the shores
of an ecologically degraded Christian eschatology. Let me suggest
that the complex reality encoded in the biblical figure of the *tehom*—
the deep, the sea, or the chaos—long ago fell victim to an in-house
tradition demonizing it as evil disobedience. Ultimately its very existence would be denied in the classical doctrine of a *creatio ex nihilo*.
The systematic abjection of the depth, the fluidity, the indeterminacy,

and uncertainty of all existence comprises, I have come to suspect, a profound fount of Christian bad faith.[2] Without the healing of this "tehomophobia," our ecotheological efforts—our efforts toward a green eschatology, toward the renewal of the creation—may remain self-defeating. So I thought it worthwhile to consider the relation of *eschaton* to *tehom*. The following meditation will therefore be drenched in scriptural and scripturally based figures. Let me clarify that I engage these symbols as layered, contested texts of one holy book of one religion (my own, as it happens) among others, to be approached with a principaled ambivalence and irreducible respect for their power to configure, disfigure, and refigure social meaning. While I read them in the light of their originative rhetorical contexts, I do not work as a biblical scholar but as a constructive theologian who considers the effects of the text within current ecosocial practices. I read these textual figurations for the sake not of their own but of the current context.

The Sea Now and Then

The tehomophobic tradition receives its strongest biblical trope in the *locus classicus* of Christian apocalyptic hope: "Then I saw a new heaven and a new earth; for the first heaven and the first earth had passed away, and the sea was no more. . ." (Rev. 21:1–4).

New creation thus inscribes itself as evaporation of the *tehom* left over from the first creation. The sea was identified with the death-tainted, threatening chaos of creation, so such a vision was meant to convert despair to hope. But for any restoration of the interactive health of earth, sea, and sky, such hope seems a counsel of despair.

Regarding the apocalypse now of planetary damage, Dan Maguire asserts that "despair is the ultimate ethical apostasy. Ethics is the progeny of hope."[3] Inspired by the socialist ethics of Ernst Bloch, Jürgen Moltmann made the case that Christian eschatology properly addresses not end things but hope.[4] Yet that hope remains as much the problem as the solution. Moltmann himself, in important ways an ecological compadre, advances an eschatological transcendence *of* transience: what is intended as an ecotheological salvation *of* nature becomes salvation *from* nature—unless, of course, you buy the premise that you can have your nature and escape from its transience too.[5]

As feminist theology has insisted, "otherworldly eschatology" has transmogrified a historical and earthy Hebrew faith into a fantasy of final escape from transience and death.[6] In the verse following the announcement of "no more sea" we read: "he will wipe away every tear from their eyes, and death shall be no more, neither shall there be mourning nor crying nor pain any more, for the former things have passed away." So the new creation entails the evaporation of the salt waters of tears and of seas. The sea as the mythical marine chaos, a roiling and rebellious materiality, had a long tradition of personification as evil sea monster. Certainly John's primary intertext in this passage, the Isaianic new heaven and earth, called eschatologically for a reproduction of a divine warrior creation myth melded with Exodus liberation motifs (Isa. 51:9; 65:17).

This tradition, which projects the hope of economic and political liberation into the future, interpreted by a twentieth-century liberation hermeneutic, has yielded its symbolism as the sine qua non of Western revolutions. Hence I emphasize elsewhere in considerable detail the needed ambivalence: an antiapocalyptic stance, however tempting from an ecological or feminist standpoint, colludes with a conservative triumphalism—the extent of whose Babylonian-Roman dominance may also be symbolized in John of Patmos's "sea."[7] Social justice Christianity, which has expressed no discomfort with the mythologem of an urban prophetic emptying of the sea, has thus only recently begun to work out meaningful coalitions with the environmental movement.

Though authorial intentions fade into a radically anterior ecological context, we may today read the contemporary plight of the earth's real oceans as a literalization of the apocalyptic tehomicide. If the seas had been primordially identified as a churning waste, a watery wilderness, we have correspondingly treated them as the ultimate sewer. Thus, they become toxic and dangerous in new ways for us. As Rachel Carson wrote thirty-six years ago: "It is a curious situation that the sea, from which life first arose, should now be threatened by the activities of one form of that life. But the sea, though changed in a sinister way, will continue to exist; the threat is rather to life itself."[8]

Does the eschatological inscription in the salt waters of a womblike monstrous past, a past that taunts us with our finitude until it is finally vaporized, have some bearing on global indifference to the death of the oceans? Does it address our likely ignorance, for example, of the dependence of the global climate on the seas, through the sheer mass, the movement of currents, oxygen production, and the climate-regulating function of the "biological pump?"[9]

Yet, in the Apocalypse, the sea, as long as it does continue to exist, is vivid, visible, and vulnerable. The sea would share the fate of the rivers and the earth, agonized zones of the creation, convulsing in the struggle with global evil: "a third of the sea became blood, a third of the living creatures in the sea died"—not evil, just ruined. Without going premillennialist, we may note the prophetic fit of this imagery: consider the increasing incidence of "red tides," toxic algal blooms caused by a variety of onshore pollutants that release deadly toxicants into the water, killing other marine life and poisoning people.[10] We will not know when we have passed the point of the death of one-third of the life of the sea, if we have not already. We do know that the opening of a recent Icelandic trawling net is large enough to trap twelve Boeing 747 airplanes.[11]

As John sharply symbolized with Babylon, economic injustice and environmental damage go hand in hand: the industrial nations put local third world fishers out of business, making off with gigantic catches for profit, or forcing third world nations to overfish for export. Moreover, fish contributes only about 8 percent of the animal protein consumed in North America and Western Europe, but over 20 percent in Africa and 27 percent in the Far East; yet, at the same time "people in the industrial world eat three times as much fish as people in developing countries."[12]

In this way John's visionary analysis remains valid: the sea offers passage to the ships bearing the bounties of a global trade which John denounced as lascivious empirial evil: "all shipmasters and seafaring men, sailors and all whose trade is on the sea, . . . cried as they saw the smoke of her burning. . . . 'Alas, alas, for the great city where all who had ships at sea grew rich by her wealth!'" (Rev. 18:17b–19).

But it is the symbolic sea, restless and roiling with rebellion, threatening boundaries, breeding monsters, habitat of Rahab and Leviathan, which John sees so definitively dispatched. The celestial dragon, called Satan, touching down on its shore, midwifes the emergence of the beast from the sea (Rev. 12:17; 13:1). The semetic polytheisms of Israel's environment had an old tradition of inscribing the sea with evil, as, for example, the female Tiamat slaughtered once and for all by her grandson Marduk, hacked up as natural resources of his new creation.[13]

The ultimate constructive question is whether there may be a tehomophilic strategy for Christian hope, which neither demonizes nor annihilates the deep. By an analogous hermeneutical principle, can we reuse, recycle, renew the text, neither demonizing nor erasing the apocalyptic heritage?

From Annihilation to *Ex Nihilo*

Genesis 1 has, with the rediscovery of the Enuma Elish and Ugaritic texts, been read in the light of the battle against the chaos.[14] Biblically speaking, this is an improvement over the classical theist tradition of reading the *tehom* as nothing at all, as the needed absence for the *creatio ex nihilo*.[15] One can also read the chaos of Genesis 1:2 as neither the nothing of *ex nihilo* nor the nothingness of a monstrous enmity to creation. One can discern there a deliberately alternative, pacific relation of the spirit hovering, blowing, or as Herman Gunkel translated, "vibrating" over the face of the *tehom,* preparing to unfold the deep into the upper darkness of outer space and the lower darkness of the terrestrial sea—a relation of interdependence by which the no-thingness of the indeterminate yields potentiality for difference and actualization. In other words, one may imagine here, rather than a replication of the warrior-deity of the military state, a relatively non-violent and nature-loving resistance to its imperial imaginary. But in times of harsh oppression by one of these military states, the appeal to a liberating warrior God can become irresistible: it shores up hope for a cosmic-revolutionary justice, for vindication and a final accounting. Dread before the global grip of imperial corruption is catalytically converted into the militant mythogram of the new creation. By the logic of apocalypse, the worse things get, the closer we are to the best.

The image of the dry eschaton concentrates in itself the solution of all suffering and death—not just unjust suffering and premature death. Paul also makes this apocalyptic gesture, which marks death itself as the ultimate enemy (1 Cor. 15:26). I submit that at such points biblical eschatology loses its edge, its very *eschaton:* the focus shifts from the human systems of domination and destruction about which the people of God might *do* something, to natural systems of mortality, requiring a supernatural solution. The possibility of prolonged activism in history thus becomes moot.

Yet, it is also true that John's Apocalypse announces—with extraordinary precognition of the environmental effects of imperial markets, such as dying seas, desertified and deforested earth, diseased air—the time "for destroying the destroyers of the earth" (Rev. 11:18). But despite this textual potentiality, human accountability for the polysystemic ecosocial injustices of the earth is swallowed by the ultimate hope for resurrection into deathlessness. Inasmuch as the unifying vision-language of apocalypse has been dogmatized, it confuses the avoidable tears of *han,* or oppression, with the unavoidable pains of life amidst finitudes. The saltwater of tears, recognized rightly as confluent with the oceanic flux of all existence, are dried up together. These saline solutions become salient symbols of the solvable, of the emotive, embodied condition, which will be dissolved. In the end, no death; no depth.

The postbiblical doctrine of *creatio ex nihilo* follows back the logic of "no more sea" quite furiously: if in the end the *tehom* is extirpated, then perhaps, really, it never was. Irenaeus had first articulated the orthodox doctrine in a direct repudiation of a gnostic creatrix, Achamoth, whose tears and other bodily emotions give rise to matter. He juxtaposes such a salty, fluid, and fleshy female origin to the dry, disciplinary word of the Father who creates with no preconditions, and thus owns and controls all his domains—and can guarantee the proper outcome, the resurrection of the dead, and the eternal reward of the obedient.[16] The eschatology of the classical Christian narrative of salvation vaporizes all traces of the *tehom.* It dries her up.

Gradually, the multiple and ambiguous effects of the Apocalypse found modern voices. For Americans, Christopher Colon (that prophetic name) offers a paradigmatic case. In 1500, having located what would soon be called South America, at the mouth of the Orinoco, which he believed to be the lost "terrestrial paradise," he wrote: "Of the New Heaven and Earth which our Lord made, as St. John writes in the Apocalypse, after He has spoken it by the mouth of Isaiah, He made me the messenger thereof and showed me where to go."[17] With this self-esteeming sleight of hand, Colon has shifted the new creation to the past tense, so that it became a matter, not of divine creativity, but of his own discovery. Henceforth, the sea functions no longer as the infinite horror, but as the tameable medium of an apocalypticized discovery—the horizontal, horizonal transcendence smoothly absorbing into its nautical conquests the vertical thrust of medieval theology. The unprecedented "ecological imperialism" (Alfred Crosby) coupled with genocidal impact suggest the aggressive carelessness toward that which comes before, toward the preconditions of the earth and its populations: toward all that is constructed as chaos. The long traditions of *ex nihilo* creation and apocalyptic eschatology join smoothly in a new gospel of annihilation. "The symbol functions," repeats Elizabeth Johnson.

Whirlwind Wisdom

Fortunately there are other biblical feelings for the *tehom* and its creatures. Let us, for example, reread the final epiphany from the whirlwind to Job. Job himself, at the nadir of his depression, cursing the day he was born, had invoked the conventional imagery of the sea as chaos, of the sea monster Rahab as an evil smitten by God (Job 3:3, 8; 26:12). In the bitterness of his loss, he not surprisingly inscribes the unpredictable, turbulent, and destructive forces of nature as the Other of creation, the evil *tehom*. I believe it is precisely this negative valorization of chaos which the whirlwind—in its blustery list of rhetorical questions—blows away.

> Do you know when the mountain goats bring forth? Do you observe the calving of the hinds? Can you number the months they fulfil, and do you know the time when they bring forth, when they crouch, bring forth their offspring, and are delivered of their young? Their young ones become strong, they grow up in the open; they go forth and do not return to them. (Job 39:1–4)

Commentators, who seem bored by the particularities of the questions, routinely signify this speech as divine one-upmanship (look at all that I made. Who are you, mere mortal, to question me?), an epiphany of the power of the Creator. Commentators feel no call to cultivate a comparable interest, feeling this bottomless and rather nonsymbolic preoccupation with the amoral intricacies of cosmic structure and animal life to fall a bit beneath the Creator's dignity—or beneath their own theodicy. Perhaps at this point in history we had better take more seriously this great interrogation of human ecological ignorance—and our correlary abjection of the *tehom*.

Not that Job should not have grieved and raged over his sufferings at the hand of natural catastrophe. After all, the intensity of his questioning persistence, if not its logic, has attracted the supreme honor of a divine disclosure—even a long-winded one. The voice does not scold him for his anger and doubt. It does, however, declare itself unanswerable to the juridical abstractions of Job's challenge: it does not recognize its work within the discourse of a ruling, interventionist transcendence. Job's outrage, depicted as brave and fair under the assumption of a controlling, anthropocentric order of creation, collapses before the divine immediacy. After exhibiting a diverse creation through the device of rhetorical questions, pulsing with the fascinated pride of the *spiritus creator* in the intricacies of its universe, the epiphany culminates with a full thirty-four-verse paean to Leviathan.

How can we read this creator's delight in the power of the sea monster but as a disturbingly amoral trope of omnipotent order subduing puny, rebellious human doubt? Of his scales, for example, Yahweh exults: "one is so near to another that no air can come between them. They are joined one to another; they clasp each other and cannot be separated" (41:17). The text offers a rare witness to God's bottomless enthusiasm for the wild and the wet—in particular for the remarkable achievement of the complex organization of this formidable organism. Yahweh's scornful invocation of Leviathan's indomitable superiority to all human order specifically stresses the creature's absolute resistance to domestication and commodification, "Will you put him on a leash for your maidens? Will traders bargain over him? Will they divide him up among the merchants? Can you fill his skin with harpoons?" (41:5b–7a). In other words, the economics of human arrogance appears ludicrous before Leviathan, the mythic embodiment of the deep, the wild energy of an all-encompassing nature which can only be exploited and battled at peril to ourselves. The text suggests divine disdain, not at human *vulnerability,* but at the delusions of human *power.* When we set ourselves apart from and above nature, hoping to transcend finitude, we only set ourselves at odds with a creator not made in our image: one who in the image of a whirlwind and a whale parodies human political economy based on the conquest and exploitation of the nonhuman.[18]

Might we rethink eschatology in the light of this radical Wisdom text? Might Job's whirlwind answer John's Apocalypse? The final verse from the whirlwind does not enunciate final judgment, let alone a brand new death-free creation (though the final frame by the folk narrative might be read as anticipating such a neatly restorative cosmic order): "he is king over all the sons of pride" (41:34b). Does it not rather warn of a quite precise ecopoetic justice? I read here a startling inversion of the troubling tradition of Genesis 1:28 inasmuch as humans have mistaken their distinction for the right to exploitation, dominion shifts to the wildest of creatures. When the "sons of pride" deny and defy our species' limits, the royal privilege which defines the *imago Dei* is forfeit. Yet, again, the whirlwind condemns not Job, the honestly suffering individual, but the multisystemic cultural illusions of invulnerability from which Job's sense of contradiction arises. God in the image of chaos—the whirlwind—offers not resurrection or afterlife, but a cosmic bestiary.

Leviathanic Revelations

Shifting again to North America, we find a homegrown Jobian Wisdom classic likewise combining apocalyptic and tehomic themes. It offers "a thorough appreciative understanding of the more special leviathanic revelations." Introducing his chapter on cetology, Herman Melville, ironic scholar of all available whale data, oddly echoes the obsessive nature descriptions of Job's revelation: "The classification of the constituents of a chaos, nothing less is here essayed."[19] Here, I can only suggest that Moby Dick, mercilessly hunted by the wounded Ahab, emerges from the deep as a full-bodied symbol of the tehomic Other. Moby Dick is portrayed as neither good nor evil but, like Job's Leviathan, magnificent in freedom and power. Ahab sails the edges of Calvinist capitalism, embodying in his complex and brilliant insanity that culture's internal contradictions—a madness only fully revealed when it hurls itself against the full force of its own otherwise repressed limits. In an incisive comment upon New England whaling practices, the white whale had taken off one of his legs. But the system cannot brook such revolt: so Ahab neglects even mercantile interest in his marine quest for a "supernatural vengeance" against what we may read as nature itself. "'Vengeance on a dumb brute!' cried

Starbuck, 'that simply smote thee from blindest instinct! Madness! To be enraged with a dumb thing, Captain Ahab, seems blasphemous'" (236). Ahab literally goes off the deep end. And takes his ship down with him.

To the rhetorical question of Job's epiphany—"Can you fill his skin with harpoons?"—Ahab gave the wrong answer. Eschatological truth, embodied in the nature that will not be controlled, answered this "son of pride." With him all the humble, multicultural crew go down as well—as the poor of all peoples suffer disproportionately in John's Apocalypse and in the devastations and depletions of our ecosphere. The *monstrum* (sign or omen) of the deep operates not in the anthropomorphic, individualist justice of classical eschatology, but rather within complex, ecosocial interdependencies.[20] Like the Book of Job, however, *Moby Dick* has not been conventionally read as an allegory for an ecosystemic theology. These prophetic voices within Yahwism or Calvinism, respectively, stretch beyond orderly theologies of supernatural reward and punishment toward symbolizations of an alternative order that appears as chaotic in substance and in form.

Surface and Depth

An ecosystemic rather than a merely systematic theology neither repeats nor shuns but rather recycles, grounds, and deepens eschatology. This is not easy, since the very gestures of grounding and deepening counter the classical directions of transcendence—the "updraft of the spirit."[21] But they resist the postmodern updraft of cultural-linguistic idealism as well. Much current thought celebrates the textual surface, blown dry of all tehomic significations—while busily "denaturing" discourse, replacing all reference to "nature" with "culture."[22]

As the opening metaphor suggests, the very dualism of surface and depth dissolves in the face of the shimmering, interfluent layers. Thus, the literal damage to the sea as the "last frontier" of environmentalism seems to me to emerge as a metaphor and effect of the damage to our culture's capacity to think, feel, and act deeply. Our flight from finitude and death, from fluidity and indeterminacy, keeps us perpetually "out of our depths." Indeed, a tehomophobic privilege, based on objectifying versions of natural and social science as well as of eschatological revelation, has dominated progressive almost as much as conservative Christianity. The terms of debate rarely exceed the androcentric imaginary of order, order as eternal law or transcendent commandment, old creation or new.

Yet order—*kosmos,* beautiful pattern—is not the problem; the problem is the habituation to an order of symmetrical, fixed identities, an order expunged of chaos. How, instead, might the polysystemic issues of ecology mesh with the plurisignifications of theological inquiry to construct, to disclose, a theology which becomes ecological in depth, not merely on its surface, in the face of the immediate crisis?

Constituents of a Chaos

The whirlwind in nature is itself a paradigmatic case of the thermodynamic principles scientists now study in the new science of chaos. Stochastic (probabilistic, rather than merely random) chaos refers to nonlinear patterns of unpredictable, assymmetrical dynamics in nature, such as the turbulence of winds and waters, tides, clouds and flames, as well as ecological and economic shifts. Such chaos evinces not mere lack of order but rather an order too complex to have been understood in terms of euclidian geometry or classical physics. I want to draw from chaos theory five figurative—not foundational—criteria for reinforcing a tehomophilic theology. For each I will first summarize the scientific characteristic, then apply it theologically.

1) Nonpredictability, or *nonlinearity:* the unpredictability in principle that has been first discovered in the science of weather, in feedback, in general thermodynamics; "chaos seems to provide a bridge between the deterministic laws of physics and the laws of chance, implying that the Universe is genuinely creative."[23] Liberation from faith in providential predetermination, of eschatology as guaranteed outcome, of divine promise as prediction, makes possible a nonlinear theology for an open universe, and thus for a responsible terrestrial *oikonomia.*

2) *Radical interrelation* involves chaotic and complex processes like the weather that seem to be inherently nonlinear and unpredictable, not because they are random, but because they function as a dynamic web: they display the effects of so many intermeshed causal

processes that the outcomes can never be precisely predicted. This connectivity, depicted so graphically in fractal geometry, is in nature described as the extreme sensitivity to initial conditions. Small causes can have major effects; thus, the belabored butterfly flapping its wings in Boston can set off an avalanche in the Himalayas. This is not magic at a distance but rather a ripple effect of the causal, ecological web of interactions. So, theologically, interrelatedness is the foundation of all ecosystemic thought and its Whiteheadian cosmological precedents. It has been formative for the particular voices of feminist relational theory and ecofeminist theology.

3) This relationalism means, as physicist Per Bak has shown in his work with sandpiles, that there is a point called *criticality* at which a system qualitatively shifts from a predictable linear process to a non-linear pattern of avalanches which, when calculated after the fact, prove to have followed rules, but cannot be predicted. As he says, all the grains seem to be in communication, behaving as an organism.[24] Because this interdependence is not a closed unity but an open system, the criticality (and the related butterfly effect) may suggest not only unpredictable outcomes, but hope—hope, for instance, that a minor movement, such as that of ecological Christianity, might, by reinforcing its own "criticality," exercise a disproportionate, indeed revolutionary, impact.

4) The fractal geometry of *self-similarity,* to be distinguished from self-identity, illustrates a kind of open-windowed Leibnizianism, in which each part at some point exhibits the morphology of the whole system in microcosm. But always with a *difference;* that difference accounts for the unpredictable interweaves of order and chaos. The form of the interrelatedness in the mode of self-similarity suggests that such relationship never takes place between two simply separate entities, but always within an intersubjective filigree including the subjects of all implicated otherkind; that the other cannot be kept outside myself and is always multiple. The complex hybridities of our cultural differences thus reflect the inextricability of nature and culture, of precondition and construction, and so perhaps of *tehom* and *eschatos*.

5) What is of interest in a more systemic sense is not chaos per se, but that layering interplay of chaos and order that has been symbolized for a decade at the Santa Fe Institute as *"the edge of chaos,"* a condition, or "phase transition," where there is enough order and

enough chaos for what is novel, interesting, creative, and complex to take place. (The edge of chaos signifies something akin to the point of criticality.) Biologist Stuart Kaufmann speculates that "life evolves to the edge of chaos."[25] If life consists of the emergence and interactions of "complex, self-organizing systems," the creation, and therefore the newness possible to the creation, has nothing to do with the defeat of chaos by order. Rather, the rich, indeterminate edges of spatio-temporality brim with potential cosmos.[26] As to the theological implications, the edge of chaos, as the evolutionary site, or critical point, at which "complex self-organizing systems" seem to emerge, suggests the site for an ecological eschatology. I believe we cannot erase the apocalyptic edge of urgency in the face of systemic collapse, or lose the eschatogical edge of irreversible historical time, and still hope. I do not want a tehomophilic theology so fluid and indeterminate that it loses its edge. But the Greek meaning of eschaton is "edge," as either spatial or temporal rim, and only derivatively "end." So, perhaps we may cultivate an eschatology of and for the edge of chaos. Does not the *rūah* of Genesis 1:2 hover, vibrate, precisely at that edge, upon that "face"—the sur/face of the deep?

"No End in Sight"

Meanwhile, species are terminating daily, in the ocean and on land. The fantasy of The End keeps these man-made terminations spiritually acceptable to the Christian mainstream. The deep, the indeterminate potentiality in which we swim, which will hold the seeds of future earth evolutions no matter what we do, does not end. We might. Perhaps the endlessness of the deep, of the spatiotemporal relatedness we call the universe, can—better than mere apocalyptic stress—motivate us to resist the violent extinctions caused by our arrogant species. The impulsion toward novel self-organization, toward greater complexity and therefore richness of experience, demands justice as its sine qua non, since injustice simplifies horrifically. The sustaining of the great wealth of species, of biodiversity and of cultural diversity, at the same time provokes a bottomless love—a love for that endlessly rotting and renewing riot of life of which we are a clever and troublesome bit. And love is its own reward, needing no final prize.

To summarize the rather nonlinear argument of this paper: I have attempted to address the Christian repression of the *tehom,* the indeterminate, the transitional, the wild. I have suggested that such symbolic tehomophobia maintains a general squeamishness toward all things mortal, fleshy, feminized, unpredictable, and complex; that this abjection works itself out as the indifference and even vengeful- ness of church and culture toward the creation—inasmuch as it resists our projects of self-immortalization and other-exploitation. Chaos theory hints at ecological wisdoms underrevealed among us all along. My own theological practice draws connections between our sacred texts and our ecology by reference to a wide range of issues resonant within my context, such as our multiform sexualities and ethnicities. After all, the tensile strength of theological practice does not weave itself from the force of single-issue and monocausal discourse. The linear logic of the old left is, as they say, history. Rather, a multiply issued and issuing feedback of hybrid, overlapping, mutually challenging, and reinforcing differences—differences heightened and held in "self-similarity"—may better ecologize our politics and our spirituality.

This essay understands theological metaphors as practical embodi- ments of an ecological struggle. But theology can only connect to specific avenues of social policy formation in interdependence with those activists, clergy, ethicists, and administrators who can better address particular liturgical, political, and economic structures. Such interdependence of theory and practice nests within the niches of academy and church, where I, like many of us, seek to foster sites of enough stability and enough chaos for systemic change to occur, for complex, self-organizing systems to find community and language. A project like the one enacted in this anthology aims, I trust, not at attaining another neat and mediocre unity of our commitments, but rather a rich, indeed oceanic, ecology of Christian practices, itself generating specific waves of interdependence with the other religions represented so munificently in this series. "Her depths peel off into innumerable thin, shining layers. And each one is the equal of the other as it catches a reflection and lets it go."

Notes

1. Luce Irigaray, *The Marine Lover: Of Friedrich Nietzsche,* trans. Gillian C. Gill (New York: Columbia University Press, 1991), 46.

2. The subject of which is the topic of my work in progress, "The Face of the Deep."

3. Daniel C. Maguire and Larry L. Rasmussen, *Ethics for a Small Planet: New Horizons on Population, Consumption, and Ecology* (Albany: State University of New York Press, 1998), 48.

4. Jürgen Moltmann, *A Theology of Hope: On the Ground and the Implications of a Christian Eschatology,* trans. James W. Leitch (New York: Harper and Row, 1967).

5. See especially Jürgen Moltmann, *The Coming of God: Christian Eschatology,* trans. Margaret Kohl (Minneapolis: Fortress Press, 1996).

6. Thus, for instance, Rosemary Ruether sets aside the very concept of eschatology in favor of "redemption": "Redemption puts us back in touch with a full biophilic relationality of humans with their bodies and one another and rebuilds social relations that can incarnate love and justice." *Women and Redemption: A Theological History* (Minneapolis: Fortress Press, 1998), 8. While her reasons make sense, one may just as subversively redefine eschatology.

7. See Catherine Keller, *Apocalypse Now and Then: A Feminist Guide to the End of the World* (Boston: Beacon Press, 1996), especially chapters 2, on the text of Revelation, and 4, "Place: De/Colon/izing Spaces." The liberationist reading of John's Apocalypse, centered around an economic analysis of the trope of Babylon, has been most forcefully set forth by Alan Boesack and Elisabeth Schüssler Fiorenza.

8. Rachel Carson, foreword, *The Sea around Us* (New York: Oxford University Press, 1991).

9. "In the process of producing a third to half of the global oxygen supply, oceans help regulate the primary greenhouse gas, carbon dioxcide, through a mechanism known as the biological pump." Peter Weber, "Safeguarding Oceans," in *State of the World 1994* (Washington, D.C.: Worldwatch Institute), 42. Tellingly, no reports on the state of the sea appear in recent *State of the World* annual reports.

10. Algae blooms are the consequence largely of nutrient runoff from sewage, from upland forestry and farming; they are also caused by nitrogen oxides from power plants and cars; and, the thousands of species in transit every day in ballast water, which outcompete native species and thus reduce biological diversity, are also associated with increased incidence of red tides.

11. Weber, "Safeguarding Oceans," 52.

12. Ibid., 53.

13. See Alexander Heidel, *The Babylonian Genesis: The Story of Creation,* 2d ed. (Chicago: University of Chicago Press, 1951). Also, for an introduction to the parallelism of Enuma Elish with Genesis, see E. A. Speiser, *Genesis,* The Anchor Bible, 1 (Garden City, N.Y.: Doubleday, 1964). For a feminist interpretation of the problematic, see Catherine Keller, *From a Broken Web: Separation, Sexism, and Self* (Boston: Beacon Press, 1986), chap. 2.

14. John Day, *God's Conflict with the Dragon and the Sea: Echoes of a Canaanite Myth in the Old Testament* (Cambridge: Cambridge University Press, 1985).

15. Karl Barth's doctrine of the chaos as the evil nothingness is informed by the rediscovery of the evil, not merely nonbeing, *tehom*. His God defeated it once and for all (*Church Dogmatics* [Edinburgh: T. and T. Clark, 1958], vol. 3, pt. 1, p. 101ff.) but it nonetheless floods the faithless who do not recognize it, who betray the order of creation with disorders such as homosexuality and feminism (vol. 3, pt. 2, pp. 77, 289ff.; vol. 3, pt. 4, p. 116ff.), and with liberal theologies which construe chaos as potentiality.

16. *The Writings of Saint Irenaeus,* vol. 2, *Irenaeus against the Heresies,* trans. Alexander Roberts and W. H. Rambaut (Edinburgh: T. and T. Clark, 1868).

17. Keller, *Apocalypse Now and Then,* 159.

18. For a lovely, widely accessible ecological Job, see Bill McKibbin, *The Comforting Whirlwind: God, Job, and the Scale of Creation* (Grand Rapids, Mich.: Eerdmans, 1994).

19. Herman Melville, *Moby Dick: Or, the Whale* (New York: Modern Library, 1982), 190.

20. Melville demonstrates an extraordinary sensitivity to issues recognizable today as capitalism, same sex intimacy, and race that attest to the polysystemic complexity of his vision. On the latter, see Toni Morrison, "Unspeakable Things Unspoken: The Afro-American Presence in American Literature," *Michigan Quarterly Review* 22 (1983): 14ff.

21. See Sharon Betcher's groundbreaking ecofeminist theology, *Grounding the Spirit* (Minneapolis: Fortress Press, forthcoming).

22. For a diversified discussion of the poststructuralist "nature" problematic in the light of ecology, see *FutureNatural: Nature, Science, Culture,* ed. George Robertson et al. (London and New York: Routledge, 1996).

23. Paul Davies, "Is the Universe a Machine?" in *Exploring Chaos: A Guide to the New Science of Disorder,* ed. Nina Hall (New York: W. W. Norton, 1991), 212.

24. Per Bak, *How Nature Works: The Science of Self-Organized Criticality* (New York: Springer-Verlag, 1996).

25. Stuart A. Kauffman, *At Home in the Universe: The Search for Laws of Self-Organization and Complexity* (New York: Oxford University Press, 1995), 26.

26. As edge of sea, or edge of chaos, the *tehom* does double semantic duty. To return to the case of the oceans, the most extraordinary evolutionary leaps have taken place, to borrow a recent title, "at the water's edge"—"from first fishy creatures to tetrapods 360 million years ago, rushing out over the landmass to become everything from turtles to dinosaurs to humans; then back again 50 million years ago from land mammal to the high intelligences of marine mammals, including our leviathan, the whale"; Carl Zimmer, *At The Water's Edge: Macroevolution and the Transformation of Life* (New York: Free Press, 1998).

Response to Catherine Keller

MARY ANN HINSDALE

Catherine Keller describes her essay as a "meditation" drenched in biblical symbolism (notably, from the Wisdom, prophetic, and apocalyptic traditions)—and that is exactly what I found it to be. In the brief space allotted to me, however, I cannot adequately plumb the depths of what Keller offers us here, so I simply hope to give impetus to us all to enter into the entire way one does theology rather than just a rethinking of Christian eschatology. In short, what most strikes me about this paper is that it serves as a model for a truly ecological theology. It is Keller's method that I found to be so exciting, and that is my main point of response.

Catherine Keller criticizes Christian eschatology for demonizing "the deep." Inspired by Luce Irigaray's metaphor of the sea (provided in the opening quote), Keller illustrates how "the very dualism of surface and depth dissolves in the face of the shimmering, interfluent layers." She does this by deconstructing the apocalyptic text of Revelation 21:1–4, a text that, ironically, is meant to convert despair to hope. Her purpose is to explore and unmask what she calls the "tehomophobic" politics that have dominated both conservative and progressive Christianity. Proceeding with this cautionary hermeneutic, she makes a constructive proposal for a tehomophilic theology, one that affirms chaos (or perhaps, better, "the edge of chaos," since she reminds us that the first meaning of *eschaton* is "edge," and only derivatively, "end").

In this project, I find that Keller is doing ecosystemic rather than systematic theology. Her theological method is truly ecological in its attempt to reuse, recycle, ground and deepen, and renew the text/ tradition. Her project is not mere retrieval of the tradition, for she remains critical of it. I agree with her reading that the contemporary plight of the earth's oceans can be read as a metaphor and foretaste of eschatological tehomicide. When allowed to be viewed as "evil," this negative-chaos tradition allows the sea to become humanity's ultimate sewer. On the other hand, the seas represent the past, the precondition of life on Earth, just as the *tehom* precedes the creation according to Genesis 1.

Classical, as well as liberationist, Christian eschatology has stressed that eschatology concerns not merely "end" but "hope." But Keller finds this hope problematic. In her estimation, to have "no more weeping" (no more death) means espousing the elimination of the sea. Thus, the new creation requires not only the evaporation of tears, but the evaporation of the seas. I find Keller's insight into how the symbol of "new creation" has fused liberation motifs with the defeat of pre-creation chaos extremely valuable for understanding the inability of what she calls "social justice" Christianity to recognize the importance of ecology. In her book *Apocalypse Now and Then,* she explores in greater detail the legacy of this fusion of motifs in Isaiah and Revelation, what Germans call its *Wirkungsgeschichte,* the effective history of these received texts, making important connections with the history of colonialism, of sexism, racism, and ecological subjugation of species—whether mineral, plant, animal, or human. But I must raise a flag here, in order that we may see the challenge Keller is putting to us. Revelation 21:1–4 was a text we chose for my father's funeral three years ago. I am sure many other Christians have also used this text in such contexts. Keller's ecological eschatology would seem to require a relinquishment that may be fraught with emotion for many Christians.

The constructive, tehomophilic eschatology that Keller proposes affirms chaos. She retrieves Job's whirlwind and finds in it a stochastic chaos that holds out the possibility for rethinking eschatology ("Leviathan is king over the sons of pride"). This leads her to appropriate chaos theory, namely its features of nonlinearity or nonpredictability, radical interrelation, criticality, self-similarity, and the interplay of chaos and order that lies on the edge (which is really what *tehom* means: the critical point of self-organizing systems is on the edge). Chaos theory offers an ecological countereschatology.

The chief insight I derive from Keller is that she is proposing something that cannot take place within the narrow limits of theology alone. And it is here that she deals with praxis implications for church and society. She reminds us that renewing eschatology in an ecosystemic way involves more than trying to make eschatology more ecological; it must address particular liturgical, political, and economic structures. As she says, there needs to be "a rich, indeed oceanic, ecology of Christian practices, itself generating specific waves of interdependence with the other religions," recalling Irigaray's sea, whose "depths peel off into innumerable thin, shining layers. And each one is the equal of the other as it catches a reflection and lets it go."

For me, personally, Keller's reflection took me back to my own experience of "the deep"—scuba diving off the Great Barrier reef and sleeping out under the stars in a wadi somewhere near Elat in Israel. These experiences reminded me that ecosystemic theology must bring together approaches that I often find are presented as mutually exclusive alternatives: the prophetic, the apocalyptic, and the mystical. As Keller suggests, we theologians need to attend to genres other than printed words in our theologizing. Unless a renewal of Christian eschatology also surfaces in art, music, and ritual, we will be perpetuating a drying up of *tehom,* no matter how many theological tomes are written on the subject. Building on the method that Catherine Keller has presented, let me suggest a concluding meditation as prelude for reflecting further on her insights. Canadian Loreena McKennitt's song, "Dante's Prayer,"[1] has been playing in my head ever since I read Catherine's essay. I'd like to share it with you. I think that in its refrain, you will recognize in another way Keller's challenge to us, not only to rethink eschatology, but to do theology ecologically, so that all symbolic mediations of Christian faith, including art, music, and liturgy, speak to the eschatological hope that lies in the depth of the universe.

> When the dark wood fell before me
> And all the paths were overgrown
> When the priests of pride say there is no other way
> I tilled the sorrows of stone.
>
> I did not believe because I could not see
> Though you came to me in the night
> When the dawn seemed forever lost
> You showed me your love in the light of the stars.

Refrain:
Cast your eyes on the ocean
Cast your soul to the sea
When the dark night seems endless
Please remember me!

Then the mountain rose before me
By the deep well of desire
From the fountain of forgiveness
Beyond the ice and the fire.

Refrain

Though we share this humble path alone
How fragile is the heart
Oh give these clay feet wings to fly
To touch the face of the stars.

Breathe life into this feeble heart
Lift this mortal veil of fear
Take these crumbled hopes, etched with tears
We'll rise above these earthly cares.

Refrain

Note

1. Loreena McKennitt, "Dante's Prayer," from *The Book of Secrets,* Warner Brothers QR Compact Disc Recording (Stratford, Ontario: Quinlan Road Music, Ltd., 1997).

River of Life in God's New Jerusalem: An Eschatological Vision for Earth's Future

BARBARA R. ROSSING

A pillar on a bridge over the Charles River in Boston has become a favorite for me. It bears an inscription about the wondrous river of the water of life in God's city, from Revelation, chapter 22: "On either side of the river there was the tree of life which bare twelve manner of fruits . . . and the leaves of the tree were for the healing of the nations (Rev. 22:2; Anderson Bridge, 1913)."

At first that bridge inscription seemed grandiose. How could Bostonians claim such an explicit link between their river and God's river, between Boston and the city of God? I have since come to see the importance of such links to a Christian ecological vision and commitment. When we can glimpse in every river the river of life flowing from God's throne in the holy city, we see ourselves as citizens of a holy city, as stewards and "priests" of Earth's waters and trees.

When I tell people I work on the Book of Revelation, I get odd responses, particularly among ecologists. Even theologically minded environmentalists have told me, "There's nothing helpful in the book of Revelation—nothing but destruction and mutant animals there." Vice President Al Gore compared South American animal deformities due to the ozone hole in the earth's atmosphere to a "nature hike through the book of Revelation." Catherine Keller argues in her essay in this volume that the end to the sea in Revelation 21:1 ("And the sea was no more") itself contributes to pollution of the oceans.

Part of the suspicion about Revelation may be due to its eschatological orientation. Like most New Testament books, Revelation was written in the expectation that Jesus would soon return and that heaven and earth would be transformed. Some Christians, such as former secretary of the interior James Watt, have interpreted this eschatological belief as permission to cut down all the trees we can, to use up the world's resources. Others, however, find an environmental mandate in the New Testament's eschatological worldview. Paul Santmire says the New Testament's theology is "thoroughly shaped by the ecological motif, albeit eschatologically construed."[1] David Rhoads, too, suggests that early Christian responses to the eschatological expectation of the end to the world can inspire us today, as we face a possible ecological end to the world as we know it. "Early Christians did not abandon the present age. On the contrary, they prepared for the salvation of the new age as a means to avoid its judgment."[2]

I will argue that the most eschatological of New Testament texts, the Book of Revelation, is also profoundly ecological. Certainly, there are a variety of ways to read Revelation. Revelation has been used to justify environmental destruction as well as intolerance, fundamentalism, war, and violence, specifically attacks against women. I seek to present a positive reading of this book as an environmentalist, a feminist, and a New Testament scholar.

This ecological reading will focus on Revelation's final two contrasting visions of *polis,* or city, Babylon and New Jerusalem. I will argue that these two contrasting visions of political economy can be a resource for the earth-centered ecological vision of the future that is urgently needed today. The Babylon vision offers a prophetic critique of environmental injustice—including global deforestation and ecological imperialism. New Jerusalem offers the promise of a totally renewed urban world, where God takes up residence on Earth, in our midst. Revelation's visions of God's future home on Earth can empower us to work to renew our cities and our world today.

It is generally understood that the Book of Revelation was written by someone named John (not the same John who wrote the gospel), around the year 96 C.E., at the end of the rule of the emperor Domitian.[3] John writes an "apocalypse" (Rev. 1:1), a favorite genre of writing in the ancient world, somewhat akin to our genre of science fiction.[4] He addresses this apocalypse to urban Christians in the prosperous port city of Ephesus and in other cities of Asia Minor.

John calls this work "prophecy" (Rev. 1:3; 22:18–19). Given the tradition of the Hebrew Bible prophets, this suggests that Revelation is not intended as a prediction or a timetable of future or end-time events. Rather, like other biblical prophecy, Revelation's purpose is to exhort and encourage people, to proclaim the judgment and the salvation of God, to provide a vision of hope and justice.

Revelation as a Critique of Roman "Realized Eschatology"

To understand the eschatological visions of Revelation and the role of the "sea" in the argument of the book, it is helpful to situate the book alongside the first century Roman eschatological propaganda that John is implicitly critiquing.[5]

The first century was a time of dueling eschatologies, of Roman boasts of its imperial eternity (*Roma Aeterna*) versus Christian hope for an end to oppression and a future in God's hands. Rome viewed itself as endless and eternal, politically and geographically, as well as temporally. The victory of the future emperor Augustus in 31 B.C.E. had brought about the *Pax Romana*. Rome now laid claim to the whole inhabited world, the whole *oikoumenē*. The poet Virgil lauded the emperor Augustus not only as a military hero but as an eschatological "son of a god [Julius Caesar], who shall again set up the Golden Age . . . and shall spread his empire . . . to a land that lies beyond the stars" (*Aeneid* 6.790–96).

A classic example of the type of Roman propaganda that the Apocalypse seeks to counter is the lengthy "Roman Oration" of Aelius Aristides, a second-century orator who was familiar with many of the same cities as the author of the Apocalypse. In Aristides's view, Rome was an empire without end: "The whole inhabited world [*oikoumenē*] speaks in greater harmony than a chorus, praying that this empire [will] last for all time" (*Orations* 26.29).

The backbone of Rome's global omnipotence was its maritime trade. Aristides praised the system by which subjugated nations supplied Rome with their products:

> The arrivals and departures of the ships never stop, so that one would express admiration not only for the harbor, but even for the sea. . . . So everything comes together here, trade, seafaring, farming . . . all the crafts that exist or have existed, all that is produced or grown. Whatever one does not see here, is not a thing which has existed or exists, so that it is not easy to decide which has the greater superiority, the city in regard to present day cities, or the empire in regard to the empires which have gone before. (Aelius Aristides *Orations* 26.13)[6]

The location of that trade was the Mediterranean Sea, lying as a "belt
. . . through the middle of the inhabited world [*oikoumenē*] and your
empire" (*Orations* 26.10). The sea is the "place where everything has
been channeled into one beginning and end" (*Orations* 26.13). This is
an example of an "eschatological" claim for the all-encompassing
and eternal dimensions of Rome's sea trade and economy.

It is to such Roman visions of omnipotence and eternity that the
Book of Revelation says "no." Revelation counters the "already" of
official imperial eschatology with the "not yet" of the reign of God.
To the question of the duration of Roman rule ("How long, O Lord?";
Rev. 6:10), Revelation responds, "just a little longer" (Rev. 6:11).

Revelation's visions are structured to offer an alternate vision both
of the *eschata,* or "end," and of the lordship (*basileia*) of Christ.[7]
Revelation subverts Roman claims to eternity and ultimacy by per-
sonifying Rome not as the goddess Roma but as a prostitute. Liturgies
of praise for God and the lamb in the heavenly courtroom surpass and
trump the grandest liturgies of Rome's imperial cult.[8] All of Revelation's visions aim to persuade the audience that God, not the emperor,
is the true divine ruler seated on the throne; that the Roman imperial
economy is coming to an end; and that any future "golden age" will
be inaugurated not by Augustus's victory but by the Lamb's victory,
in which God's saints will share in the future New Jerusalem.

Revelation's Two Contrasting Cities

Revelation is a thoroughly urban book. The principal strategy by
which John critiques Rome is the image of two rival cities, Babylon
and New Jerusalem. Both cities were familiar from the Hebrew Bible
and from Jewish literature of the second temple period.[9] Unique to
Revelation, however, is the juxtaposition of Jerusalem and Babylon
as two contrasting political economies, with the appeal to the audience to "Come out" of the one city in order to participate in the other.

A number of features set the two city visions in contrasting literary
parallelism. In both city visions the same angel of the bowl plagues
issues the invitation, "Come I will show you," and carries the author
"in the spirit" to a location where he is shown a city (Rev. 17:1; 21:9).

Both visions portray the city as a feminine figure. Especially in
light of issues of violence against women, often linked to ecological

violence, it is important to seek a reading of Babylon and New Jerusalem that emphasizes their political characterization as *polis,* or cities, not as women. While the vision of Babylon has been used to vilify women, in my view its primary polemic is political and economic, not gendered.[10] The author constructs Babylon predominantly as a city, in the tradition of classical and biblical city personifications. The Babylon critique can be a resource for critiquing injustice and ecological violence today, just as New Jerusalem can be a resource for ecological hope and justice. The political power of these visions is undercut if we read them primarily as visions of a "harlot" and a "bride," rather than political economies.

The parallel structure of the two city visions heightens the rhetorical impact of their contrasting imagery.[11] Babylon is an idolatrous city that seduces and oppresses nations and peoples with the wine of the wrath of its "prostitution." The audience must "come out" of this evil empire (Rev. 18:4). As the contrast to Babylon (Rome), New Jerusalem is the city of justice and well-being coming down from heaven, with springs of living water flowing from God's throne. The holy city's radiant beauty and open gates invite participation.

The Political Economy of Babylon

Babylon is the first of Revelation's two cities to come into view. John is brought to an *erēmos* ("wasteland"; Rev. 17:3) to view the judgment of the great prostitute city, Babylon. The "wasteland" setting for this vision foreshadows Babylon's ecological ruin. The connotation of the term *erēmos* in this context is of a landscape that has been ruined or devastated.[12] This desolate setting anticipates the "laying waste" (*erēmoō*) of Babylon which will unfold in Revelation 17:16, 18:17, and 18:19.

Revelation 17–18 depicts the Roman Empire as a powerful market economy, a great prostitute that has "seduced" and "intoxicated" rulers and nations with its trafficking.[13] The connection between the prostitute's expensive attire of "purple and scarlet . . . gold and jewels and pearls" (Rev. 17:4) and the imported cargo items in the merchants' lament (Rev. 18:12, 16) suggests that Revelation's critique of Babylon's prostitution is not sexual but is directed metaphorically against Rome's exploitive trade and economic domination. Babylon's boast that "I rule as a queen . . . , I will never see grief" (Rev. 18:7) reflects Rome's eschatological claim to dominance over the entire Mediterranean world.

Babylon is a world of buying and selling, frenetic commerce and accumulation of wealth. Three groups who have profited from Babylon's wealth—kings, merchants, seafarers—are portrayed as lamenting the loss of the cargo they can no longer buy and sell. The cargo list of Revelation 18:12–13 encompasses the span of Rome's extractions from the land and sea: gold, precious stones, pearls, exotic hardwoods and wooden products, ivory, metals, marble, luxury spices, food, armaments and war horses, and even "bodies, that is, human slaves" (Rev. 18:13). These final two items in the cargo list of Revelation 18 furnish the most explicit critique of slavery and slave trade in the New Testament.

Revelation 18:4–6 calls on God's people to "come out" of Babylon and become a sign of prophetic judgment against the exploitive empire by handing back its "cup of wrath."[14] The vision culminates with a dramatization of Babylon's fall (Rev. 18:21), modeled on Jeremiah 51:63–64. An angel takes up a large millstone and throws it into the sea, proclaiming Babylon's destruction.

Deforestation: The Landscape of Babylon as a "Denuded Wasteland" (Rev. 17:16)

Ecological catastrophe, such as the clearing and burning of rain forests, can be seen in the vivid depiction of Babylon's ruin. Some feminist scholars have interpreted one such scene, Revelation 17:16, as a gruesome scene of the torture and rape of a woman's body.[15] I suggest an English translation of the assault against Babylon that emphasizes the landscape or ecological elements of the destruction:

> they will make it a wasteland [*ērēmōmenēn*] and denuded [*gymnēn*];
> they will devour its flesh and burn it up with fire. (Rev. 17:16)

In the multivalence of Revelation's vivid imagery, such a translation is based on the primary reading of Babylon as a *polis,* a city, not as a victimized woman.[16]

Support for such an ecological reading of the devastation of Babylon in Revelation 17:16 can be found in other classical and biblical texts that use the same Greek words to describe deforestation and violence against the land. The first action against Babylon in Revelation 17:16, for example—"make a wasteland" (*erēmoō*)—employs a verb that is widely used by classical and biblical authors to describe the razing and depopulation of conquered landscapes and cities.

In his description of the Jewish War of 68–70 C.E. the Jewish author Josephus employs the term *erēmoō* to lament the horror of destruction of the landscape of Jerusalem and the surrounding countryside by the Roman armies:

> Pitiful too was the aspect of the country, sites formerly beautified with trees and parks now *reduced to an utter desert* [*erēmōto*] and stripped bare of timber; and no stranger who had seen the old Judaea and the entrancingly beautiful suburbs of her capital, and now beheld her present *desolation* [*erēmian*], could have refrained from tears. . . .
> (Josephus *Jewish War* 6.6–7)

The same verb could also refer to the plundering of wealth or property, as in the lament of the merchants (Rev. 18:17): "For in one hour all this wealth has been laid waste [*erēmōthē*]!" The semantic range of possible meanings for *erēmoō* does not encompass actions against people or their bodies, nor does it carry connotations of rape or sexual violence.[17]

The second action against Babylon in Revelation 17:16, "they will make it denuded" (*gymnos;* usually translated as "they will make her naked"), can carry similar ecological connotations of a landscape that has been stripped of its vegetation and forests.[18]

Rome's deforestation of conquered lands was notorious. Both Josephus and Aelius Aristides use the same Greek word, "make naked" (*gymnos;* verbal form, *gymnoō*), to describe Rome's stripping of forests. Josephus laments the beautiful countryside around Jerusalem that was logged by the Romans to construct massive wooden siegeworks and embankments:

> [Caesar] at once gave the legions permission to lay waste the suburbs and issued orders to collect timber. . . . So the trees were felled and the suburbs rapidly stripped [*gegymnōto*]. (Josephus *War* 5.264)

Aelius Aristides admires Rome's power to strip distant forests "bare" (*gymnos*). The huge logs that he sees arriving on ships from Asia are evidence of Rome's global commercial hegemony:

So many merchants' ships arrive here, conveying every kind of goods from every people every hour and every day, so that the city is like a factory common to the whole earth. It is possible to see so many cargoes from India and even from Arabia Felix, if you wish, that one imagines that for the future *the trees are left bare* [*gymna*] for the people there and that they must come here to beg for their own produce. (Aelius Aristides *Orations* 26.12)

In a time when global deforestation is an increasing problem, we can be attentive to hearing Revelation's astute ecological critique of Rome, together with its critique of imperialism and injustice. Two of the items in the cargo list of Revelation 18:12–13 are forest products: "all kinds of scented woods" (*xylon thyinon,* lit., citrus wood, imported from North Africa) and "objects made of ivory and of expensive wood." Could it be that John, like Aelius Aristides, had watched so many ships unload logs from the forests of conquered nations that he would agree with Aristides' diagnosis: "one imagines that for the future the trees there are left bare"?

New Jerusalem as Contrast to Babylon: No More Sea (Rev. 21:1)

God's New Jerusalem is the antithesis of the toxic Babylon with its ecological imperialism, violence, unfettered commerce, idolatry and injustice. The New Jerusalem is a city where life and its essentials are given "without money," as a gift, even to those who cannot pay for them. Babylon's idolatrous liturgy of buying and selling is replaced by the saints' hymns of praise in the New Jerusalem, where all God's people are priests and share in ruling with God and with the Lamb.[19]

It is in this sense of sharp contrast over against Babylon, rather than a Christian fear or hatred of oceans, that we should read in Revelation's declaration that "the sea was no more" (Rev. 21:1). The opening verses of Revelation 21 and 22 list a series of items that are said to be "no more" (*ouk eti*) in God's new city—no more sea (Rev. 21:1), no more death, mourning, weeping, or pain (Rev. 21:4), nothing accursed any more (Rev. 22:3), and no more night (Rev. 21:25; 22:5). These contrasts underscore the newness of Jerusalem in contrast to Babylon and all that has gone before.

The disappearance of the "sea" (*thalassa*) in Revelation 21:1 is perhaps the most pointed economic contrast between New Jerusalem and Babylon: New Jerusalem will have no sea, and therefore no shipping economy. Maritime trade in luxury goods, so prominent in Babylon's economy, will now come to an end. While many scholars interpret the pronouncement about the disappearance of the sea in terms of biblical chaos traditions and fear of the sea, as Catherine Keller does,[20] such a mythological terror is not the principal critique of the sea for Revelation. Revelation portrays the sea politically—as well as mythologically—as a location of evil (Rev. 13:1) and a place where commercial ships sail (Rev. 8:9, 18:11–17).[21]

Such a commercial critique of sea trade appears already in Revelation 8:9, after the third trumpet's blast turns one-third of the sea to blood. The author further adds the astute detail that "a third of the ships were destroyed"—a remark that stands out from the other trumpet calamities that are all nature-related and based on the Exodus plagues. The sea's commercial dimension becomes most central in Revelation 18, with the critique of Rome's rulers, merchants, and all those who "work the sea" (18:17). In the economy of Rome, "all who had ships at sea grew rich by its wealth" (18:19). It is because of this polemic against sea trade that the sea is the location of the final symbolic action against Babylon, when the angel threw the millstone into the sea (18:21).[22]

As the sequel to the dramatic pronouncement of judgment on sea trade in the Babylon vision, the eschatological end to the sea in Revelation 21:1 must be read as more economic than mythological, hailing the end of Rome's cargo ships and trade.[23] Such a harsh critique of Rome's sea-faring economy and the proclamation of the end of the sea is a perspective shared with the fifth Sibylline oracle, a Jewish text dated to the second century C.E.:

> In the last time, one day the sea will be dry,
> and ships will then no longer sail to Italy.
> Great Asia then will be water, bearing all cargo. . . .
> (*Sib. Or.* 5.447–49)[24]

In prophesying an end to the sea, both Revelation and the fifth Sibylline promise an alternate economic vision of an eschatological city where trade in luxury goods will be supplanted by an economy that provides the essentials of life "without payment" (*dorean;* Rev. 21:6, 22:17). In God's New Jerusalem there will be no ships, no maritime commerce or traffic in cargo, for "the sea is no more."

New Jerusalem: City of Life

The eschatological vision of God's radiant New Jerusalem is profoundly ecological. The powerful vision of the New Jerusalem—of a holy city with its gleaming golden street and twelve pearly gates, where death and tears are no more, on the banks of whose river of life grow luscious trees with nation-healing leaves—has given form and voice to the dreams of God's people throughout the centuries.

From Augustine's *City of God* through William Blake's "Jerusalem," the image of the holy city of Revelation has promised life and healing, reconciliation and justice. Blake used an unforgettable image to judge the hideous factories and inhuman working conditions of England's industrial revolution:

> "Was Jerusalem builded here among these dark Satanic mills? . . . I will not cease from mental fight . . . til we have built Jerusalem in England's green and pleasant land."

The vision fed early American visions of a "city on a hill" and a range of nineteenth-century utopian experiments. African American spirituals and gospel songs invoke the imagery of a holy city and the river of life. Carly Simon sings of New York City in light of the New Jerusalem vision in the opening scene of the movie *Working Girl,* as the Staten Island ferry pulls into the lower end of Manhattan.

God's love for the created, natural world is one aspect of the New Jerusalem that has received less attention in the history of interpretation, but is nonetheless important. The text can inspire us to trust God in the midst of our urban and ecological crises, the crisis of global market economy that marginalizes increasing millions of people, and the crises of loss of moral will as environmental problems become both more complex and more urgent.

God's Home (*Skene*) on Earth: A Vision for Urban Life

Contrary to current popular apocalyptic thinking, there is no "rapture" in the Book of Revelation, no vision of people snatched from the earth.[25] Instead, God is "raptured" down to Earth to take up residence and "tent" (*skēnē, skēnoō*) with us.

And I saw the holy city, the new Jerusalem, coming down out of heaven from God, prepared as a bride. . . . And I heard a loud voice from the throne saying, "See, the dwelling [*skēnē*] of God is among mortals. God will dwell [*skēnoō*] with them as their God; they will be his people, and God's very self will be with them. (Rev. 21:2–3)

This is a distinctly earth-centered vision of our future with God. Heaven no longer exists after God descends to Earth in Revelation 21. It is also a profoundly urban vision. The dwelling of God and of God's people is an enormous city, a radiant and thriving urban environment. The "holy city" (*polis*) that descends in Revelation 21 is a splendid city whose architecture, beauty, precious stones, wondrous trees, waters, and open gates invite entry and participation.

The image of "city" (*polis*) is central to the Book of Revelation, beginning with the seven opening letters to cities in Asia Minor (Revelation 2–3).[26] The New Jerusalem vision fulfills God's promises to the seven churches, including the promise to Philadelphians of citizenship in the "city [*polis*] of my God, the new Jerusalem which comes down from my God out of heaven" (Rev. 3:12).[27]

Revelation draws on both a rich biblical tradition and Hellenistic utopian ideals in describing the wondrous city of Jerusalem. The text weaves together prophetic dreams of a new creation (Isaiah 65, Ezekiel 47), a renewal of Jerusalem and the covenant (Zechariah 8, Ezekiel 37), and pilgrimage of the nations to Jerusalem (Isaiah 60), together with paradise themes (Genesis 2) and wisdom texts (Psalm 46, Sirach 15 and 24) promising lavish gifts to all who are faithful.[28]

Dieter Georgi has demonstrated that Revelation's New Jerusalem vision also invokes Greco-Roman utopian hopes about the ideal city, a landscape with a majestic processional street and abundant greenspace.[29] In our time, when so many people long to escape to the suburbs or the countryside to avoid the crisis of American cities, Revelation's proclamation of God's future and of ours in the midst of a city can renew our vision for urban ministry.

Water of Life "As a Gift" (*Dōrean*) for Everyone

One of the central images in the utopian New Jerusalem is the river or fountain of living water (Rev. 21:6, 22; 22:17; see also Rev. 7:17).

Water, freely given by God, flows through this paradisiacal landscape. When God's own voice speaks from the throne for the first
time in the book, it is to offer water to those who thirst. Twice God
extends the invitation to come and receive the water of life "without
cost" (*dōrean*):

> To the one who is thirsty I will give to drink from the spring of the
> water of life as a gift [*dōrean*]. (Rev. 21:6)

This promise is reiterated in chapter 22:

> Let everyone who is thirsty come. Let anyone who wishes take the
> water of life as a gift [*dōrean*]. (Rev. 22:17)

In the overall argument of Revelation, the invitation to drink from
the "springs" (*pēgai*) of the water of life in New Jerusalem functions
as healing imagery, a contrast to the deadly "springs" of waters that
turned to blood and became undrinkable (Rev. 16:4).[30] As a healing
contrast also to the exploitive economy of Babylon, New Jerusalem
offers a gift economy in which water and other essentials of life are
available "without cost."

The motif of the well or fountain of living water holds great possibilities for ecological interpretation. The ancient motif draws on rich
associations with life-giving fertility and wisdom in biblical traditions.[31] The author of Revelation alludes to Jerusalem's "river whose
streams make glad the city of God" (Ps. 46:4), as well as Sirach's
offer of the water of wisdom to drink (Sir. 15:3; 24:21) and Isaiah's
invitation to everyone who thirsts to "come to the waters" (. . . and
you that have no money, come, buy and eat"; Isa. 55:1).

The "living waters" of Revelation's New Jerusalem vision are not
just spiritual or theological waters. This vision can speak of life for
the real waters of our world, for rivers and groundwater sources, for
endangered wetlands and estuaries. New Jerusalem's promise of
access to pure, living water for all can offer a prophetic critique of our
damage to ecosystems, of waters polluted by industrial and agricultural waste, and of the encroachment on wetlands by developers.
At a time when waters of life on our planet are in danger of dying, the
vision of the river of life can sustain our commitment to justice and
healing for all creation.

The Vision of Ezekiel's New Temple Expanded and "Democratized" to a City

The heavenly city's descent is narrated for a second time in Revelation 21:9–27, as the angel guides the seer and the audience on a tour of the beautiful city. The same introduction as the Babylon vision, "Come, I will show you" (Rev. 17:1; 21:9), underscores the parallelism of the two city visions. This tour, like the first descent of New Jerusalem (Rev. 21:1–8), emphasizes the city's invitational character and openness, culminating in the image of nations and kings streaming into the city (Rev. 21:24–26). Gold and precious stones beckon to the audience to enter into the city through the gates, to walk on its golden street, and to explore the city's radiant beauty.

The tour and measuring of the city in Revelation 21:9–27 are modeled on Ezekiel's tour and measuring of the new temple in Ezekiel 40–48. Revelation makes important modifications in Ezekiel's vision, however, to open up the New Jerusalem to everyone. One of the most striking modifications is the statement that the city has "no temple" (Rev. 21:22). God's presence is not confined to a temple, but now extends to the entire creation. Revelation further universalizes and "democratizes" Ezekiel's elite priestly vision by extending priestly status to all God's people (Rev. 1:6; 5:10; 20:6).[32]

New Jerusalem is a welcoming city, not a gated community. Whereas Ezekiel's gate was shut so that "no one shall enter by it" into the temple or its courtyards (Ezek. 44:1–2), the twelve gates into New Jerusalem are perpetually open (the gates are "never shut by day, and there will be no night there"; Rev. 21:26). Even foreigners (*ethnē*) and those who have no money are invited to enter. The translucent wall of jasper that surrounds God's city seems to serve more for beauty and invitation than for protection.[33] The nations of the world will walk by the light of this radiant city, streaming into New Jerusalem (Rev. 21:24, 26).

The City as Paradise: The Tree of Life for the Healing of the Nations

God's water of life appears again in the concluding section of the New Jerusalem vision:

> Then [the angel] showed me the river of the water of life, bright as
> crystal, flowing from the throne of God and of the lamb, through the
> center of the street. On either side of the river stood the tree of life,
> yielding fruit each month. And the leaves of the tree are for the healing
> of the nations. (Rev. 22:1–2)

This imagery draws on the conclusion of Ezekiel's new temple
description (Ezek. 47), the wondrous river of ever-deepening fresh
water flowing from the temple, sustaining aquatic life and watering
fruit trees on the river's banks:

> Water was flowing out from under the entrance and flowing east, the
> direction the temple faced. . . . Where the river flows everything will
> live. . . . Fruit trees of all kinds will grow on both banks of the river . . .
> because the water from the sanctuary flows to them. Their fruit will
> serve for food and their leaves for healing (Ezek. 47:1, 9–12)

In Revelation the wondrous river of life flows not from the temple but
from the throne of God, through the center of the city's landscape.
One of the most beautiful ways Revelation universalizes the vision of
Ezekiel is by adding the healing of the "nations" to the reference to
the tree's healing leaves. Ezekiel's trees become the "tree of life" in
Revelation 22:2. Revelation offers the fruit of the tree of life to
everyone who is faithful (Rev. 2:7), overcoming the prohibition of
Genesis 3:22.

In the New Jerusalem vision of Revelation 21–22, the trees and
rivers of the landscape of Eden (Genesis 2) are recreated in an urban
center. In this way, as Georgi notes, the New Jerusalem vision "fulfills the ideal that the Hellenistic city aspired to, but never realized,
the reconciliation of city and countryside."[34] The city of New Jerusalem is itself a paradise, integrating nature and urban life, bringing
healing to the landscape as well as to the nations.

The New Jerusalem Vision for Today

As we face the upcoming millennium, Revelation's vision of green
space in the city, of a river of living water flowing from God through
the center of our cities, can be a vision of eschatological renewal. We
need trees of life for the healing of nations.

New Jerusalem is a vision for the future. It is a vision that we can glimpse even now: in the river flowing through the heart of Boston, from the heart of God; in a tree nursery tended by low-income gardeners in the heart of Baltimore;[35] in the tree-planting eucharistic liturgies of Christian churches in Zimbabwe;[36] in the work of community building, justice seeking, bread breaking, nation healing. In every tree, every river, every city, we can glimpse God's holy city dawning in our midst, both beyond and before the millennium.

A seminary student from the Lutheran School of Theology, Beth Utto-Galarneau, led Bible studies on Revelation 21–22 with the people of Our Saviour's Lutheran Church in a blighted neighborhood of East Boston. Her question, "What might the new East Boston look like?" is one all Christians can ask in order to envision renewal for our own cities. I quote at length from her reflection because it is an example of the kind of "imagining" of the New Jerusalem that can empower ecological ministry:[37]

> "What does our city look like?" I asked this question of our Bible study group one Wednesday evening. . . . I hardly had to wait for a response: stinky; scary; there are gangs . . . people are crying because they are hungry; . . . there is poverty; people are homeless; it's unsafe. . . . It seems a far cry from the glorious, radiant new Jerusalem.
>
> "Where is that holy city where God dwells among the people?" When I asked the Bible study folks that evening, they replied, the promised city must be describing heaven. It's something we look forward to, in the future, after we die. It's impossible now, they said.
>
> Then I asked the group, "can we try to imagine what the holy city, what the new East Boston, might look like?" Then the people were quiet . . . and in the end this is what they said:
>
> "We saw the holy city, the new East Boston, coming down out of heaven from God. . . . It has clean streets in which people can walk in safety and with peace at any time. There are no drugs . . . no fire, no fighting; no one is hungry; everyone has a place to live. People are planting flowers and trees. . . . And God is there.

During her internship Utto-Galarneau helped children in Maverick Housing Development draw pictures of their dreams. "These dreams, these hopes are important," concludes Utto-Galarneau. "We have to keep hoping, imagining a better neighborhood, a holy city."

Notes

A shorter version of this article appeared in *Currents in Theology and Mission* 25 (1998): 487–99.

1. H. Paul Santmire, *The Travail of Nature: The Ambiguous Ecological Promise of Christian Theology* (Philadelphia: Fortress Press, 1985), 200. In his survey of ecological themes in the New Testament, Santmire finds most promising Paul's vision of the reconciliation of "all things" (*ta panta;* Rom. 11:36) in Christ and the continuation of this cosmic Christ theme in Colossians and Ephesians.

2. David Rhoads, "Reading the New Testament in the Environmental Age," *Currents in Theology and Mission* 24 (1997): 259–66.

3. For an overview of the scholarship on Revelation's authorship, date, and context, see Adela Yarbro Collins, "Revelation, Book of," *Anchor Bible Dictionary,* 6 vols. (New York: Doubleday, 1992), 5:694–708.

4. On the genre of apocalypses, see most recently Margaret Mitchell, "A Tale of Two Apocalypses," *Currents in Theology and Mission* 25 (1998): 200–209. Mitchell suggested at the conference at which this paper was given that apocalypses had an entertainment function in the ancient world much as disaster movies do today.

5. See Dieter Georgi, "Who is the True Prophet?" *Harvard Theological Review* 79 (1986): 100–126, for this "eschatological" reading of Revelation 18 as countering Roman imperial propaganda of a utopic "golden age." In Georgi's view, "the power and persuasiveness of the Augustan religion finds an indirect testimony in John's polemics. . . . The seer sees himself in a dramatic competition with the prophet(s) of the Caesar religion, people like Horace and Virgil." On the Roman imperial poetry of Virgil and Horace as "eschatological," see also Helmut Koester, *Introduction to the New Testament,* 2 vols. (Berlin: Walter De Gruyter, 1982), 1:340–41.

6. Aelius Aristides *Orations* 26; trans. Charles A. Behr, *P. Aelius Aristides: The Complete Works,* 2 vols. (Leiden: E. J. Brill), 2:75–79. Klaus Wengst analyzes Revelation and other New Testament texts in light of this oration of Aelius Aristides in his *Pax Romana and the Peace of Jesus Christ* (Philadelphia: Fortress Press, 1987).

7. See, for example, the reading of the *eschata* by Vítor Westhelle as geographic as well as temporal, and as encompassing marginalized peoples; "Crises of Society—Crises of the Church? Towards an Eschatological Reading of the *Saeculum*" in *Communion, Community, and Society,* ed. Wolfgang Greive, Lutheran World Federation Studies, 1 (Geneva: Lutheran World Federation, 1998), 97–109.

8. See David Aune, "The Influence of Roman Imperial Cult Ceremonial on the Apocalypse of John," *Biblical Research* 28 (1983): 5–26, for the argument that the throne room scene of Revelation 4–5 is a deliberate "parody" of Roman imperial cult worship.

9. For the image of a heavenly or new Jerusalem as a place of future blessing, see 4 Ezra 9–10; 2 Baruch 4; *Sibylline Oracle* 5.420–27; Tobit 13–14; Galatians 4; Hebrews 12. Elizabeth Gaines analyzes these texts' New Jerusalem imagery in terms of its literary function in "The Eschatological Jerusalem: The Function of the Image in the Literature of the Biblical Period" (Ph.D. diss., Princeton Theological Seminary, 1988). For the label of Rome as "Babylon," see 4 Ezra 3:1–2, 28–31; 2 Baruch 10.1; 11.1; 67.7; *Sib. Or.* 5.143, 159; 1 Peter 5:13.

10. See my *The Choice between Two Cities* (Valley Forge, Pa.: Trinity Press International, 1999) for the argument that the feminine personifications of the two cities function in the book's argument to underscore the ethical "either/or" contrast between Babylon and New Jerusalem.

11. I follow Elisabeth Schüssler Fiorenza's "rhetorical" approach to Revelation, reading the text in terms of its argument and persuasive power, and its construction of an alternate "world of vision." See *Revelation: Vision of a Just World,* Proclamation Commentaries (Minneapolis: Fortress Press, 1991).

12. "Wasteland" is Behr's English translation for *erēmos* in Aelius Aristides' laments over Smyrna's devastation after the earthquake:

> The most beautiful city to behold . . . has been made the most unpleasant of spectacles, a hill of ruins and corpses. The west wind blows through a waste land (*erēmēn*). (*Orations* 19.3)

This usage of *erēmos* is seen also in the Gospel of Matthew, in Jesus' prophetic lament over Jerusalem's desolation:

> Jerusalem, Jerusalem. . . . Behold, your house is forsaken and desolate (*erēmos*). (Matt. 23:37–38, RSV)

13. The intoxication accusations against Babylon in Rev. 17:2 and 18:3 are paralleled by charges of deceit and sorcery (*pharmakeia*) in Rev. 18:23. See Richard Bauckham, "Economic Critique of Rome in Revelation 18," in *Images of Empire,* ed. Loveday Alexander (Sheffield: JSOT Press, 1991), 47–90, for the argument that Babylon's intoxicating wine in Rev. 17:2 and 18:3 refers to the seductive delusion of the *Pax Romana*: "Rome's subjects are . . . taken in by Roman Propaganda. They are dazzled by Rome's glory and seduced by the promised benefits of the *Pax Romana*" (p. 56). Allen Callahan calls the accusation of intoxication and *pharmakeia* a "narcotics charge," for which Babylon is guilty of "poisoning the international community" ("A Note on Revelation 18: Apocalypse as Critique of Political Economy," unpublished paper, 7).

14. This reading of the role of the community ("my people") in handing back Babylon's cup of wrath is based on the argument that the audience for the imperatives of Rev. 18:6–7 ("give back . . . double . . . and mix") is the same as that of Rev. 18:4, named there as "my people." This is a minority position. See Pablo Richard, *Apocalypse: A People's Commentary on the Book of Revelation* (Maryknoll, N.Y.: Orbis Books, 1991), 135–36; and Dagoberto Ramirez Fernandez, "The Judgment of God on the Multinationals: Revelation 18," in *Subversive Scriptures: Revolutionary Readings of the Christian Bible in Latin America,* ed. Leif E. Vaage (Valley Forge, Pa.: Trinity Press International, 1997), 88–89. I presented the text-critical argument for reading the audience as "my people" at the 1995 Society of Biblical Literature meeting in Philadelphia; a similar argument has been published by Susan Elliott, "Who Is Addressed in Revelation 18:6–7?" *Biblical Research* 40 (1995): 98–113.

15. Marla Selvidge ("Powerful and Powerless Women in the Apocalypse," *Neotestamentica* 26 [1992]: 164) refers to Rev. 17:16 as a "rape" scene. See especially the work of Tina Pippin (*Death and Desire: The Rhetoric of Gender in the*

Apocalypse of John [Louisville: Westminster/John Knox Press, 1992], 57–58) for the interpretation of Rev. 17:16 as a "sexual murder" and as "the most vividly misogynist passage in the New Testament."

16. Obviously, violence is equally as prominent in my reading as in the gendered reading which Pippin and Selvidge find problematic. While not disagreeing that Revelation's violence poses ethical problems, I argue that the violence is directed primarily against a city's landscape, not against a woman. The ethical issues raised by the text thus lie primarily in the arena of war.

17. The standard New Testament lexicon, W. Bauer, W. F. Arndt, F. W. Gingerich, and F. W. Danker, *Greek-English Lexicon of the New Testament,* defines *erēmoō* as "lay waste, depopulate a city," and offers no possibility of the verb being used to describe an action against persons. The only personal definition for *erēmoō* furnished by the standard classical lexicon, Liddell-Scott-Jones, *Greek-English Lexicon,* involves double accusative objects, "to bereave one of a thing." Otherwise, the term always describes the destruction of cities, lands, or property. This is true of the usage of the term also in the Septuagint. See the LXX of Ezek. 29:10–12 (against Egypt); Ezek. 26:2, 19 (against Tyre); Ezek. 30:7 (against Egypt); and Ezek. 33:24, 27, and 36:4, 10 (about Israel).

18. This is true also of the Hebrew word for "naked," *erevah,* which is used to describe the nakedness of the land stripped of vegetation. See Gen. 42:9, 12; Psalm 137:7–8; Lam. 1:8; Hosea 2:3, 9. See Alice A. Keefe, "The Female Body, the Body Politic, and the Land: A Sociopolitical Reading of Hosea 1–2," in *A Feminist Companion to the Latter Prophets,* ed. Athalya Brenner (Sheffield: JSOT Press, 1995), 70–100, expecially 90–95.

19. On the priesthood of all in Revelation, see Elisabeth Schüssler Fiorenza, *Priester für Gott: Studien zum Herrschafts- und Priestermotiv in der Apocalypse,* Neutestamentliche Abhandlungen, n.s., 7 (Münster: Aschendorff, 1972).

20. Catherine Keller, "No More Sea: The Lost Chaos of the Eschaton," in this volume. See also Thomas Schmidt, "And the Sea Was No More: Water as People, Not Place," in *To Tell the Mystery: Essays on New Testament Eschatology in Honor of Robert H. Gundry,* ed. Thomas E. Schmidt and Moises Silva, Journal for the Study of the New Testament, Suppl. 100 (Sheffield: JSOT Press, 1994), 233–49. See also Dieter Georgi, "Die Visionen vom himmlischen Jerusalem in Apk 21 und 22," in *Kirche: Festschrift für Günther Bornkamm zum 75 Geburtstag,* ed. Dieter Lührmann and Georg Strecker (Tübingen: Mohr [Siebeck], 1980), 353; Celia Deutsch, "Transformation of Symbols: The New Jerusalem in Rev 21:1–22:5," *Zeitschrift für die neutestamentliche Wissenschaft* 78 (1987): 115.

21. Additionally, the sea appears in formulaic constellations with other elements, such as the earth (Rev. 10:2, 5; 13:1, 11), heaven and earth (Rev. 10:6, 12:12), and rivers and fountains (Rev. 14:7). See Adela Yarbro Collins, "The History-of-Religions Approach to Apocalypticism and the 'Angel of the Waters' (Rev 16:4–7)," *Catholic Biblical Quarterly* 39 (1977): 376.

22. This is a change of location from Jeremiah 51:63–64, the author's model, where the stone is thrown into the Euphrates River.

23. Klaus Wengst suggests that the sea symbolizes the Roman Empire. The Mediterranean has become the "Roman sea" (see Aelius Aristides *Or.* 26.28) and thus

had to be destroyed; Wengst, *Pax Romana and the Peace of Jesus Christ,* 130.

24. John J. Collins, trans., "The Sibylline Oracles: A New Translation and Introduction," in James H. Charlesworth, *Old Testament Pseudepigrapha,* 2 vols. (Garden City, N.Y.: Doubleday, 1983–85), 1:393–405. Collins notes that the fifth Sibylline "has its most significant contacts with the Revelation of John" (392).

25. This idea of a rapture is found in only one biblical text, 1 Thessalonians 4:16–17, the first of Paul's letters. Paul uses the promise that those who have died will be snatched up to meet Christ in the air as a way of assuring Christians that their loved ones would not be forgotten. Paul does not return to this idea in his later letters, however.

26. See especially the commentary of M. Eugene Boring, *Revelation,* Interpretation Commentary (Louisville: Westminster/John Knox Press, 1989), which emphasizes the importance of Revelation's urban vision for ministry today.

27. Elisabeth Schüssler Fiorenza has identified the overall concentric structure of the book of Revelation in which the seven letters and the New Jerusalem vision are counterparts, B and B'. The specific promises to the "victor" (*ho nikōn*) in Revelation 2–3 find their fulfillment in the New Jerusalem vision of Rev. 21–22. See "The Eschatology and Composition of the Apocalypse," *Catholic Biblical Quarterly* 30 (1968): 537–69, reprinted in *The Book of Revelation: Justice and Judgment* (Philadelphia: Fortress Press, 1985). Schüssler Fiorenza's concentric outline is endorsed by Ugo Vanni in "L'Apocalypse johannique: État de la Question," in *L'Apocalypse johannique et l'Apocalyptique dans le Nouveau Testament,* ed. J. Lambrecht, Bibliotheca ephemeridum theologicarum lovaniensium, 53 (Leuven: University Press, 1980), 26.

28. On the use of the Hebrew prophets in Revelation 21–22, see Matthias Rissi, *The Future of the World: An Exegetical Study of Revelation 19:11–22:15,* Studies in Biblical Theology, 23 (London: SCM Press, 1972); Georgi, "Die Visionen vom himmlischen Jerusalem"; Deutsch, "Transformation of Symbols."

29. Georgi, "Die Visionen vom himmlischen Jerusalem."

30. This is reminiscent of the Exodus plague that turned water to blood (Exod. 7:18–24; see also *Wis.* 11:5–7), making the water undrinkable. See the interpretation of the plagues of Egypt by Terrence Fretheim as both acts of judgment and as "ecological signs of historical disaster. They function in a way not unlike certain ecological events in contemporary society, portents of unmitigated historical disaster"; "The Plagues as Ecological Signs of Historical Disaster," *Journal of Biblical Literature* 110 (1991): 387.

31. *1 Enoch* 48:1–2: "I saw the fountain of righteousness . . . surrounded completely by numerous fountains of wisdom. All the thirsty ones drink and become filled with wisdom." Sirach 24 likens God's law to a river that pours forth wisdom, understanding, and instruction (Sir. 24:25–27). For an analysis of this motif in biblical and Jewish tradition, see Michael Fishbane, "The Well of Living Water: A Biblical Motif and Its Ancient Transformations," in *Sha'arei Talmon: Studies in the Bible, Qumran, and the Ancient Near East Presented to Shemaryahu Talmon,* ed. Michael Fishbane and Emanuel Tove (Winona Lake: Eisenbrauns, 1992), 3–16.

32. For the argument that Revelation "democratizes" Ezekiel, see Dieter Georgi, "Die Visionen vom himmlischen Jerusalem."

33. See Georgi (ibid., 363–64), who argues that the city wall itself has an invitational quality, as expressed by the transparent jasper construction which "awakens longing" in those who see it. Georgi notes that it is typical of hellenistic cities that their walls serve not for protection against enemies but for beauty and integration. See also Rissi, *Future of the World,* 71, on the function of the wall.

34. Georgi, "Die Visionen vom himmlischen Jerusalem," 369.

35. See the work of Gloria Luster and the "Power of Hope Garden," presented at the Chicago Center for Global Ministries conference on urban ecojustice, April 1998.

36. See the essay by Marthinus Daneel, "Earthkeeping Churches at the African Grassroots," in this volume.

37. Beth Utto-Galarneau, "The New Jerusalem in East Boston," *New England Synod Lutheran,* winter 1992. Used by permission.

III. The Universal and Particular in Ethics and Spirituality

Seeking Moral Norms in Nature:
Natural Law and Ecological Responsibility

JAMES A. NASH

The peoples of this planet are now involved in a great civil and ethical struggle, testing which socioeconomic and ecological vision of the planetary future will long endure. The importance of this struggle can hardly be overstated, nor its difficulties and dilemmas be overestimated. To be a voice of moral discernment in this monumental debate, Christian ethics needs a sound ethical worldview and method. My argument here is that the natural law tradition can contribute significantly to the satisfaction of these needs.

Thus, the central questions for this essay are: 1) What are the main contributions, actual and potential, of the natural law tradition for adequate Christian social and, particularly for my purposes here, ecological ethics? and 2) What reforms are necessary in new manifestations of this tradition to fulfill its potential and perhaps to become an adequate framework or system for Christian social and ecological ethics?

Despite its well-known historical (but not inherent) deficiencies, the natural law tradition at its best offers a package of indispensable elements for viable social and ecological ethics. These include:

- an affirmation of objective moral values and norms (as an alternative to skepticism and relativism), which correspond to the conditions for flourishing among relational beings;
- a rational-experiential method—in its trajectory at least—for evaluating and justifying (or not) moral standards;

- a dependence on and dialogue with empirical disciplines in searching for "norms in nature";
- a quest for common moral grounds accessible in principle to all humanity; and
- a necessary autonomy from and yet compatibility with basic Christian affirmations of faith.

Nearly all of the diverse expressions of this tradition, however, have been strongly anthropocentric, and at best ecologically oblivious. The interpreters have *not* understood that humans are both social *and* ecological animals, that our moral responsibilities are discovered by reflecting not only on human nature but also on our interactions with the whole of nature, and that the exercise of human rights is limited by the moral claims of other life-forms.

Ecologically sensitized and otherwise reformed, the natural law approach can provide or point to an adequate framework for social and ecological ethics. The task, however, is not simply to reaffirm or reestablish one of the classical types of the natural law, whether it be a Stoic, Thomistic, Enlightenment, or one of the various Protestant versions. All of these have too many weaknesses to stand when tested. Rather, the task is to appropriate the moral wisdom embodied in each of these types and to create a new, coherent interpretation that can withstand the moral challenges of the age.[1]

Historical Diversity and Defects

What is the natural law? This question cannot be answered straightforwardly. One reason is that interpretations of the natural law have constituted a dynamic and diverse tradition. A significant variety of versions has emerged historically, including those of Cicero, Ulpian, Aquinas, Hooker, Pufendorf, Grotius, Locke, and Blackstone;[2] constant or essential features of this tradition are often difficult to discern in the midst of such diversity. Even St. Paul allegedly recognized the natural law; the classic proof text has been Romans 2:14–15 where Paul refers to the Gentiles having the law "written on their hearts." The natural law, however, is not simply a curio from the past. Indeed, it is showing signs of renewal in modern legal philosophy.[3] The natural law is accepted by most Catholic moral theologians, but contemporary Catholic interpretations are highly diverse in themselves. They include, for example, both a deductive-casuistic type in conservative Catholic circles and the revisionist versions of Charles Curran and Richard McCormick that berate the deductive-casuistic type. Many contemporary Protestant theologians reject the natural law, but many others, while critical of its historical deficiencies, are sympathetic or supportive of the tradition's main affirmations. That is true even among some who reject or avoid the term. For instance, the influence of the natural law is clearly evident in Emil Brunner's "Divine Law of Justice" and "constants of Creation,"[4] Max Stackhouse's "public theology,"[5] Walter G. Muelder's "moral laws,"[6] and Reinhold Niebuhr's "law of love" as the "law of [our] being."[7] Even Karl Barth, while condemning the very idea of natural law, finally appeals to it when discussing public policy.[8]

Another reason why it is imprudent to define the natural law directly is that some major expressions of the tradition have been associated with a variety of moral distortions and other faults. The natural law has been used both to promote and condemn democracy, imperialism, gender inequalities, racism, and slavery. Culture-bound values were expressed as timeless truths. Historical biases, antiquated worldviews, and particular social systems, such as medieval feudalism, were absolutized or eternalized. The natural law was used as a "support for the special institutional claims of the [Catholic] Church,"[9] on such issues as the political status of the church and public policy on contraception. In early-twentieth-century political thought in the United States, the natural law had become "a synonym for subjective prejudice and reactionary social views."[10]

Neo-scholastic Catholic versions abandoned experientially grounded inductive reasoning in favor of deductions from abstract assumptions about the human condition. The natural law became a code of casuistic absolutes. Charles Curran describes one dimension of this development as "physicalism," identifying the morality of an act with its physical or biological structure, without regard for relational circumstances and the demands of moral proportionality—so that contraception was conceived as a sin against nature.[11] Another major defect in some interpretations of the natural law is what John Courtney Murray called "immobilism"[12] and Curran calls "classicism"[13]—a worldview that understands humans as immutable essences, with fixed norms for all times and places, without regard for the dynamics of human culture or relational circumstances, and without allowance for evolving moral possibilities. Ironically, for an ethical framework that allegedly finds its norms by reflecting on biophysical reality, one of the perennial problems of the natural law has been an inadequate or distorted understanding of the nature of humans as living and interacting beings, let alone as an ecologically interdependent species.

In view of the diversity and defects of the natural law tradition, any normative interpretation of the natural law, including mine, is something of an idealization or ideal type. My interpretation points to the aspirations—the potential strengths—of this moral framework for social and ecological ethics, and it seeks to avoid or transcend the historical faults in this framework.

A Universal and Immanent Moral Order

The natural law is not "law" in the sense of enacted and enforceable legal codes, usually called positive law. Nor is it "law" in the sense of the dynamic order known in physics, such as the law of gravity—though an ecologically informed version of the natural law will demand a respectful adaptability to these physical processes and constraints. Rather, it is law in the sense of moral norms and obligations, which provide a basis for evaluating, challenging, and transforming human character and conduct, including legal and political structures. Similarly, the natural law is not "natural" in the sense of being instinctive or self-evident, nor in the sense of following amoral patterns in autonomous nature as a moral guide. Instead, "natural" means that moral values and norms should reflect the reality of the human condition and, as I must add, the condition of the planet's whole biota. Moreover, these norms can be discovered through "natural" reasoning capacities, without aid from special revelations. In this sense, the "natural" was often contrasted historically with the "supernatural."

The first and fundamental affirmation of the natural law is that we live in a universal moral order. Moral values and moral standards are not merely humanly constructed or created; they are discovered, independent of our preferences or opinions. Metaethically, the natural law is one form of moral realism, a philosophical category which claims that moral judgments are "truth assessable," subject to evaluation about whether they are right or wrong, objectively true or false.[14]

Authentic moral values and norms transcend our inevitable mental and social reconstructions of reality; they are more than subjective, emotional, cultural, customary, or otherwise arbitrary preferences; they are structured at least in the nature of relationships. Moral judgments deal with facts about "goodness" and "rightness"—what we ought to be and do in general and in particular situations, in view of what norms and actions contribute to the flourishing of our kind and other kinds of creatures in our relationships. Thus, the natural law rejects moral relativism and emotivism.

Within moral realism, the natural law belongs in a category generally called ethical naturalism, which affirms that norms are found in "nature." Values are grounded in facts. "Ought" can be derived from and defined and defended in terms of "is." Ethics depends on empirical inquiry to discover what enables creaturely well-being and to define the good and the right. Thus, values and norms are justified on naturalistic or empirical data and reasons. As such, the natural law defies the so-called naturalistic fallacy, which claims that ought or good cannot be defined in nonethical or naturalistic terms. Values cannot be derived from facts. For the intuitionist G. E. Moore, the good is indefinable and unanalyzable; moral principles are self-evident and need no justification.

Logically, the naturalistic fallacy makes sense: One cannot draw a moral or "ought" conclusion from strictly factual, or "is," premises, as David Hume showed. That problem can be resolved easily, however, by making explicit any implicit or hidden moral premise and enabling a valid deduction. The main question then concerns the veracity of the premise. Thus, as William Frankena argues, the alleged fallacy is at least not a logical fallacy.[15]

The naturalistic fallacy is plausible only on the positivistic assumption that "facts" are devoid of value, that "is" and "ought" are sharply separated.[16] Indeed, the argument for the naturalistic fallacy itself seems rooted in a positivistic fallacy. In reality, we do not experience facts and values as dichotomous categories. Facts are not morally neutral or value-free. Values are a constitutive part or inherent quality of the facts.[17] The movement from "is" to "ought," argues Holmes Rolston, cannot be arbitrary, but it is reasonable to value the intrinsic good of diverse life-forms and the ecologically interactive dynamics of these life-forms that enable the thriving of all life.[18] As Frankena maintains, there can be no naturalistic fallacy if values and virtues are somehow facts or truths about the conditions for human flourishing.[19] Furthermore, Jean Porter rightly argues that there is "no real understanding of the facts that is not simultaneously a knowledge of values," because knowledge of what a being really is is the same as knowledge of what is good for that being.[20] On this assumption, social and ecological ethics need strong empirical groundings to help us discern the common good for all beings in relationships.

If norms are found in nature, then the universal moral order affirmed by the natural law is not something alien or external to humans and other life-forms. Instead, this order is immanent—an "intrinsic morality"—which "advances the true self-fulfillment of the human being"[21] (and otherkind). It is a "natural order." It affirms a value system that is not necessarily built into the structure of the universe, but rather one that is built into the essential constitution of human beings as rational and relational creatures. Living by the natural law is not "following nature" per se, but rather practicing the norms of our nature, the conditions necessary for our good and that of other life-forms with whom we exist interdependently.[22]

Thus, moral reflection in the natural law tradition normally has started with human relationships. Catholic ethicist Richard Gula rightly says, "The moral person and the moral community must discover what is morally good by critically reflecting on the total complexity of human reality in all its relationships."[23] In its best forms, the natural law is a set of values and norms, patterns of goodness and rightness, that correspond to the full breadth of our relationships. Humans do not exist as isolated individualists. We are internally relational creatures—social and ecological animals, existing only interdependently. Our moral rights and responsibilities arise from this relational condition. Indeed, we are ethical animals because we are first social and ecological animals with unique rational capacities (e.g., capacities to analyze consequences and to make choices among alternatives). Thus, we are compelled by our relational nature and our rational capacities to reflect and act on questions of the good and rightness in relationships. The natural law offers universal ground rules for living together effectively, for surviving and thriving as social and ecological animals.

Yet, one of the significant defects in the natural law tradition, both classical and contemporary versions, is that it generally forgot that humans are ecological animals. Rather than succumbing to a naturalistic fallacy, the tradition was guilty of being insufficiently naturalistic, or even of succumbing to an anthropocentric or humanistic fallacy. What is striking about the tradition to the ecologically conscious is that morality is not grounded in nature per se, but almost exclusively in human nature (and in reality, a male European nature of a privileged class—though that subject is beyond the scope of this paper). Like the rest of classical Western philosophy and theology, natural law ethics has been largely anthropocentric and dualistic— focusing exclusively on human interests and segregating humanity from the rest of nature. The tradition has treated humans as if we are not parts and products of nature, as if we have not evolved in interaction with all other creatures and elements, and as if the realities of biological kinship and ecological interdependence with all the flora and fauna are irrelevant for our theological vision and moral responsibilities. As a consequence of this nonecological mindset, the tradition has had little sense of the moral claims embodied in nature as a whole, and precisely for that reason it also has had a truncated sense of the rights and responsibilities rooted in human nature.

An ecologically viable conception of the natural law, or any other ethical theory, depends on a transvaluation of values. Contemporary ecological degradation—from various forms of pollution to extinctions—confronts us with moral problems of a different order than the one perceived traditionally. The context is now biological and ecological and not simply human and social. The moral problems are not only human relationships with all other humans, but also those with all other creatures and elements.

Not Written on Our Hearts

The norms of the natural law are not known instinctively or intuitively, let alone indisputably, as the earlier tradition often suggested. We are not born with this knowledge; it is not "written on our hearts" (Rom. 2:14–15), at least not in any substantive sense. Yet, perhaps the tradition had a point: we seem to be born with some genetically shaped capacities to know the natural law and some pre-ethical inclinations to follow it, as a consequence of natural selection. Surprisingly perhaps, the arguments of sociobiology may be helpful here, despite this discipline's well-known weaknesses when applied to the human situation—for example, its tendency toward biological deter-minism or exaggeration, and its definition of "inclusive fitness" as simply reproductive success. Organisms, however, are far more than "survival machines" for colonies of "selfish genes."[24] Still, there does appear to be some "natural moral sense," consisting of innate capac-ities and inclinations for fairness, sympathy, a sense of duty, and constraints against cruelty,[25] along with a conflicting selfish or sinful sense. We are not born into cultures as moral tabula rasa; we are already moral animals, bearing not only self-regarding but also other-regarding instincts that can be both cultivated and corrupted by cul-tures. But these instincts are only moral capacities and inclinations, not full-fledged principles.

The norms of the natural law are discovered only gradually and imperfectly through the trials and errors of historical experience, as we grow in our understanding of what helps and hinders social and ecological well-being. Such moral "discovery" or discernment depends on receptivity to all cultural wisdom, including such disci-plines as psychology, sociology, physics, biology, ecology, history, and political science. To continue to make progress in ecological eth-ics, for example, we simply must take the biological and ecological sciences seriously as a necessary empirical base and, in fact, as a prime place for discerning and testing our norms. Ecological ethics must be structured in ways that are coherent with the best and fullest scientific data and interpretations available. Incidentally, we can find no better model to follow in this process than the writings of Holmes Rolston, III.

A Rational-Experiential Method

The "intrinsic morality" of natural law suggests a rational-experiential method that I will now interpret. A rational-experiential method is certainly not peculiar to the natural law tradition—though the tradition clearly contributed to it. It is, in fact, a method that is shared by several ethical theories or frameworks. Edward Long described it as the "pragmatic-empirical tradition," because it begins with the examination of experiential data and moves inductively to "moral generalization."[26] Despite the fact that some versions of natural law theory have been deductive and abstract, this method represents the trajectory of the mainstream of the natural law tradition, particularly in its Enlightenment-influenced forms. It is an indispensable method for any viable version of the natural law—indeed, for any viable ethics—for the future.

"Experience" is, deliberately and appropriately, a broad and loose category, to indicate the all-encompassing breadth of relevant data. By experience is meant far more than the personal or affective side of being, to which the word is sometimes constricted.[27] Instead, experience here covers the totality of being: past and present, emotional and rational, existential and scientific, spiritual and moral, personal and social, psychological and sociological, technical and aesthetic, cultural and ecological. Nothing is excluded as relevant data for theological and ethical reflection. This approach is a rejection, for example, of biblical and traditional exclusivism, which arbitrarily limits the subject matter of theology and ethics to past and privileged revelations and ignores the continuing revelations of God in the totality of existence.

The stress on comprehension is also a reaction against philosophical positivism, which limits relevant data to sensory perceptions—what can be seen, felt, weighed, and measured—and which determines truth strictly by what can be verified or falsified empirically on the model of the natural sciences. Again, positivism is an arbitrary limitation on potentially relevant data. It excludes vast amounts of "extrascientific" experience, such as the thinking, feeling, valuing, and choosing of the self-aware self.[28] It also excludes specifically religious experiences—those direct revelatory encounters or intuitions which are known under various names, including the "witness of the spirit," the "still, small voice," and the "sense of the heart." Such experiences must be subject to tough pragmatic and coherence tests, but they cannot be dismissed on the basis of an arbitrary principle.

Yet, despite a theoretical stress on comprehension, the vast majority of practitioners of a rational-experiential method have focused on human experience alone. This focus does not necessarily lead to ecological abuses or to an exclusively instrumentalistic view of nonhuman nature. Because humans are inherently ecological beings, they can discover in their own experience some sense of both biological kinship and ecological interdependence, as well as the moral responsibilities that arise therefrom. Still, full moral sensitivity to the interests of otherkind is likely to arise only if we give due and direct consideration to their experience, insofar as we can make inferences.

This planet's biota, from unicellular to complex creatures, are at least systemic, interactive, adaptive, renewing, reproductive, and vital forces. They are characterized by conation—aims *or* drives, goals *or* urges, purposes *or* impulses, whether conscious *or* unconscious, sentient *or* nonsentient. As such, they are good for themselves—intrinsic values—in addition to whatever systemic or instrumental values they may provide others. These intrinsic values merit respect from moral agents. By becoming biologically and ecologically informed, we can judge what is good and bad, beneficial and harmful to otherkind, and then act empathetically to promote their good[29]—indeed, the ecological common good, which is essential also for the human community. For the future, a viable version of the natural law—or any other ethical approach, for that matter—must give due consideration not only to human experience but to the whole of biotic experience.

Experience in the raw, however, doesn't tell us very much about moral truth and meaning. Experience needs to be analyzed, evaluated, and interpreted. At this point, reason becomes an imperative in the process.

"Right reason" has been central to the natural law tradition, but the concept has been badly abused by its foes and sometimes badly misinterpreted by its fans. Reason, for example, has often been used as a cold, calculative process. But as Daniel Maguire and Nicholas Fargnoli argue, moral reasoning is both art and science, the "alliance of head and heart," a cognitive and affective process that weighs matters proportionately and sensitively, judiciously and empathetically.[30] This is the essence of moral discernment.

Yet, the most serious, as well as the most irrelevant, complaint against reason is that reason is corrupted by sin and finitude. Of course, that's true! Sin distorts all reality that humans touch. That is evident in the very theories of natural law, not simply the abuses of the theory. When faith is put in reason, like all idols, reason can't deliver. Reason is "tainted"; it is not dispassionate, objective, or definitive, despite legitimate aspirations toward these goals in certain areas. The rationalizations of the self and its culture masquerade as rationality. Our use of reason is always affected by our particular social locations and other biases. We all are to some degree captives of our contexts, reflections of our conditions. Our ethical constructions are always more or less social constructions.

But the same distortions are true of every other alleged means to moral truth! The symbol of the Fall points to the corruption of all human endeavors. Rationalism is only one of the fundamentalisms that pretend to be pure and undefiled. The others include traditionalism, scientism, and biblicism. If reason is going to have ethical utility, it must be tempered by epistemological humility and informed by love.[31] Nevertheless, reason is truly indispensable for ethics and every other search for truth. The reasoning spirit is one of the "natural graces," a sign of the divine image in classical thought, the means of loving God with one's whole mind.

Reason is not really a "source" or an autonomous way of "knowing" God or moral truth, at least not in itself. The critics of reason have it right on this point. Instead, moral reasoning is the critical reflection on the givenness of experience (a posteriori reasoning), including scripture and tradition as historical expressions of Christian experience. It cannot be divorced from experience. It is primarily an inductive process in quest of moral values and norms. Understood in this way, reason and revelation are not alternatives. Rather, reason is human reflection on divine revelation—known not only in the witnesses in scripture and tradition, not only in "spiritual" experience, but also in the whole of life, including the biological and ecological sciences.

Moral reasoning is a critical process of probing and evaluating the whole of experience and interpretations of experience to discover the values, norms, and practices that promote the social and ecological common good of humans and otherkind in our interdependent relationships. The purpose is to determine what moral claims should be justified or not on the basis of their adequacy of interpretation, internal consistency, and coherence with other knowledge.

Historically, in Christian versions, the natural law was often interpreted as a parallel but partial and, therefore, subordinate source of moral truth to scripture. The "two books" of morality were the "natural" and the "supernatural," or "revealed," laws, the former accessible to all humanity and the latter knowable only through the Bible, often viewed as accessible only or fully to the redeemed. This dual track is still fairly common, but it does not seem compatible with a rational-experiential method. The problem is that the moral authority of the Bible itself needs justification, but that justification flounders on two facts. First, the Bible is embedded in ancient, culture-bound value systems, which include, for example, the acceptance of slavery, the subordination of women, and often ecological insensitivity toward wildlife and wildlands. Second, it embodies moral pluralism—in methods, values, principles, and prescriptions. Given these facts, the Bible itself can no longer be regarded as the final arbiter or the methodological norm on moral matters.[32] We cannot know what is morally true or false on the basis of internal biblical evidence alone when the final court of appeals is regularly giving split decisions and occasionally offering some malicious options. Instead, we need to introduce an independent criterion—an extrinsic justification—for selection among the multiple choices in as well as beyond scripture. That is precisely what a rational-experiential method seeks to do. It weighs the evidence from experience in order to confirm or deny any biblical perspective.

This approach clearly denies that the Bible alone should be morally normative for Christians, but it also affirms that moral norms can be derived from the Bible—after critical reflection. Indeed, for many of us, the core of our theological vision and our foundational values and norms have been discerned in this unique but human—and therefore fallible—witness to the cosmic ministry of God. In relation to scripture, a rational-experiential method has important benefits for ecological ethics: it discourages a moral etherealism that floats in a stratosphere of biblical exegesis and only bouncingly touches ecological reality, and it demands an engagement with empirical data and disciplines that can foster ecological realism and relevance.

Christian Compatibility Yet Universal Accessibility

From a Christian perspective, one of the great values of the natural law is that it can be interpreted as both compatible with Christian affirmations of faith and yet independent of these affirmations. Christians can understand the natural law as God's creation of humanity's moral constitution and/or the rational and moral order in the universe. The natural law then is an expression of the moral character of God. It can even be understood as essentially Christocentric, assuming that all things have been made through Christ the Logos. The law of nature is then ultimately the law of Christ.

Aquinas and subsequent Catholic thought described the natural law as the participation of the rational creature in the eternal law of God, insofar as it is relevant and knowable to humans.[33] In terms of human moral responsibilities, the natural law then is the divine design for the fullness of humanness—the "truly human" that fulfills our dignity.[34] Indeed, the life and death of Jesus has been morally normative for Christians because he is considered at least the model of the "truly" or "fully" human. Similarly, one can argue that an ethics of love is not distinctively Christian; it can be justified by—in my view, it can be justified *only* by—rational-experiential criteria, since that love is the fulfillment of our moral aspirations, the fundamental norm of our nature.

Yet, the natural law is not dependent on—and, for its viability, must not be dependent on—Christian assumptions. It is a "natural revelation," a "common grace," a gift of God to all people. The natural law is open in principle to all, whatever their ultimate commitments, whether evangelical or atheist. It is a morality for all humanity. Indeed, Christians should rejoice in finding moral commonalities across religious and philosophical lines, because they are "an indication that the God revealed in Christ is God of the whole world, the source of all value as all being," as well as a sign that all share in the grace of reason as part of the image of God.[35]

Universal accessibility is one of the natural law's primary appeals—in the imperial Roman world, in the cultural diversity of medieval Europe and its increasing encounters with Asia and Africa, in religiously divided post-Reformation Europe, and now in the midst of contemporary globalization. Its claim, or hope, is that common moral grounds can be found in the midst of moral pluralism.

In significant contemporary forms of the natural law, there is no distinctive Christian ethics, no substantive supplement delivered by special revelation that "perfects" natural reason. This denial of distinctiveness avoids a moral dualism of higher and lower norms, as well as a moral triumphalism typical of Christians when they celebrate their moral uniqueness and superiority vis-à-vis the rest of humanity. Thus, ethicist Richard M. McCormick argues: "Christian morality is, in its concreteness and materiality, human morality." It is not distinctive in "material content" or substance (norms, principles, virtues, goals) The Christian choice is simply the morally justified choice.[36] Certainly, Christian perspectives affect ethical choices: They can give enhanced reasons for respecting life and enhanced motivations for acting morally. They can provide illumination and inspiration. There may very well be some functionally distinctive elements in Christian ethics. Indeed, I am inclined to think there are—not least the ultimate foundations of love. But the point is that these elements are not "in principle unavailable to human insight and reasoning in the broadest sense."[37]

On these assumptions, it is critically important for Christian ethics to be in dialogue with all other moral traditions, religious and philosophical. That has been a part of the natural law tradition. Properly understood, the relationship between Christian and other moral traditions is not one of superior and inferior but rather one of mutual illumination and correction.

The natural law tradition points to the possibility of an ethical basis for making common cause with a host of worldviews in a morally pluralistic culture and global community. Moral pluralism is a prominent feature of the contemporary world. A variety of moral voices are competing for faithful followings. No dominant ethical perspective or prevailing set of values can be assumed among cultures or even within particular cultures. In this context, it is fruitless—and unfair—for religious advocates to argue for a norm or policy direction on the basis of their epistemologically privileged and parochial warrants, such as a scripture or confession of faith. A narrowly confessional method provides ethical standards which are suitable, if at all, only for ecclesiastical ghettoes, such as the "contrast model" of the church as a "political alternative" to civil government, as advocated by Stanley Hauerwas.[38] Despite the insistence of some that we do not need a "moral esperanto" for a civil public square,[39] it seems increasingly clear that we need some common ground—some shared standards of rationality or process of moral reasoning, along with some shared perspectives on appropriate means and ends—to avoid sheer babble and severe conflicts, and to achieve global solidarity.

Global solidarity is no longer an ultimate vision; it is fast becoming a social, political, and ecological necessity, because the world is becoming increasingly a holistic system of interdependent socioeconomic systems, communications and transportation networks, and ecosystems. In the midst of this rapid and radical civilizational transformation, a premium is now placed on human solidarity, as John

Paul II argued, as a moral response to the fact of human and eco-logical interdependence.[40] We are experiencing the moral reality of social and ecological indivisibility.

Thus, various social and ecological trends are forcing us to become global citizens. The nations' decisions and destinies are increasingly bound together; national isolationism and self-reliance are in many ways obsolete. Unprecedented levels of international cooperation across religious and cultural boundaries are necessary to deal with global social and ecological problems that threaten the welfare of all life-forms. The fundamental ethical task is to try to shape the actual process of globalization in accord with a moral vision of globaliza-tion (indeed, the word itself is often used in both empirical and normative senses). Hans Küng is right: there is "no survival without a world ethic"—universal or common norms, values, ideals, and goals that will optimize the social and ecological common good.[41] That will require an uncommon moral discernment, including a distinction between ethically constant functions and culturally variable forms, to allow an appropriate diversity and flexibility in expressing the same universal values. As global citizens, we need global ethics to confront global social and ecological problems in global solidarity.

Clearly, no version of the natural law yet offers an adequate global ethics, a set of universal values and norms. The world faces, as Alasdair McIntyre argues, conflicting concepts of rationality and justice, reflecting different moral and cultural traditions.[42] Disagree-ments abound on both the "good" and the "right." Yet, the fact that there is no universal agreement on the substantive formulations of the natural law does not mean that the task is hopeless.[43] Moreover, some moral norms do have universal or near-universal cultural assent, such as the social protection of human life. The task before us is to persist in the aspirations of the natural law tradition, because the search for universal norms universally accessible is not only a worthy hope, but also, in light of our global relationships, a practical necessity.

Content of Natural Law

What is the content or substance of natural law? That is a difficult question to answer, because there has been significant dissensus in the tradition. Yet, the question is important, because the value and relevance of the natural law rest in some measure on our answers.

For Thomas Aquinas, the first principle of the natural law is: to do good and avoid evil.[44] He regards this principle as self-evident; it is at least a reasonable statement of faith—unproveable and yet a necessary assumption for doing ethics as an appropriate response to encounters with value. It is comparable to Maguire and Fargnoli's "foundational moral experience": the sense of the intrinsic value of persons and all other forms of life, and the appropriate response to promote these values or goods.[45] The natural law, however, is not the principle itself, but as Maritain says, "the ensemble of things to do and not to do which follow therefrom in necessary fashion."[46] The natural law, as Aquinas claims, is those norms necessary to promote the good associated at least with our instincts for self-preservation, our animal needs, and our rational (including our social) nature.[47] For example, prima facie prohibitions against killing and theft follow from this mandate to do good.

Unfortunately, the natural law sometimes has been interpreted as precise precepts or casuistic absolutes. Perhaps as a counter to this casuistry, John Courtney Murray argued that the natural law is only a "skeleton law."[48] Similarly, John Macquarrie claims that the natural law cannot be particularized much beyond general moral principles, comparable to W. D. Ross's prima facie duties (such as doing justice and telling the truth).[49]

My own sense is that the natural law has much greater content than Murray and Macquarrie suggest, and that this content can be interpreted in ways that do not absolutize or universalize particulars or relativities, but rather allow for concrete circumstances and human variability. It can include, for example, a variety of prima facie duties and virtues, as well as Muelder's "moral laws." It also can be developed to include all the basic goods necessary for social and ecological flourishing, and the moral rights and responsibilities resulting therefrom.

The natural law often, and rightly, has been interpreted as the ground, or source, of human—or "natural"—rights. Human rights are those moral claims that concern the vital interests or basic necessities for human well-being. They are the imperative conditions for expressing our human dignity, and they, therefore, apply equally and universally to all humans. They include the following basic categories: biophysical and economic needs; physical security; spiritual and moral autonomy; mental and cultural development; full and equal participation in defining and shaping the common good; social ground rules for fair and equal consideration; environmental security as an extension of biophysical needs; and the common good itself as the "ensemble of conditions" that favors the realization of individuals in community—the total constellation of rights fairly distributed, balanced, and blended.[50] Indeed, an adequate theory of human rights will be built not on traditional individualistic assumptions, but rather on our relational nature. Understood not as absolutes but as prima facie claims (rebuttable for compelling moral reasons), these human rights can be understood as part of the natural law.

But the rest of the planet's biota cannot be ignored here, as the natural law tradition's almost exclusively humanistic focus has done. The moral claims of other life-forms on the human community also should be considered as part of the natural law. One of the fundamental ethical challenges of the time is to redefine responsible human relationships with the rest of the biota, and to ground these responsibilities not only in utility and generosity, but also in justice— the moral demands imposed on us by the vital interests of otherkind. Their intrinsic value is itself a prima facie moral claim on humans to respect the imperative conditions for their well-being. These claims include the right to participate in the natural dynamics of existence, the right to healthy and whole habitats, the right to fulfill their evolutionary potential with freedom from human-induced extinctions, the right to freedom from human cruelty or profligate use, and the right to a "fair share" of the planetary goods necessary for the well-being of all kinds.[51] Indeed, the exercise of human rights must be limited to respect these biotic rights.

Following Nature as Ecosystemic Compatibility

The idea of "following nature," or conformity to nature, has in some sense usually been associated with the natural law tradition.[52] Whether or not this idea is defensible depends in part on the definition of "nature"—and, of course, definitions differ. Cicero, for example, argued that "the highest good is to live according to nature." To him, following nature did not mean the abandonment of moral constraints. Rather, it meant a "life both temperate and virtuous," including doing the justice which is a central demand of the rational order of the cosmos.[53] Similarly, in medieval political thought, nature had a normative status, to which humans ought to conform.[54] In both cases, however, nature is understood not as the biophysical world per se, but rather as an ultimate order of reason and justice, reminiscent of the Hebraic idea of Wisdom. This metaphysical and even romanticized version of "following nature" transcends the naturalistic; it avoids the moral problems associated with conformity to nature in a biophysical sense. Oppositely, Thomas Huxley condemns a social Darwinian interpretation of "following nature," which advocates ruthless and reckless selfishness as nature's way. An amoral nature is regarded as the "exemplar for human conduct" or the "pedagogue for virtue," so that ethics becomes "applied natural history."[55]

If there is any moral validity in following nature, we will need to avoid both the transcendent and the cynical interpretations. So the question is: In what sense can following nature as a biophysical reality be a moral mandate, and a necessary component of any viable version of the natural law? I believe we find an answer in an important moral norm of ecosystemic compatibility.

Ecosystemic compatibility is part of the ethics of the fitting—in this case, adapting ecologically to natural cycles and constraints and respecting systemic values. It is closely related to sustainability, though I think it has an independent status. Ecosystemic compatibility is the norm that counters one of the fundamental failures at the roots of the ecological crisis: the failure to adapt to the limiting conditions of life—the carrying, regenerative, and absorptive capacities of the biophysical world, as illustrated by the problems of climate change and human overpopulation.

Holmes Rolston's environmental ethics is a clear example of what I mean by this norm. Rolston is seeking "inclusive *environmental* fitness"—notice: not the inclusive *reproductive* fitness of the sociobiologists—of humans on the earth. It is "following nature" not in an "imitative ethical sense" (for ethics often entails a defiance of nature's moral indifference). Rather, it is following nature, first, in a "homeostatic sense" of fitting into the stability of ecosystems and the ecosphere, and, second, in an "axiological sense" of respecting and being guided by the values we encounter in nature.[56]

Following nature in the sense of ecosystemic fitness or compatibility is evident also in the thought of Rosemary Radford Ruether.

The study of ecology, she argues, "suggests guidelines for how humans must learn to live as sustaining rather than destructive members of . . . biotic communities"—thus suggesting an important function for science in doing ethics. For her, " 'good' lies in limits, a balancing of our own drive for life with the life drives of all the others with which we are in community, so that the whole remains in life-sustaining harmony."[57] The same point pervades the work of Larry Rasmussen. Notice, for example, his discussions of "the principles of Earth's economy" and the moral dilemmas of balancing the intrinsic and instrumental values of nonhuman life.[58] Similarly, John Cobb and Herman Daly stress the importance of the "optimal scale of the economy relative to the ecosystem."[59]

The same idea of fittingness is prominent in the thought of James Gustafson. Indeed, it seems central to his theological ethics. Morality is "the task of discerning what the divine ordering requires under particular conditions in a particular time and place." "Consenting" to and "cooperating" with the "divine governance" demands recognition of the "limits and possibilities of human activity that are consonant with it." We experience a naturalistic version of judgment and wrath when we do not fit into this order.[60]

Ecosystemic compatibility is often described as "mimicking" nature. Thus, Paul Hawken argues that modern economic production is "maladaptive and predatory," and calls for a redesign of production and consumption systems to mimic natural processes, in which waste is reclaimed and only renewable energy is used. He calls this "restorative economics."[61] This mimicking applies also to forestry, agriculture, grazing practices, and so on.[62] Indeed, E. F. Schumacher's concept of "appropriate technology," adapted to relevant values and social and ecological conditions, is partly an expression of ecosystemic compatibility.[63]

In order to avoid the "judgments" of nature, ecosystemic compatibility accommodates to biological limits and cycles. As an insurance provision, it allows room for flexible responses to unpredictable but inevitable shifts in ecological dynamics, such as natural calamities or normal fluctuations in the populations of species. For instance, in biological management on the basis of "sustained yields," the "harvests" of a commercial species—say, halibut—are supposed to equal the annual or other periodic rate of increase in numbers. Yet, a sustainable "take" has often been overestimated. One reason has been that the appropriate quantities to be taken have been determined more politically and economically than ecologically. But another reason has been that allowances have not been made for unpredictable fluctuations in populations and changes in ecological processes.[64] Ecosystemic compatibility has not been taken seriously. This norm, of course, has numerous applications.

Thus, in the sense of ecosystemic compatibility, following nature makes moral sense. The natural law tradition will do well to incorporate this idea and to develop its implications for ecological norms and virtues.

Conclusion

The natural law legacy is far from antiquated. It has made, and makes, important contributions to contemporary ethics. Indeed, most of the central features of contemporary Christian social and ecological ethics are rooted in this tradition—not only its Christian versions, but also its too-much-berated Enlightenment versions. Its basic affirmations and aspirations—a rational-experiential method and a quest for universal accessibility, for example—seem to be necessary elements for adequate ethics in our time.

Yet, the ethical contributions of the tradition will be greatly enhanced if, in our approach to natural law, we change some habitual faults. For our focus here, the ecological deficiencies—especially the ecological unconsciousness—in the natural law tradition are serious. Henceforth, our search for norms in nature must reflect not only on human nature but also on the whole of biophysical nature, of which humans are parts and products, to discover our rights and responsibilities in all our relationships. Ecologically sensitized and otherwise reformed, the natural law tradition can provide, or at least point to, an adequate framework for social and ecological ethics in the emerging times.

Notes

1. My own interpretation of the natural law strongly reflects the school of Protestant liberalism, so prominent in the first two-thirds of the twentieth century and still influential in various guises, particularly in the form of Boston personalism associated with Borden Parker Bowne, Edgar Brightman, Walter G. Muelder, L. Harold DeWolf, S. Paul Schilling, and Paul K. Deats, Jr. See my "Christian Liberalism: Ambiguous Legacy, Enduring Ethos," *Unitarian Universalist Christian* 41, no. 1 (spring 1986): 9–25.

2. For useful summaries of and excerpts from many of the classical and some contemporary interpretations, see Paul E. Sigmund, *Natural Law in Political Thought* (Cambridge, Mass.: Winthrop, 1971). See also an excellent brief summary, Douglas Sturm, "Natural Law," *The Encyclopedia of Religion,* ed. Mircea Eliade (New York: Macmillan, 1987), 10:318–20.

3. Andrew A. Altman, *Arguing about the Law: An Introduction to Legal Philosophy* (Belmont, Calif.: Wadsworth, 1996), 32–60; See also *Natural Law Theory: Contemporary Essays,* ed. Robert P. George (Oxford: Oxford University Press, 1992).

4. Emil Brunner, *Justice and the Social Order* (New York: Harper, 1945), 65–100. For Brunner, the "constants" can be known by natural means, but clear knowledge is available only through scripture.

5. Max Stackhouse, *Public Theology and Political Economy: Christian Stewardship in Modern Society* (Grand Rapids, Mich.: Eerdmans, 1987), 27–28.

6. Walter G. Muelder, *Moral Law in Christian Social Ethics* (Richmond, Va.: John Knox Press, 1966).

7. Reinhold Niebuhr, "Christian Faith and Natural Law," in *Christian Social Teachings: A Reader in Christian Social Ethics from the Bible to the Present,* ed. George W. Forrell (New York: Anchor/Doubleday, 1966), 395, 401–2. First published in *Theology,* February 1940.

8. Christians must speak solely out of the "Word of God," Barth argues, and not abandon the norms of Christ by adopting "the human illusions and confusions" of the natural law. Yet, he clearly resorts to some type of natural law when he describes the role of the state, "according to the providence and ordinance of God," as "the natural, secular, and profane way of the establishment of law, the safeguarding of freedom and peace, according to the measure of human insight and capacity." Indeed, on questions involving the civil community, "the decisions of Christians should be made as though they could be decisions of any other citizens, and Christians must finally hope that they may become the decisions of all other citizens regardless of their religious profession." See *Community, State, and Society* (Garden City, N.J.: Doubleday/Anchor, 1960), 163–66, 184; also 172, 180. Barth thus illustrates that some of the grievances against the natural law are rooted in confusion, sometimes justifiable, about its meaning.

9. Muelder, *Moral Law,* 140.

10. Sigmund, *Natural Law,* 107.

11. Charles E. Curran, *Directions in Fundamental Moral Theology* (Notre Dame: University of Notre Dame Press, 1985), 129–30, 160–61; and idem, *The Living*

Tradition of Catholic Moral Theology (Notre Dame: University of Notre Dame Press, 1992), 42-43.

12. John Courtney Murray, "The Doctrine Lives: The Eternal Return of the Natural Law," in *Readings in Moral Theology,* vol. 7, *Natural Law and Theology,* ed. Charles E. Curran and Richard A. McCormick (New York: Paulist Press, 1991).

13. Curran, *Directions,* 126, 138–48.

14. Michael Smith, "Realism," in *Companion to Ethics,* ed. Peter Singer (Oxford: Blackwell, 1993), 403.

15. William K. Frankena, *Perspectives on Morality: Essays by William K. Frankena,* ed. K. E. Goodpaster (Notre Dame: University of Notre Dame Press, 1976), 4.

16. Langdon Gilkey, *Nature, Reality, and the Sacred: The Nexus of Science and Religion* (Minneapolis: Fortress Press, 1993), 110.

17. Holmes Rolston, III, *Philosophy Gone Wild* (Buffalo: Prometheus Books, 1989), 19–20; also, idem., *Environmental Ethics* (Philadelphia: Temple University Press, 1988), 214–15, 231.

18. Rolston, *Philosophy Gone Wild,* 108–15, 127; Rolston, *Environmental Ethics,* 179–91.

19. William K. Frankena, *Ethics,* 2d ed. (Englewood Cliffs, N.J.: Prentice Hall, 1973), 98–102.

20. Jean Porter, *The Recovery of Virtue: The Relevance of Aquinas for Christian Ethics* (Louisville: Westminster/John Knox Press, 1990), 43.

21. Curran, *Living Tradition,* 185.

22. Gilkey, *Nature, Reality, and the Sacred,* 23. Jacques Maritain also nicely argues this point; see *Man and the State* (Chicago: University of Chicago Press, 1951), 87–88.

23. Richard M. Gula, "Natural Law Today," *Readings in Moral Theology,* ed. Curran and McCormick, 384.

24. Richard Dawkins, *The Selfish Gene* (Oxford: Oxford University Press, 1989), 9, 21, 111, 182. For a good collection on the debate concerning sociobiology, see *Issues in Evolutionary Ethics,* ed. Paul Thompson, (Albany: State University of New York Press, 1995). Also Howard L. Kaye, *The Social Meaning of Modern Biology* (New Haven: Yale University Press, 1986).

25. James Q. Wilson, *The Moral Sense* (New York: Free Press, 1993).

26. Edward Leroy Long, Jr., *A Survey of Recent Christian Ethics* (New York: Oxford University Press, 1982), 9. My mentors at Boston University called it "comprehensive coherence."

27. For example, Margaret Farley, "The Role of Experience in Moral Discernment," in *Christian Ethics: Problems and Prospects,* ed. Lisa Sowle Cahill and James F. Childress (Cleveland: Pilgrim Press, 1996), 135.

28. Gilkey, *Nature, Reality, and the Sacred,* 63, 74, 86.

29. Paul Taylor, *Respect for Nature: A Theory of Environmental Ethics* (Princeton: Princeton University Press, 1986), 65–68.

30. Daniel C. Maguire and A. Nicholas Fargnoli, *On Moral Grounds: The Art/Science of Ethics* (New York: Crossroad Press, 1991), 34–35, 94–95.

31. D. D. Williams, *The Spirit and the Forms of Love* (New York: Harper and Row, 1968), 276–300.

32. For much of Christian ethics, traditional concepts of biblical authority—such as the inherent power of a trustworthy witness to compel consistent and even uncritical assent—are dead from the overburden of a thousand qualifications. Perspectives on biblical authority tend now to be considerably ambivalent and diluted. The work of Bruce Birch and Larry Rasmussen is representative of this widespread viewpoint in the discipline. While the Bible is a unique witness to God, who can still speak through it, they argue, its authority is not absolute, exclusive, or self-sufficient. "Christian ethics is not synonymous with biblical ethics." They deny all forms of textual inerrancy or inspiration and the prescriptive use of scriptural rules to settle moral disputes; they recognize the moral pluralism and moral faults in scripture. It is a "source of life and death, liberation and oppression, hope and despair." The Bible functions "more as exemplary guidance than comprehensive instruction." Bruce C. Birch and Larry L. Rasmussen, *Bible and Ethics in the Christian Life,* rev. ed. (Minneapolis: Augsburg, 1989), 11, 13, 143, 149–53, 175. Birch and Rasmussen express what Allen Verhey describes as a consensus among Christian ethicists on scripture: It includes not only a recognition of the moral diversity in the Bible, but also a rejection of the prescriptive use of scripture in moral judgment. "Scripture and Ethics: Practices, Performances, and Prescriptions," in *Christian Ethics,* ed. Cahill and Childress, 21.

33. Thomas Aquinas *Summa Theologiae* 1.2.91.2

34. Hans Küng, *Global Responsibility: In Search of a New World Ethics* (New York: Crossroad Press, 1991), 90–91.

35. Brian Hebblethwaite, *Christian Ethics in the Modern Age* (Philadelphia: Westminster Press, 1982), 113.

36. Richard M. McCormick, "Does Religious Faith Add to Ethical Perception?" in *Introduction to Christian Ethics: A Reader,* ed. Ronald P. Hamel and Kenneth R. Hines (New York: Paulist Press, 1989), 140.

37. Ibid., 140–45. Cf. Curran, *Living Tradition,* 175.

38. Stanley Hauerwas, *Community of Character* (Notre Dame: University of Notre Dame Press, 1981), 12, 49, 86. This vision is grounded on romantic illusions about the church and explicitly negative views of government.

39. Richard John Neuhaus, *America against Itself: Moral Vision and the Public Order* (Notre Dame: University of Notre Dame Press, 1992).

40. John Paul II, *On Social Concern* [*Sollicitudo Rei Socialis*] (Vatican City: Libreria Editrice Vaticana, 1987), 26, 38–39.

41. Küng, *Global Responsibility,* xv, 68–69. On some strategies and dilemmas, see Cristina L. H. Traina, "Creating a Global Discourse in a Pluralist World: Strategies from Environmental Ethics," in *Christian Ethics,* ed. Cahill and Childress, 250–64.

42. Alasdair C. MacIntyre, *Whose Justice? Which Rationality?* (Notre Dame: University of Notre Dame Press, 1988), 1–11, 389–403.

43. Timothy E. O'Connell, *Principles for a Catholic Morality* (New York: Seabury Press, 1978), 177.

44. Thomas Aquinas *Summa Theologiae* 1.2.94.2.

45. Maguire and Fargnoli, *On Moral Grounds,* 9–11, 19–20, 89–94.

46. Maritain, *Man and the State,* 90.

47. Thomas Aquinas *Summa Theologiae* 1.2.94.2.

48. Murray, "The Doctrine Lives," 219.

49. John Macquarrie, "Rethinking Natural Law," in *Readings in Moral Theology,* ed. Curran and McCormick, 239–40.

50. On rights in the common good, see John Finnis, *Natural Law and Natural Rights* (Oxford: Clarendon Press, 1980), 154–56, 214–18. On the symphonic or coherent organization of values and moral claims, in contrast to a scale, see Peter A. Bertocci and Richard M. Millard, *Personality and the Good* (New York: David McKay, 1963), 356–58.

51. See my "Biotic Rights and Human Ecological Responsibilities," *Annual of the Society of Christian Ethics,* 1993: 137–62. For some proposals earlier in this century for the ecological reinterpretation of natural law, see Scott Buchanan, "Natural Law and Teleology," 140–53, and Robert Gordis, "Natural Law and Religion," 265–70, in John Cogley et al., *Natural Law and Modern Society* (Cleveland: World Publishing Co.), 1962.

52. Michael S. Northcutt, *The Environment and Christian Ethics* (Cambridge: Cambridge University Press, 1996), 248.

53. "On the Laws" [*de Legibus*], bk. 1, *Selected Works of Cicero* (Roslyn, N.Y.: Walter J. Black, 1948).

54. D. E. Luscombe and G. R. Evans, "The Twelfth Century Renaissance," in *The Cambridge History of Medieval Political Thought, c.350–c.1450,* ed. J. H. Burns (Cambridge: Cambridge University Press, 1988), 335–38.

55. Thomas Huxley, *Evolution and Ethics,* in *Issues in Evolutionary Ethics,* ed. Paul Thompson (Albany: State University of New York Press, 1995), 128–29.

56. Rolston, *Environmental Ethics,* xi, 3, 34–41.

57. Rosemary Radford Ruether, *Gaia and God: An Ecofeminist Theology of Earth Healing* (San Francisco: HarperSanFrancisco, 1992), 47, 256.

58. Larry L. Rasmussen, *Earth Community, Earth Ethics* (Maryknoll, N.Y.: Orbis Books, 1996), 113–14, 107–9, 344–48.

59. Herman E. Daly and John B. Cobb, Jr., *For the Common Good: Redirecting the Economy toward Community, the Environment, and a Sustainable Future* (Boston: Beacon Press, 1989), 38–60, 141–45, 368–69.

60. James Gustafson, *Ethics from a Theocentric Perspective,* vol. 1 (Chicago: University of Chicago Press, 1981), 242–46.

61. Paul Hawken, *The Ecology of Commerce: A Declaration of Sustainability* (New York: Harper Collins, 1993), 3, 15, 54, 68.

62. For example, see John Ryan, "Conserving Biological Diversity," 23, 25, and Alan Thein Durning and Holly B. Brough, "Reforming the Livestock Economy," 66–67, 74, 81, in *State of the World 1992* (New York: W. W. Norton, 1992). For a valuable overview of the theory and applications, see Janine M. Benyus, *Biomimicry: Innovation Inspired by Nature* (New York: William Morrow, 1997).

63. E. F. Schumacher, *Small Is Beautiful* (New York: Harper and Row, 1973).

64. Robert Leo Smith, *Elements of Ecology,* 3d ed. (New York: Harper Collins, 1992).

Response to James A. Nash

CRISTINA L. H. TRAINA

James Nash has reminded us of the impossibly diverse approaches that go by the name "natural law." But he has also implied that one of these approaches promises to be the most coherent, compelling, and fruitful for ecological ethics: the Thomistic theological tradition. In unfolding this tradition of natural law, Nash has also diverted us from common misinterpretations, warned us of its flaws, and even suggested how we should correct them in light of critical Protestant reflection about what counts as legitimate authority. What remains is to reiterate the theological character of natural law—a crucial point for its most faithful contemporary revivers—and to expand on its special strengths and weaknesses as a foundation for ecological ethics.

Theological natural law is not simply the deterministic "law of nature" of reductionist sociobiology. Nor is it universal, objective Kantian duty. Rather, natural law is about ends; it is a human corollary of the principle that every being seeks its own perfection within an interdependent cosmos. Natural law is human, self-conscious participation in this divine comprehensive plan. Thus, it directs human beings to the same sorts of ends as other members of the natural world—for instance, physical and communal flourishing—but it also distinguishes human beings from these other members by steering us to the transcendent, eschatological perfection of love and knowledge. Natural law, in its most practical sense, is about fulfilling temporal ends in a way that coheres with transcendent ends. This project in turn entails recognizing flourishing and understanding how to accomplish it. Thus, natural law—human reason—subsists in delicate relationship with the laws of nature—the physical workings of beings and systems that must be respected for the sake of flourishing.

This connection among transcendent and practical ends and the given structures of earthly existence grounds both the distinct advantages and the possibly problematic character of a natural law ecological ethic. In what follows I will elaborate on additional advantages that contemporary ecological ethicists have seen in this connection, issue a theological warning, and point to a likely way of overcoming danger.

Advantages of Natural Law Approaches

To the same degree that natural law touts human capacities for the creative transformation of the world and ourselves, it respects the limits that our given, physical existence and our transcendent ends place on that transformation. As William French pointed out nearly ten years ago, ecological ethics cannot live happily with utter social constructionism, the belief that human beings in society "create" their bodies and their environments utterly freely and arbitrarily.[1] The inspiration for ecological ethics is that there exist " 'natural laws' that we disobey at our peril."[2] But a theological ecological ethic cannot accept the almost complete sociobiological determinism of an Edward O. Wilson, in whose view people are "predisposed biologically to make certain choices," so that "*ought* is the product of a material process" and religion arises "on a foundation of ethics" and in response to genetically generated needs for transcendence or desires for sacred narratives.[3] Theological ethics sees evolution as the purposeful creation of a benevolent God, and not the reverse.

The natural law tradition provides a middle path: we use our reason and creativity to shape ourselves and our surroundings within the physical limits (and according to the social possibilities) that they present to us,[4] as well as within the transcendent bounds of our ultimate telos, which we find in revelation. Certainly there can be argument over the span of these limits—say, of the appropriate characteristics of flourishing. But the point is that only from a strong common appreciation for givenness, with its ranges of possibility and its trajectories toward fulfillment, can one being make credible moral claims on other beings.

Second, environmental ethics has frequently been hamstrung by debates over which moral standpoint should anchor the conversation (animal rights, species preservation, ecosystematic balance for its own sake, or ecosystematic balance for the sake of human flourishing) and over what degree of commitment is necessary (conservation within an existing life-style versus radical social and economic transformation). Just as problematic as these impasses are authors and activists who either combine these rhetorics without acknowledging tensions among them or falsely treat them as mutually exclusive. As Drew Christiansen has pointed out, natural law thought has something to teach us here: the prudent, self-conscious, and appropriate use of multiple strategies.

For instance, there may need to be a distinction between the minimal precepts of ecological justice that everyone must fulfill and the ecological counsels of perfection embraced by deep ecology. The latter keep an inspiring, prophetic ideal before everyone but demand a level of commitment not to be expected of people for whom the goal of living as lightly as possible on the earth may need to give way slightly to other ends like basic survival or a vocation of service to others.[5] Similarly, all must adhere to public standards of justice, but there is also the order of charity in which I and those closest to me deserve my special consideration; global thinking must never preclude local action. Likewise, self-sacrifice, even martyrdom, commands a high value, but self-preservation is a basic and appropriate human inclination. Each of these rational impulses contains an invaluable insight, but none is, in practice, adequate in itself.[6] It would thus be inappropriate either to reduce the natural law tradition to any one of these elements or to minimize the potential for conflict between them. Rather, the point is to use measures of justice and urgency to blend them in different proportions in diverse situations, depending upon what is at stake, in light of the supreme criterion of charity.

In addition, ecological language about "webs" and "interdependence" would benefit from more theoretical precision. Christiansen, Christine Firer Hinze, and French have all pointed out that the natural law tradition has a theory and ethic of interdependence ready for the taking: the common good.[7] The doctrine of the common good holds that many goods essential to integral human flourishing are goods that can be accomplished only collectively, that benefit the whole society when they are in place, to which everyone has a duty to contribute, that everyone has a right to enjoy, and whose damage deserves correction—coercive, if necessary. Classically, the common good is a human good, the product of human rational activity. But because ecosystematic flourishing too requires cooperative effort and benefits all, it makes some sense to extend the image of the common good analogically to the whole biosphere. For instance, climate is corporately generated and enjoyed (or suffered) by countless organisms. Here, the common good receives some help from the expansive image of the Great Chain of Being, which, as French notes, "leads Thomas to highlight continuities and linkages throughout a conjoined cosmos pulsing with life and sustained by God's energy and love";[8] in fact Thomas Aquinas "suggests that the highest good is 'the perfection of the universe.'"[9]

The doctrine of the common good does present one invidious obstacle: Thomas Aquinas took for granted hierarchical social arrangements in which burdens and benefits were not equally shared but were distributed according to gender and social standing. Among human beings, at least, we can aim for a leveling of sacrifices and benefits. But humans—and indeed all other organisms—survive by eating some organisms and restricting others.[10] And although in this historical moment rational human use of resources is essential to ecosystematic survival, humans as a species are not; we cannot justify our existence by arguing that the ecosystem "needs" us. For both these reasons, moral arguments for our own survival and flourishing depend upon some other justification than equality of creatures or physical ecosystematic flourishing.[11]

Finally, in an era of renewed concern for the ethics of virtue, the apparently consequentialist tendency of ecological ethics runs against the grain. The particular advantage of the natural law tradition is its ability to unite character and consequences. According to the natural law theological tradition, a person's temporal goals include physical well-being, on the one hand, and natural or acquired virtue (disciplined habits of rational thought and action), on the other. Yet, because virtue is telic—it conduces to well-being, even perfection— these two temporal ends are interdependent. Infused or theological virtue in turn is the keystone between an individual's transcendent end in God and her efforts toward temporal well-being for herself and others. Grace, through charity, lifts, transforms, and perfects natural virtue rather than eradicating it. So the individual's graced journey toward God, her temporal ends, and her advancement of the common good are not merely coherent but entail each other.

James Nash's articulation of the ecological virtues in particular invites conversation with this vision of the virtues. To begin with, in the natural law tradition the virtue of justice is a habit of *actual* right relations with others; that is to say, a person falls short of true virtue *if* she is not in fact fair and respectful toward others and their goods. In addition, as Jean Porter has pointed out, for Thomas Aquinas intrinsically evil acts are simply another name for acts of injustice, or wrong relations.[12] If the virtue of justice can be extended analogically to "otherbeings" or to the global ecosystem, Nash's virtues—with their double telic and habitual reference—will fall under it: sustainability, adaptability, relationality, frugality, equity, solidarity, biodiversity, sufficiency, and humility.[13] To be a person of virtue would be to act justly within the global ecosystem, not merely toward other human beings.

A Difficulty and a Solution

Adding these advantages to those James Nash has already articulated in this volume makes palpable the power of a critically retrieved version of natural law to illumine the theological and moral meaning of our power over global ecology. But, as the "if" in the preceding paragraph reminds us, when we try to articulate these suggestions with greater theoretical precision we come to a theological crossroad that we cannot pass through without further, deeper, more difficult conversation. Embodiment, as Nash rightly points out, is one candidate for such a discussion, for the "disembodiment" of recent moral theology and revisionism is a genuine historical liability. Yet, I believe this is an intersection through which we have already begun to pass, for scholars have made significant recent headway in the "reembodiment" of natural law moral thought; recent works on the sexed and social body, sociobiology, and epistemology represent only a small sampling of efforts to update and clarify this connection.[14]

The real challenge, as I see it, also begins as a question for theological anthropology, but it cuts much deeper. It is the existential chasm that, according to the natural law tradition, divides us from all other creatures, a chasm that exists despite the similarities in our inclinations and in the requirements of our physical flourishing. Thomas points out that, unlike other creatures, we also and ultimately aspire to an intellectual and eschatological fulfillment: the beatific vision. And, unlike other creatures, we are "imprinted" with the natural law. That is, we participate consciously and reflectively in divine reason, in the eternal law, God's plan for the cosmos. This participation—this exclusive ability to act consciously and reflectively for ends, as God does—is the substance of the natural law, and also of the *imago Dei* (the image of God) in human beings. And it is this rational conception of the *imago Dei,* not any general claim about creation or creaturehood, on which the twentieth-century natural law doctrine of human dignity and human rights rests. In sum, although all existents (even rocks, in a sense) have inclinations, only we have the natural law. And because we are also the only ones with transcendent ends, in cases of conflict our transcendent ends trump all natural ends, our own and others'.

These beliefs create a few sticky problems even for anthropocentric theology—how we think of children before the age of reason, or of retarded adults, or "irrational" women—but these can be solved without too many anthropological gyrations. The real difficulties arise when we begin to think of "otherbeings" as subjects—if not as full moral subjects exactly, at least as makers of moral claims or in some sense possessors of dignity or rights. Surely we can all tell stories of "intelligent" mammals who have "virtues" and "vices" and "choose" ends—not just with respect to us but with respect to other animals as well.[15] What is their theological standing? What is their ultimate good? What sort of weight do their experiences (not communicable to us) and their ends have in our moral deliberation? Are there only two theologically significant classes—human and nonhuman— or is there a continuum? And if the latter, how do we explain it theologically? As Thomas Berry and Elizabeth Johnson argue so eloquently and enthusiastically in this volume, we would have to alter entirely our doctrine of God, our soteriology, our anthropology, our doctrine of the *imago Dei,* and our metaphysics in order to accommodate this transformation of perspectives.[16]

We can get a sense of the profundity of this challenge by framing it another way. When Sir Isaac Newton measured the behavior of objects in motion he came up with simple and straightforward relations, like $d = vt$ and $f = ma$. A few centuries later, Albert Einstein noticed that when velocity approaches the speed of light, none of these simple relations of force, mass, time, and distance quite holds—in fact, Newton's simple equations turn out to be special cases of the more complex formulae of relativity theory, valid only when velocities are so low that the effects of relativity are negligible.

The question we need to answer is whether natural law really is a guide for all time, already possessing the ethical concepts and theological justifications we need to handle the challenge of life on Earth, needing only to be refined and extrapolated in light of new knowledge. Perhaps historical natural law thought is actually like Newtonian mechanics: a special, simplified mode of discerning justice and right among human beings, a method of reasoning that works when "all other things are equal," and animals, plants, and eco-systems drop out of the equation. If so, we face the daunting task of developing our own equivalent of the theory of relativity, of discover-ing the general standard of relations between beings of which the natural law tradition of ethics is only a special case. But if we did, would we also erode natural law theology's advantages for ecological ethics? This is the real challenge of offering a critically retrieved ver-sion of natural law as the basis for environmental ethics.

The work of Daniel Cowdin begins to dissolve the dilemma. Cowdin, like French, points out that the similarity and interdepen-dence of human beings with other organisms and systems is still not an identity: nature is neither "a mere 'thing'" nor something we should treat "like we treat each other."[17] Rather, our responsibility is to understand the places of human beings and all other systems and entities within the global ecosystem and then to "fit into its basic di-rectionality and order,"[18] in short, to "subordinate ourselves to a wider moral reality" than the human.[19] The human mandate is "to be *human in nature*," rationally to understand and "respect everything for what it most fully is and treat it as far as possible in accordance with that perception."[20] Then, as Cowdin suggests, "nonpersons warrant moral consideration *as nonpersons* by persons" analogically, in "a frame-work appropriate to them";[21] "human dignity thus becomes one in-stance of this overarching imperative," and yet a peculiar and distinct one.[22]

Finally, I close these reflections with the hope that proponents of biblically based environmental ethics will take seriously the natural law arguments of James Nash and the other authors cited in these comments. Nash's frustration with scripturally grounded ecological ethics is as genuine as his relief at finding a Christian moral language that can be employed and understood in secular circles. But neither sentiment should obscure the fact that natural law is a theological tradition firmly grounded in scripture. For Nash as for Thomas Aquinas, "reason and revelation are not alternatives"; they are compatible foundations for ecological ethics, inadequate on their own but indomitable when paired.[23]

Notes

1. William C. French, "Ecological Concern and the Anti-Foundationalist Debates: James Gustafson on Biospheric Constraints," in *The Annual of the Society of Christian Ethics, 1989,* ed. D. M. Yeager (Washington, D.C.: Georgetown University Press, 1989), 113–30; and idem, "Subject-Centered and Creation-Centered Paradigms in Recent Catholic Thought," *Journal of Religion* 70 (1990): 48–72. For more comprehensive references to treatments of the following themes in Thomas Aquinas's *Summa Theologiae* see Cristina L. H. Traina, *Feminist Ethics and Natural Law: The End of the Anathemas* (Washington, D.C.: Georgetown University Press, 1999), chapter 2.

2. French, "Paradigms," 72.

3. Edward O. Wilson, "The Biological Basis of Morality," *Atlantic* 281, no. 4 (April 1998): 53–70, at 58, 65, and 70. Italics in original.

4. Daniel M. Cowdin, "Toward an Environmental Ethic," in *Preserving the Creation: Environmental Theology and Ethics,* ed. Kevin W. Irwin and Edmund D. Pellegrino (Washington, D.C.: Georgetown University Press, 1994), 127; and Cristina L. H. Traina, "Creating a Global Discourse in a Pluralist World: Strategies from Environmental Ethics," in *Christian Ethics: Problems and Prospects,* ed. Lisa Sowle Cahill and James F. Childress (Cleveland: Pilgrim Press, 1996), 260. See also James A. Nash, *Loving Nature: Ecological Integrity and Christian Responsibility* (Nashville: Abingdon Press, 1991), 63.

5. Drew Christiansen, "Ecology and the Common Good: Catholic Social Teaching and Environmental Responsibility," in *"And God Saw that It Was Good": Catholic Theology and the Environment,* ed. Drew Christiansen and Walter Grazer (Washington, D.C.: United States Catholic Conference, 1996), 192–93.

6. See, for example, James M. Gustafson, *Varieties of Moral Discourse: Prophetic, Narrative, Ethical, and Policy,* The Stob Lectures of Calvin College and Seminary, 1987–88 (Grand Rapids, Mich.: Calvin College and Seminary, 1988).

7. Christiansen, "Ecology and the Common Good"; Christine Firer Hinze, "Catholic Social Teaching and Ecological Ethics," in *"And God Saw That It Was Good,"* ed. Christiansen and Grazer, 165–82; William C. French, "Beast-Machines and the Reduction of Life: A Creation-Centered Perspective," in *Good News for Animals? Christian Approaches to Animal Well-Being,* ed. Charles Pinches and Jay B. McDaniel, Ecology and Justice Series (Maryknoll, N.Y.: Orbis Books, 1993), 39. Rosemary Radford Ruether makes implicit use of this doctrine; see Cristina L. H. Traina, "An Argument for Christian Ecofeminism," review of *Gaia and God: An Ecofeminist Theology of Earth Healing,* by Rosemary Radford Ruether, *Christian Century* 10, no. 18 (June 2–9, 1993): 600–603.

8. French, "Beast-Machines," 37.

9. French, "Paradigms," 71; French cites Thomas Aquinas *Summa Theologiae* 1.22.4 and 1.47.1.

10. See, e.g., Cowdin, "Toward an Environmental Ethic," 117.

11. See Daniel Cowdin, "Toward an Environmental Ethic," and "The Moral Status of Otherkind in Christian Ethics," in this volume.

12. Jean Porter, *The Recovery of Virtue: The Relevance of Aquinas for Christian Ethics* (Louisville: Westminster/John Knox Press, 1990), 141–43.

13. Nash, *Loving Nature,* 63–67.

14. See, respectively, Lisa Sowle Cahill, *Sex, Gender, and Christian Ethics,* New Studies in Christian Ethics (Cambridge: Cambridge University Press, 1996); Stephen J. Pope, *The Evolution of Altruism and the Ordering of Love,* Moral Traditions and Moral Arguments (Washington, D.C.: Georgetown University Press, 1994); and Daniel Westberg, *Right Practical Reason: Aristotle, Action, and Prudence in Aquinas* (Oxford: Clarendon Press, 1994).

15. See also French, "Beast-Machines," 33.

16. See also Michael S. Northcott, *The Environment and Christian Ethics,* New Studies in Christian Ethics (Cambridge: Cambridge University Press, 1996), 266–67.

17. Cowdin, "Toward an Environmental Ethic," 119.

18. Ibid., 124.

19. Cowdin, "The Moral Status of Otherkind," 285.

20. Cowdin, "Toward an Environmental Ethic," 134, 131.

21. Cowdin, "The Moral Status of Otherkind," 263.

22. Cowdin, "Toward an Environmental Ethic," 132.

23. James A. Nash, "Seeking Moral Norms in Nature: Natural Law and Ecological Responsibility," in this volume, 237. On the inadequacy of reason, see Drew Christiansen, "Nature's God and the God of Love," in *Preserving the Creation,* ed. Irwin and Pellegrino, 148–53.

The Moral Status of
Otherkind in Christian Ethics

DANIEL COWDIN

The problem, and necessary challenge, is how to theologize Aldo Leopold.[1] His land ethic is one modern source, along with Albert Schweitzer's reverence for life and originally utilitarian concern for animal sentience, of what I will term the moral status question.[2] The question is relatively straightforward. Does otherkind (meaning the nonhuman realm) call forth from us a moral response? Is our behavior in relation to otherkind in itself subject to moral evaluation, that is to say, judgments of right and wrong, justice and injustice, virtue and vice? If so, on what basis? Which members, levels, or dimensions of otherkind, and what about them, call forth such a response? And what sort of moral language best articulates it? Moreover, should there be just one or a diversity of approaches? Or, in the end, is the attempt to attribute a moral status to otherkind a mistake?

The Philosophical State of the Question: Recalcitrant Humanism

The question of the extent to which humans should give moral consideration to the health of ecosytems and to other species and their members has received a good deal of attention in the last twenty years from moral philosophers.[3] I am persuaded by the overall dynamic of that conversation not only that some form of moral status for otherkind is required, but that the shape of the question itself is morally significant. Some philosophers argue that the attribution of moral status to nonhumans remains an absurdity, an ultimately unnecessary and misguided abuse of language. Luc Ferry levels this critique in *The New Ecological Order* from the standpoint of his nonmetaphysical humanism.[4] His overall project is to defend a critical version of modern society, which pits him against deep ecologists whose project he sees as fundamentally (and fundamentalistically) opposed to modernity. Ferry believes that concern for otherkind can adequately and coherently be addressed within a sensitive yet unabashedly anthropocentric framework.[5]

He offers a new, dual typology of radical ecology. The first strain is a nostalgic rejection of modernity in favor of the past, advocating a recovery of traditional life-styles. It is a right-leaning antimodernism reminiscent of fascism. The second strain is a utopian rejection of modernity in favor of a new future, advocating revolutionary new experiments in eco-integrated life-styles. It is a left-leaning antimodernism reminiscent of socialism. In spite of his sometimes off-putting polemics, his approach has an illuminative power at the broad level of political ideology. One cannot read the two most substantial recent contributions in Christian ethics (Michael Northcott[6] and Larry Rasmussen,[7] respectively) without being struck by how closely they fit his typology. Northcott is strikingly premodern, while Rasmussen is strikingly post-; yet large stretches of their respective social-political-economic critiques are almost identical. Radical ecology has become a kind of velcro onto which both "traditionalists" and "progressives" can adhere (particularly in the absence of other alternatives), the commonality being the judgment that "anthropocentrist modernity is a total disaster."[8]

Within this overall project, Ferry attacks the philosophical attempt to forge a nonanthropocentric ethic. He portrays such attempts as ultimately applying the status of "legal subject" to otherkind, by which he means the capacity of entering into reciprocal contracts and/or the possession of "absolute value in and of itself."[9] The attribution of legal subject status to nonhumans, however, is both false and a performative contradiction. It is false because animals, much less insects and trees, simply cannot be treated as subjects in any moral-legal sense without reverting to unsubstantiated metaphysical assertions such as those underpinning medieval animal trials. It is a performative contradiction, because the claim itself is contradicted by the very conditions of its enunciation. Since "all valorization, including that of nature, is the deed of man . . . all normative ethics is in some sense humanist and anthropocentrist." Because it is we, "as human beings, who value nature, and not the reverse . . . it is impossible to disregard this subjective or humanist moment and project into the universe itself an 'intrinsic value.'"[10]

There is in this, I think, a deep conceptual confusion which conflates moral capacity with the object of moral concern. On what basis does Ferry assume that morality's focus can only be self-referential, that is to say, can only be moral agency itself? Within the moral status discussion the argument has been that our moral capacity is capable of valuing things outside itself. Not all moral patients— objects of moral considerability—need be moral agents.[11] As Holmes Rolston, III, puts it: "Man may be (in some advanced senses) the only *measurer* of things, but it does not follow that man is the only *measure* of things."[12]

Similarly, Christopher Stone argues that otherkind's "considerate-ness is in doubt only if we suppose that the moral fabric that connects us with them has to be embroidered with the same governance that embroiders our relations among ourselves, as Persons."[13] But that it has to be so is far from self-evident. The point is not to force non-persons into a persons framework (by construing them as subjects, for instance), but to explore whether nonpersons warrant moral consider-ation *as nonpersons* by persons, thus having a framework appropriate to them.

In the end Ferry does not want to disregard otherkind. "[W]e cannot entirely dismiss our impression that nature possesses a certain value *in and of itself.* . . . This 'lived experience' seems immediate, independent, at least, of our goals."[14] He acknowledges that higher animals seem to belong to an order different from plants and stones, not human but still capable of some goals, of suffering, and even a degree of freedom analogous to ours. He also acknowledges the "finality" and beauty of nature. "We, therefore, must do justice to the feeling that nature is not devoid of value, that we have duties toward it, though it is not, for all that, a legal subject."[15] Ferry proposes find-ing a path that is neither Cartesian dualism nor radical ecology as he has portrayed it.

But again, the lack of real contact between Ferry's analysis and the moral status question in recent analytic moral philosophy becomes clear. For it has been precisely the task of philosophers wrestling with the question for the past several decades to find just such a path. Leopold knew full well that the passenger pigeons would not have mourned us had we become extinct first, and never sought to attribute to them (or any other nonhuman) the status of legal subject as Ferry construes it.[16] Nor have many (any?) of the major environmental ethicists or animal welfare theorists of recent note taken the legal subject route.[17] There is a spectrum between treating otherkind as persons on the one hand and with no moral consideration whatsoever on the other. The majority of reflection on moral status in the past several decades has taken place within that spectrum, without appealing to unverifiable metaphysical qualities.

Moreover, ecosystemic thinkers like Leopold, Rolston, and Stone, as well as most animal welfare philosophers, believe that their task "need not refute and displace rivals that govern interpersonal behavior."[18] As a result, the relationship between democratic humanism and moral status for otherkind has remained (not without criticism) an open one for such thinkers. I would argue, then, that Ferry leaves off quite close to where the moral status conversation began decades ago, a conversation his overly broad analysis, reacting primarily to continental philosophy, has failed to engage. Ferry's concern for animal characteristics "analogous" to human qualities seems hardly different operationally from a prima facie respect for animals as such.

The moral status question expands ethical conversation beyond a strictly humanist perspective. Humanism nevertheless makes an appropriately serious demand, forcing claims of moral status to be well-defined and sensible. It protects us from conceptual absurdity and the political specter of ecofascism. But a solely humanistic approach, even if stretched and kneaded, "has in some ways lost contact with the predicaments we are interested in resolving" at this point in history.[19]

The Theological State of the Question

What is noteworthy, but perhaps in retrospect not surprising, is how much Christianity has had to say to this question and in how many different ways. The moral status of otherkind is tied into the entire theological meaning of creation. A seemingly discrete and precise question thus brings with it a vast history of reflection about one of the foundational topics of Christian theology.

There seems to be scholarly consensus at this point on two aspects of the question. First, theologically positive views of creation lie deep in the tradition, beginning with the Hebrew affirmations in Genesis 1 and continuing through Wisdom, covenantal, and prophetic sources. Although the New Testament is at times ambiguous in this regard, the first few centuries of Christian existence involved a theological struggle to reaffirm the basic goodness of creation. Against various dualisms, patristic theologians defended "the material realm as an expression of God's creative and redemptive purposes" and thus "fundamental to the whole structure of Christian moral teaching."[20] This affirmation continued into and through the Middle Ages as part of what Louis Dupré has termed an "ontotheological synthesis," which began to break down in the face of late medieval nominalist and voluntarist influences.[21]

Insofar as Western culture generally and Christianity in particular bear a "huge burden of guilt" for the ecological crisis, the locus of such blame exists more in the early modern thought of Descartes, Newton, and Bacon, as well as in the rise of industrial capitalism, than in the core affirmations of traditional Christianity. Descartes's mind-body dualism, Newton's inert mechanistic view of the physical world, and Bacon's manipulative scientific domination of nature all combined to form the uniquely modern view of nonhuman nature as simply a valueless field to be exploited for human benefit.[22] Industrial capitalism alienated individuals from traditional communities, and both from the land.[23] Deep Christian resources have been accessed to criticize these phenomena as divergent from rather than an expression of traditional Christianity.

Second, however, the precise question of moral status seems far less solidly grounded. Even Thomas Aquinas failed to attribute direct moral status for otherkind in his otherwise theologically positive view of the created order. For Aquinas, "animals are irrational. . . . [T]hey exist to serve human ends by virtue of their nature and by divine providence. . . . [T]hey therefore have no moral status in themselves save in so far as some human interest is involved. . . ."[24] Moreover, the affirmations of such status that do exist in Christian history have been fragmentary, minority viewpoints, and at times shot through with other religious themes such that the moral status question itself was obscured. James Nash's account of the Desert Fathers, Celtic saints, and monasticism bears this out.[25] Nash is therefore correct to construe the question as calling for an extension of the tradition rather than the recovery of a directly applicable, previously mainstream view.

Not surprisingly, the various Christian traditions are today employing their historically particular approaches to creation in an attempt to address this question. In Orthodox approaches, for example, environmental concerns revive the micro/macrocosm imagery of patristic theology, in which human beings reflect the entire world and the Incarnation therefore links Christ to the whole of creation.[26] Some Roman Catholics and Anglicans attempt to "repristinate" natural law[27] while others explore sacramental approaches to the universe,[28] and some combine both. Those rooted in Calvinism have developed theocentric approaches revolving around the sovereignty of God and the divine purposiveness that can be gleaned from the created order.[29] Other Protestants depend primarily on the scriptural witness as the source for establishing respect for creation, which of course becomes a multifaceted project given the pluralism of biblical context and authorship.[30]

In many of these tradition-extending approaches, however, the specific question of moral status is elusive, tucked within complex symbolic folds, or insufficiently addressed at all. For example, a micro/macrocosm approach, while certainly establishing a profound connection between God Incarnate, humans, and the created order, leaves questions as to the independent moral status of that order.[31] Sacramental approaches view the creation as mediating God's self-manifestation, but this manifestation seems general and diffuse, leaving questions of more particularized moral discrimination within creation unaddressed.[32] A radically theocentric approach stresses fitting into God's broad purposes so strongly that questions are raised about the moral status of anything, human or nonhuman, in this view. The danger is that the created order (humanity included) essentially becomes diaphonous, not really able to carry moral claims in itself. Direct scriptural appeals, for their part, do indicate some sort of specific moral status, but tend to provide at best very generalized moral direction. W. Sibley Towner, for example, proposes a biblically based moral imperative for "a functional, modest, loving relationship with nature that prefigures the way it will be in God's new age . . . a style of ethical living in the present that is holistic, interdependent, non-hierarchical, and one that does not reject flesh and matter as corrupt because God does not reject them."[33]

Nevertheless, most traditional approaches are capable of embedding direct moral status for otherkind, providing a religious background within which such claims would fit, even if the background itself does not fully specify them. They in effect provide a symbolic habitat within which more discriminate ethical speciation can occur.

The question quickly becomes more complex as various traditional bents intersect with particular contemporary methodologies, theological commitments, and ideological frameworks. Here, process,[34] eschatological,[35] and feminist[36] theologians work through the question across denominational lines. As with the various traditional approaches, most are capable of embedding first-order moral status within the general background of their methodology, though the specific question of moral status can be elusive in these cases as well.[37]

Additional levels to the question emerge with direct appeals to philosophical, scientific, and experiential sources (the "much living in and with" that Leopold insisted was necessary).[38] Scientific understandings of the natural world shift, as do approaches in moral philosophy and epistemology. Moreover, experience of nature is mediated through culture, itself a dynamic reality.[39] Yet, any account of moral status cannot bypass these realms and still remain fully credible.

The theological response to the moral status question thus becomes kaleidoscopic. Different combinations of traditional commitments, theological methods, and scientific-philosophical-experiential engagement will yield varying patterns of human-otherkind relationship. This in turn raises the question whether the tradition itself, more generally understood, grounds and sets boundaries to the play of various patterns. Can a foundational affirmation of the moral status of otherkind be attributed to Christianity generally such that all other more particularized approaches would be judged by it?

This, I take it, is the force of James Nash's widely successful book *Loving Nature*. In 1967, historian Lynn White indicted the Christian tradition as such, charging it with "a huge burden of guilt" for espousing an ensemble of ultimately creation-disregarding beliefs: God is not nature, only humans are in the image of God, creation exists for the sake of humans and nothing else.[40] For a Christian, argued White, nonhuman nature "can be no more than a physical fact," with no intrinsic moral or religious significance except insofar as it can be used for our benefit.[41] In 1991, Nash defended Christian faith against White's portrait of it. The moral status of nature can and must be seen to dwell at the very heart of Christianity, he argues, beneath all particular methodological and traditional approaches. "The faith contains all things necessary, all the values and virtues, for ecological integrity. Indeed, nothing short of that integrity is compatible . . . with authentic representations of the Christian faith."[42] In successfully showing the depth and breadth of the tradition concerning creation, and the possibilities of extending it to more contemporary circumstances, Nash makes a strong case that there is an ecumenical bottom line to this question. If Nash is correct, the kaleidoscopic designs can and ought to occur within the traditional theological boundary of a loving Creator who values the creation, who charges human beings to do the same, and who promises to retain, even if transformed, all that is lovingly valued.[43]

The Individual versus the System: A Theological Problem

The moral status question has been explored along a spectrum ranging from individual organisms as exclusively considerable, on the one side, to species, ecosystems, and natural processes as exclusively considerable, on the other. Animal welfare as well as broader reverence for life approaches fall on the individualistic side of the spectrum, while a land ethic approach falls on the systemic side. A variety of philosophical and scientific considerations can tilt thinkers toward one side or the other, and some of those will be briefly indicated in what follows. My own position is that these considerations lean significantly, though nonexclusively, toward the systemic side. That is to say, the moral status of otherkind should primarily be understood through a land ethic. Yet this poses a theological problem, for a land ethic rests far less easily within a framework of natural evil, cosmic redemption, and eschatological visions of nonpredatory peace than do more individualistic approaches. This section surveys several recently influential Christian approaches to the moral status question, starting on the individualistic end and working progressively toward the systemic, where a variety of theological options will be explored.

Andrew Linzey uses a provocative mix of Barthian and patristic theologies to construct his *Animal Theology,* which stands firmly on the individualistic side of the spectrum. His Barthian roots are evident in his rejection of any sort of natural theology: "there can be no straightforward moral or theological appeal to the way nature is. . . . [It] can in no way be an unambiguous referent to what God wills or plans for creation."[44] Remarking on Leopold's land ethic, he finds it "astonishing that contemporary eco-theologians should be so eager to incorporate this naturalistic principle into their systems."[45] As a corollary, he insists that purely philosophical animal rights approaches are insufficient.

A genuinely theological approach must be "grounded in the nature of God itself."[46] We know, through Revelation, that 1) creation exists for God; 2) God is for creation; 3) God's for-ness is dynamic, inspirational, and costly; and 4) we therefore must be for the creation. Linzey attributes "theos-rights" to animals, "by virtue of their Creator's right."[47] Since God's creation does not belong to us, we certainly have no rights over it.

What then is our role? The only right we have relative to animals is the right to serve them. And that service—indeed, that liberation—consists in freeing them from the suffering brought by the fall, which has encased the created world in bondage and decay. Here patristic and Orthodox leanings as to the importance of the Incarnation for the whole of creation emerge. Through the Incarnation, God enters into all suffering, including that of nonhuman creatures; and ultimately the cosmos as a whole will be redeemed from that suffering. The proper human role becomes one of priestly "participation in God's redeeming presence in the world."[48]

The moral implications of this are radical. It is not simply a matter of avoiding "needless" suffering when convenient. There is a Christian imperative for merciful and generous, at times even costly and sacrificial, action toward animals, on the model of the higher serving the lower. Linzey "rejects the idea that the rights and welfare of animals must always be subordinate to human interests, even when vital human interests are at stake."[49] We are to condescend, in effect, placing ourselves kenotically at the service of otherkind. Such action is a participation in the work of the Holy Spirit, partially but truly operative in creation. Linzey defends vegetarianism and the renunciation of all animal experimentation as a moral-theological witness to the order of redemption, in which life will no longer be parasitic on life.

The primary strength of Linzey's approach is its effectiveness in placing concern for animal sentience into a wider and transformative theological framework that is both scriptural and creedal. Although his theological methodology involves scholarly tensions, his substantive ethical position attains a powerfully coherent simplicity. Expressed narratively, one can understand animal suffering in terms of creation, sin, incarnation, and redemption. Creation was originally good and sentient life was not parasitic on other sentient life (Eden). After the Fall, enmity erupted between human- and otherkind, and all of life was put into the bondage of decay (humans and nonhumans groaning, in St. Paul's image, for release). God entered into this bondage through the Incarnation and suffers with all who suffer until the end of time. The Incarnation also decisively began the final process of salvation, which will ultimately eliminate suffering and death (lions laying with lambs), transforming the current disordered structure of the world. Christian action for animal welfare thus becomes a participation in the eschatological fulfillment that is not as yet fully realized. Suffering and death, then, are at odds with God's ultimate purpose for all creatures, and it is on that axis which Christian animal rights turn.

The drawback to this approach is that our contemporary understanding of nature as a whole, and current ecoevolutionary insight, seems to lack *moral* relevance. An animal-based or even a more broadly organismic approach to moral status tends to function independently of scientific perceptions of collectivities and systems. Yet, such perceptions impact our basic understanding of individual animals in the natural world.

Consider the swallows of western Nebraska, for example, through the eyes of biologist John Janovy: "There is no such thing as a single cliff swallow. The individual is subordinate to the colony, and it is the colony that grows, occupies the available space, and reproduces, amoebalike, new colonies. . . . The individual cliff swallow is the philosophical equivalent of a single cell of the multicellular colony-organism."[50] And the colony, in turn, is involved in a set of wider biotic relationships on which it depends. Consider in this regard the ecological state of a mountain devoid of wolves, as does Leopold in his famous essay "Thinking Like a Mountain."[51] Humans may fear wolves, but the mountain fears deer. This is anthropomorphizing, but tethered to scientific reality: no wolves means an explosion of deer, which in turn means a mountain that is eaten into biotic austerity.

Linzey and others on the individual side of the spectrum can concede that all of this is important and should be appreciated on many levels (scientific, instrumental, aesthetic), but the moral level is simply not one of them. The concrete problem with this response, however, is that exclusive moral concern for individual animals becomes incoherent at the level of land management. One thinks immediately of animal rights activists protesting the reduction of deer populations running ecologically rampant for lack of predators. Should the moral status question be broadened?

Enter Aldo Leopold who proposed just that, and in so doing did something genuinely new. He was a forester, but not confined to the anthropocentric conservationism of Gifford Pinchot. Leopold was a preservationist, but not simply a disciple of Muir; he valued the land as farmed as well as recreationally enjoyed (hunting and fishing). He drew from romanticism, transcendentalism, and Frederick Jackson Turner style nationalism, but he moved past them. He was an ecologist and founder of professional wildlife management. He understood land as biotic community, and humankind "as plain member and citizen" of that community.[52] This in itself was cutting edge at the time, but the truly new thing he did philosophically was to extend ethics into the relationship by giving land moral status.

The land ethic is a complex, critical, moral-scientific modern insight.[53] Land is understood not just as a collection of individual elements but as an ecological pyramid of interdependencies within a broader evolutionary process. Human beings are understood as essentially connected to the land, but unique within it: we are the only species which can value beings and systems beyond our own kind for their own sake. We not only need the land, but are capable of respecting it as such. Hence, a land ethic is both "an evolutionary possibility and an ecological necessity."[54]

A land ethic means that our use of the land in itself becomes subjected to moral analysis. Land has moral status; it is no longer simply "property." The criterion for judgment is whether our land use "tends to preserve the integrity, stability, and beauty of the biotic community" or the reverse.[55] One aspect of this is a scientific judgment of systemic health, understood as the capacity of the land for self-renewal, or its elasticity. This in turn is based on its diversity. The less diverse, the more fragile and hence unstable the pyramid of relationships, and the more constricted the energy flow.[56]

Leopold did not seek to include the land within our community of moral deliberation and reciprocal obligations; he sought to extend our moral deliberation and obligation to the land. He hoped for an ethical inclusion of the land into our assessment of the common good. The land ethic should be factored into our decision making along with other cultural pursuits, needs, and values. Leopold was painfully aware that gaining any space for the land as such in ethical and policy discussions would be a difficult task.

Under a land ethic, the moral status of otherkind, organismically considered, is subordinate to the overall functioning of the system. The moral assessment of a deer population must be embedded in a deeper concern for the underlying conditions that make the deer, as well as the diverse others in the ecosystem, possible in the first place. The normative implication, as Rolston and others have argued, is that "[n]o duty to sentient life overrides the carrying capacity of an ecosystem. . . ."[57]

Note that this does *not* preclude all sensitivity to individual organisms. Janovy is still careful not to kill birds recklessly, releasing those he can. Rolston still accords certain prima facie moral duties toward organisms, appreciating them for what they are. A thoughtful and coherent approach is possible between systemic and organismic approaches. Yet the scale of values is clear. "The appropriate unit for moral concern is the fundamental unit of development and survival."[58] The ethical apex when considering otherkind is what Rolston terms systemic value, which "is the productive process: its products are intrinsic values woven into instrumental relationships."[59]

Why not, then, a Christian land ethic, turning on the axis of systemic value? One could, at this point, press Linzey's incarnational immanentism against his Barthian theocentrism. If we are to respect, and even serve God's creation, why only the creatures and not the creation's operating principles? If Christ as Logos "inheres" in all creation, does not its ecoevolutionary process become a subject of legitimate theological respect? What makes its theological incorporation any more naturalistic, in the pejorative sense, than that of animal sentience?

The short answer, from a Linzeyan perspective, is that the eco-evolutionary system is comprised of suffering and death, from which

God has promised to free us (human and nonhuman). A land ethic thus presents Christianity with a problem, something of a theological knot. Those processes that from an ecoevolutionary perspective are necessary parts of the natural system are, from a theological perspective, precisely the dimensions of the world in need of redemption. The death and decay praised by a land ethic as recycling in service of homeostasis and equilibrium are castigated in traditional Christian theology as "bondage"; the predation and competition praised by a land ethic as relationships in service of fitness, adaptation, and speciation are construed in Christian theology as "groaning." If we reconceive our assessment of suffering and death, viewing them no longer as evils but as parts of God's good ecoevolutionary system, are we not (as Linzey would have it) naturalistically reconciling ourselves to huge portions of the world that traditionally we have seen God as freeing us from? Are we not prematurely reconciling ourselves to a world that has not yet fully been reconciled to God through Christ? Simply put, what of the eschatological vision of lions laying with lambs?

It is helpful to return to James Nash briefly to appreciate the depth of the problem. Nash includes both the individual and collective dimensions of otherkind in his approach, insisting that a rights ethic and a land ethic are complementary.[60] Yet, within this affirmation of collectivities lies a simultaneous moral rejection by Nash of the competitive systemic relationships Leopold respected. Natural "evil is an inherent part of the system," making "the classical theological propositions that the Creator and the creation are 'very good' . . . virtually indefensible . . . apart from an eschatological expectation."[61] This expectation must include cosmic rather than merely human redemption. "The key issue in [this] hope . . . is the moral character of God in relation to God's valuation of creatures as ends in themselves. . . ."[62] Death cannot be the final word without making creation itself tragic and God's character immoral.[63] Even if natural processes produce biological diversity amidst stability over time, they do so at great cost, and the Christian imagination hopes ultimately for another sort of system, and for redemption for all who have suffered through this one. How then can Christian ethics incorporate a land ethic?

Michael Northcott attempts a middle path, incorporating respect for ecosystems as well as individual organisms, but theologically endorsing the former only in their cooperative (rather than competitive) dimensions. He argues that "it is precisely the modern scientific method of empirical observation . . . which allows us to dare to believe that the non-human world . . . still contains within it marks of the moral order, as well as the physical design, of the creator God who first affirmed its goodness."[64] Within that order as it now stands are not only individual animals, each with a *telos,* but ecosystems as well. These have a certain *telos* of their own toward diversity, balance, cooperation, and beauty. We have, Northcott argues, "duties to the ecosystem which sustains life."[65] As the Hebrews extended the covenant to animals and the land, and as medieval natural law saw the wider world as a significant moral order, so contemporary Christians can and should relate to the ecoevolutionary earth.

There is, however, natural evil due to the Fall, which consists of predation and parasitism among living things. Northcott takes the eschatological image of lions laying with lambs realistically: noncooperative ecoevolutionary mechanisms must ultimately be redeemed. Here he sides with Irenaeus, who questioned whether the killing in nature was part of God's eternal intention, rather than with Aquinas, who accepted it for the sake of the whole.[66] Even so, Northcott retains an interim affirmation of the system in its positive dimensions, a system that will ultimately be vindicated by the Resurrection.[67]

One can ask, however, to what extent, or even whether, a land ethic has truly been incorporated into his Christian environmental ethic. Is "ecology" for Northcott really just a placeholder for relationality, which in turn is implicitly limited to the nonconflictual? Yet, as Leopold had it, the land's "competitions are as much a part of the inner workings as the cooperations,"[68] and therefore they must be respected—given moral status—in a land ethic. Empirically, conflictual processes are *intrinsically* related to the very natural order and its diverse products, which Northcott affirms. A scientifically based land ethic simply cannot detach one from the other. As Rolston urges: "Loving lions and hating jungles is misplaced affection. An ecologically informed society must love lions-in-jungles, organisms-in-ecosystems, or else fail in vision and courage."[69] Remarking directly on Northcott's work, Rolston wonders: "Perhaps [he] needs to take another look at these fierce dimensions of nature; they too may be among the primal elements loved by God."[70]

As stated at the outset, the problem and necessary challenge is how to theologize Aldo Leopold. There are of course more options than can be covered here, but three will be explored briefly. The first is to retain a theological framework of natural evil, cosmic redemption, and visions of nonpredatory peace, but to invoke a severe eschatological proviso with regard to our ecological behavior at present. James Nash takes this route, arguing that our Christian responsibility to otherkind "is to approximate the harmony of the New Creation to the fullest extent possible under the constricted conditions of the creation."[71] In other words, competitive natural systems ("constricted conditions") must by and large be worked with rather than abrogated prior to the eschaton. Any foundational rearranging of natural systems along the lines of eschatological imagery would be hubris, an assertion of power we cannot claim for ourselves.[72]

This solution allows Christians to work with a land ethic operationally, while hoping ultimately for God to bring a new sort of noncompetitive land into existence. Arguably, this is more a theological compromise than a genuine incorporation of a land ethic. There is at best a begrudging relationship to competitive processes, tolerating without theologically endorsing them. In this it is reminiscent of Augustine's approach to the state, and in fact Nash invokes just war theory in an attempt to navigate our competitive relationship to otherkind. [73]

A much more direct resolution can be found in Rosemary Radford Ruether's *Gaia and God*. Ruether limits redemption to human sin, which she defines as "distortion of relationship, the absolutizing of the rights to life and power of one side of a relation against the other parts with which it is, in fact, interdependent."[74] Redemption is understood as a social reality free from such distortion, but not freedom from our natural context. Sin is thus dissociated from finitude and mortality. The roots of this view are Hebrew: "mortality is our natural condition, which we share with all other earth beings, and . . . redemption is the fullness of life within these finite limits. . . ."[75] The acceptance of finitude allows us to consider the earth our home in the deepest sense, which in turn removes the "phobic relations to the death side of the life cycle" which have underpinned the anti-body, antiwoman, antinature dimensions of Christianity and other worldviews.[76] "Finitude is not our fault, nor is escape from it within our capacities. Mature spirituality frees us from ego-clinging for acceptance of the life processes of which we are inescapably a part."[77]

Here the theological knot is untied by separating the natural system from redemption. A land ethic can be embedded here; ecosystemic

relations are affirmed. Our biotic membership is essential and permanent. The theological price, however, is daunting: salvation in eternal
or supernatural terms, both for humans and otherkind, has been
thoroughly redefined or given up entirely. From the web we are, and
to the web we shall return. Christianity has become not merely earth-
inclusive (recognizing direct moral relationships to otherkind), but,
taking a term from Rasmussen, "earthbound."[78]

Ruether's approach reveals that theologizing the land ethic
involves several questions. The first, as we have noted, is whether
Christianity can endorse systemic value. The second is how radically
to understand human membership in the biotic community. Must we
be earthbound as a condition for genuine endorsement of the land
ethic, or can we in some sense transcend that membership without
forfeiting Leopold? Can the ecoevolutionary process (humans included) be understood within a transformative eschatological vision
that is not a form of immature escapism?

John Haught offers another option. If ecological concern is to have
an essential connection to Christian faith, he argues, it *must* be incorporated into a full eschatological vision. In this vision "the whole universe is somehow shaped by God's gracious promise. . . . Indeed, in a
very literal sense it *is* promise. . . . [I]t carries in its present perishable
glory the seeds of a final, eschatological flowering."[79] The construal
of creation as promise retains a cosmic eschatological connection, but
the connection is conceived primarily in terms of fulfillment rather
than redemption.

The change is crucial for the incorporation of a land ethic. The ecoevolutionary system is not essentially evil, and hence our concern for
it can be more than simply an operationally necessary concession.
Nonhuman nature retains an inherent goodness. Mistreatment of
creation not only violates its goodness at present, but cuts against its
promised future. Ecological degradation becomes "fundamentally an
expression of despair."[80] At the same time, creation as we know it is
not "the full and final context of our lives."[81] It beckons us toward the
ultimately transformative (though not discontinuous) mystery of
God's love for the world. Eschatological hope "draws us out of complete servility to the rhythms and cycles" of creation.[82] The resulting
ethic therefore recognizes in creation genuinely "intrinsic but by no
means ultimate value."[83] It further recognizes our biotic membership
as genuine but, like creation as a whole, dynamically transcendent.

Questions remain. Whether Haught escapes Ruether's concern is one; how he can justify a much more robust endorsement of creation's goodness than Nash allows is another. Other theological options could be explored, but the nature of the overall problem has been sufficiently exposed. The Christian endorsement of systemic value and human biotic membership must pass through an intersection of traditional issues, including the nature of evil, the scope of redemption, and the shape of eschatological expectations. It is, I believe, much easier for animal welfare and reverence for life advocates to navigate the intersection than those who seek a Christian version of the land ethic, for the basic reason that the last requires a transvaluation of death, certainly with regard to otherkind and perhaps with regard to us. Insofar as a Christian soteriological framework seeks to conquer death, a land ethic becomes theologically problematic.

The foundational nature of these issues makes genuinely critical leverage difficult to come by, and most decisions with respect to them seem grounded either in moral intuition or theological predisposition. Arguably, the likes of Leopold and Rolston gain some critical leverage in their valuationally sensitive reflection on the ecoevolutionary world, thus posing a genuine challenge to those Christian thinkers who would reject competitive natural processes as simply evil. Though it does not eliminate the problem of natural evil, an ecoevolutionary land ethic contextualizes it in such a way as to reduce its severity. If this reduces the scope of Christ's redemption, it nevertheless increases the scope of God's original goodness. And this in turn would be a gift to monotheism, within which natural evil has tended to present an even more difficult theodicy problem than human sin.

Post Moral Status

Some see the moral status question as having been helpful in the transition toward ecological concerns but as now essentially passé. Fifteen years ago, perhaps, one could have argued that the fulcrum of the contemporary environmental question was moral status. But now the wave of thought has crested over the ethical question and broken onto the shores of social-political-economic structure and cosmology. The two foci are often conjoined, but for the sake of this analysis will be distinguished.

The first challenge is implicit in some versions of eco-justice. Eco-justice arose from the recognition that ecological degradation can at points intersect with social injustice, as when a dangerous landfill is located in an impoverished area. From points of specific policy overlap arose deeper reflections on the economic and political nexus in which all land and water use takes place. Finally, ideological connections between abuse of nature and abuse of people were exposed, particularly by ecofeminists, who documented the historical and ideological connections between the subordination of women by men and the subordination of nature. Eco-justice has thus expanded into an overall framework, insisting that a full and genuine resolution of the ecological crisis necessarily entails a reevaluation of our patterns of production and consumption, political participation, and gender relationships. The relevant focus becomes the entire economic-political-gender-nature nexus.

Dieter Hessel conveys the grounding theological vision of eco-justice as follows: "all beings on earth make up one household (oikos), which benefits from an economy (oikonomia) that takes ecological and social stewardship (oikonomos) seriously."[84] Eco-justice "fosters ecological integrity and the struggle for social and economic justice. It emerges through constructive human responses that serve environmental health and social equity together—for the sake of human well-being *with* otherkind."[85] Hessel further articulates four basic norms of eco-justice ethics: solidarity with other people and creatures in the earth community; ecological sustainability; sufficiency as a standard of organized sharing; and socially just participation in decisions about the earth household. The norms reinforce and qualify one another.

Christine Firer Hinze argues for a similarly integrated approach within a Catholic variation of eco-justice. In combining ecological ethics and Catholic social teaching (a primarily anthropocentric justice framework), she argues that "human dignity can be realized only in the midst of ecological respect. . . . Conversely, an ecological ethics that fails to give particular attention to the welfare of . . . those who are poor, marginalized or powerless, will not suffice."[86] She concludes: "the two, in fact, entail one another."[87] The explicit affirmations of eco-justice, then, combine moral status concerns with issues of social justice.

Yet eco-justice, as a relatively new and ambitious framework, is in the early stages of articulating the full dynamics of the combination. While rhetorically pointing toward an equal and reciprocal relationship between moral status and social justice concerns, there are indications in some of the literature that moral status concerns are less significant than first appears. At least three implicit challenges to the significance of the moral status question can be gleaned from recent eco-justice work:

1. Much of the philosophical discussion of moral status appears socially naïve and ineffectively abstract. A project like Rolston's, which focuses primarily on otherkind as such, assumes that such analysis can take place independently of reflection on political, economic, and ideological location.[88] The sequence seems to be: do the primary moral analysis of otherkind first, then apply it to the wider context. Arguably, an eco-justice approach rejects such a sequence. To take one example: Rolston devotes a great deal of thought to the defense of endangered species, yet questions such as who, economically and racially, actually pays for and benefits from their protection still remain in the background. They would be at the foreground in an eco-justice framework.

Moreover, spending too much time on the fine points of moral status begins to seem like an academic (in the pejorative sense) indulgence in the midst of a massive, concrete threat to the globe.[89] One gets the sense from some eco-justice advocates that the moral status question is little more than a helpful prelude to the real task at hand, and ultimately dwarfed by it. Rasmussen, for example, ends his specific treatment of the moral status question by asserting: "The biggest rub is the grind of the human economy against the economy of nature."[90] Similarly, Northcott asserts: "Ultimately the problems of environment and development . . . are problems of human political economy."[91] He criticizes Nash's *Loving Nature* "for a certain lack of system," meaning "an unwillingness systematically to critique the real roots of the ecological crisis in modern civilisation . . . the actual procedures and processes of modern human and social economic life."[92] He also criticizes Rolston as insufficient precisely at this point as well.[93]

2. A moral status approach potentially cuts against what Hessel calls "essential habits of mind" for eco-justice, namely, thinking relationally. The moral status question perhaps carries with it an us-them dynamic, with one foot still in what Rasmussen terms "apartheid"

thinking, whereas the image of household moves past that. This concern motivates Rasmussen's choice of "earth" rather than "environmental" ethics. We will return to this challenge in the next section.

3. There is some question in the literature whether moral status, though initially recognized, becomes absorbed by some into what in effect is a humanistic approach. A recent issue of *Theology and Public Policy* containing five case studies concerning the population-consumption-environment nexus is interesting in this regard.[94] The first three cases definitively turned on humanistic axes. Women's rights to contraception dictated the analysis of one case, equity in the burdens and benefits of labor another, racial and economic factors a third. The final two engaged ecological concerns more directly. Overall, this might suggest the comprehensiveness eco-justice seeks. Yet it may also indicate a certain problematic malleability in the framework.

A great deal rides, one suspects, on whether a given author comes to eco-justice originally from the eco or the justice side. One can question whether those who come from the justice side incorporate otherkind's moral status in any significant manner. Ecodegradation can become merely an indicator of social injustice, sustainability a more egalitarian and participatory version of Pinchot conservationism, and environmental health a byproduct of solving other social injustices. But none of these indicate real moral status for otherkind.

The justice side of the framework is a crucial and necessary dimension of any adequate environmental ethic. Leopold's awareness that a land ethic would be at best one consideration among others should be embraced but changed in tone. Its one-among-others status should not be seen as a regrettably realistic concession but an expansion of view, a deepening of systemic analysis to include sociopolitical realities that in turn impact the land and waters. The wave has crested over the moral status question as such; the issue is whether the moral status question has been brought in with the wave or simply passed over.

I would argue against a version of eco-justice that uses the moral status question in the rhetorical foreground while shunting it to the background in actual case study, or absorbing it into such a vast economic-political-gender nexus that it effectively becomes lost. As Stone argues, it remains worthwhile to retain and explore the various distinct domains of moral considerateness, from animals to ecosystems to persons, each with their own moral texture and governance.

Or, as Rasmussen argues, we must "respect . . . otherkind *as* differentiated other."[95]

A serious endorsement of this requires an acceptance of and willingness to work within complex conflicts of values. If harped on, conflict of value questions can become paralyzing, and eco-justice supporters rightly stave off what amounts to premature closure. Yet eco-justice rhetoric can at times approximate a variant of the invisible hand: social justice will necessarily create ecological health and vice-versa. Empirically, it is not always so, and unexamined value conflict leads to the unreflective sacrificing of one side of the term to the other. One indicator of the genuine incorporation of moral status will be the level of tension within the list of norms. Analyses such as Stone's of the various complexities (such as "cycling" and "agenda dependency") faced by any multivalue approach must be taken seriously.[96] A faith stance affirming the ultimate coherence of eco-justice requires this for credibility.

The second challenge to the relevance of the moral status question asks whether contemporary scientific knowledge requires radical alteration of Western philosophical and theological commitments. Some thinkers construe our current ecoevolutionary-cosmic situation in terms that essentially blow us out of anthropocentric humanism and redemption-centered Christianity altogether; our new awareness of the universe and the earth's history creates a foundational religious prism of its own. These approaches tend to be genuinely postmodern, in that (following Dupré) they relocate primary meaning outside the human subject and in a larger vision of worldly or cosmic holism. There are arguably elements of this in Ruether's approach,[97] even more so in Rasmussen's,[98] and a straightforward defense of the view by Thomas Berry and Brian Swimme.[99] The entire question becomes reconfigured in the attempt to usher in a fundamentally new world-view, one in which the moral status question becomes, if not obsolete, then drastically subsidiary.

At the heart of the new worldview is the claim that the human species is fundamentally a function of the earth, which in turn is a function of the vast cosmological process of the universe. The moral status question, in this view, arose at a point when an alienated humanity was attempting to (re)connect with the rest of the world. The new worldview, however, dissolves the barrier between us and the earth to such an extent that "moral status" becomes a virtually

inappropriate category. Once the depth of our intersubjective communion with the earth is realized, moral status becomes superfluous
(similar to the role of legal rights within a genuinely loving friendship
or family situation). "Reverence will be total, or it will not be at
all."[100] In this view, the moral status question was a transition from
alienation to intersubjective communion. To continue to dwell on it
misses the end point of the transition and the much vaster change in
mind-set at work here.

The case that our ecoevolutionary cosmic situation requires a
drastic revamping—or even jettisoning—of humanism and/or Christianity has yet to be definitively made or definitively resolved. The
moral status question may be part of such a transition in worldview,
but by itself does not trigger it. It is possible to incorporate direct
moral concern for otherkind into traditional Christianity, and, in my
view, is strategically more promising at the popular level than a
radical change in worldview.

Moreover, even if such a transition is in process, the moral status
question still has a critical role to play. The relationship between
cosmology and morality is complex. Making sense of the relationship
is in part a question of moral point of view. One could argue that
attempting to address specific moral questions about human relationships to otherkind from the point of view of the cosmos is dysfunctional. It suffers from the same liability that impartial observer
theories carry when they become exaggeratedly abstract: If our
perspective goes too far out, we lose touch with who we are here and
now.[101] The task then is how to connect cosmology in an authentic
way to the more immediate human scale.[102] Granted, a view from "the
universe story" is not a view from nowhere; it inspires religious awe
and a sense of humble connection. But it is so vast a thing to compre-
hend that it is hard to see how it directly translates into axiology,
norms, and casuistry—the stuff of determinative guidance—without
a great deal of additional input.

Assessments of moral status do not necessarily, or even usually,
hinge directly on vast cosmological assertions. To some extent the
moral status question takes place at what Rolston calls "native range,"
meaning that it turns in large part on our empirically informed
experience of otherkind on a human scale. The analytic question of
moral relevance arises here. Does the fact that I share stardust with
stones constitute a morally relevant reason for changing my behavior

toward them? No. Does the fact that plants are alive and birds migrate—whereas a stone is neither alive nor mobile—make a moral difference? Yes. Is a stone's microlevel participation in spontaneity morally relevant? No. Is the fact that elk are sentient and chimpanzees can use language morally relevant? Yes. This is not to say that stardust and microspontaneity are irrelevant to overall perception, or that such perception plays no role at all in constructing morality. But it is important to avoid a potentially confusing conflation of levels (by contending, for example: you must respect the spontaneity of the stone!). There exist boundaries to moral relevance.

It thus remains worthwhile to articulate cogent, focused moral arguments with regard to nonhuman nature. The values of rigorous attention to the moral status question include protecting against its overextension, as well as bringing critical reason to bear on any attempt to draw direct human guidance from the cosmic story as we currently grasp it. And within eco-justice ethics, the moral status question plays a critically constraining role. Primarily, this consists of keeping the "eco" in eco-justice, but it can also protect against claims for otherkind that are ill-defined or overly casual. The meaning of shared membership in moral community is one such example, to which we now turn.

Conclusion: Membership and Moral Status

Northcott argues "the land is not just the context on which Israel works out her covenant, but a part, a vital part, of the covenant community itself."[103] Rasmussen claims that "all life, not just human life, shares a common moral universe. Aboriginal traditions have assumed this. Most modern ones have not."[104] Eco-justice approaches, as Hessel articulated above, envision the earth as a single household.

Stone nicely articulates the background sensibility that generates such claims. "Throughout civilization, the more 'we' have recognized that another person, family, or tribe is like us, both in the properties 'it' possesses and the common fate we share, the readier we have been to connect our common relations with moral filament. By extension of the same process, the more we are learning about animals, plants, and, in its way, all of existence . . . the more we have been struck with the sorts of similarities that stir empathy . . . and the often unanticipated interdependencies that cause concern."[105] Our increased awareness of commonness has in turn heightened (and revived) intuitions that we are more than merely next to otherkind, but perhaps form a community in a meaningful sense.

But what do such claims mean? What specifically about our inter-relationship constitutes shared moral community? A combination of intuitions and verbal fiat will not do, even if we become comfortably habituated into the notion. On the other hand, it is equally fair to require that otherkind not be excluded from moral community simply by definition.

I think the question is clarified by asking, "Who or what is joining what or whom?" There seem to be two versions at work in much of the literature that are often conflated but that the moral status question helps distinguish. One version incorporates otherkind into the moral community traditionally reserved in the West to human persons. Another version incorporates humanity into the biotic community, with consequent moral ramifications for humans. In the first version, they are joining us, while in the second we are joining them. The first version raises questions concerning otherkind's participation in mutual reflection and obligation. The second version, a land ethic version, does not raise such questions (though of course it raises others). Humans remain the only moral agents, but our fully appreciated biotic membership engenders moral requirements toward otherkind that might otherwise be ignored.

The conflation of the two versions is evident in John Passmore's influential rejection of the idea of shared moral community. Passmore argues: "Ecologically, no doubt, men form a community with plants, animals, soil, in the sense that a particular life-cycle will involve all four of them. But if it is essential to a community that the members of it have common interests and recognise mutual obligations then men, plants, animals and soil do *not* form a community . . . [i]n the only sense in which belonging to a community generates ethical obligation."[106] To be a member requires that one be able at least to share self-consciously in the purposes, and thus the benefits and burdens, of the community (the first version). Yet, the position he intends to refute with this argument is Leopold's, quoted by him as follows: "When we see land as a community to which we belong . . . we may begin to use it with love and respect."[107] This is clearly the second version, and Passmore's critique fails to engage it.

It is easier in a contemporary scientific Christian framework to defend version two than version one. Version one seems to require the projection of some sort of unverifiable agency onto otherkind. Though less rich spiritually, a land ethic retains a certain honest modernity in comparison. There is wisdom, I think, in Joseph Epes Brown's call to respect the integrity of primal worldviews in the face of the ecological challenge rather than attempt to pull elements from them into a Christian or post-Christian context.[108] Native Americans share a community with the land because various elements of the land are spiritually alive, active, and personal in a way that they are not in Christianity. One can, nonmetaphorically, enter into reciprocal relationships with them. To make shared moral community intelligible in this sense requires a quite specific "metaphysic of nature," as Brown terms it, that neither contemporary Christianity nor postmodern thought can provide.[109]

This does not, of course, close the conversation. Northcott, for example, understands shared covenantal community not only in terms of extending moral status but in terms of a broader moral framework rooted in Christianized natural law. We must "imagine ourselves as members of the community of life which includes humans and non-humans,"[110] which in turn has moral ramifications (first version). But even beyond this, "nature itself can or should exercise moral authority over the moral goods and purposes of human life."[111] We do not simply extend our moral concern in light of our biotic membership, but rather subordinate ourselves to a wider moral reality. It is a reality, according to the Hebrew Bible, "which is redolent of the purposes and providence of the creator God, though it is ontologically distinct from the being of God."[112] This is perhaps a third version of the claim and deserves further scrutiny.

Notes

1. See Aldo Leopold, *A Sand County Almanac* (New York: Ballantine Books, 1970).

2. Representatives of a land ethic approach include Holmes Rolston, III, *Environmental Ethics: Duties to and Values in the Natural World* (Philadelphia: Temple University Press, 1988), and J. Baird Callicott, "Animal Liberation: A Triangular Affair," *Environmental Ethics* 2, no. 4 (winter 1980). Paul W. Taylor, *Respect for Nature: A Theory of Environmental Ethics* (Princeton: Princeton University Press, 1986), develops an organismic, life-based approach. Animal-oriented approaches include, in order of ascending radicality, Bernard Rollin, *Animal Rights and Human Morality* (Buffalo, N.Y.: Prometheus Books, 1981); *Animal Rights and Human Obligation,* ed. Tom Regan and Peter Singer (Englewood Cliffs, N.J.: Prentice-Hall, 1976); and Tom Regan, *The Case for Animal Rights* (Berkeley and Los Angeles: University of California Press, 1983). Finally, Christopher D. Stone offers a version of moral pluralism in which the various approaches, along with intrahuman moral concerns, each constitute distinct realms of moral meaning that cannot be univocally reconciled; see *Earth and Other Ethics: The Case for Moral Pluralism* (New York: Harper and Row, 1987).

3. Much of the conversation can be traced in the journal *Environmental Ethics*, which began in 1979, though the animal welfare side of the question has a much broader history of its own.

4. Luc Ferry, *The New Ecological Order,* trans. Carol Volk (Chicago: University of Chicago Press, 1995).

5. "The question here is whether the civilization of uprootedness and innovation is utterly irreconcilable with a concern for nature. . . . I do not believe so." (Ibid., xxii).

6. Michael S. Northcott, *The Environment and Christian Ethics* (Cambridge: Cambridge University Press, 1996).

7. Larry L. Rasmussen, *Earth Community, Earth Ethics* (Maryknoll, N.Y.: Orbis Books, 1996).

8. Ferry, *The New Ecological Order,* xxvii.

9. Ibid., xxiii; also 139–40. I say "and/or" because his precise claim was not clear to me. At times he seems to mean both, at times one or the other.

10. Ibid., 131.

11. The seminal article in this regard for environmental ethics was written by Kenneth Goodpaster, "On Being Morally Considerable," *Journal of Philosophy* 75, no. 6 (1978): 308–25.

12. Rolston, *Environmental Ethics,* 32, emphasis his.

13. Stone, *Earth and Other Ethics,* 147.

14. Ferry, *The New Ecological Order,* 128.

15. Ibid., 141.

16. See "On a Monument to the Pigeon," in Leopold, *A Sand County Almanac,* 116–19.

17. Even Regan's "experiencing subject of a life" criterion does not imply legal subject status in Ferry's sense, i.e., animals entering into contractual relationship to humans.

18. Stone, *Earth and Other Ethics,* 93.

19. Ibid., 19.

20. J. Philip Wogaman, *Christian Ethics: A Historical Introduction* (Louisville: Westminster/John Knox Press, 1993), 27.

21. Louis K. Dupré, *Passage to Modernity: An Essay in the Hermeneutics of Nature and Culture* (New Haven: Yale University Press, 1993), is essentially an account of the gradual unraveling of this synthesis.

22. See Rosemary Radford Ruether, *Gaia and God: An Ecofeminist Theology of Earth Healing* (San Francisco: HarperSanFrancisco, 1992), particularly 194–99.

23. For an account of this, see Northcott, *The Environment and Christian Ethics,* chap. 2; also Rasmussen, *Earth Community, Earth Ethics,* pt. 1.

24. Andrew Linzey, *Animal Theology* (Urbana: University of Illinois Press, 1995), 13–14.

25. James A. Nash, *Loving Nature: Ecological Integrity and Christian Responsibility* (Nashville: Abingdon Press, 1991), specifically 79–88.

26. See, for example, Philip Sherrard, *Human Image: World Image: The Death and Resurrection of Sacred Cosmology* (Ipswich, England: Golgonooza Press, 1992).

27. See Northcott, *The Environment and Christian Ethics.* Also see Daniel Cowdin, "Toward an Environmental Ethic," in *Preserving the Creation: Environmental Theology and Ethics,* ed. Kevin W. Irwin and Edmund D. Pellegrino (Washington, D.C.: Georgetown University Press, 1994), 112–47.

28. Michael J. Himes and Kenneth R. Himes, *Fullness of Faith: The Public Significance of Theology* (New York: Paulist Press, 1993), specifically chap. 5.

29. James M. Gustafson, *A Sense of the Divine: The Natural Environment from a Theocentric Perspective* (Cleveland: Pilgrim Press, 1994).

30. See, for example, *Interpretation* 50, no. 1 (January 1996), which is devoted to the theme of theology and ecology.

31. Northcott, for example, argues that "it is doubtful that [such a] humanocentric concept . . . is productive of an environmental ethic which allows nature apart from human purposes the space to *be.*" (*The Environment and Christian Ethics,* 132, emphasis his).

32. Northcott asks "how we can construct a theory of values in creation . . . when . . . God as Spirit is in everything including presumably the smallpox virus and the louse" (ibid., 142).

33. W. Sibley Towner, "The Future of Nature," *Interpretation* 50, no. 1 (January 1996): 32, 33.

34. See, for example, Jay B. McDaniel, *Of God and Pelicans: A Theology of Reverence for Life* (Louisville: Westminster/John Knox Press, 1989).

35. John F. Haught, *The Promise of Nature: Ecology and Cosmic Purpose* (New York: Paulist Press, 1993). Also see his "Ecology and Eschatology," in *"And God Saw That It Was Good": Catholic Theology and the Environment,* ed. Drew Christiansen and Walter Grazer (Washington, D.C.: United States Catholic Conference, 1996).

36. In addition to Ruether, see, for example, Elizabeth A. Johnson, *Women, Earth, and Creator Spirit* (New York: Paulist Press, 1993).

37. Again, Northcott's review of the literature is incisive. See *The Environment and Christian Ethics,* chap. 4.

38. Leopold, *A Sand County Almanac,* 180.

39. Roderick Nash, *Wilderness and the American Mind* (New Haven: Yale University Press, 1967), remains very helpful in this regard. It has since been expanded in later editions.

40. Lynn White, Jr., "The Historical Roots of Our Ecologic Crisis," originally appeared in *Science* 155 (10 March 1967): 1203–7. My citations are from a reprint in *Environmental Ethics: Readings in Theory and Application,* ed. Louis P. Pojman (Boston: Jones and Bartlett, 1994), 13.

41. Ibid.

42. James Nash, *Loving Nature,* 93.

43. See ibid., chapters 3–6, for the full defense of this multifaceted claim.

44. Linzey, *Animal Theology,* 81.

45. Ibid., 187.

46. Ibid., 48.

47. Ibid., 27.

48. Ibid., 57.

49. Ibid., 44.

50. John Janovy, Jr., *Keith County Journal* (New York: St. Martin's Press, 1978), 60, 65.

51. Leopold, *A Sand County Almanac,* 137–41.

52. Ibid., 240.

53. A land ethic is quite similar in this regard to John Courtney Murray's conception of religious freedom under constitutional governance; see "The Problem of Religious Freedom," *Theological Studies* 25 (December 1964): 503–75. One could argue along parallel lines that a land ethic has emerged as a human and planetary exigency at this point in history, and that its incorporation into Christian ethics is necessary because it is a grounding insight into the human role on Earth, an insight that promises to endure. Its theologization, however, cannot simply be deductive; it requires a new integration with past Christian sources.

54. Leopold, *A Sand County Almanac,* 239.

55. Ibid., 262.

56. Ecology has developed since Leopold's day, presenting critical challenges to the shape of a land ethic. For a recent philosophical defense of a systemic approach, focusing on the idea of integrity, see Laura Westra, *An Environmental Proposal for Ethics: The Principle of Integrity* (Lanham, Md.: Rowman and Littlefield, 1994).

57. Rolston, *Environmental Ethics,* 87.

58. Ibid., 176.

59. Ibid., 188.

60. James Nash, *Loving Nature,* 185.

61. Ibid., 98, 100.

62. Ibid., 132.

63. Ibid., 131.

64. Northcott, *The Environment and Christian Ethics,* 132–33.

65. Ibid., 187.

66. Ibid., 231–32.

67. Ibid., 165ff. Here he relies on the work of Oliver O'Donovan, *Resurrection and Moral Order: An Outline for Evangelical Ethics* (Leicester: InterVarsity Press, Grand Rapids, Mich.: Eerdmans, 1986).

68. Leopold, *A Sand County Almanac,* 190.

69. Rolston, *Environmental Ethics,* 188.

70. From Holmes Rolston, III, review of *The Environment and Christian Ethics,* by Michael Northcott, *Theology Today* 54, no. 4 (January 1988): 550.

71. James Nash, *Loving Nature,* 133.

72. Karl Barth takes this approach (see John Passmore, *Man's Responsibility for Nature* [New York: Scribner, 1974], 122–23), as does Gustafson, *A Sense of the Divine,* 106.

73. James Nash, *Loving Nature,* 190.

74. Ruether, *Gaia and God,* 142.

75. Ibid., 139.

76. Ibid., 140.

77. Ibid., 141.

78. Rasmussen, *Earth Community, Earth Ethics,* 281.

79. Haught, "Ecology and Eschatology," 52.

80. Ibid., 52.

81. Ibid., 58.

82. Ibid., 56.

83. Ibid., 57.

84. Dieter Hessel, "Ecumenical Ethics for Earth Community," *Theology and Public Policy* 8, no. 1-2 (summer/winter 1996): 18.

85. Ibid., emphasis his.

86. Christine Firer Hinze, "Catholic Social Teaching and Ecological Ethics," in *"And God Saw That It Was Good,"* ed. Christiansen and Grazer, 170–71.

87. Ibid., 176.

88. It is perhaps telling in this regard that Rolston's review of Northcott's book does not even mention the systemic social-political-economic dimension, arguably at the heart of his treatment.

89. The social-political irrelevance of the philosophical discussion of moral status has been raised by Michael Bruner and Max Oelschlaeger, "Rhetoric, Environmentalism, and Environmental Ethics," *Environmental Ethics* 16 (winter 1994): 377–96.

90. Rasmussen, *Earth Community, Earth Ethics,* 110.

91. Northcott, *The Environment and Christian Ethics,* 32.

92. Ibid., 144.

93. Ibid., 104–5.

94. *Theology and Public Policy* 8, no. 1-2 (summer/winter 1996): 30ff.

95. Rasmussen, *Earth Community, Earth Ethics,* 106, emphasis his.

96. Stone, *Earth and Other Ethics,* 176–79. Cycling points to the nontransitive relationship among multiple values, such that valuing A over B and B over C may not imply A over C. Agenda dependency points to different possible outcomes in multiple value conflicts depending on the order of resolution.

97. Northcott categorizes Ruether as humanistic, but her understanding of death certainly places the human person within the wider ecological web.

98. Rasmussen's defense of loyalty to the earth, of a religious kind, his affirmation of earthboundedness, and his attempt to draw human guidance directly from nonhuman nature merit his inclusion here.

99. See Brian Swimme and Thomas Berry, *The Universe Story* (San Francisco: HarperSanFrancisco, 1992); see also Berry's *The Dream of the Earth* (San Francisco: Sierra Club Books, 1988).

100. Berry, *Dream of the Earth,* 134.

101. For an entry into the contemporary debate in moral philosophy over impartiality, see Thomas Nagel, *The View from Nowhere* (New York: Oxford University Press, 1986), and Bernard Williams, *Ethics and the Limits of Philosophy* (Cambridge, Mass.: Harvard University Press, 1985).

102. None of this is to say that impartiality as such is unimportant to ethics, including and especially concern for otherkind. Though the current emphasis on localism is politically and economically important, it is not a sufficient basis of concern for otherkind. And this because one of the essential dynamics of the ethical problem posed by the environmental crisis is that "the harm we do . . . can stretch across the earth and linger well into the future. . . . These distances dilute the forces that animate and direct moral thought in kinship groups and small communities— shame, guilt, empathy, anxiety, and the prospects of retaliation and reciprocity." Stone, *Earth and Other Ethics,* 30.

103. Northcott, *The Environment and Christian Ethics,* 187.

104. Rasmussen, *Earth Community, Earth Ethics,* 107.

105. Stone, *Earth and Other Ethics,* 34.

106. Passmore, *Man's Responsibility,* 116, emphasis his.

107. Ibid.

108. See Joseph Epes Brown, *The Spiritual Legacy of the American Indian* (New York: Crossroad Press, 1992), esp. 110–11 and 116–18. Brown urges Christians and Jews to recover the premodern elements of their own traditions.

109. Ibid., 4 and 37ff.

110. Northcott, *The Environment and Christian Ethics,* 129.

111. Ibid., 238.

112. Ibid., 164.

Behemoth and Batrachians in the Eye of God: Responsibility to Other Kinds in Biblical Perspective

CALVIN B. DEWITT

My paper's title is designed to catch your eye and raise your curiosity. I am a zoologist, with a deep interest in animals. My early work in this field—grade school through college—was focused largely on reptiles and amphibians. Hence my use of the word batrachians in the title. This is the name zoologists have given to the order of frogs and toads,[1] and these, along with turtles, lizards, and snakes, are among the creatures that first held my interest. Batrachians are animals not often loved or shown affection by people. This became apparent to me in my youth, as I saw how people behold frogs and toads. People's lack of love and affection for these creatures made me wonder about what made some creatures lovable and others not. Sharing with batrachians a lack of human love and affection is Behemoth (from Hebrew, *bĕhēmōth,* plural of *bĕhēmāh*), a creature of a different order.

While I identify Behemoth with the hippopotamus, its name was not available to us until the seventeenth century. The hippopotamus was reliably reported, according to zoologist F. S. Bodenheimer, from the Orontes River in Syria around 1500 B.C.E. and was in the lower Nile until the twelfth century C.E. It was hunted using harpoons with barbed hooks and was well known in biblical times. In Egypt, the Romans reduced its population greatly to eliminate the damage it was doing to crops.[2] The name by which this creature has been known in these last few centuries literally means "river horse," even though it is an even-toed hoofed mammal that is anatomically nearer to pigs.[3] Bible translators have chosen not to use the word hippopotamus, perhaps because it comes so late in usage, because they are not zoologists, and because some scholars—including Bodenheimer—have preferred using the name Behemoth for beasts generally.[4] In any case, Bible translators have decided not to translate the Hebrew word, but simply to transliterate it "Behemoth." However, as I "behold Behemoth" with you in this paper, I join with most other zoologists, and with Job scholar Robert Gordis,[5] to behold the hippopotamus.[6]

It is clear from the Creation story that the creatures are of many kinds and that each one of them, as individuals and kinds, has its own context. This context includes the habitats of its individual members as well as the larger creation of which these habitats are part. The context of every creature also includes those of kinds other than their own. From the perspective of any kind of creature, all those besides their own can be referred to as "other kinds." From the perspective of a zoologist, "other kinds" thus refer to other than human, and that is the perspective I take here. I also use the word "otherkind" but do so sparingly, only when all other kinds have more in common among themselves than with humankind on a given point being considered. This restricts the use of "otherkind" to situations in which humankind's distinctiveness is empirically evident. I also use the words "other creatures" in order to recognize that "other kinds" are comprised of individual creatures. In so doing I indicate that I am not restricting my consideration to taxa higher than the individual, but include individuals as well. I also use the words "human creatures" in order to recognize that "humankind" is comprised of individual human beings. In this paper I also restrict my usage of "other kinds" to biotic kinds and thus exclude for my purposes things that are more exclusively physical, such as rocks and machines. I also will be thinking here largely of animal kinds, although not to the exclusion of other biotic kinds.

There is, of course, more than biophysical context to be considered here: there also is scriptural context. As a student of the Bible, I am interested not only in passages dealing with living creatures, but also with the context of these creatures, particularly as this context relates to their Creator. More specifically, I am working in this paper to see the creatures through the eyes of their Maker. I do so because of my conviction that insights on how the creatures might be viewed by their Creator may have profound implications for human relationship with living creatures. I know of no better place to begin than Job 40:15–24. I present it here with a preface and running commentary designed to slow us in our reading, to elicit reflection on the text, and to build wonder. Here, then, is God's speech to Job on Behemoth.

Behold Behemoth!

We human beings seem to have some natural affinity to some creaturely kinds: the soft furry ones with big round eyes, the flashy feathery ones with docile beaks, the colorful scaly ones with whiskery fins. But those with flabby flesh and oozing pores (hippos), with bulging throats and acrid warts (batrachians) are "horses of a different color." In the eyes of individuals of *our* kind there is likely to be an asymmetry in the affection we bestow across the creatured spectrum. In parallel with this spectrum of affection also come differential awareness, dissimilar appreciation, divergent respect, divagating consideration, and varying treatment. Koalas and cockatiels are more likely to be loved, cuddled, and cared for. Toads and hippopotami are not.

Perhaps it is for this reason that God praises the unlovely, uncuddled, and little cared for kinds in the presence of Job. God's psalm to the hippopotamus is wondrous in this regard. From it we gain insight into respecting creatures that may not attract us. From it we are helped to understand our proper relationship with kinds other than our own. Here we see what people may see as monstrous and ugly, but we see it through the appreciative eyes of God.

> "Behold Behemoth which I made along with you
> and which feeds on grass like an ox."

This giant herbivore is my Creation! I who created you with all of your remarkable qualities, I also made this great beast! Behold! Open your eyes! And see!

> "What strength he has in his loins,
> what power in the muscle of his belly!"

My marvelous hippo is strong and powerful! Look at those flanks! See its massive frame, woven with powerful muscles. Admire its capacity to contain its massive bulk.

"His tail sways like a cedar
the sinews of his stones are close knit."

While you may not want to admire the perfection and wonder of this creature's reproductive organs, I—their Creator—am proud of my wonderful provision for their reproduction and fruitfulness. Do you see the problem female and male could have in joining their germ cells together to continue their kind? See my provisions for their procreation!

"His bones are tubes of bronze
his limbs like rods of iron."

What architecture! Look how those "pillars and beams" are harmonized with the mass to which they give support and provide articulated strength. They do so even while subtracting and adding bone here and there to counter new and changing strains and stresses. Osteoclasts and osteoblasts dynamically reforming these tubes and rods to meet challenges of life and growth, while never weakening! Dynamic support for dynamic mass. Beautiful!

"He ranks first among the works of God."

Not that you people are not important, of course! But my hippo ranks first among my works. Why do you think I would tell you that I rate my hippo "number one?" You know! It is to crack you out of your anthropocentrism for a moment to get you to see my creations as I do. I want you to know the importance of this creature in my sight. I rate my hippo number one so that you will take notice, and so that you will be inspired to wonder!

"Only I, the Maker of this beast can approach it with a sword."

Only I have the *author*-ity to destroy this work of art, and I alone. I say this not to tell you I am going to destroy it. I say this to tell you: Put down your arrow and gun. Do not be so foolish as to think that you are powerful if you destroy what through my power I have made. Real power, after all, belongs to the Maker, not the destroyer. This work of art belongs to its Creator alone. Only I have the right to destroy what I have made.

> "The hills bring him their produce,
> and all the wild animals play nearby."

The hippo in my view is not one with its flesh spread out over a concrete slab at one of your zoos. Neither is it one who works at dusk to raise its bulk to the top of the wall to graze awkwardly on Kentucky blue grass in the National Zoo. Nor is it one confined to a pen on Noah's Ark. I see my hippo in its proper habitat. My giant herbivore lives in concord with the other creatures, plants and animals, reeds and batrachians; at dusk it grazes on the vegetation that borders the wetlands and rivers and extends to the hills.

> "Under the lotus plants he lies,
> hidden among the reeds in the marsh."

Its wetland habitat, while not very well suited for people, is nicely suited for the hippo. And the hippo is nicely suited for its aquatic habitat. It is fully integrated into the dynamic fabric of its lush and watery world. Great floating and emerging leaves attend the water surface. Batrachians sing their nocturnes there under cover of darkness. Herons collect their dinner, conspicuous at the water's edge. And the hippo?

> "The lotuses conceal him in their shadow;
> the poplars by the stream surround him."

Giant as it is, this great creature can be inconspicuous. It fits into its habitat in a marvelous beastly harmony. The wetland vegetation embraces hippo habitat with spreading boughs and concealing leaves. Moored in its marsh, even great currents do not sweep it away.

> "When the river rages, he is not alarmed;
> he is secure, though the Jordan
> should surge against his mouth."

And so, as the hippo's ecological relations are maintained with integrity within the framework of its habitat, so is its psyche. The hippo is secure in its wetland habitat. It is at home in the marsh and the river torrent!

> "Can anyone capture him by the eyes,
> or trap him and pierce his nose?"

This is a creature that might not respond to your beckoning! It is not one you could put on a leash and show it off around town! It is God's creature and praises God in its being; it is not yours. It is not even yours in the sense that some of your pets are. My hippo has strength and a will that can overwhelm you. Respect it!

A Three-Party Relationship

"Only a great poet could paint this vivid picture of the Hippopotamus, lying at his ease in the Nile among the lotus leaves, swallowing an entire river in one mouthful (40:24)!"[7] writes Robert Gordis. My representation of the text here, therefore, should not substitute for reading the uninterrupted text. Instead, it should be seen as preparatory to its reading. It also is preparatory to introducing two basic ways that humankind can view other kinds.

The first is as a two-party, human creatures–other creatures relationship. It is a relationship of us with them and them with us. Much can be derived from such a visualization, of course, as we have learned from the many who have seriously worked to do this. Such work recognizes benefits conveyed by other kinds to humankind, such as provision of 1) oxygen and consumption of carbon dioxide through the photosynthesis by green plants; 2) food for human use by plants and animals and their fruits; 3) materials for clothing and construction; 4) medicines and pharmaceuticals; 5) companionship; and 6) aesthetic benefits in human environments. It also recognizes detriments brought to humankind by creatures, such as 1) disease, parasitism, and predation; 2) degradation of human clothing and structures; 3) consumption of food produced for human use; and 4) human discomforts. There are benefits and detriments conveyed by humankind to other kinds as well. Among the benefits are 1) seed and organism dispersal (sometimes detrimental); 2) habitat creation and protection; and 3) land restoration. Among the detriments are 1) seed and organism dispersal (sometimes beneficial); 2) habitat degradation and destruction; and 3) land degradation.

The two-party relationship can be represented thus:

Other Creatures — Human Creatures

When the Creator of the creatures is recognized and incorporated, however, a three-party, human-creature-Creator relationship can be envisioned.[8] It is one in which human beings and other beings are coordinated with their Creator; the importance of this is illumined by hearing and studying God's speech to Job. This three-party relationship can be represented thus:

Creator

/   \

Other Creatures — Human Creatures

Incorporating this third dimension brings greater robustness to the human creatures—other creatures, or humankind–other kinds, relationship. It co-orders both human and other creatures to their Creator.[9] As we have seen for Job, viewing other creatures through the eyes of their Creator can transform our perspective. In beholding Behemoth, in the manner God would have us, we discover the beauty, integrity, and habitat-fitness for what at first glance we might have considered monstrous and repulsive. We see as beautiful what we first thought to be ugly. We come to view a wetland no longer as wasteland but as home and habitat for God's creatures. We transform our belief that power is measured by one's capacity to kill or to tame into one that sees real power as one's demonstrated capacity to create and sustain. We discover that real power in relation to God's creatures is not in the human capacity to extinguish life with arrow, bullet, or barbed harpoon, but in God's creating it and sustaining it as something marvelous and wonderful. We find that authority over things belongs to the Author of those things: we have no authority to destroy what we ourselves did not create; destruction of a grand master's work by its onlooker, beholder, or curator may be a disgrace to their Creator.

Reading the broader context within which the hippopotamus is described, we gain even more of the force of scriptural teaching here. Before describing the hippopotamus and the crocodile, God's first speech describes the mountain goat, ostrich, and hawk. "To be sure, they were not created for man's use," writes Robert Gordis, "yet they do possess a beauty and a grace that man can appreciate." And then, observes Gordis, "The poet goes one step further. The Hippopotamus and the Crocodile can lay no claim to beauty, but on the contrary, are physically repulsive. When the poet glorifies these beasts he is calling us to rise completely above the anthropocentric point of view which, however natural for man, distorts his comprehension of the world."[10] God's second speech "represents a higher level in the argument, an ascent from God's creative power as manifested in creatures that are independent of man, to God's creative joy in creatures that are positively dangerous and repugnant to man."[11]

In biblical Christianity, the value of creatures derives ultimately not from their utility, market price, cuteness, or charm. Instead, their value derives from their Creator. All things owe their life and breath to their Creator who not only has created them and declared them good but also sustains them through divine love and power. Basing their understanding on the teachings of the Bible, people of the Christian faith acknowledge God's gift of life (*zoe*) and breath (*pnoe*) to all things (Ps. 104:27–30; Acts 17:24–25); God's repeated declaration of the goodness of Creation and all the creatures (Gen. 1 and Gen. 1:31; 1 Tim. 4:4); and God's caring and sustaining of all things (Ps. 104; Col. 1:15–20; Heb. 1:3).

Incorporation of the divine dimension in a three-part model illumines humankind's relationship with other kinds. It also illumines the relation of other kinds with God and God's relationship with us. But there is much more than this small part of the book of Job that is available to us in the Bible. We now turn to the rich biblical heritage of which God's speech to Job is a small part.

Heritage and Prejudice

A geneticist and counselor in human genetics some years ago helped me and my students to understand and address the problem of prejudice. It is his observation that gave me permission to begin this paper with a passage of scripture, rather than zoology. My colleague explained how understanding genetics helps one to discover that it is no one's fault that they look ugly or beautiful, are tall or short, male or female, yellow or black. Instead of thinking them responsible for their looks and form, we can simply appreciate and respect them for what they are. Our cultural heritage is similar: each of us comes with a cultural heritage we have not initially chosen. We enter the stream of life when and where we do through no plans of our own. None need to feel responsible for being born into a family that is religious or irreligious, Hindu or Christian, bond or free.

And so I began this paper with the Bible, because that is my cultural heritage. Even though the Bible, Christianity, and even "religion" have come into disfavor in many quarters and can be associated with murderous cults, bigotry, brutal warfare, oppression, and doctrinaire imposition, this does not change the circumstances of my birth and my growing up in a Christian community that nurtured me in a cultural matrix of story, song, and exposition. This matrix respected science heartily, yet did not hold it up as arbiter of absolute truth. It promulgated a system of ethics, yet continuously reformed this system as knowledge from the Word, and the world increased and was clarified.[12] It sought to bring goodness and integrity to human life, yet did not pursue happiness or other by-products of goodness and integrity for their own sakes. It sought wholeness and care for creation, yet was not afraid to take from creation what was needed to sustain human life and achieve contentment as this was biblically defined in 1 Timothy 6:6–21.

The exposition of these stories and songs was brought to me by disciplined and highly educated scholars who taught in sanctuary, classroom, laboratory, and field. The practical exposition of these stories and songs was published in the lives of people around me, many of whom were exemplary in upgrading the poor, visiting the sick, rehabilitating prostitutes, singing in prisons, doing daily labor, and tending the land and its creatures.[13]

My love for plants and animals, and my love for creation, derives from this matrix of story, song, and exposition. It is out of this love that I became a zoologist. The Behemoth speech opens one window to this much larger matrix. Another window can be opened by looking at a distillation of this matrix. I move with considerable reservation and caution, because it is impossible to compose such distillates adequately or even respectfully.[14] Nevertheless it is helpful for our topic. This distillation, to whose numbered distillates I refer, is found at the end of this essay.[15]

Human Beings in Relation to Other Kinds

In Christian perspective, the value of creatures derives ultimately not from their utility, market price, cuteness, or charm. Instead, their value derives from their Creator. The biblical passage on Behemoth in Job 40:15–24 is but one illustration. A Christian matrix of story, songs, and exposition, it brings one closer to understanding that the worth of the creatures is not so much in the eye of the human beholder as in the eye of the divine Beholder. The Beholder is also the Author and Owner of all things (distillates 1 and 2).

Creator-based value has profound consequences. It makes it necessary to see other creatures and other kinds through the eyes of their Creator. It brings us to ascribe intrinsic value to the creatures and to creation (distillate 3). The primary relationship is that between the Creator and the creatures, which for our purposes I have resolved along two lines: the Creator in relation with human creatures, and the Creator in relation with other creatures.[16] In this primary relationship, the creatures—human and other—owe their being to their Creator. They bring glory and praise to their Creator by being the dynamic beings they have been created to be.

It is the relationship between Creator and creature that establishes the human relationship of humankind with other kinds. In this view, a human being does not first ask, concerning the hippo: Can I eat it? How can I shoot it? How can I market it? How can I get it out of my way? Instead, the questions are: What does the Creator think of this creature? How in my relationship to it should I honor its Owner? How might I learn to live with it? How does it fit into the larger system of which it is part?[17] Even if a person has the opportunity to buy a hippo, thereby gaining legal title to it, the responsibility to its Owner remains. The individual may have bought the privilege of having a hippo under his care, but it must be care under the eyes of its Owner and Creator. There would be little doubt that this would require keeping this creature in its native habitat, "Under the lotus plants . . ., hidden among the reeds in the marsh."

This, of course, strongly affects a human being's relationship with other kinds. The Creator-creature relationship controls the humankind–other kinds relationship. Among other things, we come to discover the beauty, integrity, and habitat fitness for a creature that at first glance we might have declared ugly.

Clearly, human beings in this view are creatures (distillate 4). But we are distinctively different from otherkind. Humans differ greatly at least in this: humans have the capacity to destroy their own kind, otherkind, and the creation on a grand scale. No texts are needed to support this statement.[18] It is apparent from empirical observation in the present. And it has been apparent from empirical observation over recorded human history and on to the present. Human beings are distinctive in this: we are the only kind that has the capacity to destroy the earth. Moreover, this capacity appears to be joined with a proclivity and even a will to do so.[19] Even in our time, when human beings know what environmental integrity means, we still degrade the earth. This is the human predicament (distillate 12). In seeking a solution to this problem, historian of science Colin Russell evaluates the prospects for addressing the human predicament by the conventional reductionist view and the postmodern organismic view of Earth, but finds that alone, or in combination, they fall short. In seeking a third way, Russell finds that the scriptures provide an answer, and it is to this he directs our attention. It is a way that comes from perceiving Earth unified with the universe under its orderly Creator, as God's footstool; the earth is not the center of all things (distillate 1).[20]

The capacity and proclivity to destroy the earth has a correlative distinction. Human beings are also distinctive in this: we are the only kind that can make the decision not to exercise our capacity to destroy our own kind, other kinds, otherkind, and the earth. While having the capacity for domination and destruction, human beings can recognize this capacity and prevent its actualization. Human beings have the capacity to take care of the earth and its creatures (distillates 4 and 5). Again, no texts are needed here; we know this from empirical observation. Human beings have the capacity to mirror God's love for the world (distillate 5).

While it is interesting to probe the Christian tradition for reasons for this capacity, proclivity, and will, it is for our purposes more pressing to probe it for solutions. This brings a text from the matrix, Genesis 2:15. Here are five English translations from the Hebrew:[21]

The LORD God took the man and put him in the Garden of Eden to work it and take care of it. (NIV)

And Jehovah Elohim took Man, and put him into the garden of Eden, to till it and to guard it. (DBY)

The LORD God took the man and put him in the garden of Eden to till it and keep it. (RSV)

> And the Lord God took the man, and put him into the garden of Eden
> to dress it and to keep it. (KJV)

> And Jehovah God taketh the man, and causeth him to rest in the garden
> of Eden, to serve it, and to keep it. (YLT)

Lest we be distracted by concern for inclusion of women and children
here, the Hebrew word translated in the King's English as *man* is the
word *'adam—the* word for humankind; it is *'adam* of *adamah*. Just as
these five translations do not convey this well, neither do four of the
five render adequately another important word in this well-known
biblical text: the word translated "to work it," "to till it," "to dress it."
For present-day gardeners, of course, "dressing" is not far from what
we actually do—and it is not far from its Hebrew meaning. The
Hebrew here is *'abad,* perhaps best known from the book of Joshua:
"Choose ye this day whom you shall serve (*'abad*). As for me and my
house, we will serve (*'abad*) Jehovah." Wherever this word is used
outside of agriculture in the Bible, it is translated "to serve." When it
is used for gardens and agriculture, it is translated "dress," "till,"
"tend," or "cultivate," except here in Young's Literal Translation. Human beings are expected to serve the garden. (distillate 4).

Beyond our service to the garden, expected in this text, we also can
discover that the garden in many ways also serves human beings and
the rest of creation. If we acknowledge that the garden and the wider
creation serves us with its fruit, aesthetic beauty, reciprocating the
exchange of oxygen and carbon dioxide, we can come to the conclusion that the garden, through the eyes of God, might be seen as
engaging in reciprocal service with its gardeners.

Thus, whatever we do in company with the various individuals and
kinds of creatures in the garden, and in some sense also the wider
creation, we do as acts of con-service. The Latin prefix, *con-*, applied
to the word "serve," can convey this. "Con-service" can be used to
indicate *service with*. It appears that the biblical expectation—or, if
we will, the expectation of the garden in the eyes of God—is that
people, its many creatures, and its many kinds of creatures are
engaged in reciprocal service, or con-servancy.[22] We creatures, human
and other, are creatures in relationship. It is a relationship in which
we reciprocally serve each other (distillate 4).

People are expected not only to con-serve the garden but also to
keep it. The Hebrew word for *keep* used in Genesis 2:15 is not

natsar—a word that describes the "keeping" of pickles in a jar—but the Hebrew word *shamar,* a word used in another well-known passage, Numbers 6:24, "The Lord bless you and keep you."[23] When this blessing is invoked, the expectation is that God would keep us not merely in a kind of preserved, inactive, uninteresting state. Instead, God would keep us in all of our vitality, with all our energy and beauty. Our expectation is that God's keeping will be keeping that nurtures all of our life-sustaining and life-fulfilling relationships—physiologically, psychologically, socially, ecologically. Our internal functioning, our relationship with family and community, and our interfacing with the land and creatures would be sustained so that we would be kept in all integrity.

When people "keep" the creation in this deep, full, and dynamic sense, they confess in deed that the creatures being kept must be able to maintain their proper connections—with members of their own kind, with the many other kinds with which they interact, with the soil, air, and water upon which they depend for their life and fruitfulness. The rich and full keeping invoked in the Aaronic blessing is the kind of keeping that should be confessed by keepers of God's garden, the keepers of God's creation. As God keeps us, so should we keep God's earth (distillate 5).

This brings us to the confession of the con-server. As beholder of the creatures, the con-server mostly needs to do no more than join the creatures in bringing praise to their God. There is, however, a principal task: in beholding, the con-server must also name what is beheld (distillate 5). The hippo or batrachian must not just be called "beast" but must be given a name by its human beholder. And it interests God what names we give. Naming is necessary for becoming aware of the numbers and qualities of the myriad of kinds; it is necessary as we describe and teach about plants and animals; it is necessary when human actions threaten to degrade or destroy the creatures or creation. These things we know from experience. And, should we have to counter the pain and destruction inflicted by people upon individual creatures, kinds of creatures, and all creation, the con-server will have to know more than their taxonomy. The con-server will also have to know the creature—its individuals and its kind, its dynamics and its niche requirements—in order that their flourishing can be re-established in the wake of their abuse, degradation, and destruction.[24] The con-server/keeper must not be satisfied with existing ignorance of the names, needs, and requirements of the creatures, their various kinds, and of creation; neither must the keeper participate in the efforts to create, promote, and preserve such ignorance.

The con-server (human or other) is a creature in relationship with other creatures and in relationship to all creation. It is a relationship for which the entities have contributions and responsibilities to others, beyond self, including such things as production or consumption of oxygen and reciprocal provision of food and habitat.[25] It is a relationship that necessarily transcends the grammar of atomistic individualism and atomistic justice. It is a relationship that is not one of independent peers, and thus not limited by the grammar and principles of atomism.[26] When we consider others of our kind and other kinds, we see ourselves in relationship rather than as independent entities, peers or not. This means that we address others within the relationship of reciprocal service, however direct or indirect that service might be. For creatures under domestication this means reciprocal provision of needs between con-servers, based upon knowledge and seeking God's will on Earth by the human keeper. For the wild creatures this may mean a benign beholding by human onlookers.[27] For threatened creatures and kinds it will involve rescue work, considered incomplete until the rescued are liberated from human keeping into self-sustaining habitats.[28] The con-server is not satisfied until the domestic animals on the ark are restored to full con-serving relationship and wild creatures are restored to natural habitats where they can flourish once again (distillates 7 and 12).[29] In all of this the keeper-server sees the creatures not as strangers but creatures in relationship.[30]

Keepers or con-servers must also guard against greed and arrogance and their degrading effects on creatures, other kinds, and creation. Caring for these is a humble privilege, not the pursuit of one's own security or reputation (distillate 8). And in this faithful con-service—in this imaging of God's love for the world—con-servers not only make others aware of the creatures and our caring,[31] but also warn them that without responsible con-service and keeping of creation and its creatures, human beings themselves are threatened with destruction (distillate 6). The goal for people in creation is to achieve contentment rather than maximization, to do God's will and sustain God's economy of creation (distillate 9).

The keeper/con-server must be on guard, ready to sound the alarm, ready to confront the establishment of ignorance. The keeper/con-server must be a persistent, diligent, and discerning truth-seeker. The keeper/con-server must be fully aware of the human predicament and the need to fight and overcome evil that is manifest in the abuse of creatures, of other kinds, and of creation. The keeper must pray for deliverance from evil (distillates 10 and 12).

The scriptures tell us that all creation, every creature, praises God. Every creature reflects back something of the love God pours out through all creation. The heavens and all creatures declare the glory of God. The chief end of each creature, the communities of creatures, and all creation is to glorify God and enjoy God's blessings.[32] The scriptures further tell us that this praise, testimony, and witness to God leaves every person without excuse for not knowing God's divinity and everlasting power. And the keeper/con-server of creation, mirroring God's love for the world, confesses this love in deed. The keeper/con-server of creation admires and sustains the world in beauty.[33] Praise, testimony, and witness are proclaimed to the world "loud and clear" by human beings and all other creatures; their publication pours forth over all the earth. God's love for the world is published in life and landscape. And the keepers, the con-servers, sing: Praise God from whom all blessings flow! Praise God all creatures here below!

Conclusion

How ought human beings regard Behemoth and other kinds? In the Christian and biblical view, they must be regarded as the works of the Lord. To so regard God's creatures identifies a person more with the biblical Noah than with the destroyers of the earth. To so regard Behemoth places one among those who respect God's command and blessing to the creatures to be fruitful and multiply; those who would provide the conditions for a fruitful and flourishing biosphere; those who would be sensitive and responsive to any dangers facing other kinds; those who would join in with other creatures in praising their Maker. Such respectful people behold the batrachians and Behemoth, con-serve and keep the creatures, and, confessing creation's integrity in word and deed, hold them and their habitats together, assure their periodic self-enjoyment and rest, rescue them from human onslaughts, and restore the rescued to full and fruitful life.[34] In so doing, they mirror the One the scripture tells us is the namesake of Christians, the One by and for whom all things were created, in whom all things hold together, and through whom all things are reconciled to God. As they image God and behold the creatures through God's eye, they not only are better able to behold the creatures; they are better able to behold the beauty of the Beholder.

Distillates from a Christian Cultural Matrix

1. Authorship and Integrity of the Cosmos

There is but a single just and loving Author of all that is, including temporality and chance, who creates all creatures good and declares all creatures good, who holds all things together, and who reconciles all things.[35] This means that all things are consistent, justly ordered, and have integrity, whether apparent or not. This is captured by Einstein, for example, in his exclamation, "Raffiniert ist der Herrgott, aber boshaft ist er nicht!"[36] This also means that the just and discoverable consistency within the world and universe makes science possible, including discovery of principles and laws.

2. The Creation and All the Creatures Belong to Their Creator

Neither the creation, nor any of its creatures belong to human beings, but to their Creator, who cares for all of it. The earth (*ge*) and its fullness is the Lord's, the biosphere (*oikoumene*) and everything that lives in it.[37] God has established a covenant with the earth, with every living creature, with all living creatures of every kind on the earth.[38] Thus, God respects and sustains the creatures and the earth,[39] we hold these things in trust, and they must be treated with respect and cared for. Beyond the other creatures, we too belong to God,[40] who cares for us;[41] thus, we need not be anxious about our lives or sustenance.

3. Intrinsic Worth of the Creatures

The divine authorship of all things means that creation and all its constituents have intrinsic worth apart from their utility or perceived pleasantness, and thus the whole creation and every creature must be respected.[42] God loves the world and cares for it,[43] and imaging God,[44] we must love the world and take care of it.[45] This also means that while we may make responsible use of the fruits of creation we may not destroy its fruitfulness.[46] Thus, the prerogative of destruction and extinction lies only with the Creator, not with people.[47] And, while we may employ creatures in responsible ways, we must not press them relentlessly;[48] we must assure repeated opportunity for the creatures of Earth to enjoy their rest and creation's blessings.[49]

4. Human Beings as Part of Creation

Because we also are creatures, we human beings do not stand apart from "environment" but are part of the whole.[50] Neither are we the center of things, nor is our dwelling place—the Creator's footstool we call Earth.[51] The biosphere and the earth, together with everything in the universe is identified as the creation and its totality is beyond our comprehension.[52] The integrity of the whole creation must be confessed in word and deed, cherished in whole and in part. Furthermore, as the rest of creation serves us, so should we serve the rest of creation.[53] "Con-service" and con-servation is the rule.

5. Human Beings as Imagers of God

Yet, as con-servants with creation, human beings have a special honor of imaging God's love to the world.[54] It is a special honor with special responsibility. God is love; and we should image God's love. Imaging the Creator's love and care for the creatures sustains us as their appreciative beholders, prevents us from abusing them or their kind, compels us to have compassion for the biosphere and all it contains, and brings us to con-serve creation. Thus, human beings are responsible to God as earthkeepers.[55] Earthkeeping is an important way of imaging God's love for the world. Human beings must give names to the creatures.[56] And describing and teaching about plants and animals is honorable and wise.[57]

6. Penalty for Eschewing Our Reflection of God's Love

While expected to image God's love for the world out of love and gratitude to God, people who destroy the earth will themselves be destroyed.[58] Yet, people who believingly practice God's love for the world will live everlastingly.[59]

7. Creation Is a Powerful Teacher

The just and discoverable consistency of creation is rooted in God's order and thus, for those who study the works of creation, creation is a powerful teacher.[60] Therefore, having been created justly and rightly by God, the creation is in many ways normative, and its normativity should be "ob-served" in ways that inform its ob-servers how it works and (for correcting human degradation of creation) how it ought to work.[61] For example, creation teaches that biological death is basic to life, contrary to what might be assumed by people who failed to ob-serve natural ecosystem functions.

8. Mindless Selection Should Be Constrained in Mindful Society

Darwinian principles may operate creatively and thoughtlessly in the biotic world. However, when thoughtless Darwinian principles are found to operate in the thoughtful world of human beings, they must be constrained and even countered in order to assure sustainability of human society and the creation.[62] Thus, fitness of human culture comes not from seeking the supremacy of the individual, race, nationality, sex, or economic status but from con-service in God's creation, including God's other creatures and their kinds, and other people and their communities. Self-interest is always secondary to seeking God's rule. Therefore, whatever benefits accrue to one's self come as by-products of confessing in word and deed the integrity of creatures and the whole of creation.[63]

9. Contentment Rather Than Maximization Is a Worthy Goal

Given God's ownership of all things and human responsibility to God, the aim of human beings and human societies should be contentment, not the maximization of things, pleasure, or accomplishments.[64] Thus, whatever things we hold in trust, whatever joy we experience, and whatever accomplishments we achieve should come as by-products of our loving and self-giving con-service. Contentment is worth far more than money, possessions, wealth, or fame—to us and to the rest of creation.

10. Truth Must Always Be Sought

In whatever human beings do or say, in whatever they learn and teach about the world and how things ought to be, and in whatever actions they take in the world, human beings must consistently be truthful and seek the truth, never misrepresenting the world or what is happening within and to the world.[65] Thus, when there is danger people must sound the alarm;[66] when there is no danger they must not be alarmist. When there is need for prophets, they should prophesy; when corrective actions result from the warning of prophets, the prophets should rejoice and not grumble.[67] Moreover, when there is need to know, people should seek knowledge. And, when there is confusion people should seek clarification. Thus, truth must be defended and consistently be sought.

11. The Whole Creation Praises Its Creator

In understanding God's world human beings should know that the whole creation gives testimony to God's divinity and everlasting power.[68] Thus, in our life and work we should help others share in receiving creation's testimony and we should assure that the testimony of the creatures and of creation to their Creator is not diminished or extinguished.

12. Humankind Must Recognize the Human Predicament and May Commune in Dialogue with the Creator

Human beings must acknowledge and deal with the problem that the good we want to do, we often fail to do and the evil we do not want to do, we often do. This is the human predicament and one of our primary reasons for seeking dialogue with God in prayer. When we do, we model this on the prayer of our Lord, that God's name be revered, that God's economy be established and God's will be done on Earth, that God provide for our modest daily needs, that God forgive us as we forgive our friends and enemies, and that God deliver us from evil. This is a prayer that we put our belief into practice on Earth in our daily lives, God helping us.

Notes

A popular version of this paper has been published as "The Beauty of the Beast: Behemoths and Batrachians in the Eye of God," *Green Cross* 4, no. 1: 8–9.

1. Batrachia is the "leaping order" of the class Amphibia, an order more commonly known as the order Salientia. Thus, members of this order may be called Batrachians. See G. K. Noble, *The Biology of the Amphibia* (New York: McGraw-Hill, 1931; reprint, New York: Dover, 1954), 485 (page citations are to the reprint edition).

2. F. S. Bodenheimer, *Animals and Man in Bible Lands* (Leiden: E. J. Brill, 1960), 101.

3. George S. Cansdale, *Animals of Bible Lands* (Exeter Devon, England: Paternoster Press, 1970), 101.

4. Ibid., 101.

5. Robert Gordis, *The Book of God and Man: A Study of Job* (Chicago: University of Chicago Press, 1965), 119–22.

6. Behemoth and Leviathan as treated here in God's second speech to Job are sometimes considered to be mythological. Robert Gordis, however, tells us that the writer "is not interested in imaginary creatures from the dim mythological past—he is concerned with the actual present, with the vast universe as it is governed by its Maker. The hippopotamus and the crocodile are real beasts and their choice for inclusion in the paeons of praise is by no means accidental" (ibid., 120).

7. Ibid., 122.

8. This three-party diagram addresses Richard Griffiths's criticism of Andrew Linzey. Linzey writes that "Perhaps I deserved the trenchant criticism of Richard Griffiths to the effect that the 'search for an adequate secular basis for animal rights is bound to fail because of the overriding difficulty of establishing any rights at all (even human rights) on a purely two-dimensional plane, without including some notion of God.'" Andrew Linzey, *Christianity and the Rights of Animals* (New York: Crossroad Press, 1987), 71.

9. Note should be made here of the fact that I use "other creatures" and "human creatures" in this diagram. Thus, based upon my earlier discussion of how I am using these terms, the reference here is to individual creatures. With due consideration to the fact that all creatures are individuals, these terms can be replaced with the terms "other kinds" and "humankind" respectively when one wishes to reference the relationships of taxa higher than the individual. However, I would not support their replacement with the terms "otherkind" and "humankind," respectively, because it diminishes the particularity to such an extent that its practical outcomes no longer are evident and because the anthropocentrism that comes from this overwhelms careful and reflective thought on creatures other than those of our own kind.

10. Gordis, *The Book of God and Man,* 120.

11. Ibid., 123.

12. A phrase I learned in my youth that expresses this is *Ecclesia reformata semper refermandum est,* "the reformed church is ever reforming."

13. See, for example, C. B. DeWitt, "Life as a Psalm to the Lord: Thanking God for Holsteins and Coyotes," *Reformed Worship* 35 (1995): 24–25.

14. I am reminded to put things this way by a Navajo graduate student in my laboratory whose doctoral research is based upon understanding the wisdom of his own culture. He too has the problem of being disrespectful and even sacrilegious by attempting to distill the teachings of his tradition devoid of sacrament, ritual, customary reflection, and praxis. For him, this is compounded by his tradition's not conveying some of the heritage to him until he will have gained understanding as an elder. Both he and I risk being sacrilegious toward our heritage by having to reprocess and "box" cultural knowledge and wisdom for rapid consumption. This, of course, is a problem for all cultures, not just Navajo and Christian ones.

15. A good way to begin to understand the tradition to which I refer is to read and study each of the texts cited, and read them directly in their contexts in one or more versions of the Bible, and then perhaps also to read or sing the psalms and hymns of the "blue" *Psalter Hymnal* (Grand Rapids, Mich.: CRC Publishing House, 1959).

16. Clearly, here we can have more than two lines between Creator and creatures, even as many as there are kinds or as many as there are individual creatures. However, our purpose here is to deal with the relationship between human and other creatures, and thus the two lines create the space for relating us to other kinds, shown by the basal horizontal line in the triangular diagram.

17. C. Dean Freudenberger tells the story of his experience in Africa during which soldiers engaged in Cold War activities shot hippos for food in the river where his family swam and bathed. Removal of the hippos eliminated grazing on the marsh grasses, reeds, and sedges. Growing tall, these plants captured silt and slowed water flow at the river margins, creating habitat suitable for snails, and with the snails also schistosomiasis (liver fluke). The hippo was eliminated and schistosomiasis established. A member of their community died from schisto and their community no longer could swim and bathe in the river (Freudenberger, personal communication, 17 April 1998).

18. However, Rev. 11:18 recognizes this: "The time has come for . . . destroying those who destroy the earth."

19. Abraham Joshua Heschel puts it this way: "Man rarely comprehends how dangerously mighty he is. . . . The realization of the dangerous greatness of man, of his immense power and ability to destroy all life on earth, must completely change our conception of man's place and role in the divine scheme." Heschel, *God in Search of Man: A Philosophy of Judaism* (New York: Farrar, Straus and Giroux, 1955), 171. This is the human capacity recognized in Revelation 11:18.

20. Colin A. Russell, *The Earth, Humanity, and God,* Templeton Lectures, Cambridge 1993 (London: UCL Press, 1994).

21. Abbreviations use for the various Bible translations are: NIV, New International version; DBY, Darby Version; RSV, Revised Standard Version; KJV, King James Version; and YLT, Young's Literal Translation.

22. The verb "con-serve" as compared with "serve" better indicates the relational connections between creatures and human beings. Use of "serve" can allow for the possibility of an "us-them" administration that conceivably can lead to "humble arrogance"—an arrogance of unidirectional service. If we use instead the word and concept of "con-service" we are continually reminded of the reciprocal service among the creatures that recognizes that otherkind also serves humankind. Thus, as

human beings we never achieve the status of "lords of creation," not even "servant-lords," but affirm only Jesus Christ or God triune as Lord of Creation, under whose eye we both behold the creatures and engage in con-service in creation. This differs somewhat from Andrew Linzey who, in responding to Keith Ward, writes: "given our God-given power and lordship over Creation it is *we* who should *serve creation.* The inner logic of Christ's lordship is the sacrifice of the higher for the lower; not the reverse. If the humility of God in Christ is costly and essential, why should ours be less so?" (Andrew Linzey, *Animal Theology* [Urbana: University of Illinois Press, 1995], 71). This appears to be a development from an earlier work in which he writes, "Slowly but surely, having grasped that the notion of dominion means stewardship, we are now for the first time capable of seeing how demanding our lordship over creation is really meant to be. . . . [O]ur power cannot be understood as legitimate except as service, which is necessarily costly and sacrificial. Lordship without service is indeed tyranny." (Linzey, *Christianity and the Rights of Animals*, 29).

23. Harvard Hebrew scholar Krister Stendahl notes that the use of the Hebrew word *shamar* is largely used in relating God's keeping, not as much the keeping of things by human beings (personal communication, 17 April 1998). This, linked with consideration of human beings as made in the image of God may have significance in Genesis 2:15 in the sense that this keeping by human beings reflects God's keeping.

24. See Rolf Bouma, "Creation's Persistent Voice: Critiquing the Secondary Status of Creation as Revelation," *J. Faith and Science Exchange,* 1977: 1–6. He asks "what the result would be if the Christian community allowed creation to be taken out of the children's section and off the secondary reference shelf and moved to a place of genuine engagement. What if the natural sciences were truly allowed a dialogue with theology, and Christian theology were to resist the impulse to cut the conversation short?"

25. "The kinship relationship suggests a reciprocity rather than a competition. . . . competition is not the basic social dynamic of the environment. . . . If this is our home, then measuring costs and benefits is not the basic moral logic. Rather, it is a concern for the health of all the creatures belonging to a given place, from the creatures of the soil and water to the humans and other creatures of the land surface to the birds of the air." L. Shannon Jung, "Animals in Christian Perspective: Strangers, Friends, or Kin?" in *Good News for Animals? Christian Approaches to Animal Well-Being,* ed. Charles Pinches and Jay B. McDaniel (Maryknoll, N.Y.: Orbis Books, 1993), 59.

26. Here, I am reflecting the thought of Elizabeth H. Wolgast (*The Grammar of Justice* [Ithaca: Cornell University Press, 1987]), who deals with the "inadequacies in the atomistic model of human society derived from Hobbes and Locke and embodied in the U.S. Constitution." She "demonstrates that traditional liberal theory, with its emphasis on individual rights and self-defined interest, cannot by itself give an adequate picture of community, morality, or justice." (Quotes from outside back cover.) This accords with Jung, for whom rights language can be seen, at best, as "the lowest secular common denominator of gracious love" ("Animals in Perspective," 57), and with Hauerwas and Berkman, for whom "this use of the language of rights embodies the very anthropocentrism that is antithetical to the goals of those who participate in the movement known as 'Animal Rights'" and who conclude "that to

ascribe rights to an animal may in the short run be a strategy for its survival, but in the long run this language will simply maintain the current understandings of and practices in relation to other animals that continually bring about their destruction" (Stanley Hauerwas and John Berkman, "A Trinitarian Theology of the 'Chief End' of 'All Flesh,'" in *Good News for Animals? Christian Approaches to Animal Well-Being,* ed. Charles Pinches and Jay B. McDaniel (Maryknoll, N.Y.: Orbis Books, 1993), 66. In his *Animal Theology,* Andrew Linzey makes some concession to the direction of these other authors by writing, "The concept of rights, I suggest is fully compatible with moral theology and should be properly extended to include animals. At the same time, I resist the idea that rights language is exhaustive of everything that should be said from a theological perspective about animals. In my view, there are good theological grounds for respecting the worth of animals, accepting responsibility *and* recognizing their God-given rights" (Linzey, *Animal Theology,* 19).

27. See Exod. 20:10; Deut. 25:4; Prov. 12:10; Luke 13:5, 14:5.

28. Liberation from human keeping does not mean animal liberation in the sense that animals are given freedom to overcome their human companions in creation, as is becoming the situation for people in the village of Banpukele at the edge of the Réserve de Fauna à Okapi (RFO) in northern Congo. Here, one of the village elders, reflecting on the new RFO regulations against killing animals, observed: "now the animals are oppressing us. If it was still like it was in the past, they would kill them. Now, the animals—elephants, every type of animal, baboons—they have made their way even all the way into our houses!" Another elder added, "Elephants were people who would go way off into the forest. . . . But now, at this time, elephants are right here in the village. In the village!" And others: "You see, the animals have gotten their independence." "Now the animals are simply destroying our food. And you can look at them, but you better not kill them." "Just like people in the village, they have begun eating all the foods that people are planting in addition to their foods of the forest . . ." (Richard B. Peterson, personal communication, 21 April 1998).

29. As Noah did, for example. On the ark each creature required that its individual needs be attended to, but Noah's purpose was not to meet all of these needs from then on; instead, it was his purpose ultimately to free these animals into habitats that would sustain them without additional human help.

30. It is this consideration that brings Shannon Jung to say: "The approach to right relations which invokes animal rights is, at best, inappropriate. It operates on the basic perspective of seeing animals as strangers, and short-circuits its own manifest intent to encourage humane treatment for animals. It basically undermines relationality" (Jung, "Animals in Christian Perspective, 55–56.) Shannon does concede, however, that "In defense of rights language, it does seem necessary in those situations in which basic human regard for the other has been grievously violated. Rights tend to get expressed in law, and there is a genuine place in law to establish minimum standards of right conduct among equals" (56).

31. This can be given the name stewardship. And if this is properly understood as con-service and earthkeeping that includes beholding named creatures and creatures to be named, then stewardship is a good descriptive term. It is in this sense, I believe, that Colin Russell employs stewardship. Russell (*The Earth, Humanity, and God*), concludes that stewardship offers both the best practical understanding and the best

prospects for our world. He tells us that, at the conceptual level, stewardship makes a great effort to understand the complex systems of the planet and biosphere. It recognizes that in times of environmental degradation the need for public understanding of science is greater than ever. At the perceptual level, stewardship leads people to value the earth highly as a treasure held in trust. This includes development of empathy with nature and sympathy with those who work for environmental integrity. At the relational level, stewardship elicits practical strategies for relating people to the earth as responsible members who are obedient to the dictates of conscience.

32. See H. Richard Niebuhr's supplementary essay entitled "The Center of Value," in H. Richard Niebuhr, *Radical Monotheism and Western Culture* (New York: Harper and Row, 1943), 100–113. In it he writes: "vitalistic or evolutionary value systems beginning with life of the community of living beings can make rational judgements about what is good for life—the fitness of an environment, the mutual limitations of living beings in right relations of the struggle for existence—but it cannot or does not raise the question what the community of the living is good for."

33. Stephen R. L. Clark concludes his book: "Our duty is to admire and to sustain the world in beauty, and not to impose on others pains and penalties we could not bear ourselves. . . . We ought to live by those laws that an ideal observer or Creator-God would make (maybe has made) for the world: to respect the integrity of every creature, and not to seize more for ourselves and our immediate kin than would be granted under such a dispensation." Stephen R. L. Clark, *Animals and Their Moral Standing* (London and New York: Routledge, 1997), 168.

34. Andrew Linzey identifies six main ethical theories of the status of animals: Humanocentric, Contractualist, Humanitarian, Welfare, Rights, and Generosity theories. In Paul Barry Clarke and Andrew Linzey, *Dictionary of Ethics, Theology, and Society* (London and New York: Routledge, 1996), 29–33. The theory presented in this paper does not fall into any of these categories neatly. This is due largely to the three-party Creator-creature-human construct that characterizes the present work. However, it has some of the character of the Generosity theory espoused by Linzey in that it has generous costly service at its heart.

35. Gen. 1; Col. 1:15–20; Apostles' Creed; Nicene Creed; Athanasian Creed; Belgic Confession, article 2. See *The Creeds of Christendom,* ed. Philip Schaff (Grand Rapids, Mich.: Baker, 1931).

36. "Subtle is the Lord, but malicious is he not." For further insight on this, see the frontispiece in Abraham Pais, *"Subtle is the Lord": The Science and Life of Albert Einstein* (New York: Oxford University Press, 1982).

37. Ps. 24:1; Our World Belongs to God: A Contemporary Testimony (pp. 1019–38), "This is My Father's World" (no. 374), and "The Earth and the Fullness with Which it is Stored" (no. 41) in the *Psalter Hymnal* (Grand Rapids, Mich.: CRC Publications, 1987).

38. See Gen. 9:8–17.

39. See Job 38–40; Ps. 104.

40. 1 Cor. 3:23 and Titus 2:14.

41. Matt. 10:29–31.

42. See Job 38–40; Ps. 104. "Hallelujah, Praise Jehovah," *Psalter Hymnal* (1959), no. 304.

43. John 3:16; Ps. 104; "My Soul, Bless the Lord!" (no. 206), "Hallelujah, Praise Jehovah" (no. 301), and "Joy to the World" (no. 337) in the *Psalter Hymnal* (1959).

44. See Gen. 1:26–27, 9:6.

45. "Of course not in its sinful strivings and unholy motions," writes Abraham Kuyper of God's love for the world—the love for the world that we human beings are to mirror (Abraham Kuyper, "God So Loved the World!" chap. 7 of his *Keep Thy Solemn Feasts: Meditations,* trans. John Hendrik de Vries [Grand Rapids, Mich.: Eerdmans, 1928], 70–71).

46. Ezek. 34:18; Deut. 20:19–20, 22:6–7.

47. See Job 40:19.

48. See Exod. 20:10; Deut. 5:14.

49. See Exod. 20:10; Deut. 5:14.

50. Gen. 2:7. "The Tender Love a Father Has," *Psalter Hymnal* (1959), no. 205.

51. Isa. 66:1; Acts 7:49; Matt. 5:34–35.

52. Job 38:4–40:2.

53. Gen. 2:15.

54. Gen. 1:27.

55. Gen. 2:15.

56. Gen. 2:19.

57. 1 Kings 4:33.

58. Rev. 11:18; cf. Isa. 33; 1 Cor. 15:24.

59. John 3:16; 1 Cor. 15:22.

60. See Ps. 112:2; Job 12:7–10.

61. Gordon J. Spykman, *Reformational Theology: A New Paradigm for Doing Dogmatics* (Grand Rapids, Mich.: Eerdmans, 1992).

62. See Matt. 6:33.

63. The phrase sometimes used for the wholeness and integrity that should be sought is "the Kingdom of God," which has its expression, for example, in Matt. 6:33.

64. 1 Tim. 6:6–21. "On the Good and Faithful," *Psalter Hymnal* (1959), no. 7.

65. Prov. 14:5; John 8:31ff.; and "Who, O Lord, with Thee Abiding" (no. 20), "Grace and Truth Shall Mark the Way" (no. 45), and "Be Thou My Judge" (no. 47), *Psalter Hymnal* (1959).

66. Ezek. 33:1–6.

67. Jon. 3–4.

68. Ps. 19:1; Acts 14:17; Rom. 1:20. "O Lord, Our Lord, in All the Earth" (no. 12), "The Spacious Heavens Declare" (no. 28), "The Heavens Declare Thy Glory" (no. 31), "Sing a New Song to Jehovah" (no. 190), "Exalt the Lord, His Praise Proclaim" (no. 282), "Give Thanks to God for Good is He" (no. 284), and "Great is Thy Faithfulness" (no. 408), *Psalter Hymnal* (1959).

Words beneath the Water:
Logos, Cosmos, and the Spirit of Place

DOUGLAS BURTON-CHRISTIE

Introduction

Deep in the heart of a sandstone canyon, in what is now southern Utah, an unknown figure daubs pigment against the stone. Again and again until a slender, ghostly figure emerges, its deep auburn hues radiant, its gaunt silhouette gesturing forth. Thousands of miles away, at almost the same moment, an old man on the island of Patmos in Greece pauses to wonder at the marks drying on the parchment before him: "When all things began, the Word already was. The Word dwelt with God, and what God was, the Word was. . . . Through the Word, all things came into being" (John 1:1).

Of those mysterious figures in Barrier Canyon, Kiowa writer N. Scott Momaday notes: "they are invested with the very essence of language, the language of story and myth and primal song."[1] Here, he suggests, we are at the root of American literature. A literature emerging from and bound to a particular place. A literature that speaks *of* the natural world, *through* the natural world, through the geologic shape of the canyon, bird song, the play of sun and moonlight among the cottonwoods, the shifting currents of floodwater, the wind. As does early Christian literature. The evangelist makes this clear: *Panta. All things*. Apart from the Word, "not one thing came into being." Here, close to the source of Christian life, arises another myth, another primal song, giving expression in its own terms to the intricate dance between Word and world. A song full of wonder and amazement at the notion that God has been speaking to us from all eternity through everything that exists. Wonder, too, that the creative Word through whom the cosmos exists has taken on human flesh and dwelt among us, has made all things whole again.

Does the world have a voice? Does it speak a language we can understand? Does it, perhaps, beckon to us, call us toward an intimate encounter? Both the American literary tradition and the Christian theological tradition have long been haunted by such questions. I want to ask here whether reading these two traditions together might help us deepen our capacity to attend to, respond to, and care for the natural world. Can the Christian understanding of the Word incarnate—in all its cosmological and sacramental fullness—illuminate our experience of the natural world on this continent and our poetic expression of that experience? And can the American experience of the natural world and its various literary expressions—with its acute sensitivity to the language of this land—deepen the Christian understanding of the Word incarnate? This theopoetic work seems not only possible but necessary if we hope to rediscover the living world as charged with the presence of the holy. But to realize this will require us to learn again how to listen. "I have come to feel," says Alaska writer John Haines, "that there is here in North America a hidden place obscured by what we have built upon it, and that whenever we penetrate the surface of the life around us that place and its spirit can be found."[2] If we learn to listen, we may yet come to hear the voice beckoning to us from that hidden place.

Logos and Cosmos

Christian belief and practice is rooted in the Word. One of the most significant and elastic root metaphors within the Christian tradition, *logos* possesses a seemingly endless reservoir of significance, catching and giving expression to a constellation of Christian mysteries, all grounded in the sense that God comes to us as a kind of utterance.[3] Nor is this metaphor limited to its linguistic roots: like the cottonwood tree deep in the desert canyon that draws into its branches wrens, juncos, hawks, and ravens and pulses with their movement and color, so the Word has attracted to itself diverse symbols and metaphors, many drawn from the natural world, that have deepened and enriched the Word's expressive power. The redemptive power of the Word has been understood as having come to expression not only through the person of Jesus and the scriptures, but also through the varied expressions of the cosmos itself. There is a reciprocal process at work here: the natural world informed the Christian understanding of *logos;* and the evolving sense of the pervasive presence of the *logos* helped the Christian imagination see and understand the world as charged with ultimate significance.

Already in the New Testament one can see the Christian imagination beginning to reflect upon the cosmological significance of the *logos.* In the prologue of John's gospel and in the letter to the Colossians especially, Christ the Word is understood as the utterance through whom the world has come into existence. Redemption and creation are understood as part of a single, continuous process. The world is incomprehensible apart from the Word. And the Word is apprehended in and through the world. This potent cosmological sense of *logos* comes into Christianity through an eclectic range of influences, including the Jewish understanding of *sophia* (wisdom), the feminine creative principle through whom the world comes into being, and *dabar,* the divine Word of Yahweh that effects what it says. Also present in this unfolding process are traditions of Greek philosophical speculation on *logos* as mediating principle between God and the world.

Among the most important of these latter traditions was the Stoic tradition of Word as seed that proved so fruitful for the evolving Christian understanding of theology, soteriology, and cosmology. The Stoics believed that the universe was governed by the divine *logos,* was in some sense identical with the *logos,* and must therefore be rational and bound by rules of cause and effect. But how to account for the inexplicable changes and developments that occur in nature that are not easily predicted by such rules? The answer the Stoics arrived at was the notion of the *spermatikos logos*, the seed of the *logos* which contains within itself the germ of everything it is eventually to become. *Logoi spermatikoi* exist as seeds planted, as it were, in the divine *logos* waiting to germinate and unfold at some later, divinely ordained moment.[4] The *logos* is not merely an idea, a philosophical principle. It is a kind of palpable substance. Zeno likened it to fire. It is "as it were a seed, possessing the *logoi* of all things and the causes of events, past, present, and future."[5] The cosmos is alive with this word. The metaphor of the Word as seed not only helped to address a pressing philosophical question—did the universe cohere? It also suggested the deep and significant continuity between the *logos* as generative principle of the universe and the *logoi* that quickens every human person and the entire living world. It is in this sense that the Stoics could say, as philosopher Erazim Kohák suggests, that: "The *logos* is the order of the *kosmos,* guiding alike the flight of the sparrow and the life of the sage."[6] From such a perspective, the human is anything but a stranger in the cosmos.

Here is an understanding of the Word that early Christian thinkers found immensely helpful to their own attempts to articulate a theologically and cosmologically meaningful Christology. Tertullian, for example, draws upon the Stoic understanding of the *logos* in responding to those like Hermagoras who claim that God is remote from the created world. To the contrary, he says: the Stoics remind us "that God permeates the world in the same way as honey in the comb."[7] Elsewhere, he addresses the question of how the divine *logos* can be said to permeate the sensible world without losing its divinity: it is like the sun's relations with its own rays, he says, which are a portion and extension of their source.[8] Both analogies draw upon the idea of *logos* as generative principle immanent in the cosmos. Tertullian also voices his support for the Stoic idea that everything which exists, including the *logos,* is a kind of body: "All things have one form of simple corporeality, which is a substantial thing."[9]

Other theologians, such as Clement of Alexandria, give more attention to the transcendent character of the *logos,* all the while seeking to discover an understanding of the Word supple enough to encompass both the transcendent reality of God and the immanent particularity of the living world. Drawing upon an eclectic mix of Jewish-Alexandrine philosophy, Stoicism, Middle Platonism, and Neoplatonism, Clement articulates an understanding of the *logos* capable of reaching into the hidden depths of the transcendent Godhead while also stretching out across the whole universe. According to Clement, the *logos* has three distinct but related dimensions. It is utterly transcendent, being identical with the totality of the ideas or powers of God. It is also the principle or pattern of everything that has been created. And it is the *anima mundi,* or world soul, the law and harmony of the universe, the power which holds it together and permeates it from the center to its most extreme boundaries.[10]

Subsequent Christian reflections on this idea unfurled like so many seeds scattered by the winds, flowering, cross-pollinating, and spilling their seeds again into the dark loam of the earth. The Word's cosmic expressions within the Christian tradition are, to borrow a phrase Paul Ricoeur uses to describe the revelatory character of scripture, irreducibly polyphonous and polysemous.[11] Light, darkness, seed, garden, tree, bread, wine are but some of the palpable realities of the world through which the *logos* was believed to have gestured forth.[12] So too were the modes of its expression diverse, arising not only within Christian theological discourse, but also in art and architecture, in biblical commentary, in mystical literature, in ascetic practice, in music, in poetry.

Consider how in the *fiat lux* of the Genesis Creation account and in the luminous gold background of ancient Christian and later Byzantine mosaics, *logos* comes to expression through light.[13] Or consider how the Word that speaks through the cross also gestures forth across the cosmos. According to Irenaeus, "because [Christ] is Himself the Word of God . . . who in His invisible form pervades us universally in the whole world, and encompasses its length and breadth and height and depth . . . the Son of God was also crucified in these, imprinted in the form of a cross on the universe." In the Mausoleum of Galla Placida in Ravenna this cosmic cross is given exquisite artistic expression, appearing on a dark blue shallow dome in the midst of stars arranged in concentric circles, whose diminishing size toward the center gives one the impression of gazing into a heavenly vault.[14]

Consider the power of the *logos* who, according to Origen of Alexandria, rises up to meet us in the biblical text as ardent lover and who kindles within us a passionate love for the world: "If a [person] can so extend his thinking as to ponder and consider the beauty and grace of all things that have been created in the Word," he claims, "the very charm of them will so smite him, the grandeur of their brightness will so pierce him as with a chosen dart . . . that he will suffer from the dart Himself a saving wound, and will be kindled with the blessed fire of His love."[15] Here is a sensual, palpable Word, present to us, says Origen, as touch, fragrance, sound, vision, and taste.

Within the Christian monastic tradition, tasting and chewing upon the Word became a way of life. For the monks of the Egyptian desert, the Word arose from the silence as a powerful and numinous presence. To ruminate, digest, and absorb such a Word into the marrow of one's being was to be brought into the very presence of the Holy One. Nor was the desert landscape itself an insignificant part of this process. According to Athanasius's *Life of Antony,* the Word of God not only beckoned Antony to withdraw into the desert, but called him to a particular place, *from* a particular place. It was a wild and beautiful spot in the remote Arabian desert known simply as "the inner mountain." Athanasius tells us that it exercised a powerful pull on Antony's imagination and that, upon seeing it for the first time, he "immediately fell in love with the place." The entire subsequent tradition of monastic stability, or devotion to place, owes much to this early sense that places do indeed speak with a particular voice, that rumination upon the Word and the spirit of the place are integral elements in a larger rhythm.

Rhythm and movement, form and color are also important to the expression of the *logos* within the long tradition of manuscript illustration, in which the Word was often set—actually and figuratively— within an entire constellation of living beings, suggesting the sense in which the Word is virtually embedded within and arising out of the living world. In the Lindisfarne Gospels, for example, one finds surrounding its illustration of the opening words from John's gospel, *In principio erat verbum:* "trumpet-patterns, whorls, triangles and lozenges, and birds and animals interlaced, as though foreshadowing the whole wealth of forms and life that was to issue from the Word; and this whole microcosm is highlighted by the interplay of colours used for the illumination . . . green, mauve, yellow, red and pink."[16] To gaze upon this intricate dance of Word and world is to be drawn more deeply into the mystery of the Word's generative power. It is also to be asked to listen more carefully to the eloquence of the world.

It is to be invited to listen, as twelfth-century mystic and visionary Hildegard of Bingen apparently did, for traces of the *prima vox,* or "voice primordial," the animating principle everywhere present in the world.[17] It is to feel the redemptive, healing transformative power of the incarnation as "a blossoming of a beautiful flower / that gave fragrance / to all the spices / which had been dry."[18] It is to listen intently for the music in that flowering, a music that is the redemptive power of the Word present at once in the soul and the cosmos. And it is to be invited to respond, in song, to that music. As Hildegard did, her *symphonia* refracting and giving voice to the celestial harmony that was revealed to her through vision and through the palpable world. Or as Francis of Assisi did, praising God in his renowned Canticle to the Creatures, not *because* of the creatures but *through* them, his own voice rising, as it were, through theirs: "All praise be yours, my Lord, through Sisters Moon and Stars. . . . All praise be yours . . . through Brothers Wind and Air."[19]

Certainly, the Christian tradition does not speak with a single or unified voice regarding the presence of the *logos* at the heart of creation. I have focused my attention here on some of the ways the Word comes to expression through the palpable, material reality of the natural world. But there are significant countercurrents in the tradition, more radically transcendent, interior expressions of the Word that are also important to the Christian understanding of God, self, and cosmos. A full and adequate Christian understanding of the Word would require taking seriously the continuous, often creative, often irresolvable tension between its immanent and transcendent expressions. It might even require us to find new language for this tension, to pursue more vigorously the sense of "transcendence downwards" that appears so powerfully in the poetry of Wallace Stevens. Still, I *do* mean to call attention to a tendency, a pattern within Christian thought and practice that binds world and Word together as part of a single, continuous whole, a pattern that can instruct us regarding how we might begin articulating a Christian theopoetics of the natural world.

I think we need to take seriously the irreducibly poetic character of these ruminations on the Word. The natural, physical, spatial metaphors and analogies alluded to here—the long-germinating seed, the drenched honeycomb, the permeating warmth of the sun, the lover's embrace, spatial depth and breadth, embodiment—are more than merely decorative. They create the medium, the tensive space, in which the often paradoxical, richly allusive meaning of the *logos* gradually unfolds. Nor is this meaning grasped only or even primarily as an idea. Mediated by these tensive metaphors and symbols, drawing on the mythic depths to which this language refers, *logos* beckons the imagination, draws us in at every level of our being. Here is an exemplary instance of the theopoetic process at work, the Christian theological imagination weaving materials old and new into a fabric of immense and lasting significance. If we follow Clement, who introduced the term *theopoesis* into the Christian vocabulary, we begin to realize that this process involves at its most profound level nothing less than divinization, being taken up into the life of God—in and through the life or *logos* of everything that exists.

When refracted through the experience of the risen Christ, this understanding of the *logos* becomes a way of articulating the ultimate personal and cosmic significance of Christian faith. "Were we to imagine," says Sallie McFague, "'The Word made flesh' as not limited to Jesus of Nazareth but as the body of the universe, all bodies, might we not have a homey and awesome metaphor for both divine nearness *and* divine glory?"[20] Such a full-bodied reading of this metaphor would allow, even require, the Christian imagination to search out and become conversant with every language of every place and every being through which God comes to expression in the universe.

Lingua Vernacula and the Spirit of Place

But how to learn this language? How to recover the capacity to hear the subtle music, the voice of the world? We will need to begin, I think, by working to cultivate what Barry Lopez calls a "more particularized understanding" of place, an understanding alert to the infinitely subtle, delicate, and varied life of particular places. In the ancient pictographs of the Southwest, in the myths, stories, and songs of so many indigenous peoples of this continent, and in the literature and poetry of nature that has flourished in this country during the past one hundred and fifty years, one finds language deeply rooted in particular places, responsive to the life and movements of plant and animal species through those places, intricately woven into the patterns of sky, rock, and wind.[21] One finds vivid traces, that is, of an incarnate Word. To listen to this Word is to hear a language arising from the shape and texture of the living world, a Word as old as the world itself. It is to be brought around to dwell in a silence beyond and beneath all language, from which language and the world itself arise.

This "more particularized understanding" of place arises, as does all understanding, through language, which is why the careful attention to language that one finds in this literature is so significant. Through precise description, apt metaphor, and vivid narrative, language acts as a medium through which the voice of a place can emerge. But language is not only medium. It is also a metaphor. The metaphor of the Word arises as a question: is the natural world itself a kind of language, speaking to us, beckoning to us? Living with this question leads to others. If we listen carefully enough, can we learn this language? Will we begin to find our own voices inflected with the language of the living world? Will we find ourselves taken up into the world in an intimate embrace?

Such questions seem to have been much on the mind of Henry David Thoreau during his sojourn at Walden Pond. To listen, to learn the language of the place—these were his central concerns. "We are in danger," he says in *Walden,* "of forgetting the language which all things and all events speak without metaphor, which alone is copious and standard." This is the fundamental language, of which the language of books is but a pale reflection. Which is why, he says, he spent his first summer at Walden not reading books but hoeing beans, giving himself over to what he called "the bloom of the present moment," to "the discipline of looking always at what is to be seen."

> Sometimes, in a summer morning, having taken my accustomed bath, I sat in my sunny doorway from sunrise till noon, rapt in a revery, amidst the pines and hickories and sumachs, in undisturbed solitude and stillness, while the birds sang around or flitted noiseless through the house, until by the sun falling in at my west window, or the noise of some traveler's wagon on a distant highway, I was reminded of the lapse of time.[22]

Here, as throughout his work, the language of consciousness or awareness seems to occupy Thoreau's interest every bit as much as the language of the world. What does it mean to pay attention? To abandon oneself so fully to observing the world that one is no longer "a reader, a student merely, but a seer?" Such questions haunt the pages of *Walden* and remind us how intent Thoreau was not only on listening to the language emerging in and through the texture of the world but also on attending to that profoundly interior moment when "a fact flowered into a truth." At times in *Walden,* the language of the world becomes absorbed into and even eclipsed by the language of awareness.

Still, one catches hints elsewhere—in *Walden,* in the *Journal,* and in other late works—that Thoreau never lost interest in trying to hear and respond to the distinctive voice of his own place. In *Walden*'s "Winter Animals" chapter, he notes:

For sounds in winter nights, and often in winter days, I heard the for-
lorn but melodious note of a hooting owl indefinitely far; such a sound
as the frozen earth would yield if struck with a suitable plectrum, the
very *lingua vernacula* of Walden Wood, and quite familiar to me at
last, though I never saw the bird while it was making it.[23]

Here, again, the metaphor of the Word mediates the terms of the encounter. It is language Thoreau is listening for, a language rooted in,
arising from, particular to this place. And he hears it in the cry of the
owl, which speaks in "the very *lingua vernacula* of Walden Wood." It
is not clear why the owl is seen as being the quintessential voice of
this place. But the precise reason for this choice is less important here
than the fact that Thoreau thinks of the owl's sounded presence as a
kind of "vernacular language," a local language or dialect. And that
he notes that this language has become "quite familiar to me *at last.*"
It takes time to learn the language of a place, time and careful
attention to the intricate patterns of the place.

The language of nature, Thoreau suggests here, comes to us intimately and incrementally, through our growing familiarity with a
particular place. This is why he gave himself over, with ever greater
acuteness and precision, to the study of Concord's botanical, zoologi-
cal, and geological forms. This is particularly apparent in his great
study of seed dispersal, a study Thoreau hoped would reveal to him
the true language of the forest. This study led him, as one commentator has noted, to move "past the mere naming of trees—the nouns of
the forest—to track its verbs: the birds, rodents, and insects that pol-
linate flowers or disperse seeds, and all other agents that shape the
forest's structure."[24] He was intent on uncovering the subtle dynamism of his home place in all its complexity, not only as it presented
itself in a given moment but also as it unfolded across time. Careful
observation, scientific precision, and literary expression converged to
create a powerful and compelling poetics of nature, as in this
description of maples' keys, part of a much longer account of the life
of maple trees within the local ecosystem:

About the middle of May, the red maples along the edges of swamps,
their fruit being nearly ripe, are among the most beautiful objects in
the landscape, especially if seen in a favorable light with respect to the
sun. The keys are high colored, a sort of pink scarlet commonly,
dangling at the end of peduncles three inches or more in length and

only a little darker shade than themselves. The lit masses of these double samarae, with their peduncles gracefully arching upward and outward a little before they curve downward in order to spread the fruit and give it room, are unequally disposed along the branches, where they tremble in the wind and are often tangled by it. Like the flower of the shadbush, this handsome fruit is seen for the most part against bare twigs, it is so much in advance of its own and other leaves.[25]

Are we drawing closer here in this spare, lyric language to the language of the forest itself? Thoreau seemed to think so, seemed to feel he was gradually moving toward a more adequate means of evoking and encompassing the life of the place he called home. As his language grew both more precise and more intricate, the complex dynamism of Walden's entire life world gradually came into clearer focus.

Not that he ever stopped believing in the transcendentalist idea of correspondence, in which the truth of the physical world is understood as always corresponding to a hidden, transcendent truth. But as Daniel Peck has shown so clearly, the patterns of correspondence that most interested Thoreau toward the end of his life were not vertical ones, between the seen and unseen world, but horizontal ones, between one thing and another in the natural world.[26] Thoreau's sense of transcendence became increasingly grounded, increasingly focused on the unfolding relationships *within* the natural world. The language of his later work, which can seem relatively lacking in literary style compared with *Walden,* may in fact reflect a more difficult and sharply focused literary accomplishment: the evocation of the world as it is. By 1857, already deep into his study of seed dispersal, Thoreau could declare confidently but also with humility: "If a man is rich and strong anywhere, it must be on his native soil. Here I have been these forty years of learning the language of these fields that I may better express myself."[27]

Self-expression here becomes a means of bringing the natural world itself to expression, an expression which, if transparent enough, if supple and imaginative enough, can help us rehabilitate our capacity to hear and understand the language of the world. Which is one of the reasons why the sustained conversation about language and landscape currently unfolding among writers and poets in this country is so significant and encouraging. Here we have a literature that is itself a kind of conversation with the living world, a conversation characterized by a remarkable willingness to listen, to pay attention—to the color, fragrance, and texture of the living world, to its intricate life; and by a conviction that such attention can facilitate an encounter—with the living world and with the numinous presence that speaks to us in and through the world. No wonder, then, that the poetry and prose issuing forth from this encounter so often feels like prayer, like a response to a word already spoken by the living world.

One can sense this in the lyric evocation of place one finds throughout this literature. Through delicate and precise description, the *lingua vernacula* of particular places is brought to palpable expression. An example is the work of Denise Levertov, in which the voice of the Pacific Northwest, and of Mt. Rainier in particular, can be heard so clearly:

> clear gold
> of late summer, of opening autumn,
> the dawn eagle sunning himself on the highest tree,
> the mountain revealing herself unclouded, her snow
> tinted apricot as she looked west,
> tolerant, in her steadfastness, of the restless sun
> forever rising and setting.[28]

For Alaska writer Richard Nelson, the *lingua vernacula* is discerned in the "shrill voices" of oyster catchers "punishing but beautiful, a pure incantation of this northern shore, arising from the dark rocks, the chill gray waters, and the slick fronds of kelp."[29] For Robert Hass, a Californian, it is in the intricate delicacy of a Sierra Nevada mountain meadow on a late afternoon that one senses the local language:

> So many wildflowers
> tangled in the grass. So many grasses—reedgrass, the bentgrass
>   and timothy, little quaking grass, dogtail, rip-gut brome—
>   the seeds flaring from the stalks
> in tight chevrons of green and purple-green
> but loosening.[30]

To name and describe with such care and precision is to open up a space within the self in which the minute particularities of the living world can sound and take hold. It is, as Mary Oliver suggests, "To learn something by being nothing / A little while but the rich lens of attention."[31]

But attention here means more than looking and listening. It means working to cultivate empathy. As Oliver says elsewhere, it means trying

> . . . to enter the long black branches
>   of other lives—
> . . . to imagine what the crisp fringes, full of honey,
>   hanging
> from the branches of the young locust trees, in early summer,
>   feel like[.][32]

It means working to discover within oneself the capacity for deep engagement, for encounter, working to kindle a sense of relationship between one's own life and those "other lives." It means learning to give oneself over, unstintingly, to these other lives, dwelling among them, ardently seeking and listening.

> Only last week I went out among the thorns and said
>   to the wild roses:
> deny me not,
> but suffer my devotion.
> Then, all afternoon, I sat among them. Maybe
>
> I even heard a curl or two of music, damp and rouge-red,
> hurrying from their stubby buds, from their delicate watery bodies.[33]

Is this not the language of prayer, the most intimate and probing of all languages? Certainly the audacity of the direct address—"I . . . said / to the wild roses"—and the boldness of the imperative voice—"Deny me not"—suggest something akin to prayer. So does the note of humility: "*suffer* my devotion," the poet implores; "allow me," that is, "permit me." Such language reflects a reverential respect, even awe, a sense that one is approaching the numinous other. So, too, does the language of devotion. To devote oneself is to vow oneself, conse-crate oneself to the Holy One. And if the object of one's devotion should turn out to be wild roses? Then, seek there the voice, the presence of the numinous. Significantly, the most eloquent expression of devotion here comes not through spoken words, but through an extravagant, deeply contemplative gesture: "all afternoon I sat among them." Saying nothing at all, apparently. Listening, rather, for the voice of these wild roses, hearing—"maybe"—a kind of music, "damp and rouge-red," arising from their "delicate watery bodies."

Poetry here becomes a kind of prayer, a response to a word arising in and through the living world. The language of prayer, it turns out, is necessary and integral to the contemporary experience and poetic expression of the Word incarnate. But this poetic expression, like so much of our experience of the natural world, is fraught with uncertainty and doubt. We are not sure whether we hear and understand the voice of the living world. "*Maybe* / I . . . heard a curl or two of music," says the poet. Prayer and the poetry of prayer become a means of probing this uncertain terrain, of asking the most difficult questions, such as whether the world speaks at all, whether we can discern the meaning of its signs, whether we possess the capacity and courage to respond.

Nowhere in contemporary literature have these questions been subject to a more searching inquiry than in Annie Dillard's *Pilgrim at Tinker Creek*. Signs abound in the natural world, she suggests, including signs hinting at a transcendent presence. There is a language speaking in and through the world. But it is ambiguous and immensely difficult to read. She describes waking one morning to discover her cat has kneaded her chest while she slept and left her covered in blood, as though she had been painted with roses. But she wonders: "what blood was this, and what roses? It could have been the rose of union, the blood of murder, or the rose of beauty bare and the blood of some unspeakable sacrifice or birth."[34] And so it continues, the universe speaking now as an "inrush of power and light," now as a "thick darkness"; now as an Osage orange tree lighting up as though kindled from within by fire, now as a tiny frog suddenly imploding, its muscles and organs dissolved by the venom of a giant water bug; now as the gratuitous free fall of a mockingbird, now as the grotesque pressure of fecundity. To attend to such a world, to inquire into its meaning requires the courage and devotion of a pilgrim, Dillard suggests. It also requires the capacity to live with ambiguity, to respond to the world with something like faith. Not blind faith, for the world is not utterly bereft of signs. But a naked faith, able to carry us deep into the darkness of a *via negativa,* beyond signs, beyond language where the world and the Word speaking through the world are encountered, as mystics have always understood, in both knowing and unknowing.

But perhaps we are lacking in faith. Perhaps we do not really believe the world speaks to us or that we know how to listen. These troubling questions form the heart of Louise Glück's remarkable book-length prayer-poem, *Wild Iris*. More than one-third of the fifty-four poems in this collection are set within the ancient ritual context of Matins and Vespers and are themselves prayers. With profound longing and an often painful sense of uncertainty, they address a God who may or may not be listening, who may not even exist. But the world exists and it is the world that speaks, that responds to these prayers, mostly in the language of flowers—trillium, lamium, snow-drops, scilla, violets, clover, a red poppy, a white rose—but also in the language of a clear morning, retreating wind, early darkness, September twilight. Each has its own subjective presence, each its own distinctive voice. Each calls out to the lonely supplicant, seeking through a gesture of some kind, through a word, to touch, maybe to heal. Glück invites us to enter imaginatively into the life of these beings, to consider what their voices might sound like, what they might be saying to us. What might we hear if we really listened to the sunset?

> My great happiness
> is the sound your voice makes
> calling to me even in despair; my sorrow
> that I cannot answer you
> in speech you accept as mine.
>
> You have no faith in your own language.
> So you invest
> authority in signs
> you cannot read with any accuracy.
>
> And yet your voice reaches me always.
> And I answer constantly,
> my anger passing
> as winter passes. My tenderness
> should be apparent to you
> in the breeze of the summer evening
> and in the words that become
> your own response.[35]

Like the words of this poem, perhaps.

Here Glück struggles with one of the most fundamental questions of prayer, indeed of all theology: do we share the same language? Can we hear and understand what the "Other" is saying to us? Can we respond? There is a profound sense of brokenness at the heart of this exchange. The sunset here speaks as a lover longing for intimacy with her beloved, an intimacy mediated through an exchange of voices. But there is no exchange. A voice calls out, its despair-tinged sound sufficient to fill the other with happiness. It is our voice. But we do not hear the voice of the other. We do not know how to listen. Or we are perhaps unwilling to listen. Which is why the sunset also feels sorrow, why it is mute: "I cannot answer you / in speech you accept as mine." So the world falls silent—because we lack faith in our own language, because we don't believe we are heard when we call out. But the silence is only apparent: "your voice reaches me always. / and I answer constantly." Perhaps we already believe this. Perhaps we already hear the tenderness, the voice of the other: "in the breeze of the summer evening / and in the words that become / [our] own response."

Conclusion

Louise Glück's poem catches well the pathos and ambiguity at the heart of so much contemporary writing about the natural world. One finds in it expressions of profound fear, that the world itself has gone silent, or that something in us has died leaving us unable to hear the world's subtle and delicate music. But one also finds myriad expressions of faith: faith in the presence of a voice beckoning to us in and through the living world, and faith in the power of "our own responses"—that is, our own poetic evocations of the living world— to bring this voice to clear and vivid expression. In its honest exploration of this rich and troubling ambiguity and in its careful attention to the intricate relationship between Word and world, the contemporary literature and poetry of nature can help us recover a sense of the Word as incarnate in every living being—as creative, renewing presence in the world, as the source of all language, all storytelling, community, the cosmos itself.

It can also help us recover the inescapably poetic character of Christian theological reflection on the Word incarnate. Twenty years ago, poet and New Testament critic Amos Wilder called for Christian theology to overcome its "long addiction to the discursive, the rationalistic, and the prosaic . . . [and do more] justice to the role of the symbolic and . . . mythopoetic dimension[s] of faith."[36] To retrieve, that is, a sense of the theopoetic. If we listen carefully to the literature and poetry of nature, we will discover, I think, the elements of a theopoetics of the natural world. To be drawn into the spell of this literature is to find oneself beckoned to listen to the language, the idiom of the natural world, to discern how the Word comes to expression through particular places, in the stories, poems, and living communities that take root in those places. It is to be brought to a heightened awareness of what it might mean to live more deeply into the truth of the Word and the living world.

This means learning to remythologize the Word in the idiom of our own native places. This is what Priest of the Sun does in N. Scott Momaday's *House Made of Dawn,* reimagining the Christian Creation story in light of ancient Kiowa myth:

> In the beginning was the Word. . . . There was nothing. There was *nothing!* Darkness. There was no end to it. . . . There was only the dark infinity in which nothing was. And something happened, and everything began. The Word did not come into being, but *it was.* It did not break upon the silence, but *it was older than the silence and the silence was made of it.* . . . And from that day the Word has belonged to us, who have heard it for what it is, who have lived in fear and awe of it. In the Word was the beginning; *In the beginning was the Word.* . . .[37]

Or, as father and son do in Norman Maclean's *A River Runs through It,* perched at the edge of the Big Blackfoot River in Montana, listening:

> Then [my father] told me, "In the part I was reading it says the Word was in the beginning, and that's right. I used to think water was first, but if you listen carefully you will hear that the words are underneath the water."
>
> "That's because you are a preacher first and then a fisherman," I told him. "If you ask Paul, he will tell you that the words are formed out of the water."
>
> "No," my father said, "you are not listening carefully. The water runs over the words. Paul will tell you the same thing."[38]

Are we listening carefully enough? Can we discern this Word, older than the silence, deeper than the water, woven into both?

I think of that unknown artist at the bottom of Barrier Canyon and of that old man on the island of Patmos. Did they know that deep, archaic silence woven into the very fabric of the world? Did they stand, trembling, in that silence, listening to the world, before finally giving voice, in word, in song, to what they had heard? Can we recover a sense of world so pregnant with Word, a sense of Word so intimately bound up with the very life of the world? Such attentive listening may well be the only way for us to begin rekindling a deeper sense of relationship with the places we inhabit. It may also be necessary to the long-term survival of those places.

Notes

1. N. Scott Momaday, "The Native Voice in American Literature," in his *The Man Made of Words: Essays, Stories, Passages* (New York: St. Martin's Press, 1997), 14.

2. Cited in *The Wilderness of Vision: On the Poetry of John Haines,* ed. Kevin Bezner and Kevin Walzer (Brownsville, Oreg.: Story Line Press, 1996), 28.

3. For the idea of root metaphor, see Paul Ricoeur, *Interpretation Theory: Discourse and the Surplus of Meaning* (Fort Worth: Texas Christian University Press, 1976), 64. For the Word of God as a root metaphor, see Sandra M. Schneiders, *The Revelatory Text: Interpreting the New Testament as Sacred Scripture* (San Francisco: HarperSanFrancisco, 1991), 27–33.

4. Marcia L. Colish, *The Stoic Tradition from Antiquity to the Early Middle Ages,* vol. 1, *Stoicism in Classical Latin Literature,* 2d impression with addenda and corrigenda (Leiden: E. J. Brill, 1990), 31–35.

5. J. van Arnim, *Stoicorum Veterum Fragmenta* (Leipzig, 1903–5), 1.98; cited in David E. Hahm, *The Origins of Stoic Cosmology* (Columbus: Ohio State University Press, 1977), 60.

6. Erazim Kohák, *The Embers and the Stars: A Philosophical Inquiry into the Moral Sense of Nature* (Chicago: University of Chicago Press, 1984), 10.

7. Tertullian *Adv. Herm.* 44.1; in Marcia L. Colish, *The Stoic Tradition from Antiquity to the Early Middle Ages,* vol. 2, *Stoicism in Christian Latin Thought through the Sixth Century,* 2d impression with addenda and corrigenda (Leiden: E. J. Brill, 1990), 19.

8. Tertullian *Apol.* 18.11–13, 21.10–14; in Colish, *The Stoic Tradition,* 2:19.

9. Tertullian *Adv. Herm.* 36.4; in Colish, *The Stoic Tradition,* 2:20.

10. Salvatore R. C. Lilla, *Clement of Alexandria: A Study in Christian Platonism and Gnosticism* (London: Oxford University Press, 1971), 199–212.

11. Paul Ricoeur, *Essays on Biblical Interpretation,* ed. with an introduction by Lewis S. Mudge (Philadelphia: Fortress Press, 1980), 92.

12. On the cosmic symbolism of the Word incarnate, see Gerhart B. Ladner, *God, Cosmos, and Humankind: The World of Early Christian Symbolism,* trans. Thomas Dunlap (Berkeley and Los Angeles: University of California Press, 1995), 65–154.

13. Ibid., 84.

14. Ibid., 99.

15. Origen of Alexandria, *The Song of Songs: Commentary and Homilies,* trans. and annotated by R. P. Lawson (Westminster, Md.: Newman Press, 1957), 29.

16. Donald Nicholl, *The Beatitude of Truth: Reflections of a Lifetime* (London: Darton, Longman and Todd, 1997), 18.

17. Hildegard of Bingen, *Symphonia,* with introduction, translations, and commentary by Barbara Newman (Ithaca: Cornell University Press, 1988), 102–3: "O Pastor animarum" (Antiphon for the Redeemer).

18. Hildegard of Bingen, *Symphonia,* 126–27: "O viridissima virga" (Song to the Virgin), translation adapted.

19. Francis of Assisi, "Canticle to the Creatures," in Paul M. Allen and Joan deRis Allen, *Francis of Assisi's* Canticle of the Creatures: *A Modern Spiritual Path* (New York: Continuum, 1996), 87–89.

20. Sallie McFague, *The Body of God: An Ecological Theology* (Philadelphia: Fortress Press, 1993), 131.

21. *This Incomperable Lande: A Book of American Nature Writing,* ed. Thomas Lyon (Boston: Houghlin Mifflin, 1989), provides a critical, historical introduction together with a representative anthology of classic nature writing. For an assessement of the cultural, aesthetic, and political significance of this literature, see Lawrence Buell, *The Environmental Imagination: Thoreau, Nature Writing, and the Formation of American Culture* (Cambridge, Mass.: Belknap Press of Harvard University Press, 1995).

On the religious significance of American nature writing, see Douglas Burton-Christie, "Interlude: The Literature of Nature and the Quest for the Sacred," in *The Sacred Place: Witnessing the Holy in the Physical World,* ed. W. Scott Olsen and Scott Cairns (Salt Lake City: University of Utah Press, 1996), 165–77; "Mapping the Sacred Landscape: Spirituality and the Contemporary Literature of Nature," *Horizons* 21, no. 1 (spring 1994): 22–47; "A Feeling for the Natural World: Spirituality and the Appeal to the Heart in Contemporary Nature Writing," *Continuum* 2, no. 2-3 (spring 1993): 154–80; Lynn Ross-Bryant, "Of Nature and Texts: Nature and Religion in American Ecological Literature," *Anglican Theological Review* 73, no. 1 (winter 1991): 38–49; Catherine L. Albanese, *Nature Religion in America: From the Algonkian Indians to the New Age* (Chicago: University of Chicago Press, 1990).

22. Henry David Thoreau, *Walden* (Princeton: Princeton University Press, 1971), 111.

23. Thoreau, *Walden,* 271–72

24. Gary Paul Nabhan, foreword to *Faith in a Seed: The Dispersion of Seeds and Other Late Natural History Writings,* by Henry David Thoreau (Washington, D.C.: Island Press, 1993), xvi.

25. Thoreau, *Faith in a Seed,* 51.

26. H. Daniel Peck, *Thoreau's Morning Work: Memory and Perception in* A Week on the Concord and Merrimack Rivers, *the Journal, and* Walden (New Haven: Yale University Press, 1990), 39–114.

27. Cited by Nabhan, foreword to Thoreau, *Faith in a Seed,* xvi.

28. Denise Levertov, *Evening Train* (New York: New Directions, 1992), 3.

29. Richard K. Nelson, *The Island Within* (New York: Vintage, 1991), 150.

30. Robert Hass, *Sun under Wood* (Hopewell, N.J.: Ecco Press, 1996), 18–19.

31. Mary Oliver, "Entering the Kingdom," in *New and Selected Poems* (Boston: Beacon Press, 1992), 190.

32. Mary Oliver, "Have You Ever Tried to Enter the Long Black Branches," in *West Wind: Poems and Prose Poems* (Boston: Houghlin Mifflin, 1997), 61.

33. Ibid., 62

34. Annie Dillard, *Pilgrim at Tinker Creek* (New York: Harper's Magazine Press, 1974), 1.

35. Louise Glück, "Sunset," in *The Wild Iris* (Hopewell, N.J.: Ecco Press, 1992), 57.

36. Amos Wilder, *Theopoetic: Theology and the Religious Imagination* (Philadelphia: Fortress Press, 1976), 1–2.

37. N. Scott Momaday, *House Made of Dawn* (New York: Harper and Row, 1968), 97.

38. Norman Maclean, *A River Runs through It, and Other Stories* (Chicago: University of Chicago Press, 1976), 95–96.

A Christian-Chinese Version of Ecotheology: Goodness, Beauty, and Holiness in Creation

PETER K. H. LEE

This paper represents a personal spiritual-intellectual journey to explore both the Christian theological world and Chinese cultural treasures concerning ecology. I am a Christian by religious conviction and a Chinese by ethnic origin, with the cultural background to go with my ethnic identity. Hence, the expression "Christian-Chinese" in the title. To help you visualize what I intend to do here, imagine that on my journey I am gathering weaving materials from both Christian and Chinese sources. I am going to interweave strands of Christian beliefs and Chinese thoughts to make a tapestry. The tapestry will have the design motifs of goodness, beauty, and holiness, with creation as the background. Interwoven into these motifs are strands which will reveal a Christian character together with strands having a Chinese texture.

Goodness

In an exploration in ecotheology, it seems only natural to begin with the biblical idea of creation. That idea is announced in chapter 1 of the Book of Genesis. God effected a series of creation acts, and after each act God saw that what was created was good. What does the goodness of creation mean? If we ponder the Creation account, it is not difficult to gain an impression of the elements of which goodness in creation consists.

First, what is created has orderliness. Day and night alternate. The sun, the moon, and the stars follow well-regulated paths. The seasons rotate. So creation is good in that it has orderliness, and God sees to it that this is so. The opposite of orderliness is chaos. Chaos cannot be good.

There is splendor in the created order. The movement of the heavenly bodies, the growth of plants and trees which bear fruit, and the land, sea, and sky, with living creatures walking, fish swimming, and birds flying, all are scenes of splendor, even if in a primitive state. Hence, creation is good in that it is splendid to behold.

The last act of Creation is the creation of human beings in the representative man, Adam, and the representative woman, Eve. God is said to have created them in God's image. This means in man and woman, above all, is reflected the likeness of God. That gives humans a special kinship with the Divine.

Chinese cosmological thinking does not have the concept of a personal God who created Heaven and Earth. The Chinese sages from antiquity have spoken of *t'ien* (Heaven) and *ti* (Earth) as the unitive cosmological components out of which the myriad things are created. "Heaven" (*t'ien*) is not a spiritualized place. *T'ien* and *ti* paradigmatically represent *yang* (male) and *yin* (female) forces, which intermingle with the five agents, metal, wood, water, fire, and earth, to produce the multitude of things. Chinese cosmology does give ample room for the pluriform of things within unitive principles (besides *t'ien* and *ti*, there is *Tao,* or Way). In the end the cosmos is seen in its grand harmony. *T'ai-chi* (Great Ultimate) is the symbol of such grand harmony; it is not abstract harmony but harmony with rich content in specific circumstances in constant change and hence dynamic, infinitely rich harmony.

The *I ching* (Book of changes), the ancient classic of cosmology, is a collection of sixty-four symbolic paradigms (represented by hexagrams, six-line diagrams), each of which gives rise to a number of typical situations. It is up to a wise person to interpret what each situation portends for an individual or nation involved.

Natural phenomena are represented in the sixty-four hexagrams, which are symbolic representations of paradigmatic situations. The five agents are mixed in a variety of ways, and *yang* and *yin* forces are present in various proportions up to a limit, beyond which disharmony results. For instance, thunder roars, foretelling a great happening ahead. *Yang* predominates. A wise person is well-advised not to have excessive self-confidence and to rely on propriety for judgment. *Yin* modulates.[1] And where there is too much water and there are scanty trees in the land, it is an excessively *yin* situation, and flood will occur. A responsible person in power should be prepared to do something about the flood.[2] What is out of harmony is not good. What is in harmony is good. This is true in nature as in human events. Indeed, nature's forces and human affairs interact to attain dynamic harmony. Certainly, from numerous instances in the *I ching,* lessons can be drawn for ecological considerations.

The proverbial *yin-yang* balance in the *I ching,* though, has been called into question by feminist critique. Admittedly, patriarchalism has crept into the "texts" (which, over the centuries, have been piled high with layers upon layers of interpretations). However, the pristine vision could only have held a genuine gender balance. This is not the place to go into the gender issue in the *I ching.* For me, it is ever so helpful to keep before one's awareness the twin prime images for Heaven (prototype *yang*) and Earth (prototype *yin*), respectively, which are perfectly in balance:

> Heaven proceeds vigorously. The superior person
>   strengthens the self ceaselessly.
> Earth is in proper order. The superior person
>   through abiding virtues carries the world to prosperity.[3]

Confucius (sixth century B.C.E.), who admitted that he was deeply indebted to the *I ching* and himself wrote commentaries for it, was the preeminent founder of the Confucian tradition, which is chiefly concerned about the morally good. Benevolence (*jen*) is the cardinal virtue, and it is realized in reciprocity (*shu*) in person-to-person relations. Other virtues, like righteousness (*i*), propriety (*li*), wisdom (*chih*), and trustworthiness (*hsin*), are not just talked about but exemplified in typological personal relationships: ruler-minister, father-son, husband-wife, brother-brother, friend-friend.

Confucius was aware of orderliness in nature, as is testified by his saying, "Does Heaven need to speak? The four seasons march on!" Yet, he was mainly concerned about putting human affairs in good order. When good order prevails in the human world, you can be sure that it is in accord with the ways of Heaven (*t'ien*).

Indeed, all Confucians lift up the ideal of "Heaven-humanity harmony" (*t'ien-jen-ho-i*). "Heaven," not to be spiritualized in the Christian sense, is transcendent, yet it is within reach of humanity through virtue (*t'e*). Virtue is lived by humans in harmony with Heaven.

Returning to biblical thought, we want to trace creation back to its linkage with covenant. God in the Bible is not only the God of creation but also the God of covenant-making. Karl Barth made a great deal of this dual relationship between creation and covenant. He approached the two Creation narratives (Gen. 1 and 2) to expound his thesis that "creation is the external basis of the covenant" and "the covenant is the internal basis of creation."[4] Even if we question Barth's theological overloading in his exegesis, we are indebted to his reminder to link creation with covenant as far as biblical thought is concerned.

Let us follow the sequence of the biblical story, as Christians have told it. There is the Fall of humanity through disobedience to God's will. There is the flood, destroying all life on Earth, save Noah, his family, and the creatures that went into the ark. After the flood God made a new covenant of peace with humans. Then came the covenant with Abraham and its renewal in the Sinai covenant, making the worship of the one true God and obedience to God's moral commandments more explicit. These commands encompass care for and renewal of the land, through practices such as observance of the Sabbath that allows the land to rest. In modern times Jürgen Moltmann has called attention to this.[5]

Then came the prophets, calling the people back to the covenantal relation with Yahweh and the practice of justice. Finally, for Christians, came Jesus Christ, the embodiment of God's forgiving love, the New Covenant personified.

Chinese thought does not have distinct doctrines of creation and covenant as in biblical thought, but it has enough appreciation of the richness of the created world and lays ample emphasis on moral goodness as a responsible act accountable to Heaven. The Chinese are apt to connect virtue with the earth's productivity. I repeat the memorable image of the hexagram for Earth: "Earth is in proper balance. The superior person through abiding virtue, carries the world to prosperity."

Taoist ethos exudes humans' contented communion with nature, as Chinese paintings of nature sceneries eminently show. The point to be noted here is that a Chinese, if he or she is a Christian believer, would find little irreconcilable opposition between the Christian view toward nature spoken of thus far and the Chinese worldview on the same subject. Or, rather, the Christian view of nature provides a theological framework which can be enriched by the Chinese worldview.

The Bible—and Christian thought—does not relish sheer romanticism toward the natural environment. The subtitle of a book entitled *The Travail of Nature* reminds us of "the ambiguous ecological promise of Christian theology."[6] The ambiguity is undoubtedly traceable to the perceptions of theological and biblical writers, but is it not also inherent in nature? Biblical writers are not always clear whether natural disaster is brought on by human folly or is a judgment of God. Theodicy remains an unresolvable issue in rationalistic terms. The Book of Job demonstrates the inadequacy of the conventional law of moral retribution. The book's answer is that, after making allowance for vehement protest against the undeserved suffering of the innocent, in the end a finite human being, however righteous, bows down in utter humility before the marvel of God's creation as pronounced by the matchless eloquence of God's speech (Job 37–41).

Upon reading biblical literature, one has an enhanced sense of the wonderment of nature, while being left with a sober awareness of "nature in travail": "We know that the whole creation has been groaning in labor pains until now; and not only the creation, but we ourselves, who have the first fruits of the Spirit, groan inwardly while we wait for adoption, the redemption of our bodies" (Rom. 8:22–23).[7] The "travail," or "groaning in labor pains," is in creation as well as experienced by human beings. In part, the travail is due to human "fallenness"; it is also due to inexplicable "metaphysical fallenness."[8]

How is the travail, the labor pains, to be assuaged? Continuing in a metaphorical vein, Paul counseled, "wait for adoption, the redemption of our bodies. For in hope we were saved. Now hope that is seen is not hope" (Rom. 8:23b–24). The concluding chapter of *The Travail of Nature* gives suggestions for "an ecological reading of biblical theology." Addressing Romans 8, which contains the "nature in travail" (or "groaning in labor pains") metaphor, author Paul Santmire refers to Jesus' apocalyptic proclamation in terms of the renewal of the whole creation in the last days. Santmire seems sympathetic to J. Christian Beker's interpretation that Paul is overwhelmingly concerned to show the particular meaning of the lordship of Jesus Christ for every concrete historical situation realizable apocalyptically.[9]

A Christian worldview, coupled with a Chinese view of things, equips one with a positive but realistic attitude toward the created order. Intelligent judgment and responsible action are called for. Concrete responses to ecological situations may lead to a variety of actions: enjoyment of the natural scenery coupled with its tender care; the opening of national parks and conservation of plant and animal species; correcting damaging conditions and effectively carrying out engineering plans; bold vision supported by shrewd political action.

Chinese philosophers and scholars, perhaps in their predilection for the ideal of harmony, are less likely to take into serious account disasters and destructions caused by natural forces. But those in positions of public responsibility, thanks to Confucian teachings, are forced to view the world more realistically. Famines, plagues, and floods fill the living pages of Chinese history. Government officials and persons of action who succeeded in turning the tides of destruction have been made folk heroes or even deified. One of the legendary sage-kings, the Great Yü, is remembered not only for his virtuous wisdom but also for his effective control of flood. Is there a correlation between the flood in Noah's time and the flood in Yü's?[10] This question has ecological implications and will be taken up at the end of my essay.

Beauty

In our consideration of goodness in creation, it was already suggested that there is splendor in God's creation. Another word we might use is "beauty." The Bible is by no means short on passages praising creation's beauty or grandeur:

> The heavens are telling the glory of God;
> and the firmament proclaims his handiwork. (Ps. 19:1–2)

> Let the heavens praise your wonders, O Lord,
> Your faithfulness in the assembly of the holy ones.
> For who in the skies can be compared to the Lord? (Ps. 89:5–6.)

It was Jonathan Edwards (1703–1758), a leading preacher of the Great Awakening in colonial America, who developed the category of beauty to characterize God and to highlight religious sensibilities. As a youth he felt close to nature, and he was drawn to its beauty. After his conversion he experienced intense delight in the natural world. He recalled:

> God's excellency, his wisdom, his purity and love, seemed to appear in everything; in the sun, moon and stars; in the clouds, and blue sky, in the grass, flowers, trees; in the water, and all nature; which used greatly to fix my mind. I often used to sit and view the moon for continuance; and in the day, spent much time in viewing the clouds and sky, to behold the sweet glory of God in these things; in the mean time, singing forth, with a low voice my contemplations of the Creator and Redeemer.[11]

Edwards went on, during the course of his life, to give further thought to the subject of beauty. Thanks to recent scholarship, Edwards's significant contributions to theological understanding of beauty and psychological analysis of aesthetic sensibility are reaffirmed.[12]

Let us turn from the biblical-theological world to Taoist thought for an apprehension of beauty of another kind. Let me first invoke Lao Tzu and Chuang Tzu, the two great masters of Taoism. Lao Tzu (sixth century B.C.E.?) says:

> The great Tao flows everywhere. . . .
> The myriad things owe their existence to it. . . .[13]

All Taoist-inspired Chinese paintings have a flowing quality, but the innermost of what flows is hidden, which is the Tao, the mother of everything.

> It [the Tao] is called formless form, thingless image.
> It is called the exclusive, the evasive. . . .[14]

Objects in Chinese landscape paintings, like mountains, rocks, rivers, are never shown in sharp-edged forms but as elusive "images," which suggest the spirit of the Tao:

> The most yielding of things outruns the most unyielding.
> Having no substance, they enter into no-space.
> Hence I know the value of non-action (*wu-wei*).[15]

The flowing river, the waving willow, the floating clouds are yielding objects in action, or rather, non-action or non-self-assertive action (*wu-wei*), yet they can outlast the unyielding, stubborn forces, as water wearing away rocks. Non-action occupies no-space. Empty space is most important in a painting; it is not really emptiness but inner spaciousness through which a sense of fullness is suggested. The sense of fullness can be best conveyed by beauty perceived in the painting—beauty in the shading of lightness and darkness; beauty executed by the brush strokes and lines; beauty delighting the senses, evoking imagination, and stirring the soul.

Chuang Tzu (fourth century B.C.E.) turned the elusiveness of the Tao into unbound playfulness. Chapter 1 of the *Chuang-tzu* is entitled "The Carefree Excursion." It is the carefree flight of a huge bird which spreads its wings over no one knows how many miles. The bird soars into the sky miles and miles upward, with clouds as companions, and flaps its wings over thousands of miles of ocean, churning up water to rock large ships and small boats alike. Chuang Tzu loved to play on the imagination and wanted to set the mind free. Isn't this essential to the artistic spirit?

Chuang Tzu and Hui Tzu were once strolling on a bridge over a river. Chuang Tzu, looking down into the water, exclaimed, "See how the minnows are darting about! Such is the pleasure that fish enjoy." Hui Tzu said, "You are not a fish, how do you know what fish enjoy?" "You are not I," retorted Chuang Tzu, "So how do you know that I do not know what fish enjoy?" "I am not you," Hui Tzu conceded, "and so evidently I do not know what you know. But it is also evident that you are not a fish, and so it is certain that you do not know what fish enjoy."[16]

The difference between the two men is that one was trapped in a one-track mind, while the other had lively empathy. An artist, to paint a beautiful picture of such a scene, must have empathetic powers to enter into an enjoyment of both the fish and the beautiful scenery. Whereas Confucianism has sought to strengthen the moral fabric of the Chinese cultural heritage, Taoism lifts up its aesthetic soul. The Taoist spirit finds its best expression in Chinese painting and poetry, in which the quality of beauty reaches great heights.

People who have nurtured such a sensibility for beauty naturally see beauty in nature's sceneries (mountains, streams, rocks, trees, and flowers) and living creatures (horses, cats, fish, shrimp). Listen to poet and painter Wang Wei (415–443 C.E.) discoursing on painting:

Gazing upon the clouds of autumns, my spirit takes wings and soars. Facing the breeze of spring, my thoughts flow like great, powerful current. Even the music of metal and stone instruments and the treasure of priceless jades cannot match [the pleasure of] this. . . . The wind rises from the great forest, and foaming water rushes in the stream. Alas! such paintings cannot be achieved by the physical movements of the fingers and the hand, but only by the spirit entering into them. This is the nature of painting.[17]

In the contemporary ecological movement, the aesthetic factor is not often highlighted, and the religious or spiritual dimension of the experience of beauty is even more conspicuously underplayed. Actually, appreciation of beauty and grandeur in nature is implied in any ecological concern and celebration of nature's beauty is found in the religious classics of Christians and Jews. St. Francis of Assisi's "Canticle of the Sun," "Sermon to the Birds," and other writings are gems that delectably capture creation's beauty and help awaken a sense of nature's beauty as holiness. "The Sermon to the Birds," more than anything else, has heightened my own awareness of the sprightliness and delightfulness of birds as lovable creatures of the living God.

Holiness

In considering both goodness and beauty, we have alluded to the religious or spiritual dimensions. I would now like to invoke Rudolf Otto, who wrote the classic *The Idea of the Holy,*[18] to lead us further into the subject. The key word in Otto's book is numinous, which is derived from the Latin *numen,* meaning divinity or a divine being. Otto conceived of the numinous as a category of value or a state of mind which is *sui generis* and irreducible to anything else in relation to the supernatural. The numinous is objective, outside the self, but its nature is such that it grips or stirs the human mind. The numinous is rendered "the holy" in English. Otto hastened to explain that "holy" does not mean simply "completely good," nor is it used to describe a perfectly moral person.

Rather, the numinous has a quality that belongs to the mysterious, indeed, the tremendously mysterious—hence the expression *mysterium tremendum.* The *mysterium tremendum* of the numinous is characterized by the following elements: awe, overpoweringness, energy or urgency, the "wholly other," and fascination.[19] Otto's

expositions of the numinous in the Old and New Testaments are illuminating. From the earliest days of Yahweh's covenant with Israel,
through Moses' mission, the prophets' call to return to God's ways,
the prayers of the Psalms, to Jesus' incarnation and the apostles being
"captured" by the resurrected Christ, God reigns supreme. God is
awe-inspiring and mysterious, yet God is unmistakably clear in giving directions to God's people.

Otto included the other great world religions, besides Judaism and
Christianity, in his explanation of the numinous. He cited numerous
instances from Hinduism, Buddhism, and Islam. *The Idea of the Holy*
makes no mention of Lao Tzu or Chuang Tzu. But, in a footnote, Otto
indicated that he thought that Taoism had elements that could belong
to the *mysterium tremendum*.[20] He devotes a small section of his book
to the numinous character of Chinese art. Otto, speaking on the numinous as expressed in art, showed keen appreciation for the landscape
and religious painting of China in the classical period of the T'ang
and Sung dynasties. He quoted a sinologist, Otto Fischer, on Chinese
paintings:

> These works are to be classified with the profoundest and sublimest of
> the creations of human art. The spectator who, as it were, immerses
> himself in them feels behind these waters and clouds and mountains
> the mysterious breath of the primeval Tao, the pulse of innermost
> being. Many a mystery lies half-concealed and half-revealed in these
> pictures. They contain the knowledge of the "nothingness" and the
> "void," of the "Tao" of heaven and earth, which is also the Tao of the
> human heart.[21]

Note that the spectator is drawn into the work of art. That is so
because the artist first of all immerses himself or herself in nature's
scene.

Otto linked the words "religious" and "landscape" when referring
to paintings of China. Chinese painting is not religious in the sense
that religious figures are the subject matter. By "religious," he meant
the numinous. The best of Chinese landscape paintings do have
elements of awe and mystery, and they fascinate the human mind and
soul. It is not enough to say that Taoist-inspired paintings are
"naturalistic"; they contain mystery and fascination. Taoist-inspired
paintings induce a sense of communion with nature, not just the
outward phenomena but the inner essence.

Chinese poetry and painting, with a touch of the Tao, have been a tonic enhancing my appreciation of nature's beauty and even inviting me into communion with nature. Here, let me cite a poem, "The Temple at Yung Lake Mountain," by Chang Shuo (667–730 C.E.):

> In the silence of boundless space
> is born the heart that knows the Tao:
> From the depth of the valley
> echos the cry of the wild bird from afar.
>
> The zen chamber delights in what's beyond worldly cares;
> incense on the altar offers up not passions of the world.
> Between clouds to the east pile up a thousand peaks;
> Behind trees in the south hides a lake pure and clear. . . .[22]

Chang Shuo was a high government official with public responsibilities, but, a poet, he found refreshment from visiting the mountains and meditating in a zen temple. The meditation was inward, while the mind was in communion with the typical "mountain and water" scenery of clouds floating around peaks, trees lining a lake, such as an artist would paint.

The concluding lines of the poem have a twist:

> If only Ch'ao and Yu
> had beheld such a scene as this,
> they would not have turned in the official's robe
> and gone on to wear coarsely knitted garb.

Ch'ao and Yu were legendary recluses, who turned to primitive, rustic living after a stint of public service. The poet-official Chang Shuo mused: supposing Ch'ao and Yu had experienced this kind of spiritual communion in a lovely natural setting, need they have forsaken official responsibilities and become recluses? In other words, meditation is good for a public official too. Chang Shuo seems to have entertained this as a possibility.

What about moral goodness at its noblest? Earlier I said that Otto did not want to limit "the holy" to moral perfection. He avoids talking about moral goodness. However, if he had known of the Confucian ideal of "Heaven-humanity harmony," he probably would have accepted that as a legitimate instance of the numinous.

In Confucian thought the morally good (*shan*) is also beautiful (*mei*). In fact, *mei-shan* (beautiful-good) is a familiar expression in the Chinese language. These lines from the *Book of Odes* speak of the combination of moral principle and beautiful character under the approving eyes of Heaven:

> Heaven so produced the teeming multitudes
> that everything there is has its principle.
> The people will keep to the constant principles,
> and all will love a beautiful character.[23]

Confucius's *Analects* has an aphorism which can be used as a motto for ecological education: "Neighbors benevolent [*jen*], [neighborhood] beautiful [*mei*]." In a full sentence it would read: "Where the people are benevolent, there you have a beautiful neighborhood."

In biblical thinking, goodness and beauty are inseparable in the holiness of God. For example:

> In that day the Lord of hosts will be a
> garland of glory, and a diadem of beauty,
> to the remnant of his people;
> and a spirit of justice to the one who sits in judgment. . . .
> (Isa. 28:5–6.)

Jonathan Edwards spoke the same kind of language. Edwards conceived of beauty in two forms: secondary, or natural beauty, and primary, or spiritual beauty.[24] Spiritual beauty belongs to moral agents—to persons who think and act morally and, above all, to God, who is morally perfect.

> He that sees the beauty of holiness, or true moral good, sees the greatest and most important thing in the world, which is the fullness of all things without which all the world is empty, no better than nothing, yea, worse than nothing. Unless this is seen, nothing is seen, that is worth the seeing: for there is no other true excellency or beauty.[25]

Edwards is unparalleled in giving beauty primacy in our approach to God. The beauty of God, the holiness of God, the beauty of holiness, divine moral perfection, all these attributes are God's. They certainly qualify to be called the numinous, in Rudolf Otto's language. The moral beauty of God is perceived by those who have a sensibility for it. Such sensibility is not just a natural instinct, but a divine endowment, following a regeneration of the heart:

> The first effect of the power of God in the heart in regeneration is to give the heart a Divine taste of sense; to cause it to have a relish of the loveliness and sweetness of the supreme excellency.[26]

Jonathan Edwards has done us the great favor of enriching our understanding of God by adding on the attribute of beauty and pointing to the manner of awakening our sense of beauty. The beauty of holiness is the quality that is the immediate object of human awareness in experiencing the Lord. It is when we sense the beauty of the moral perfection of God that we can accept Jesus Christ as the mediator, reconciling us to God.[27] Regeneration, reconciliation, or renewal in Christ is a prerequisite for the perception of the beauty of holiness, thereby opening up a new heaven and a new earth before our eyes.

In this paper, I am concerned with ecology rather than Christology. Approaching the subject of ecology as Christians, however, we open the christological question. Not that we are dogmatically bound to be christocentric. Personally, as I am swept off my feet by the beauty of nature on many an occasion, I cannot close my ears to the groans of "nature in travail," or shut my eyes to the deterioration (by natural process) and pollution (by human folly) in the natural environment. I have taken to heart the Confucian "Heaven-humanity harmony" ideal. Yet, after hearing the sages and scholars in China talk about it for two and a half millennia, I see how human beings have again and again violated the will of Heaven, resulting in violence and tragedy. Where is the real answer to bringing about harmony? It is not by mere verbal repetition of a cliché but after a hard search in the depth of my soul that I have found the necessary but effectual mediator or reconcilor of Heaven, humanity and Earth to be Jesus Christ, the living New Testament.

What if Christ is not in the historical experience of the Chinese people? No matter; the cosmic Christ is "before all things and in him all things hold together" (including the Chinese people's historical experience and other peoples' experiences), all brought together in the church's historical experience:

> He is the head of the body, the church; he is the beginning, the firstborn from the dead, so that he might have first place in everything. For in him all the fullness of God was pleased to dwell, and through him God was pleased to reconcile to himself all things, whether on earth or in heaven, by making peace through the blood of his cross. (Col. 1:18–20)

The christological hymn of the Letter of Paul to the Colossians (1:15–20) has been the subject of lively debate in recent New Testament scholarship.[28] It is relevant to our ecological reflection to point out that one of the issues over which the debate is conducted involves the phrases "the body, the church" and "by the blood of the cross," which were apparently added on to a mystical hymn known to the Colossian church. In other words, the Letter to the Colossians meant to hold together both the importance of the church and the reality of the cross in the final consummation.

There are two divergent trends of interpretation on the question of whether the author-didactor is justified in holding such a unified view. One trend takes the conjunctive position in Pauline thought: both exalted Lord and crucified Saviour, both cosmos and church, both creation and redemption. Another trend takes the disjunctive view: either one or the other. Paul Santmire is sympathetic to a critical continuity between the original hymn and the Pauline Christology of Colossians.[29] This allows an apocalyptic distance between Christ the first fruits and the future general resurrection. And, this harks back to J. Christian Beker's interpretation of Romans 8 from an apocalyptic perspective, which leaves room for concrete realization of the redemptive power of Christ.

This discussion of Christology is relevant if we take seriously the ruptures and cracks in creation and yet seek a way of reconciliation. Assuming that one can take a critical continuity position on the Colossian hymn, it has a "high" ecclesiology and a "high" Christology, too high perhaps for the Chinese people's historical experience in which Christians have always been a minority and the Christian church not well established. Nevertheless, it is possible to hold a "low" view of the cosmic Christ and a "low" view of the Christian church. In my own experience the cosmic Christ does speak to me in the Chinese context, while he also has universal validity. But he can assume a low profile, a humble, even unknown position, until his identity is revealed in unexpected circumstances. The Christian community is indeed small and fragmentary among the Chinese people, whether in mainland China or overseas, but the power of regeneration for the people can be out of proportion to the church's size.

Turning to ecology, I begin with the theme of regeneration, re-creation, or renewal. These words are not exactly synonymous. Whether taken each by itself or all together, the words, regeneration, re-creation, and renewal, are ambiguous in English; translated into

Chinese they are even more confounding—but let us capitalize on ambiguity. In Colossians 1:21–22, we read:

> And you who were once estranged and hostile in mind, doing evil deeds, he has now reconciled in his fleshly body through death, so as to present you holy and blameless and irreproachable before him. . . .

The author of Colossians did consider human estrangement from God a serious matter, and he saw the death of Christ as the pivot in reconciling humans to God, whereby the followers of Christ will present themselves as holy and good and beautiful.

Further on in the letter, the author adjured:

> As God's chosen ones, holy and beloved, clothe yourselves with compassion, kindness, humility, meekness, and patience. Bear with one another and . . . forgive each other. . . . Above all, clothe yourselves with love, which binds everything together in perfect harmony. (Col. 3:12–14)

Jonathan Edwards would have endorsed such refined religious affections.

We can extend this love to ecological concerns. James A. Nash has titled his book *Loving Nature*.[30] Indeed, loving nature, not just the objective analysis of love of nature, is the live energy behind ecological commitment. But loving nature need not be wooly sentimentalism. It holds together the firm foundations of ecological integrity and Christian responsibility.[31] It expresses itself in multiple dimensions, as beneficence, esteem of others, receptivity, humility, understanding, and communion—all ecologically felicitous virtues.[32] These are not just individuals' virtues but virtues translatable to public life, too.

Finally, Nash interprets cosmic redemption in an ecological perspective:

> The expectation of universal or cosmic redemption is a necessarily vague vision of the consummation of shalom—reconciliation among all creatures (Isa. 11:6–9). . . .
>
> Ecologically, this vision gives ultimate meaning and worth to the cosmic ecosphere. It is the confirmation of nature's ultimate value to God. Nothing is any longer valueless or meaningless or irrelevant. Every living creature counts for itself and for God ultimately.[33] Is this talk about cosmic redemption and the cosmic Christ too high-flown for down-to-earth ecological concerns?

Both Noah and the sage-king Yü were involved in floods. Noah and his family were accompanied by the pairs of living creatures. After the flood subsided they walked out of the ark to be greeted by a new creation, with the promise of the sign of the rainbow from God. By contrast, the Great Yü performed wise deeds to control the flood and has thereafter been immortalized. Representing two different traditions, what each did was not mutually exclusive in ecological terms but could be taken to be complementary to each other. How can this be accomplished? I think of the Three Gorges Dam Project on the Yangtze River. This is a colossal engineering project to build a dam for the dual purpose of flood control and generation of electric energy. The national leaders behind the project probably like to think that they will be remembered by generations to come as other Great Yüs of flood-control fame. But the project is highly controversal from an engineering and an ecological point of view. Even if it is intended to serve a good end, the end result is questionable. Where is their sense of beauty? The breathtakingly beautiful scenery of the Three Gorges will be gone forever. Of course, those in charge have no sense of the holy in creation. The whole subject is too vast to be discussed here. Instead, I only refer to a small scenario as an illustration of a Christian-inspired way, however modest, to redeem destruction done by flood, if not to control or prevent floods.

The flooding of the Yellow River has been a continuous menace in northern China. Not long ago (1995) another flood occurred in Honan Province, leaving thousands homeless and many buildings damaged. As may happen in times of disaster, various groups in Hong Kong (notwithstanding their proverbial individualism and materialism), were moved to donate money generously for aid and even went to the mainland, this time to Honan to help with relief and repair work. Christian organizations also joined in. Under a church-related voluntary organization, a group of students went to a village in Honan for a summer camp experience as volunteer workers. The students took part in rebuilding a damaged clinic and saw the need in the clinic for new medical equipment. After returning to Hong Kong, they started a campaign to raise money for the medical equipment and for further work in health services—hence their name "Heaven Neighbors" (with the implication of being neighbors bordering on *t'ien*).

A student testified that it was during the group's work with the people in need that he understood for the first time the real meaning of Immanuel ("God with us"), not only for himself but for those who had not before heard the name of Christ. Is this not the work of the cosmic Christ, albeit a low-key manifestation? And, is it not the evidence of cosmic redemption at work? As I write these words in Canada, I cannot wait to return to Hong Kong to talk to the people connected with Heaven Neighbors to find out if they would also be concerned with flood control. If they could indeed help in that way, they would be following in the tradition of the sage Yü and, like Noah and his family who entered a new creation, they would be working to build a new city with the beautiful rainbow on the horizon as a sign of divine promise.

Notes

1. The *I ching,* hexagram 36, "Great Confidence." The most reliable English translation of the *I ching* is probably the one translated by C. F. Baynes from the German text by Hellmut Wilhelm (5th ed., Princeton: Princeton University Press, 1995).

2. Ibid., hexagram 30, "Great Error."

3. Ibid., hexagram 1, "Heaven," and hexagram 2, "Earth."

4. Karl Barth, *Church Dogmatics,* trans. J. W. Edwards, O. Busser, Harold Knight (Edinburgh: T. and T. Clark, 1956–59), vol. 3, bk. 1, sec. 41.

5. Jürgen Moltmann, *God in Creation: An Ecological Doctrine of Creation,* trans. Margaret Kohl (London: SCM Press, 1985), chap. 11.

6. H. Paul Santmire, *The Travail of Nature: The Ambiguous Ecological Promise of Christian Theology* (Philadelphia: Fortress Press, 1985).

7. All biblical quotations in this paper are from the NRSV.

8. My own expression, to cover a wide variety of thoughts, philosophical and theological, on the falling away of nature from divine perfection. St. Augustine's Neoplatonic theory of evil as the absence of good is an eminent example.

9. Santmire, *The Travail of Nature,* 202.

10. I am indebted to Archie Lee for this suggestion. See Archie Lee, "The Dragon, the Deluge, and Creation Theology," in *Frontiers in Asian Christian Theology: Emerging Trends,* ed. R. S. Surgirtharajah (Maryknoll, N.Y.: Orbis Books, 1994), 97–108.

11. Jonathan Edwards, *Selections,* ed. Clarence H. Faust and Thomas H. Johnson (New York: Hill and Wong, 1962), 61. Quoted in Richard Cartwright Austin, *Beauty of the Lord: Awakening the Senses* (Atlanta: John Knox Press), 97.

12. See, especially, Roland André Delattre, *Beauty and Sensibility in the Thought of Jonathan Edwards: An Essay in Aesthetics and Theological Ethics* (New Haven: Yale University Press, 1968).

13. *Tao-te-ching,* chap. 34. All the passages from Lao Tzu are taken from "Selections from the Lao Tzu (or *Tao Te Ching*)," in *Sources of Chinese Tradition,* comp. Wm. Theodore de Bary, Wing-tsit Chan, and Burton Watson, 2 vols. (New York: Columbia University Press, 1964), 1:58.

14. *Tao-te-ching,* chap. 15, p. 54.

15. *Tao-te-ching,* chap. 43, p. 59.

16. "Selection from Chuang Tzu," chap. 17, in *Sources of Chinese Tradition,* 68.

17. Wang Wei, "Introduction to Painting," in *Sources of Chinese Tradition,* 255.

18. Rudolf Otto, *The Idea of the Holy,* trans. John W. Harvey (London: Oxford University Press, 1926).

19. Ibid., chaps. 5 and 6.

20. Ibid., 206, n. 2.

21. Ibid., 69.

22. *Sources of Chinese Tradition,* 90–91.

23. The English rendition is mine.

24. Roland Andre Delattré, "Beauty and Theology: A Reappraisal of Jonathan Edwards," in *Critical Essays on Jonathan Edwards,* ed. William J. Scheick (Boston: G. K. Hall, 1980), 138.

25. Jonathan Edwards, *Religious Affections,* ed. John E. Smith (New Haven: Yale University Press, 1959), 274.

26. Jonathan Edwards, *A Treatise on Grace.* Quoted in Austin, *Beauty of the Lord,* 146.

27. Edwards, *Religious Affections,* 273.

28. Paul Santmire gives a summary of the debate. See Santmire, *The Travail of Nature,* 205–6.

29. Ibid., 264–66, n. 46.

30. James A. Nash, *Loving Nature: Ecological Integrity and Christian Responsibility* (Nashville: Abingdon Press, 1991).

31. Ibid., chap. 5.

32. Ibid., chap. 6. The phrase "ecologically felicitous virtue" is mine.

33. Ibid., 132–33.

Response to Peter K. H. Lee

HEUP YOUNG KIM

I am deeply honored to respond to the inspiring paper by Peter Lee, a pioneer and leader in the field of comparative study between Christianity and Chinese religions for several decades. From the Christian-Chinese vantage point, he has formulated an illuminating intrareligious dialogue, engaging in an imaginative hermeneutics of retrieval in and through both Christian and Chinese religious traditions. Although it certainly deserves a more extensive discussion, I will focus on three points.

First, Peter Lee is not ashamed to identify himself as a Christian-Chinese, that is, as being simultaneously a Christian and a Chinese. He argues that this hyphenated identity can enrich theological discussions on ecology: "a Chinese, if he or she is a Christian believer, would find little irreconcilable opposition between the Christian view toward nature . . . and the Chinese worldview." "A Christian worldview, coupled with a Chinese view of things, equips one with a positive but realistic attitude toward the created order."

I will argue even further that an integrated, conjunctive perspective, such as Christian-Chinese or Korean-Christian, is more appropriate than the divisionist, disjunctive attitude of traditional Christian churches. These latter attitudes are subtly hidden even in some of the recent discussions under the rubrics of interreligious dialogue, religious pluralism, and comparative theology. Adopting the philosophy of others, they still maintain epistemological and essentialist vestiges which divide "I" (the subject) from "others" (the object). However, we are no longer living in culturally or religiously isolated, monolithic, and homogenous societies, but in complexly interrelated, pluralistic, multicultural, and multireligious societies. Today, no one can isolate clearly the essence of his or her religious or cultural identity. In this global world, an integrated (hyphenated or "hybridized") identity so conceived can be more real and paradigmatic than those disjunctive attitudes of the "either-or" developed from the modern myth of an isolated self.[1] Furthermore, the present ecological crisis urgently demands that we move beyond such a disjunction toward an all-embracing, conjunctive attitude of "both-and," embracing not only the horizon of co-humanity but also cosmos and the transcendent.

We East Asian Christians living in traditionally non-Christian cultures are particularly situated in the historical fusion of two great hermeneutical horizons, the "theohistorical vision" (salvation history) of Christianity and the "anthropocosmic vision" (the cosmos and humanity being interrelated) of Asian religions.[2] Hence, I argue, it is imperative for East Asian Christians to thematize a "theanthropocosmic vision," a holistically integrated vision of God, humanity, and cosmos.[3] In his paper Lee illuminates poetically and powerfully a plausibility of the "goodness," "beauty," and "holiness" of this theanthropocosmic vision.

Second, Lee rightly points out: "In the contemporary ecological movement, the aesthetic factor is not often highlighted, and the religious or spiritual dimension of the experience of beauty is even more conspicuously underplayed." To overcome this shortcoming, he accentuates the aesthetic dimension of Taoism (in comparison to the ethical dimension of Confucianism): "Whereas Confucianism has sought to strengthen the moral fabric of the Chinese cultural heritage, Taoism lifts up its aesthetic soul. The Taoist spirit finds its best expression in Chinese painting and poetry." And he revalidates the value of empty space in Chinese painting: "Empty space is most important in a painting."[4]

Without doubt, Taoism offers fruitful contributions to the ecological discourse.[5] Specifically, the emphasis on emptiness is important. Compare Western paintings with Chinese paintings. While the accent of the former lies in the fullness of images artificially drawn by the hands of a human author, the real value of the latter is in the natural look of empty space unoccupied by a human painting. The *Tao-te-ching* says: "We make pots of clay, but it is the empty space in them which makes them useful. We make a wheel with many spokes joined in a hub, but it is the empty space in the hub which makes the wheel go round. We make houses of brick and wood, but it is the empty spaces in the doors and windows that make them habitable."[6]

This motif of empty space is a legitimate and necessary corrective to this systematic age of mechanization, containerization, and cementation. In this age, when people cannot experience living without intentionally doing something (*yu-wei*), the Taoist insights of *wu-wei*, nonbeing, and vacuity reveal a most profound way of life that we should pursue. But *wu-wei* here is not merely a passive nonaction; it is "actionless activity," "a state of passivity, of 'non-action,' that is totally active, in the sense of receptivity."[7]

Nevertheless, Lee's treatment of this fascinating area is not as persuasive as it might be, because he has chosen three Reformed theologians as Christian partners for the dialogue. (Perhaps Reformed theology is more comparable to Confucianism than to Taoism.) Taoist motives seem to have closer affinities with the apophatic, kenotic, contemplative, and mystical traditions of Catholic spirituality (Gregory of Nyssa, Dionysius the Areopagite, Francis of Assisi, Meister Eckhart, and Julian of Norwich). Rather, Lee makes use of positivistic, kataphatic, rational traditions of Protestant Logos theologies. Without doubt the theology of Karl Barth (uniting "covenant and creation" for goodness) is their towering representative, and yet Jonathan Edwards ("religious affection" for beauty) and Rudolph Otto (for holiness) have not transcended the kataphatic Logos tradition.

No longer do we East Asian Christians need to look elsewhere to inherit such a Logos-centric theology. Instead, we may need to appreciate emptiness and nothingness as they are, free from the Western obsession of fullness. Taoist emptiness does not refer to a positivistic space to be paved with the fullness of higher truth, such as the numinous in the analysis of Otto. Rather, it is vacuity, an empty space for genuine freedom and carefreeness. This Taoist spirit of freedom can embody a creative space for an East Asian theology to make a significant contribution in the reformation of Christian theology in the third millennium.

The great trajectory of the third millennium seems to be pointed toward the East. According to the reversal principle of *t'ai-chi,* the *yang* side of history reaches its extreme, and the trajectory of the Tao begins to revert toward the *yin* side. The following statement by Bede

Griffiths, a Benedictine mystic who lived many years in Indian ashrams, is very illuminating:

> This may sound very paradoxical and unreal, but for centuries now the western world has been following the path of *Yang*—of the masculine, active, aggressive, rational, scientific mind—and has brought the world near destruction. It is time now to recover the path of *Yin*, of the feminine, passive, patient, intuitive and poetic mind. This is the path which the *Tao Te Ching* sets before us.[8]

The traditional theological root metaphor, *logos,* the genius of fourth-century Christianity (the old wineskin), is no longer adequate and viable, but life threatening and ecologically disastrous. Now we need to adopt boldly a new life-affirming and truly ecological root metaphor (a new wineskin) for Christian faith: an apophatic, kenotic, mothering, all-inclusive metaphor, such as Tao.[9]

Third, Lee suggests that the cosmic Christ can be formulated by a constructive engagement in and through the metaphysics of *t'ai-chi* and the *I ching*.[10] Although this is an enormously important suggestion, I would like to make two critical comments.

First, an East Asian Christian integrated vision needs to be constructed in such a way that it tells its new, coherent story, while re-visioning not only Christian but also East Asian traditions. This story should be more than an a priori comparison in a simple juxtaposition of the similarities between the two traditions. Such a revisioning should call for a serious engagement with the hermeneutics of suspicion. Historically, Chinese cosmology has been manifested in unfortunate forms of an ethnocentric worldview, manipulated and used in ideologies for sinicizing and colonizing people in neighboring countries, such as Korea, Manchuria, and Vietnam, so-called barbarians on the peripheries of the sinic center. Furthermore, although we argue that Taoism and Confucianism have a lot to offer to the ecological discourse, in reality we are living in the most ecologically disastrous areas of the world. Why? We should be critically involved in answering this question

Second, the metaphysics of *t'ai-chi* and the *I ching* are not innocent, but fully loaded. We must not excessively romanticize old ideals (the onto-cosmology of the *I ching*), such as "natural naturalization" ("to-make-natural"), but need to demythologize and revision them for a new situation.[11] The exclusive and closed metaphysics of *t'ai-chi* and the *I ching*, historically manifested in sinocentric and patriarchal ideologies, should be renovated and opened up to become fully inclusive. Overall, Lee's paper tends to neglect the justice (social) side, focusing excessively on the ecological (metaphysical) side. However, a proper East Asian Christian ecotheology should be both ecologically sublime and justly emancipatory.

Hence, a new hermeneutics of the integrated vision should be not just aesthetic-mystical but also prophetic-practical.[12] Speaking in the Christian way, the goodness, beauty, and holiness of the old East Asian metaphysical cosmology needs a process of *metanoia* (crucifixion and resurrection) that involves serious theological scrutiny. The *Chuang tzu* quotes Confucius as saying: "Only the Tao gathers in emptiness. The cause of emptiness is the fasting of the mind-and-heart."[13] Speaking in the Taoist way, all wonderful theanthropocosmic visions in the triad of Heaven, humanity, and Earth can be acquired first and foremost through the fasting of the mind-heart.

The Tao of East Asian Christian theology unfolds, not so much in the participation of the anthropocosmic festival of the celestial universe, as in sociocosmic dancing of the exploited lives on the planet Earth for survival and reversal. We may need to make the socio-ecological interpretation of the revolutionary return of exploited life in the communicative power of spirit (*ch'i*) a preferential option. This I call the "serendipitous pneumatosociocosmic trajectory."[14]

Notes

1. Wai Ching Wong makes an interesting proposal based on her postcolonial experiences in Hong Kong. She argues for "hybridity" and "hybridization" as a new site and a strategy of politics for "doing" theology in Asia. See Wai Ching Wong, "Asian Theology in a Changing Asia: Towards an Asian Theological Agenda in the 21st Century," in *Proceedings of the Congress of Asian Theologians* (Hong Kong: Christian Conference of Asia, 1997), 1:30–39.

2. Neo-Confucianism developed this "anthropocosmic vision" of cosmic togetherness in an organismic unity with Heaven, Earth, and the myriad things. This vision is beautifully expressed in Chang Tsai's *Western Inscription,* quoted in Lee's paper. Also see Tu Weiming, *Centrality and Commonality: An Essay on Confucian Religiousness,* rev. ed. (Albany: State University of New York Press, 1989), 102–7.

3. See Heup Young Kim, *Wang Yang-ming and Karl Barth: A Confucian-Christian Dialogue* (Lanham, Md.: University Press of America, 1996), 175–88.

4. However, Lee understands this emptiness in a very positivistic way: "it is not really emptiness but inner spaciousness through which a sense of fullness is suggested."

5. See Roger T. Ames, "Putting the *Te* Back into Taoism," in *Nature in Asian Traditions of Thought: Essays in Environmental Philosophy,* ed. J. Baird Callicott and Roger T. Ames (Albany: State University of New York Press, 1989), 113–44. Also see Mary Evelyn Tucker, "Ecological Themes in Taoism and Confucianism," in *Worldviews and Ecology: Religion, Philosophy, and the Environment,* ed. Mary Evelyn Tucker and John A. Grim (Maryknoll, N.Y.: Orbis Books, 1994), 150–60.

6. Translation from Bede Griffiths, *Universal Wisdom: A Journey through the Sacred Wisdom of The World* (London: Fount; San Francisco: HarperSanFrancisco, 1994), 27. Also see *Tao-te-ching,* chap. 11, in *A Source Book in Chinese Philosophy,* trans. Wing-tsit Chan (Princeton: Princeton University Press, 1963), 144–45.

7. Griffiths, *Universal Wisdom,* 26–27. In his paper, Lee translates *wu-wei* as "non-self-assertive action."

8. Griffiths, *Universal Wisdom,* 27–28.

9. See my article, "A Tao of Asian Theology in the 21st Century," *Proceedings of the Congress of Asian Theologians* (Hong Kong: Christian Conference of Asia, 1998), 2:60–72.

10. Jung Young Lee made significant contributions in this enterprise: see his *The Theology of Change: A Christian Concept of God in an Eastern Perspective* (Maryknoll, N.Y.: Orbis Books, 1979); *Marginality: The Key to Multicultural Theology* (Minneapolis: Fortress Press, 1995); and *The Trinity in Asian Perspective* (Nashville: Abingdon Press, 1996). For a criticism and further formulation, see my "Toward a Christotao: Jesus as the Theanthropocosmic Tao" (paper presented at the annual meeting of the American Academy of Religion, San Francisco, 22 November 1997).

11. Cheng Chung-ying makes a helpful comparison between Chinese philosophy and Western philosophy, namely, "natural naturalization" and "human immanentization" versus "rational rationalization" and "divine transcendentalization." See his *New Dimensions of Confucianism and Neo-Confucian Philosophy* (Albany: State University of New York Press, 1991), 4–22.

12. I borrowed "mystical-prophetic" from David Tracy. See his *Dialogue with the Other: The Inter-religious Dialogue* (Louvain: Peeters Press; Grand Rapids, Mich.: Eerdmans, 1991), 7.

13. *Chuang-tzu,* chap. 4; see *The Complete Works of Chuang Tzu,* trans. Burton Watson (New York: Columbia University Press, 1968), 58.

14. I borrowed "serendipitous" from Gordon D. Kaufman, though I do not fully agree with his vision of the cosmic evolutionary-historical trajectory, which still is more or less linear, pragmatist, and historicist. See Gordon D. Kaufman, *In Face of Mystery: A Constructive Theology* (Cambridge, Mass.: Harvard University Press, 1993), 264–80. "Pneumatosociocosmic" is my term to denote the unified vision of social justice and cosmology mediated through the work of *ch'i* (vital energy). I argue that the pneumatosociocosmic vision will overcome the dichotomy between social and cosmological concerns laid between liberationists and inculturationists among Asian theologians, parallel to the dichotomy between justice and ecological issues (see my papers, "Tao of Asian Theology" and "Toward a Christotao"). For an ecological implication of *ch'i,* see Mary Evelyn Tucker, "The Philosophy of *Ch'i* as an Ecological Cosmology," in *Confucianism and Ecology: The Interrelation of Heaven, Earth, and Humans,* ed. Mary Evelyn Tucker and John Berthrong (Cambridge, Mass.: Harvard University Center for the Study of World Religions, 1998).

Deep Ecumenicity versus Incommensurability: Finding Common Ground on a Common Earth

PAUL F. KNITTER

The goal of the series on religions of the world and ecology is as urgent as it is bold: to gather the religious communities of the world together on the common ground of our threatened earth. In pursuing this goal, the series seeks, like the Buddha, a middle path: on the one hand, avoid the illusion of establishing a grand "unified worldview or a single global ethic." But on the other hand, be unsatisfied with "a simple bricolage or bland fusion of perspectives" from the different religions. Rather, the task is to gather the "multiperspectival" and "distinctive ecological attitudes and values" of the individual religions, and then to identify and assemble "commonalties" and "grounds for common concern."

In other words, this project of the Center for the Study of World Religions intends to promote an ecological interreligious dialogue—a dialogue among religious communities that takes as its common ground (its starting point and its reference point, its source of motivation and evaluation) the physical world, in both its nature and its needs. This is what I mean by the image of deep ecumenicity: the more the religions of the world can ground themselves in this earth and the more deeply they can connect with the nature and the needs of this planet, the more they will find themselves interconnected. The more deeply religious persons become ecologically attuned, the more effectively they will become ecumenically connected.

A Warning: Proceed with Caution

With so many others, I endorse and join this call for an ecological dialogue, or deep ecumenicity, among the religions. But such an endorsement must, I believe, be tempered with caution. As necessary, urgent, and promising as such an ecumenical call to the religions is, it is also complex and dangerous. To ignore the complexity of this project is to succumb to its dangers. Most of the warnings about the dangers of an interreligious dialogue that seeks its common ground in the environment come from a familiar (and perhaps nearby) source: the postmodern academy. There is no need, nor space, for me to rehearse the details of these reservations and admonitions. They take their source not only from epistemology and the sociology of knowledge, but also from the clear, but often ignored, witness of history (that is, when history is written not by the victors but by the vanquished): every time "common ground" is staked out, every time a universal project based on universal need is proclaimed, it either starts as, or ends up as, the "ground" or the "need" that is much more "common" to one group then to others. Usually the group who determines what ground is common and what truth is universal will be the one with more money—or guns—than the others. Common ground, all too easily, becomes a tool for political or economic domination.

And it does so because, according to our postmodern critics, such calls for universal projects based on common ground are not sufficiently aware of how much our ability to know is determined, or at least profoundly limited, by our ability to speak. Language—or our cultural-linguistic systems—determines not just how we speak of what we know, but how we know what we know. It determines, in other words, *what* we know. Truth is much better served and protected, therefore, when it is recognized to be inherently, ineluctably, diverse. The truth of humanity, like the beauty of flowers, will grow only when we allow ten thousand blossoms to bloom. A universal flower, able to grow in soil common to all parts of the world, is an artificial creation which requires the importation of this common soil and which usually ends up stifling local flowers. *Truth* therefore will always be *truths*. Diversity outweighs universality. Or, diversity will always mean incommunsurability—the impossibility of reducing the diverse truths to a common, universal truth. Thus, the tension, if not contradiction, between our program of "deep ecumenicity" and "incommensurability."

And so projects such as this one on religions and ecology are deemed by postmodernists to be highly suspect and deceptively dangerous. To proclaim nature, as understood by science, to be the source of a common creation myth, or as the new text for a universal revelation, or as the universal locus for encountering the Divine, or as the generator of universally binding ethical norms—such moves, our critics admonish, are but renewed and veiled attempts to carry on the Western-based, hegemonic project of modernity. They are still driven by "a Kantian motor"[1] in their resolve to find one text—this one discovered by natural scientists or environmentalists—that cannot be "deconstructed" and that will either subsume or be the higher norm for all the others. John Milbank sees this turn to nature already present in the earliest movements of modernity but today grown much more robust:

> After the collapse of the medieval consensus, faced with the difficulties of containing the conflicts amongst communities of diverse beliefs, the early modern age already fled to the arms of nature as support for a new objectivity. . . . Displacement towards nature was therefore in place from the outset of modernity, although 'nature' was also from the outset a cultural construct: initially a disguised projection of a new mode of human power.[2]

So projects such as ours have been described as a "divinization of the earth" based on a "sacralization of 'science,'" a "new ecologism" that becomes an eco-olatry. All this is a "Trojan Horse," we are told, within which hides a new metanarrative that is not only theologically suspect as idolatry but that can easily take the form of an "eco-fascism" proclaiming one unified, universal, authoritative voice—now the voice of the earth—over all other voices.[3]

In no way am I suggesting that we should succumb to such postmodern reservations or roadblocks. I believe that in many ways they are profoundly flawed and propelled by their own "motors." But I *am* saying that the reservations have to be taken seriously. If they are not, the dangers that they signal are all too likely to infect or impede our project.

In what follows, I would like to suggest reasons why an ecological interreligious dialogue, or deep ecumenicity, is not only necessary but possible. While such a dialogue has its inherent dangers, there are resources both within the present environmental "state of the world" and within the religions themselves with which these dangers can be warded off. I hope to lay the foundation for an effective procedure or methodology by which the religions can realize a dialogue that will discover or create common ecumenical ground on our common earth, but in such a way that diversity is preserved and fostered, and no one religion or nation is allowed to own more stocks of that common ground than others.[4] Naturally, I am doing this from my Christian, Catholic, Western, male perspective; but in trying to do that dialogically, I trust that my perspective can speak to other perspectives.

The Common Ground of "Metaproblems"

Respectfully but firmly, I would first of all like to say to my postmodern colleagues in the academy that if, as they insist, there are no such things as "metanarratives," there are such things as "metaproblems." We may not have universal, particular solutions that work for everyone, but we do have, it seems to me, universal particular problems that affect everyone. And some of the most evident and most pressing of these universal particular problems are to be found among the list of environmental woes and crises that scientists and environmentalists have been describing since the second half of this almost-ended century. Though I sound judgmental and very unpostmodern, I must say that to ignore these ecological metaproblems is, at best, naïve and, at worst, immoral. And regarding my brothers and sisters of the South who express their fears that the environmental agenda can be, and is being, exploited by the Northern powers,[5] I first listen to the details of their case; but then I respectfully respond that the danger and reality of exploitation does not remove the urgency of the agenda. To the necessity of pursuing the environmental agenda, we add the necessity of pursuing it with these dangers of exploitation in mind. But the reality and the urgency of the deteriorating environment is raising ethical issues and making ethical demands that apply universally, to all of us. Pace postmodernism, we do have metaethical problems.

So I do not think that Suzi Gablik exaggerates: "Despite claims by social critics like Jean-François Lyotard and Frederic Jameson that our society reflects the absence of any great integrating vision or collective project, the great collective project has, in fact, presented itself. It is that of saving the earth—at this point, nothing else really matters."[6] If the reality of ecological peril is providing us with a common ethical project, that project also provides us with the raw materials and the heuristic context for a universal ethical discourse. The ethical challenges of the environment offer us possibilities of a "metadiscourse of the universe" which can link our individual ethical discourses and enable us to talk to each other across our incommensurabilities.[7]

With Baird Callicott, who evinces a marked postmodern consciousness and sensitivity, we can speak of the need and possibility of a universal environmental ethic. Such an ethic, Callicott points out, would be thoroughly postmodern in that it recognizes the ineradicable diversity of cultural perspectives, the danger of any final or absolute worldview, and the necessity of openness to further ethical evolution; but at the same time, this environmental ethic would serve as an "intellectual global commons" on which fidelity to the earth serves as the connector and adjudicator between our diversities.[8] While Callicott often seems to understand this environmental "global commons" in terms of a vision of "the ecological relationships binding the myriads of species into hierarchically nested ecosystems,"[9] I would see it more in terms of ethical challenges to elaborate a way of acting in the world. I suspect that the shared vision will grow out of shared praxis, informed by an ethic of sustainability and justice.

The Necessity of an Interreligious Contribution to an Environmental Ethic

If, then, the state of the earth is presenting us with "metaproblems" that call for a concerted effort toward "metasolutions" based on "meta-ethical" values and policies, those people who are trying to respond to these problems are recognizing more and more, often to their own surprise, that the religious communities of the world have an important, if not essential, role to play in fashioning such responses.

As I survey and sift the many reasons why religious spokespersons are being invited to the table of environmental discussions, I find two dominant themes, different yet complementary: the "vision thing" and the "political thing."

First, the vision thing might also be termed the "feeling thing," for it recognizes that if we are really going to respond to the environmental crisis, we not only have to see and understand the earth differently; we have to feel it differently. What we call "nature" has to touch us, or enter into the network of our sensitivities, more deeply and more engagingly than it has in the past. Even crusty, "facts-only" environmentalists are starting to admit (I know it's not yet a general consensus) that we cannot regard the things of the earth as mere "things." We cannot pick up a rock or plant or animal and simply hold it in our hands as something we measure, weigh, and put to use. Somehow, when we touch it, it has to touch us. When we perceive it, the perception has to affect not just our brains but also our hearts. That means that each "it," in some strange but real sense, has to become a "you." Our relationship with the beings of the earth—animate and inanimate, sentient and insentient—has to be more than an instrumental relationship; it must also become—again this may sound strange to some of us crusty types—an interpersonal relationship. The beings of the earth cannot be only objects that we use; they must be persons or beings which we love. "Love your neighbor as yourself" must include also our earth-neighbors. We need a bigger neighborhood.

And here is where the religious dimension must contribute to the foundations of an integral, effective environmental program. To perceive and feel and affirm our interpersonal relationship with rocks and plants and animals is to feel that which connects them with us and grounds their value and sacrality. It is to feel what some religious persons would want to symbolize as "Spirit" or "Tao" or "Dharma" or "Buddha-nature" or "Wakan-Tanka"—that which *grounds* everything and *connects* everything and indeed makes us family. I'm not saying that a religious belief or perspective is necessary to feel the sacredness of the earth and our connection with it; but I am saying that it certainly can help. If environmentalists are concluding that in order to protect the earth we have to love it, religious persons are suggesting that they can help in fostering such love.

So, environmentalists are starting to ask themselves the question: "does not an effective ecological ethics, if it is to be more than an abstract set of principles, rest on a spiritual attitude toward the larger natural community to which we belong? Must not a serious and effective ecological ethics be grounded and founded upon a deeper and wider spiritual vision of life than seems available in the modern consumer societies. . . ?"[10] In their open letter to religious communities, thirty-four internationally known scientists answer that question: "Efforts to safeguard and cherish the environment need to be infused with a vision of the sacred."[11]

Second, the help that religions can provide the environmental agenda is, however, not only a vision of the sacred; it is also political. Here, I signal another growing recognition within the environmentalist movement: the global fire that is consuming the life and life-sustaining capacity of the planet is not just abetted by the lack of a spiritual vision of the earth; it is also positively fed by another kind of vision that measures well-being in terms of the graph of growth-production-consumption. "I consume, therefore I am. And the more I can consume, the better-off I will be." It is this vision, or worldview, or philosophy—or really, *religion*—that pervades the economic and political life and practice of our so-called new, neoliberal world order. Timothy Weiskel describes this dominant ideology as "growthism": "Without any exaggeration . . . it is fair to say that in practical terms the most pervasive form of this religiously held belief in our day is that of growthism founded upon a doctrine of techno-scientific salvation."[12] For Max Oelschlaeger, it is the new and thoroughly ecumenical church of "utilitarian individualism": "Utilitarian individualism reigns supreme as the *public philosophy*. So absolute is its power, hiding from view anything that does not conform with its description of the world and institutional imperatives that some doubt our ability to escape."[13]

The tactical or political response to this dominant religion of growthism or utilitarian individualism must be twofold: one of preaching and one of organizing. In a sense, we must "fight spiritual fire with spiritual fire."[14] In the context of the United States and perhaps Europe, it would seem that only the churches have another Gospel to counteract the gospel of utilitarian individualism—and the means to deliver that Gospel. As Oelschlaeger somberly points out: "the ethical theory of the professional environmental ethics community is powerless to overcome the pervasive influence of utilitarian individualism, an ideology institutionalized in political and economic institutions."[15] Each week millions assemble in the churches and synagogues of the land; if all these people could hear from their pastors and rabbis how diametrically opposed this new, earth-and-people-consuming religion of growthism is to the Gospel and the Torah (that's a big "if," I know), we would have a message and mechanism to bring people back to their religious and planetary senses.

And, politically speaking, this is perhaps the only kind of message that will give them the required prophetic courage and chutzpah to speak and act against the assumed and dominant orthodoxy in the world of business and politics. To question growthism is to take a thoroughly, and often lonely, counterculture stance. Most citizens of the United States find that extremely difficult—unless they feel they have Isaiah, Jeremiah, Jesus (and I think I can add Muhammad) on their side. Religious prophets can be both brave and ornery.

But what we're envisioning, and what is needed, is not just that each religious congregation assemble its environmental prophets and lobbyists; we need a joining of ranks, a common front built on common ground, for an interreligious prophetic voice and lobby! We might expand Hans Küng's well-known rally-call, "No world peace [peace among nations] without peace between the religions,"[16] to also proclaim, "No peace with the earth without peace between the religions." The earth needs the help of the religions; and the religions will not be able to provide this help effectively unless they "get their act together"—both their intrareligious act, as they retrieve and refurbish their own ecological messages, and their interreligious act, as they seek to join their ecological voice with that of other religious communities. Can we realistically hope for this?

The Possibility of an Interreligious Contribution to an Environmental Ethic

We are asking the religious traditions of the world to endorse and respond to Dean James P. Morton's sobering announcement: "the environment is not just another issue but an inescapable challenge to what it means to be religious."[17] Can we expect persons from *all* religions to affirm that challenge? Here we feel the postmodernist monkey on our back: we are setting up a "meta-agenda" that could end up as an imperialistic imposition; we are crossing the "no trespassing" signs of incommensurablity. I've already offered one, rather pragmatic and emotional response to such accusations: an interreligious contribution to the environmental project is necessary. And what is necessary must, somehow, be possible. In what follows, I would like to show *why* such an interreligious effort *is* possible, why an ecumenical agenda is not an imposition on the religions, why the faithful in all the religious communities can feel not only able but required to respond to the need for a shared environmental ethic.

I am not suggesting that all the religious communities of the world have ready-made environmental ethics or theologies tucked away in their scriptures or teachings, which they can simply look up, maybe dust off, and then announce to the world. Many religions, especially those of the family of Abraham, do not have a well-elaborated ecological theology and ethics. For many traditions the "inescapable" environmental challenge that Dean Morton talks about is a wake-up call—like an unexpected challenge to the stability of a good marriage. Like all such challenges, it is both unsettling and renewing. What Rita Gross says about her own Buddhist tradition can apply to most others: "The question is not what *has* Buddhism said about ecology and the environment, but what *could* Buddhism have to say about these subjects."[18] What I'm suggesting to the postmodern skeptics is that all religions *can* respond to the environmental challenge; they all can feel the will, the desire, to do so. The environmental challenge has the power to leap across incommensurable chasms and to touch the religious sensitivities of persons no matter what their cultural-linguistic systems. And once touched by this challenge, members of diverse religions will use it as a search-light to discover old or new environmental messages in the treasure-chests of their scriptures and traditions.

Let me offer a few considerations that will, I hope, ground the "metaclaims" I have just made—that persons in *all* religious communities can feel called to respond, as religious persons, to the environmental challenge:

1. Outside the World, No Salvation

I begin with what I think is a phenomenological claim—something that can be seen throughout the religious world, no matter what socially constructed glasses one is wearing. In all the historical, still-living religious traditions (and that certainly includes the primal religions), one finds affirmed, in differing ways and to differing degrees, Edward Schillebeeckx's rather jolting dictum, *Extra mundum nulla salus*—"Outside the world, there is no salvation."[19] He is trying to turn on its head the age-old Roman Catholic claim, "Outside the church there is no salvation." In doing so, he offers a broad description of what one can find, somewhere, within all religious traditions. But note, in saying there is no salvation outside the world, he is not reducing the content or the object of religious experience to the finite realm. Rather, he is asserting that whatever the "transcendent" or the "more-than-human" or the "deeper" ultimate content of religious experience may be, it is to be found in, and through, and generally transformative of, this finite world.

Religion or religious experience, therefore, seeks or contains many things; and one of them—an essential ingredient in the mix of religion—is to enable people to live more adequately in this world and thus to fashion, either historically or psychologically, a better world. Salvation, or whatever the goal of a religion may be, intends, in some way and degree, to affect or to better or to change this world. Therefore, no salvation lies completely outside of this world.

Thus, Gordon Kaufman, from the cultural-linguistic perspective of Harvard University, makes an assertion which I trust will find sympathetic vibrations among followers of religious paths distant from Cambridge: "Every religious tradition promises salvation in some form or other, i.e., promises true human fulfillment, or at least rescue from the pit into which we humans have fallen. Every religious tradition thus implicitly invokes a human or humane criterion to justify its existence and its claims."[20] From his Buddhist perspective, Robert Thurman would seem to agree with Kaufman: "Real religion is nothing but the energy to help sentient beings; all religions were originally founded to promote happiness and reduce suffering."[21]

If, therefore, there is no salvation outside this world, no salvation that does not somehow touch and transform finite surroundings, then we can expect "persons of faith" within religious families across the world to respond to the new and menacing ecological threats to the world. We can also paraphrase the well-known statement of Gandhi, "I can say without the slightest hesitation, and yet in all humility, that those who say that religion has nothing to do with politics do not know what religion means," to read "those who say that religion has nothing to do with the environment do not know what religion means."[22]

2. The Dipolarity of the Mystical and the Prophetic

Another way to elucidate the inherent way religion relates to the environment, or what religious salvation has to do with this world, is to examine another claim that comparative religionists are advancing nowadays. In the past, theologians and historians of religions, mainly those housed in Western universities, traced a vertical line between the religions of the world, with "mystical," or inner-oriented, religions (usually Indic) on one side and "prophetic," or world-involved, traditions (usually Semitic or Abrahamic) on the other.[23] Today, it is generally recognized that the line should be drawn horizontally rather than vertically; mystics and prophets populate, in differing proportions, *all* (or at least most) of the religious communities of the world. This means that the force or dynamism released in persons and communities by what we call religious experience is *dipolar.* Religion might be compared to an energy field with two different but profoundly complementary poles; to move within this field, or to let it move oneself, is to oscillate back and forth between these two poles. Neither pole is primary; neither is more important than the other. Indeed, one cannot exist or function without the other.

Western scholars have tried to identify these poles with terms such as "the mystical and the prophetic," or "contemplation and action," or "faith and good works," or "manifestation and proclamation." Aloysius Pieris, from his Buddhist-Christian context in Sri Lanka, finds more engaging terms in *gnosis* (or *prajna*) and *agape* (or charity):

> What must be borne in mind is that both *gnosis* and *agape* are *necessary* precisely because each in itself is *inadequate* as a medium, not only for experiencing but also for expressing our intimate moments with the Ultimate Source of Liberation. They are, in other words, complementary idioms that need each other to mediate the self-transcending experience called "salvation." Any valid spirituality, Buddhist or Christian, as the history of religions attests, does retain both poles of religious experience—namely, the gnostic and the agapeic.[24]

To be—or better, to grow—religiously is to find a rhythm between these two poles (a rhythm adapted, necessarily, to one's personal or social context); it is to move between the within and the without, between the transformation of inner consciousness and social consciousness, between efforts to bring forth peace of the heart and peace within the world, between engagement in spiritual praxis and political praxis, between fleeing to the desert and plunging into the marketplace. Undeniably, in both individuals and in communities, this rhythm has not always been maintained. When that happens, we have self-absorbed mystics whose search for the Mystery within blinds them to the terrestrial misery all around them; or we have rudderless prophets whose political programs easily become intolerant or even violent. Unprophetic mystics or demystified prophets easily turn religion into either an opium to avoid the world or a concession to exploit it.

And so David Tracy urges a "new hermeneutical practice" for the study of religion that he describes as "mystical-prophetic." And he adds immediately: "The hyphen is what compels my interest."[25] To understand the nature of religion, its relevance for today's world and the possibilities of cross-cultural conversations between religious communities, we must explore this "hyphen"—the life-giving dipolarity between the mystical and the prophetic. But not only scholars are coming to realize the importance of the hyphen. As Tracy also recognizes, "in all the major religious traditions, there is a search for new ways to unite those mystical and prophetic trajectories."[26] What that means for this project is, I think, clear: the "prophetic trajectory" that stirs within each religious family will not be adequately understood, nor will its mystical moorings be adequately grasped, unless this prophetic, world-involving and world-transforming energy is aroused and directed by the environmental challenges of our age. Simply stated: if the scholars are right that prophets are essential to the balance and well-being and relevance of religion, today they will have to be environmental prophets. A religious prophet without a concern for this earth would be an "other-worldly prophet"—which, of course, is a contradiction in terms.

3. From Self-Centeredness to Reality-Centeredness

I offer one more consideration why it is possible for all religious communities to participate in an ecological interreligious conversation—or, why to call on all religions to contribute to an environmental ethic is not an imperialistic imposition but a fitting invitation. What many environmentalists are proposing as the crucial and unique contribution that religions must make to an environmental ethic is precisely what many scholars and practitioners of religion are saying is an essential "family characteristic" of all religions. In other words, what environmentalists want from all religions, all religions can provide (again, in different ways and degrees).

What they want from religion happens to be, many would say, the most decisive ingredient in an effective environmental ethic: the ability to move from an anthropocentric to a biocentric understanding of the world and our human place in that world. Environmentalists have long recognized this shift as essential; recently, many are also recognizing—some with consternation, others with hope—that this shift is really "a religious question." This is how Bill McKibben puts it:

> Who is at the center of affairs? We have behaved for quite a long time as if we were, and it is this assumption that drives most of the environmental dilemmas we face. . . . Now we need somehow to discover an old formula: that the tribe, or nature, or God, or most likely some amalgam of the three, is at the center of things. In such a world it becomes possible to imagine certain limits, to imagine fulfilling our unique ability as a species to limit ourselves.[27]

McKibben then goes on to offer the sobering suggestion that it is "only churches, synagogues, mosques (and the campfires of those who do their worshipping outdoors)" that can stir people to affirm this unique ability to limit ourselves and so realize ourselves.[28] "Religious awareness, then, may be absolutely indispensable in such an awakening, by integrating our lives in a wider reality beyond our own anthropocentric needs. . . ."[29] Timothy Weiskel makes a similar move from environmental demands to religious supply to meet the crying need for "a new vision of community and a compelling theory of human limit." He recognizes that the call to humans to "de-center ourselves and recenter our awareness around the logic of a larger system of which we are a part" is "at the heart of . . . religious experience." He proposes that every "theology is in essence a theory of human limit."[30]

And I think he's right. Some years ago, well before I encountered such announcements as these of McKibben and Weiskel, I formulated what other religious scholars and I might call the "shared diagnosis and remedy for the human predicament" that is found in most, if not all, religious communities.

In many different ways, most (all?) religions seek to convert the energies of one's self from a centripetal to a centrifugal movement and so to broaden the focus of concern from not only me or us (egocentricity) to Other or others (altruism). We have to find ourselves outside of ourselves; to realize who we are, we have to experience ourselves as part of something that is greater than what we understand ourselves to be right now. John Hick, using Western terminology, seeks to summarize all this by describing the analogously common goal of most religions as a shift from self-centeredness to Reality-centeredness.[31]

When Hick and others describe the ethical dynamism that can be identified commonly across religious boundaries as this "shift from self-centeredness to Reality-centeredness," he is assuring us that differing religious communities, at least in their "good news" if not in their "good practice," can provide what the environmentalists are asking of religions: the call, and the energy, to move away from anthropocentrism.

A case can be made that all the living religious communities—if we look carefully or anew at their original experience, visions, and sacred scriptures—are inherently and essentially antianthropocentric. In the multiple and vast forms of religious experience, we can find this movement away from self-centeredness to Reality-centeredness in an awareness that whatever our true selves are, they can be realized only in a decentered relationship with other selves. Traditionally, these other selves have been the human Other and, for most traditions, the Divine Other. Today, religious communities are recognizing that the "Other" must also include the earth Other. One cannot truly be Other-centered or Reality-centered unless one is life-centered, biocentric. All living religions, I believe, can deliver this message, even if they are not actually doing so at the moment. To discover and deliver this message they may need to be shaken by the challenge the environmentalists are formulating; but it is a message that comes from the heart of religion and religious experience.[32]

Interreligious Dialogue Starts with Ethics

If the considerations stitched together in this essay really do hold together—that our environmental plight calls for a religious contribution and that all the religions have the ability (at least potentially) to offer such a contribution—then what we have constructed is an ethical springboard, or starting point, for a more effective interreligious conversation. In order to guard against all the valid warnings that the postmodernists make about incommensurabilites and the danger of one religion dominating the discourse, let the discourse begin with earth ethics rather than particular religious beliefs, with moral praxis rather than mystical reflection, with acting together for the earth rather than elaborating a common religious story about the earth. The first steps toward determining common ground for our deep ecumenicity will be interethical more than expressly interreligious. I think it can be shown that, if we start with ethics, we will, necessarily and happily, find ourselves closer together as religious persons. Ethical "first steps" enable and require religious "second steps." The door, or the guide, to a deep mystical ecumenicity among the religions can be found in an ethical ecumenicity. An earth ethics can be an effective key to opening the door to an interfaith earth mysticism and a common creation story.[33]

Notes

1. Gavin D'Costa, "Critical Questions of the Pluralistic Theology of Religions with Reference to the Work of Paul Knitter" (paper presented at a conference on pluralistic theology, Bildungshaus St. Virgil, Salzburg, Austria, May 1996), 4.

2. John Milbank, *The Word Made Strange: Theology, Language, Culture* (Oxford: Basil Blackwell, 1997), 258.

3. D'Costa, "Critical Questions," 1–5, passim.

4. In this chapter, I am primarily laying this foundation for such an ecological dialogue; in the original, much too lengthy, paper prepared for the project, I also went on to trace the methodology of dialogue that can be developed on this foundation. This second part will be published as another essay.

5. An excellent summary of such concerns is offered by Ramachandra Guha, "Radical Environmentalism: A Third-World Critique," in *Ecology,* ed. Carolyn Merchant, Key Concepts in Critical Theory (Atlantic Highland, N.J.: Humanities Press International, 1994), 281–91.

6. Suzi Gablik, *The Reenchantment of Art* (New York: Thames and Hudson, 1991), 26.

7. Charlene Spretnak, *States of Grace: The Recovery of Meaning in the Postmodern Age* (San Francisco: HarperSanFrancisco, 1991), 81, 105.

8. J. Baird Callicott, *Earth's Insights: A Survey of Ecological Ethics from the Mediterranean Basin to the Australian Outback* (Berkeley and Los Angeles: University of California Press, 1994), 197, cf. 187–88.

9. Ibid., 187.

10. Paul Brockelman, "With New Eyes: Seeing the Environment as a Spiritual Issue," in *The Greening of Faith: God, the Environment, and the Good Life,* ed. John E. Carroll, Paul Brockelman, and Mary Westfall (Hanover, N.H.: University Press of New England, 1997), 38.

11. "An Open Letter to the Religious Community," issued in January 1990 and available from the National Religious Partnership for the Environment, 1047 Amsterdam Ave, New York, NY 10025.

12. Timothy C. Weiskel, "Some Notes from Belschaz'zar's Feast," in *The Greening of Faith,* 21.

13. Max Oelschlaeger, *Caring for Creation: An Ecumenical Approach to the Environmental Crisis* (New Haven: Yale University Press, 1994), 218

14. Brockelman, "With New Eyes," 39.

15. Oelschlaeger, *Caring for Creation,* 186.

16. Hans Küng, *Global Responsibility: In Search of a New World Ethic* (New York: Crossroad Press, 1991), xv.

17. Dean of the Episcopal Cathedral of St. John the Divine, New York, as quoted in the introduction to *The Greening of Faith,* 5.

18. Rita Gross, "Toward a Buddhist Environmental Ethic," in *Visions of a New Earth: Religious Perspectives on Population, Consumption, and Ecology,* ed. Harold Coward and Daniel Maguire (Albany: State University of New York Press, forthcoming).

19. Edward Schillebeeckx, *The Church: The Human Story of God* (New York: Crossroad Press, 1990), 5–15.

20. Gordon D. Kaufman, *The Theological Imagination: Constructing the Concept of God* (Philadelphia: Westminster Press, 1981), 197–99.

21. Robert A. F. Thurman, "Tibet and the Monastic Army of Peace," in *Inner Peace, World Peace: Essays on Buddhism and Nonviolence,* ed. Kenneth Kraft (Albany: State University of New York Press, 1992), 79.

22. Mohandas K. Gandhi, *An Autobiography: The Story of My Experiments with Truth* (Boston: Beacon Press, 1957), 504.

23. See, for example, Hans Küng, *Christianity and the World Religions: Paths of Dialogue with Islam, Hinduism, and Buddhism* (Garden City, N.Y.: Doubleday, 1986), 174–77.

24. Aloysius Pieris, *Love Meets Wisdom: A Christian Experience of Buddhism* (Maryknoll, N.Y.: Orbis Books, 1988), 111.

25. David Tracy, "God, Dialogue, and Solidarity: A Theologian's Refrain," *Christian Century,* 10 October 1990, p. 904.

26. David Tracy, *Dialogue with the Other: The Inter-Religious Dialogue* (Grand Rapids, Mich.: Eerdmans, 1991), 100.

27. Bill McKibben, foreword to *The Greening of Faith,* vii.

28. Ibid., viii

29. Introduction to pt. 1, *The Greening of Faith,* 9.

30. Weiskel, "Notes from Belschaz'zar's Feast," 25, 27.

31. Paul F. Knitter, *One Earth, Many Religions: Multifaith Dialogue and Global Responsibility* (Maryknoll, N.Y.: Orbis Books, 1995), 107. Reference to Hick is from John Hick, *An Interpretation of Religion: Human Responses to the Transcendent* (New Haven: Yale University Press, 1989), 299–309.

32. Admittedly, as feminist critics point out, such ideals of a selfless self have been fashioned by patriarchal religions—that means, by men whose primary "sin" has been an inflated self that abuses other selves, and not by women whose primary sin has been a deflated self that allows itself to be abused by others. Thus, what I am proposing here as a diagnosis common to all religions requires a feminist hermeneutics of suspicion that will assure that the selfless self does not become the enslaved or subordinated self. Valerie Saiving, "The Human Situation: A Feminine View," in *Womanspirit Rising: A Feminist Reader in Religion,* ed. Carol P. Christ and Judith Plaskow (San Francisco: Harper and Row, 1979), 25–42. Still, I think feminists would agree that the "saved self" or new self is one that is sustained in the web of mutuality rather than in the cell of egocentricity. Catherine Keller, *From a Broken Web: Separation, Sexism, and Self* (Boston: Beacon Press, 1986).

33. A promising step in this direction is being made in the Earth Charter process of the Earth Charter Commission headquartered at the Earth Council in Costa Rica. In April 1999, it issued Benchmark Draft II of the Earth Charter, being offered to the planet's people and the United Nations. It presents general principles of respect and care for Earth and all life, rooted in religious sensibility, followed by ethical guidelines to achieve sustainability with justice.

IV. Toward Global
Security and Sustainability

Scientific and Religious
Perspectives on Sustainability

IAN G. BARBOUR

Other contributors to this volume have documented the fact that the world of nature has received relatively little attention in the life and thought of the Christian community. Divine transcendence has historically received more emphasis than divine immanence. The doctrine of redemption has been celebrated in liturgy and preaching far more often than the doctrine of creation. My own concern is that the neglect of nature has been accompanied by the neglect of science and technology in theological and ethical reflection and in seminary education. Our new awareness of environmental degradation and the depletion of natural resources should lead us to not only to reexamine our attitudes toward nature but also to ask about the relationship between scientific and religious perspectives on sustainability.

Members of the scientific and religious communities have been working together in recent years in a common concern for the environment and the future of life on planet Earth. Starting in 1990, a series of conferences of prominent scientists and religious leaders was held under the title "Joint Appeal of Science and Religion for the Environment." It culminated in 1992 in a meeting in Washington which included a Senate committee hearing and a press conference organized by then Senator Albert Gore. In 1994 the National Religious Partnership for the Environment was established by denominational leaders to continue this project, with scientific advice from the Union of Concerned Scientists. A conference in 1995 on consumption, population, and the environment was jointly sponsored by the

American Association for the Advancement of Science and the Boston Theological Institute.[1]

Such collaboration is in part the result of pragmatic considerations; people who share a concern can be more effective in education and political action if they work together. But I believe there are also deeper reasons why the scientific and religious communities should cooperate on these issues. Each of us is a whole person and our ideas are indebted to diverse sources; we cannot divide up our lives into watertight compartments. Interdisciplinary dialogue is also motivated by the recognition that the problems of the real world cut across the boundaries of academic disciplines. But if we are to learn from each other, we must examine both the common ground and the distinctive contribution of each community.

In looking at sustainability, I will first consider some contributions from science, then contributions jointly from science and religion, and finally some distinctive contributions from religion. I will be discussing the Christian tradition, but a similar analysis could be made in the case of other religious traditions.

Contributions from Science

Science can give us a better understanding of the environmental impacts of our current agricultural, industrial, and personal practices. In more general terms, the sciences (especially ecology and evolutionary biology) offer a new view of the place of humanity in nature and our interdependence with other forms of life; this new perception of ourselves will affect our practices if we take it seriously.

Understanding Environmental Impacts

During the 1960s and 1970s scientists achieved greater knowledge of the impact of our actions on the environment, particularly in the pollution of air, water, and land. They also proposed ways of reducing those impacts. Many of these pollutants were relatively localized, and we have made some progress in regulating and controlling them. In the 1980s and 1990s scientists have made us aware of more long-term global impacts, such as climate changes and the loss of endangered species.[2] Topsoil around the world is being eroded by intensive agriculture, overgrazing, and deforestation. World population is growing by 80 million each year. Industrial growth and the consumption of global resources by affluent nations have raised additional questions of long-term sustainability, which we have hardly begun to address.[3]

In relation to such scientific evidence, the main task of members of the religious community is to listen to scientists, to become better informed, and to help in spreading the word. But religious participants also have a responsibility to raise questions. They can ask scientists to indicate the assumptions and the uncertainties present in their interpretation of data. In the case of global warming, there is virtual unanimity among experts that increases in carbon dioxide and other greenhouse gases will lead to significant warming, though there is a range of estimates of probable temperature changes and their effects on climate, agriculture, and coastal areas.[4] In other cases there may be greater disagreement among experts. Assessments of risks often depend on assumptions that should be made explicit since they may be influenced by a scientist's ethical or political convictions.

A scientist's recommendation of a particular policy of action is based in part on scientific estimates of the consequences of that policy. But policy recommendations inescapably involve value judgments in weighing the relative importance of diverse kinds of consequence. Furthermore, the main benefits of a new technology or economic policy may accrue mainly to one group of citizens, while another group carries the main burden of risks or indirect costs, so that issues of distributional justice are at stake. In addition, policy recommendations are the result of comparison with the alternatives that a person thinks are feasible and realistic—which introduces political and economic considerations. Policy decisions thus require ethical analysis and input from the social sciences and the wider culture as well as input from the natural sciences, even when the latter are as crucial as they are in decisions affecting the environment and sustainability. In short, we need to rely heavily on the work of scientists without expecting them to have the last word on policy choices.[5]

Awareness of Ecological Interdependence

A more indirect contribution of the scientific community to sustainability is an awareness of the interdependence of all forms of life. The study of ecosystems shows the complex interconnections in the web of life. While some ecosystems are quite resilient, others are fragile and vulnerable to the repercussions of human actions. Diversity in the biosphere allows for both stability and adaptation to new conditions. Beyond the study of specific interactions among life-forms, ecology has led to a new understanding of our dependence on our environments. Evolutionary biology has also given us a new perception of our place in nature. It has shown our kinship with other creatures. We are united in a common cosmic story that goes back to the early stars in which were formed the atoms in our brains and in all plants and animals. Life on Earth is the story of our family tree of descent from common ancestors. More than 99 percent of the active genes in humans and chimpanzees are identical—though, of course, the remaining 1 percent make an enormous difference. Scientists see humanity as part of the natural order, even as they acknowledge human capacities not present in other forms of life.

Scientific work in evolutionary biology and neurobiology has been an important influence on recent theologians in their writing about human nature. In the Bible itself, persons are viewed holistically as integrated centers of thinking, feeling, willing, and acting. The Bible portrays the social and bodily character of selfhood. While humanity is given a special status, kinship with other forms of life is also asserted. But under the influence of late Greek thought, the early church came to view a human being as a separate soul temporarily inhabiting a body. This dualism continued in Descartes's distinction between mind and matter as radically different substances. Only humanity was said to have an immortal soul or a rational mind, establishing an absolute line between humans and all other beings. The recent writings of theologians describing a person as an integral psychosomatic being, a bodily self in community, reflects an indebtedness to science as well as a return to biblical roots.[6] As science helps us to see ourselves in a new way, both our attitudes and our actions will be affected.

Contributions from Science and Religion Jointly

Let us consider some cases in which very similar ideas are found in the scientific and religious communities even though they are derived from differing sources. Three such themes are 1) a long-term global view, 2) respect for all forms of life, and 3) concern about population growth.

A Long-term Global View

Degraded land, eroded soil, and decimated fisheries and forests will take many decades to recover. We have been living off biological capital, not biological income. Many of the impacts of our technologies will be felt by future generations. Radioactive wastes from today's nuclear power plants will endanger anyone exposed to them ten thousand years from now. The world of politics, however, takes a very short-term view. Political leaders find it difficult to look beyond the next election. Elected officials receive campaign contributions and heavy lobbying from business and industry whose attention is directed to short-term profits. Economic calculations give little weight to long-term consequences because a time discount is applied to future costs and benefits.

Scientists, by contrast, typically think in terms of long time-spans. Biologists study the history of evolution, and ecologists study populations over many generations. They are keenly aware that population growth in any species puts increasing pressures on the environment and jeopardizes the welfare of future generations. Without the work of scientists we would never have had the 1987 Brundtland Report, which elaborates the idea of sustainable development and the importance of the needs of future as well as current generations. Scientists from around the world helped to develop the agenda for the 1992 United Nations Conference on Environment and Development in Rio around the theme of sustainable development.[7]

Religious traditions also take a long-term view. Stewardship requires consideration of the future because God's purposes include the future. The Bible speaks of a covenant from generation to generation "to you and your descendants forever." The land, in particular, is to be held as a trust for future generations. This long time-perspective derives from a sense of history and ongoing family and social life, as well as accountability to a God who spans the generations. So it is not surprising that sustainability has been a major theme in statements of the World Council of Churches, several Protestant denominations, and the U.S. Conference of Catholic Bishops.[8]

In addition, both the scientific and the religious communities at their best have advocated a global perspective. Science itself is international. Scientific meetings and journals ignore national boundaries. Scientists have a global viewpoint on environmental and resource problems. They recognize that impacts on the environment at one point have far-reaching repercussions at distant points. CFCs released in repairing an air-conditioner in Boston will contribute to the depletion of ozone and the risk of skin cancer in Berlin or Bangkok. Scientists have insisted that an adequate response to global warming can be achieved only by international agreement on the reduction of greenhouse emissions. They have been aware of the destructiveness of nuclear war and have been prominent in the arms control and peace movements and in supporting the UN. However, we must acknowledge that scientists are subject to the same nationalistic viewpoints as other citizens, and a large fraction of applied scientists has been working directly or indirectly on military projects.

Our religious traditions have also held up a vision of world community, though they have too often themselves succumbed to intolerance and religious imperialism. The biblical writers affirm our common humanity and assert that we have been made "one people to dwell on the face of the earth." The religious communities of the United States have been active in working for peace and for support of the UN. They have organized famine relief and lobbied for foreign aid and agricultural and technical assistance. Most religious groups have been urging a reduction in military expenditures and have criticized reliance on nuclear weapons. Religious leaders can join scientists in asserting that future threats to the nation's security are likely to be economic and environmental rather than military. Our response to these threats must be global and international rather than narrowly national, for we live in an interdependent world. The end of the Cold War and the emergence of global environmental crises presents an unprecedented opportunity for international cooperation.[9]

Respect for All Forms of Life

I noted above the scientific evidence for the ecological interdependence of all forms of life and the evolutionary understanding of our kinship with other creatures. Human self-interest requires that we consider the impact of our actions on other life-forms. But many scientists are critical of a purely anthropocentric viewpoint. They are concerned for the wider web of life and they value other creatures in themselves, not simply for their usefulness to us. Some scientists, such as Aldo Leopold, Loren Eiseley, and Rachel Carson, have given eloquent expression to their experience of unity with and participation in the world of nature. Others respond to the cosmos with a sense of awe and wonder, and regard the earth as in some sense sacred. Such personal and reflective responses go beyond science itself, but they provide strong motivation for action to preserve the environment.

Biblical writings also affirm the value of the natural world. The creation story asserts the goodness and unity of the created order. It acknowledges our common status as creatures, even though humanity alone has capacities for personal relationships and moral responsibility that are uniquely in God's image. According to Genesis, humanity is called to till and keep the garden and to exercise careful stewardship of the earth. The covenant after the flood includes all living creatures, and the Deuteronomic law specifies humane treatment of animals and a day of rest for land and animals as well as humans. Many of the Psalms celebrate the beauty and order of nature and its intrinsic value quite apart from its usefulness to us. In subsequent Western history, however, many forces resulted in the increasing alienation of humanity from nature. Medieval thought gave more emphasis to redemption than to creation, and referred more often to salvation in a future life than to stewardship of the created order. With the rise of capitalism, nature was viewed as simply a resource for human use. With the growth of technology, human power over nature increased dramatically, and it was assumed that there are no limits to our ability to manipulate it for our own purposes.

But this separation of humanity from nature is now being questioned by theologians as well as scientists. Some of them speak of evolution as God's way of creating, and they see humanity as part of nature, though a unique part. Others seek more frequent celebration of nature in worship and liturgy. Most of the religious denominations in the United States have made statements elaborating the theological and ethical grounds for care of the earth. But local churches and synagogues are only beginning to take these ideas seriously, and much more needs to be done to implement them in practice.[10]

I suggest that the biblical idea of the Holy Spirit is particularly helpful in bringing together concerns for the environment and for social justice. It also allows us to integrate the doctrines of creation and redemption, which have often been separated in Christian history. In the opening verses of Genesis, "the Spirit of God was moving over the face of the waters." Several of the psalms speak of the presence of the Spirit in nature. In Psalm 104 the Spirit is the agent of continuing creation in the present: "Thou dost cause the grass to grow for cattle and the plants for man to cultivate. . . . When thou sendest forth thy Spirit, they are created." The Spirit also represents God's activity in the inspiration of the prophets and their message of social justice.

Jesus opened his public ministry in Nazareth by quoting from Isaiah: "The Spirit of the Lord is upon me because he has anointed me to preach good news to the poor . . . and to set at liberty those who are oppressed" (Luke 4:18). And of course the activity of the Spirit marked the birth of the church at Pentecost. Within the Bible, then, reference to the Spirit ties together God's work as Creator and as Redeemer. Only later was the Spirit institutionalized in the sacraments and teaching of the Catholic Church, or restricted to individual experience in pentecostal and charismatic groups which have neglected the biblical association of the Spirit with nature and with social justice.[11]

Concern about Population Growth

Population growth is outpacing growth in agricultural production and is putting increasing pressure on erodible soils, grazing lands, water, and fuelwood supplies. The average number of children per couple has been slowly falling in most of the third world, but the total population is growing faster than ever because of the large number of young people entering childbearing years. No problem is more urgent, but none is more complex, because human reproduction is related to so many variables, including cultural and religious beliefs, family patterns, health services, and economic and educational policies.[12]

Scientists were in the forefront in alerting us to the seriousness of population growth. Ecologists had studied the effects of animal populations on environments of limited carrying capacity, and their work was extended into human ecology. Experts in agronomy and forestry in the third world observed the ways population pressures led to harmful practices. Social scientists observed the consequences of population growth in urbanization and the perpetuation of poverty. They also studied the relation of fertility rates to education, the role of women, and the provision of health services, as well as specific programs for family planning.

At the UN conference in Cairo in 1994, women were for the first time strongly represented in both governmental and nongovernmental delegations. The Program of Action adopted by the conference gave major emphasis to the empowerment of women through access to education, health care, and political and economic equality. The document recognized that birth rates fall when women have more control over their lives. It also called for access to "safe, effective, affordable and acceptable methods of family planning of their choice." Moreover, it pointed to the importance of economic development both as a goal in itself and as a way of encouraging population stability. But the funds pledged to further these goals were quite incommensurate with the magnitude and urgency of the program recommended.[13]

Many church groups were active participants among the nongovernmental organizations at the meetings preparing for Cairo, though the Vatican alone had official standing because of its status as a state. At Cairo the Vatican and some conservative Muslim nations stood virtually alone in totally opposing contraception as well as abortion. On this issue the Vatican does not have the support of most Roman Catholics; nine out of ten Catholics in both the United States and Mexico reject the church's teaching, and they practice contraception in almost exactly the same proportion as non-Catholics. Conservative Protestants do not object to contraception, but they have been afraid that the UN would promote abortion as a means of controlling family size, and on those grounds they persuaded the Reagan and Bush administrations to withdraw U.S. support for UN population programs. U.S. funding was restored under the Clinton administration but drastically cut in the 1996 budget agreements, in part out of deference to the religious right.

Mainline Protestant groups have tried to separate the questions of contraception and abortion. They have also insisted that family planning must be included in the wider context of socioeconomic development in the third world and disproportionate consumption and pollution by industrial nations. Most Protestant leaders hold that human sexuality serves not only the goal of procreation but also that of expressing love and unity in marriage, so contraception is an acceptable means of responsible family planning.[14] There is little recognition, however, that in addition to the welfare of individual families, global justice and the integrity of creation are at stake in personal and social decisions about family planning. This is an issue that urgently needs the best joint efforts of the scientific and religious communities.

Contributions from Religion

Let us turn finally to some distinctive contributions of the religious community in relation to applied science and technology, under four headings: 1) commitment to social justice, 2) a realistic view of human nature, 3) an attitude of humility, and 4) an alternative vision of the good life that is less consumptive than current patterns in industrial nations.

Commitment to Social Justice

Consumption by industrial nations is responsible for a highly disproportionate share of global resource use, greenhouse gases, and other pollutants. Our dogs and cats are better fed than most of the children in Africa. Many developing nations use their best land to produce export crops in order to pay the interest on their national debts. Poor farmers are forced onto marginal or hillside land that is vulnerable to erosion. Brazil cuts tropical forests mainly for timber export and for agriculture, but also to grow feed for cattle for beef sent to American fast-food chains. But the soil is low in nutrients and will support agriculture for only four or five years, so half the Brazilian land cleared for agriculture has already been abandoned. In many third world countries the pattern of export crops is a legacy of colonial imperialism in which the colonies supplied the raw materials for the industrialization of the colonial powers and provided markets for their manufactured goods. The current international economic order tends to perpetuate the third world's role as a supplier of raw materials and cheap labor.

Within our own nation the effects of environmental damage fall very unevenly on different groups. The urban poor are exposed to higher levels of air pollution, water pollution, noise, and lead poisoning than citizens with higher incomes, and they have little economic or political power to defend themselves from such risks. Environmental injustice is a product not only of economic differences but also of social and racial inequalities. For example, African American children from middle-income families are three times as likely to have lead poisoning as children from white families of identical income. Companies looking for a site for a new waste facility are likely to choose an already polluted area in which they expect to encounter little opposition. There is evidence of discrimination in government decisions as to which toxic waste sites will be cleaned up first, which has led to legislation seeking to enforce equal environmental protection. Another example of unequal risks is the high exposure to pesticides among migrant farm workers, who are predominantly Hispanic.[15]

Many scientists do indeed have a deep personal commitment to social justice. Some scientists, for example, have been active in working for the health and safety of workers and citizens and for greater equity in resource consumption. But I suggest that their commitment to justice did not arise directly from their scientific work, nor can it be supported by scientific evidence. To be sure, in the practice of science itself certain ethical principles are promoted, such as honesty, co-operation, universality, freedom of thought, open communication, and acknowledgment of indebtedness to the work of others. But the actual motives of scientists, like those of all human beings, are mixed. Secrecy, rivalry in seeking recognition, and support of nationalistic or militaristic goals are not uncommon. Moreover, ideals applicable within science do not provide an adequate basis for social ethics in general. I would argue that a scientist's dedication to social justice is a reflection of his or her philosophy of life, whether secular or religious. It is also the product of cultural ideals and of a person's life experiences, exposure to role models, and personal decisions about priorities.

Members of religious communities are equally subject to mixed motives, cultural influences, and life experiences. But in regard to social justice they do have the support of the Western religious traditions. Ever since the prophets of ancient Israel, the call for justice has been based on the idea of the fundamental equality of all persons in the sight of God. The God of the Bible is portrayed as being on the side of the poor and oppressed. Religious leaders had a major role in the abolition of slavery, the establishment of hospitals, women's suffrage, and, more recently, the civil rights movement and protest against the Vietnam War. Today, environmentalists often neglect social justice, and social activists often neglect the environment, but the religious community can bring these values together.[16] The National Council of Churches has had a Task Force on Eco-justice. The Catholic Bishops' environmental statement cited earlier advocates both solidarity with the poor and respect for nature, and it explores the links between them.

A Realistic View of Human Nature

Technology is both a product and an instrument of social power. It tends to reinforce existing social structures. In the third world, the Green Revolution favored large landowners who could afford tractors and fertilizer, and this led to the further concentration of landownership. In Western nations, absentee or corporate farm ownership is common, and food processing companies sometimes control the whole food cycle (from farm inputs and crop or feedlot contracts, to food processing, marketing, and restaurant chains). Economic power translates into political power through election campaign contributions. Strong lobbies have promoted policies and subsidies favorable to oil and coal, while solar energy and conservation measures have received little support. The same institutions often result in harm to the environment and human beings. For example, the monopolies held by coal companies, and their influence on the legislatures of Appalachian states, encouraged both the destruction of valleys and rivers and the high incidence of lung disease among coal miners.[17]

Technology is a source of power, and power tends to corrupt those who hold it. Abuse of people and abuse of the earth are in large part products of the self-interest of nations, corporations, government bureaucracies, and other organizations. For this reason, religious ethics looks at economic and political institutions as well as individual behavior. Large-scale capital-intensive technologies often result in a concentration of economic and political power that is difficult to control through democratic processes. When human errors occur in large-scale technologies, or when organizations cut corners on safety measures, the consequences can be tragic, as we saw in the Chernobyl accident, the Bhopal disaster, the Challenger explosion, and the Exxon oil spill.

The biblical tradition is realistic about the abuse of power. The concept of sin refers to the actions of groups as well as the attitudes of individuals. Every group or nation tends to rationalize its own self-interest. In policy decisions, technical experts often use a narrow range of criteria and have a vested interest in a particular technology, so we need input from a wide range of people who might be affected by a decision. But the biblical tradition is also idealistic in its affirmation of creative human potentialities. Through technology, we can use our God-given intellectual capacities to promote human and ecological welfare within a more just social order. The biblical view of human nature would lead us not to reject technology but to seek to redirect it toward the basic needs of all people and the flourishing of other creatures.

An Attitude of Humility

The legends of Prometheus, Faust, and Frankenstein all point to the dangers in the search for unlimited power. The attitude of manipulation and control that is associated with technology is harmful when it affects human and nonhuman life. It is tempting to seek "technical fixes" for social and environmental problems to avoid making basic changes in social institutions. Unqualified reliance on technology as the source of salvation is the modern form of idolatry. Technical rationality and obsession with things can impoverish our experience and our human relationships. I submit that awareness of the sacred and recognition of human limits can provide antidotes to the arrogant search for technological omnipotence. Receptivity and acknowledgment of grace are correctives to the dangers in control and manipulation, but they run against the dominant outlook of a technological society.

Religious faith has no quarrel with technology when it serves human needs and its benefits are equitably distributed. Agricultural and medical technologies, for example, are a valid response to the biblical injunction to feed the hungry and care for the neighbor. However, our society has been confident that all problems can be solved by technological ingenuity, and that there are no limits to our power over nature. But in the last two decades we have seen that a technical solution to one problem often creates unexpected new problems—like the ozone-depleting effects of CFCs, which no one had anticipated. And religious faith insists that technological improvements are not a substitute for a more humane social order and a more just world.[18]

Humility requires recognition of limitations in human character and social institutions as well as ecological limits. It would lead us to respect the evolutionary wisdom and the divine activity embodied in the order of nature, and to be sensitive to the far-reaching and often unpredictable repercussions of our interventions. This does not mean that genetic engineering, for example, should be ruled out. Genetic defects cause great suffering in human life and we should correct them when we can, with provisions to ensure justice in access to such therapy. But we should be particularly cautious about irreversible changes, such as germ-line alterations in human genes, because we do not know enough to predict all the consequences. We should also be more cautious in seeking positive improvements in human nature than in trying to remove impediments to normal functioning, because our ideals for human improvement are so strongly influenced by the ideologies of our culture.[19]

A Less Consumptive Vision of the Good Life

As a start, stronger conservation policies in industrial nations would be a significant step toward a more just and sustainable world. Greater efficiency, waste recovery, and cleaner technologies can cut down on both pollution and resource use. But I believe we must go beyond efficiency and look at our basic patterns of consumption. In our society there are powerful pressures toward the escalation of consumption. By the age of twenty, the average American has already seen 350,000 television commercials. The mass media hold before us the images of a high-consumption life-style. Self-worth and happiness are identified with consumer products. Our culture encourages us to try to fill all our psychological needs through consumption. Consumerism is addictive, and like all addictions it involves the denial of its consequences.[20]

Now, I do not think science itself offers us goals for our lives, though it offers the means to achieve some of our goals. But the biblical tradition does offer a vision of the good life, and it is one that is less resource consumptive than prevailing practices. It holds that, after basic needs are met, true fulfillment is found in spiritual growth, personal relationships, and community life. This path is life-affirming, not life-denying. Religious faith speaks to the crisis of meaning that underlies compulsive consumerism. We should seek a level of sufficiency that is neither ever-growing consumption nor joyless asceticism. A vision of positive possibilities and an alternative image of the good life are likely to be more effective than moral exhortation in helping people to turn in new directions. For most people in our nation, restraint in consumption is indeed compatible with personal fulfillment. We can try to recover the Puritan virtues of frugality and simplicity, both in individual life-styles and in national policies. For the third world, of course, and for low-income families in industrial nations, levels of consumption must rise substantially if basic needs are to be met.[21]

To sum up: I have asked why members of the scientific and religious communities should cooperate on issues of population, consumption, and the environment. In the most general terms, they should cooperate because they are human beings concerned about the future of planet Earth. Each of us is a whole person and we cannot divide our lives into watertight compartments. But we also bring distinctive contributions from the communities to which we belong. Scientists bring specific information about environmental impacts and a new understanding of the relation of humanity to nonhuman nature. Members of both communities share a long-term global view, respect for all forms of life, and concern about population stabilization. The Christian community brings a history of commitment to social justice, a realistic view of human nature, an attitude of humility, and a vision of the good life that is less resource consumptive than current patterns in industrial societies. Hopefully, we can learn from each other and move together toward the action that is so urgently needed.

Notes

1. An earlier version of this paper was given on 10 November 1995 at a conference sponsored by the American Association for the Advancement of Science and the Boston Theological Institute. It will appear in *Consumption, Population, and Sustainability: Perspectives from Science and Religion,* edited by Audrey Chapman and Rodney Petersen (Covelo, Calif.: Island Press, in press).

2. *Tropical Deforestation and Species Extinction,* ed. J. Sayer and Timothy Whitmore (London: Chapman and Hall, 1993); *Biodiversity II: Understanding and Protecting our Biological Resources,* ed. M. L. Reaka-Kudla, D. E. Wilson, and E. O.Wilson (Washington, D.C.: Joseph Henry Press, 1997).

3. Lester Brown et al., *State of the World 1998* (New York: W. W. Norton, 1998); World Resources Institute, *World Resources, 1998–99* (New York and Oxford: Oxford University Press, 1998); *Global Ecology: A New Arena of Political Conflict,* ed. Wolfgang Sachs (London: Zed Books, 1993).

4. *Second Assessment Report of the Intergovermental Panel on Climate Change* (Geneva: IPCC, 1995); World Council of Churches Study Project, *Climate Change and the Quest for Sustainable Societies* (Geneva: WCC, 1998).

5. Ian G. Barbour, *Technology, Environment, and Human Values* (New York: Praeger, 1980), chaps. 8 and 9; also *Ethics in an Age of Technology* (San Francisco: HarperSanFrancisco, 1993), chaps. 2 and 3.

6. On the relation of scientific to religious views of human nature, see Ian G. Barbour, *Religion and Science: Historical and Contemporary Issues* (San Francisco: HarperSanFrancisco, 1997), chap. 10; Philip Hefner, *The Human Factor: Evolution, Culture, and Religion* (Minneapolis: Fortress Press, 1993); Arthur Peacocke, *Theology for a Scientific Age: Being and Becoming—Natural and Divine,* enlarged ed. (Minneapolis: Fortress Press, 1993), chap. 12; Malcolm Jeeves, *Human Nature at the Millennium: Reflections on the Integration of Psychology and Christianity* (Grand Rapids, Mich.: Baker Books, 1997).

7. World Commission on Environment and Development, *Our Common Future* (Oxford: Oxford University Press, 1987); *The Global Partnership for Environment and Development: A Guide to Agenda 21* (New York: United Nations Publications, 1992).

8. United States Catholic Conference, "Renewing the Earth," *Origins* 21 (1991): 425–32; Presbyterian Eco-Justice Task Force, *Keeping and Healing the Creation* (Louisville: Presbyterian Church USA, 1989); Environmental Task Force, Evangelical Lutheran Church in America, "Caring for Creation" (Minneapolis: ELCA, 1991). On the World Council of Churches, see Welsey Granberg-Michaelson, *Redeeming the Creation: The Rio Earth Summit: Challenges for the Churches* (Geneva: WCC Publications, 1992).

9. Norman Myers, *Ultimate Security: The Environmental Basis of Political Stability* (New York: W. W. Norton, 1993).

10. James Nash, *Loving Nature: Ecological Integrity and Christian Responsibility* (Nashville: Abingdon Press, 1991); Max Oelschlaeger, *Caring for Creation: An Ecumenical Approach to the Environmental Crisis* (New Haven: Yale University Press, 1994); Larry L. Rasmussen, *Earth Community, Earth Ethics* (Maryknoll, N.Y.: Orbis Books, 1996).

11. G. W. H. Lampe, *God as Spirit* (Oxford: Clarendon Press, 1977); Alasdair Heron, *The Holy Spirit* (Philadelphia: Westminster Press, 1987); Mark I. Wallace, *Fragments of the Spirit: Nature, Violence, and the Renewal of Creation* (New York: Continuum, 1996).

12. *Beyond the Numbers: A Reader on Population, Consumption, and the Environment*, ed. Laurie Mazur (Washington, D.C.: Island Press, 1994); Benedicta Musembi and David E. Anderson, *Religious Communities and Population Concerns* (Washington, D.C.: Population Reference Bureau, 1994).

13. United Nations, *Report of the International Conference on Population and Development: Cairo, 1994* (New York: United Nations, 1995); "Linking Population and Development in Cairo," *Ecojustice Quarterly* 15, no. 1 (winter 1995).

14. Susan Power Bratton, *Six Billion and More: Human Population Regulation and Christian Ethics* (Louisville: Westminster/John Knox Press, 1992); James B. Martin-Schramm, *Population Perils and the Churches' Response* (Geneva: World Council of Churches, 1997).

15. *Confronting Environmental Racism*, ed. Robert Bullard (Boston: South End Press, 1993); *Faces of Environmental Racism: Confronting Issues of Global Justice*, ed. Laura Westra and Peter Wenz (Lanham, Md.: Rowman and Littlefield, 1995).

16. *Ecology, Justice, and Christian Faith: A Critical Guide to the Literature*, ed. Peter W. Bakken, Joan Gibb Engel, and J. Ronald Engel (Westport, Conn.: Greenwood Press, 1995).

17. Barbour, *Ethics in an Age of Technology*, chaps. 4 and 5.

18. Robert L. Stivers, *Hunger, Technology, and Limits to Growth: Christian Responsibility for Three Ethical Issues* (Minneapolis: Augsburg Publishing House, 1984); Herman Daly and John Cobb, Jr., *For the Common Good: Redirecting the Economy toward Community, the Environment, and a Sustainable Future* (Boston: Beacon Press, 1989).

19. Ronald Cole-Turner, *The New Genesis: Theology and the Genetic Revolution* (Louisville: Westminster/John Knox Press, 1993); Ted Peters, *Playing God: Genetic Determinism and Human Freedom* (New York and London: Routledge, 1997).

20. Alan During, *How Much Is Enough? The Consumer Society and the Future of the Earth* (New York: W. W. Norton, 1992); Paul Wachtel, *The Poverty of Affluence: A Psychological Portrait of the American Way of Life* (Philadelphia: New Society Publishers, 1989); Lester Milbraith, *Envisioning a Sustainable Society* (Albany: State University of New York Press, 1989).

21. James Nash, "Toward the Revival and Reform of the Subversive Virtue: Frugality," *Annual of the Society of Christian Ethics*, 1995: 137–60; James Martin-Schramm, "Population-Consumption Issues: The Debate in Christian Ethics," in *Theology for Earth Community: A Field Guide*, ed. Dieter T. Hessel (Maryknoll, N.Y.: Orbis Books, 1996); Wesley Granberg-Michaelson, "An Ethics of Sustainability," *Ecumenical Review* 42 (January 1991): 120–30.

Population, Consumption, Ecology: The Triple Problematic

DANIEL C. MAGUIRE

While speaking recently to a group of Ford Foundation program officers in Greece, I made reference to "the common good." They asked that, after the break, I return to "the common good" and tell them precisely what it is. For my break I took a walk down a dirt path toward the lovely Aegean Sea. Ahead of me was what looked from a little distance to be a black ribbon stretched across the path. As I got closer I saw that it was not a ribbon, but two columns of ants moving back and forth in single file. Those in one row were all carrying something; the others were going back for a new load. A real estate change was in process. Every ant was committed to the project. There were no shirkers or apostates from the effort. There were no special interest groups. All these insect citizens were bonded to the common good of that community.

What a pointed illustration nature had given me to take back to the program officers. The needs of the common good are inscribed on the genes of the ants. Human genes have no such inscription. We, like the ants, have need of common good considerations, since the common good is the matrix of minimal livability within which individual good can be pursued.[1] With our species, this need for which our genes do not provide is met by ethics and by cultural motivators like religion. Our genes, in fact, seem more disposed to egoistic good in opposition to the common good. Since the common good includes the good of the whole of nature and not just human good, this fatal flaw in our composition portends our planetary undoing. Ethics and religion are, apparently, no match for the efficacy of genetic inscription. The current state of the planet suggests what a dangerous mix humanity is, with its prodigious talents and its enfeebled ecological and social conscience.

It is hard to focus on our ecocrisis. We shy from its data as we do from looking at the sun. But let us dare for a moment to look at a short primer on the state of our planet.

Water, Soil, and Air

Our species is a threat to all of the foundational elements of life on earth: water, topsoil, and air. Similarly, the fundamentals of our political economy are being dangerously transformed. This is the sun we have to look at for a moment.

This water planet lives on water or it dies. Less than 1 percent of the earth's water is usable by humans, and this treasure is unevenly distributed. Pure water is becoming scarcer than gold. The two dangers to water are threatened supply and pollution. The Middle East illustrates the supply problem. Tony Allan, a water expert at the University of London, says the Middle East "ran out of water" in 1972 when its population stood at 122 million. At that point the region began to draw more water out of its aquifers than the rains could replenish. Today the population has doubled and the politics of water has grown intense. Water wars could be in our near future. Jordan's King Hussein once said that water was the only issue that could lead him to war with Israel.[2] Most of Africa, the Near East, northern Asia, and Australia suffer from chronic water shortages. On the pollution side oysters and mussels, nature's water-purifying kidneys, are becoming dangerously depleted. Meanwhile, farm and chemical wastes borne by land, sea, and air invade our precious sources of usable water.

All life depends on cropland and on that thin but indispensable treasure called topsoil. In just thirty years, China, where one of five humans lives, lost in cropland the equivalent of all the farms in France, Germany, Denmark, and the Netherlands. In fact, 43 percent of the earth's vegetated surface is to some degree degraded, and it takes from three thousand to twelve thousand years to develop sufficient soil to form productive land.[3] Our corruption reaches even to the skies. As Peter Barnes puts it: "At the rate we are burning fossil fuels—and moving carbon from beneath the ground to the atmosphere—we'll double-glaze the planet by early next century, with unknowable consequences."[4]

Not surprisingly, people, in solidarity with an agonized earth, are dying too. When it comes to impoverishment, the rule seems to be "women and children first!" Four million babies die yearly from diarrhea in the euphemistically entitled "developing world." Noeleen Heyzer of the United Nations says: "Poverty has a female face." Women constitute 70 percent of the world's 1.3 billion absolute poor, own less than 1 percent of the world's property but work two-thirds of the world's working hours.[5] Microbes and viruses that found a life for themselves in the forests are deforesting humans as their new hosts. As Joel Cohen says: "The wild beasts of this century and the next are microbial, not carnivorous."[6] More than thirty new diseases have been identified since 1973, many of them relating to our new and ecologically dangerous life-styles.[7]

The elitist illusion is that we can make nations, or parts of them, into gated communities, veiling from our eyes the decay and the huddled and hungry masses, but we can't. Poisons are as globalized as capital. They come to us in the strawberries and the rain. David Orr gives us some of the scary data: male sperm counts worldwide have fallen by 50 percent since 1938. Human breast milk often contains more toxins than are permissible in milk sold by dairies. At death some human bodies contain enough toxins and heavy metals to be classified as hazardous waste.[8] Jeremiah warned us that it is hard to escape the effects of moral malignancy: "Do you think that you can be exempt? No, you cannot be exempt" (Jer. 25:5, 29).

More People, Less Earth

Meanwhile, there are more, and in many places far too many, of us. It took ten thousand generations to reach the first 2.5 billion; it took one generation to double it. World population is like a triangle, with the reproductive young at the wide base and the old at the narrow top. Until the model comes closer to a rectangle, with a more balanced distribution of young and old, the growth will not stop, nor does anyone expect it to. Because the population of the industrialized nations is expected to decline over the next fifty years and because the world annual rate of increase has slowed in the last two years, we begin to hear a gospel of consolation proclaiming the end of the population problem. This is illusory. As Jennifer Mitchell says:

> Over the next 25 years, some 3 billion people—a number equal to the entire world population in 1960—will enter their reproductive years, but only about 1.8 billion will leave that phase of life. Assuming that the couples in this reproductive bulge begin to have children at a fairly early age, which is the global norm, the global population would still expand by 1.7 billion, even if all of those couples had only two children—the long term replacement rate.[9]

Since most of that increase will occur in the overstressed poor world, the proclamation of the end of the population crisis is strategic myopia. The United Nations projects that world population will reach 9.4 billion by 2050 and nearly 11 billion eventually.[10]

Note that I refer to the "poor world," not to "the third world." It is no longer meaningful, I submit, to divide the world up numerically into first, second, and third. If we insist on the numbers, we would have to admit that there are third world sections, often based very much on color lines, in our first world. Also, the propaganda terms "developed" and "developing" pull a "tissue of lies" over the facts of life, since the masses of the undernourished living in absolute poverty live in the world that is not developing for them, and the "developed nations" are overdeveloped ecological barbarians. Neither term, "developing" or "developed," is descriptive of reality. Development language is not on a mission of truth.

The big lie in development parlance—we affluent folks are developed; the others are on their way to being like us—is that there are enough resources for all peoples to go on gorge mode. As Gro Harlem Brundtland said, "if 7 billion people were to consume as much energy and resources as we do in the West today, we would need 10 worlds, not one, to satisfy all our needs."[11] If China ate fish at the rate the Japanese do, it would take the whole world's supply to feed them. There are limits and we are there.

The true picture of modern aristocratic economics is seen in the following figure.

Population pressures and consumption patterns interact malignantly. For one thing, the overconsumption of the few impoverishes the many. Poverty and lack of education and health care motivate

World
population
arranged
by income

Distribution of income

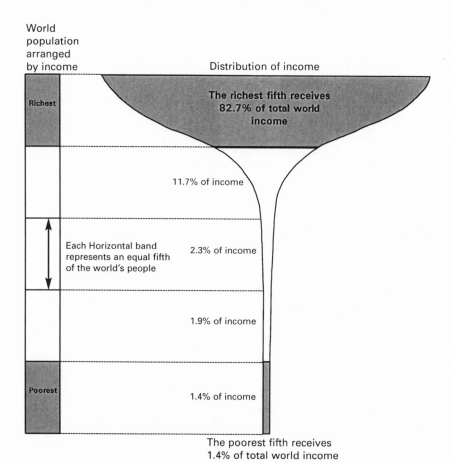

FIGURE 1.
(*Source: UNDP,* Human Development Report 1992
[New York: Oxford University Press, 1992]).

people to reproduce. When many or most of your children die, having more children is an insurance policy. My father, born at the end of the last century in Donegal, was one of thirteen children in his family. His family was poor. Nutrition and medical care were deficient. Only five of those children lived to become adults. His condition mirrored that of the poor world today. Poverty, intensified by today's accelerated movement of wealth to the top, is a force for overpopulation.

The limitation of fertility is essential to honoring the earth's carrying capacity and for eliminating poverty. Since 1950 there has been a fivefold increase in global output. During that time population has doubled, but so too has the number of people living in absolute poverty.[12] Statistical improvements in poverty rates are an abstract consolation when the reality is that there are more poor people. Population and poverty have grown together. This does not allow for a simplistic one-rubric analysis of earth woes—we'd be fine if there were not so many people. Overconsumption by the elite is the prime demon. Still, a finite earth cannot hold infinite numbers. Thomas Aquinas saw and wrote that the number of children should not exceed the resources of the community. He even added that this should be assured by law as needed. Thomas said that if the generation of children exceeds what we call today the "carrying capacity" of the territory, civil chaos would result. That makes it state business since the preservation of public order is essential to governance. Aquinas did not enter into the details of sanctions, incentives, or coercion, but obviously law does not simply make suggestions.[13] The insight into the need for the restriction of procreation is not new; indeed, Thomas was commenting on Aristotle who was making the same point.

The entrance of government into population policy when the common good is at stake is also not new. Depopulation was often the concern. It led to legislation under Emperor Augustus which penalized bachelors and rewarded families for their fertility.[14] Small wonder. Augustus presided over a society with an average life expectancy of less than twenty-five years. It was a society where, as Peter Brown says, "death fell savagely on the young."[15] Only four out of every one hundred men—and fewer women—lived beyond their fiftieth birthday. As a species, we formed our natalist habits in worlds that were, in John Chrysostom's words, "grazed thin by death."[16] Such instincts are deep-rooted. If, as Teilhard de Chardin sagely says, nothing is intelligible outside its history, this reproductive thrust, especially in stressful conditions, is the defining story of our breed. It also affected the religions that were spawned in this kind of world.

Overpopulated and overconsuming rich nations can deflect the crisis and transcend the limits of their plot of earth by importing what they need. The International Monetary Fund (IMF) and the World Bank have aided this by pressuring poor nations to move from self-supporting farming communities to cash crops for export. As a result, the Netherlands, for example, would require fourteen times the amount of land they have to meet their consumption levels. They make up the difference by appropriating by trade the resources of poorer nations. All this is done in the name of "free trade," but, as John Cobb points out, once the conversion to export farming has been put in place and debt burdens are driving these poor economies, they are no longer free to regroup and simply get back to feeding themselves in a largely self-sufficient economy. If they could make that choice, they would be enjoying truly "free" trade.[17]

The opposite of "free" is "slave." Poor nations shackled into export to meet the needs of the affluent are our modern slaves. The "sweat shops" which intermittently make news are only minute examples of a slave economy that grips the poor world. In this aristocratic global economy, therefore, overpopulation and overconsumption are luxury items that are supported by exploitative wealth. The poor nations are the new plantations, or *latifundia,* which unwillingly underwrite this excess. They are largely overpopulated but they cannot afford to deflect their crises by adequate import; there are no plantations they can exploit. Injustice rolls downhill, exploiting those below. The poor nations where population increase is mainly occurring are at the bottom of that hill.

Gated Communities

Green racism is a virus that is infecting legitimate ecological and population concerns in the United States. Charts indicting immigration as the single nemesis lead to calls for its drastic reduction, especially from the South. There is no balancing concern for why these refugees are fleeing their homes and how we and globalizing capitalism contribute to their plight. Illustrative of this is Virginia Abernethy. After rehearsing our ecological disasters, she gives a one-rubric diagnosis: all are "symptoms of one cause: overpopulation."[18] Echoing Garrett Hardin, "large scale international aid" is faulted and seen as contributing to the fertility of the poor.[19] We should close our generous pockets as well as our borders. This is simple patriotism and "patriotism does not have to be justified." There is too much concern about "abuses and want abroad." Our motto should be "God save America."[20] The worry over immigration is color coded. Abernethy speaks of "the ongoing reconquest of the Southwest," the erosion of the Gadsden Purchase, and the emergence of a "bronze continent" reclaiming California "in due course by sheer weight of numbers."[21]

What must be avoided in the Abernethy view is "further downgrading of our standard of living" so we can pass on to our children "the opportunities and freedoms we have long enjoyed."[22] The enemies to this dream of a gated United States are the "globalists," a "generation raised on the idea of a shared planet" for whom the only aliens are the creatures "from outer space." These are the purveyors of a "one-world ideology which implies that resources will be shared." Such delusional thinking results in "the persistently high fertility of the third world."[23]

Seductively, the flag that flies over the Hardin/Abernethy lifeboat is green and is stitched with legitimate threads of concern about lost topsoil and the pollution of water, land, and air. What can be lost amid the self-serving simplisms of this view is the major impact on ecology and the poor of global corporations.

The Corporate *Coup d'Etat et d'Eglise*

It seems a fact of history that power develops before critical social theory can address it. The "divine right of kings" was well ensconced and long tenured before it got critiqued. This, we thought, taught us a lesson, and when the democratic nation states emerged as a new economic-political configuration, we set out to civilize them with laws and constitutions and a balancing of powers. We have been at that daunting task with only some success for more than two centuries, without adverting to the darkness of an ongoing eclipse. Statistics sometimes tell a truth. Of the one hundred largest economies in the world, at least fifty are corporations, not nations.[24] The civilizing of these colossuses is a task scarcely addressed. Investment banker Roger Altman compares this new corporate power to the atom bomb. He calls it "a similarly awesome force, one capable of overthrowing governments and their policies almost overnight. And there are no systems in place for controlling it."[25] But these rampaging juggernauts, often in collusion with nation states, are becoming the main ecological actors. And corporations are not conscientized by democratic structures, laws, or constitutions. They are driven by the need to increase production, which depends on increased consumption.

Euphoria clogged thought as the Second World War moved to a close. In this mood a group of economic planners convened at Bretton Woods. Henry Morgenthau, U.S. Secretary of the Treasury presided at the conference. In his speech he spoke dulcetly of "the creation of a dynamic world economy in which the peoples of every nation will be able to realize their potentialities in peace and enjoy increasingly the fruits of material progress on an earth *infinitely blessed* with natural riches." He asked the participants to embrace the "elementary economic axiom . . . that prosperity has *no fixed limits*. It is not *a finite substance to be diminished by division*" (emphasis added).[26] This almost psychotic lack of any sense of limit—along with a glaringly unmet need for a theology of original sin—set the tone for the creed of postwar global capitalism. From this utopian womb emerged the IMF, the World Bank, the General Agreement on Tariffs and Trade Organization (GATT), and now the Multilateral Agreement on Investments (MAI). Through these powerful initialed agencies and arrangements, the democratic and ecological concerns of nations can be overridden by corporate despotism. Bretton Woods was an aristocratic call to earth-unfriendly gluttony with the self-serving pretense that it would benefit "the peoples of every nation."

But, as David Loy, a Buddhist social critic points out, this corporate subversion of democracy and earth-care has another dimension, a religious dimension, and religion always thickens the plot. Loy, using a functionalist definition of religions, says that religion teaches us what the world is and what our role and status in the world are. The major religions have defaulted in this their traditional task, yielding much of this function to the new religion of market capitalism. "The Market," says Loy, "is becoming the first truly world religion, binding all corners of the globe more and more tightly into a worldview and set of values whose religious role we overlook only because we insist on seeing them as 'secular.'"[27] This new religion, says Loy is "winning more converts more quickly than any previous belief system or value-system in human history."[28]

The major religions look moribund, or at least senile, in comparison. What help can they be in our ecological crisis? Says Loy: "Although it may offend our vanity, it is somewhat ludicrous to think of conventional religious institutions as we know them today serving a significant role in solving the environmental crisis. Their more immediate problem is whether they, like the rain forests we anxiously monitor, will survive in any recognizable form the onslaught of this new religion."[29] Here is the challenge boldly stated. To Loy's challenge I now turn.

Religion: A Definition

Upon the face of the earth there is a delicate, tenuous, precarious film. It weighs as little as one-billionth the weight of the planet. It is, however, not negligible. The name we give to this film is life. When we respond to the goodness of this film, we call it ethics; our response to its holy and mysterious wonder, we call religion. Religion is essentially a response to the sacred. Sacred is the superlative of precious. When we move beyond excellence to ineffable, awe-full good, we reach for the ultimate encomium and speak the language of the religio-sacred. Religions, when formalized and expressed in poetic imagery, get names like Hinduism, Judaism, Buddhism. Some of these religions express themselves in the imagery of theism; others do not. But all are helpful and positive responses to life—culturally rich, poetically pregnant, historically conditioned responses to the sacred.[30]

This definition is not functional, nor is it merely descriptive, i.e., fitting any old thing that calls itself "religion," which is the way the term is despairingly used in much of social science. This is a normative definition describing as genuine religions only those responses to the sacred that are classics of cherishing, that rise from respectful, enhancing reactions to the life mystery in this universe. And, it should be sharply noted, religions are powerful. John Henry Cardinal Newman said people will die for a dogma who will not stir for a conclusion. In parallel insights, Albert Camus noted that people will not die for scientific truth, and the poet Alexander Pope, reaching to the nether side of religion, said that the worst of madmen is a saint gone mad. All three gentlemen are onto the same point. The tincture of the sacred yields power and effaces limit, for good or for ill.

Realistic social analysis should recognize that two-thirds of the world's peoples affiliate with some religion and the other one-third are affected by the gravitational pull generated by these symbol-filled cultural powerhouses. Religions, in a word, must be taken seriously. I look now at two of them.

Judaism and Christianity

Can Judaism and its offspring Christianity meet the Loy challenge? It won't be easy, but Judaism gives us a great start.[31] Early Israel saw itself as nothing less than a workshop for a new humanity. This ragtag group of literarily gifted cultural revolutionaries had tried the status quo and found it wanting, and so dreams exploded among them of "new heavens and a new earth" (Isa. 65:17–25). This was not an otherworldly vision or a dream of postmortem bliss. The Isaian plan was of this earth and earthy. It involved child raising, housebuilding, the planting of vineyards, and the eating of fruit; an earth where "weeping and cries for help shall never again be heard." The Israelites would not have called this social experiment a "religion." They didn't even have a word for it. The closest to it, according to Morton Smith, was what Hellenists would call a philosophy of life.[32] They were rethinking everything from the bottom up. They were not concentrated on personal conversions or therapy, but on structural, political, and economic metamorphosis. Their main critique was of what Pope John Paul II calls "structural evil." Their audience was "kings" and "nations." Their immodest goal was not national, but global. Other nations, as Deuteronomy crows, will see this experiment and their jaws will drop in admiration: "What a wise and understanding people this great nation is!" (Deut. 4:6). Jeremiah claimed "authority over nations and over kingdoms to pull down and to uproot, to destroy and to demolish, to build and to plant"—everything that needs to be done right now to reverse our terracidal thrust (Jer. 1:10). Isaiah was supremely confident that if Israel would be true to its vision (a vision that in today's language would be called radical and left-wing), "the nations shall march toward your light, and their kings to your sunrise" (Isa. 60:3). One dares to wonder how the courts of surrounding nations reacted to the boast that these upstart and maverick Hebrews had a sunrise toward which they and all of history should march. The Israelites' gall was not without foundation. They did become, as Morton Smith says "the seedbed of the subsequent religious history of the Western world."[33] And, as I would argue, they reshaped modern Western political and economic theory and practice.

I submit that with all the messes that attend these history-battered religions, there are renewable moral energies in Judaism and in its Christian and Muslim progeny. There is food here, and we could walk many days and turn important corners on the strength of that food.

Dissecting classics is perilous, but I dare to pluck out just some of the "theopolitcal dynamite" (Pinchas Lapide's term) that lies in the scrolls and history of Israel. These rebels rethought 1) power and authority; 2) status; 3) ownership and property; 4) they linked social and distributive justice to peace; and 5) they fashioned a social psychology of shock therapy and raised it to the level of high art.

This prophetic religion was not facing ecological challenges so much as human concerns with oppressive political and economic power. I submit, however, that their five key ideas just cited are open to creative expansion into the ecological domain, relating to 1) our power and authority over the rest of nature; 2) the status we give to the rest of earth life; 3) how much we dare commodify natural resources; 4) how rights language applies to all of nature; and finally 5) how to shock humankind into a new reverence for other species of life in the earth community.

Power

The concept of power is a supreme challenge to ethics. Power ranges from violent to nonviolent and is moralized as it moves from the former to the latter. Israel's former slaves, escapees from sweat shops, were eloquent witnesses to the abuse of power. They indicted the violence of royalty not just in its pharaonic and priestly forms but as a permanent human temptation. Their condemnation of it, they were beamingly convinced, would serve as "a light to the nations" shining "to earth's farthest bounds" (Isa. 49:6). Royalty was knavery and they would have none of it. The royal temptation is the vile temptation to establish a privileged elite built on oppression and greed. Those not in the elite are grist for the royal mill. The structure of royalty is pyramidal, something the Hebrews knew a bit about. The top is for the rapacious few; the huge base is the exploited foundation. In proof of their convictions, Israel stunned their world by dethroning royalty. For two hundred years they banned kings and settled for judges. Eventually they succumbed and brought the kings back, but then the prophets struck out after the kings and blamed the people of Israel for a vision lost.

Royal power is vicious and contains no respect for those who are there to be used. The kings are "mere brutes" and "stupid," says

Jeremiah (10:21). Ezekiel agrees: "I am against the shepherds (their term for princes)" (24:10). Isaiah joins the tirade. Kings are "blind . . . unaware . . . dumb dogs . . . lovers of sleep," "greedy dogs that can never have enough and who understand nothing" (56:10, 11). Zephaniah sees them as "roaring lions" and "wolves of the plain" (1:8). And Jesus saw royalty as "snakes . . . vipers" who spill "innocent blood" (Matt. 23). Our pundits are Milquetoast in comparison to these social critics.

The disgust for royalty has a broad and perennial target. It has, as classic insights do, an eternal contemporaneity. Those are royal today who live in the top of the champagne glass (figure above), who wear clothes woven in sweat shops, who consume profligately while the hungry die, who bear titles such as CEO and require tens of millions of dollars a year for the "incentive" to do their job. Powerful over-consuming nations, and many of their people, are royal. Chicago, a city of 2.9 million people, consumes more than the 97 million peoples of Bangladesh. The castles of royalty were always big on consumption and short on distribution. The corporations are royal, as are the nations who consort with them to ravage the earth. Today's royals export pollution, using poor lands as their garbage disposal units. Today's technology is modernity's gift to exploiters. It allows them to savage the earth as well as people in ways that were never imaginable. The nonhuman life-forms of the earth are the new members of the *anawim*. The production of high-grade copper cathodes, for example, is a dirty business, so Japan, Inc., exports the operation to the places made vulnerable by poverty, like the Philippines. There they acquire four hundred acres appropriated from the poor, and the emissions from the plant spew out high levels of boron, arsenic, heavy metals, and sulfur, contaminating local water, reducing fishing and rice yields, killing forests, and sickening the people.[34] The ongoing globalization requires victimization as it enriches the few at the expense of the weak and of the victim earth.

Religions who would be the moral heirs of the prophets should target these greedy dogs, wolves, snakes, and vipers. Preaching and religious education should be building prophetic lobbies fueled by scriptural study and burning indignation at the ongoing rape. Jews, Christians, and Muslims, the alleged descendants of the prophets, are pathetic. The royal wreckers of the earth have little to fear from them. Distracted by lesser issues and internal disputes, these self-described "people of faith" are not the massive moral lobby they could be. Prophetic critique will not come from the news media. They are corporate courtesans, bought into silence. Have the "people of faith" also been bought, bought by their privileges? The poor of the earth and the earth itself have a right to know.

Status

The Hebrew revolution redefined status. The survival needs of evolution taught us to identify with the powerful to be saved. Israel turned this wisdom on its head, saying that identification with the poor is essential for survival and for peace.[35] God-talk is the window to one's philosophy of life. For the surprising Israelites God became a "God of the humble . . . the poor . . . the weak . . . the desperate . . . and the hopeless" (Judg. 9:11). That's not the way Tacitus saw it. The Gods, he was sure, are with the mighty. "Godliness is in league with riches," intoned Bishop Lawrence of Massachusetts.[36] Not at all, says that great Jewish mother, Mary. "The rich are sent away empty" and the "arrogant of heart" and the "monarchs" are routed by her son's God (Luke 1:46–55).

Jewish idealism was never unpractical. The payload of identifying with the poor is peace. Even the selfish should want to do it. "The poverty of the poor is their ruin," says Proverbs 10:15. Now we can go beyond Proverbs and say that the poverty of the poor is our ruin too, as the poisons of poverty cross borders and gates. Because of the rampage of the royal gluttons, the air, the water, the soil, the flora and the fauna have joined the ranks of the "humble . . . the poor . . . the weak . . . the desperate . . . and the hopeless" (Judg. 9:11). Scriptural spirituality would have us bond with them out of reverent collegiality and joyful awe—or at least out of fear of our undoing.

Owning

Ownership is the root concept of all economic theory, and Judaism and the Jesus movement targeted it as a basal source of moral rot. They did indeed believe in absolute property rights, but only the Lord had such. As Luke Johnson says: "The Israelites could no more lay ultimate claim to the land than they could to their own life breath; it came as a constantly renewed gift."[37] "The land is mine," said the Torah God (Lev. 25:23). "The earth is the Lord's" and all the beauty that grows from it (Ps. 24:1–2). The right to cherish it is absolute; the right to own it is relative. We humans are after all made of the same stuff as the rest of the earth, from surface to torrid core. To add cosmic sense to the Catholic Ash Wednesday mantra: "Stardust thou are and unto stardust thou shalt return." The earth and its life-community—including us, the birds, bees, earthworms, and humus—are reconfigured stardust and to stardust we shall return when our solar star completes its mission and ends this lovely story. We, being many, are ontologically "one body" (1 Cor. 12:12) more truly than Paul knew.

Ṣĕdaqâ

Israel, the land that has never known peace, first dreamed of it as a practical possibility. There was a one-word formula to bring it about: *ṣĕdaqâ*. Israel shared with Buddhism the insight that existence is a shared glory, and *ṣĕdaqâ* says that. Mercy for the powerless and the exploited ensouls *ṣĕdaqâ*. The word should never be translated as "righteousness," a word with pompous cousins. It may be translated as justice, especially social and distributive justice, but take care, for our word justice is feeble beside it. The other-respecting, mercifully sharing social force of *ṣĕdaqâ* is a solvent of alienating differences and the only route to peace. The effect of *ṣĕdaqâ* "will be peace" (Isa. 32:17). Weaponry will not bring peace. Indeed, the song of the military will be silenced (Isa. 25:2, 5). We cannot really be saved "by force of arms or brute strength" (Zech. 4:6), and nations that count on military strength for security "will be ashamed of all their might" (Mic. 7:16). *Ṣĕdaqâ* is an alternative theory of national security. *Ṣĕdaqâ* is also tough-minded and biased. It is partial to the poor and virulently suspicious of the rich, based on the conviction that security and wealth chill the heart. *Ṣĕdaqâ* theology is a rich and neglected broth. It is also an invitation to clarify the cardinal category of social ethics, the common good.[38]

Where are the collective well-organized voices of the people of *ṣĕdaqâ* faith, when the U.S. government spends almost 300 billion dollars a year on the military, while all of the prospective enemies of the United States spend only 17 billion?[39] According to David Korten, most countries could eliminate the worst effects of poverty simply by "reallocating the resources now devoted to military purposes."[40] What would the prophets think of their pusillanimous children in Judaism, Christianity, and Islam who offer no effective protest against this unholy waste?

No prophetic protest can come against U.S. military spending from Congress since the Pentagon spread out its weapons production over most of the jurisdictions of the land. Jobs are thus at stake everywhere, and a compromised Congress is subdued into paralytic compliance. People of faith, where are you, as 30 million dollars an hour, nine thousand dollars a second go to feed this sacred military cow, while school teachers work in old buildings for a pittance and 40 million people lack health insurance? On top of this, the military are master polluters, basking in the immunity that comes from the propagandistic word "defense." Where there is no prophecy, people and the earth perish.

Shock Therapy

The important concept of conversion has fallen victim to individualism. Conversion of socially entrenched valuations is an area needing attention if this earth is not to die, and our religions are not yet even amateurs at it. Old Israel drew the broad lines for a social psychology of conversion. The foundation is prophecy. The effort to supplant the dominant consciousness with an alternative social consciousness seeks a revolution in affect. The target is "the heart" (Isa. 51:7; Jer. 4:4; 4:14; 31:35; Amos 6:6). Israel knew that moral knowledge is born in the affections. The foundational moral experience is to know the value of persons and of this precious earth.[41] Valuational patterns anchored by interests, real or imagined, will not be changed by information or reasons unless these move the heart. Technical intelligence has so impressed us Westerners that our epistemology is distorted. We think of *knowing* in fleshless terms and wonder if computers can do it. The ancients were not so shallow.

For major cultural change—culture being what people love and hate collectively—there must be seismic affective shifts. For suggestive starters we can follow the prophets through four doorways into the heart: *delight, anger, tears,* and *mind-blowing shock.*

Delight is a form of pleasure shock. Aquinas mistakenly traced it to *dilatatio* in Latin, which means stretching or broadening.[42] It was a happy mistake. Delight stretches us so we can receive a new and congruent good. When delight stretches us to new awareness, the stretching is sometimes so great it produces tears. Orgasm and pain produce the same grimace. There are practical conclusions to this. Without the stretching caused by delight there is no learning. Theology, preaching, or liturgy that does not delight leaves us as it found us, or worse. No delight, no growth was Thomas's point. The literary power that pulses from Micah to the Psalms to the Sermon on the Mount gives us lessons on delight-filled, passionate teaching. *Cor ad cor loquitur;* only the heart speaks to the heart. All true learning is a passionate *eureka!* Neurophysicists tell us that emotion is the key to lasting memory. It is also the key to moral growth. Boring, pedantic theology, dry sermons, rote religious education *anathema sitis!*

Anger bristles through the prophets, and why not? The biblically astute Thomas said that anger looks to the good of justice, so that those who do not have it in the face of injustice love justice too little.[43] Thomas loved John Chrysostom's dictum: "Whoever is not angry when there is cause for anger, sins!" Therapeutic culture sees anger as a malady to be cured. Prophecy sees it as the awakening of the soul and the passionate key to conversion.[44]

Tears. We have everything to fear from the tearless. The old Catholic liturgy had a prayer begging the gift of tears. This prayer used to befuddle me as a young victim of our jejune Anglo-Saxon culture. The prayer begged divine power to break through the *duritiem,* the impenetrable hardness of our hearts, and bring forth a saving flood of tears. Unless "our eyes run with tears and our eyelids be wet with weeping," we will come to a "fearful ruin" (Jer. 9:18–19).

Finally, *shock.* Shock specialists are what the prophets were. Simple, sensible approaches won't do it and so the prophets turned bizarre and eccentric. Isaiah wandered around "naked and barefoot" for three years (20:2–4). Micah was also drawn to the streaker tactic: "Therefore I must howl and wail and go naked . . ." (1:8). The nudity caught on. When Saul stripped himself naked, the people asked: "Is Saul also among the prophets?" (1 Sam. 19:24). Jeremiah harnessed himself to a yoke and was seen, understandably enough, as a "madman" (27:2–3; 29:26). Ezekiel cut off his hair with a sword and scattered it to the winds (5:1–2). Jesus was so intemperate he was seen as "a prophet like one of the old prophets" (Mark 6:15). He was a scandal because, as Walter Brueggeman says, he violated "propriety, reason, and good public order."[45] And so did they all.

To what end? And how could it apply to our as yet unborn psychology of societal conversion? The prophets intuited that only outrage speaks to outrage. Outrageous insensitivity is thick-shelled. Only shock gets through. The Berrigans spoke and no one listened; they burned government records and were heard. Martin Luther King, Jr., preached and enjoyed anonymity; he led a boycott and was killed by the overwhelming impact. Notice that it is not either/or, but both/and. The Berrigans continued to speak, and King continued to preach with even more effect until he met a prophet's death. Prophecy is essentially eccentric, coming from the Greek, outside the center. The center is where the addicts of comfort and safety dwell. Prophecy leaves them and pushes to the edges where new horizons can be seen. Resistence to the dominant consciousness anchored in ill-gotten privilege is the essence of prophetic eccentricity.

These four hints on how to move the tectonic plates of our cognitive affectivity present huge challenges to our inbred stoicist epistemology. They threaten our confidence in logic and technique. They call attention to our almost total neglect of the constitutive role of affect in all moral and religious understanding and hence in all religious and moral education.[46] They reveal our poverty in the realm of ritual and liturgy. We are queasy when we hear that Hindu ecologists use dance, song, art, and drama more than lectures to raise ecological literacy.[47]

In my *A New American Justice,* I explored social conversion in a racist and sexist society. First, on the principle that societies need to see gain to accept pain, to see that doing good will be doing well, the "justice for profit" theme must be explored with the sagacity of serpents and the honesty of doves. Also fear, guilt, and a summons to appear before the court of candor and face our avowed ideals can move the mountain of societal conscience.[48] With all the justice theory and motivational resources that religious groups have in their scrolls and stories, they do not seize opportunities to mainstream their strengths in the social order. Entering debates on justice and environmental issues through the powerful medium of *amicus curiae* briefs infuses one's strengths into the political and journalistic processes. Ideas thus entered become, as it were, legal tender in public discourse. This is but one of the neglected opportunities in the Acropolis.

Confession of Debits

None of the religions of the world is perfect. All of them were heavily patriarchal. As Buddhist Rita Gross asks indictingly: "Can a religion founded by a man who abandoned his wife and newborn infant" to go seek enlightenment "possibly serve women's interests and needs?"[49] Similar laments could be registered for all the world's religions.

Judaism and Christianity are especially guilty of anthropocentric hubris, as Lynn White famously reminded us. They also suffer from amnesia, forgetting some of their past good sense. An example: the Catholic bishops must have cut class when it was taught, but their tradition is pro-choice on abortion. The first systematic ethics on abortion was done by St. Antoninus, Archbishop of Florence and a Dominican. He approved of early abortions to save the life of the woman, a huge allowance given the medicine and hygiene of that day which made most pregnancies dangerous. Everyone accepted this limited pro-choice position, and Antoninus was canonized a saint, not stripped of his post like a Charles Curran. Thomas Sanchez, S.J., who died in the early seventeenth century, could find no Catholic theologian in his day who did not approve of and teach St. Antoninus's view. Thomas Aquinas, and almost everyone in the tradition right into this century, held that early fetuses (before three months) were not humanly ensouled and were not candidates for baptism. Augustine said they would not be there at the resurrection of the dead. Neither, he added, would all the sperm of history rise in that final triumph, for which we can all be grateful.[50] The claim to a "clear and constant" church teaching on the wrongness of all abortions is either disingenuous, uninformed, or mendacious. Catholics, bishops and pope included, would do well to learn their own history and to begin all their deliberations on this subject with a prayer to St. Antoninus.

The bonding of all the world religions to counter our terracidal thrust is an imperative.[51] An obstacle to that is the symbol systems developed over the centuries by these religions to image and poetize their experience of the sacred. How theistic and nontheistic religions will relate as they face our common planetary plight is a delicate subject usually politely ignored. Chun Fang Yu writes that in the Chinese religions "there is no God transcendent and separate from the world and there is no heaven outside of the universe to which human beings would want to go for refuge."[52] That raises two issues—what we believe about God and afterlife—on which the three Abrahamic religions are not open to much dialogue. If an angel from heaven came around questioning these ideas, she or he would be sent packing. And yet, the theistic and afterlife hypotheses are serious and influential and they do not bask in self-evidence. There is an understandable reluctance to raise issues that would offend the pews. Those pews, however, have been emptying and it is worth questioning whether a mutating sense of the sacred accounts for some of the exodus.

If we have afterlife insurance and the rest of nature does not, that tilts toward an ecologically unfriendly *fuga mundi* (flight from the world) spirituality. The scientific "creation" story on the origin of the earth and its place in the universe, has led to what Rosemary Ruether calls "the breakdown of the Christian Creation Story."[53] This story, as the First Vatican Council saw it at the end of the last century, led to a becalming confidence that God was "protecting and governing" all things with "sweetness and with strength."[54] Such a statement of belief underplays our earth-wrecking potential and resonates poorly with scientific accounts of the formation and demise of stars and galaxies. Astral science indicates that it is not order but chaos that has the last word in the universe. All of this has led to theistic slippage in modern sense-making that Abrahamic religious theorists have visited with too little scrutiny.[55]

The question of how much of God-talk is anthropocentrism writ divine is worth critical reflective attention. Some cognitive assumptions are like waves; some, like tides; and some are like currents (such as the Gulf Stream) that carry both waves and tides. The currents of theistic assumptions that move the Abrahamic religious traditions carry waves and tides of related presuppositions that in turn shape both helpful and unhelpful attitudes on the issues of population, consumption, ecology. Given this triple problematic, and the insights of current cosmology, the contours of our beliefs about God and afterlife need to be reexamined.[56]

Conclusion

A recent study, *Religion: The Missing Dimension of Statecraft,*[57] presents case studies of how U.S. foreign policy was bungled by ignoring the religious dimension of international problems. American political faith believes that the First Amendment took religion out of public life; and acting on that faith we have bungled repeatedly. Any analysis of our consumerist binging and our ecological and demographic crises that ignores both the noxious and the critically helpful possibilities of religion will stumble in a self-imposed darkness. Gandhi said: "As human beings our greatness lies not so much in being able to remake the world—that is the myth of the Atomic Age—as in being able to remake ourselves."[58] Don't try that without attending to what people find sacred.

Notes

1. For a fuller definition of the common good, see n. 38.

2. See Jennifer D. Mitchell, "Before the Next Doubling," *Worldwatch* 11, no. 1 (January/February 1998): 22. See Population Reports, ser. M, no. 10, Population Information Program, Johns Hopkins University, May 1992, pp. 8, 16.

3. Gretchen C. Daily, "Restoring Value to the World's Degraded Lands," *Science* 269 (21 July 1995): 351.

4. Peter Barnes, review of *The Ecology of Commerce,* by Paul Hawken, *Nation* 258, no. 5 (7 February 1994): 172.

5. Noeleen Heyzer, *The Balancing Act: Population, Development, and Women in an Era of Globalization* (Chicago and New Delhi: A publication of The John D. and Catherine T. MacArthur Foundation, 1996), 16–17.

6. Joel E. Cohen, "Population Growth and the Earth's Human Carrying Capacity," *Science* 269 (21 July 1995): 34.

7. See Anne E. Platt, *Infecting Ourselves: How Environmental and Social Disruptions Trigger Disease,* Worldwatch Paper, 129 (Washington, D.C.: Worldwatch Institute, 1996).

8. See David W. Orr, *Ecological Literacy: Education and the Transition to a Postmodern World* (Albany: State University of New York Press, 1992), 3–5, and *Earth In Mind: On Education, Environment, and the Human Prospect* (Washington, D.C.: Island Press, 1994), 1–3.

9. Mitchell, "Before the Next Doubling," 23.

10. John Bongaarts of the Population Council, letter in *New York Times,* 9 November 1997.

11. Gro Harlem Brundtland, "The Challenge of Sustainable Production and Consumption Patterns" (keynote address, Symposium on Sustainable Consumption, mimeographed).

12. See David C. Korten, *When Corporations Rule the World* (West Hartford, Conn.: Kumarian Press, 1995), 39.

13. Thomas Aquinas, *Omnia Opera: Sententia Libri Politicorum* (Rome: Ad Sanctae Sabinae, 1971), bk. 2, chap. 15; also, chap. 6, 13, 17. On the thorny problem of governmental regulation of fertility, see Daniel C. Maguire and Larry L. Rasmussen, *Ethics for a Small Planet: New Horizons on Population, Consumption, and Ecology* (Albany: State University of New York Press, 1998), 10–18, for my comments entitled "China and the Draconian Critical Mass."

14. See Peter Brown, *The Body and Society: Men, Women, and Sexual Renunciation in Early Christianity* (New York: Columbia University Press, 1988), 6.

15. Ibid.

16. John Chrysostom *De Virginitate* 14.1.

17. John B. Cobb, *Sustainability: Economics, Ecology, and Justice* (Maryknoll, N.Y.: Orbis Books, 1992), 47. Truly free trade occurs when "a country is free either to trade or not. Its people can survive without it."

18. Virginia D. Abernethy, *Population Politics: The Choices That Shape Our Future* (New York: Insight Books, 1993), 27.

19. Ibid., 36, 294–95.

20. Ibid., 297.

21. Ibid., 303.

22. Ibid., 299, 309.

23. Ibid., 127, 228.

24. David C. Korten gives a Patrick Henry indictment of corporate tyranny in his *When Corporations Rule the World*. In the list of the one hundred largest economies, Malaysia was number 53, bigger than Matsushita (54) but smaller than IBM (52). Mitsubishi was number 22, the largest of the corporations on the list.

25. Roger C. Altman, "The Nuke of the 90's," *New York Times Magazine,* 1 March 1998, 34.

26. Quoted by David C. Korten in his opening plenary presentation to the Environmental Grantmakers Association, October 1994, at Bretton Woods, New Hampshire: "Sustainability and the Global Economy: Beyond Bretton Woods." Korten is president of the People Centered Development Forum, 14 E. 17th St., Suite 5, New York, NY 10003.

27. David R. Loy, "The Religion of the Market," *Journal of the American Academy of Religion* 65, no. 2 (summer 1997): 275.

28. Ibid., 276.

29. Ibid. In this article and in his other writings, Loy does not despair about the possibility of revitalizing the slumbering religious giants so that they might meet the challenge of the misdirected sense of what is sacred. It is the challenge of this "false religion" of the market that might awaken them.

30. I develop this notion of religion in my *The Moral Core of Judaism and Christianity: Reclaiming the Revolution* (Minneapolis: Fortress Press, 1993), chap. 3, "Religion and Common Weal," 31–57. I discuss the common root of religions as moral classics.

31. In part two of *The Moral Core of Judaism and Christianity* ("Scripting a New Humanity," 111–279), I trace the principal and innovative themes of Israel and the Jesus movement.

32. Morton Smith, "Palestinian Judaism in the First Century," in *Israel: Its Role in Civilization,* ed. Moshe David (New York: Harper and Brothers, 1956), 67–81.

33. Ibid., 81.

34. See Korten, *When Corporations Rule the World,* 31–32.

35. See Gerd Theissen, *Biblical Faith: An Evolutionary Approach* (Minneapolis: Fortress Press, 1985).

36. Quoted in Walter L. Owensby, *Economics for Prophets* (Grand Rapids, Mich.: Eerdmans, 1988), 19.

37. Luke Johnson, *Sharing Possessions: Mandate and Symbol of Faith* (Minneapolis: Fortress Press, 1981), 89.

38. I developed the meaning of the common good in a way that builds on *tsedaqah* theology; see Daniel C. Maguire, *A New American Justice* (San Francisco: Harper and Row, 1980), chap. 5, "What's So Good about the Common Good?" See also Daniel C. Maguire and A. Nicholas Fargnoli, *On Moral Grounds: The Art/Science of Ethics* (New York: Crossroad Press, 1991), 27–32, 68–69. Briefly, the common good is both a descriptive and normative category. It *describes* the fact that the conditions for surviving and some thriving are to some degree present, but it *prescribes* our

common obligation to meet the indispensable needs that make our communal existence possible. Humanity's absolutely indispensable needs, I submit, are respect and hope. The opposite of respect is insult, and insult is the root of all rebellion. The opposite of hope is paralysis. The common good is a context in which minimal amounts of respect and hope are available to all. Social justice is simply our ongoing obligation to contribute—with taxes, obedience to just laws, civic participation, breakup of monopolies, voting, affirmative action, and so on—to creating a context where no one will lack the essentials of life.

An ecological expansion of this theory shows that just as respect and hope are the two irreducible human needs, parallelly, reverence and expectancy are the appropriate attitudes toward the rest of nature. Indeed, reverence and expectancy are the soul of sound science and ecological ethics.

Social and distributive justice dictate the sharing we must do, not just with humans, but with the rest of the biotic community.

39. See the publications of the Center for Defense Information: 1500 Massachusetts Avenue, NW, Washington, DC 20005; 202-862-0700; fax 202-862-0708. This center, consisting mainly of retired military people, targets the profligacy of useless military spending.

40. Korten, *When Corporations Rule the World,* 41.

41. See Maguire and Fargnoli, *On Moral Grounds,* 7–25.

42. Thomas Aquinas *Summa Theologiae* 1.2.33.1. Actually, Thomas's word for delight, *delectatio,* comes from *diligere,* to love, so the true etymology would be helpful but not as helpful as Thomas's mistake.

43. Thomas Aquinas *Summa Theologiae* 2.2.158.8.

44. In the crudity of modern parlance, this would mean that the only just woman is "a bitch." Sexist society reserves this term for angry women; significantly, there is no parallel word for angry men.

45. Walter Brueggemann, *Prophetic Imagination* (Minneapolis: Fortress Press, 1978), 102.

46. See Daniel C. Maguire, "*Ratio practica* and the Intellectualistic Fallacy," *Journal of Religious Ethics* 10, no. 1 (spring 1982): 22–39.

47. As Wilfred Cantwell Smith points out, the Abrahamic religions place prime stress on law and theological formulation, whereas "in Africa . . . a tribal dance, and not a set of doctrines (nor of laws) might be the central pattern." *Modern Culture from a Comparative Perspective* (Albany: State University of New York Press, 1997), 26.

48. Maguire, *A New American Justice,* 99–124. This book was published in a new edition under the title *A Case for Affirmative Action* (Dubuque: Shepherd, 1992).

49. Rita Gross, "Buddhism after Patriarchy?" in *After Patriarchy: Feminist Transformations of the World Religions,* ed. Paula M. Cooey, William R. Eakin, and Jay B. McDaniel (Maryknoll, N.Y.: Orbis Books, 1991), 65.

50. See Daniel C. Maguire, "The Catholic Legacy and Abortion: A Debate," *Commonweal* 114, no. 20 (20 November 1987).

51. The Religious Consultation on Population, Reproductive Health and Ethics, of which I am president, is a collegium of some one hundred religious scholars from many of the world's religions. In its projects, the consultation brings groups together,

representing some ten religions in each project, and addresses issues such as population, ecology, and consumption, men's obligations to women, women's religious wisdom on human sexuality, and the right to family planning, including contraception and abortion. Each participant seeks to mine the renewable moral resources of his or her tradition and apply them to the topic. The State University of New York Press and Fortress Press will publish the results and efforts will be made to reach on-the-ground workers and nongovernmental organizations with our data. The address of the consultation is 2717 E. Hampshire Ave., Milwaukee WI 53211; 414-962-3166; fax 414-964-9248.

52. Chung Fang Yu, "Chinese Religions on Population, Consumption, and Ecology," in *Visions of a New Earth,* ed. Harold Coward and Daniel C. Maguire (Albany: State University of New York Press, forthcoming).

53. Rosemary Radford Ruether, *Gaia and God: An Ecofeminist Theology of Earth Healing* (San Francisco: HarperSanFrancisco, 1992), 32.

54. *Universa vero, quae condidit, Deus providentia sua tuetur atque gubernat, attingens a fine usque ad finem fortiter et disponens omnia suaviter* (Wisdom 8:1); Constitutio Dogmatica de Fide Catholica, chap. 1. The view that God's providence is protecting and governing everything with strength and sweetness (*fortiter et suaviter*) can ease the burden of human responsibility.

55. Since many Christian theologians do their theology *quasi deus non daretur,* they in effect sidestep the question.

56. Daniel C. Maguire, "More People: Less Earth: The Shadow of Man-Kind," in Daniel C. Maguire and Larry L. Rasmussen, *Ethics For a Small Planet: New Horizons on Population, Consumption, and Ecology* (Albany: State University of New York Press, 1998), 21–48.

57. *Religion: The Missing Dimension of Statecraft,* ed. Douglas Johnston and Cynthia Sampson (New York: Oxford University Press, 1994).

58. Quoted in Larry L. Rasmussen, *Earth Community, Earth Ethics* (Maryknoll, N.Y.: Orbis Books, 1996), 87, n. 40. Rasmussen's book won the Grawemeyer Award in Religion, and understandably so.

Response to Daniel C. Maguire:
The Church Should Call not Just Prophets
but Environmental Deacons

SUSAN POWER BRATTON

Daniel Maguire invokes the prophetic calling of the Abrahamic faiths as a powerful instigator or irritant in the process of social change. Yet, Christianity has hardly shown consistent or courageous leadership in confronting demographic dilemmas or environmental degradation. Although a handful of socially conscious Christians have exhorted their denominations and congregations to greater environmental responsibility, Christianity thus far has been barely a follower, much less a leader, in engaging international environmental concerns. The first great forthtelling may indeed be past, with little Christian presence in the schools of the green prophets.

In his presentation, Maguire identifies the megacorporations and their extravagantly salaried CEOs as the new Goliaths. I have the strong suspicion, however, that while Goliath has been pillaging the global countryside, I have been sleeping in the giant's bed, or bouncing up and down on it and tossing his foam-filled pillows about. Before we cast the expanding corporate economy as an exterior evil, we must reflect on how entangled we are in its multidimensional web. Thoroughly trapped would, in fact, be a better description.

Since I am employed by a small college, I may be less involved in spreading corporate hegemony. But, by means of confession, I first have to recognize that my students' families work for Kaiser Aluminum, Boeing, Microsoft, the U.S. Air Force, and the Presbyterian

Church. (The latter is an old-fashioned form of an international fran-
chise, which appears to be badly in need of restructuring and better
advertising strategies. Presbyterianism is still, however, a dependable
brand name, much like Quaker Oats.) Many of my students have federal loans and some participate in ROTC (the military Reserve Officer
Training Corps). Most will ultimately find employment in federal or
state government, public school systems, large institutions such as
universities and hospitals, or corporations.

I personally have an American Funds retirement account which
invests in European and Asian companies. The electricity running my
Hewlett Packard computer is provided by Washington Water Power
(of the Grand Coulee Dam and the Woody Guthrie song "Roll on Columbia, Roll On"), and I used a mix of Shell, Texaco, and off-brand
gasoline to propel my Ford Escort along Interstate Highway 90, so I
could drink Diet Coke and eat Georgia peanuts while flying cross-
country on Boeing jets to Boston.

Every time I put a dollar in my savings account (money market, of
course), I am encouraging electronic banking in Mexico and helping
establish McDonald's restaurants in China. While I am busy speaking
or writing about the environment, my savings, retirement investments, and taxes aren't sitting innocently in the bank or in government vaults; they are out roaming the planet, engaging in totally
unsupervised activities, and acting as support troops for Goliath. I
worry that the moola may be building roads and dams in the Amazon
watershed or purchasing pornographic Internet sites in Brooklyn—or,
geographically, vice versa—without leaving detectable fingerprints. I
lie awake at night, fraught with anxiety that I may be unknowingly
contributing more than one dollar to the Republican presidential
campaign coffers, or that I am adding nickels to Bill Clinton's legal
defense fund through a Hong Kong bank.

Cutting CEOs salaries by 50 or even 90 percent will not terminate
our participation in a massive global reorganization. It isn't that our
individuality is limiting our ethics, it is our sharing in industrial
society that confines our spiritual responses. We army ants are all
marching together down a plastic highway, as we carry silicon chips
instead of leaf fragments toward our great, sprawling nest at the mall.
As the German sociologist Ulrich Beck has pointed out, we fail to
recognize the extent to which we are entrenched in institutions and
social organizations which arose in response to the industrial

revolution.[1] Our universities and seminaries are the product of a long partnership with corporate and government sponsors and interests.

We Christians must contend with seven realities, or inevitabilities:

1. technological ascendancy in postmodern culture;
2. globalization of economies and the continuing growth of megacorporations;
3. globalization of communications networks;
4. expanding human population;
5. urbanization as a national and global process;
6. continued habitat and ecosystem degradation; and
7. American Christianity's continued dedication to middle-class values and life-styles.

These seven inevitabilities, perhaps with the exception of environmental degradation, are not pure "evils." Greater global availability of pharmaceutical products, for example, is saving millions of critically ill patients each year and is greatly improving the lives of children, including many who are poor. Better communications networks will provide wonderful educational opportunities for folks at all phases of life. Demographic shifts may strain our resources but may originate in blessings. The population of the United States is aging, which is partially the product of safer working conditions and better medical services for the average citizen—what a change from the ravages of nineteenth-century toil in factories and mines! The twenty-first-century church, rather than withdrawing in an ascetic muddle, should turn and confront these unrelenting processes affecting almost every aspect of our daily lives and make them more humane, less unjust, and less degrading.

In the realm of environmental and demographic crisis, we already have a long list of unsolved or partially solved problems to tackle. To meet them, I propose that, though a few very irritating prophets could elicit heartfelt penance, what we really need is a great cadre of deacons—environmental deacons, or ecodeacons—to lead us in day-to-day environmental service. When we think of deacons, too often we visualize a group of middle-aged men wearing frumpy Sunday suits, who seat elderly ladies in back pews, calculate church budgets, and locate a new pastor when the old one burns out. Or, we imagine a trainee for the priesthood or pastorate, working his or her way up through the ecclesiastical ranks. Our contemporary concept of deacon is far too narrow; the New Testament model of the διακονος, from the word διακονια, which means "to serve" or to "minister to,"[2] implicitly incorporates mature Christians who are neither theologians nor professional preachers.

Why environmental deacons? First, the early church conflict resulting in the call of the first deacons in Acts 6 is a fitting analog for our twenty-first-century environmental and demographic needs for service. As Christianity began to grow after the outpouring of the Holy Spirit at Pentecost, the expanding fellowships incorporated both the wealthy and the needy, those who were from Jewish backgrounds and those who were not. The Hellenized Roman Empire was cosmopolitan, yet strongly stratified by social class and economic inequities, as well as rife with ethnic strife. Acts 6:1 reports: "Now in these days when the disciples were increasing in number, the Hellenists murmured against the Hebrews because their widows were neglected in the daily distribution."[3] Eleven of Jesus' original apostles plus Matthias, who were leading the budding faith, did not wish to "give up preaching the word of God to serve tables." Therefore, they called all the disciples together and had them select from amongst themselves "seven men of good repute, full of the Spirit and of wisdom" to provide a fair distribution to the widows, regardless of their ethnic origin.

Environmentally, our most critical difficulties center on unjust distribution of economic benefits and environmental risks and degradations. The core ethical issue is sharing, or equitable or just distribution of the basics of life. Those stalwart first deacons, such as Stephen and Philip, would be seriously challenged by our diverse collection of the needy, sitting at a table where the bread is tainted with pesticides, the fish is laced with methylmercury, and the wine is diluted with trichlorethylene. Even the preaching-centered apostles, such as Peter and James, might stop to lend a hand in a dining room where one end is stacked with low-calorie microwavable treats and the other end has only handfuls of insect-infested rice and wheat.

Deacons present some further advantages. First, it is easy to be a false prophet and difficult to be a completely unfaithful deacon. In becoming a deacon, or a servant of the Christian community, you can do good despite yourself. Second, a prophet exhorts others to action (Deborah's ride into battle aside), while a deacon engages in direct ministry to her sisters and brothers, and thereby sets an example to the local community. Deacons may fill the role of prophets, and they may serve as healers, administrators, teachers, and even busboys. Third, we can easily imagine ourselves as prophets speaking for the nonhuman cosmos, but to picture ourselves as environmental deacons requires a deeper conversion of mind and heart, more difficult to attain because we have to serve not just marginalized humans, but the degraded and abused nonhuman. Imagine washing the feet of zebra or pouring olive oil (and, I repeat, *olive* oil) on the brow of an otter. Far more godly than piloting the Exxon Valdez into a rocky shoal! Fourth, service as deacons will provide "lay" leaders who are more aware of how environmental inequities and degradation arise from our lifestyles, sins, and prejudices. Rather than just blame the CEOs for our consumerism, we should encourage them to Christian service in the business sector and challenge them to spread the blessings of new technologies, while mitigating the negative impacts of industrial expansion and avoiding all unnecessary environmental damage.

The Book of Acts and the New Testament epistles offer useful clues to the spiritual formation of dependable green Philips and earth-friendly Phoebes. The names of the seven deacons listed in Acts 6:5 are Greek. This implies the Christian community appointed those who were from the same cultural background as the victims of injustice, and that they trusted these distributors of daily bread to be fair to the Hebrew faction as well. The calling of ecodeacons, therefore, should particularly encourage those who are from environmentally stressed communities, such as inner cities engulfed in air pollution and poor neighborhoods next to leaking dumps, to constructive ministry. Women are frequently the victims of toxic exposure, loss of land rights, food and fuel shortages, or inadequate medical and family planning services. As a result, women often have great sympathy with those who suffer due to want or structural violence and greatest passion for combating these injustices. A genuinely environmentally sensitive deaconry should have no difficulties with diversity.

Acts 6:6 records that the apostles "prayed and laid their hands on them." The early church honored those willing to serve, and by formally commissioning them for the task, encouraged other disciples to recognize their authority concerning food distribution. These actions also ritually linked the deacons to the church's daily involvement in prayer, worship, and preaching. Acts 6 also notes the good repute, wisdom, Spirit indwelling, and strong faith of those selected. In our contemporary context, we should avoid drafting spiritual laggards who have been slow to sign up for choir practice or to provide salad for covered dish suppers and coercing them to become wardens of the light switches and the recycling bins. We should look instead for those with a desire for service and the potential for becoming environmentally "wise."

Home congregations rarely acknowledge environmentally conscious Christians for their ministries to their human neighbors and to creation. Formal commissioning should follow a successful apprenticeship and a demonstration of long-term commitment. (And, for faith traditions that limit the deaconry to one gender or to those who have formal theological training, some other title such as "servant" or "elder" can acknowledge the type of ministry described in Acts 6. We will never be able to respond to the most critical environmental needs if we cannot find imaginative ways to compromise with denominational polity.) Acts 6, in fact, suggests a reversal of status surrounding the first church "table servers." Elsewhere in the New Testament, women seem to be the primary meal providers. In Luke 5:39, after Jesus healed Simon Peter's mother-in-law, "she immediately rose and served them," and in Luke 11:40, Martha is "distracted with much serving." The first seven post-Pentecost deacons care for women who, lacking husbands and adequate means of economic support, are presumably of lower social status than themselves.

The text of Acts 6 does not actually designate the dedicated seven as holding a specific office, but discusses their "service" or election "to serve." The emphasis is not on a position in a religious hierarchy but on the process of ministry. (Although, when Paul commends Phoebe in Romans 16:1, he calls her sister and minister—διακονον.)[4] In providing an appropriate Christian response to environmental degradations, the emphasis should be not on new social roles and professionalization, but on stimulating practical, effective service from the greater community of "disciples."

The New Testament epistles present varieties of ministry as Spirit-inspired. Paul suggests, in 1 Corinthians 12, that the Spirit may provide such gifts as wisdom, knowledge, discernment, prophecy, and healing. Administration and teaching are as legitimate Christian vocations as preaching. All of these gifts are applicable to environmental problem solving. The church as a whole is undoubtedly ignoring a call to leadership in environmental healing and ministry to the poor, both of which would bloom if based on the general principles of New Testament ethics. Further, we miss the diversity of virtues shown by early Christians that could underpin distinctively Christian environmental ministry. Paul comments (Rom. 16:1), for example, that Phoebe has been a "helper," or perhaps better, a "protectoress of many" (προστατις).[5] The Greek implies a person of some social authority, such as a "chief" or "patron."[6] What would an environmental *prostatis* be like? Could a twenty-first-century Phoebe protect children from pollution-induced asthma or provide safe places for inner-city children to play or experience nature?

Christian ecodeacons can lead the church in constructive and loving responses to the seven inevitabilities by tackling a diversity of tasks, including:

- sound, caring environmental management of church-related structures and properties, including not just over-heated sanctuaries and construction paper strewn Sunday schools, but cemeteries, lawns, parking lots, camps, hospices, office buildings, publication plants, retirement complexes, food banks, secondhand shops, day care centers, high schools, and homeless shelters;
- education at all levels and development of activities for youth (helping to turn the home church into a "creation awareness center" or leading "creation-sensitive" camping trips);
- seeking legal protection and medical service for those suffering from environmental injuries or illnesses, such as victims of air pollution, radiation, or pesticide exposure;
- assisting and acting as advocates for the poor and marginalized who may suffer disproportionately from environmental degradation, such as lack of clean water and fuel wood shortages;
- ministering to the needs of environmental refugees—those driven off their land by environmental degradation—and sponsoring programs to reestablish those so displaced;
- initiating environmental healing, including clean up and restoration of oceans, lakes, and rivers, making inner-city environments more life-friendly, planting trees in eroded or overgrazed landscapes, and reducing atmospheric pollution;

- protecting the habitats God has provided for our fellow creatures, as an acknowledgment of God's loving creative acts
  and the blessings of providence;
- assisting in environmental conflict resolution and acting as
  peace-keepers in battles over land use, development, and
  natural resource access;
- working to mitigate the impacts of population growth and
  urbanization, including raising money to provide better
  health services for poor women and families and to make
  health care and education universally available to children of
  both genders;
- encouraging sensible and woman-sensitive family planning.

The deacon may do very mundane tasks, and minister in very
quiet, unassuming ways, yet truly express the heart of God. By
distributing justice, deacons also become part of Christianity's conscience. Most of us, including environmental theologians, will find
ourselves bound by our "middleclassness." Our first mandate is to
recognize and repair the environmental harm we ourselves are causing. Engagement in ministry will not only generate healing, it will
foster discernment and repentance.

A constructive way to deal with Goliath may well be to ask him to
dinner and then to point out that the Philistine widows have not all
been fed. Or, one might meet him in the valley of Elah[7] and invite him
to serve as the Philistine champion in the stream bank restoration
competition, where he races that whimpy teenager, David, in install-
ing erosion-reducing fences and planting tree seedlings. Or, challenge
him to use his stature and prowess to develop a water pollution abate-
ment plan for the Tyre and Sidon coast.

While finishing this essay, I called L. L. Bean and Company and
asked if they had any environmental hair shirts available. The clerk
said they did not stock them, and then he wanted to know if real environmentalists actually needed the extra itch. So, a last advantage to
deacons: they are easier to outfit than prophets, as deacons can wear
coveralls, jeans, hiking shorts, and aprons while answering their God-
given calling.

Notes

1. Ulrich Beck, *Risk Society: Towards a New Modernity* (London: Sage Publications, 1992).

2. Harold K. Moulton, *The Analytical Greek Lexicon Revised* (Grand Rapids, Mich.: Zondervan Publishing House, 1977), 91–92.

3. All quotations are from *The New Oxford Annotated Bible: Revised Standard Version,* ed. Herbert G. May and Bruce M. Metzger (New York: Oxford University Press, 1973).

4. *The Interlinear Greek-English New Testament,* trans. Alfred Marshall (Grand Rapids, Mich.: Zondervan Publishing House, 1970).

5. The latter translation is from Marshall, cited above, although the RSV uses the less authoritative "helper."

6. Clinton Morrison, *An Analytical Concordance to the Revised Standard Version of the New Testament* (Philadelphia: Westminster Press, 1979), 273, distinguishes this Greek word from two others translated as "helper" in the RSV.

7. Here, the Israelite army faced off with the Philistines and David eventually slew the giant (1 Sam. 17:19).

Incentives, Consumption Patterns, and Population Policies: A Christian Ethical Perspective

JAMES B. MARTIN-SCHRAMM

After some opening remarks responding to Daniel Maguire's paper about the persistent challenge of global population growth and the issue of poverty, this paper explores the role incentives might play in changing human patterns of production, consumption, and repro-duction.[1] While incentives and disincentives are common tools in economic and environmental policy, they raise areas of significant moral concern for those interested in the intersection of Christian ethics and population policy.[2]

Population and Poverty Growth

First, Daniel Maguire does well to challenge those like Ben Watten-berg who proclaim that we no longer need to worry about global pop-ulation growth.[3] It is true that some populations in Western Europe and Scandinavia are experiencing below replacement rate fertility. It is also true that great gains have been made over the last forty years in slowing the rate of population growth around the world. But the fact remains that the current global population of 5.9 billion is projected to reach 9.4 billion by 2050 and 10.4 billion in 2100, before stabiliza-tion at nearly 11 billion around 2200.[4] Over 90 percent of that growth will take place in nations that are already struggling with poverty.

Moreover, while fertility is declining in every other major industrialized nation, fertility is increasing in the United States, the largest industrialized nation in the world.[5] At our current rate of growth, the United States will double in size in a little over sixty years.[6] Given the disproportionate ecological impact which U.S. citizens have upon the planet, data like this should give rise to significant concern, not consolation.[7] Not only should we be concerned about the social and ecological impact of high rates of global population growth among the poor, we must also be concerned about the social and ecological impact of high rates of consumption among the rich.

Elsewhere, I have argued that the metaphor of justice as right relationship can provide a foundation for Christian moral reflection about these interrelated issues.[8] This notion of justice is rooted in God's love for the world. That is to say, God's love for all of creation confers intrinsic value to all of God's creatures and creations. It is this fundamental measure of worth which serves as the foundation of justice.[9] Christians are called by God to love what God loves, to value what God values, and to join with God in the process of redemption—to restore the right relationships of a good creation in a fallen world. Justice understood in this light is not simply "rendering to each their due," but is more profoundly understood as "rendering to each their dignity as a creation of God." Christians are called by God to restore dignity by remedying the injustices that violate the dignity of God's creation.

Faced with the problems created by overconsumption and population growth, Christians rooted in God's justice as right relationship should be empowered by the vision of a world where all pregnancies will be desired and welcome, where children and their parents will have all they need to live full and productive lives, and where the human species will live in harmony with each other and with the rest of God's creation. But this vision has been shattered. Significant numbers of wealthy people and growing numbers of the poor are both contributing to social and ecological degradation. Any effort to address these realities requires seeing the reciprocal relationship between ecological integrity and social justice.

In this vein, Maguire argues that the ecological jeopardy which the world currently faces is grounded in an unjust distribution of wealth and power between the affluent few and the numerous poor. The sad truth is that the growing gap between the rich and the poor is reaching new heights. In 1960, the ratio of the income of the top 20 percent to that of the poorest 20 percent was 30 to 1; by 1994 it had risen to 78 to 1.[10]

Data like this leads Maguire to conclude that the "overconsumption of the few impoverishes the many."[11] He notes that, since 1950, the number of people living in absolute poverty has doubled (as has the global population), while world economic output has increased fivefold. This is true. In absolute numbers, more people live in absolute poverty than ever before. The World Bank estimates that 1.3 billion people live on less than one dollar a day.[12]

This reality is tragic, but it needs to be seen in historical perspective. While more people are poor than ever before, a smaller percentage of the world's population lives in poverty today. According to the United Nations Development Programme (UNDP): "While nearly 70% of humanity survived in abysmal conditions in 1960, only 32% suffered such conditions in 1992."[13] Similarly, the Food and Agriculture Association (FAO) reports that the percentage of those who suffer from chronic malnutrition has decreased from 24.4% of global population in 1970 (920 million) to 13.7% in 1996 (840 million). At the end of the twentieth century, a larger percentage of human beings enjoys greater access to education, health care, sanitation, potable water, and other key human services than ever before.[14]

Many of these gains are the fruits of hard work within the relief and development community, but much can also be ascribed to the fivefold economic increase that has taken place in the latter half of this century. While this "wealth" has been poorly distributed (a notorious, if not fatal, flaw of capitalism) and was garnered at significant social and ecological cost, it does appear that this rising tide has lifted the welfare of many—at least those who have boats or access to them. While I agree that there are unjust systems and practices that privilege the wealthy and function so as to harm the poor, poverty has fallen more in the last fifty years than in the previous five hundred.[15]

Incentives and Disincentives

This brings me to the primary focus of this paper. With Maguire, I agree that the production and consumption patterns of the rich currently pose the greatest threat to the planet's carrying capacity. In the near future, however, the near doubling of the world's population among those living in poor nations will pose a comparable threat to the welfare of those living in those nations as well as to the planet itself. These dual realities have led some to propose ways that various incentives or disincentives might alter human patterns of production, consumption, and reproduction. Drawing upon personal experience, I want to comment on two of these proposals. The first pertains to my involvement with a task force associated with the President's Council on Sustainable Development. The second experience relates to my opportunity to attend the 1994 United Nations International Conference on Population and Development in Cairo, Egypt.

In 1993, President Clinton appointed twenty-five leaders from business, government, environmental, civil rights, and Native American organizations to the President's Council on Sustainable Development (PCSD). The council was charged with the task of developing a sustainable development plan for the United States. In 1994, I was invited to serve on the Population and Consumption Task Force of the PCSD. This task force was one of eight created by the council. Together, the task forces comprised more than 450 experts from around the country. Like other task forces that focused on energy or agriculture, we grappled with a broad range of issues that fall under the categories of population and consumption. As we discussed these issues over the course of fourteen months, we focused first on matters relating to individual choice and responsibility and then on the larger social, economic, and cultural conditions that shape and constrain choices and responsibilities.

Each task force was asked to prepare a set of goals and policy recommendations for the council. On the population side, we developed two goals. The first was to stabilize U.S. population early in the twenty-first century "by providing universal access to a broad range of information, services, and opportunities that enable individuals to plan responsibly and voluntarily the number and spacing of their children."[16] There were four policy recommendations related to this goal. The first two focused on increasing information and access to services that prevent unintended pregnancies, particularly among adolescents. The third outlined various measures to reduce poverty, eliminate discrimination in public policy, and increase opportunities for women in society. The fourth policy recommendation dealt with the controversial political issue of legal and illegal immigration to the

United States: the task force suggested that the United States "should develop comprehensive and responsible immigration and foreign policies that reduce illegal immigration and mitigate the factors that encourage immigration."[17]

The second goal the task force adopted with regard to population was to achieve a geographic distribution of the U.S. population "consistent with the long-term ability of environmental, social, and economic systems to support those populations."[18] To achieve this, the task force recommended that the president and Congress appoint a national commission to study transportation, tax, land use, and development policy in order to develop a national strategy that would reduce the adverse impacts of settlement patterns in the United States.

Turning to the role incentives might play in these policy recommendations, the task force noted that many think that financial incentives might encourage use of contraception, delayed childbearing, or smaller families. Nevertheless, the task force concluded:

> Several factors suggest that reliance on financial incentives is not appropriate, with limited exception, in a wealthy country with as much unintended fertility as this one. People already want fewer children; the difficulty is matching outcomes with intentions. Broader access to family planning services and more education about sexuality and contraception seem more appropriate than financial incentives.[19]

For reasons I will discuss later, I shared the task force's consensus with regard to the role of incentives or disincentives in U.S. population policy. The task force did discuss, however, the symbolic value of limiting the federal tax deduction for dependents to two children, but we could not reach consensus on this issue. Since then, President Clinton has proposed and Congress has approved a $500 tax credit per child that will be phased in beginning with the 1998 tax year. While intended as a way to bring tax relief to families in the United States, this measure will likely function as a pronatalist population policy that increases fertility at a time when the task force suggests the nation should seek to stabilize its population.

Shifting to the consumption side, while the task force was reluctant to embrace financial incentives with regard to population policy, it eagerly embraced them when it considered ways to change U.S. consumption patterns. In fact, the principle that most guided our conversations was the maxim that "we should put our incentives where our objectives are." The task force developed five goals. The first was to reduce the amount of primary materials utilized in the U.S. economy through increased efficiency during the extraction, production, consumption, and disposal of these resources. The second goal was to shift taxes from income and investments to consumption of natural resources and those goods and services that pose significant environmental risks. The third goal was to empower consumers with the information they need to make informed and intelligent choices in the marketplace. The fourth goal was to encourage research and development of cleaner and more efficient technologies. Finally, the fifth goal was to promote an ethic of stewardship through various means to individuals and communities in the country.[20] All of these goals were accompanied by a host of policy recommendations. Here, I want to comment on the various incentives and disincentives linked with the second goal of shifting taxes from income and investment to consumption.

Among the many things that make the status quo ultimately unsustainable in the United States is our dependence on fossil fuels. Through consumption of these fuels in the energy and transportation sectors, the United States leads the world in both total and per capita greenhouse gas emissions. With data like this, it quickly became clear to the task force that reduced consumption of fossil fuels would have to be an essential component of any plan for sustainable development in the United States. Recalling the relationship between higher prices and decreased consumption that was proven during the energy crises in the 1970s and early 1980s, the task force began to discuss the relative merits of imposing a carbon tax on fossil fuels.[21] During this discussion, representatives from the Departments of Commerce and State insisted that new taxes were not feasible politically. Instead, they encouraged the task force to proceed with a proposal for a carbon tax but to make the tax revenue-neutral. To achieve this goal, they proposed that revenues from a carbon tax be offset by reductions in federal taxes on income and investment. Noting that taxes function as disincentives, they suggested that taxes should be placed primarily on human activities that harm the common good and not on income and investment that tend to increase economic prosperity.

This proposal prompted a vigorous discussion in the task force about the moral implications of reducing federal taxes on income and investment and the regressive nature of consumption taxes. With regard to the former, concern was expressed that the progressive nature of the federal tax code be preserved. Currently the tax code is grounded primarily in the moral principle of equity and not equality. Rather than each citizen paying an equal percentage of income in taxes, the burden of taxation is distributed according to the ability to pay taxes. On a percentage basis, the rich pay more taxes than the poor. Given the cry for a "flat tax" among several conservatives, the task force should have given more attention to this issue. Instead, it folded this concern into its response to the broader issue of the regressive nature of consumption taxes:

> Similar treatment of taxpayers in similar situations and taxation according to ability to pay are of particular concern to the Task Force. Provisions of any tax shift can compensate for regressivity through a number of measures: rebates to individuals and businesses disproportionately affected by a tax; income and payroll tax credits or deductions; and investment of revenues in worker training or other appropriate compensatory programs, particularly for the poor who do not pay taxes.[22]

I was encouraged when the task force developed and adopted this stance. As one of two ethicists on the task force, I emphasized the "preferential option for the poor" in the Christian tradition. While I am a Protestant, I affirmed and endorsed the following claim by the National Conference of Catholic Bishops in their 1986 pastoral letter on the U.S. economy:

> [Economic] decisions must be judged in light of what they do *for* the poor, what they do *to* the poor, and what they enable the poor to do *for themselves.* The fundamental moral criterion for all economic decisions, policies, and institutions is this: They must be at the service of *all people, especially the poor.*[23]

This brings me to the conclusion of this brief review of the task force debate concerning the role of incentives in changing U.S. patterns of production, consumption, and reproduction. I want to turn my attention now to appeals by a few for the use of various incentives and disincentives in the population policy of nations struggling with high rates of fertility and population growth.

Implications for Population Policy

The situation in Africa is particularly dire. Globally, the fertility rate has declined from 4.5 (children per woman over the course of her reproductive life) in 1970–75 to 3.1 in 1990–95. The fertility rate in Africa, however, is much higher and has declined less rapidly. In 1970–75, the average fertility rate in Africa was 6.6 and in 1990–95 it had only declined to 5.8. While 60 percent of the nations in Africa have seen fertility decline over the last twenty-five years, 23 percent have the same rates of fertility today as they did in 1975, and 17 percent have seen their fertility increase. Taken together, this means that most nations in Africa will see their populations double over the next twenty to twenty-five years.[24]

Data like this have led some scholars and population experts to argue that the goals of gender equity, reproductive rights, and universal access to the means of family planning adopted at the 1994 United Nations International Conference on Population and Development (ICPD) are necessary but insufficient steps to curtail global population growth.[25] In addition to these indirect routes of reducing fertility, some propose that more direct methods may be necessary, particularly in countries with high rates of fertility and population growth. These direct measures involve various incentives and disincentives aimed at individuals and communities to impact decisions and behavior regarding fertility. Various incentives might include free sex education and family-planning services, free sterilization or contraceptive implantation, cash or material payments, tax breaks, or housing privileges. Various disincentives might include fewer tax deductions, monetary penalties, or the revocation of various social privileges for fertility above the stated goal.[26]

The *Programme of Action* that was approved at the ICPD opposes coercion and is reluctant to embrace various incentive or disincentive schemes. The document distances itself from measures like these because of significant human rights violations that have occurred through the implementation of various population policies over the last thirty years. For example, local government officials eager to enforce China's one-child policy have coerced many women into abortions and sterilizations against their will. China's set of disincentives and incentives has also contributed to an increased rate of female infanticide and girl child mortality as families exercise their preference for sons under a one-child policy. In Puerto Rico, India, and a few other developing countries, some women who entered hospitals to give birth left with intrauterine devices (IUDs) implanted against their will or were involuntarily sterilized. Given these kinds of abuses, the approach which the *Programme of Action* has taken toward incentives, disincentives, and more direct forms of coercion is understandable.

The reality remains, however, that some nations with high rates of fertility, population growth, and demographic momentum may not see these rates drop fast enough through the means proposed in the *Programme of Action* to avoid social, political, and ecological collapse. Faced with the doubling of their populations in approximately twenty years, lacking the resources either to grow economically or to trade for food, and faced with the reality that mass internal migration or international emigration is not an option, nations like Rwanda and Malawi may face "demographic entrapment."

The concept of a demographic trap was first developed by Lester Brown at the Worldwatch Institute.[27] Across the Atlantic, Maurice King, a research fellow at the Institute of Epidemiology and Health Services Research at the University of Leeds, has further developed the concept and its policy implications. In order to avert social, political, and ecological disaster, King argues that nations like Rwanda and Malawi should implement a one-child policy or a substantial mix of incentives and disincentives to reduce fertility and slow demographic momentum.[28]

When I met King at the ICPD in Cairo, I was alarmed by these policy recommendations and what I perceived to be his cold, consequentialist approach to moral reasoning. Since then, I have discovered that some of my colleagues in Christian ethics and some population experts are sympathetic with King's views. They are reasonably concerned that if actions are not taken now to curtail fertility in high-growth nations, then a much greater magnitude of hunger, suffering, and death will be experienced in the near future.

King's arguments raise the issue of whether governments can legitimately limit an individual's reproductive rights so as to protect the common good. While the power of the state to limit the free exercise of rights is clearly established and practiced throughout the world, the burden of proof falls upon the state to prove that limitation of individual reproductive freedoms is necessary to protect the common good. As I survey the global demographic scene, it seems to me that a one-child policy or aggressive incentives and disincentives would be unjustified in most nations in the world. The problem, however, is that nations like Rwanda and Malawi do appear to fit King's definition of demographic entrapment.

In the past, moral philosophers and theological ethicists have evaluated population policies that contain various types of incentives, disincentives, and forms of coercion by considering their impact on four primary human values: freedom, justice, general welfare, and security or survival. While responsible moral evaluation of specific population polices involves reflection on all four of these primary values, ethicists have arranged these values in different orders of priority. For example, some have made the values of general welfare and security or survival subordinate to the more fundamental values of freedom and justice. Ethicists like Ronald Green and Daniel Callahan have argued that efforts to maximize freedom and equality are more effective means of securing the common good than coercive means that violate human dignity.[29] Callahan warns that "[t]he end—even security-survival—does not justify the means when the means violate human dignity and logically contradict the end."[30] Others have taken the opposite approach and have emphasized that without a fundamental measure of general welfare and security it is impossible to experience the values of freedom and justice. Ethicists like Michael Bayles and James Gustafson have argued that it may be necessary and justifiable to limit certain individual rights and regulate human fertility out of a concern for the common good of present and future generations.[31] Bayles writes: "inequality and lack of freedom are acceptable if without them people would lack welfare or security."[32]

This difference in the ordering of primary moral values is reflected in more recent moral reflection on population issues as well. I have summarized those discussions elsewhere and will not do so here.[33] Instead, I want to offer some initial guidelines to use when considering the kinds of measures King proposes.[34]

First, it must be demonstrated that voluntary measures to reduce fertility, such as those described in the *Programme of Action,* have been tried and found insufficient.

Second, it must be demonstrated that efforts to permit international migration and achieve food security have been attempted through the international community and have failed.

Third, any decision to implement such drastic measures as a one-child policy, or a similar set of incentives and disincentives to reduce fertility, must result from a democratic process that spreads the burdens and responsibilities equally across the entire population.

Fourth, measures must be taken to prohibit sex selection and discrimination against girl children.

Fifth, reversible means of contraception also should be utilized, and forced contraception, sterilization, and abortion must be considered anathema.

Finally, if incentives or disincentives are considered, they should be designed, implemented, and evaluated by those most directly affected by them. In almost all cases, this will be women. It may, in fact, be possible to distinguish *supportive* or *empowering* measures from *coercive* incentives or disincentives.[35] Some incentives actually increase the moral agency of women rather than undermine it. The key is that those who are most affected should have the power to decide.

Given the past abuses of various incentive and disincentive schemes, it is certainly not wise, nor is it necessary, to pursue them in any aggressive fashion in international population policy. Moreover, appeals to such measures on the grounds of ecological well-being tend to miss entirely the devastating impact of relatively stable populations in the developed world that are wreaking havoc on the earth through their unsustainable patterns of production and consumption. Proponents of "direct" measures should focus their attentions there.

Notes

1. In his most recent book, co-authored with Larry Rasmussen, Daniel Maguire suggests that China's controversial population policies represent "an urgent invitation to revisit the question of the proper role of public policy and government in population matters"; see Daniel C. Maguire, "More People, Less Earth," in *Ethics for a Small Planet: New Horizons on Population, Consumption, and Ecology* (Albany: State University of New York Press, 1998), 13.

2. I try to outline the basis for this concern in *Population Perils and the Churches' Response* (Geneva: World Council of Churches Publications, 1997).

3. Ben J. Wattenberg, "The Population Explosion Is Over," *New York Times Magazine*, 23 November 1997, 60–63.

4. These figures represent the 1998 revision of the medium fertility projection of the United Nations Population Division. This widely used scenario assumes that total fertility rates will stabilize at approximately 2.1 children per woman in the year 2055. Slight variations in the fertility stabilization rate, however, could produce quite different results. For example, the UN's high projection, based on a fertility rate of 2.5 in 2050, points to a population of 11.2 billion by 2050, 17.5 billion by 2100, and 27.0 billion in 2150. On the other hand, the low fertility scenario assumes that fertility will stabilize at 1.6, resulting in a projected population of 7.7 billion in 2050, 5.6 billion in 2100 and 3.6 billion by 2150. See "United Nations World Population Projections to 2150," *Population and Development Review* 24, no. 1 (March 1998): 183–89. See also J. Mayone Stycos, "Population, Projections, and Policy: A Cautionary Perspective," *Population and Environment* 16, no. 3 (January 1995): 205–19.

5. The total fertility rate in the United States in 1995 was 2.1, up from 1.8 in 1980. The World Bank, *World Development Report 1997* (New York: Oxford University Press, 1997), 225.

6. Ibid., 221. The annual rate of population growth in the United States is 1.1 percent.

7. To be sure, if the international community takes appropriate measures over the next two decades we could "stabilize" the human population below the projected near doubling forecast for the end of the next century. See John Bongaarts, "Population Policy Options in the Developing World," *Science* 23 (11 February 1994): 771–76. The reality, however, is that the international community, and the United States in particular, are not following through on the financial commitments they made in Cairo. While the 1994 International Conference on Population and Development (ICPD) set some new and important directions for population policy for the next twenty years, implementation of the goals outlined in Cairo is lagging for lack of full financial support and sufficient political will. See Josh Hamilton and Robert Ivker, "Donor Fatigue Hits Family Planning in Developing World," *The Lancet* 349 (24 May 1997): 1530.

8. James B. Martin-Schramm, "Population Growth, Poverty, and Environmental Degradation," *Theology and Public Policy* 4, no. 2 (summer 1992): 26–38.

9. See Daniel Maguire, *A New American Justice: Ending the White Male Monopolies* (San Francisco: Harper and Row, 1980), 58.

10. United Nations Development Programme, *Human Development Report 1997*, http://www.undp.org/undp/hdro/overview.html.

11. Daniel Maguire, "Population, Consumption, Ecology: The Triple Problematic," in this volume. I suspect Maguire would agree, however, that there are clearly various factors that give rise to poverty and or perpetuate it. Race, gender, and class distinctions all play important roles. So too do congenital health problems, illiteracy, and family size. It would be unfair and inaccurate to blame the rich as the sole cause for poverty.

12. *Finance and Development,* March 1997, http://www.worldbank.org/fandd/english/0397/articles/0180397.html.

13. United Nations Development Programme, *Human Development Report 1994* (New York: Oxford University Press, 1994), 1.

14. United Nations Development Programme, *Human Development Report 1997,* http://www.undp.org/undp/hdro/overview.html.

15. Ibid.

16. President's Council on Sustainable Development, *Population and Consumption Task Force Report* (Washington, D.C.: President's Council on Sustainable Development, 1996), 59.

17. Ibid., 65.

18. Ibid., 59.

19. Ibid., 22.

20. Ibid., 59–60.

21. Carbon taxes are only one type of market incentive or disincentive that was discussed by the task force. For a fuller description of a broad range of incentives and disincentives discussed by the task force and proposed by the President's Council, see *Sustainable America: A New Consensus for Prosperity, Opportunity, and a Healthy Environment for the Future* (Washington, D.C.: President's Council on Sustainable Development, 1996), 44–51. For a review of the impact of a $100 and $300 carbon tax on OECD emissions of carbon dioxide, see Daniel Finn, *Just Trading: On the Ethics and Economics of International Trade* (Nashville: Abingdon Press and the Churches' Center for Theology and Public Policy, 1996), 177–200.

22. President's Council on Sustainable Development, *Population and Consumption Task Force Report*, 40.

23. National Conference of Catholic Bishops, *Economic Justice for All* (Washington, D.C.: United States Catholic Conference, 1986), 12.

24. World Resources Institute, *World Resources 1996–97* (New York: Oxford University Press, 1996), 192.

25. For example, see Charles F. Westoff, "International Population Policy," *Society* (May/June 1995): 11–15; and Maurice King, Charles Elliot, et al., "Does Demographic Entrapment Challenge the Two-Child Paradigm?" *Health Policy and Planning* 10, no. 4 (December 1995): 376–83.

26. For a more specific discussion of the types of incentives and disincentives offered by nations, see Nafis Sadik, *Population Policies and Programmes: Lessons Learned from Two Decades of Experience* (New York: United Nations Population Fund, 1991), 120–23; see also Robert M. Veatch, "An Ethical Analysis of Population Policy Proposals," *Population Policy and Ethics: The American Experience,* ed. Robert M. Veatch (New York: Irvington Publishers, 1977), 445–75.

27. Lester Brown, "Analyzing the Demographic Trap," *State of the World 1987* (New York: W. W. Norton, 1987).

28. Maurice King, "Health Is a Sustainable State," *Lancet* 336 (15 September 1990): 664–67; "Public Health and the Ethics of Sustainability," *Tropical and Geographical Medicine* 42, no. 3 (July 1990): 197–206; "Lessons from Rwanda: The Case for a One-Child World" (paper presented at the NGO Forum during the United Nations International Conference on Population and Development in Cairo, Egypt, 5–13 September 1994), 1–4; "To the Point of Farce: A Martian View of the Hardinian Taboo—The Silence That Surrounds Population Control," *British Medical Journal* 315 (7120) (1997): 1441–43. See also Maurice King and Charles Elliott, "Legitimate Double-Think," *Lancet* 341 (13 March 1993): 669–72; "Cairo: Deep Squib or Roman Candle?" *Lancet* 344 (20 August 1994): 528; "Double-Think—A Reply, *World Health Forum* 116 (1995): 293–98.

29. See Ronald Michael Green, *Population Growth and Justice: An Examination of Moral Issues Raised by Rapid Population Growth,* Harvard Dissertations in Religion, no. 5 (Missoula, Mont.: Scholars Press for Harvard Theological Review, 1976); and Daniel Callahan, "Ethics and Population Limitation," in *Ethics and Population,* ed. Michael D. Bayles (Cambridge, Mass.: Schenkman Publishing Co., 1976).

30. Callahan, "Ethics and Population Limitation," 34–35.

31. See Michael D. Bayles, *Morality and Population Policy* (Birmingham: University of Alabama Press, 1980); and James M. Gustafson, "Population and Nutrition," *Ethics From a Theocentric Perspective,* vol. 2 (Chicago: University of Chicago Press, 1984).

32. Bayles, *Morality and Population Policy,* 35.

33. See James B. Martin-Schramm, "Population-Consumption Issues: The State of the Debate in Christian Ethics," in *Theology for Earth Community: A Field Guide,* ed. Dieter T. Hessel (Maryknoll, N.Y.: Orbis Books, 1996), 134–40.

34. I was pleased to discover, after the fact, that the guidelines I propose here are quite similar to those proposed by Stephen Isaacs at Columbia University's School of Public Health; see Stephen L. Isaacs, "Incentives, Population Policy, and Reproductive Rights: Ethical Issues," *Studies in Family Planning* 26, no. 6 (November/ December 1995): 363–67.

35. See Sonia Correa and Rosalind Petchesky, "Reproductive and Sexual Rights: A Feminist Perspective," in *Population Policies Reconsidered: Health, Empowerment, and Rights,* ed. Gita Sen, Adrienne Germain, and Lincoln C. Chen (Boston: Harvard Center for Population and Development Studies, 1994), 116.

Climate Change: Ethics, Justice, and Sustainable Community

DAVID G. HALLMAN

Introduction

The public debate about climate change is evolving from scientific questions about whether it is a real phenomenon to the even more challenging level of political, economic, and social issues regarding what should be done.[1] The United Nations Climate Change Conference[2] held in Kyoto, Japan, in December 1997 raised the profile of climate change as an issue of substantial global conflict between industrialized and developing nations, within the block of countries belonging to the Organization for Economic Cooperation and Development (OECD), and between environmentalists and large economic interests.

The World Council of Churches (WCC) and many of its member communions have been engaged in the issue for almost ten years. We see the ecological, scientific, political, economic, and social debates within a larger context of ethics and justice. In the churches' analysis, human-induced climate change is primarily the result of anthropogenic greenhouse gas emissions from industrialization and transportation based on the burning of fossil fuels by powerful interests and societies to increase their wealth, consumption, and mobility. The consequences of climate change will be experienced disproportionately by the poor in developing countries, island states and low-lying regions, and future generations.

Moreover, climate change can be seen as a metaphor of the fractured relationship between human societies and God's creation, the broader earth system of which we are a part. Not only will people suffer as a result of climate change, but many ecosystems will be disrupted and species threatened.

It is not just Christians who have become concerned about climate change as an issue of their faith. During the UN Climate Change Conference in Kyoto, several moving interreligious events took place involving Buddhists, Christians, Hindus, Jews, Muslims, members of New Religions in Japan, and Shintos.

Science, religion, and economics have played their own respective roles in the evolution of the model of development dominant in industrialized countries over the past two centuries,[3] which is the source of the emissions of greenhouse gases leading to climate change. Each discipline, to varying degrees, now offers elements of a new vision that could help reorder human societies so as to function in a more harmonious relationship with the rest of the biosphere. Within ecumenical discussions, we are coming to articulate this vision as one of "sustainable community" characterized by peace, social justice, and ecological integrity. Climate change increases the urgency in making this vision a reality.

The Science of Climate Change[4]

There continues to be some scientific debate about various aspects of climate change. It is important however to distinguish among several layers of this debate.

The vast majority of the meteorological and related scientific community agrees that human-produced emissions are accumulating in the atmosphere and causing a slow warming of the atmosphere's mean temperature. This global atmospheric warming is in turn predicted to lead to climatic changes.

In 1988, the World Meteorological Organization and the UN Environment Programme formed the Intergovernmental Panel on Climate Change (IPCC) to assess the science related to climate change and its implications for policy. The IPCC involves over twenty-five hundred scientists in more than one hundred countries and uses rigorous peer-review processes to vet the syntheses which they produce based on primary research that has itself gone through peer-review processes. Their reports are then reviewed by the more than 120 governments which are involved in the climate change negotiations. The Executive Summaries are reviewed, line-by-line, and approved by representatives of those governments.

In its modeling of possible climate change to come, the IPCC projects future temperature increases using a number of scenarios with varying assumptions as to population, economic growth, and energy supplies. These will influence the emission of greenhouse gases. The range of scenarios may lead to a one- to three-degree Celsius temperature increase by the end of the next century, compared to the present climate state. The midrange scenario projects a two-degree Celsius increase, on average, with a greater increase at high latitudes.

The climatic consequences of this global warming of the atmosphere are likely to include the following effects:

- patterns of weather, in particular rainfall, are likely to change significantly and have a severe impact on water resources and water availability in many places;
- droughts and floods are likely to be more frequent and more severe than in the past, especially in subtropical regions where many developing countries will be particularly severely affected;
- atmospheric warming would increase the temperature of oceans, leading to an expansion in the volume of the water and a rise in sea level. Already it has risen ten to twenty-five centimeters in the past one hundred years. The IPCC's best estimate is a further rise of fifty centimeters by the end of the twenty-first century. Such a rise would have severe consequences for people and ecosystems in such vulnerable areas as the Pacific and Caribbean Islands, countries with populations and agriculture on river deltas (for example, Bangladesh, Egypt, and the state of Louisiana in the United States), and many coastal regions. Any contribution from the ice caps to sea level rise is likely to be small.

The Second Assessment Report of the IPCC, released in December 1995, concluded that:

the observed warming trend is unlikely to be entirely natural in origin . . . the balance of evidence suggests that there is discernible human influence on global climate.[5]

The debate about whether climate change is a real phenomenon or not occurs more in the media than in academic journals. There are some well-publicized dissenters who dismiss the scientific consensus reflected in the work of the IPCC. One must note several qualifications which raise questions about the critiques of at least some of these dissenters. Much of their work has not gone through the rigorous peer-review process to which all of the IPCC's analysis is subject. Secondly, there have been some disturbing revelations about the links between some of the detractors and the fossil fuel industry lobby, which has so vigorously opposed action to address climate change. An article in the December 1995 issue of *Harper's Magazine* described those links.[6] The manipulation of science for the explicit purpose of supporting vested economic interests is ethically reprehensible, especially when the results postpone action, thus jeopardizing the lives and well-being of many vulnerable people and other species.

I do not wish to dismiss everyone who objects to the IPCC consensus. That could imply a type of scientific tyranny. Indeed, some scientists have voiced a justifiable concern about the political correctness of supporting the IPCC position and have expressed reservations about raising questions for fear of being labeled reactionary. Nevertheless, it must be noted that there is only a very small minority of reputable scientists who challenge the IPCC consensus.

Legitimate scientific debate is focused now not so much on whether climate change is a real phenomenon but rather on the details of such a change. While the IPCC's Second Assessment Report affirms the reality of human-induced climate change and represents increased scientific consensus, it acknowledges that further work is needed to reduce uncertainties in various areas and increase predictability. These areas include the timing, magnitude, and regional patterns of climate change, the interaction of clouds with greenhouse gas build-up, the response of the polar ice sheets to climate change, and other possible feedback mechanisms. The rise in global mean temperature could be less but, of course, it might also be more drastic than currently projected.

Climate change is an illustration of the complex relationship between science and economics. For both detractors and believers of the IPCC consensus on climate change science, scientific research and economic analysis are intertwined, raising a wide range of ethical questions. Clearly it is wrong to skew science to protect the rich and powerful interests which are threatened by proposals to reduce fossil fuel use. But those who endorse the IPCC consensus have also been subject to their own ethical complexities. Because of the economic disparities which exist among nations, there have been fewer scientists and economists from developing countries who have had the opportunity to do research or to participate in the IPCC deliberations than from the richer nations. The IPCC has done its best to find the financial resources to facilitate involvement of researchers from the economic South, but it continues to be a problem. Not only is the meteorological and social research not as available from the South, but the IPCC's whole approach to analytic design has tended to be dominated by Western economic models, with their emphasis on the monetization of everything possible.

The report of IPCC Working Group III, "The Economic and Social Dimensions of Climate Change," has been of particular interest to the World Council of Churches. Among other issues, the report discusses equity considerations, especially concerning the differing responsibility for, and impact of, climate change in various regions of the world. It also looks at issues of equity between generations, given that future generations will have to pay a heavy cost for the problems being caused by current generations. One of the more problematic parts of the report discusses the "applicability of cost benefit assessments." In economic modeling, there is an attempt to place a quantifiable value on many things that do not lend themselves easily to such reduction. Furthermore, comparisons have been made in the preparatory work of Working Group III between the economic value of a life in an industrialized country and the value of one in a developing nation. These discussions produced a great deal of controversy, and the final report of Working Group III is written in a more nuanced way as a result. There is still reason for concern about how the report is so heavily dominated by Western approaches to economic analysis.

Christianity and the Western Economic Development Model

Scientists estimate that over 80 percent of the anthropogenic greenhouse gas emissions that have accumulated in the atmosphere have come from industrialized nations over the past two hundred years of their development. The Western model of economic development has been based on the exploitation of natural resources, the expansion of capital, and a continuous growth in production and consumption. Fossil fuels, especially coal and oil, have been the primary energy source supporting this industrial development. The burning of fossil fuels is the main source of emissions of carbon dioxide (CO_2), which is the major greenhouse gas leading to a warming of the atmosphere. (Natural gas is also a fossil fuel, but its more recent use does not pose as big a problem because it emits considerably less CO_2 than coal and oil.)

Climate change is not just a matter of the ecological impact of economic development. It also has elements of religious responsibility. In my book *Ecotheology: Voices from South and North,* I note that

> churches in the North have not yet come to grips with the degree to which Christian theology and tradition are implicated in the Western capitalist development model that has dominated our countries since the industrial revolution, many other countries through the colonial periods, and more recently every part of the world that is touched by the new "global economy". This goes well beyond the famous critique of Lynn White Jr. and the theological responses to it. It has to do with economics, cultural values, worldviews and even understandings of faith. A sign of our lack of progress here is our limited impact on the materialism and consumption which pervade North America and Europe and are the source of many of our ecological problems including toxic wastes, exorbitant energy consumption, and greenhouse gas emissions.[7]

Christianity has had a complex interaction with science and economics in the evolution of the Western economic development model. Though we tend to focus on the conflicts between religion and science during the early periods of the scientific revolution, in fact, Christianity provided important sources of support for science. From the beginning of the Middle Ages, monasteries had been a secure refuge in which classical Greek and Roman culture were preserved and scholarship encouraged. Without this data base, modern intellectual development and scientific progress would have been immeasurably slowed. When the Protestant Reformation spread across Europe, it added several important conceptual building blocks for science. In emphasizing the distinction between the Creator and the creature, the Reformers desacralized the natural world. This made it possible for the budding sciences to study and manipulate it. Francis Bacon maintained that all creation had meaning only in relation to humanity:

> Man, if we look to final causes, may be regarded as the centre of the world insomuch that if man were taken away from the world, the rest would seem to be all astray, without aim or purpose.[8]

Ian Barbour observes that

> The "desacralization" of nature encouraged scientific study, though it also—along with other economic and cultural forces—contributed to subsequent environmental destruction and the exploitation of nature.[9]

Christian theology provided a moral legitimacy for human ascendancy over nature, which had become the accepted goal of human endeavor. According to Keith Thomas,

> The dominant religious tradition had no truck with the 'veneration' of nature which many Eastern religions still retained and which the scientist Robert Boyle correctly recognised as 'a discouraging impediment to the empire of man over the inferior creatures'.[10]

Though one should not draw direct causal relationships between the scientific revolution and the first industrial revolution that followed, there are some significant interconnections between the science of the day and the emerging discipline of economics—interconnections in which Christianity is also implicated. Economists Adam Smith and David Ricardo provided the theoretical basis for the tremendous growth of the industrial revolution. Smith argued that economic life was governed by objective laws, just as Newtonian physics described the laws of nature. Ricardo used the rigor of the scientific method to derive logical theories from well-specified assumptions.

Early Protestants believed that industrious, disciplined work would yield benefits to those who were predestined for salvation. Economic success was an outer sign of inner faith. But material luxury was considered unacceptable for the truly devout. The accumulation of money for its own sake, rather than for the purchase of goods, thus became legitimized. This was to prove critical to the rise of capitalism and liberal economic theory.

There was a shared sense of religious fervor among those involved in the early scientific and economic pursuits: God was beckoning humanity to use all of its intelligence to usher in a new day of enlightenment and prosperity. The natural world was seen as yielding its long-held secrets to the rigor of scientific experimentation. Economic theories were formulated to describe the unseen laws that governed supply and demand. There was a genuine conviction among the theologians, scientists, and economists that God's will was being realized in their efforts. In *The Passion of the Western Mind,* Richard Tarnas observes:

> With Calvin, a Christian's worldly vocation was to be pursued with spiritual and moral fervour in order to realise the Kingdom of God on earth. . . . On a larger social scale, the Protestant call to take this world more seriously, to revise society and to embrace change, served to overcome traditional religious antipathy both to this world and to change, and thereby gave the embryonic modern psyche the religious sanction and internal restructuring it required to propel the progress of modernity and liberalism in many spheres, from politics to science.[11]

Theological attitudes which viewed the natural world primarily as a God-given resource whose utility related to exploitation for human purposes continued as a dominant perspective until relatively recently. A document from the 1961 Assembly of the WCC states that

> the Christian should welcome scientific discoveries as new steps in man's domination of nature.[12]

The pastoral constitution *Gaudium et Spes* of the Second Vatican Council expressed a general expectation that

> [human beings], created in God's image, received a mandate to subject [to themselves] the earth and all that it contains . . . thus, by the subjugation of all things to [humanity], the name of God would be wonderful in all the earth.[13]

The Western economic development model of industrialization with its consequential despoiling of the environment, including the emission of greenhouse gases, has progressed within a value system endorsed by the dominant mainstream of Christian theology.

Two qualifications are worth noting at this point. First, environmentally polluting industrialization has not been limited to Western, capitalist countries. The socialist countries of the former Soviet Union were even less attentive to the ecological consequences of their exploitation of natural resources and fossil fuel–based economies. Second, other religions whose sacred writings and traditions reflect a concern for the earth have not demonstrated much more success in restraining pollution than has Christianity within the West. Both of these qualifications, however, do not mitigate the responsibility of religion in the West for contributing to the value base which allowed for economic development to proceed with little regard for the environmental consequences. Moreover, this responsibility has increased as the Western economic development model has gained predominance throughout the world over the past decade, with the collapse of the Soviet regime and the growth in economic globalization.

Fortunately, providing moral support for Western economics is not the whole of the story of the Christian relationship to the Western economic development model. There have been significant occasions challenging various aspects and impacts of the development model. Much of the reform legislation in England from 1750 to 1850, which addressed such economic exploitation as child labor was based on the proposals of religious leaders, such as Wesley and Wilberforce. In our century, the social gospel movement raised major questions about the economic disparity in Western, capitalist countries. These precedents provided a conceptual and strategic heritage on which theologians and ethicists could build over the past thirty years as awareness grew of the devastating environmental consequences of industrialization.

Climate Change as an Issue of Justice

Given this Christian culpability, we are called to at least two responses: challenging the injustice and contributing to alternative approaches.

No one would deny the very considerable benefits to human well-being that have resulted from scientific and economic development over the past century. But the Western economic development model has also bequeathed destructive socioeconomic and environmental legacies, human-induced climate change being one of them. The ethical dimensions of climate change come to the fore as we recognize that human choices have led to the propagation of the Western development model, with its unintended negative consequences, and human choices can change it for the better. This human responsibility is one dimension of the ethics of climate change; it is supplemented by the fact that the problem is caused largely by those who are rich and powerful in the world and the consequences will be suffered the most by those who are poor, politically weak, or voiceless as a function of being yet unborn. In a World Council of Churches statement delivered to the plenary at the Kyoto Climate Conference in December 1997, we integrated these two ethical dimensions and spoke of climate change as an issue of justice. (The WCC statement to the High-Level Segment of the Kyoto Climate Summit is attached as an appendix.)

The WCC statement in Kyoto articulated several implications of viewing climate change as an issue of justice, with dimensions of both retributive and distributive justice. Justice means that as individuals and as societies, particularly in the overdeveloped parts of the world, we must be held responsible for the destructive impact of our actions, which are leading to climate change and threatening vulnerable human communities, other species, and broader ecosystems. Justice implies that we must be accountable for promises that we make to limit the emission of greenhouse gases. Justice demands truth and an end to the campaigns of misinformation whose purpose is to protect powerful economic interests. Justice requires honesty in international relations so that rich oil-producing countries are not allowed to masquerade their interests by appealing to their technical status as belonging to the category referred to as "developing nations."

In addition to these dimensions, which we might refer to as retributive justice, there is also a significant distributive justice aspect to the climate change issue. Justice means an equitable sharing of access to the earth's resources and the right to use resources for ecologically sustainable human development. The major conflict between North and South in the international negotiations on climate change has stemmed from the concern among developing nations that global treaties might place restrictions on their economic development and thus hamper their ability to deal with the poverty in their countries. They see this possibility as unjust because the climate change problem has been caused by the industrialized nations, which have grown rich pursuing a development model powered by fossil fuels. The poorer nations have thus argued that they must be allowed to develop so that their people can enjoy a good quality of life. Ethicist Henry Shue has proposed the helpful distinction between the "luxury emissions" of the rich, which are produced in support of life-styles of consumption and transportation, and the "survival emissions" of the poor, who use fossil fuels primarily for the essentials of food and shelter.[14]

In the final hours of negotiations in Kyoto, India and China provided a dramatic illustration of the distributive justice dimension of the climate change issue. The point being debated was a concept called "emission trading." The industrialized countries wanted the Kyoto Protocol to include provisions allowing them to buy and sell emission credits. A credit would be the difference between a country's actual emission level and the level that it would be allowed to emit under the treaty. Theoretically, emission trading is supposed to lead to an overall reduction in emissions by assigning a market value to emission credits whereby more efficient countries could receive money by selling their credits to more polluting countries who would need them in order to meet their target. Using the market in this way is supposed to be beneficial environmentally by making it costly to pollute, thus inducing countries to reduce their emission levels.

There is considerable skepticism about emission trading among some observers of the Kyoto Protocol because the former Communist bloc countries, at least in the near future, will have credits to sell, not because they are more efficient, but because their economies have collapsed and many polluting industries have closed since the baseline year of 1990 against which the reduction targets are set. The buyers of these credits will likely be industrialized countries, such as the United States, Japan, Canada, and Australia, and some fear that the net impact would be to diminish the pressure on these countries to make changes that would reduce greenhouse gas emission levels in their own countries.

The objections voiced by India and China during the Kyoto negotiations were related to these concerns but were stated on a more general level, using terminology of ethics in viewing the atmosphere as a global commons. The delegates from these two countries were upset that the industrialized countries were preparing to launch a bartering system for a commodity which no country or corporation owns—the atmosphere. The Indian representatives demanded that before emission trading is allowed, there needed to be agreement on "an equitable distribution of emission entitlements," that is, an agreement on how much emissions each person should be allowed.[15] Their basic ethical foundation was that all members of the human community should have the same right to a sustainable quality of life. They argued that only when a global agreement is reached on emission entitlements can a system be devised for assigning monetary value and initiating an emission trading system. The Chinese articulated the issue as one of human rights. A compromise was arranged by the chairman that avoided the collapse of the negotiations by basically postponing the hard decisions on emission trading until a future meeting. The drama of that debate, at 3:00 A.M. on the last night of the negotiations, illustrated that the ethical dimensions of the climate change issue, both in terms of retributive and distributive justice, are not hypothetical but carry very real force in the economic and political hardball of international negotiations.

Toward Sustainable Community

This is a dynamic time to be engaged in issues of ecological theology and ethics. Within the disciplines of religion, science, and economics, one perceives a passion not only for critiquing the current policies and practices that have led to problems such as climate change but also for exploring concepts, experimenting with new models, and entering into interdisciplinary dialogue toward the creation of more ecologically sustainable approaches to the economic organization of our societies. Much of this work focuses on reducing consumption patterns, particularly energy use, and thus has direct implications for addressing climate change.

Collaborative endeavors between science and economics are leading to the development of many new energy-efficient technologies and renewable energy alternatives. Supporters of international environmental negotiations have long maintained that technological development would be stimulated more by the setting of ambitious standards and targets than by the reverse argument that such international agreements should only be made once technology was available for implementing them. That seems to be confirmed by the significant momentum stimulated by the negotiation of the Kyoto Protocol and is evident in many areas, including experimentation with alternate fuel sources for cars, improvements in the energy efficiency and the attendant reduction of greenhouse gas emissions in many industrial operations, and innovations in alternate energy sources, such as biomass, wind, and solar.

Beyond the technological innovations, there are thinkers addressing the larger questions of economic models and systems. Herman Daly has been a leader in this field for several decades and the 1989 book that he co-authored with John Cobb, Jr., *For the Common Good,*[16] translates theories of sustainability into proposed policies and practices in many areas, including trade, land use, agriculture, and industry. Vandana Shiva bases her insightful analyses on the life experience of women within economic and social systems.[17] Economist Paul Hawkin has taken a different but also very creative approach with his book *The Ecology of Commerce,* which proposes structuring economic systems on the principles that guide ecological systems.[18] Ernst Ulrich von Weizsäcker, president of Germany's Wuppertal Institute for Climate, Energy and the Environment, has made important conceptual contributions in his writing and policy work, including an essay in *Earth Politics* and *Factor Four,* a book co-authored with Amory and Hunter Lovins of the Rocky Mountain Institute that shows how our societies could function without a loss of standard of living while using a fraction of our current energy consumption.[19] The Intergovernmental Panel on Climate Change has focused considerable effort on articulating economically viable policies and measures that could substantially reduce greenhouse gas emissions without compromising standards of living.

At a more foundational level, theologians and ethicists are making contributions that reinforce this exploration of alternate economic models of development and go beyond to propose value systems that integrate ecological sustainability and social justice. The current Earth Charter discussions are an attempt to revitalize efforts prior to the 1992 Rio Earth Summit to articulate a set of global principles for the relationship between human societies and the broader ecosystem. The World Council of Churches hosted an interreligious consultation in 1991 to develop suggestions for an earth charter. My denomination, The United Church of Canada, adapted WCC ideas in a policy statement entitled *One Earth Community: Ethical Principles for Environment and Development.* The preamble to the principles reads in part:

> The vision of One Earth Community is a call to live in harmony with all life, to draw on the earth's sustenance responsibly and to care for the planet that all may benefit equitably now and in the future. . . .
>
> The way forward will require a turn towards restoration and renewal. We need to reaffirm the importance of justice, frugality, humility and reverence for life and nature. To live within such a holistic relationship requires our rediscovering the spiritual connection that unites us to the land and that nourishes our souls as well as our bodies.[20]

One of the important contributions that the WCC and member churches are making to the climate change discussions is to emphasize the indispensable interconnection between ecological sustainability and social justice.[21] We argue that not only do we need to pursue an "efficiency revolution" in terms of our use of energy, but we also need a "sufficiency revolution." By this we mean that our consumption-oriented societies must be challenged to reflect on what is really enough, or sufficient, to provide a good quality of life. The overconsumption of the wealthy societies must be reduced because it is threatening the well-being of all. Similarly, the poverty of much of the world must be eliminated if all are to enjoy access to adequate nutrition, health, education, and security. Sufficiency implies significant changes in life-styles for both the rich and the poor, with the consumption patterns of the former being reduced and those of the latter being increased.

In our work in the World Council of Churches, we are coming to utilize the terminology of "sustainable community" as an articulation of this vision, which integrates ecological integrity and social justice.[22] We understand community in a broad sense. Community includes the centrality of the local setting in which people meet their needs and find meaning. Beyond that, we seek to discern principles of community that apply to relations among nations, particularly when addressing issues such as climate change, where we are reminded that we live in a global village. Further, community encompasses our relationships beyond the human family—the web of life in which we are only one of the many interrelated members.

The churches are proposing that we rediscover the virtue of simplicity, that we break our addiction to ever more consumer products, and that we challenge the economic system that seeks to feed this addiction. We need to distinguish between our needs and our greeds.

Moving away from life-styles that are defined by their material wealth would allow us to move toward life-styles that are defined by their attention to relationships. We need the time and the economic freedom to focus our energies on nurturing our relationships within our families, within our communities, with the natural world around us, and with God, or however we understand the spiritual dimension of life. For us in the churches, two sources of inspiration for moving in this direction have been insights from native spirituality and analyses from ecofeminist thought.

Climate change poses a challenge to the whole global community. Christianity has significant contributions to offer and responsibilities in which to be actively engaged. In collaboration with living faiths around the world, religion has an important role to play in the pursuit of sustainable community.

Appendix: Statement by the World Council of Churches to the High-Level Segment of the Third Session of the Conference of the Parties (COP3) to the UN Framework Convention on Climate Change, Kyoto, Japan, December 9, 1997

Mr. President, Distinguished Delegates, Observers,

We recognise that the COP3 negotiations are at a difficult point. We make this statement on behalf of the World Council of Churches with a combination of humility and prayer, wanting to assist the process and yet needing to speak the truth as we discern it.

For us in the World Council of Churches, the core of the COP3 agenda is *justice*.

Justice means being held responsible for one's actions.

The rich of the world, through promotion of the current economic model, have been and continue to be responsible for the vast majority of emissions causing human-produced climate change but seem unwilling to honestly acknowledge that responsibility and translate it into action. It is ironic that countries which exult in their domestic legal principles feel themselves above the law when it comes to their international obligations on climate change.

Justice means being held accountable for promises you make.
The rich of the world have broken their Rio promise to
stabilise emissions by 2000 at 1990 levels and yet seem to
exhibit no embarrassment at their failure.

Justice means being held responsible for the suffering you cause to
others.
Small island states, millions of environmental refugees, and
future generations will suffer as a result of the callous exploitation of the Earth's resources by the rich.

Justice means being held accountable for abuse of power.
Human societies, particularly in the over-developed countries, are damaging the environment through climate change
with little respect for the inherent worth of other species
which we believe to be loved by God as are we.

Justice means an equitable sharing of the Earth's resources.
Millions of people lack the necessities for a decent quality of
life. It is the height of arrogance to propose that restrictive
commitments be placed on the poor to make up for the
delinquencies of the rich. Over-consumption of the rich and
poverty of the poor must both be eliminated to ensure quality
of life for all.

Justice demands truth.
Destructive misinformation campaigns are being used by
groups with powerful economic self-interest with the intention of preventing meaningful action on climate change.

Justice requires honesty.
The world is not so easily divided into the rich North and the
poor South as we used to think. There are a few wealthy and
powerful countries and elites within the category referred to
as developing countries who sometimes misuse this classification of nations to disguise their economic self-interest.

God's justice is strict but it is not cruel. We are all here in Kyoto as
brothers and sisters equal before God within the community of

creation—a creation which we all want to be healthy and thriving for future generations. In affirmation of the goodness of creation (Genesis 1:25), God beckons us to respect all forms of life. In what we do at COP3, we must not betray life.

Confidence-building measures are needed so that together we can reduce the threat of climate change:

- Industrialised countries must demonstrate, in the near future, real and significant reductions in domestic greenhouse gas emissions which many studies have shown to be possible with a considerable net benefit to their economies.
- Though developing countries should not be subject to formal emission limitation commitments yet, many of them are pursuing measures and can continue their efforts to become more energy-efficient and to limit greenhouse gas emissions.
- The sharing of finance and technological resources is needed but it is also very important to exchange experiences from both South and North including those of indigenous cultures, women's organisations and others which can offer lessons and tools for learning to live in a socially just, equitable and ecologically sustainable manner.

In these remaining days of COP3, let us shift our energies away from trying to figure out how to attain the minimum and channel them instead toward creative risk-taking options for accomplishing the maximum. Thank you.

Notes

1. For more information about the work and resources of the World Council of Churches regarding climate change, including the new 1998 discussion document *Climate Change and the Quest for Sustainable Societies,* contact:

• WCC, Unit III, 150 route de Ferney, P.O. Box 2100, 1211 Geneva 2, Switzerland; tel. 41-22-791-6111; fax 41-22-791-0361; e-mail: mro@wcc-coe.org
or

• Dr. David G. Hallman, WCC Climate Change Co-ordinator, c/o The United Church of Canada, 3250 Bloor St. W., Toronto, Canada M8X 2Y4; tel. 1-416-231-5931; fax 1-416-232-6005; e-mail: dhallman@web.net

2. Officially, the Kyoto meeting was called "The Third Session of the Conference of the Parties to the UN Framework Convention on Climate Change," COP3 for short. A copy of the treaty negotiated during the meeting is entitled the "Kyoto Protocol" and is available from me or through the web page for the UN Climate Change Secretariat (www.unfccc.de/).

3. See David G. Hallman, *A Place in Creation: Ecological Visions in Science, Religion, and Economics* (Toronto: United Church of Canada Publishing House, 1992), for an analysis of the interconnections between science, religion, and economics in the genesis of today's ecological crises and for an identification of new models from the disciplines for living more sustainably.

4. Some of the material in this and other sections is drawn from the WCC's new study document, *Climate Change and the Quest for Sustainable Societies* (Geneva: World Council of Churches, 1998), of which I am also one of the main authors and principle editor.

5. *Second Assessment Report of the Intergovernmental Panel on Climate Change* (Geneva: IPCC, 1995), 22. The IPCC web page contains the reports at www.unep.ch/ipcc95.html.

6. Ross Gelbspan, "The Heat Is On: The Warming of the World's Climate Sparks a Blaze of Denial," *Harper's Magazine,* December 1995, 31–37.

7. David G. Hallman, *Ecotheology: Voices from South and North* (Geneva: WCC Publications; Maryknoll, N.Y.: Orbis Books, 1994), 5.

8. Keith Thomas, *Man and the Natural World: Changing Attitudes in England, 1500–1800* (London: Allen Lane, 1983), 18.

9. Ian Barbour, *Religion in an Age of Science* (San Francisco: Harper and Row, 1990), 17.

10. Thomas, *Man and the Natural World,* 22.

11. Richard Tarnas, *The Passion of the Western Mind: Understanding the Ideas That Have Shaped Our World View* (New York: Harmony Books, 1991), 245.

12. Wesley Granberg-Michaelson, "Creation in Ecumenical Theology," in *Ecotheology: Voices from South and North,* ed. David G. Hallman (Geneva: WCC Publications; Maryknoll, N.Y.: Orbis Books, 1994), 97.

13. Second Vatican Council, *Gaudiem et Spes.*

14. Henry Shue, "Subsistence Emissions and Luxury Emissions," *Law and Policy* 15, no.1 (January 1993).

15. Several years ago, India held a position in the negotiations that a per capita emission entitlement should be established. Their terminology in Kyoto of "equitable distribution of emission entitlements" is more ambiguous and would allow, presumably, for broader considerations of geography, history, culture, etc. Their basic point remains, however, that the atmosphere is a global commons and the more wealthy and powerful countries should not be allowed to claim it and buy and sell it on their own.

16. Herman E. Daly and John B. Cobb, Jr., *For the Common Good: Redirecting the Economy toward Community, the Environment, and a Sustainable Future* (Boston: Beacon Press, 1989).

17. Vandana Shiva, *Staying Alive: Women, Ecology, and Survival in India* (Delhi: Kali for Women, 1988), and *Let Us Survive: Women, Ecology, and Development* (New Delhi: Sangarsh, 1986).

18. Paul Hawken, *The Ecology of Commerce: A Declaration of Sustainability* (New York: HarperCollins, 1993).

19. Ernst Ulrich von Weizsäcker, *Earth Politics* (London: Zed Books, 1994); and Ernst Ulrich von Weizsäcker, Amory B. Lovins, and Hunter L. Lovins, *Factor Four: Doubling Wealth, Halving Resource Use* (London: Earthscan Publications, 1997).

20. United Church of Canada, *One Earth Community: Ethical Principles for Environment and Development,* a policy statement of the thirty-fourth General Council of The United Church of Canada, 1992.

21. See David G. Hallman, "Ecumenical Responses to Climate Change," *Ecumenical Review* 49, no. 2 (April 1997).

22. Canadian churches prepared a document for the 1997 five-year review process of progress on agreements since the 1992 Rio Earth Summit entitled *Toward Sustainable Community: Five Years since the Earth Summit.* The report is available from me, at the address in n. 1. In addition to reflections on the general issue of sustainability, the report reviews progress (particularly from a Canadian perspective) in such areas as climate change, forests, mining, biodiversity, gender equity, globalization-trade-transnational corporations, aboriginal issues, agriculture, and oceans.

Ecological Security and Policies of Restraint

WILLIAM C. FRENCH

In order to understand the human condition at the beginning of the twenty-first century, we might try, as E. O. Wilson suggests, to imagine what watchers from space would have observed occurring on the surface of the earth over the last few centuries. He asks us to imagine a space station on a moon of Jupiter constructed by a benevolent civilization from beyond our solar system whose mission is one of silent observation of the evolution of life on Earth. For centuries they have recorded climate cycles, mapped forest growth and animal and plant ranges, tracked population fluctuations, and noted the advance and retreat of glaciers. But these watchers have been waiting for what Wilson dubs "the Moment," the evidence of the development in one animal species of intelligence and its breakthrough to planetary dominance. The watchers from space would have seen increasing signs that the moment has arrived over the last three centuries—forests cut back to half their original range, atmospheric carbon dioxide surges upward, stratospheric ozone layer thins. Where once only forest fires could be seen from space breaking the blackness of the earth's surface at night, now the watchers observe the increase of "millions of pinpoints of light, which coalesce into blazing swaths across Europe, Japan, and eastern North America."[1]

Humanity via our surging numbers and advancing industrial and agricultural powers has become, as Wilson puts it, "a geophysical force, swiftly changing the atmosphere and climate as well as the composition of the world's fauna and flora." As more of the earth's surface is brought under the domination of humanity, natural habitats are transformed and simplified and increasing numbers of species are forced into extinction. Wilson, noting that "during the past 500 million years there have been five great extinction spasms," argues that "human expansion" is promoting a tragic sixth extinction. If current trends continue, he projects we will loose 20 percent or more of the rain forest species by 2020 and 50 percent or more by 2050.[2] By 2050, United Nations' projections estimate that global human population will reach 9.4 billion.[3]

Wilson's image of the celestial watchers is helpful for framing life on Earth in a wide historical expanse. We, however, do not observe night on Earth from the heavens, but mostly from within the constrictions of the circles of light in cities, suburbs, and villages. Where from the watchers' and Wilson's vantage the last century has been an awesomely revolutionary century, for most of us it has been simply our familiar home. Our attention is captured by events and dramas framed in narrower historical scales—months, years, decades. Our eyes are so accustomed to the tempo of the productive and consumptive practices that dominate developed and developing societies today that we feel the pace of change as normal, not problematic or revolutionary.

In the following essay I examine some of the forces driving the global growth agenda, some of the ecological threats it poses, and some of the reasons why Christian communities have been relatively slow to commit sustained attention and energy to public policy change promoting ecological sustainability. The moral convictions of diverse Christian communities have pushed forcefully for policy reform in areas ranging across the political spectrum—from civil rights, nuclear arms reductions, and economic justice to activism against abortion and for prayer in the public schools. However, Christian communities have generally been slow to take seriously the threats posed by global ecological degradation. I examine current ecologically centered thinking that is helping to suggest the stake that religious communities have in promoting ecological sustainability.

Christianity, like other religions, can play a critical role in the development of broad-based national and global efforts to institutionalize policies that will stop the unfettered growth agenda that is undercutting the powers of life on Earth. Even as a healthy ecosystem requires biodiversity, the global community is gifted with cultural and religious diversity. Each religious community can help draw the attention of its adherents to the stakes involved in our emerging ecological threats and can help mobilize powerful energies of care and commitment for the earth and its living creatures and a willingness to sacrifice for the planetary good. Although Christianity has too often accommodated itself to the culturally dominant values of the day, nevertheless Christianity, like other religions, holds promise of vital countercultural energies that can help encourage its members to join hands with other communities around the globe working for policies of environmental sustainability and social justice.

Global Growth Agenda

The current default in the public policies of almost every nation is set on a powerful growth agenda. People worldwide seek better jobs, increasing income, better living standards, swift transportation, and myriad consumer items. In addition, very few want higher taxes. Governmental competence around the globe is measured by rising gross national product (GNP) levels, national productivity growth, job creation, and low unemployment rates. Corporations want expansion of sales, increasing market share, and increasing quarterly profit margins and are often willing to engage in expensive advertising campaigns to thwart potential environmental legislation that might diminish sales and earnings. A recent example was the $13 million ad campaign by the gas, coal, and automobile industries in the fall of 1997 before the Climate Conference in Kyoto, Japan, urging that climate change data is too uncertain to warrant any United States' policies designed to diminish domestic fossil fuel consumption or automobile usage.[4] Electorates, governments, and national and multinational corporations together push a powerful juggernaut of economic growth in all countries today, which escalates the practices of unsustainability.

Rising GNP is commonly taken as a basic indicator of economic growth and, hence, of increasing national well-being. It is the sum of the value of all goods and services produced in a country in a given year. However, this index is tremendously crude for it overinflates the benefits of growth by failing to deduct the social and ecological costs of certain types of production and consumption that are passed on beyond the market transaction to third parties—human, animal, and plant—and often to future generations. Logging off a forest and selling it for lumber gets factored in as an addition to GNP, but there is no deduction for a loss of ecological capital and potential productive capability. Perversely, ecological disasters like the Alaskan oil spill caused by the Exxon Valdez that bring significant ecological harm generate pollution clean-up campaigns whose costs are included in the GNP ledger as a positive addition of services to the nation's economy. Similarly, there is no attempt to monetize the negative impact of soil erosion and habitat loss and additions to our atmospheric buildup that increase global warming threats, so human productive and consumptive practices that generate these typically are accounted for on the GNP tallies as unqualifiedly good. As Al Gore has put it, our current GNP accounting system is "partially blind," for it sees only certain aspects of our relationships with the natural world and it obscures tremendously significant costs of such common practices as auto driving, industrial farming, and jungle clearing.[5]

Christian Slowness in Response to Ecological Concerns

The Christian community, like many of the world's religions, has been slow to grasp what is at stake in ecological degradation. Christian ethics has historically focused closely on human decisions and actions which impact directly on human life and interests, but has typically not viewed decisions and actions that impact on the nonhuman world—animals, plants, ecosystems—as subject to close moral review. Rather, such actions of transforming and using nature were held to be subject to evaluation according to the canons of efficiency, not those of ethics. Dominant traditions of Christian thinking have held that actions on, and relations to, the nonhuman world do not constitute a sphere of genuine religious or ethical significance.[6] As Immanuel Kant summarized this general ethical view, rational beings are "persons" and thus valued "ends-in-themselves," whereas other sorts of living beings who lack rationality are designated "things" having worth only as a "means" of service to the life and interests of humans.[7]

Where language of "sin" comes readily to mind in Christian thinking about actions and policies that kill and damage humans, there has not yet developed any widespread view that notions of "sin" might also rightly name actions and policies that degrade the earth and thereby threaten both human and nonhuman lives and interests. Given the anthropocentric focus that dominates modern Christianity, it is not surprising that many Christian communities have been slow to see working for ecologically oriented policy change as a central practice of Christian responsibility.

Remarkable theological and ecclesiastical attention is also absorbed by denominational identity issues. Concerns for institutional boundary-maintenance pull many in different Christian denominations to focus intensely on their doctrinal, liturgical, and ethical distinctiveness, leaving little sense of a broader loyalty to an earth community in great need. The noted theologian H. Richard Niebuhr has argued that Christian obsession with identity issues has too often directed the sense of the holy toward narrow ritual, doctrinal, and theological formulations and hence "toward the symbols of a closed society," thereby eclipsing notions of God's universal engagement in the entire created world of being. He has chastened Christians regarding what he has dubbed the idolatry of "henotheistic faith," a "social faith which makes a finite society, whether cultural or religious, the object of trust" and absolute loyalty.[8] Distinctiveness and particularity of expression and tradition are taken as key signs of theological integrity, but, for Niebuhr, this inward-curving focus narrows attention and makes Christians forget an outreach of love and responsibility to a wider world that characterizes traditional Christian understandings of religious and spiritual integrity.[9]

Yet another obstacle to the engagement of Christian communities with ecological concerns is a reticence to risk asserting views on complex environmental policy issues. As James Gustafson has noted, there are different modes of moral discourse, each with its own distinct strengths and limits.[10] While theologians, pastors, and the churches in general feel more comfortable with prophetic discourse that expresses passion and indictment, and with ethical discourse that weighs general value claims and principles, only rarely are policy issues elaborated in their concreteness and detail. However, this generates the unfortunate result that the churches' educational outreach to members regarding ecological issues is rendered generalistic and vague. Abstract appeals to "love creation" and "care for the earth" are preached, but the details of concrete ecological problem areas often are left undiscussed. Accordingly, parishioners typically receive little sustained guidance regarding concrete steps for achieving "sustainability" or for implementing direct practices of care for creation.

Ecologically Centered Christian Thinking

In the last two decades a growing number of Christian theologians and ethicists have begun to emphasize God's and humanity's relationship to the nonhuman natural world by reconceiving God as centrally manifest in the world of creation and humanity as thoroughly embedded in the matrix of natural creation. Thomas Berry argues that Christians have for too long concentrated spiritual attention on scriptural texts and failed to attend sufficiently to the immediacy of God's presence in the remarkable narratives disclosed in the natural world. For Berry, modern Christianity has overemphasized divine transcendence and placed an excessive concentration on the redemptive energy in the Christ event. These block, he believes, Christians' ability to attend to divine presence as he perceives it to be embodied in processes of nature and the divine energies that he sees as creating and sustaining life on Earth. Berry wants Christians to understand the natural world as "the primary revelation of the divine, as primary scripture, as the primary mode of numinous presence."[11] The recovery of Christian notions of divine grace and presence in the natural world suggested by Berry has also directed his attention toward issues of ecological degradation. In habitat destruction and species extinction, Berry sees humanity destroying "modes of divine presence," which he argues should evoke a powerful sense of loss and concern among all religious people.[12]

Corresponding to the recovery of a broader account of divine action, relation, and presence, many suggest the need to rethink the ethical core focus of Christian ethics in light of emerging ecological data. Recently, James Nash has helpfully situated the requirements of the Christian ethic of love in "an ecological context." He holds that Christians must now ecologize their understanding of the range of individuals whose needs "neighbor-love" now obligates them to serve: "our neighbors who are to be loved are all God's beloved creatures."[13] Liberation theology has also made an ecologically helpful contribution to Christian ethical analysis through its examination of how systems of oppression and injustice harm individuals and communities through processes of systemic or "structural violence."[14] Habitat degradation, climate forcing, and biodiversity loss suggest an expanded range of structural violence with harmful impact on both human and nonhuman communities. If Christians come to recognize an ecologically expanded sense of systemic violence, the affirmation "Blessed are the peacemakers" in the Sermon on the Mount (Matt. 5:9) could help them see public policies designed for ecological sustainability as institutionalized mechanisms for extending the range of peacemaking and neighbor-love. The Christian injunction to feed the hungry could also be perceived as entailing protection of habitat integrity and climate conditions that make possible a sustained nourishing of the planetary community across the generations.

Environmental public policy appears to many to be a "cold," analytical field, where details and statistics overwhelm patience and feeling. Thus, to many religious people it seems distant from the core of faith, compassion, or commitment. But public policy does not just shape collective behavior. It can also empower new occasions of seeing by breaking old habits of inattention, thus encouraging new sensitivities, commitments, and loyalties to grow. Public policy change can be an engine of societal renewal based less in prophetic emotional appeal and more in the concrete reinforcement of new practices and new perceptions. Policy discourse may appear initially to be a "cooler" medium than other modes of religious ethical appeal. Yet if, as many Christians hold, the core of Christian ethics lies in its affirmation of the obligation to "love the neighbor" through service of their basic needs, then policy formulation that promotes justice and ecological sustainability deserves to be seen as a critical institutionalization of "loving service" to the wide array of human and nonhuman neighbors both in this generation and in future ones.[15]

Policy Change and Moral Vision

Some on the radical environmental wing occasionally lapse into antihuman arguments deriding humanity as a "cancer on the earth." Neoconservatives, on the other hand, often make too much of environmentalism's purported antipathy for humanity in favor of animals and ecosystems. In fact, the animating vision of most environmentalists is that humanity is a part of the greater natural ecosystem and our well-being is dependent on its continued integrity, stability, and health.

Biocentric ethics need not be antihuman, nor need it undercut concerns for human rights and social justice, which are central concerns in many religious traditions, including Christianity. Rather, biocentric ethics usually affirms those traditional valuations of human worth and wishes to expand the circle of valuing and direct moral concern to nonhuman living entities and ecosystems. Environmentalists point out that the brunt of environmental damage falls on the back of the world's poor and will fall on future generations, so that concerns for human life and interests remain among the core values of biocentric thinking.[16] Concern for policies of sustainability is consonant with core emphases of traditional Christian ethics on social justice. By situating justice concerns in the context of potentially severe planetary ecosystem harm, Christian communities can begin to mobilize their moral energies to help focus attention on the need for public policies to promote ecological stability.

The discipline of ethics is usually viewed as primarily an educational enterprise; the power of ethical reflection lies in its ability to persuade individuals and communities to act in certain ways. Policy, on the other hand, imposes legal constraints on behavior, thus enforcing compliance through institutional means. While guided by ethical considerations, as well as political, scientific, and economic considerations, public policy is, in the end, thoroughly practical. Public policy formation is centrally guided by considerations of constraints on the feasibility of actual implementation.

Relegating educational power primarily to ethics, however, does not account for the full range of influence generated by public policies. Like ethics, public policies can also function as powerful educational vehicles. While human values shape our practices, our habits of practice also come to shape our values, our notions of normality, and what counts as the good life and proper action.[17] By restructuring practices, public policies can help shape new patterns of attention and sensitivity, generate new sorts of care and concern, and hence transform societal and group values. For example, the passage of the Civil Rights Voting Act in 1965 clearly did not end racism, but it did undo certain practices that entrenched racism in place. Passage of the act changed habituated behaviors, and over time this change, combined with others, came gradually to help transform many hearts and minds.

Sustainability, Social Justice, and Fossil Fuel Consumption

While the global economy is a system of surging power, some reap its benefits more than others and some cause more ecological disruption than others. No environmental ethical or policy analysis can leave out the remarkable disparities between and among people in terms of wealth, levels of fossil fuel consumption, levels of meat eating, level of overall ecological impact, and level of numbers of offspring.

Alan Durning, formerly of the Worldwatch Institute, has noted that the bulk of global ecological degradation is caused by the wealthiest one-fifth—the global consumer class—and the poorest one-fifth. The consumer class receives roughly 64 percent of the world income—thirty-two times what the poorest one-fifth receives.[18] The poor have few options and therefore cannot be expected to rectify habits that cause habitat degradation. Nor, given the constraints that poverty imposes, should the poor be held morally culpable for the degradation they cause. It is from the rich—those to whom much has been given —that much is required. The global differential between rich and poor requires that we design policies to restrain the overconsumption of the rich and quite different policies designed to empower enhanced, but ecologically more appropriate, consumption for the global poor.

Different countries have different sorts of "occasions of ecological sin." So it is incumbent upon rich nations to curtail their own ecologically unsustainable practices if they are ever to have any credibility when they call on poorer countries to change their policies, such as when the United States and Europe ask Brazil to halt its development of the Amazon region or call on India to stabilize its population size or on African nations to protect habitat for wild animal preserves. No nation by itself can insure global ecological security; therefore, it is necessary that nations work together in coordinated efforts to achieve the goal.

While Brazil bears a heavy burden of responsibility for the current damage to the Amazon ecosystem, and Japan bears responsibility for overhunting whales in the Pacific, the United States clearly bears a heavy responsibility as the planet's highest emitter of greenhouse gases, which help push climate change concerns. The United States will have little ability to provide ecological leadership in the world if it fails to restrict its own surging fossil fuel consumption rates. Since it is impossible to cover the range of policies needed to promote ecological sustainability, I will simply illustrate how one policy—fuel taxes—might help resolve the problem of fuel overuse in the United States.

Currently the United States, with roughly 5 percent of the global population, contributes almost 20 percent of global greenhouse gas emissions and 23 percent of global carbon emissions.[19] The average U.S. citizen pushes climate change roughly 17 times more than the average Indian, 7.6 times the average Chinese citizen, and 13 times the average Brazilian. While in 1995 U.S. per capita tons of carbon emission equaled roughly 5.3 tons annually, the average per capita use for Germany was 2.9 tons, for China 0.7 tons, and for India 0.3 tons annually.[20] The average per capita use for Europe, a continent with a standard of living similar to the United States', is roughly half the U.S. rate.

One important factor in pushing high U.S. fuel consumption is the way Americans have, since World War II, allowed our daily transportation and commuting patterns to become dominated by the automobile. Globally, auto use is surging, but nowhere has the auto come to dominate a society as much as in the United States. While the world's motor vehicle fleet totals almost 650 million, 198 million of these—over 30 percent—were registered in the United States in 1996.[21] European rates of fuel use are much lower in good part because European countries have used high gas tax rates as disincentives for auto usage and the suburban growth patterns that make high auto usage a necessity. Where many European countries levy a tax per gallon of gas around the $2.50 mark, the current United States' gas tax (state and federal) averages only thirty-six cents per gallon—one of the industrialized world's lowest rates. European countries also have continued to subsidize public transit to encourage high ridership and high urban density patterns to help keep people from opting for high rates of auto usage.[22]

The rise of the American suburbs after World War II is directly tied to the rise in auto ownership and the decline of governmental support for more energy-efficient, ecologically friendly mass transit systems. The auto is commonly said to overcome distance via its high speed, but, in fact, the auto has been the creator of distance, for only with the auto and highway system would individuals choose to buy homes, or developers choose to build malls, factories, and housing developments, at the edge of the suburban ring. It is the auto and the highway system that make suburban low-density sprawl patterns possible, and these in turn make high rates of auto usage and fossil fuel consumption a daily necessity.

Some environmentalists have suggested that, in addition to focusing on the goods and resources we derive from nature, we should expand our attention to the full range of services that natural systems provide us. Where we have tended to focus on forests in terms of resource management to maximize lumber output sustained over time, we need also to attend to and attempt to monetize the value of the soil erosion mitigation and watershed flood control offered by the forests' network of root structure and undergrowth. Likewise, we need to remember that forest growth increases biomass, which functions as a sink for pulling carbon dioxide out of the atmosphere and sequestering it in tree growth, thus working against global warming build-up. Complex and critical services are provided by soil systems, by pollinators—honey bees and other insects—and by natural pest control relations. As Gretchen Daily notes, the earth's natural "life-support systems" require protection and this requires "that their value be explicitly incorporated into decision-making frameworks" to help guide individual, national, and global behavior.[23] Only through incorporating the value of ecological costs and services can we develop an adequate ecological hermeneutics to guide our assessments of responsible decision and action.

Ecologists accordingly are trying to suggest ways to calculate the hidden social and ecological costs of different human activities and to impose taxes on certain products and services to get the actual price paid to reflect more accurately the real costs of that consumption. This approach of using taxes to help draw people's attention to genuine ecological costs of common consumptive activities, often dubbed "green taxation," is increasingly being explored in discussions in the United States about how to reduce high American rates of fossil fuel use.

Increasing fuel costs via tax additions would immediately function as a disincentive for driving and an incentive to explore alternative transit modes or to purchase more fuel efficient cars with higher gas mileage. A fifty cent gas tax increase per gallon of gas has been estimated to cost the average American family roughly $550 per year and to generate about $46 billion per year of federal revenue, money that could be used to increase the extension of adequate mass transit systems throughout urban and suburban America.[24] Such fuel tax additions could help change the whole default system that now encourages suburban sprawl via edge development and low-density zoning and the need for parking spaces surrounding every commercial establishment. Gas taxes would shift incentives for investment back to retrofit suburban and urban regions and to increase land-use density along bus and rail lines.[25] It would also help generate political pressure to build and sustain better mass transit options that would allow Americans to begin to reduce high rates of auto usage and consequent high levels of fossil fuel consumption and carbon dioxide emission.

Concerns for social justice, which are central to both philosophical and religious ethics, must also play a central role in the development of green taxation schemes. Gas and energy taxes are regressive, for they fall with equal weight on the rich and poor. Disproportionate burdens on the poor and middle class can be balanced by, for example, progressively increasing the overall income tax reduction rates on those classes. Hence, while some voters might see their fuel costs go up, those with the most limited resources could see their overall tax burden held constant or reduced. Many worry also that increasing gas taxes would lay a disproportionate burden on the inner-city poor who must drive far for employment opportunities. Low gas taxes, however, have been one of the prime factors in encouraging decades of edge development in the suburban periphery, which has in turn pulled investment and job creation energies away from many inner-city districts. Higher gas taxes and shifts to better mass transit could well prompt a revitalization of inner-city regions, which could help bring jobs and neighborhood stability back to the urban poor.

A key difficulty with all green taxation schemes is their unpopularity with the general electorate (particularly in the United States and Canada) and thus their current political unfeasibility. Green taxation approaches are unpopular because they raise individuals' costs and raise elected officials fear of the voters' wrath. Public policy realism requires thinking through concrete steps that might help mobilize peoples' willingness to bear some economic costs for the sake of ecological sustainability. One step toward increasing popular support for green taxation is to couple such taxes with corresponding income tax reductions. Another step lies in examining analogous cases where people are persuaded that future risks are high enough to warrant buying insurance now to mitigate the potential threat of future loss.

The argument that we should not bear any economic sacrifice now for ecological insurance in the future loses force as more people gain a sense of the potential scale of the ecological threat looming ahead.

The Clash of Superpowers and the Moral Equivalent of War

Ecologically unsustainable rates of human population, economic production, and consumption growth deserve recognition as among the central national and global security concerns in the century ahead. The Cold War conditioned many Americans to view security threats only as those posed by hostile nation-states, making it difficult for us to perceive threats that come in unfamiliar guise, such as climate change. Accordingly, national leaders find the American public willing year after year to accept the governments' spending of vast tax dollars on military preparedness but quite unwilling to pay taxes for ecological preparedness. While it has long been a standard assumption that security in the military sphere requires being prepared to handle the worst-case estimate of potential threat, in the environmental sphere today worst-case estimates of impact from climate change and biodiversity loss are dismissed as "doomsday" fantasizing, and the rosiest of projections are appealed to in order to justify delay, low levels of spending or commitment of resources, and policies of business as usual favoring short-term corporate, governmental, and electorate interests in sustaining the surging growth and high consumption agenda.

This asymmetry of threat recognition leads to a remarkable asymmetry in the application of the prudence principle. When the stakes are vastly high and outcomes uncertain, nations have historically opted to reduce risk even if that meant spending much for military defenses.[26] Because the stakes involved in ecological threat potentials are not yet broadly enough recognized, most electorates balk at increasing taxes or bearing other economic burdens to promote ecological and climate stability.

In public policy discussions the most potent appeal for top priority of response is an argument based on national security claims. By long-standing tradition, whenever a consensus emerges that a threat constitutes a genuine security risk, then citizens are expected to bear sacrifices willingly to deter such a danger. National security discourse remains a privileged national policy idiom for speaking about value, priority, and justified sacrifice, and it is critical that ecological security be framed in the center of national and global security considerations in the century ahead.

It helps to see how central ecological security is to national and global security concerns when we recognize that the global biosphere is a vast superpower. We are often told today that with the end of the Soviet Union, the United States stands as the world's only superpower. However, superpowers need not always come packaged as nation-states. The planetary biosphere is the only primordial and foundational superpower. It is the material nexus that gives rise to all life and to all resources and energies that sustain life. It is the ultimate source of material and productive processes from which all the goods and services of the world's national economies are derived. When humanity's numbers were fewer and the scale of our economic activity smaller, our actions tended to be easily contained within the field of immense productive energies of the planetary ecosystem. But over the course of the last century the fiftyfold expansion of the global economy and the tripling of human population has begun to cause increasing harm and degradation to the global ecosphere.

Nature is a superpower in another sense, too. As the ecological sciences are now tracking, nature has, in a manner of speaking, a retaliatory capacity against human ecological irresponsibility.[27] This can be seen when deforestation promotes soil erosion crippling a community's agriculture, when CFC emissions lead to ozone depletion and increases in skin cancer rates, and when greenhouse gas emissions increase threats of climate change and extreme weather. Even in its vulnerability, nature retains massively strong biological, climatological, and chemical capacities of reaction to human actions which cross biospheric thresholds and upset critical balances. Nature's reactive capabilities to increasing rates of human abuse pose a significant threat of potentially high rates of human casualties caused by pollution, increasing skin cancer rates, and famine pushed by biodiversity loss, water shortage, climate shifting, and extreme weather events.

Only when enough citizens of each nation come to understand ecological degradation as posing direct threats to communal, national, and global security will they be able to impose sacrifices on themselves by passage of policies of sustainability.[28] Because environmental degradation has typically not yet been so recognized, ecological concerns regularly are trumped in national policy formation and resource allocation decisions by military security, economic growth, and job creation interests. In this regard, one problem with much of Christian ecologically oriented theology and ethics is that it stresses nature's emerging vulnerability and humanity's intimacy of relationship with nature, underplaying the massive strength of nature's reactions to human abuse. The refrain about nature's emerging fragility is not always well balanced with a similarly needed stress on nature's awesome power and humanity's vulnerability in the context of nature's demise. Humanity is said to hold stewardship over nature, but too little is said about nature's power over humanity.

In his 1910 essay "The Moral Equivalent of War," William James argued that although modern war must be jettisoned—he dismissed it as too gruesome, given the rise of modern weaponry—the practice of war sustains valuable "martial virtues" like courage, honor, discipline, and willingness for self-sacrifice, virtues that he hoped could be preserved by finding a moral substitute for war. James imagined this "moral equivalent" to lie in engaging the youth of the nations in a common effort "in the immemorial human warfare against nature."[29] He had in mind road building, tunnel making, canal digging, fishing, mining, and the like. James imagined this "war" as a bloodless enterprise, for he viewed nature as a passive sphere subject to human transformative agency.

As a new century begins we now know in ways that James could not that when we adopt a stance of war against nature, we clash with a system of energy that is not passive, but dynamic and potent. The ecological sciences are helping to inform us of the myriad ways damage to nature redounds back to cause damage, suffering, and death to humans. We now see that conflict with nature is the "moral equivalent of war" in ways that James did not anticipate. If we insist on adopting a stance of conflict with nature, there will be much carnage and many casualties, as in any war. Ecosystem degradation, species extinction, climate forcing, soil erosion, deforestation patterns, and similar trends are indicators highlighting the need for the moral equivalent of planetary peacemaking found in a turn to regional, national, and global policies of sustainability.[30]

While one of the greatest dramas of the twentieth century was the Cold War, the superpower clash between the United States and the

Soviet Union, it is likely that one of the greatest dramas of the twenty-first century will be a similar superpower clash. This time, however, the clash will be between the surging growth agenda of the global economy and the limits and balances of the global biosphere, and this clash will put us at war with ourselves as human desires for ever-increasing consumption and production collide with ecological thresholds necessary to sustain human (and nonhuman) well-being. Policies of planetary peacemaking must be enacted to restrain global population and energy consumption growth, increasing habitat degradation, and climate change potentials. Enacting such policies is the way the earth's peoples "make peace with the planet" and therefore should be of central concern to the world's religious communities.[31]

In his classic essay "The Land Ethic," Aldo Leopold suggested that ethics is best thought of as "a kind of community instinct in-the-making."[32] This implies that a core challenge for religious communities is to help inculcate in their members a vivid sense of their simultaneous participation in different communities of varying scale —regional, national, religious, and planetary communities—and of the distinct loyalties and responsibilities owed to each. Like other religions of the world, Christianity is an intergenerational community and thus a vehicle sustaining deep memory and powers of anticipation. It, therefore, is able to help educate people about nature's fragility and nature's potent retaliatory capacity against human abuse by highlighting the need for gratitude for the gifts given to us by previous generations—both human and nonhuman—and the need for responsibility and loyalty extended to generations yet to be. Despite particular differences of belief, almost all religious communities enshrine traditional affirmations that meaning in life is less tied to unfettered material accumulation than to sacrifice for the community's good and compassionate service to others. Christianity can affirm in common with most other religions, as Max Oelschlaeger has noted, a shared responsibility to "care for creation."[33] And the institutional means of extending such care lies in the enactment of regional, national, and global policies which restrain ecological un-sustainability and promote environmental stability and security.

Notes

I would like to thank Tracy Pintchman of Loyola University of Chicago and Preston Williams of Harvard University for their many helpful suggestions regarding this essay. Also I must thank Walt Grazer and the United States Catholic Conference for their support of my initial effort to write about ethics and climate change concerns.

1. Edward O. Wilson, "Is Humanity Suicidal?" *New York Times Magazine,* 30 May 1993, 24. This is reprinted in Edward O. Wilson, *In Search of Nature* (Washington, D.C.: Island Press, 1996), 183–99.

2. Ibid., 24, 29.

3. Lester R. Brown et al., *State of the World 1998* (New York: W. W. Norton, 1998), 174.

4. See John H. Cushman, Jr., "CNN Halts Companies' Ads Attacking Administration on Warming Treaty," *New York Times,* 3 October 1997, Midwest edition. See generally Ross Gelbspan's fine book, *The Heat Is On: The High Stakes Battle over Earth's Threatened Climate* (Reading, Mass.: Addison-Wesley Publishing, 1997); David Helvarg, *The War against the Greens* (San Francisco: Sierra Club Books, 1994); and Andrew Rowell, *Green Backlash: Global Subversion of the Environmental Movement* (London and New York: Routledge, 1996).

5. Al Gore, *Earth in the Balance: Ecology and the Human Spirit* (Boston: Houghton Mifflin Company, 1992), 182–87. See also Herman E. Daly, *Beyond Growth: The Economics of Sustainable Development* (Boston: Beacon Press, 1996), 40–42; and Robert Repetto, "Accounting for Environmental Assets," *Scientific American* 466, no. 6 (July 1992): 94–100.

6. See Hans Jonas, *The Imperative of Responsibility: In Search of an Ethics for the Technological Age,* trans. Hans Jonas in collaboration with David Herr (Chicago: University of Chicago Press, 1984), 4. For an important critique of Christian anthropocentrism, see James M. Gustafson, *Ethics from a Theocentric Perspective,* vol. 1 (Chicago: University of Chicago Press, 1981), 86–113.

7. Immanuel Kant, *Foundations of the Metaphysics of Morals*, trans. Lewis White Beck (Indianapolis: Bobbs-Merrill, 1959), 46.

8. H. Richard Niebuhr, *Radical Monotheism and Western Culture* (New York: Harper Torchbooks, 1960), 51, 11.

9. Ibid., 56–60. See also Thomas Berry, *The Dream of the Earth* (San Francisco: Sierra Club Books, 1988), 126, where he critiques the dominant "sectarian" move in Christian theology with its "intensive preoccupation with the personality of the Savior, with the interior spiritual life of the faithful, and with the salvific community."

10. James M. Gustafson, *Varieties of Moral Discourse: Prophetic, Narrative, Ethical, and Policy* (Grand Rapids, Mich.: Calvin College and Seminary, 1988), 7–14, 19–21, 39–42, 46–47.

11. Berry, *Dream of the Earth,* 105.

12. Ibid., 11.

13. James A. Nash, *Loving Nature: Ecological Integrity and Christian Responsibility* (Nashville: Abingdon Press, 1991), 143.

14. Robert McAfee Brown, *Religion and Violence* (Philadelphia: Westminster Press, 1973), 34–37. See also Steven Bede Scharper, *Redeeming the Time: A Political Theology of the Environment* (New York: Continuum, 1997).

15. See Nash, *Loving Nature*.

16. On environmental ethics as an extension of the moral concerns of liberalism, see Roderick Frazier Nash, *The Rights of Nature: A History of Environmental Ethics* (Madison: University of Wisconsin Press, 1989), 3–32, 55–86. On heightened impact of ecological degradation on the poor, see Tom Athanasiou, *Divided Planet: The Ecology of Rich and Poor* (Boston: Little, Brown, 1996). On the impact of global warming on the poor of developing nations, see the report by the Intergovernmental Panel on Climate Change, *Climate Change 1995: Impacts, Adaptations, and Mitigation of Climate Change: Scientific-Technical Analyses,* ed. Robert T. Watson et al. (Cambridge: Cambridge University Press, 1996), 24–25, 33.

17. See Pierre Bourdieu, *Outline of a Theory of Practice,* trans. Richard Nice (Cambridge: Cambridge University Press, 1977), 78–95.

18. Alan Durning, *How Much Is Enough? The Consumer Society and the Future of the Earth* (New York: W. W. Norton, 1992), 23–36.

19. See Nicholas D. Kristof, "Japan's Goal of Leading on Climate Is in Doubt," *New York Times,* 5 October 1997; Robert B. Sample, Jr., "Mr. Clinton and Global Warming," *New York Times,* 6 October 1997; and Lester R. Brown et al., *Vital Signs 1997* (New York: W. W. Norton, 1997), 58.

20. Lester R. Brown et al., *State of the World 1997* (New York: W. W. Norton, 1997), 11. See also Klaus M. Leisinger and Karin Schmitt, *All Our People: Population Policy with a Human Face* (Washington, D.C.: Island Press, 1994), 79–83.

21. See *Motor Vehicle Facts and Figures 1997* (Detroit: American Automobile Manufactures Association, 1997), 2; Steve Nadis and James J. MacKenzie, *Car Trouble* (Boston: Beacon Press, 1993); and Brown et al., *Vital Signs 1997,* 74–75.

22. Christopher Flavin and Seth Dunn, "Responding to the Threat of Climate Change," in Brown et al., *State of the World 1998,* 115, 117–19.

23. *Nature's Services: Societal Dependence on Natural Ecosystems,* ed. Gretchen C. Daily (Washington, D.C.: Island Press, 1997), 372.

24. David Hage and Sara Collins, "Driving Down the Deficit," *U.S. News and World Report,* 18 January 1993, 58–60.

25. See my article, "The Auto and the Earthly City: Gas Taxes and Civic Renewal," *Theology and Public Policy* 5, no. 1 (summer 1993): 15–28.

26. For example, a recent study concludes that since 1940 the United States has spent trillions of dollars just on building and maintaining its nuclear arsenal. See Matthew L. Wald, "Total Cost of U.S. Nuclear Arms Is Put at $5.48 Trillion," *New York Times,* 1 July 1998.

27. See my essay, "Contesting Energies: The Biosphere, Economic Surge, and the Ethics of Restraint," in *The Challenge of Global Stewardship: Roman Catholic Responses,* ed. Maura A. Ryan and Todd David Whitmore (Notre Dame, Ind.: University of Notre Dame Press, 1997), 119–34.

28. On ecological security issues see Norman Myers, *Ultimate Security: The Environmental Basis of Political Stability* (New York: W. W. Norton, 1993); Michael Renner, *Fighting for Survival: Environmental Decline, Social Conflict, and the New*

Age of Insecurity (New York: W. W. Norton, 1996); and Jessica Tuchman Mathews, "The Environment and International Security," in *World Security: Trends and Challenges at Century's End,* ed. Michael T. Klare and Todd David Whitmore (New York: St. Martin's Press, 1991), 362–80.

29. William James, "The Moral Equivalent of War," in *War and Morality,* ed. Richard A. Wasserstrom (Belmont, Calif.: Wadsworth Publishing, 1970), 11, 13.

30. See Barry Commoner, *Making Peace with the Planet* (New York: Pantheon Books, 1990), 3–18.

31. Ibid.

32. Aldo Leopold, *A Sand County Almanac* (New York: Ballantine Books, 1966), 239.

33. Max Oelschlaeger, *Caring for Creation: An Ecumenical Approach to the Environmental Crisis* (New Haven: Yale University Press, 1994).

Response to William C. French

PRESTON N. WILLIAMS

I would like to thank William French for his well-reasoned and careful attention to some of the considerations we must have in mind as we act and encourage others to act on matters related to ecology and public policy.

I hope, with William French, that we will survive the sixth great extinction spasm, and I believe with him that in order to do that we must give greater religious significance to nature. I, like him, would affirm that the effort to prevent the extinction should appeal to anthropocentric interests because it is, in my view, humans, not nature, that are concerned with their own survival as well as that of nature.

African Americans, and I think a number of other modern and postmodern people, have not lost a concern for the world of nature. Howard Thurman points this out in many of his works, among them *Deep River*. Consequently, I would, like French, not only appeal to anthropocentric interest, but w fWld seek to relate these interests more clearly to the reasons why most persons and groups should be involved in the effort to prevent a sixth great extinction.

French's paper properly begins with an underscoring of the several levels at which policy needs to be made: communal, national, global. This is important and needs further development because different strategies will have to be employed in order to create effective policies. "Not in my background" is present at everyone of these levels, and the ethical and religious orientation must be sensitive to them. More important, it needs to be sensitive to those peoples in Brazil, Asia, and elsewhere who, like African Americans, have nature as a part of their religious experience and find that experience to be compatible with notions of transcendence and a personal God. How one reaches these people and how one persuades them must be related to an understanding of Christianity shaped by more than Western cultural traditions. The complexity of religious understanding and policy making at these several levels must not be underestimated.

The policy problem, then, is how to influence by means of Christian theology and churches politicians in Brazil, India, North America, Europe, and Africa. This can be done, I believe, only in a marginal manner and through the coercive powers of such bodies as human rights groups, ecological organizations, and the several units associated with the United Nations. Such action or policy making, even if ecologically beneficial to the poor and oppressed, will not spur greater participation by the poor in efforts to restrain in large ways the exploitation of nature. Nonetheless, attempts to learn more about the belief systems and practices of the poor, the blacks, the Hispanics, the Native Americans, and others and the introduction of such understandings into the formation of public policy will be wiser and more useful than seeking to change the vocabulary of Western Christians in respect to reward and blame. The latter may help to develop the character of a few but it will contribute little, I think, to public policy.

The difficulty here is related not only, as French points out, to the reluctance of religion to deal in policy debates, but also to the fact that successful policy making occurs only when prophetic discourse, with its passion and indictment, and ethical discourse, with its weighing of general value claims and principle, drive and direct policy making. Few theologians, pastors, and churches will be able to marshal these resources. The consequence of their failure most likely will be the heavy-handed paternalism of some persons of good will and intention.

I agree, then, with French that the churches' involvement in policy making will be general and vague—this is better than no policy at all—not because policy making is abstract and cool, but rather because it must embody both prophetic and ethical discourse as well as concreteness and specificity.

We, and French, need also to reflect a bit more on why the African Americans and the poor have not lost wholly a concern with the world of nature. The absence of such reflection is due, I suspect, to the fact that Thomas Berry and some ecologists have not spoken fully about nature. Nature not only nurtures and supports us, it also crushes and destroys us. The notion of survival of the fittest accompanies that of nurturance and sustenance. The natural world is not only the primary revelation of the Divine but also that which we call evil. It is the poor and oppressed, whether in Brazil, India, or the United States of America, whether black, Hispanic, or Native American, that are most related to these two faces of nature and thus cannot forget nature. Their embeddedness in nature most often prevents them from realizing their human fulfillment as persons. Too frequently they are not only related to nature and animals; they are also regarded in like manner. Life is sustained for briefer periods of time and under conditions of great hardship and pain.

Vigorous efforts are needed, therefore, to extend justice to the oppressed and neglected humans as well as to our biotic neighbor. Failure to do both may result in increasing the gap between the rich and the poor and further diminishing our efforts to forestall the sixth great extinction. A concern for racial and ethnic diversity must accompany our concern for biodiversity and world religious diversity.

I agree with French that, properly understood, a biocentric model is not antihuman and should not undercut concerns for human rights and social justice. The necessity for this dual emphasis needs to be stressed by theologians and policy makers in this area, especially at a time when notions of justice are being eroded by the increasing stress upon market orientations.

I applaud the effort to make the reporting of the GNP more sophisticated. The real cost of growth in our society and the world needs to be understood. At the same time ecologists (and I seek to be one) need to be aware of the burdens placed upon the poor by the limitations to growth and the utilization of consumption taxes. The rich need to pay their fair share and ecological policy should in some immediate ways benefit the living poor, blacks, Hispanics, and Native Americans. If it can be made to do that, then these persons might see more clearly the face of God in nature and work to help the Sustainer of nature and their own person.

Christianity, Economics, and Ecology

JOHN B. COBB, JR.

Christian thinkers and church leaders have come a long way in recognizing the importance and intrinsic value of all creatures. The declaration of the 1982 Vancouver Assembly of the World Council of Churches on the integrity of creation was a milestone. Many denominations have made fine statements. In gatherings of concerned Christians there is considerable agreement that we should repent of our anthropomorphism and our dualism. There is also a growing sense of urgency about changing the direction our society is going.

Given this remarkable movement toward a new consensus, the question arises why so little real change results. Why does the voice of the church sound so uncertain in relation to the critical environmental issues of the day? No doubt one answer is that our entrenched habits do not yield easily to the implications of the new understanding. Another answer is that we Christians share with society as a whole the short-term selfishness that we deplore.

But the problem is deeper than that. Even Christians who cease to be anthropocentric and dualistic, and recognize the intrinsic value of nonhuman creatures, often remain committed to the technology that drives the progressive deterioration of the natural world. As Lynn White noted, the development of technology in the West, even during what are called the "Dark Ages," shows how the understanding of Christianity led to the exploitation of nature.[1] The positive support of technology by Western Christians continues to this day even among those who are ecologically concerned.

One of White's followers, David F. Noble, has recently published a book, *The Religion of Technology,* in which he traces the history of this Christian teaching and its transformation into a secular faith. Augustine described the technology of his time as an astonishing achievement, but he stressed that it related only to mundane matters. It was of no help in spiritual matters.[2] Perhaps the first signs of a change came with Benedict in the early sixth century. He "made the practical arts and manual labor in general vital elements of monastic devotion, alongside liturgical praise of God and the meditative reading of Scripture, . . . and it was this overriding spiritual motivation that inspired such unprecedented performance."[3]

> Charlemagne imposed the Benedictine Rule on all religious houses in his realm, and his son Louis the Pious, an earnest advocate of useful innovation, was the original patron of the monastic-reform movement which was to sweep through Europe in the tenth and eleventh centuries. Under first imperial, and then feudal and papal auspices, the Benedictines eventually turned their religious devotion to the useful arts into a medieval industrial revolution, pioneering in the avid use of windmills, watermills, and new agricultural methods. In the process, the monastic elevation of technology as means toward transcendent ends gained wider currency.[4]

During the same period there was a change in the understanding of the *imago Dei*. In the patristic period it had been seen as purely spiritual. In the writings of the ninth-century philosopher John Scotus Erigena,

> the notion of image-likeness for the first time incorporated the corporeal—the body and the external senses—as a necessary correlate of reason and spirit. If the spirit required the corporeal, in this new view, the corporeal was in turn spiritualized, and matter became linked with the transcendent. It is likely that the Carolingian advances in, and heightened regard for, the useful arts reflected and reinforced such a transformed vision of the image-likeness of God to man.[5]

Erigena called the useful arts "the mechanical arts," and he gave them equal standing with the classically established liberal arts. His term became standard by the twelfth century. Erigena argued that the mechanical arts were among the original endowments of humankind, so that the effort to recover our original nature entailed their development. Noble quotes him as saying that these arts are "man's links with the Divine, their cultivation a means to salvation."[6]

Technology is in many ways the link between economics and ecology. Terminologically, they are much more directly related. One is the *nomos* of the *oikos,* and the other the *logos* of the *oikos.* The difference, terminologically, is that economics is more the practical ordering of the household and ecology is its structure. One might expect the former, as the practice, to follow from, or at least be consistent with, the more theoretical *logos.* But, as we know, the former has evolved into a study of how to increase market activity and the latter into a study of the way different species of living things interact with one another. They have developed quite independently and, until recently, with little thought about their relationships. Their implications often appear to be in conflict.

One main function of technology is the transformation of the natural into the artificial. In this role there is an obvious tension with ecology. Yet the line is far from sharp. When a bird builds a nest it employs technology to this end, but we consider this natural. Human actions that adapt the natural environment to make it more supportive of human life are also natural. Ecology does not exclude technology.

At some point, however, human technology ceased being part of nature and began to change nature into an artificial world. One plausible place to draw a line is with the domestication of plants and animals, that is, with the beginning of farming and herding. The biblical story draws a line between the pre-fallen life of gathering in the Garden and the farming and herding that followed.

Locally, these technologies made possible a growth of population which in turn led to unsustainable practices that began the process of degrading the land. The ecology of the Middle East has been disrupted for thousands of years. But until recent times, on a global scale, wilderness continued to dominate. We should not underestimate the ecological havoc wrought in previous centuries, but it is the century now coming to an end, with its tremendous technological achievements and global population growth, that has transformed local destructiveness into global destructiveness.

If Christians recognize the destruction associated with technological advance, why do we continue to support it? First, we take the meeting of human needs very seriously; we rejoice as people become more prosperous. One cause around which Christians of diverse theological positions can rally in the United States is the reduction of poverty. This means that Christians are committed to the production of sufficient goods to meet the needs and satisfy many of the desires of the growing global population. We also call for economic policies that provide employment as widely as possible.

Since overall economic growth seems to be the easiest way to attain full employment and the goods needed by the poor, Christians are easily persuaded to support policies that bring about such growth. Since this is the province and goal of economists, Christians supply a natural constituency of support for them. Concern about the ecological consequences of such growth is usually subordinated to concern for the poor.

A second reason Christians find it difficult to criticize the policies that lead to the devastation of the earth follows from this closeness of our values to those of the economists. We have noted our shared commitment to technology. Economists point out that the other main element in the industrial system that has so greatly increased production is organization. Whereas previously artisans individually took raw materials and transformed them into humanly useful artifacts, industrialization involved giving one highly specialized job to each worker. The same number of people organized in this way could produce far more goods.

Organization extended far more widely. One large factory could produce more goods with fewer workers than several small ones. The unneeded workers could produce other goods. Thus, through economies of scale total production rose. This required reorganizing society into larger markets. These became national, then international, and now global. Hence, policies aimed at growth consistently break down barriers to the free movement of capital and goods. Although this is destructive of the communities Christians prize, as well as of the environment, we share the goal of meeting material needs and, hence, find it difficult to be critical.

Third, alongside technological and economic advance, another major reason for the acceleration of destruction is growth in population. Christians have always celebrated human life and taught its sanctity. We have celebrated the family as the context for bringing children into the world and nurturing them. We have valued large families.

These teachings, and similar ones in other traditions, have had a positive social and evolutionary role in most of human history.

Without them, whole communities might have vanished. But with advances in medical science and technology, the same teachings have supported the population explosion and placed obstacles in the way of slowing it down. For example, there is virtually unanimous support among contemporary Christians for making modern medical care available to everyone, with particular efforts to prevent the death of infants and young children. But there are still many thoughtful and progressive Christians who belittle the population problem and oppose most practical efforts at control. Saving human life has deep roots in our heritage and in our psyches. Limiting human life does not.

For reasons such as these, we must acknowledge that the overall weight of Christian opinion and effort supports policies that lead to the continuing degradation of the earth. But this does not mean that Christians are happy to find themselves in this position. We articulate our commitment to the preservation of the natural world at the same time that our better-established commitments indirectly support actions that destroy it.

Our first line of response is to turn for help to the technology that is so extensively responsible for the problem. Our technology developed in a time when human labor was short and natural resources and sinks for pollution were plentiful. As a result, technology's effect has been to exhaust resources and increase pollution. The situation is now reversed. Globally, labor is plentiful and resources and sinks are scarce. Today, what should be conserved is nature. The productivity we should aim to maximize is not that of labor but that of resources.

Technology, therefore, has a new task—to produce sufficient useful goods while using fewer resources. Most urgently, we must learn to supply the same amount of goods with much less use of fossil fuels and other sources of energy. Since the production processes developed when fossil fuels seemed inexhaustible were quite inefficient in their use of energy, there is room for enormous improvement along these lines, especially in the United States. And since this does not lead to any reduction in the availability of goods and services, Christians can support this shift without hesitation. Amory and Hunter Lovins have given extraordinary leadership in this regard.

If the industrialized world moves vigorously in this direction, it may develop forms of production that can be employed also in the third world. That may make possible increasing production dramatically without the catastrophes that are otherwise foreseeable. For example, a modern communications system can now be created without the use of telephone poles and metal wires. This is, for the most part, what is meant by the sustainable development we desire.

A second step is to construct individual buildings and whole cities in such a way as to require much less use of energy and other scarce resources. Buildings can be constructed so that very little energy is required for heating and cooling, and this energy can be provided by the sun alone. Cities can be constructed in such a way that private automobiles become superfluous. Indeed, Paolo Soleri has shown that they can function without any form of motor transportation at all.

A third step is to reduce our use of virgin materials. The part of this that is furthest advanced now is recycling paper, plastics, and metals. In some countries there have also been significant efforts to reduce packaging. A second feature would be to shift from the throwaway style, into which we have been drawn so far, back to one of repairing. This would be connected with changes in manufacturing design and franchising that would make repairs easier and reduce the pressure to update. It would also require changes in attitude toward clothing that would reduce the need to have elaborate wardrobes and would make the wearing of repaired clothes acceptable.

A fourth step is to develop sustainable forms of producing food and other agricultural products. Much is happening in this sphere. Organic methods are being revived along with less tillage. The Land Institute under the leadership of Wes Jackson is seeking long-term solutions through the substitution of perennials for the annual grains on which humanity is so dependent.

A fifth step would involve influencing land use by a change in eating habits. Some land is well-suited to grazing animals for meat consumption, and the meat thereby produced is healthful. Some land is well-suited to grain production, and this can feed many people when directly consumed. Unfortunately, much grain is now fed to cattle, and much grazing land is being converted to grains. This results in food shortages, unhealthful meat, and the degradation of the land. We can help by restricting ourselves to grass-fed animals, even if this means a considerable reduction of meat in our diets.

A sixth step, however, would be the renewal of an ancient Christian virtue—the willingness to make personal sacrifices for the sake of the well-being of others. In this case, the others are all the living creatures that share the earth with us. Personal sacrifices can take the form of withdrawal from our consumer-oriented society on a personal basis. More important on a global scale is the willingness of those of us who already participate in affluence to forego increase (or even to accept a decrease) in our income and wealth in favor of allowing any further increase in goods and services to go to those in need. In short, the major expression of personal sacrifice will be on the part of the affluent and will take the form of supporting public policies that re-distribute income and wealth.

If we have consensus on the desirability of such moves, what steps can be taken to achieve them? Probably the one that will be most effective in the short run and has the best chance of gaining Christian support is changing tax policies. The highly regressive sales tax and payroll tax (social security) should be replaced by taxes on the use of those things that are most scarce. For example, oil should be taxed heavily. This would make benign sources of energy competitive and speed their development. The situation with minerals that are growing scarce is the same. Similarly, where forests are being unsustainably used, their exploitation should be taxed. And taxes should discourage unsustainable exploitation of agricultural land and fisheries.

Alongside resource taxes would be pollution taxes. We could cal-culate the social cost of pollution and charge polluters accordingly. This would make the reduction of pollution economical and direct technology more strongly toward that reduction.

As the cost of conventional sources of energy rose, building homes and even cities that required little use of these would become more attractive. Even if initial costs were somewhat higher, the savings would become apparent in a few years. As other raw materials rose in price, repair and recycling also would become more obviously profitable.

A common objection is that the poor cannot afford to pay more for energy and for other resources. Some of those who raise the objection do not oppose the existing regressive taxes that could be replaced by resource and pollution taxes. The effect of the proposed shift would be that the poor would pay less in taxes and for some of their purchases but more for others. In general, it would ease their burden rather than worsen it. Nevertheless, if we are genuinely concerned for the poor, and as Christians we must be, other steps can be taken.

Income taxes were originally introduced for redistributive purposes. Only the rich paid them. We could return to this system, removing all income taxes from the poor and the middle class. We could also adopt a negative income tax for those falling below certain income levels. The redistributive use of taxes is quite possible. It requires a national will to which Christians should be contributing.

Another important change in the tax system would be to stop taxing buildings and improvements and to tax only the land. Removal of taxes on improvements would encourage new building and repairing existing buildings. A heavy tax on land would deter land speculation and lead to more efficient use. Henry George and his followers argue that profits on land belong to the community as a whole since they result from population shifts rather than from work on the part of owners. They believe that if society received this income from rising land values, other taxes could be greatly reduced. They also believe that this policy change would improve the lot of the poor.[7]

Tax and budgetary policies can make some contribution to slowing population growth as well. Taxes on resource use and on land can provide funds to ensure security in retirement for all. This can reduce the need for offspring in countries where such social security is not now in place. But many other changes in the social and economic systems are required in those countries whose populations are still growing rapidly. The most important change is probably in the status of women and in their access to roles in society other than motherhood.

If total population and per capita consumption continue to rise, then measures to make the use of natural resources more efficient and less polluting can, at best, prevent the increase of pressure on the earth system. But that does not suffice. We are already well beyond the limits of sustainable use. We must slow both population growth and unnecessary increase in per capita consumption.

It is at this point that, for the sake of the health of the planet, Christians should critique the dominant economic practices and the theories that support them.[8] Since these practices and theories are oriented to the promotion of economic growth, we can do so only if we ourselves give up our addiction to economic growth. This is both a personal matter of internalizing Christian values supportive of frugality and an intellectual matter of finding ways of achieving Christian goals apart from overall economic growth.

A distinction is important here between growth as such and policies aimed to achieve it. Growth of many kinds is benign and desirable. Much of this growth is economic. Economic growth as such is not the enemy of ecology. To adopt policies directly designed to stop growth or reverse it could have horrible consequences both for humanity and for the rest of the natural world.

But while many kinds of growth, including many kinds of economic growth, are desirable, aiming at economic growth in general leads to policies that are destructive both for humanity and for the rest of the natural world. Growth-oriented policies aim to increase the productivity of labor, break down community barriers to the global market, and give free rein to technology. Furthermore, they require growth in countries that are already affluent at more or less the same rate as growth in countries that desperately need it.

Christians should distinguish between the specific goals that we cannot give up and the generalized economic growth that calls for measures destructive of human community and the natural environment. Devotion to the latter is too much like the worship of Mammon to be acceptable. And it is this worship of Mammon that is destroying our planetary biosystem as well as so many human communities.

The Christian goal identified earlier is that all people have the material means for a good life. Given a growing population, this does require a great deal of production. Accordingly, we have supposed that we must support overall economic growth as the means of meeting the recognized need. What we have been slow to recognize is that enormous overall global growth has been accompanied by an increase in the most degrading forms of poverty. Further, where there has been a decrease of poverty, this has not been accomplished by the policies aimed at growth. It has required policies aimed directly at the reduction of poverty.

These statements are often challenged. The World Bank, for example, agrees that it is important to have policies directed specifically to the reduction of poverty, but it claims that these can be effective only in the context of overall economic growth. And no doubt there are many places where a growing population can have sufficient goods for a healthy and happy life only with an increase in the supply of goods. There is certainly some correlation between the abundance of available goods and services and the relief of poverty. But instead of making the relief of poverty incidental to growth, growth should be incidental to the relief of poverty.

Especially since the collapse of the Soviet Union, most of the world has been organized, through structural adjustment and the

World Trade Organization, into a global market. The currently promoted Multilateral Agreement on Investments is designed to remove many of the remaining obstacles to the smooth functioning of this market. Most alternative experiments in development styles have been crushed. Hence, there are few examples of countries that have overcome poverty in a different way.

In any case, most poverty reduction outside the global market has been by authoritarian methods that Christians find unacceptable. The chief argument for growth-oriented policies as the means of overcoming poverty is that they reduce conflict and the need for compulsion by enabling all segments of society to gain.

Despite the paucity of examples of communities that have worked to overcome degrading poverty without adopting either growth-oriented policies or authoritarian compulsion, there are some. The most impressive in recent years has been the state of Kerala in India. Although the per capita income of Kerala has been no higher than that of India generally, Kerala has virtually wiped out hunger and homelessness. Infant mortality has decreased while population growth has been slowed. Reduced fertility is chiefly due to the education of women by women.

From our point of view, almost everyone in Kerala is poor. But the people of Kerala are probably, on the whole, as happy as the people of the United States. Far fewer are degraded by their poverty. Theirs is not the kind of poverty which Christians must commit themselves to overcoming.

Again, this does not mean that the people of Kerala should be denied economic growth. If this growth is shared by all instead of being concentrated in the hands of a few, and if it does not involve undue pressure on the environment, we could rejoice that the people had more of this world's goods. No doubt some such growth is possible.

Unfortunately, what is actually happening is that India as a nation has opted to join the global market after years of resistance. This has opened Kerala to "development" by transnational corporations. The remarkably successful experiment in popular democracy, political and economic, is threatened. But this should not discount the value of the model as an indication of what is possible.[9]

One very important need within the Christian community is to emphasize that the earth is God's creation, that we are part of that creation with special responsibilities for the rest of it, and that we find

God in and through it. In short, we need to repent of the theology that has allowed us to exploit the earth with little regard for its well-being, supposing ourselves somehow to stand above it or outside it. We are making some progress in these respects. Without much further advance, without changing habitual anthropocentric patterns of thinking and feeling, we will not have the context and grounding for challenging destructive theories and practices in the public world. The assumptions underlying these theories and practices are too much like our own.

In addition, if Christians are to carry forward our historic role of bringing our faith to bear on public policy, we must recover a sense of social responsibility and of the importance of social analysis. Black theologians, liberation theologians, and feminists, in different ways, have been encouraging us to move in this direction. Recently, more of them have come to recognize that this analysis should be related also to ecological issues. Those of us with strong ecological concerns must reach out to connect with this social analysis and deepen its ecological dimension. Together, perhaps, we can draw the church into serious reflection about the changes that would be required to save the earth from desolation.

The change that must be sought is the reconnection of economics and ecology according to their original meanings. If ecology is the study of the whole household, human and other, and if economics becomes the rule for ordering this household, and if our actual economic practices conformed to this rule, then humanity could flourish alongside other species in a sustainable way. This may be dismissed as a utopian fantasy, but the alternative is too horrible to accept.

Rethinking economic theory on the basis of ecology would not require the abandonment of all the achievements of current economics. It *would* require several deep changes in assumptions. These are, for the most part, analogous to changes that we Christians have been making in our theology only quite recently.

First, *Homo economicus* must be rethought as person-in-community. This means that what happens to communities as communities must enter into the measure of authentic economic progress as it now does not. If increasing production and consumption requires the destruction of community, this changed understanding of goals would often show that it is not economically positive.

Second, the community of which *Homo economicus* is a part must be understood as not limited to human beings. Human beings cannot flourish in isolation from other creatures. The degradation of the natural environment must count against human economic well-being, not only because eventually it reduces the possibility to produce, but also because it immediately impoverishes us. The improved state of other creatures will, then, be counted as an economic gain.

Third, the community extends into the future. There can be no discounting of the well-being of our grandchildren and great-grandchildren. This applies also to the future well-being of the other species with which we share the earth.

Fourth, every member of the larger community, human and non-human, has intrinsic value as well as value for others. This intrinsic value can be enriched through the provision of adequate goods and services but, beyond a certain point, added goods and services are a minor contribution to well-being. Mutually supportive and appreciative relations among individuals contribute more, as do the health and beauty of the natural surroundings.

Fifth, the diversity of creatures, human and nonhuman, adds to the aesthetic richness so important for the human beings who can appreciate it. This adds to the importance of avoiding the extinction of species and also of preserving cultural diversity, and varieties of styles and personalities within cultures. The tendencies to homogenization of crops and cultures that results from currently dominant economic practices should be ended.

Sixth, technology would be just as important in this context as in the current one. But it would become ecologically fitting,[10] and it would be used to minimize the cost to other species and to the earth of meeting human needs. It would also seek to reduce monotonous and routine work in favor of that which involves more human capacities.

Seventh, many of us Christians believe that God cares for all the creatures. God suffers with them and rejoices with them. This heightens the importance, for us, of working for the relief of suffering and the enrichment of enjoyment, especially among human beings, but among other creatures as well. It heightens also the importance of the diversity of life, since God appreciates that diversity far beyond what any human observer can know or understand.

What would a global economy based on such principles be like? We need wide discussion among Christians. My own judgment is that it would accent local economies, that is, that people in rather small areas would once again produce most of their own goods. This would not preclude trade, but for the most part local communities should not depend on trade for what is necessary for survival. Thus, while they would be free to trade, they would also be free not to trade if others manipulated the terms of trade against them.

Economic autonomy would make possible meaningful political autonomy. Ordinary people could play a significant role in shaping the policies that governed their lives. But local political autonomy can certainly not be absolute. No community can be allowed to solve its problems by exporting its pollution or by monopolizing the water of a river on which other communities downstream depend. Furthermore, the more powerful people in a locale cannot be allowed to impoverish or disenfranchise others. To do so is to deny community.

Local communities should be in community with their neighbors to constitute communities of communities. These larger communities should ensure that policies in each community support the well-being of other communities as well. They should also ensure that communities not be hijacked by powerful members at the expense of the weak. The degree of economic self-sufficiency would be greater at this larger level.

In this ordering of global society, communities of communities would also need to be in community with other such communities. This structure would continue up to the United Nations. The principle of subsidiarity would hold, that is, whatever issues can be dealt with at the smaller level will be assigned to that level. But in our world, there are more and more problems that can be treated only globally. The United Nations would need to be strengthened.

At present, the political order everywhere is expected to serve the economic one. This involves an enormous transfer of power to the great economic actors, chiefly the transnational corporations but also such international organizations as the International Monetary Fund (IMF), the World Bank, and the World Trade Organization (WTO). The fate of the earth is largely in the hands of organizations designed to serve stockholders or to encourage overall global economic growth. Some of them are somewhat responsive to concerns of environmentalists, but with the partial exception of the World Bank, saving the earth is not part of their basic mission.

One goal of the reorientation I am proposing is to bring the economic order back into the control of the political one. That would make it possible for ordinary people to participate in shaping the rules under which they live. There is no guarantee that people will care for their local environment, but the chances are greater than when such control is vested in institutions designed for quite different purposes. At the global level, this principle would lead to the subordination of the IMF, the World Bank, and the WTO to a strengthened United Nations, another reversal of current trends.

One claim that we Western Christians have made is that our faith has led us to go beyond a purely individualistic expression of love to social analysis and social ethics. A major disappointment I have felt during the time since White called our attention to our responsibility for the ecological crisis is that we have engaged in so little of this. We have reflected together about how our tradition calls on us to care for the earth. That is a great gain. But we have done much too little to consider the social and economic structures that lead to the continuing degradation of the planet and to move from such analysis to proposals for changed directions.

I do not believe that our failure results from anything inherent in the Christian faith. It results more from our acceptance of the progressive fragmentation of thought that has characterized the last two centuries. We are far too much in awe of "experts" in the several disciplines and far too reticent to examine their assumptions. We who believe so strongly in the interconnection of all things have an opportunity and a responsibility to break out of our compartmentalization of ecology and economics and to think through their relationship. We are called to offer a new vision that could draw the whole society toward a human way of being on this planet that is not only sustainable but also regenerative.

Notes

1. Lynn White, Jr., "The Historical Roots of Our Ecologic Crisis," *Science* 155 (10 March 1967): 1203–7.

2. David F. Noble, *The Religion of Technology: The Divinity of Man and the Spirit of Invention* (New York: Alfred A. Knopf, 1997), 11–12.

3. Ibid., 13.

4. Ibid., 13–14.

5. Ibid., 14–15.

6. Ibid., 17.

7. See Henry George, *Progress and Poverty* (New York: Random House, 1879).

8. See Carol Johnston, *The Wealth or Health of Nations* (Cleveland: Pilgrim Press, 1998), for a theologically informed critique of modern economic theory.

9. See William M. Alexander, "A Sustainable Development Process: Kerala," *International Journal of Sustainable Development,* May 1992: 52–58.

10. See Sim Van Der Ryn and Stuart Cowan, *Ecological Design* (Washington, D.C.: Island Press, 1996).

V. Christian Praxis for Ecology and Justice

Global Eco-Justice: The Church's Mission in Urban Society

LARRY RASMUSSEN

There is a middle-aged book by a city pastor who addressed the rancid conditions of a neighborhood on my little island. The neighborhood was "Hell's Kitchen," just west of Times Square. The pastor was Walter Rauschenbusch. The book is *Christianity and the Social Crisis,* published in 1907. A remarkable passage in that book leads off this chapter.

Centennial Spirits

The passage portrays a gathering of centennial spirits. Imagine yourself gathering at century's close, and listen in.

"When the Nineteenth Century died," Rauschenbusch writes, "its Spirit descended to the vaulted chamber of the Past, where the Spirits of the dead Centuries sit on granite thrones together."[1] There the Spirit of the Eighteenth Century asks for the mandated report: "Tell thy tale, brother. Give us word of the human kind we left to thee."[2] The Spirit of the Nineteenth Century obliges.

> I am the Spirit of the Wonderful Century. I gave men mastery over nature. Discoveries and inventions, which lighted the black space of the past like lovely stars, have clustered in the Milky Way of radiance under my rule. One man does by the touch of his hand what the toil of a thousand slaves never did. Knowledge has unlocked the mines of

wealth, and the hoarded wealth of to-day creates the vaster wealth of to-morrow. Man has escaped the slavery of Necessity and is free.

I freed the thoughts of men. They face the facts and know their knowledge is common to all. The deeds of the East at even are known in the West at morn. They send their whispers under the seas and across the clouds.

I broke the chains of bigotry and despotism. I made men free and equal. Every man feels the worth of his manhood.

I have touched the summit of history. I did for mankind what none of you did before. They are rich. They are wise. They are free.[3]

The Spirits of the dead Centuries sit in silence for awhile, "with troubled eyes." Eventually the Spirit of the First Century speaks. It poses a series of searing questions about the Nineteenth Century claims that "You have made men rich. . . . You have made men wise. . . . You have set them free. . . . You have made them one."[4] The Spirit of the Nineteenth Century listens carefully. Soon its head sinks to its breast. Then it says:

> Your shame is already upon me. My great cities are as yours were. My millions live from hand to mouth. Those who toil longest have the least. My thousands sink exhausted before their days are half spent. My human wreckage multiplies. Class faces class in sullen distrust. Their freedom and knowledge has only made men keener to suffer.[5]

Pensive, and now with troubled eyes of its own, the Spirit of the Nineteenth Century can only issue a request: "Give me a seat among you, and let me think why it has been so."[6]

Thinking "why it [was] so" for the Nineteenth Century was the work of many. Rauschenbusch and his colleagues in the Social Gospel joined to give voice in the final third of that century to what Ernst Troeltsch at about the same time called "the social question" or "the modern social problem." Troeltsch's own rendition of that is among the conclusions of his opus, *The Social Teaching of the Christian Churches* (1911).

> This social problem is vast and complicated. It includes the problem of the capitalist economic period and of the industrial proletariat created by it; and of the growth of militaristic and bureaucratic giant states; of the enormous increase in population, which affects colonial and world policy, of the mechanical technique, which produces enormous masses

of materials and links up and mobilizes the whole world for purposes of trade, but which also treats men and labour like machines.[7]

"The social question" or "the modern social problem" was the effort to name the exploitative character and massively dislocating effects of rapidly developing industrial society. Troeltsch himself found Marx's treatment descriptively powerful and persuasive even though he rejected Marx's conclusion that economic forces created religious consciousness in such degree that religious impulses could not be considered independent, culturally creative forces in their own right. But Marx had the upending and downside effects of modernity largely right. I cite a passage now one hundred fifty years old (1848):

> Modern industry has established the world market. . . .
>
> The need of a constantly expanding market for its products chases the bourgeoisie over the whole surface of the globe. It must nestle everywhere, settle everywhere, establish connections everywhere.
>
> The bourgeoisie has through its exploitation of the world market given a cosmopolitan character to production and consumption in every country. . . . In place of the old wants, satisfied by the productions of the country, we find new wants, requiring for their satisfaction the products of distant lands. . . . In place of the old local and national seclusion and self-sufficiency, we have intercourse in every direction, universal inter-dependence of nations. And as in material, so also in intellectual production.[8]

To Marx's mind this dynamism means a tumultuous, permanently destabilized world and an epoch that sets modernity apart from all preceding ones.

> Constant revolutionizing of production, uninterrupted disturbance of all social conditions, everlasting uncertainty and agitation distinguish the bourgeois epoch from all earlier ones. All fixed, fast-frozen relations . . . and opinions are swept away, all new-formed ones become antiquated before they can ossify. All that is solid melts into air, all that is holy is profaned, and man is at last compelled to face, with sober senses, his real conditions of life and his relations with his kind. . . . The bourgeoisie, during its rule of scarce one hundred years, has created more massive and more colossal productive forces than have all preceding generations together. Subjection of Nature's forces to man, machinery, application of chemistry to industry and agriculture, steam-navigation, railways, electric telegraphs, clearing of whole

continents for cultivation, canalization of rivers, whole populations conjured out of the ground—what earlier century had even a presentiment that such productive forces slumbered in the lap of social labor?[9]

Marx was wrong in his prophecy that the proletariat would dig the graves of the bourgeoisie and the coming socialist revolution would upend global capitalism itself. But he was right, as were Troeltsch and Rauschenbusch, that society was being atomized by the new economics of capitalism and that industrialized orders were humanly exploitative and alienating.

Still, the initial point here is that the last third of the nineteenth century gave voice to "the modern social problem," graphically reported by the otherwise triumphalist Spirit of the Nineteenth Century.

The social question persists. Indeed, the most extraordinary fact a century later may well be the simplest one; namely, that both the tally of unprecedented accomplishment and the litany of steady shame that Rauschenbusch penned could simply be repeated in 2007, adjusted for extremes at certain notable points. After all, the Twentieth Century both promised more than the Nineteenth and delivered on it. Goods and services increased fiftyfold. Lifetimes for millions, even billions, doubled. Equal numbers—millions and billions—were lifted from misery. Children lived better than their parents. Education became a common treasure, as did better health. And the gifts of innumerable cultures, together with the amazing discoveries of science and inventions of technology, moved far beyond their home borders and at higher velocity.

At the same time, the Nineteenth Century's domestic problems of industrializing nations have now gone global with a vengeance. Mass unemployment, the bumpy ride of casino capitalism's rapid-fire investment and mobile business, the spreading distance between rich and poor in a confrontation of limousine plenty and homelessness, and limited revenues for limitless needs now afflict most societies, albeit in drastically different proportion. Not least, violence has been both common and extreme, and the twentieth century stands as easily the deadliest to date—something like 187 million lives lost to the waste of warfare alone, not to mention intimate violence and periodic spasms of genocide.

So perhaps the gathering of centennial spirits now would only rachet up the tally of weal and woe this particular immigrant urban pastor witnessed as he walked the streets of his Hell's Kitchen parish.

Something Old, Something New

But I think not. There is a new dimension. The Spirit of the Twentieth Century would have to testify to a reality about which the spirits of previous dead centuries were silent. To put that into perspective, we must of needs return briefly to Rauschenbusch and the Social Gospel.

As noted, in the nineteenth century, progressive clergy and social theorists in the West joined popular movements of reform, especially workers' movements, to voice "the modern social problem" as one way of naming the results of the exploitative character of rapidly developing industrial society. These allies developed an extensive critique of the capitalist order and the political and economic efforts to govern it, envisioned the outlines of a more just and humane civilization, and took on an array of interlocking issues: the use and abuse of wealth, racial reform, tenement housing, women's rights, "machine" politics, police corruption, taxes, immigration policy, and political reform. Such issues were all matters of rapidly growing cities and industrial relations.

The chief difference from its nineteenth-century form is that the social question has now gone both global and urban. Indeed, one of the most stunning shifts in human demographics in history has happened in this century. For the very first time since we stood upright to sniff the air somewhere on the savannahs of East Africa, the majority of human beings now live in urban centers. As recently as a century ago, the vast majority lived in rural environments dominated by village and small town life.

Yet, the second salient point is not the global and urban dimensions of the social question, important as that is. The new factor is that, in the final third of the twentieth century, "the social question" has been joined by "the ecological question." The degradation of Earth's lifeforms and life systems threatens the habitats of human and other creatures, habitats all of us depend upon for every breath we take, every morsel we chew, every song we sing, every right we claim, every enjoyment we cherish. While the causes are multiple, "the ecological question" is chiefly the result of the destructive downside of modern industrialized society, whether in the form of corporate capitalism or state socialism.

The social question is essentially the social justice question. The ecological question is essentially the question of sustainability. They must now be addressed together as the global eco-justice question.

Globalization

The effort of these pages is to argue that global eco-justice—addressing the social and ecological questions together for the sake of comprehensive sustainability[10]—is the proper frame for the churches' urban mission. To put the normative concerns in the proper historical framework we will identify the ecosocial consequences arising from three consecutive waves of globalization, consequences largely ignored by dominant cultures and most churches.

"Globalization," as awkward a term as we can muster, is associated with many things: the information society, the erosion of borders and national sovereignty itself, footloose corporations hopscotching the planet, growing premiums for skilled workers and a growing plight for unskilled ones, and the free flow of finance capital.

But this late-twentieth-century rendition is too narrow a gauge. Globalization as it impacts cities and the biosphere itself and as it creates the need for global eco-justice has long been underway. It has been underway in the three waves of colonialism, development, and free trade global capitalism. These successive waves deeply altered not only human society, to give us "the social question" in its modern and largely urban form; they also upended the biotic community locally, regionally, even globally, to give us the present "ecological question." And (we will return to this) these waves largely sucked away any remaining sense of Earth itself as a living community in the churches' theology, liturgy, and mission. The present point, in short, is that all life's communities, human and nonhuman alike, have been and are being dramatically recast, not separately but together, as a single, enormously complex Community of Life comprised of the socio-communal, the biophysical, and the geoplanetary simultaneously.

The major outcome of all three waves of globalization, then, is not only what social scientists have documented from the rise of the new economy of the bourgeoisie to the present; namely, that globalization has been and is disruptive of intact local community and corrosive of settled traditions and ways of life. The waves of globalization have always been transformative, and sometimes destructive, of life-forms themselves, together with the ecosystems that comprise their lifelines and matrix. Moreover, the waves of globalization continue to institutionalize the conquest of nature as the key to progress, just as they continue to live off nature's capital for the sake of human well-being, rather than off nature's income only.

We need not tarry long with the first wave of globalization: conquest, commerce, and Christianity as a mission faith self-identified by its (European) bearers as the "spread of civilization." If your genes are "Euro," you are part of by far the highest population growth rates and by far the largest and most dispersed emigration in recorded history—fifty million people left Europe in the long century, 1820–1930. You are also part of the greatest upending of both culture and nature in history, the greatest exchange and transformation of flora and fauna and crops and diseases the planet has experienced. That happened over the centuries trailing in the wake of Columbus's embarkation from Cadiz.

To underscore the matter again: globalization is about the socio-communal, biophysical, and even geoplanetary simultaneously in an upending of nature and culture together. Yet, the churches' urban mission has never taken account of this, preferring only the domain of the social question in the realm of the sociocommunal. This conceives justice in intrahuman terms only and circumscribes the moral world in a way that excludes human power's effects on the more-than-human world. Any church urban mission now that is not about the sociocommunal, biophysical, and geoplanetary together is truncated, blinded by its own anthropocentrism, and ignorant of its actual historical legacy.

Conquest and colonization in the name of a globalizing civilization effected chiefly through commerce is far from dead. But it merged some time ago with the second wave, development.

Consider a citation from the newspaper, *Perfil de la Jornada,* Mexico City, January 27, 1994. The date is important. The North American Free Trade Agreement went into effect at midnight, January 1 of that year. That very day, and by design, a hitherto unknown movement emerged from the forests of the state of Chiapas to challenge the Mexican government. But not only the national government; it intended—and still intends—to challenge the whole process by which Earth is now unified. The leader, Subcommandante Marcos, wrote a letter to the editor. It begins as follows:

> Suppose you want to travel to the South East of the country, and suppose you find yourself on one of the three roads which lead to the state of Chiapas. . . . Our wealth leaves this land not just on these three roads. Chiapas is bleeding to death in a thousand ways: through oil and

gas pipelines, power supply lines, railway cars, banking accounts, trucks, ships and air planes, clandestine paths and paved roads. This land continues to pay its tribute to the empire: oil, electricity, cattle, coffee, maize, honey, tobacco. . . . Primary resources, several billion tons with various destinations, flow out to . . . the USA, Canada, Holland, Germany, Italy, Japan, but always with the same destination: the empire.[11]

The citation from *Perfil de la Jornada* moves us from globalization as colonization to globalization as development. The message from Chiapas was a call, says Gustavo Esteva, for an end "to 500 years of oppression and 40 years of development."[12] An end to "40 years of development?" What's behind *that* Indian demand?

"Development" once meant "evolution from within." It was "synonymous with evolution as self-organization,"[13] a process in the hands of those who were developing. It was internally rather than externally guided. But, at least since President Harry Truman's inaugural address of 1949, development has come to mean the way of life of capitalist democracies as defined by modern economic progress and advanced science and technology. In Wolfgang Sachs's words: "The degree of civilization in a country could from now on be measured by its level of production. This new concept allowed the thousands of cultures to be separated into the two simple categories of 'developed' and 'underdeveloped.' [Modulated somewhat, 'developed' and 'developing'; or, to use the present term of the International Monetary Fund, "societies in transition."] Diverse societies were placed on a single progressive track, more or less advancing according to the criteria of production."[14] So, on one winter day in 1949, two-thirds of the planet's space and two billion of its peoples became "underdeveloped" and in need of another way of living, whether or not they had considered themselves so or not.

Globalization's third wave is post–Cold War free trade liberalization. Here, globalization is effected less by nation states, including those "societies in transition" in the South, than by global economic powers mastering global markets. I mention one characteristic only, the extension and intensification of market society in a capitalist mode. The market is not only the place of economic exchange now; it is a model of society itself and a logic for it, a determiner of relationships of all kinds. In that form it continues to do what colonization and development did; namely, further modernity's assault on intact local community and transformation of the land. People are largely shorn of "their self-organizing, self-governing, and self-provisioning capacities" in the places they live and on the terms and with the resources indigenous to those places, peoples, and traditions.[15]

But beyond this expanded reach there is corporate capitalism's deeper reach into nature, to life's fundamental building blocks themselves, and into the world of ideas and the knowledge banks of cultures. There is also the spectacular growth of global financial markets in which vast sums of financial capital change hands (about 1.4 trillion U.S.$ daily as of this writing), not in the interests even of development or any real exchange of goods and services, but in the search for speculative profits.[16]

Nature itself is increasingly colonized by capital. Life-forms are more and more the organic plastic of engineering and patents as rights *to* nature are favored over the rights *of* nature, if indeed the rights *of* nature get any hearing at all. And biodiversity, the source of all future life possibilities, is under assault most everywhere—by bioprospecting, biotechnology, the spread of global monoculture and mass production and consumption, not to mention the habitat intrusions of an expanding human economy. Third world, not only first world, agriculture is drawn into the orbit of colossal agribusiness firms. Farmers may in fact lose the right to produce and use their own seeds to commercial capitalism and governmental allies.[17]

In a closely related manner, information and knowledge itself are increasingly rendered commodities in a kind of enclosure of the intellectual commons. Intellectual property rights have become private rights rather than common rights as international trade talks, pushed by corporate interests and their governmental allies, proceed.

In short, the vertical reach of global free trade capitalism into nature, knowledge, and culture matches its intensified and extended horizontal one.

Allow a summary and commentary from the *Nation*. Recent economic globalization is arguably the most far-reaching redesign and centralization of the planet's political and economic arrangements since the Industrial Revolution itself. Yet the profound implications are not given genuine public airing by elected officials, by educational institutions, by the media, or by faith communities. So the advocates of globalization have free reign at the same time that they lump the dissenters together as "protectionists" and dismiss them as out-of-touch throwbacks to pre-1989 worlds. But, of course, what we really have is corporate protectionism that fails to protect jobs, communities, effective democracy, and nature.[18] We have the triumph on a new scale of the mobility and investment of corporations and banks, the technologically enhanced acceleration of global development and commerce, a profound, rather abrupt shift in political power that "liberates" even currency from many nations' control, and, in fact, the elimination of most regulatory controls over global corporate activity.[19]

The point above, and Jerry Mander's in the *Nation,* is not only the dimensions of the new; it is the failure of corporations, elected officials, educators, media powers, and faith communities to see and air critical connections among issues. These issues—crowded urban megapolises, accelerated climate change, the growth of global poverty amidst unprecedented wealth, the stagnation and sometimes lowering of wages while stocks soar, the privatization and sometimes elimination of social services, the destruction of plants, wildlife, wilderness, wetlands, and vast amounts of habitat, and the protests of Chiapan Indians—are not presented as complex outcomes of interacting global policies. They are not understood as part of the vast transformation of nature and society together on this end of three cumulative waves of globalization. So the *New York Times* can carry two front-page stories side by side, "As Boom Fails, Malaysia Sends Migrants Home"[20] and "One in Every 8 Plant Species Is Imperiled, a Survey Finds,"[21] and can spell out the terms of the largest merger in history to that date ($70 billion), of Citibank and the Travellers Group, without a hint of any kind in these stories, on the editorial or the op-ed page, that they belong together in any way. Eyes to see and ears to hear Earth as factually a comprehensive community without an exit seem utterly to fail us. We don't recognize the linkages, from the inside out, of the social and the environmental.

A Proposed Framework

Given these waves of globalization, the task of addressing the social question (social justice) and the ecological question (sustainability) simultaneously as the global eco-justice question requires far-reaching changes. These changes frame any consideration of Christianity itself as a positive force for the next period of history. The changes are those that move us from a presently unsustainable Earth to a sustainable one. The changes entail eight transitions: an *economic* transition that lives off nature's "income" instead of "capital" and builds into all economic activity, including the cost of goods, that which is required for nature's regeneration and renewal indefinitely; a *social* transition to a far broader sharing of nature's income and human wealth, together with increased opportunities for sustaining and sustainable livelihoods for all; an *institutional* transition that combines greater cross-national cooperation in order to address global problems with greater attention to what makes for sustainable local and regional communities; an *informational* transition in which research, education, and global monitoring allow large numbers of people to understand the interrelated problems they face and offer them the means to address these problems; a *demographic* transition from an unprecedented population explosion to a roughly stable world population; a *technological* transition which effectively means minimal environmental impact per person; a *moral* transition to a framework that includes the societal, the biophysical, and the geoplanetary—the whole Community of Life—as the arena of responsibility; and a *religious* transition to earthkeeping as the religious calling and vocation common to all the world's religions.[22]

These transitions in turn require their own institutional and policy vision and framework. That vision and framework should not be that of "sustainable development," if by that is meant what most people mean; namely, how to "green" the growing global economy so as to make it environmentally sustainable. Such a course assumes, and leaves, the powerful forces of centuries-deep globalization in command. The result will likely be a hard, brown world tinged with soft, green edges for the rich and aspiring-rich. Trying to wrap the beseiged environment around the ever-expanding global economy is not the way to go.

The way to go is "sustainable community." Its basic question is how we wrap both economy and environment around healthy local and regional communities. The proper goal of an economy is not increased production and consumption as such. It is materially healthy communities, for the long haul. To this end, sustainable community in our kind of world requires a considerable devolution of economic and political power as well as strengthening certain international networks and institutions. It requires a heightened status and respect for all life and a sphere of responsibility that includes the whole Community of Life. In the phrase of one author, this is "cosmopolitan localism." It refers to "new ways of revitalizing and protecting local communities while participating in wider associations to check the growing domination of economic globalization"[23] and offer politically acceptable ways for the social protection of land, labor, local capital, and culture.

Closing

Too little has been said in these pages. The discussion has only now brought us to the proper query: What presently makes for sustainable community in the great urban areas that presently form a global necklace, and what roles might churches play in alliances that would help create sustainable cities? Instead of answering that question, I have framed it. I have conceptually staked out an ungainly territory encompassing the sociocommunal, the biophysical, and the geoplanetary together. While that is necessary, it is only a beginning.

The specific roles churches and other religious communities might play is being addressed in several metropolitan areas.[24] This brings me to the topic mentioned in passing and postponed: the churches' loss—in theology, liturgy, and mission—of Earth itself as a living community.

The constructive ecclesial task is both long-term and immediate. The pressing immediate task is to address, one by one, the downside effects in city neighborhoods of the global economy's impacts and to try to find, in practice and policy, those incremental changes that slowly build toward sustainable communities. The closely related long-term task—give it a century or so—is liturgical, theological, educational, and practical (referring here to church-institutional practices). The long-term task, succinctly put, is the conversion of Christianity to Earth. That means overcoming, in an urban setting, the collective estrangement from the numinous powers that create, sustain, and, yes, extinguish human life itself. It means recovering in new forms, fitted to urban living, of deep genetic and ancestral reciprocity with the animate earth. It means sensing in our own senses that all forms of life are *experiencing* forms that have their own indispensable agency in the wonder and mystery we call life.[25]

It means experiencing the presence and power of none other or less than God incarnate in the more-than-human universe that surrounds and surpasses the burning mysteries of our own fragile and precious lives, wherever they are lived. It means the embrace of Earth as the providing ground that is bone of our bone and flesh of our flesh and the only habitat for living the lives we can and desire to have. It means the vision of the city where, though the temple is no longer there, fruited trees of life line the banks of rivers of crystal water flowing from the throne of God located right downtown. It means a practical everyday mysticism, an aesthetic, and an ethic that knows in gut and heart as well as head that the redemption of each creature is required for the redemption of all and that the borders of all life, indeed of inorganic being and the galaxies themselves, all leak into the presence of God and bespeak the power of the same. It means conversion to urban ground, and all ground, as holy ground and the land of promise. It means cities that are green and are, in fact, food-producing regions.

Finally, then, conversion to Earth on this end of the waves of globalization is the church's eco-justice urban mission, both short- and long-term.

Notes

1. Walter Rauschenbusch, *Christianity and the Social Crisis* (New York: Macmillan Co., 1907), 211.

2. Ibid.

3. Ibid.

4. Ibid., 212.

5. Ibid.

6. Ibid.

7. Ernst Troeltsch, *The Social Teaching of the Christian Churches* (Chicago: University of Chicago Press, 1960), 2:1010.

8. Karl Marx, *The Communist Manifesto* (Chicago: Henry Regnery Co., 1954), 20–21.

9. Ibid., 20, 23.

10. The subject of my book, *Earth Community, Earth Ethics* (Maryknoll, N.Y.: Orbis Books, 1996).

11. Cited in Wolfgang Sachs, *The Political Anatomy of "Sustainable Development,"* The Wuppertal Institute, Occasional Papers, no. 35, May 1995: 23. The translation is Sachs's.

12. Gustavo Esteva, "Basta!" *Ecologist* 24, no. 3 (May/June 1994): 83.

13. I draw here from Vandana Shiva, *Biopiracy: The Plunder of Nature and Knowledge* (Toronto: Between the Lines Press, 1997), 107.

14. Wolfgang Sachs as cited by Wesley Granberg-Michaelson, *Redeeming the Creation: The Rio Earth Summit: Challenges for the Churches* (Geneva: WCC Publications, 1992), 1.

15. Shiva, *Biopiracy,* 115.

16. David Korten, "Economic Globalization: The War against Markets, Democracy, People, and Nature," in *A World That Works: Building Blocks for a Just and Sustainable Society,* ed. Trent Schroyer (New York: Bootstrap Press, 1997), 232.

17. Hans Leenders, former secretary general of the International Association of Plant Breeders for the Protection of Plant Varieties, argues for this: "Even though it has been a tradition in most countries that a farmer can save seed from his own crop, it is under the changing circumstances not equitable that farmers can use this seed and grow a commercial crop out of it without payment of a royalty; the seed industry will have to fight hard for a better kind of protection." Cited from Shiva, *Biopiracy,* 53.

18. Jerry Mander, "The Dark Side of Globalization: What Media Are Missing," *Nation* 263, no. 3 (15/22 July 1996): 10.

19. Mander, "The Dark Side of Globalization," 10.

20. To Indonesia, chiefly. "If we must grow calluses on our hearts, so be it," an editorial in the *Straits Times* of Singapore responded. Reported in the *New York Times,* 9 April 1998, A1.

21. *New York Times,* 9 April 1998, A1.

22. An adaptation from the discussion in M. Mitchell Waldrop, *Complexity: The Emerging Science at the Edge of Order and Chaos* (New York: Simon and Schuster, 1992), 350–51.

23. Trent Schroyer, "Introduction: Working Alternatives for a World That Works," in *A World That Works: Building Blocks for a Just and Sustainable Society,* ed. Trent Schroyer (New York: Bootstrap Press, 1997), 1.

24. E.g., see *One Creation, One People, One Place,* a statement of the Interreligious Sustainability Project of Metropolitan Chicago, initiated by Stephen A. Perkins, Center for Neighborhood Technology, 2125 W. North Ave., Chicago, IL 60647. In New York City, I coteach seminary courses entitled "Ecology and Ethics in the 'hood" and "Environmental Racism" that explore local/global eco-justice.

25. These lines are suggested by David Abram's *The Spell of the Sensuous: Perception and Language in a More-Than-Human World* (New York: Random House, 1997), 7–11.

Earthkeeping Churches
at the African Grass Roots

MARTHINUS L. DANEEL

"The church is the keeper of creation," said Bishop Nhongo of the Zion Christian Church. "All churches now know that they must empower their prophets to expose the wizards [*varoyi*] who kill the land. These people who wilfully defile the church through their destruction of the earth should be barred from participation in the holy communion. If I was the One who owned heaven I would have barred them from entry. The destroyers of the earth should be warned that the "blood" they cause to flow will be on their own heads. . . ."

The Bishop's son, evangelist Samuel Nhongo, concurred: "Jesus said to Simon Peter: 'I give you the keys to lock and unlock!' It is in this light that I see the earth-destroyers whom we expel from the church. . . . The tree-fellers who persist in their evil ways should be locked out of the church. . . . This war [of the trees] must be fought on all fronts and with severity. The church's new ecological laws should be universally known and respected. Otherwise we will be merely chasing the wind."[1]

To a casual passerby the conversation between father and son would appear like any other between two peasants in an African village. Clad in plain khaki clothes, seated in their courtyard in the shade of a *muchakata* tree, next to a couple of nondescript mud-and-pole huts, the two men are likely to be talking about their crops or livestock, the source of their livelihood. At least so one would think. Surely this is not the context for profound statements on ecotheology, statements that would be taken note of in the distant halls of fame where much of the business of the world church is being conducted. After all, these are the radical statements of only barely literate leaders of the African Independent Churches,[2] considered by some of the so-called mainline churches in Africa as heretical splinter groups of dubious Christian nature, if not syncretistic throwbacks to traditional religion. To propose the purging of the church of the wizards of the land and debarring such evildoers from heaven, sound rather like the idiom of the witch-hunt and the imposed legalism of medieval patriarchs. Until, of course, one sees the devastation of deforestation in the immediate vicinity of Bishop Nhongo's village; until one feels the helplessness of villagers observing the mindless onslaught on the remaining trees by those who have no hope of earning the necessary school fees for their children unless they sell firewood; until one listens to the sighs of tired village women who have to walk miles each day to gather firewood and fetch water! Then the radical and irritated attitudes of earthkeepers in relation to those who refuse to heed the environment—and, by implication, their communities—start making sense.

The conversation between father and son obtains even more meaning in the light of their earthkeeping ministry. For, like thousands of their fellow believers in Zimbabwe's peasant society, they have decided to stand up and fight the war of the trees, to combat soil erosion, deforestation, the depletion of wildlife, and the misuse of wetlands. Although they did not have the benefit of listening to Joseph Sittler's call for united action in the face of earth destruction, at the third assembly of the World Council of Churches in New Delhi in 1961,[3] or have access to subsequent ecumenical literature on the development of an ethic which integrates ecology, liberation, justice, and peace, they did respond to their own intuition and reading of scriptures in relation to the deteriorating conditions of their own local environment. Empowered by ZIRRCON—the Zimbabwean Institute of Religious Research and Ecological Conservation[4]—they formed a green force of some 150 African Independent Churches with a total combined membership of an estimated two million followers. This body is called the AAEC—Association of African Earthkeeping Churches. From the outset it collaborated with its traditionalist counterpart, AZTREC—Association of Zimbabwean Traditionalist Ecologists—

comprising a host of chiefs, headmen, and spirit mediums who engage in the environmental liberation struggle in terms of their traditional religious worldviews and ritual praxis. During the past decade this ecumenical peoples' movement, comprising two distinct green armies, Christian and traditionalist, has succeeded in establishing tree nurseries throughout the Masvingo Province of Zimbabwe and planting between three and four million trees, exotic and indigenous, in the country's central and southeastern regions. Currently, this is probably the largest grassroots ecological movement in all of Southern Africa, operating on the basis of religious motivation and mobilization.

In this paper I shall attempt to trace briefly the profile of a grassroots ecclesiology as it emerges or lies dormant in a green ministry which seeks to establish eco-justice in accordance with local African insights and convictions. African earthkeepers keep turning out in hundreds and thousands year after year, to perform their *maporesanyika* —earth-healing—ceremonies of tree planting at the behest of Mwari, the creator, keeper, and savior of creation. This they do regardless of the disheartening, repeated losses in tree seedlings wiped out by black frost, the low rate of tree survival in years of drought, the monotony of repetition, and many more setbacks encountered in the green struggle. This they do, too, as the poor and relatively underprivileged members of society, dependent on an oft capricious subsistence economy, yet deriving meaning and pride from sustained ecological service.

AIC theology at best eludes written definition and the industry of bookmaking. Enacted and lived, it finds expression in the throb of celebration, spontaneous proclamation, holistic cleansing of body, spirit, and earth, in rousing song and the rhythm of dancing feet. The attraction and relevance of this theology in the local setting derives from a literal, if at times fragmented, reading of scriptures, which allows for uninhibited and direct identification with biblical characters. At the same time it allows for in-depth interaction between the world of the Bible and the cosmologies of Africa without the interference of Western ecclesial leadership or dogmatism. Hence it is with some hesitation that I, as fellow earthkeeper yet as a privileged white missiologist, attempt to unravel and analyze the ecotheology underlying the activities of an essentially black African peoples' movement.

The Mission of an Earthkeeping Church

Bishop Wapendama, leader of the Signs of the Apostles Church, defined the mission of AAEC churches, during a tree-planting Eucharist, as follows: "Mwari saw the devastation of the land. So He called his envoys [ZIRRCON/AAEC leaders] to shoulder the task of delivering the earth. Together with you, we, the Apostles, are now the *deliverers of the stricken land. . . .* We, the deliverers were sent by Mwari on a sacred mission. . . . Deliverance, Mwari says, lies in the trees. Jesus said: 'I leave you my followers, to complete my work!' And that task is the one of healing! We, the followers of Jesus, have to continue with his healing ministry. So, let us all fight, clothing and healing the earth with trees! It is our task to strengthen this mission with our numbers of people. If all of us work with enthusiasm we shall clothe and heal the entire land with trees and drive off affliction. I believe we can change it."

Taken together with Bishop Nhongo's statement above, Wapendama's portrayal of the church's mission illuminates two dominant themes which are evolving from the AAEC's tree-planting ministry. First, the mission of the church comprises earth healing as an extension of Christ's healing activities (Wapendama); and second, the church, in so doing, functions as the keeper or guardian of creation (Nhongo). The good news proclaimed and enacted by the earthkeeping church clearly extends beyond and complements soul salvation and the healing of human beings, as formerly envisaged by the AICs. However, this trend does not supersede or replace the rich evangelistic tradition within the prophetic AICs which focused the church's outreach in conversion, the promise of salvation to converts both in this existence and in a kingdom of heaven yet to come and the baptism of converts in the name of the triune God, as prescribed in the classic missionary text of Matthew 28:18–19.[5] For the AICs involved in the AAEC continue with their missionizing strategies of old. Yet, decidedly new is the preoccupation with the inclusion of the deliverance of Mwari's stricken land in the church's mission. Bishop Wapendama, as many other church leaders, is neither a naïve optimist nor an opportunist, merely riding the wave of the latest fad. A surprising amount of his time is spent in the cultivation and planting of tree seedlings at the church headquarters. Moreover, his interpretation of conversion as condition for church entry increasingly includes an emphasis on individual change from earth-destructive to earth-care activity.

Although Wapendama did not specifically mention Holy Communion in his call to mission, his message in the context of a tree-planting Eucharist implies that at the point where the union between Christ and his disciples (cutting across denominational boundaries) is sacramentally confirmed, the mission of earth healing integral to it, is visibly acknowledged and revitalized. In this view the dialectic between summoning and mandating God and responding human earth-keepers remains focal. God certainly takes the initiative to deliver and restore his ravaged earth, in what remains essentially *missio Dei*. Wapendama, in the same sermon quoted above, repeatedly reminded his audience that they were facing a formidable task, one which could only be accomplished in full recognition of dependence on God. "I beseech you," he said, "to place yourselves in the hands of Mwari. He alone can give us the strength to endure in this struggle." But the responsibility to deliver the stricken earth from its malady here and now lies with the Christian body of believers, the church. Membership to this institution, the head of which extends his healing ministry through grace to the entire cosmos, therefore implies active earth stewardship.

Wapendama's understanding of the church's mission may be limited. Yet, it signals one of the ways in which ecologically active AICs update their sacramental-cum-missionary tradition in the face of environmental needs.[6] It also hints at Africa's understanding of the church's comprehensive missionary task in this world, not as a privileged community of mere soul-savers, but in terms of Bishop Anastasios of Androussa's vision that "the whole world, not only humankind but the entire universe, has been called to share in the restoration that was accomplished by the redeeming work of Christ."[7]

The function of the church as guardian of creation, as depicted by Bishop Nhongo, hinges on an emergent Christology which increasingly interacts with Shona cosmology. Christ in a sense absorbs for the Christian earthkeepers that part of the spirit world which traditionally provided the sanction and incentive for customary conservationist laws and practice. This is the domain of the founder ancestors of tribes and clans popularly referred to as the "guardians of the land" (*varidzi venyika*). They are the protectors of the holy groves and sanctuaries in the territories they once ruled. Their environmental commands are mediated through spirit mediums and implemented by the local chief's court. These are the senior ancestors who, during

Zimbabwe's liberation struggle, were considered to operate in unison in the "council of war" (*dare rechimurenga*), providing spirit guidance and support to the guerrilla fighters in their quest to retrieve the "lost lands" from the colonial power. These, too, are the spirit forces considered by the chiefs and mediums of AZTREC—the AAEC's counterpart—as the inspiration and sanction behind the "war of the trees."

Although the AAEC earthkeepers refrain from calling Christ *mudzimu,* or ancestor, the tendency to proclaim his lordship over all creation and to envisage him as the controller of all cosmic and life-giving forces strengthens the perception of an earthkeeper who, as part of the human family of necessity, also relates to the ancestral world. And the analogy which immediately comes to mind in such interrelatedness is that Christ is the universal *muridzi venyika* (guardian of the land). I have myself, in a number of tree-planting ceremonies, compared Christ's earth care with that of the Shona guardian ancestors. The theological assumption behind such portrayal is that the traditional guardian ancestors have through the ages sensed and accepted their responsibility for the land politically under their jurisdiction through their closeness and response to Mwari, the Creator. As such, they prefigured as earthkeeping prototypes of Christianity among the Shona. Christ's role as *muridzi venyika* therefore fulfills and transforms the old guardianship. Christ, the earth guardian, somehow inspires and holds sway through his Spirit over generations of Shona *varidzi*. Through them he appeals to *all* their living descendants, whatever their religious persuasion, to share and extend their responsibility for the earth. As John Pobee would say, Christ shares ancestorship with the living dead on account of his *kra* (soul) linking him to God.[8] However, he also transcends the regional and kinship limitations of the African senior ancestors in linking the local Shona environmental and kingroup with the universal cosmos and family of humankind. Such extension is already manifest in AAEC praxis: widening ecumenical horizons and financial and moral support from the Christian earthkeeping community inhabiting the global village.

This contextualized Christology undergirds in AIC circles the image of the church as guardian of the land, locally, and keeper of creation in the more universal sense. The proximity of the ancestral guardians also broadens the understanding of a people-oriented redemption to include salvation of all the earth. Sundkler has correctly pointed out that Africans invariably understand redemption and the forgiveness of sins in terms of Christ's revelation of such truth both to the living and the living dead.[9] Christ's *descensio* into the spirit world, to the Shona believer, not only signifies salvific proclamation to the entire human community—the living, the dead, and the unborn —but it also validates and absorbs for them the ecological concerns of the guardian ancestors into the ministry of the church, where it finds expression in liberative environmental activity, symbolizing the holistic concreteness of God's salvation in this existence.

It is at this point, in the emergence of the church as guardian or keeper of creation, that an understandable and realistic ethic of the environment takes shape. Bishop Nhongo's preoccupation with earth destruction as a form of wizardry, *uroyi,* reflects the new idiom. Sin no longer concerns only the antisocial acts committed directly against fellow human beings or against God, but also and particularly offenses against the environment. These include the indiscriminate felling of trees, refusal to participate in curative conservationist activities, riverbank cultivation and related agricultural activities, such as the use of sledges, which promote soil-erosion, pollution and misuse of water resources, and so forth. The dire implications of such activities for the entire earth community—people, animals, vegetation, and all animate or inanimate objects belonging to creation—are considered in such a serious light that willful perpetrators are indeed branded as destroyers, or wizards, of the land. Prophets of earthkeeping AICs are becoming "guardians of the land" in their own rights, in that they are instrumental in detecting environmental sins in fellow church members and urging public confessions prior to church services and a variety of earthkeeping rituals. Their green ministry enables the church to identify the enemy outside and within its own ranks. Identification of the wrongdoers illuminates the church's concern for eco-justice and concretizes its ethical code and control system. This development is reminiscent of the *chimurenga* struggle prior to Zimbabwean independence, during which the counterrevolutionaries and collaborators with the Smith regime were branded as wizards. The task of the AIC war prophets, alongside the traditionalist spirit mediums, was to elicit confessions from suspects during the secret *pungwe* vigils as part of the process of exposing the wizard-traitors and singling them out for punitive measures.

"Earthkeeping is part of the body of Christ," the Reverend Davison Tawoneichi of the Evangelical Ministry of Christ Church told his followers in a sermon. "It is so because we as humans are part of his body and the trees are part of us; they are essential for us to heal to breathe. So trees, too, are part of Christ's body. Our destruction of nature is an offense against the body of Christ. . . . It hurts Christ's body. Therefore the church should heal the wounded body of Christ."

This view complements Bishop Wapendama's assertion about mission as an extension of Christ's healing ministry. Only, in this instance, Christ's body is understood as being itself afflicted by the abuse of nature.[10] This statement underscores the growing tendency in AAEC tree-planting Eucharists to view Christ's body in both its ecclesiastic and its cosmic connotations: first, through partaking in the elements of the sacrament the earthkeepers witness to their unity in Christ's body, the church, and derive from it strength, compassion, and commitment for their environmental struggle; second, they subsequently set out on their healing mission of tree planting to restore the cosmically wounded body of Christ.

An earthbound Christology of this nature cannot but have far-reaching implications for the structure and program of the church. The prophetic AICs have all along communicated a gospel message of wholeness in healing, whereby the people of God could find well-being, peace, and belonging in a hostile world. The black "Jerusalems" and "holy cities" epitomized the presence of God where prophetic leaders and their bands of healers mirrored as icons the healing powers of Christ and of the Holy Spirit. Healing in this context encompassed all of human life. Not only were assailing spirits exorcised, wizardry banished, barren women cured and socially reinstated, and all kinds of ailments treated, but those without spouses or jobs were taken care of, entire congregations in drought-ridden areas were fed, and the mediation of rain and sound farming methods secured. Hence, from the outset a comprehensive healing ministry turned the predominant image of the Spirit-type churches, mainly the Zionists and Apostles, into that of a "hospital" (*hospitara*).

Preoccupation with Christ, both as earthkeeper and as the broken earth, introduces a revolutionary new dimension. With this in mind Wapendama's call to mission aims at mobilizing the entire church membership as active earth healers, instead of only a number of specialized evangelizers and/or healers. It is as if he and the Reverend Tawoneichi anticipate in the healing of creation and of Christ's body the liberation of the church itself—liberation from an overriding preoccupation with the human condition. In healing the earth, by reaching out beyond the vexing physical and mental ailment of human beings and by setting aside internal leadership and interchurch conflicts—the very illness of the church itself—for a higher, God-given purpose, the earthkeeping church, and the earthkeeper, is healed. In such liberation unto earth service, the apostolate of the church obtains prominence and meaning.

Sacraments of Healing

Look at the stagnant water
where all the trees were felled
Without trees the water-holes mourn
without trees the gullies form
For, the tree-roots to hold the soil—
are gone!

There were forests
abundance of rain
But in our ignorance and greed
we left the land naked.
Like a person in shame
our country is shy
in its nakedness.

Our planting of trees today
is a sign of harmony
between us and creation
We are reconciled with the earth
through the body and blood of Jesus
which brings peace.
He who came to save
All creation.
[Col. 1:17–20]

In these excerpts, taken from the liturgy of the AAEC's tree-planting Eucharist, we find the themes of confessing ecological guilt, recognizing the plight of landscapes stripped bare, anticipating the cosmic dimension of Christ's atoning death, and the determination of celebrant earthkeepers to relate the salvific message within the sacrament

to the cosmos as a form of therapeutic restoration through tree planting. Rousing sermons usually underscore the significance of confessing ecological guilt, implicit in the liturgy. Christ is proclaimed as the
One, who in the midst of ecological devastation, holds everything
together (Col. 1:17), as the one who atones for ecological sins. "As
the recipients of Christ's salvation," Bishop Marinda, author of the
liturgy, would repeatedly insist, "*humans have the duty to extend salvation to all of creation as Christ's co-workers!*" (my italics). What
this imparting of salvation essentially means in the earthkeeping
church is the symbolic fusion of healing humans and healing earth in
the sacramental reenactment of Christ's death and resurrection as
found both in baptism and Holy Communion.[11]

Baptism in the green movement is preceded by the kind of conversion which highlights the relationship between humans and Mother
Earth. The individual's change of heart in rebirth will remain incomplete if it does not include a deliberate move from earth destruction to
earth care. Acceptance of this responsibility surfaces in the novice's
public confession of ecological *uroyi* (wizardry) against the Creator
and the earth community, immediately before entry into "Jordan"
(any dam or river where baptism is conducted). Baptism thus acquires
the meaning of rejecting illicit exploitation of the environment and
obtaining Christian discipleship in a community of earth healers.
Subsequently, spiritual growth of the individual believer no longer
derives exclusively from worship, Bible study, and prayer in the
conventional sense. It also results from the encounter with God in the
protective stewardship of his garden.

It makes sense for novices to confess ecological guilt and obtain
earthkeeping discipleship at "Jordan," where a barren landscape, erosion gullies, and unprotected riverbanks will in most cases be in full
view. With its focus on Christ the wounded healer, the earthkeeping
church is rendering the broken environment that "holds" the
baptismal pool or river party to the sacrament of baptism, in similar
fashion as the trees to be planted are made to participate as brothers
and sisters in the Eucharist. The barren plains and erosion gullies, so
to speak, enter the waters of life to be baptized into a future of healing
and recovery, in the person of the novice who, in crossing "Jordan,"
gives witness to his or her transition from earth abuser to earthkeeper.

To most Independents, baptism has always held the connotation of
healing. Here, the life-giving water of "Jordan," filled for the

occasion according to popular belief by the power and presence of the Holy Spirit, is drunk by the baptisands and afflicted church members for cleansing and curative purposes. Thus, the ceremony offers a unique opportunity for interpreting the Holy Spirit as healer of both the people and the land. In this instance the drinking of "Jordan" water symbolizes the shift from personal, individual benefit of the baptisand by the Holy Spirit's healing and salvific powers to a ritual statement of divine and human solidarity with all creation; an affirmation of new commitment through conversion to a vocation aimed at eco-justice. As the Spirit-filled water of "Jordan" heals and empowers the newly converted earthkeepers, it also touches the wounded earth where it courses down a riverbed troubled by siltation —in itself a reminder to those with eyes to see that they have to be more than mere spectators in the realization in this existence of the new heaven and new earth.

The sequence of activities in the healing tree-planting Eucharist is briefly as follows:

Preparation starts with the digging of holes in the vicinity of AIC headquarters of the hosting church. The prospective woodlot may be fenced, named "the Lord's Acre," and placed under the surveillance of a church committee responsible for watering the newly planted seedlings and for general aftercare. While the communion table is being prepared near to the new woodlot, robed dancers, representing the region's ecumenically united churches, dance around the seedlings stacked nearby. Dance and song bring praise to Mwari, the Creator, recognize his presence, encourage the green fighters and even exhort the young trees to grow well. The sermons of AAEC bishops and ZIRRCON staff members are augmented by speeches delivered by government officials and representatives of the Forestry Commission, Parks and Wildlife, or other ecological institutions. Thus, the outdoor setting, religiously pluriform audience, and varied sermons and speeches cause the tree-planting Eucharist to be an open-ended, inclusive rather than strictly exclusive, in-group event.

The opening to the Sacrament itself is the public confession of sins. All the celebrants, church leaders and dignitaries included, line up behind a band of prophesying prophets to confess their guilt in earth destruction. The idea is that the Holy Spirit reveals through the prophets the still-hidden sins of communicants lest they partake of the bread and wine in an unworthy manner. Thus, divine intervention and opposition to wanton exploitation of the earth is vividly enacted in a ceremony which recognizes no individual status or privilege. My own position as founder of the movement, for instance, does not exempt me from public admission of the excesses I have committed as a big game hunter in my youth.

After confession each communicant picks up a tree seedling and carries it to the communion table as if to draw all the members of the earth community symbolically into the inner circle of communion with Christ, the Redeemer. Establishing communion with Christ in this manner gives recognition to his role as Healer-earthkeeper and is a way of focusing the sacramental union between him and his disciples, the church, on the earth-healing activity to follow. Meanwhile, one of the AIC bishops blesses the stretch of land to be healed by trees, by sprinkling holy water and scattering holy soil over it—yet another way of drawing the earth community into sacramental participation. Subsequently, all the tree planters converge on the new woodlot where they "converse" with their "fellow communicants"—the seedlings—as they plant and water them. The liturgical formula for communication with the trees at this juncture is as follows:

> You, tree, my brother . . . my sister
> today I plant you in this soil
> I shall give water for your growth
> Have good roots
> to keep the soil from eroding
> Have many branches and leaves
> So that we can:
> —breathe fresh air
> —sit in your shade
> —and find firewood.

In conclusion, many of the tree planters themselves kneel in queues in front of the prophetic healers for the ceremony of laying on of hands and prayer, in the hope of a cure of their own afflictions. Thus, the healing of barren earth and of a crippled humanity blend into a single sacramental ceremony which witnesses poignantly to the reign of Christ, crucified and resurrected Savior of all the earth.

The AAEC's tree-planting Eucharist paves the way for significant developments in local African theologies and interreligious dialogue. I mention but a few aspects worthy of consideration.

First, the AAEC tree-planting Eucharist is in itself the witnessing event, the proclamation of good news unto all the earth! It is enacted in and with nature and in the presence of non-Christian fellow-fighters of the war of the trees. In a sense this is the Christian equivalent of the attendance of the traditionalist high-god oracles, when Christian representatives of the AAEC accompany their AZTREC counterparts to the distant shrines in the Matopo Hills near Bulawayo, to observe them commune with their creator-god and receive directives for the further conduct of the war of the trees. Likewise, the traditionalist earthkeepers at the Eucharist do not partake of the sacramental elements—bread and wine—but they assimilate the message, observe the proceedings, and assist with the tree planting. In treading the holy ground of their Christian friends, as the latter are allowed to approach the ancient oracular holy of holies, where Christians normally will not venture, a new tone for interreligious tolerance and dialogue is set. The traditionalist earthkeeping brother or sister is no longer an "opponent" but a fellow-pilgrim in the joint quest for eco-justice, someone whose religiosity is seen and respected in the reverencing of creation and creator. Not that ecological endeavor supersedes the call for repentance, conversion, human salvation, and church formation—the essential missionary dynamic of all prophetic AICs! For the tree-planting Eucharist, in essence, also highlights the difference between Christian sacrament and traditional beer libation for the ancestors. Yet, it is as if the green struggle through the newly planted trees breathes the message: you cannot afford the luxury of religious conflict if it causes the wounded earth to suffocate! Ultimately, therefore, the Christian *maporesanyika* (earth-healing) and the traditionalist *mafukidzanyika* (earth-clothing) ceremonies, for all their religious differentiation, hold hands in the greening of God's earth.

Second, the christological significance of the tree-planting Eucharist lies in its ritualized blending of the wide-ranging tenets of Christ's healing ministry. Observations of villagers of different religious persuasions, who participate in the *maporesanyika* ceremonies, reflect a growing awareness of the comprehensive nature of this ministry. Said a villager during one of these ceremonies: "The protection of trees is a holy matter. The land is barren. The blanket of vegetation which should cover it has been torn away. In its nakedness the land is ill. We too, the people of Mupakwa, are ill. We have come to be healed, together with the land. In Jesus' time you only needed to touch his garment to be healed. In clothing the land with trees we, too, are being healed." Here an unpretentious peasant shows understanding of the fact that Christ had come to heal the sickness of the entire world and that care for the environment is part of the therapy of one's own malady. Such observations not only illustrate the effectiveness of the *maporesanyika* event as a means of communicating the good news of Christ's incarnation in current peasant society, but they also corroborate Aylward Shorter's views that all healing, sacramental healing in particular, is directed toward eternal life and wholeness, and that healing facilitates harmony with the natural environment as condition for human well-being.[12]

Third, the *maporesanyika* Eucharist convincingly qualifies the uniqueness of Christ's image as healer in its adaptation to transformatory fulfillment of the African *nganga*—traditional healer—paradigm.[13] During the tree-planting confession, for example, the prophetic healer, as icon of Christ, probes for and exposes the perpetrators of wizardry as the traditional *nganga* does in his or her witchcraft eradication practice. In this instance, however, the self-confessed, or divinely exposed, ecological offender, the *muroyi venyika* (wizard of the earth), is not ostracized from the community or permanently stigmatized, as the *nganga* would tend to recommend. In the event of an unrepentant spirit, the person may be temporarily barred from sacramental participation. But, despite the calls for the excommunication of willful tree fellers by such radicals as Bishop Nhongo and his son, the green prophet opens the door of reconciliation by keeping the *muroyi* in the church community. Hence, the prospect remains of Christ's forgiveness and grace being enacted in the *muroyi*'s eventual change of heart. Holistic healing in this respect seeks to establish respect for life and mercifully stays final judgment of the as yet heartless exploiters of creation.

Fourth, Christ's healing of the land also contains a spiritual and ecumenically empowering dimension, because his cross and resurrection transcend the barriers of rivalry between ancestral guardians of the land, opposing churches, Christians and non-Christians, and related societal afflictions. The concern for the traditional spirit provinces and the conflicts associated with histories of conquest of the land are, for the duration of the *maporesanyika* Eucharist at least, pushed into the background. The presence and cordial interaction of chiefs and headmen, together with a wide range of AIC members, all from the surrounding territories and all of them representing different and oft conflicting histories, myths, and ancestral bonds with the soil, point at a spirit of mutuality and reconciliation at the expense of recurrent land feuds of the past. It is at this juncture that Christ, who mends things fallen apart (Col. 1:17), interacts with the ancestral guardians of the land. His lordship over all creation relativizes territorial divisions as the contesting representatives of those divisions are drawn into united action for environmental restoration.

Fifth, the incarnation of Christ as healing earthkeeper in his fellow healers at the African grass roots goes a long way in overcoming the image of an alien, white Christ belonging to the Western world. Cécé Kolié complains about Christologies in the mission churches of Africa, which do not function convincingly in the existential reality of African believers.[14] "Our liturgies" he contends, "do not celebrate human beings fighting disease, or struggling so hard to get up on their feet, or striving to be free. . . . To give Christ the face of the healer in Africa will not be feasible until the manifold gifts of healing possessed by all of our Christian communities have begun to manifest themselves." Kolié's criticism correctly signals a serious limitation in Western-oriented Christianity in Africa. However, the AAEC's blending of a ministry of human and environmental healing illustrates that in liturgy, sacraments, and individual experience the healing features of Christ are being unmasked and revealed. The "manifold gifts of healing" *are* in fact emerging forcefully and understandably in the African context where Christ encounters and guides his fellow "wounded healers." He does so in the prophetic diagnosis of all afflictions, cleansing confessionals, tree-planting hands, exorcising hands—much of which follows the rhythm of dancing feet and song, where the inner struggle for life, dignity, and wholeness is fierce and relentless.

The Good News of Justice and Liberation

"There is absolutely no doubt about the connection [between our war of the trees and the former liberation struggle, *chimurenga*]," said Zionist Bishop Machokoto, first president of the AAEC. "I will go so far as to say that this is the most important war, following the first

chimurenga. We are all committed to this struggle to restore the vanquished land through afforestation. . . . *Trees are our life-line!* We say,
'A ward with dense forests knows no death!' Even President Mugabe
and the government know that the earth cannot be the earth, and we
cannot be people without trees."

Bishop Machokoto's assertion about the connection between the
country's erstwhile political liberation struggle and the current war of
the trees is no coincidence. The quest for justice and liberation in
colonial Zimbabwe has always been integral to the good news propa-
gated by the AICs. Soul salvation and eternal life for believers in
heaven as antithesis to "the pit of fire" remained focal in the drive for
conversion and church growth. Yet, one of the major characteristics of
AIC eschatology is its emphasis on a *visible salvation* in the present
dispensation. This requires the realization of God's saving grace in
this existence, in the creation of black "holy cities," or "Jerusalems,"
where security, health, and well-being can be experienced tangibly in
closely knit communities of believers. Salvation, therefore, to many
Independents has strong connotations of holistic healing, as suggested above, and of justice and liberation.

The good news of eco-justice in the tree-planting Eucharist signals
much more than environmental care. It repeatedly underscores social
justice in the empowerment of the poor and marginalized people—
two-thirds of the world—to make a contribution which will be of
such significance that it captures, for once, the imagination of the
nation, the recognition of the government. To a large extent, the earthkeepers engaged in these ceremonies are similar to those in Brazil
who flock to the popular religious movements and are described by
Leonardo Boff as:

> Impoverished people who are of no account socially, who are wanted
> by no one, not even by the politicians whom they have elected; people
> who are anonymous, disoriented in a society that ejects and marginal-
> izes them . . . [those] who discover in these popular celebrations some
> measure of dignity, as well as a purpose in continuing to live, hope and
> struggle.[15]

Probably the most convincing example of the comprehensive
nature of eco-justice evolved in ZIRRCON praxis is to be found in the
movement's Women's Desk, with its seventy-five rural women's
clubs. Less rigidly organized along lines of religious affiliation than

AZTREC and the AAEC, the women's clubs—each comprising on average thirty to forty adult women—combine the objectives of earth care, socioeconomic advancement through income-generating projects, and the promotion of female emancipation. In compliance with ZIRRCON policy, women's clubs develop their own nurseries and woodlots as a condition for some form of sponsorship for their community development programs, such as sewing, bakeries, soap-production, agricultural projects, vocational training, and water schemes.

The combination of ecological repair and economic advancement in a poverty-ridden peasant society, is especially good news for women who bear the brunt of collecting firewood and attempt to keep their households going in an abused countryside. Considering, in addition, that some 80 percent of all adults in the AICs are women and that the majority of them have little or no access to the top leadership offices of bishop, priest, or minister in their respective churches, then the magnitude of relatively unfettered opportunity in their new clubs becomes apparent. Ms. Raviro Mutonga, chairperson of the Women's Desk, comments on the changed status of ZIRRCON women as follows: "They [the women] still constitute the bulk of marginalized and oppressed people in rural society. . . . They were deprived of the basic rights of self-determination, co-responsibility and shared authority. Here in ZIRRCON the women are now redefining their status. . . . They are treated as equals by the men and they have their own insights and plans in the movement without interference or domination from the side of men." The relief felt by women, to be engaged in and to receive recognition for their own struggle against poverty and ecological degradation without interference from their male counterparts in the movement, is reflected in Mutonga's address to club members during a women's tree-planting ceremony. "We women have our own things [green activity] here. I am so happy because we know these things are really ours. How satisfying to know that no human being will be coming here to interfere, to ask what it is we are doing. You fathers, who have come here today are in support of *our* endeavors. You have come here because of genuine interest."

Mutonga's words confirm feelings of self-worth, dignity, and commitment in the ranks of neatly uniformed female tree planters as they set an example of orderly, emancipated militancy in the green struggle. Ms. Mangombe, one of the local club leaders, concluded the ceremony with a prayer that summed up the good news for women in rural peasant society:

> "We thank you Lord for mercy, bestowed on us women. You have be-
> stowed a seven-fold grace on us. We were an oppressed "tribe" [*rudzi*],
> always criticized, even to the end of our days. A woman was given
> little space, even within her own home. A woman was not allowed to
> undertake a journey, without her father or husband following with a
> *tsvimbo* [club]. A woman was not allowed to attend court proceedings.
> A woman was never allowed to hold high position [lit., "to sit on high
> seats"]. But, we now see with our own eyes, Lord, that you change all
> this; as you yourself have said: 'Let the old things go by. Set your
> minds on the new things that will appear these days!' We place these
> new things in your hands, Lord, as we ask you to bless the Women's
> Club at 'Wadzanai Doroguru.' You have allowed us to plant trees and
> vegetables as you have planted in your own garden, Eden, where you
> allowed your representatives to live. We thank you that you have
> reintroduced that privilege for us women; we, the stewards of your
> creation. We thank you for male support, for the good men who have
> dug the holes for our trees. Bless the people [of ZIRRCON] whom you
> have sent here. Bless them as they traverse *all of Zimbabwe* to plant
> trees. Mwari, let this task have your full endorsement. . . . Strengthen
> us in our earthkeeping quest and let the message within the sermons
> keep motivating us. Amen."

In this prayer Mwari is not explicitly called "Mother," but in the thought world of the women tree planters he or she certainly is the "God of the mothers," the One who liberates women from bondage and sets them free to serve "Eden," the earth, from a position of dignity and equality with males. There is no overt militancy here, as if all existing patriarchal structures should be destroyed before women can come into their own—but assertive, courageous activity born of the conviction that Mwari is near and that he or she guides the struggle of restoring the earth in a new mode of equality and justice. The prayer includes a vision for earthkeeping throughout the entire country and is suggestive of gender harmony in a cause which ideally should transcend oppressive hierarchical authority in a new communion of all important yet humble service.

I have been able here to highlight only one or two features of what could be termed a contextualized form of "African ecofeminism." As yet, the story of women earthkeepers is lived at the grass roots by the growing numbers of women's clubs. Hopefully, the creative theology implicit in such development will yet be documented by the women concerned themselves to enrich and give impetus to the crucial labors of the "healing mothers of Eden" worldwide.

Challenge in Action

The strength of the earthkeeping churches of Zimbabwe lies in their willingness to respond to the needs of the earth community. They work in a spirit of sacrificial yet celebratory service despite discouraging ecological set-backs. Eco-justice in these churches takes shape as a life-style rather than a written code of conduct. We have briefly traced how this life-style in Zimbabwean peasant society translates into a spontaneous reinterpretation of the church's mission. Attempts at realizing this mission of earth care lead to structured, ritual, and symbolic change within the church. Here, the Gospel finds expression in wholeness, therapy, and liberation relevant to the needs of African society. It is based, moreover, on an incarnational Christology, conversant with and easily understood within the framework of indigenous African worldviews. In the development of their earth-healing ministry, which includes the struggle against poverty, the AICs promote eco-justice as a process which seeks balance rather than competition in the treatment of both human and ecological afflictions. Eco-justice thus stands as the sign of a deliberate shift in emphasis from human dominion over to human service of nature.

In pioneering new forms of ecological outreach, as an integral part of church life, the AAEC is challenging the world church to put its earthkeeping mission into practice. This means giving substance to ecotheological theories and ethical considerations which abound in the literature on creation of recent years. The AAEC derives its mandate for earthkeeping from an intuitive reading of scriptures on themes dealing with environmental stewardship. Scriptural truths are applied literally to the locally observed condition of an ailing earth community. This dialectic stimulates calls for mobilization of the entire church in earth care. As an instrument of earthkeeping the church is obviously better placed to revision its task, institutional shape, worship, and service from within the struggle rather than from a position of discreet, controversy-free distance.

Sacramental healing in an African earthkeeping church includes, as we have seen, afforestation as therapy for a denuded and soil-eroded landscape. Should the urban church in the global village accept its environmental responsibility, it could fruitfully celebrate the sacraments in confrontation with the evils of the urban context: water and air pollution, toxic waste, mountains of garbage and the need for proper recycling procedures. Remedial action in the urban situation is bound to be more complex than tree planting in rural wastelands. Nevertheless, inventive, city-cleansing pastorates could contribute substantially toward the protection and quality of life in the metropolis.

Regional ecumenism between Christian communities undoubtedly strengthens combined ministries of earth care. The Zimbabwean case study also illustrates that interchurch ecumenism in ecological stewardship is complemented and enriched by a broadened form of interreligious ecumenism that includes traditional religious collaboration and dialogue. Interfaith encounter in this instance does not lead to religious relativism, as some Christians may fear. For, the cooperation between Christian and traditionalist earthkeepers in the Zimbabwean war of the trees illustrates quite clearly that pluriform religious identities obtain clarity and tolerant acceptance where diverse religious partners direct their activity at the well-being of God's earth. Conflicts do arise at times. However, Christian witness on the whole is kept in a healthy and creative tension with the goodwill and respect shown the ecological partner of a different faith.

Notes

1. This and the other narratives derive from my interview discussions with ZIRRCON participants or are quotes from tree-planting sermons. They will appear in a forthcoming publication: M. L. Daneel, *African Earthkeepers,* vol. 2, *Environmental Mission and Liberation in Christian Perspective* (Pretoria: Unisa Press, 1999).

2. The African Independent Churches, also known as the African Initiated Churches (AICs), are found in large numbers throughout sub-Saharan Africa. In Southern Africa they represent vigorous, fast-growing movements varying in size from a few relatives in a small family church to several million adherents in the largest churches (e.g., the Zion Christian Church of Bishop Lekganyane, with its headquarters at Pietersburg, South Africa, and the African Apostolic Church of John Maranke, centered near Mutare in eastern Zimbabwe). Leadership in these churches is based on spiritual experience, charisma, a sense of vocation, and kinship ties, rather than on educational qualifications and theological training. To date, theological training programs for the AICs have barely touched the tip of the proverbial iceberg.

Typologically, the AICs can be classified in two main categories: the Ethiopian-type, or nonprophetic, churches whose patterns of worship and doctrines reflect those of the Western-oriented Protestant mission churches from which they have evolved; and the Spirit-type, or prophetic, churches (the vast majority)—mainly Zionist or Apostolic movements—with indigenized Pentecostal traits, focused on Holy Spirit manifestations, glossololia, and prophetic healing. Some of the latter churches develop leadership patterns with "messianic" or "iconic" features. See Marthinus L. Daneel, *Quest for Belonging: Introduction to a Study of African Independent Churches* (Gweru: Mambo Press, 1987), 38–42.

3. Joseph Sittler's call for the integration of ecology, justice, and Christian faith in his significant address, "Called to Unity," to the third assembly of the WCC, marked the beginning of intensified ecotheological reflection in the Christian ecumenical movement. Sittler considers a doctrine of redemption meaningful only when it swings within the larger orbit of a doctrine of creation. Joseph Sittler, "Called to Unity," *Ecumenical Review* 14 (1962): 178.

4. ZIRRCON evolved from an empirical research unit which facilitated my study of the religious factor in Zimbabwe's liberation struggle. As founder of the movement, I have admittedly influenced its religio-ecological activities. Yet, my contribution at the outset was more that of stimulating motivation for environmental reform and providing financial empowerment through fund-raising than attempting to provide a theological blueprint for all activities. Instead, I encouraged local initiative and contextualization. Consequently, there was no question of the imposition of ecological models from above.

5. In Bishop Mutendi's Zion Christian Church, for instance, the celebration of the Eucharist during the Easter paschal festivities became the pivot for an annual reconsideration of the classic mission command as found in Matthew 28:18–19. Zionist identification with this text stimulated country-wide missionary campaigns involving the majority of ZCC officeholders and resulting in consistent church expansion; Marthinus L. Daneel, "Missionary Outreach in African Independent Churches," *Missionalia* 8, no. 3 (1980).

6. John Carmody, *Ecology and Religion: Toward a New Christian Theology of Nature* (New York: Paulist Press, 1983), 78.

7. Quoted in Donald E. Messer, *A Conspiracy of Goodness: Contemporary Images of Christian Mission* (Nashville: Abingdon Press, 1992), 69–70.

8. John S. Pobee, *Toward an African Theology* (Nashville: Abingdon Press, 1979), 81–98.

9. Bengt Sundkler, *The Christian Ministry in Africa* (London: SCM Press, 1960), 292.

10. See also the attempts of ecotheologians to describe the world as God's or Christ's body; Sallie McFague, *Models of God: Theology for an Ecological, Nuclear Age* (London: SCM Press, 1987), 69f.; Messer, *A Conspiracy of Goodness,* 67f.

11. Aylward Shorter considers the Eucharist to be "the pre-eminently healing sacrament," the symbolism of which heralds social healing and reconciliation. "The Eucharist," he correctly suggests, "also brings about our organic involvement with the physical environment and the interaction of every level of our existence. If human beings are the synthesis of the universe, the Eucharist makes them even more clearly the priests of creation." Aylward Shorter, *Jesus and the Witchdoctor: An Approach to Healing and Wholeness* (Maryknoll, N.Y.: Orbis Books, 1985), 206.

12. Charles Nyamiti, "African Christologies Today," in *Faces of Jesus in Africa,* ed. Robert J. Schreiter (Maryknoll, N.Y.: Orbis Books, 1991), 10.

13. Several African theologians have pointed out that the traditional African healer, the *nganga,* has provided the primary paradigm for an indigenous Christology since the inception of African Christianity. Gabriel Setiloane believes that an authentic Christology should be sought in the healing practices of the *bongaka*; Gabriel M. Setiloane, *The Image of God among the Sotho-Tswana* (Rotterdam: Balkema, 1979), 64. According to John Pobee, the similarity between the *nganga* and Christ lies in both being "ensouled" by God during the process of healing; Pobee, *Toward an African Theology,* 93. Buana Kibongo in turn describes Christ's ministry as the fulfillment of *nganga*'s work. He stated that *"Ngangas* willed to save man, but did not succeed in doing so; Christ did so fully once for all. Christ has therefore accomplished the work of *Nganga*"; Buana Kibongo, "Priesthood," in *Biblical Revelation and African Beliefs,* ed. Kwesi A. Dickson and Paul Ellingworth (London: Lutterworth, 1969), 55. For a detailed discussion of the *nganga*-Christ paradigm, see J. Matthew Schoffeleers, "Christ in African Folk Theology: The *Nganga* Paradigm," in *Religion in Africa: Experience and Expression,* ed. Thomas D. Blakely, Walter E. A. van Beek, and Dennis L. Thomson (London: James Currey; Portsmouth, N.H.: Heinemann, 1994), 72–88.

14. Cécé Kolié, "Jesus as Healer?" in *Faces of Jesus in Africa,* ed. Robert J. Schreiter (Maryknoll, N.Y.: Orbis Books, 1991), 141–42.

15. Leonardo Boff, *Ecology and Liberation: A New Paradigm* (Maryknoll, N.Y.: Orbis Books, 1995), 66.

Response to Marthinus L. Daneel

MARTIN ROBRA

Marthinus **Daneel's** essay offers a very interesting and inspiring case study on a vital and important segment of contemporary Christianity: the growing family of African Independent Churches. Bishop Moses, as Daneel is called in Zimbabwe, leads us into new territories. To understand the landscape in front of us more fully, it might be of help to look at it from different viewpoints. I want to highlight two perspectives based on results of programmatic work undertaken by the World Council of Churches (WCC) in recent years: the Gospel and Cultures study and the Theology of Life program. My response, therefore, is structured in three sections:

1. The Gospel and Cultures approach, concentrating on the fact that Christian communities are constantly interacting with other living faiths and ideologies, with their symbols, rituals, worldviews, and cosmovisions.
2. The Theology of Life approach, starting from the level of social and religious practices and experiences.
3. Conclusions, highlighting certain aspects that are of particular importance within the Theology of Life framework and the context of globalization.

The Gospel and Cultures Approach

No doubt, Christianity in Africa is a religion that is very much alive. Christian symbols are not dying. What Marthinus Daneel tells us about God and Mwari, the Creator, and about Jesus and the *varidzi venyika,* the guardian ancestors of the land, shows that even very basic Christian symbols are adaptable to African cultures. The African Independent Churches operate within the environment of local traditional cultures. The relationship between the two is not simply one of either accommodation or opposition or radical critical revision, but a complex mixture of those three basic relations, described by H. Richard Niebuhr.

With changing configurations of basic symbols, Christianity has shown a tremendous capacity to take root in very different cultural environments. Christians living in the historical centers of Christianity tend to overlook that what they like to call a Christian culture is really just one of the many forms in which this encounter between the story of Christ and cultures has taken shape. The majority of Christians in the North still speak of syncretism in the pejorative sense when they are confronted with expressions of Christian faith embedded in a culture that is different from their own. But they are blind to how deeply intertwined their religious practices are with their cultural way of life. A vivid example of that was and still is the conflict caused by Chung Hyun Kyung's presentation at the WCC's seventh assembly in 1991 at Canberra.[1] I mention this for two reasons:

1. When we talk about interfaith dialogue, it is necessary to recognize that Christianity does not form one cultural block (Christendom) but is operating in different cultural environments that are shaped by different faith traditions. Interfaith dialogue, therefore, is not an option for ecumenism; it is a necessity to develop and qualify the dialogue among Christians themselves, coming from different cultural backgrounds. Ecumenism without interfaith dialogue is partially blind and paralyzed.

2. Many of the problems that are addressed in this volume can be traced back to the culture of domination that developed in Europe and North America. This culture successfully integrated Christian symbols and, in providing new context, influenced their interpretation. Daneel's essay, however, proves that there are other options. Analyzing them, we Christians in the North probably better understand how to reimagine and reshape a Christian way of life that is no longer condemned to

dominate but opens up an alternative, not just for ourselves. What we need to do is to delink the story of Christ from the culture of domination and complete the process of decolonization, driving home the lessons learned in mission history.

The Theology of Life Approach

If we are committed to do so, we necessarily embark on a project of social and cultural transformation. This implies that we move beyond the level of theoretical reflection and start to introduce transformative impulses on the level of social and religious practices, for example, on the level of practical consciousness that is fundamental for any culture. Public relations people, not by accident, emphasize that the image of the commodity has to be present in daily life activities of the people. Advertisements conquer the landscape in order to dominate the landscape of the mind. Concentrating on rituals like the tree-planting Eucharist and on healing ministry, which is exercised in environmental hospitals to accommodate the wounded earth, Marthinus Daneel gives convincing examples for an approach that is more sensitive to the practical consciousness and the link between social and religious practices. To quote Daneel: this ministry "takes shape as a life-style rather than a written code of conduct. . . . It is based, moreover, on an incarnational Christology, conversant with and easily understood within the framework of indigenous African worldviews."

The WCC started to explore the dimension of the practical consciousness in a study process on Ecclesiology and Ethics.[2] Influenced by Larry Rasmussen, this process introduced the language of the church as moral community and looked at processes of moral formation and malformation linked to the religious and social practices of a given community.[3] The Theology of Life program further explored this dimension. Twenty-three contextual case studies addressed basic ethical challenges, listening to peoples' stories, poems, songs, and drama. Crosscultural exchange between different case-study groups helped them to better understand commonalities and differences. Representatives of the group met in a culminating event, modeled after a *sakoni,* a traditional African market, which took place one year ago in Nairobi. During this process, we learned to appreciate methodologies attentive to people's practices and focused on expressions of the practical consciousness that constitutes their experiences.

Just to add another example different from the African context, I want to show how the experience of a small Guatemalan community can be interpreted with Gospel and Cultures and Theology of Life approaches. Part of the Theology of Life process was a meeting of representatives of indigenous peoples involved in the program. The meeting was held in Guatemala City. On the second day, participants visited a small village in a rural area. The community of this village had suffered a lot in the struggle for human rights, dignity, and self-determination. They had started to reorganize their lives based on Christian convictions and their Mayan traditions. But, in doing so, they were confronted with an ethical dilemma. Responding to a question concerning their agricultural practices and the use of pesticides and fertilizers, they shared with us the following insights:

> "Yes, we know we are doing harm to Mother Earth. We don't treat her well, using pesticides and fertilizers. This is not what our Mayan traditions tell us to do. But look, we have no other choice. If we want education for our children, we must earn the money we need to run the school and pay the teacher. We only have some income, however, if we sell cash crops at the city-market which look very nice. Unfortunately, we never get a fair price that reflects our real production costs and the value of our labor. We simply cannot compete with very, very cheap imports of agricultural products subsidized by the U.S. government. It is money of taxpayers in the North that is used against us. What are Christians, what are churches in the North doing to change this situation?"

This statement combines in an interesting way a basic concept of the traditional Mayan culture with ethical considerations and an ecclesiologically motivated plea for solidarity by Christian communities in the United States. The conflict between a traditional cultural concept of agricultural practices and the mechanisms of a globalized market economy that has its strong power base in the North creates an ethical dilemma which has its own cultural and ecclesiological implications.

Conclusions

Gospel and Cultures and Theology of Life reflect on the complex relationship of Christian symbols, other faith traditions, and cultures, as well as the economic and political systems. The expansion of transnational corporate activity, the integration of the global financial system, and the intensification of world trade in coevolution with a global communication and media networks have their effects on the lives of people, their cultures, and religions in any part of the world. A multiplicity of linkages develops, transgressing old boundaries and forcing people living in different and distant places into interaction.

At the same time, people learn to appreciate the hidden sources of their very identities and begin to revitalize ethnic, religious, and cultural traditions—for example, the old symbols of belonging and solidarity. But this, very often, creates new tensions. The reverse side of increasing interdependence in a world where both political and economic power are distributed unequally are ethically unacceptable situations of political, economic, and cultural domination, fragmentation of old patterns of life in community, and deeply felt insecurity. Churches as well as theological seminaries will need to address those challenges.

But how to overcome fragmentation and build community from the bottom up when power is concentrated globally? A method conducive to building up local and regional cultures of life and articulating theologies indigenous to them commends itself in this situation.[4] Theology of Life went beyond the Gospel and Cultures approach when it embarked on a process of community building and theological reflection across boundaries and cultures. The twenty-three case studies in different parts of the world began to interact. The methodology of the process was based on the assumption that theological commonalities and differences, when raised up in local, regional, and worldwide interconnected processes, can deepen understanding in each place and for all involved together. The journey started in 1994 and culminated in a meeting of representatives of the different groups in 1997 in Nairobi. The journey continues. Exciting perspectives are opening up. For a project like that, the WCC provides a unique and wonderful platform. Working on this project, I feel privileged and, please forgive me when I say this, I am proud to work for the World Council of Churches.

Notes

1. See *Signs of the Spirit. Official Report, Seventh Assembly, Canberra, Australia 7–20 February 1991,* ed. Michael Kinnamon (Geneva: WCC Publications; Grand Rapids, Mich.: Eerdmans, 1991), 37–47 and 15–16.

2. See *Ecclesiology and Ethics,* ed. Thomas F. Best and Martin Robra (Geneva: World Council of Churches, 1997).

3. Ibid. 42, par. 62: "This process takes place within the ethos or environment of a particular society, community or church. The songs we sing, the stories we tell, the issues we debate, the instruction we offer, the persons thought worth emulating, the common habits and practices of a culture—these are the sources and 'signatures' of 'our' ethos. And the 'moral environment' is marked not least by the way a community, society or church is ordered—who does what, by what means, and with what kind of authority. Thus it is the whole *way of life* which morally forms and educates (or malforms and miseducates), and this way of life both creates and reflects a particular moral ethos."

4. Larry Rasmussen, unpublished document on the work of Unit III (Justice, Peace, Creation) of the World Council of Churches.

Social Transformation through Environmental Justice

VERNICE MILLER-TRAVIS

This narrative focuses on securing eco-justice in community and building civil society partnerships for earth community. We will consider: what environmental justice is, the church's role as a partner in social transformation, and how to strengthen community links for global and local sustainability. Those concerns have animated my own work, first with the United Church of Christ, then with West Harlem Environmental Action, and most recently with the Natural Resources Defense Council.

What Is Environmental Justice?

Environmental justice embraces the principle that all people in communities have a right to a safe, healthy and sustainable environment. No person, group or community should be denied the protection of environmental health, employment, housing, transportation and civil rights laws, either due to race, ethnicity, gender, or social and economic disempowerment. The linkage between disempowerment and environmental degradation constitutes fundamental human rights issues.

Charles Lee and I, working with several others, wrote this definition as part of a United Church of Christ report on the struggle for environmental and economic justice in St. James Parish.[1] There, in Convent, Louisiana, the local community successfully resisted and actually stopped a PVC plant, owned by Shintech, a Japanese company.

Quite a set of issues in the broad context of societal transformation intersected in this one local community experience. The purpose of environmental justice activism is to help such impacted communities to survive and flourish.

This is not just our own view of environmental justice. Bunyan Bryant of the University of Michigan, who has done extensive research and writing on the subject, proposes similarly that:

> Environmental justice refers to those cultural norms and values, rules, regulations, behaviors, policies, and decisions to support sustainable communities where people can interact with confidence that their environment is safe, nurturing, and productive. . . . Environmental justice is supported by decent paying and safe jobs; quality schools and recreation; decent housing and adequate health care; democratic decision-making and personal empowerment; and communities free of violence, drugs and poverty. These are communities where both cultural and biological diversity are respected and highly revered and where distributive justice prevails.[2]

When we talk about issues of environmental justice, we are really talking about what makes it possible to live sustainably in community, globally as well as locally.

At the center of most environmental justice issues is a pattern of racial discrimination, or "environmental racism." Again, in Bunyan Bryant's terms:

> Environmental racism refers to those institutional rules, regulations, and policies of government or corporate decisions that deliberately target certain communities for least desirable land uses, resulting in the disproportionate exposure of toxic and hazardous waste on communities based upon certain prescribed biological characteristics. Environmental racism is the unequal protection against toxic and hazardous waste exposure and systematic excⸯusion of people of color from environmental decisions affecting their communities.[3]

Communities of color and low-income communities are taking stands about *not* wanting particular waste facilities or policies to go forward in their own communities. But that is just the most obvious surface reality. The bigger picture is that all of these communities have been joining together for the last fifteen years to bring about some fundamental transformation both in this country and abroad. I want to focus on what we have done and on how the church has been involved. Oftentimes, I think this is a very unique partnership; the churches—particular congregations of various denominations and ecumenical bodies such as the National Council of Churches and the World Council of Churches—have been very strong ongoing partners in working with communities and with regions on specific issues of environmental injustice. Often their role is subtle and unpublicized as they go about building principled partnerships for societal transformation.

UCC Research on Environmental Racism

My work has concentrated on environmental justice since 1986, when I was hired by the United Church of Christ (UCC) Commission for Racial Justice (CRJ) to serve as principal research assistant for their "Special Project on Toxic Injustice." This research project grew out of a series of complaints received from, and actions taken by, UCC congregations, first in the Deep South. These local church leaders wanted advice about how to deal with state agencies, local municipalities, and waste management companies or industries that were trying to place or expand waste facilities in small rural communities, mostly populated by people of color. The initial locus was predominantly African-American Warren County, North Carolina, which the state chose as the site for a landfill to store polychlorinated biphenyls (PCBs), hazardous organochlorine compounds that have toxic effects on humans and wildlife. The UCC helped to mobilize protests that led to the arrests of more than five hundred activists who nonviolently blocked the trucks entering the site. This nonviolent protest was one of the first times that civil rights and environmental agendas were merged.

In light of that experience, the UCC Commission for Racial Justice continued to explore the relationship between race and toxic exposure. This special research project became the bell weather job of my life. I am a civil rights advocate by training and all I ever wanted to do was work on civil rights issues. So I was introduced to Ben Chavis, the CRJ's national executive director. At the time I was a Columbia University student and Ben was a Ph.D. candidate at Union Theological Seminary. I encountered Ben one day on the corner of 122nd Street and Claremont Avenue and said, "Well, what are you doing at the commission, and why don't you hire me, because I have the capacity to help you." Such conversations went on for awhile before Ben finally relented and said, "Why don't you come and talk to Charles Lee. He's working on a very interesting research project on toxic injustice, funded by offerings received from UCC congregations."

I met Charles Lee, and he described the special project, including how local community groups were running up against very serious problems with state environmental regulatory agencies making decisions about siting and building hazardous waste facilities in predominantly African-American and Latino communities. At first, in the early 1980s, the CRJ would receive one phone call a month, then two or three calls a month, then a call a week, and then a call every day. The calls reached a point where one couldn't just give people information over the phone about what they could do. It became necessary to look cohesively at what was happening in that particular region of the country and elsewhere. So Charles Lee decided to undertake this special project on toxic injustice, in which I became a partner.

In our research, we identified every residential zip code in the United States—at the time numbering about thirty-five thousand. Then we determined the zip codes of the U.S. Environmental Protection Agency's list of hazardous waste sites (superfund sites and sites identified under the Comprehensive Environmental Response, Compensation, and Liability Act of 1980), and we correlated this information with the racial composition of all the zip codes that had two or more hazardous waste sites. We found that *race* was the most statistically significant indicator of where those facilities were located.

We tested not only for the indicator of race, but also for such class indicators as per capita income, median income, home value, community land value, and level of education. Among dozens of variables, race proved to be the most statistically significant indicator. The strength of our data indicated that this phenomenon was *not* a random occurrence. We saw that there was intentionality in how these sites came to be located in these particular communities.

We then began to speak to people in other parts of the country who were having similar experiences. We confirmed that this was truly a national phenomenon, affecting many states, municipalities, and tribal lands. It was happening on Native American reservations, in urban and rural areas, and there was no community of color that was not touched by it.

We also *dis*proved our initial hypothesis that economic class would be a strong, if not the strongest, factor in locating hazardous waste sites. Instead, we found to our surprise that upper- and middle-income communities of color were equally as impacted as were poor and low-income communities of color. So, in 1987, we wrote and issued the report *Toxic Wastes and Race in the United States*.[4] Its gathered data and statistical analysis codified for the first time the reality that many communities in this country were experiencing. The report wasn't hypothetical, emotional, or exaggerated. It illumined the daily reality of peoples' lives and, coincidentally, my own life in New York City.

Environmental Action in West Harlem

As we were editing *Toxic Wastes and Race,* I was introduced to some people in West Harlem, in upper Manhattan, the community where I lived. These community residents organized to protest the North River sewage treatment facility that had recently gone "on line, producing an incredibly offensive odor that most affects those who live or work near the plant." Keep in mind that this is an extraordinary place architecturally—a federal historic district, where Alexander Hamilton once lived in a house that still exists (hence the name Hamilton Heights). In 1994 the average home in this historic district was appraised at $350,000, and the average family income was $72,000. It is a mixed-income urban community of color, with poor, working-class, middle-income, and business and professional people all living together, which is typical of most sections of Harlem. About ninety-eight thousand people live in the community immediately adjacent to that sewage treatment plant.

Why was the sewage treatment plant located there? What kinds of public health impacts would it have on our lives? We wanted to know, but we could get no information. So we began to organize around the principles that we lifted up in *Toxic Wastes and Race*. It is well known that sewage treatment plants may create public health consequences, and those public health consequences are intentionally being visited on a certain subset of the population here in New York City and in the State of New York. This is unjust, it is inhuman, and it is a violation of everything we hold dear as principles of justice. Such action would not be sanctioned as an official act of the government of the State of

New York and the United States.

The sewage treatment plant was originally to have been built on the upper West Side of Manhattan, as is well documented in the archives of the New York City Planning Commission. But the planners of the mid-1950s concluded that the upper West Side, thirty blocks south of Harlem, should become a cultural center in which such a plant would not be aesthetically pleasing. So the power structure chose West Harlem as the site for the facility. It fit their master plan of land use and zoning. They had already placed six out of seven of Manhattan's bus depots in Harlem, two of them in West Harlem, which was zoned as a "mixed-use" development area and therefore a ready candidate for environmental injustice. In other words, I was living with this community problem, not just researching it. It became a focus for organizing that took years to bear fruit.

It took the West Harlem organization until 1993 to prevail on that issue. By prevail, I do not mean that the sewage treatment plant has gone away. But we brought litigation and caused the city and state of New York to take serious action to fix that plant so that our community would no longer smell like a giant toilet bowl.

Larger Patterns in the Movement

Our experience in West Harlem is emblematic of the experience of communities across the United States, particularly communities of color. These communities have determined that enough is enough. Environmental impacts (both negative and beneficial) must be distributed fairly, and the costs must be shared equitably. Oftentimes, the media categorize struggles for environmental justice as mere demands of NIMBY—"not in my backyard." But the movement is so much bigger. What the environmental justice movement has grown to encompass are issues of long-term sustainable economic development that involve questions of public health, land use, and zoning. Struggles for environmental justice highlight the nexus between community empowerment and decision making and the respect that government must show for the voices and rights of local communities.

This was expressed dramatically when an unprecedented number of grassroots nongovernmental organizations (NGOs) attended the 1992 Earth Summit in Rio de Janeiro. There, leaders of environmental justice groups and scholars of the movement, such as Robert Bullard[5] and Dana Alston, articulated its current activity and underlying theory, in response to the environmental injustices being experienced in poor, indigenous, or lower-caste communities around the world.

The movement had already begun to coalesce around the Principles of Environmental Justice that were articulated by delegates who attended the First National People of Color Environmental Leadership Summit, 27 October 1991. As Jim Schwab, a Lutheran layman, described it, this unique summit "drew more than 600 activists, combining the colors of the rainbow in one giant sharing and strategizing meeting that has literally and permanently changed the complexion of the U.S. environmental movement."[6] That gathering challenged mainstream environmental organizations, which had previously involved few persons of color and paid little attention to environmental colonialism, to give racial and social justice direct attention in their policy advocacy and educational programs. Thanks to the initiative of the Eco-Justice Working Group of the National Council of Churches of Christ in the U.S.A., formed in 1986 with Chris Cowap as staff director, a large proportion of participants in the 1991 Environmental Leadership Summit received subsidies from mainline church agencies that enabled them to attend.

The comprehensive set of principles, articulated at the 1991 Leadership Summit "to build a movement of all peoples of color to fight the destruction and the taking of our lands and communities . . . and to secure our political, economic, and cultural liberation," state that environmental justice:

- affirms the sacredness of Mother Earth, ecological unity, and the interdependence of all species;
- demands that public policy be based on mutual respect and justice for all peoples, free from any discrimination or bias;
- calls for universal protection from a range of toxic threats and demands cessation of the production of highly toxic materials, as well as military exploitation of lands, peoples, and cultures;
- demands the right to participate as equal partners at every level of decision making, including needs assessment, planning, implementation, enforcement, and evaluation;
- affirms worker rights to a safe and healthy work environment;

- recognizes a special legal and natural relationship of Native Peoples to the U.S. government in agreements affirming sovereignty and self-determination;
- emphasizes the need for urban and rural ecological policies to clean up and rebuild cities and rural areas in balance with nature;
- protects the right of victims of environmental injustice to receive full compensation and reparations;
- calls for education on social and environmental issues and life-styles of reduced consumption and less waste to ensure the health of the natural world.

These Principles of Environmental Justice have now achieved wide international support among NGOs and in some governmental structures. This consensus is evident, for example, in the shared vision of basic values to be implemented in sustainable development that were set forth in the 1999 Benchmark Draft II of The Earth Charter. Principle eleven enjoins individuals, organizations, business enterprises, communities, and nations to "honor and defend the right of all persons, without discrimination, to an environment supportive of their dignity, bodily health, and spiritual well-being." Specifically this means to:

1. Secure the human right to potable water, clean air, uncontaminated soil, food security, and safe sanitation in urban, rural, and remote environments.

2. Establish racial, religious, ethnic, and socioeconomic equality.

3. Affirm the right of indigenous peoples to their spirituality, knowledge, lands and resources and to their related practice of traditional sustainable livelihoods.

4. Institute effective and efficient access to administrative and judicial procedures, including redress and remedy, that enables all persons to enforce the environmental rights.

At the same time that environmental justice became a worldwide focus, it also became a common focus of the churches. In late 1993, the NCC Eco-Justice Working Group, staffed by Dr. Jean Sindab, organized a Black Church Environmental Summit that brought together pastors and community organizers from communities experiencing the effects of environmental racism. That gathering also helped to place environmental justice prominantly on the agenda of the newly forming National Religious Partnership for the Environment.

Church agencies and community groups became partners in local and regional organizing for environmental justice on other continents as well as in North America. Denominational bodies passed important resolutions that commit the churches to continue working in partnership with local and regional environmental organizations, and to support sustainable development projects around the world. They have also produced educational materials to teach congregations within each denomination about struggles for environmental justice and against environmental racism. The church has actually assumed a pivotal role in educating itself, its members, and segments of the larger public about these important issues and in explaining how to participate in multiracial, grassroots expressions of the environmental justice movement.

A majority of the community organizations that express concerns for environmental health with social justice have been, and continue to be, led by women. As Dorceta E. Taylor documents, "In no other sector of the environmental movement (not even in the more progressive or radical sectors) can one find such high percentages of women of color occupying positions as founders and leaders of organizations, workshop and conference organizers, researchers, strategists, lawyers, academics, policymakers, community organizers."[7] And the churches, often at the initiative of women, have continued to play a central role in addressing those issues by empowering grassroots groups to gain a voice and claim their rights.

The Task of Social Transformation

Environmentalism that takes racial and social justice seriously raises fundamental questions about how we in the privileged sectors of "developed" countries envision moving toward a just and sustainable society and how we affect global environmental health and environmental quality. There is an urgent need to rethink our modes of production, our industrial processes, the way we live as communities, still much too segregated, and the way we decide to respond. If we do not begin to grapple with some of these very hard issues, then we are likely to go down a sinkhole together, collectively. It would be the one thing on which we unite: *not* being able to survive as a society. If, or when, we finally figure out what is going on, it might be too late to do much about it.

Consequently, the task we are called to undertake is not just transforming our realities where we live, but seeking social transformation comprehensively. With that in mind, eight years ago I spent a lot of time working internationally in preparation for the Earth Summit, organizing nongovernmental organizations in the United States and around the world to be able to have some fundamental impact on decision making at the 1992 United Nations Conference on Environment and Development—the Rio Earth Summit. I staffed a group called the U.S. Citizens Network for Sustainable Development. What we were able to do in this process was to create for the first time a formal role for a large number of NGOs at international UN conferences.

Prior to Rio, only a smattering of NGOs would be invited to participate in UN conferences. At the Earth Summit, we charted the participation of fifteen hundred NGOs from around the world. From that point forward, we have never had less than one thousand NGOs at major UN conferences, such as the Beijing Conference on Women, the Cairo Conference on Population and Development, and the Istanbul Conference on Sustainable Urban Development. My involvement in that process grew out of my environmental justice work in the United States, which was about opening up the process of decision making and expanding the roles of those who live and experience these issues at the most local level so that they are a part of public decision making.

No matter what the forum, those who have been living the experience have every right to be at that table and to determine the direction of decision making. As someone who lives in an underdeveloped community within one of the richest nations on the face of the earth, I know that the most important thing for those of us who live there is to have a voice, to feel that we have something meaningful to say about our future and our lives. Essentially, that is what environmental justice is about. Those who have not been at the table, those whose lives have been turned upside down by people making decisions for them, have a right to be at the table, have a right to know what the discussion is about, and have a right to shape the discussion.

My more recent role as director of Environmental Justice at the

Natural Resources Defense Council (NRDC) was to get invited to just about every environmental table there is, both internationally and domestically, and to take a lot of people with me to those tables. Now, I eventually get up from the table and leave a group of people where I once stood, so they can make decisions for themselves. The goal is to involve those most affected in direct conversation with those who have decision-making power over policy.

A decade after its initial report, the United Church of Christ Commission for Racial Justice began a conversation with the White House Council on Environmental Quality, to plan for a series of environmental justice briefings of the highest ranking federal officials in communities across the United States. The first two in a series of such briefings occurred in Los Angeles in July 1998 and in New York City in March 1999, with the aim of bringing people who live these experiences daily face-to-face with high-level federal officials who ultimately make the decisions about what happens in their lives. How vigorously are we going to enforce federal law? Are we going to make the linkages between issues of housing and food supply, and food quality and water quality, and land use? To what extent and in what ways are we going to allow our society as a whole to see the connected ways that people live?

As long as we can continue to maintain racial distinction and separation in this country and abroad, as long as we allow race and class and income to really drive how we view and work with each other, or whether or not we can even sit at the same table, we are never going to see either the real connections or the bigger picture. We need to have one conversation about earth community in its local manifestations. It cannot be a conversation just among environmentalists or, for that matter, just among church people. We must cross the lines of race, class, creed, and special interest that have kept us separate for so long.

Of all the work that Charles Lee has done, his most poignant publication is a book, co-edited with Robert Bullard and J. Eugene Grigsby, III, entitled *Residential Apartheid: The American Legacy* (1994). It highlights the continuing legacy of racial segregation in housing and land use in the United States, where we continue to be a society of people who are separate from each other. As long as we remain separate from each other, issues of environmental injustice will continue frequently to present themselves.

Making the Connections

In addition to the importance of bridging the separation, the other big lesson I learned over the last fifteen years is that it is very inadequate to look at environmental policy in this country or to export this concern internationally as single issues. Much of the press coverage is about single issues of water pollution, air pollution, soil destruction, crop loss, or deforestation. Somehow, those issues are seldom seen to be interrelated. I have yet to visit a community anywhere in this country or anywhere in the world that does not experience several of those issues together and simultaneously. But this agency deals with water quality. That ministry deals with other environmental issues. None of us can really provide the answer to the complex problems found in these communities. Isolating issues doesn't work because nobody lives like that. Nobody is affected by only one issue.

Consequently, we have been trying to bring the executive leadership of government at federal and state levels to the view that people who have poor housing also probably have poor health. They probably lack access to a good food supply. They probably are impacted by a range of different environmental assaults and threats. So public officials need to have a common conversation and to hear from these communities about what their reality is. The church can be a midwife to this process.

National and international environmental organizations are not very good at working with and in communities. They don't spend much time listening to voices from local communities, because they are working at the macro policy level. But environmental justice groups remind us that issues at the macro level are still about what affects people locally, at the micro level, on a day-to-day basis. If our hypotheses, analyses, and solutions do not capture the most local aspects of those issues, then they lack focus.

Here is a classic example. A number of my former colleagues at the NRDC had been working on global climate change, when I received a call from a network of groups in Kentucky, which included churches active in CORA, the Coalition on Religion in Appalachia. They pointed out that the NRDC was having a conversation about global climate change but had somehow neglected to invite to the conversation those people who live and work in the coal mining industry and those communities that are dependent on coal mining for their very survival. They asked, "Who are you talking to?" I said, "Oh, boy, isn't that a good question. Let me call my colleagues in Washington and find out who we are talking to." The response I got was: "We haven't gotten to them yet. We're dealing with the big picture issues. We haven't gotten down to that level yet. But when we get there, we'll invite them."

My response to that was: "How can you have a conversation at *any* level without the people whose lives are ultimately going to be destroyed by what we are recommending as fundamental policy changes, both domestically and internationally? Have we been thinking about them? We're asking for a 40 percent reduction in coal production and the burning of coal by a date certain, just a few years from now." In order to achieve this, we are going to have to close down a lot of coal-powered plants. A lot of coal is not going to be mined anymore, a goal that I completely support. But, in the interim, don't we have a public responsibility to help coal miners and their families make the transition? Attention must be paid to what happens to their lives, given the fact that half of Appalachia's rather unhealthy economy is still dependent on coal production and coal mining.

Clearly, that was not a point we had thought much about. As usual, that kind of concern is not a prominent focus in environmental policy analyses that emphasize the big picture. But the environmental justice view is that there is no big picture that is not essentially about how both nature and people can thrive interdependently *in each place*.

Environmental issues are *not* distinguishable from, but rather are woven into, the fabric of racial, social, and economic justice. In response to this reality, the environmental justice movement mobilizes community, regional, and national coalitions involving various interest groups across racial, ethnic, and class lines. Such coalitions, at their best, challenge economic practices that threaten vulnerable groups and ecosystems, while they support policies that serve the common good. This, of course, is quite consistent with the expectation of social transformation expressed in the biblical vision of the Kingdom of God coming on Earth.

Notes

1. See *From Plantations to Plants: Report of the Emergency National Commission on Environmental and Economic Justice in St. James Parish* (Cleveland: Commission on Racial Justice, United Church of Christ, 1998).

2. Bunyan Bryant, introduction to *Environmental Justice: Issues, Policies, and Solutions,* ed. Bunyan Bryant (Washington, D.C.: Island Press, 1995), 6.

3. Ibid., 5.

4. Commission for Racial Justice, *Toxic Wastes and Race in the United States: A National Report on the Racial and Socioeconomic Characteristics of Communities with Hazardous Waste Sites* (New York: United Church of Christ, 1987).

5. See Robert D. Bullard, *Dumping in Dixie: Race, Class, and Environmental Quality* (Boulder: Westview Press, 1990); and his essays in *Toxic Struggles: The Theory and Practice of Environmental Justice,* ed. Richard Hofrichter (Philadelphia: New Society Publishers, 1993).

6. Jim Schwab, *Deeper Shades of Green: The Rise of Blue-Collar and Minority Environmentalism in America* (San Francisco: Sierra Club Books, 1994), xxii.

7. Dorceta E. Taylor, "Women of Color, Environmental Justice, and Ecofeminism," in *Ecofeminism: Women, Culture, Nature,* ed. Karen J. Warren (Bloomington: Indiana University Press, 1995), 58ff.

Partnership for the Environment among U.S. Christians: Reports from the National Religious Partnership for the Environment

The Eco-Justice Working Group
of the National Council of Churches

William Somplatsky-Jarman

Eco-justice, or the integration of ecological wholeness with social and economic justice, has been the unifying theme of the National Council of Churches of Christ Eco-Justice Working Group since its inception in 1984. The origin and subsequent history of the Working Group mirrors the evolution of the ecumenical discussion on how to integrate one's experience and knowledge of God, who is both Creator and Redeemer. While each member communion may define eco-justice with different words or phrases, essentially it can be seen as "the well-being of all humankind on a thriving earth," as the Restoring Creation for Ecology and Justice policy of the Presbyterian Church (USA) puts it.

In large measure, this is because the NCC Eco-Justice Working Group brought together individuals and denominations which have played an integral role in the discussion. People such as Bill Gibson, Owen Owens, and Dieter Hessel come to mind. Or the Presbyterian Church (USA), which developed a policy in 1971 entitled "Christian Responsibility for Environmental Renewal," and another on energy in 1974 as part of a larger ecumenical effort to respond to the energy crunch in the United States in the 1970s. The Board of National Ministries of the American Baptist Churches and its staff wrestled with integrating justice and ecology in 1971 (see *Foundations* 17, no. 2

[April/June 1974]). Also, note that the first Earth Day was in 1970; several denominations updated previous statements or adopted new ones shortly after the twentieth anniversary of Earth Day in 1990.

Some members of the NCC Eco-Justice Working Group were participants in earlier pivotal ecumenical and international events, including the fifth assembly of the World Council of Churches in Nairobi, where the concept of a "Just, Participatory and Sustainable Society" was established as a council-wide theme, and its follow-up conference at MIT in 1979 entitled "Faith, Science and the Future." As the ecumenical agenda shifted to the next stage with a focus entitled "Justice, Peace and the Integrity of Creation," working group members remained active and participated in the worldwide gathering in Seoul in 1989. Since that time, the focus has been on ensuring a religious presence at major international events, such as the Earth Summit in 1992, and its spin-off conferences, such as the Cairo conference on population.

While the ecumenical discussions often focused on theology and ethics, the NCC Eco-Justice Working Group sought as well to engage the churches in the struggle for ecology and justice together. This has meant addressing pertinent environmental issues, such as acid rain, energy production and efficiency, and toxic poisoning of communities. Efforts were made to ensure that eco-justice themes were integrated into the lives of congregations through worship and preaching, education and leadership development, congregational and individual lifestyle change, public policy advocacy, and community involvement.

The Eco-Justice Working Group also served an important role in prodding the mainstream environmental organizations to broaden their agenda to embrace the social and economic justice aspects of environmental issues. An example would be the letter in 1988 to the "Big Ten" environmental organizations expressing concern about the relative absence of people of color on their staffs and addressing environmental racism as an integral part of their agendas.

We have also prodded the church-based social justice groups to look beyond their frequently very anthropocentric views to encompass ecological wholeness. Much of this has occurred in the context of developing church policies or in the internal struggles within the World Council of Churches as it has sought to define programmatic agendas, given dwindling resources. Also, the Eco-Justice Working

Group, with its broad agenda, has challenged some in the church who seem to believe that a technological "fix" exists for all environmental problems.

At the same time, we have established, and try to maintain, strong ties to community groups involved in local struggles for environmental justice, and we help them find a platform in the religious community for their concerns. Here, the Eco-Justice Working Group partnered with the SouthWest Organizing Project to cosponsor interfaith hearings and a toxic tour in Albuquerque, New Mexico, and El Paso, Texas. It also produced a video entitled "For Our Children," which focused on the chemical poisoning of Louisiana communities and their people.

For the first several years of its existence, the Eco-Justice Working Group brought together several of the mainline Protestant denominations around a common table. The National Council of Churches provided part-time staff support. Working Group members pooled rather limited funds to cover program initiatives. Very few of the denominational representatives could give major attention to environmental issues. They frequently carried additional portfolios of responsibility for their denominations.

With the advent of the National Religious Partnership for the Environment (NRPE) in 1993, the Eco-Justice Working Group received a major shot in the arm. The infusion of significant funding permitted hiring full-time staff and undertaking major program work. In addition to two full-time staff at the National Council of Churches, the Eco-Justice Working Group has part-time staff for a Black Church Network and funds a public policy intern in Washington, D.C.

Outreach to other communions was increased, and the membership grew. A Black Church Summit drew 160 leaders and led to the creation of the Black Church Network. Twenty-five congregations have received grants to establish local environmental programs. An Orthodox Summit on the Environment was attended by seventy Orthodox Christian clergy and lay leaders. Currently, the Eco-Justice Working Group has twenty-two communions and ecumenical bodies in its fold. These include the African Methodist Episcopal Church, African Methodist Episcopal Zion Church, American Baptist Churches, Antiochian Orthodox Church, Armenian Orthodox Church, Christian Church (Disciples of Christ), Church of the Brethren, Episcopal

Church, Evangelical Lutheran Church of America, Friends United Meeting, Greek Orthodox Archdiocese of America, Moravian Church in America, National Baptist Convention/America, Orthodox Church in America, Philadelphia Yearly Meeting of Friends, Presbyterian Church (USA), Reformed Church in America, Swedenborgian Church, United Church of Christ, United Methodist Church, and the Commission on Religion in Appalachia. It truly is a "working" group. Members meet three times yearly and serve on subcommittees and task forces. Programs are designed and developed with members sharing responsibility along with staff.

Currently, congregational mobilization is a centerpiece of the work. This is promoted through an environmental justice covenant program where congregations pledge officially to incorporate eco-justice into the warp and woof of their life. An eco-justice ministry occurs through worship and preaching, education and learning, congregational and individual life-styles, and involvement in public policy, work, and community issues. Resources to assist congregations have been developed and distributed. For example, in 1998, seventy-five thousand congregations received a worship resource packet, including bulletin inserts, for Earth Day Sunday. In 1996, the Earth Day Sabbath mailing focused on endangered species, and in 1997 global climate change was the theme. Ten thousand congregational resource packets, entitled "God's Earth Our Home," edited by Shantilal Bhagat of the Church of the Brethren, were produced and distributed. Training events on how to use the packet's thirteen study sessions, worship and biblical resources, and bibliography were held in several cities. The Evangelical Lutheran Churches of America produced a video entitled "Faithful Earthkeeping: The Church as a Creation Awareness Center."

Congregations, middle governing bodies, and ecumenical groups are being assisted by Eco-Justice Coordinators (EJC). These volunteers might be described as field outreach workers to help with eco-justice activities. The United Methodist Church and the Presbyterian Church (USA) have had several years of experience with such a concept. Other denominations are moving to incorporate it in their networks of local church activists. An EJC is recognized officially by a conference, synod, or presbytery and promotes eco-justice concerns at every opportunity. In reality, the work of each EJC is different in emphasis and amount of time available, but generally, the amount of eco-justice activity in congregations and church bodies increases greatly when an EJC is in place. Training events for EJCs have been held at three national conferences and within some regional gatherings. A task description and manual have been written. Working with local and regional bodies, the NCC Eco-Justice Working Group has cosponsored smaller regional leadership training events with an average participation of 120 persons. These events usually include worship, a keynote speaker, workshops, and an opportunity for networking on local environmental issues. In 1998, a toxic tour of Louisiana for Black church leaders was held, as was a conference in Mississippi for women from community and religious groups.

Education for public policy advocacy has been a focus from the beginning. Several members of the Eco-Justice Working Group are based in Washington, D.C., and carry primary responsibility for coordinating such issues in their denominations. These staff gather twice monthly to review pending legislation and develop action strategies. Legislative briefings have been held for grassroots activists, and each EJC is trained in public policy advocacy. The issues vary, but the Eco-Justice Working Group has concentrated on Superfund, clean air and water, endangered species, wetlands, and climate change.

Recently, major time and effort has been devoted to climate change. This work has been coordinated internationally with the World Council of Churches. Eco-Justice Working Group members have been part of conferences sponsored by the WCC and European churches, where policy and study documents were developed. A similar event was held in New York City. A five-part study booklet on climate change, entitled "It's God's World: Christians, the Environment and Climate Change," was sent to fifty thousand congregations and local church activists.

In addition, efforts to influence the U.S. government's approach to the issue have garnered attention. Eco-Justice Working Group members have been present at major United Nations meetings, such as the Berlin and Kyoto Climate Summits in 1995 and 1997. A WCC-initiated petition campaign in the industrialized countries was led in the United States by the Eco-Justice Working Group, and the petitions were delivered to then-Undersecretary of State Timothy Wirth at a national ecumenical conference. A public service announcement on climate change, with poet Maya Angelou doing the voice-over, was circulated to over 250 television stations.

In the area of theological and ethical reflection, the Eco-Justice Working Group continues to support the activities of Theological Education to Meet the Environmental Challenge (TEMEC). Meetings have been held in conjunction with TEMEC conferences to encourage collaboration and interaction. Eco-Justice Working Group members have led workshops and spoken on panels. In addition, a booklet entitled "And the Leaves of the Trees" was produced. Written by Carol Johnston, it reviews for general church audiences the theological and biblical underpinnings for eco-justice concerns.

Significantly, the Eco-Justice Working Group differs from the typical ecumenical committee in important ways. Members who were "present at the creation" are still active in its life. Many others have belonged long enough that the group has lived through births, marriages, divorces, serious illnesses, deaths—the whole array of human experiences. We are in many ways like a family which really enjoys being together, and hopefully does a good job of caring for each other. Little of certainty can be known about the future. The significant funding enjoyed during the past few years may or may not continue. However, the eco-justice mission of faithful response to God, who is at once both Creator and Redeemer, appears to be securely fastened to current denominational structures and agendas. That alone is a significant accomplishment.

Strategy for Environmental Engagement: Building a Catholic Constituency

Walter E. Grazer

Introduction

A central question facing Christianity in dealing with ecological and environmental challenges is: how, as believers and followers of Christ, do we go about the task of linking our faith to ecological and environmental concerns? One answer is to formulate a pastoral strategy. Such a strategy must complement the developing theological reflection among Protestant, Orthodox, and Catholic theologians on the theological dimensions of the ecological question. There is a need for both the theoretical and the practical. Because of differences in theology, ecclesiology, and administration, Protestant, Orthodox, Evangelical, and Catholic churches must necessarily approach the pastoral challenge in their own distinctive but complementary ways.

Ecological and environmental problems, at least in their recent manifestations, present new challenges to the Christian churches. The freshness of the challenge offers a unique opportunity to create new pastoral strategies that express prophetic insight and develop pedagogical and practical expression in forms that resonate with the deepest religious aspirations and understandings of most believers. If not, our deepening theological-ethical reflection risks falling on deaf ears and can be dismissed as mere ideology or idealism. Hopefully, the developing collective pastoral experiences of the churches in helping their members begin to tackle ecological and environmental issues will provide some guidance in the formation of an adequate pastoral strategy.

Pope John Paul II in his 1990 World Day of Peace message, *The Ecological Crisis: A Common Responsibility,* states that "in our day, there is a growing awareness that world peace is threatened not only by the arms race, regional conflicts and continued injustices among peoples and nations, but also by a lack of *due respect for nature.*" He further goes on to issue a direct challenge: "Christians, in particular, realize that their responsibility within creation and their duty towards nature and the Creator are an essential part of their faith. As a result, they are conscious of a vast field of ecumenical and interreligious cooperation opening up before them. . . . I should like to address directly my brothers and sisters in the Catholic Church, in order to remind them of their serious obligation to care for all of creation." Pope John Paul II's challenge, which is echoed by the U.S. Catholic bishops in their 1991 statement, *Renewing the Earth,* provides the charter, mandate, and direction for a Catholic pastoral strategy.

History

The upsurge in society's environmental awareness began in the early 1960s with Rachel Carson's *Silent Spring.* While the secular environment movement got a full head of steam after this, the Catholic community, with some exceptions, was not part of this movement. This is not to suggest that there was no prior concern. The National Catholic Rural Life Conference (NCRLC), which for several decades represented the U.S. Catholic Bishops' Conference on rural issues, has a very memorable history of concern for environmental matters. The NCRLC, which was formed right after World War I, always linked a pastoral strategy with its public policy concerns. There were other Catholic actors, like the *Catholic Worker,* which did not refer specifically to "ecological" matters in its writings, but did live out the social justice values and explicit linkage between the city and rural life that served as a precursor to some of the Church's work on the environment today. Also, religious orders, such as the Franciscan, but particularly women religious, have been addressing this issue more broadly by using their properties and facilities to model various environmentally sound projects.

In the late 1980s, as a natural outgrowth of their work in agricultural and rural concerns, the bishops began to address environmental issues more directly. At that time, Cardinal Roger Mahony of Los Angeles, who chaired the bishops' International Policy Committee, suggested at a joint meeting of the Domestic and International Policy Committees that the U.S. Catholic Conference take up this issue of ecology and the environment. A special symposium was held on 30 November–1 December 1990. Also, in 1990 Pope John Paul II issued his statement on the environment, *The Ecological Crisis: A Common Responsibility,* which forms the foundation for further reflection and action within the wider Catholic Church. The U.S. Catholic bishops issued their own pastoral reflection, *Renewing the Earth*, in 1991. It is necessary to mention this brief history to emphasize that current program efforts to expand significantly the Catholic voice in environmental matters is built on earlier efforts to lay out a serious theological framework.

This initial work by the U.S. Catholic Conference intensified and expanded as a result of the USCC formally joining the National Religious Partnership for the Environment. This mutual endeavor on the part of organized religion (Protestants, Evangelicals, Jews, and Catholics) in the United States has enabled the religious community to speak more readily on their own and together on these matters and made it possible to develop a more focused pastoral strategy for engagement by local parishes and congregations.

Mission and Strategy

The mission of the USCC's Environmental Justice Program is to help develop the U.S. Catholic Church's capacity to address emerging concerns about ecology and the environment. To implement this mission, the USCC has designed a threefold pastoral strategy: 1) integrate the concern; 2) link environmental concerns with social justice; and 3) develop the concern at the local diocesan and parish levels. It is important to realize that underlying this pastoral strategy is a conviction that, for Catholics, working within the framework of the Catholic tradition is a better avenue for engagement than trying to work outside of it or stretching the boundaries of theological reflection in ways unrecognizable to most Catholics.

But it is also important to embed this threefold strategy within the spiritual and sacramental context of Catholic theology in order to understand this pastoral strategy. Prayer, liturgy, and scripture are primary experiential vehicles for Catholic engagement. Worship of our Creator, our life in Christ, and creating a spiritual underpinning for ecological and environmental concerns are the entry points and foundation for any effort to engage lay Catholics in addressing this concern. If we do not understand that creation reveals God's presence, beauty, and wisdom and that we have an obligation to our Creator to care for God's gift of creation, it is unlikely that the religious community can be moved to deal with ecological and environmental challenges.

Integration

The goal of the USCC program is to help Catholics realize their religious obligation to care for and protect God's creation. Since humans are a part of nature, the U.S. Catholic bishops explicitly link "social and natural ecology." This linkage serves as the basis for a strategy of integration. The idea is not to ask Catholics, dioceses, and parishes to drop everything they are doing and run to a new issue (the environment), but rather to try to integrate this theme into the everyday fabric of their lives. Or, in other words, do not throw away your existing camera, but just use a wide angle lens to see a more comprehensive view that now includes a concern for one's physical environment.

We use this strategy because most Catholics are urbanites who occupy the broad center of our society. There are many demands made upon parishes to develop the religious life of Catholics as well as to minister to a wide variety of needs in the larger society. These multiple demands militate against having the resources to focus programs too exclusively on any single issue. While the USCC's Environmental Justice Program hopes it is supportive of Catholics who are already addressing environmental concerns, the intent of the program is to widen the circle of engagement and appeal to Catholics who are open to assuming more responsibility but who have not yet had the theological and program resources to respond.

The first three years of the USCC program were spent establishing the base for a network—integrating the environment into diocesan social justice work, providing educational resources (parish education kits, videos), conducting leadership retreats and training, and promoting scholarship on the theological and moral implications of the ecological and environmental challenge.

Link with Social Justice

The U.S. Catholic Bishops' Conference ties ecological and environmental concerns directly with its strong commitment to human life, human dignity, and social justice. These ties are rooted in scripture and in Catholic social teaching. Practically, this means linking environmental matters to four areas: 1) race and poverty—because, as the bishops say, "it is the poor and the powerless who most directly bear the burden of current environmental carelessness"; 2) work, labor, jobs, and the environment—because work lies at the center of our human vocation, and too often the environment issue is cast as one of jobs versus the environment; 3) sustainable development, which, while not a very precise term, does orient us to a development model that protects the environment while providing for human social and economic needs today and for future generations; and 4) the global commons—the concern for those things that sustain life itself for all creatures and are to be shared by all: air, water, the oceans, and land. The churches' strong social justice teachings provide the foundation for the USCC's approach to environmental concerns.

Local

The third major strategy is to develop this issue on a local and regional perspective. While the church is both local and universal, most Catholics live their religious lives as members of parishes or local Catholic organizations. Since everyone has "a physical environment" in which they live, there is a greater possibility of engaging them locally, because they can experience their environment more readily in the space in which they live. They can feel it, smell it, and taste it. They are more likely to sense the beauty as well as the pollution of their immediate surroundings than they are an environment that is distant or that they can only know by watching the television. Assuming responsibility for one's local environment makes eminent sense. Also, as more political decisions in the U.S. context move from the federal level to state and local decision making, it is important for the religious community to deal with environmental agendas locally as well as nationally.

Program

To implement this threefold pastoral strategy, the USCC's Environmental Justice Program (EJP) has established four programs. The first is education. The EJP has produced a number of resources, including parish resource kits and videos. The first kit was intended to help Catholics understand the Church's concern for the environment and to familiarize them with basic Catholic teachings about this issue. The second kit provided suggestions for establishing parish-based programs. The third kit highlighted practical examples of what Catholic parishes and organizations are doing to address environmental concerns and lifted up the international dimensions of this issue. Each of the kits also provides feature articles, parish bulletin quotes, and other helpful program ideas. The three kits have been distributed to all eighteen thousand Catholic parishes.

Scholarship is a critical program component. Without a firm footing in Catholic social teaching, the environmental issue is not likely to take root or be on solid theological ground. The EJP has hosted four Catholic scholars' consultations to encourage research, publication, and scholarly debate. One book has been published thus far,

"And God Saw That It Was Good": Catholic Theology and the Environment, as a result of these consultations. While the church has a rich spiritual, theological, and ethical tradition to bring to this issue, there is a need to examine emerging ecological and environmental concerns from the perspective of this tradition, both to discern its contributions and to challenge it. If the Catholic community is to make a contribution to resolving these issues, its concern must be grounded in its own experience and history and its theological and moral teachings. The EJP is currently making efforts to encourage Catholic universities to begin to offer symposia, courses, and curricula.

Leadership development is necessary to have any sustained contribution on the part of the Catholic community. The EJP has conducted several national retreats for key Catholic leaders, including diocesan social action directors, state Catholic conference directors, and other national church leadership, to lift up the theological dimensions of environmental themes and introduce these leaders to the issues. These retreats are traditional in that they focus on prayer, liturgy, and spirituality rather than serving as organizational planning meetings. The retreats are quite successful in fostering commitment and significant local follow-through. At this time, one-third of the state Catholic conferences and over thirty dioceses are involved in follow-up activities.

One of the most successful facets of our EJP leadership development effort has been its small and regional grants programs. The small grants program provided grants to help parishes, dioceses, schools, and other Catholic groups to address environmental concerns in innovative and creative ways. Among the 110 funded projects are efforts to develop environmental curricula for Catholic schools, training for grassroots environmental organizing, environmental justice projects, and diocesan leadership conferences on social justice and the environment.

The regional grants program, which provides direct support for diocesan and state Catholic conferences initiatives, is leading to an expanded network of diocesan projects. Most of these projects are a direct outgrowth of the attendance of these local church leaders at EJP retreats. The regional grants are intended to help build local Catholic leadership and impact state and local environmental public policy in light of Catholic social teaching. Awards have been given to develop a bishops' pastoral on the Columbia River in the Northwest; to conduct priests' and lay retreats to help address the destruction of the Mississippi Delta in Louisiana; to address land ethics problems in North Dakota; to build an ecumenical approach to public policy in Montana; to foster a role for the church in mediating disputes between environmental advocates and ranchers in Texas, Kansas, and Oklahoma; to promote a support role for Catholic universities and seminaries for the Florida Catholic Conference's public policy environmental initiatives; to address water problems of the Rio Grande basin in New Mexico; and to begin to address urban sprawl problems in the Archdiocese of Detroit.

The EJP also engages in partnerships with other major Catholic organizations. These include the Campaign for Human Development (CHD—the U.S. Catholic Church's antipoverty effort), Catholic Relief Services (CRS—the U.S. Catholic Church's overseas development agency), the National Council of Catholic Women (NCCW), and the National Catholic Rural Life Conference (NCRLC). It is estimated that the CHD provides between $750,000 and $1,000,000 annually to environmentally related antipoverty projects. CRS has projects in over seventy countries, focusing on basic sustainable development projects to assist the poor. The NCCW, with a membership of one million Catholic women, has its own environment program focusing on children's environmental health. The NCRLC has fostered a major public policy effort to promote sustainable agriculture here in the United States. Any collective picture of the U.S. Catholic Church's involvement in environmental matters must include these and other organizations. The EJP's strategy of integration is oriented to coordination and encouraging other Catholic organizations to assume some responsibility for ecological and environmental concerns, rather than to concentrate all efforts with the national program.

Finally, as part of its leadership effort, the EJP has focused on the problems poor and minority communities face as a result of environmental degradation. The EJP has sponsored a meeting of Catholic Hispanic, African American, Native American, and Asian leaders on the specific concern of environmental justice. This issue will receive increased attention as the program develops.

Public policy is the fourth program area. Just as the organizing principle to develop a Catholic constituency was integration, this principle also holds for the formation and selection of public policy issues. Over the years the U.S. Catholic Church has developed its teaching and commentary on a variety of major societal issues, including its stand against abortion, its support for economic reforms that can lift people out of marginality and poverty, its care for refugees and immigrants, its promotion of programs that support families and children, and its adoption of policies that foster the protection of human rights and equitable development for poorer nations. The EJP seeks to build on this policy base and to integrate and graft environmental concerns onto this existent set of policy concerns. The specific choice of issues to address is based on salient environmental concerns, Catholic social teaching, and a determination of issues to which the Catholic Church can make a distinct and unique contribution.

In *Renewing the Earth,* the bishops stated: "Above all, we seek to explore the links between concern for the person and for the earth . . . avoiding false choices between the people and the planet. It is the poor, here and in the developing countries, who suffer first and most from damage to the environment; they are the prime victims of a global system that degrades them and the rest of god's creation." Consequently, the selection of initial policy areas to develop include urban sprawl and brownfields, children's environmental health, pesticides and farmworkers, renewable energy, private property and environmental regulation (the so-called takings issue), and sustainable development (development, trade, debt).

Conclusion

While the mission is easy to state—to help the Catholic Church in the United States begin to address ecological and environmental concerns in a more integrated and effective way—its implementation is complex. It requires consideration of the unique characteristics and organizational structure of the Catholic community. It demands that the mission be approached in a way that the Catholic community can understand how these environmental concerns relate to their daily life of prayer, worship, and ministry, particularly at the parish and local levels. Finally, it means that any effort has to be rooted in scripture and the church's rich social teachings. Only if all of these elements are integrated into a strategy can we hope to help the Catholic community take up the challenge posed by Pope John Paul II and the U.S. Catholic bishops "to keep ever alive a sense of 'fraternity' with all those good and beautiful things which Almighty God has created."

Evangelicals and the Environment

Stan L. LeQuire

When describing the many ways in which the Evangelical Environmental Network (EEN) is helping evangelical Christians engage environmental issues, I could mention our various ways of reaching out to churches, individuals, and Christian organizations. As you might expect, we minister through our publications, conferences, and online services, but you might not expect another ministry that we offer. It is equally effective for outreach and certainly intriguing. We have a ministry of making people angry! There is something about our efforts that is as irritating as a pesky mosquito in the bedroom.

The EEN has found its own biological niche. Although similar to mosquitoes, we are more like gadflies. We have a unique ability to get on people's nerves. We have attracted the ire of our political leaders in Washington, D.C. The conservative media and several think tanks are carrying out their own private battle against us. Those who would gut our nation's environmental laws do not favor our advocacy on behalf of God's creation. In addition, even a few of our own brothers and sisters in the evangelical community have seen fit to prophesy about the eternal state of our souls. As you can imagine, these people believe that members of the EEN are bound to be sniffing sulfurous pollution throughout eternity.

Evidence of this anger and irritation can be seen in a variety of documents that can be downloaded from the web. One of these is a "dossier" from the National Center for Public Policy Research. It describes what a dangerous group we are, much to be avoided.

Several articles have been written against us. One of these is titled "Deforestation of the Truth" (in the magazine *WORLD,* 22 April 1995), which describes us as prone to lies. Another article is titled "It Isn't Easy Being Green: Meeting Mixes Bad Theology with Pseudoscience" (*WORLD,* 11 May 1996). This article lambastes not only our theology and our science, but also our politics. The article carries an unnecessarily large photo of the president and the vice president, as if to locate us with, in their minds, pagan Democrats.

Our ministry of irritation also includes members of the United States Congress, particularly Congressmen Don Young (Republican, from Alaska) and Richard Pombo (Republican, California) from the House Committee on Resources. Apparently, our stand on supporting and strengthening the Endangered Species Act hit a raw nerve with these two legislators.

In January 1996, the EEN took a delegation of eight evangelical leaders to Washington, D.C., to advocate on behalf of the Endangered Species Act. The highly successful event included a packed press conference, television appearances, and materials distributed to every member of Congress. The next day, Congressmen Young and Pombo issued a press release titled "Congressmen Request 'Honesty' and Fairness in Evangelical Network's . . . Effort." In the press release, the congressmen stated that "All Americans do expect religious leaders to abide by a higher standard and this is all we are asking—keep the debate honest and don't use the pulpit to mislead people." Later, they said, "We hope that you will be honest. . . . As religious people, you have a high obligation to seek the truth, even in the political arena."

In a letter to the congressmen, we responded: "You raise the question of honesty and advise us not to use our pulpits to mislead people. If this is a subtle suggestion that we return to some sort of private religious world and ignore the relationship between public policy and our deepest religious commitments, we cannot accept that." We also requested a private meeting with the congressmen where we might discuss our various concerns. We never heard from them again. I am going to take the liberty of interpreting this anger and hostility as a high compliment. This irritation must say that our challenges to the status quo must be accomplishing something. As gadflies, we can look the evangelical community in the eye and say, "Are we really doing what is right? Do our actions for or against creation conform to the will of God?" Furthermore, we are able to look political leaders in the eye and say, "Slow down your attempts to gut America's environmental laws. More is at stake here than politics and economics."

However noticable and worthy may be our unique ability to anger people, I am also baffled by these events. Of all our contributions to the national debate on environmental issues, we would most want to contribute a rich measure of hope, joy, and a sense of worship. We want our many activities to inspire rather than irritate. Yet, we do have a sobering sense that our message strikes at cherished idols and our country's rebellion against the ways of God. In many ways, we have challenged some basic precepts of our American culture. It may be that we are an irritating group of Christians precisely because we seek to remind people just how far we have drifted from God.

Paul, writing in 2 Corinthians 10:5, says, "We demolish arguments and every pretension that sets itself up against the knowledge of God, and we take captive every thought to make it obedient to Christ." In this scholarly volume on Christianity and ecology, much has been made of deconstructing and/or reconstructing theology. The EEN seeks to minister by deconstructing many cherished ideals which tear at the fabric of God's creation. Then, we seek to reconstruct a joyful, God-centered response to the environment. We call it "creation care."

In spite of our ministry of anger, others find our ministries constructive rather than contentious. Here are a few brief examples.

We seek to provide hope by engaging some of the tougher environmental issues of our day. Our Amos Initiative program is working to bring together government, business, and religious leaders to address the problems associated with dumping toxics in poor neighborhoods. This new approach is one which the Environmental Protection Agency has not been able to accomplish. We also work with evangelical relief and development agencies in addressing the many regions around the world where environmental degradation causes human suffering.

We seek to inspire joy among those who follow Christ by providing encouragement and support for activities that demonstrate that biblical faith can make a significant contribution to solving environmental problems. Our members are excited to show that faith works. Some of these activists include a Presbyterian church group in Media, Pennsylvania, which has a study group and roadside clean-up project; a Mennonite church in Harrisonburg, Virginia, which has adopted their local stream for clean-up; and a group in Bozeman, Montana, which leads worship services and speaks in local churches.

The greatest distinction that we have to offer is our commitment to worship the Creator and Redeemer God. To this end, we publish resources that provide worshiping congregations with ideas on making environmental activism an act of worship. Our anthology of sermons is titled *The Best Preaching on Earth*. We welcome plagiarism of the sermons included in that volume. In addition, some forty-three thousand kits with worship ideas have been circulated to congregations throughout the United States and Canada.

We hope that the various ministries of the EEN will serve as an inspiring call to biblical Christians who wish to serve Christ by caring for God's handiwork. However, if our ministries also irritate and confound, we consider that our privilege and our calling as well!

The Integrity of Creation:
Challenges and Opportunities for Praxis

PATRICIA M. MISCHE

Spirituality is a journey undertaken to grow closer to God. To make progress, one needs to walk on two feet: both reflection and action, contemplation and practice (praxis). The authentic spiritual journey cannot be an escape from life and its problems. Spiritual growth ultimately requires engagement and struggle with the challenges and opportunities life and the God of history put before us. Today, at the dawn of the twenty-first century, life is putting before us some unprecedented challenges and opportunities related to care of the earth. We need to respond at local, national, and global levels if we are to assure ecological health for present and future generations. In struggling to find an adequate response we can grow more spiritually mature—closer to God and God's work, ongoing creation and redemption.

Awareness and commitment to the integrity of creation is a core part of the Christian spiritual journey and mission in the world. This article focuses on the need and potential of Christian praxis to contribute with other religions toward: 1) developing a culture of ecological responsibility (applying the teaching mission of the churches to nurture among members an ecological ethos and ethic); and 2) advancing more effective systems for assuring ecological integrity at local, bioregional, national, and global levels (enabling church networks to be effective actors in the development of effective policies and structures for environmental protection).

Developing a Culture of Ecological Responsibility

The most fundamental challenge for achieving ecological security is the development of a global culture of ecological responsibility. Religious institutions are especially equipped to contribute to this development.

Scientists point to abundant evidence that serious environmental damage has already occurred and that, unless our behavior changes, more is to come, with dire consequences for myriad species as well as for human health and economic and social well-being. They have also recommended steps to prevent further damage. As a result, most people now know that we have serious ecological problems. But there is a lingering gap between knowing that we face serious ecological problems and acting on this knowledge in our personal, political, social, and economic choices. While more people have taken some modest steps, such as recycling, changes in peoples' worldviews, attitudes, and behavior have not been commensurate to the gravity and global scale of the problems. Moreover, when in conflict, economic concerns and desires usually trump environmental ones. The integrity of creation is not yet a true priority for most people, including Christians. It has not yet been integrated as a serious part of the Christian ethos (guiding beliefs) and ethics.

Science and technology alone cannot resolve ecological threats. Nor can governments or the laws they promulgate. Governments alone have not caused the problem. Every person is part of an ecological system and for good or ill affects the health of the natural world. Many environmental problems are an effect of everyday patterns of consumption by ordinary citizens, or of their apathy or inertia about systems and patterns of behavior that perpetuate poverty and environmental degradation. Sustaining the integrity of creation thus requires not only the external laws governments enact to deal with belligerent behavior, but also inner governance—laws internalized in our own hearts and minds and a movement of our wills to live by them. The need for inner governance is relevant not only to personal behavior, but also collective behavior through the economic, social, and political systems we create and help maintain.

Church praxis has special relevance for the development of inner governance and a culture of ecological responsibility. Religions carry the archetypes, symbols, meanings, values, and moral codes around which a people coalesce and define themselves, their sense of the sacred, and their relationships with each other and the natural world. Religions also affect people's concepts and perceptions of what is just and unjust, right and wrong, and hence their sense of the moral legitimacy or illegitimacy of any system of thought and patterns of behavior that tolerate or contribute to the degradation of nature.

Thus, religious institutions, including Christian churches, should not overlook their normative role with regard to the integrity of creation. Through their education and formation programs the churches can help their members develop a consciousness, conscience, and codes of behavior regarding their relationships with the natural world as an integral part of their spiritual development and practice. This entails helping members to revisit, and where necessary reinterpret, important sources within the tradition—scriptures, symbols, beliefs, and ethical principles—that affect attitudes and practices related to the natural world. Christians who have not seen the relationship of their faith to ecology may need help uncovering new or deeper layers of understanding and meaning at the core of their tradition in terms of their relevance for today's global environmental imperatives.

The churches have many ways to help their members grow in sensitivity and responsiveness to the sacredness of creation and to celebrate their connectedness and participation in the larger community of life, including through spiritual formation, liturgical, sacramental, pastoral, and education programs. Touchpoints in the Judeo-Christian tradition are many, ranging from the Genesis account of Creation with the repeated reminder "and God saw that it was good" (how can Christians help sustain that original goodness?); through the Psalms that help us rejoice in the glory of the Creator and creation by offering images so vivid one can touch and smell the earth; through the Old Testament mandate to "let the land rest" at regular Jubilee intervals, and in all years to share the harvest of its bounty with the poor and hungry; through such New Testament symbols as Christ's call to be the salt of the earth or references to himself as the vine and his followers the branches for bringing new life into the world.

Overconsumption is nowhere endorsed, and is often chastised, in the Bible. Addressing the needs of those hungry for food, thirsty for clean water, homeless and in need of shelter is a requirement for entering the kingdom of God—and also integral aspects of environmentally sustainable development. Earth elements and symbols—water, air, soil, oil, bread, and wine—are employed in Christian sacraments and rituals as holy and symbols of divine presence.

The Ten Commandments also need revisiting with an eye to codes of conduct for ecological praxis. As traditionally taught, the ten on which Judeo-Christian ethics are built seem to lack ecological content or application. Perhaps this seeming ommision is a factor in the lack among many Christians of a well-developed ecological ethic or strong sense of moral responsibility for the integrity of creation. They do not see it as a sin to harm or degrade the environment in the same way that harming or killing or stealing from another human being is a sin. But, if one looks deeper at the two great commandments and at many of the ten, one can find implicit in them relevant principles to guide our relationships with the natural world. To violate the earth and the integrity of creation is in some way to dishonor the Creator and desecrate the holy. Conversely, honoring and sustaining the integrity of creation is a way to honor and revere the Creator. Celebrating and rejoicing in creation is a way of celebrating and rejoicing in God's goodness.

To love our neighbors as ourselves also has implicit ecological content. Who is our neighbor? Christ called followers to grow in love by extending the boundaries of their sense of community and kinship beyond immediate family, friends, race, or nation and to embrace all peoples, even their enemies. Loving one's neighbors prohibits harming them by lying, stealing, coveting, killing, or in other ways depriving them of the fullness of life. By extension, loving one's neighbor also includes respecting their need for and right to water, food, shelter, and adequate resources. By further extension one can see that loving one's neighbors includes respect for the rights and needs of future generations. Those yet to come depend on our proper stewardship of resources on a finite planet.

By further extension the call to love one's neighbor can be seen to include a sense of kinship with the entire community of life. Albert Schweitzer exemplified this kind of Christian consciousness and praxis. The minister and man of medicine who committed his life to serve others acted from a very deep reverence for life that was part of an ecological as well as humanitarian sensitivity. The reverence and sense of community that led him to save many human lives also would not allow him to kill ants or any creature. His sense of community and reverence for life extended not only to all peoples, but also to all creation. While not everyone is an Albert Schweitzer, all Christians are called to practice respect and reverence for life. Such praxis is aided by church programs that help the faith community develop and live by a sense of kinship with nature and an ethic of ecological responsibility.

The Ten Commandments were given to a people in a particular place and time in which population density was not a concern and many of the ecological problems we face today were unknown. Although the commandment principles remain very relevant today, new threats, such as climate change and ozone depletion, and the imperatives that we learn to live and share diminishing resources with six billion people that will sometime in the next century reach ten billion, suggest that we now need a more explicit elaboration of, and commitment to, an ecological ethic than is now articulated in any of the great religions. Some Christians have been working with people of other traditions and secular humanists to meet this need. Since the late 1980s, more than one hundred declarations of ecological principles have been developed, including the following: the Assisi Declaration; the Earth Covenant (initiated by Global Education Associates in 1988 and used in many church settings, it now has more than two million signatories); and the 1992 Earth Charter developed by the International Coordinating Committee on Religion and the Earth. At the turn of the century, Christian networks are also contributing, along with other networks, to the development of an Earth Charter, building on the ethical content of earlier ecological declarations and covenants, which is intended to complement the UN charter.

In addition, many churches have initiated Environmental Sabbath celebrations, often around Earth Day. Through special liturgies, worship services, and related education programs congregations have an opportunity to grow in ecological awareness and to link their faith commitment to ecological practice. The churches can also utilize Sunday school, church circles and study groups, and other education programs to help members grow in awareness and commitment to the integrity of creation.

Acting Locally and Globally for Ecological Security

Besides being *sources* of inspiration and motivation for developing an ethos and ethic of ecological responsibility, the world's religious traditions also have important *resources* in the form of their institutions, agencies, and networks to help advance systems for ecological security. The Christian churches, for example, have in addition to their church buildings, many thousands of schools and universities; publishing and media arms; health-care and social-service agencies; human rights and social-justice advocacy groups; and other structures through which they contribute to the larger community at local, national, and global levels.

At local levels the churches can often reach people more directly and effectively than can national governments or international agencies. The same is often true internationally. With members in almost every country and region of the world, churches often work across national boundaries more effectively than many governments, and with greater freedom to promote values and systems of peace, human rights, and the integrity of creation. Protestant and Orthodox communions in the United States do this through Church World Service, an arm of the National Council of Churches. It exemplifies religious networks working cooperatively with one another across denominational lines and in solidarity with poor people and victims of war, human rights violations, or natural catastrophes. This same kind of cooperation and solidarity can be—and in some cases is being—employed in defense of the integrity of creation.

Christian churches have the potential to form a virtual greenbelt around the planet. They possess land, buildings, properties in almost every region and country of the world. They can use these resources to develop models demonstrating and promoting environmental sustainability and to be a leaven in the local communities for environmentally sustainable policies, practices, and systems.

Acting Locally

The process of developing systems of ecological security can begin with the churches themselves adopting policies and developing environmentally sustainable practices and systems within their own structures. From there, environmentally responsible practices can be spread by members to their homes, work places, and into the public policy arenas of the local community and bioregion. Churches can improve their practices related to the conservation of energy, water, land, and other resources. They could develop their own church's *Agenda 21* (the program of action adopted by governments at the 1992 Earth Summit in Rio), modeled on agenda items in the intergovernmental plan of action, but with attention to church commitments. They could also make awards or give recognition to the best environmental practices in the church or local community.

Churches with investment portfolios can assure that their investments: 1) do no harm (i.e., do not go to enterprises that damage the environment); and 2) do some good (e.g., the South Shore Bank's Eco-Deposit program that supports conservation-based community development). Churches and religious communities with land can use it for eco-programs, such as community-sponsored organic gardens to demonstrate sustainable agricultural practices and possibly also grow food for the hungry. Many Catholic religious orders are now establishing centers for sustainable agriculture and environmental education on their lands with outreach to local communities. And, to note a Protestant example, the Environmental Stewardship Program of the Evangelical Lutheran Church in America supports congregation-based agriculture projects. Congregations and church-related groups could also use their extensive properties to run eco-camps for youth or to involve members in environmental restoration.

Churches can also initiate, or join, local community efforts to clean up rivers and community lands and establish sound local environmental practices, policies, and systems related to recycling, toxic waste, land use, and conservation of forest, soil, and agricultural resources. Churches can provide education, leadership, meeting facilities, organizational resources, and ways for communities to build solidarity, commitment, and collaboration on projects, and to celebrate their communal efforts for present and future generations and the integrity of creation.

Acting Bioregionally and Nationally

Beyond work in their local communities, churches can work together across denominational lines and with secular groups to improve environmental practices and systems in a whole bioregion or country. For example, Catholic religious orders with property along the

Hudson River in the United States have pooled efforts for environmental protection and restoration in their bioregion. They also work with other denominations and secular networks on environmental issues in the Hudson Valley. Sisters of Earth is a network begun by Catholic religious women which provides a forum for sharing and learning from one another and for promoting activities and policies related to the integrity of creation.

In the Philippines, Catholic bishops issued a courageous and eloquent 1988 pastoral on endangered Philippine ecology, entitled *What Are We Doing to Our Beautiful Land?* In one diocese of Mindanao, the bishop and churches acted to secure a government ban on further logging of upland forests—logging which had left behind not only denuded mountains, but also led to soil erosion, flooding, the destruction of lowland rice paddies, and a depressed local economy. Despite the ban, illegal logging remained rampant with some military and police suspected of aiding illegal loggers. Government funding for forest rangers was inadequate to patrol and protect the forests effectively. In this vacuum, priests and religious joined in solidarity with local farmers to try to block illegal loggers from taking out more trees. For their efforts, one priest and a number of farmers were killed and others threatened by illegal logging interests. In response, the bishop, working with the minister of environment, had all his priests deputized with authority to arrest illegal loggers. In addition, the church responded to the wood and housing shortage in the region that had followed in the wake of deforestation and organized through the churches the training of people in brickmaking, the building of brick houses, and promotion of brick enterprises.

Elsewhere in the Philippines local churches and religious orders have used their institutions and networks to engage youth and others in environmental activities, such as reforestation, cleanup of dump sites, restoration of wetlands and coastal ecologies, and other activities that contribute to long-range sustainable development for their neighborhoods, provinces, and country. Although not all church-related initiatives at regional and national levels may be as dramatic as the above Philippine examples, courageous action for environmental protection is being undertaken by Christians in many communities, from work against radioactive contamination of water and soil near nuclear plants and military installations, to advocating for national policies and laws for environmental protection.

Acting Globally

Global cooperation, norms, and structures are essential to resolve problems that exceed local, regional, or national competencies. Local and national remedies will not suffice, for many threats are trans-boundary, such as ozone depletion, global warming, acid rain, and toxic emissions into air or water. Environmental problems that are global in scale require global solutions. National borders are no barrier, and national systems of security offer little protection against such threats.

Christian churches have significant potential to act globally, but currently this is the weakest area of their praxis. For many, the need and means to act globally is not as well understood or developed as the need and means to act locally and nationally. Their international memberships, structures, and activities give the churches some of the same capacities as multinational organizations. But, unlike multinational companies, the churches have not been utilizing their international capacities as effectively as they could to affect global policies and structures. Many denominations, as well as international church and ecumenical agencies, have representation as nongovernmental organizations (NGOs) at the United Nations and can speak on behalf of their members at UN meetings and conferences open to NGOs, or at parallel world conferences organized by NGOs and civil society.

Global Education Associates (GEA) is an NGO that in the 1980s began promoting partnerships between NGOs and UN agencies to achieve mutual goals related to peace, poverty alleviation, human rights, and sustainable development. In 1990 a partnership between four UN agencies and sixteen NGOs was formalized at a meeting in Vienna. Under the name Project Global 2000 (PG2000), the partners undertook shared work on a number of projects, including one on religion and world order, which seeks to bring the wisdom, values, experience, and networks of the world's religious traditions to the work of global systems transformation, including reform and strengthening of the UN system to meet twenty-first-century challenges. Long before PG2000, GEA had already been developing partnerships with religious institutions and networks, including 165 Catholic religious orders. GEA works with the religious partners to help them envision and apply their values, charisma, and professional competencies to the development of more effective, just, peaceful, and ecologically responsible global systems. Among partnership activities currently underway are pilot projects in Kenya and South Africa involving GEA, UNICEF, and local religious orders in efforts with sixteen local communities. A goal is to develop replicable models demonstrating effective partnership between NGOs, religious networks, local communities, and UN agencies to alleviate poverty and advance sustainable development. Although these projects were begun with Catholic religious orders, plans include the participation of other religious traditions in the region as well.

A goal of the partnership is to increase the chances for success by effective use of the strengths each partner brings to the project. NGOs and religious networks work on the ground with local peoples and have more direct and ongoing involvement in local communities than national governments or UN agencies. In contrast, UN agencies, by their mandates, must work with governments. This has certain benefits for urging improvements in government policy related to sustainable development. Such improvements can benefit a whole country or region. But it also has limitations. When governments are corrupt, inept, or inefficient, monies intended for sustainable development may not reach the people. Thus, some UN agencies are seeking ways to work more directly with people through NGOs, including religious NGOs.

A few churches have been involved in interfaith work with the United Nations Environment Programme (UNEP) to promote moral and ethical dimensions of *Agenda 21* and other international environmental agreements, and to promote the celebration of environmental holy days in the world's religious traditions. But much more could be done. There is a great need to strengthen UN capacities and structures related to the environment and to make ecological security a core part of the UN's work for peace and security. When the UN was founded in 1945, its founders did not foresee today's ecological threats and did not include ecological security in the organization's mandate for peace and security in the way that human rights and economic development were. Subsequently, the kind of development programs promoted through UN agencies (indeed, through bilateral aid agencies as well) were often not environmentally sustainable, and were sometimes actually harmful. However, the UN has proven it is a living organism that can learn and adapt and evolve in response to new needs. Once scientific evidence of environmental harm was brought to the

UN's attention, the UN helped lead the way toward the development of global environmental norms and policies. The first world conference on the environment was convened by the UN in Stockholm in 1972 and resulted, among other things, in creating the United Nations Environment Programme (UNEP) with a mandate to undertake environmental research and education and to infuse and coordinate environmental programs throughout the UN system. UNEP and the subsequent Commission on Sustainable Development (CSD) (which was established after the Rio conference in 1992 to monitor the implementation of *Agenda 21*) have made significant contributions to the advancement of ecological security. However, their mandates and resources are not commensurate to the environmental challenges we face at the dawn of the twenty-first century. UNEP's budget, which depends on voluntary contributions from member states, has suffered serious cutbacks by the United States and some other states. Moreover, their mandates are too limited in the face of serious ecological challenges ahead.

The churches could bolster UN efforts for ecological security by: 1) promoting increased and more stable funding sources for UNEP; 2) working in partnership with relevant UN agencies in promoting environmental sustainability; 3) joining other NGOs and civil society groups to upgrade UNEP to an agency with authority and resources at least equal to those of the global economic and financial institutions such as the World Bank, International Monetary Fund, and World Trade Organization; 4) promoting further environmental accountability in IMF, World Bank, and World Trade Organization policies and programs.

There is a new openness among many UN-related institutions to input and involvement from the world's religious traditions. For example, under the leadership of its new president, James Wolfensohn, the World Bank jointly sponsored with the archbishop of Canterbury at the Church of England's Lambeth Center, an unprecedented conference with religious leaders to explore areas of collaboration. The Lambeth Declaration laid out some first steps for what is intended as ongoing efforts of cooperation between religions and the World Bank to alleviate poverty worldwide and advance sustainable community development.

The Christian churches are positioned to make a major contribution to more just, humane, and environmentally responsive global systems. They can bring not only the power of their respective denominational networks, but also their collective strengths through interdenominational organizations of which they are a part, such as the World Council of Churches. Important foundations have been laid for work in the twenty-first century by the WCC and other inter-denominational and interreligious networks. The WCC, for example, has been a significant actor on many global issues, including human rights, the elimination of racism and apartheid, nuclear disarmament, climate stabilization, and other issues of justice, peace, and creation that require global partnership. Through the WCC, member churches have made a collective commitment to the integrity of creation and, in solidarity with one another, can do much more to forward international environmental norms and structures than any one church could do acting alone. Local congregations, national church bodies, and member denominations need to help support and encourage such interdenominational work for global systems of environmental protection. The solidarity of the churches can make a major difference in moving governments to strengthen global structures for ecological security in the twenty-first century.

In conclusion, we come to our starting focus on the spiritual journey. History has given those of us who live now some exciting challenges and opportunities for working with God in assuring the integrity of creation and, along the way, to grow, through reflection and praxis, closer to our Creator.

Conclusion: Eco-Justice at the Center of the Church's Mission

ROSEMARY RADFORD RUETHER

Many traditional Christians feel a deep suspicion toward the ecology movement, particularly when it lays claim to theological and religious meaning. They see the movement as the rise of a new "nature worship," to be regarded as totally contrary to "biblical faith." Here I wish to show, following up on other chapters in this volume, that the Church's mission of redemption of the world cannot be divorced from justice in society or from the healing of the wounds of nature wrought by an exploitative human industrial system. I also wish to emphasize that this wholistic perspective is central to the biblical vision of redemption. What is unbiblical is a Christianity that divorces individual salvation from society and society from creation.

This does not mean that we should ignore the questions directed at the biblical and Christian tradition by deep ecologists and ecofeminists.[1] The biblical and Christian traditions do have elements that sacralize domination and negation of body, earth, and woman. But they also struggled against what they perceived to be injustice and evil and sought to vindicate the goodness of creation and the body and their ultimate redemption against extreme dualists that saw in the material world only the manifestation of the demonic. We can reclaim these more wholistic traditions on which to ground an eco-justice vision of redemption.

In saying this, I am *not* asserting that the biblical and Christian traditions are the sole source of religious truth, the only way of access to true divinity, and that, therefore, only here is religious truth to be found. The great Asian religious traditions, as well as the unjustly scorned nature religions of indigenous peoples, have precious resources that need to be cultivated. An ecological crisis of global proportions calls for nothing less than a true dialogue and mutual enrichment of all spiritual traditions.

Nor am I claiming that the biblical and Christian traditions are adequate. They need critique and reinterpretation. But I suspect that this is true of all human spiritual heritages—and all the more so in our new situation of global ecological crisis. Until now, humans assumed that nature's power far transcended puny humans. Even biblical apocalyptic thought did not put the power to destroy the earth in human hands. The notion that our power has grown so great that we must now take responsibility for preserving the biotic diversity of rain forests and the ozone layer of the stratosphere was unimaginable in past human experience.

Although the biblical and Christian tradition is not the only source for ecological theology and ethics, it is a source that must be central for us of Christian background. First, there are magnificent themes here to inspire us. Second, Christian people and their institutions are a major world religion and world power. They have been a major cause of the problems. But they will not be mobilized to conversion unless they can find the mandates for it in those traditions which carry meaning and authority for them. Third, I suspect that none of us work in a healthy way if we operate merely out of alienation from our past. We need new visions. But new visions have power, not when they are rootless, but when they are experienced as gathering up and transforming our heritage.

The ecological theologies of Christian inspiration at this time seem to fall into two different types, which I call the covenantal and the sacramental. (In part one, above, Sallie McFague utilizes the same categories when discussing critical features of an ecological Christology.) The covenantal type is represented by the writings of Paul Santmire, James Gustafson, James Nash, Dieter Hessel, and others, such as the contributors to *Covenant for a New Creation,* edited by Carol Robb and Carl Casebolt. As typifies covenantal ecotheology, Richard Austin, in *Hope for the Land,* draws strongly from Hebrew scripture and claims the Bible as the primary source of ecological theology.[2]

A second type of ecological theology is that of Matthew Fox's *The Coming of the Cosmic Christ* and Thomas Berry's *The Dream of the Earth*.[3] Fox claims a biblical basis for his thought in the cosmological Christology of the New Testament. He also draws on patristic and medieval mysticism and casts a wide net of ecumenical dialogue across world religions. Other examples of sacramental ecotheology are offered by Sallie McFague, Jay McDaniel, Carol Adams, Paulos Gregorios, and Sean McDonagh.[4]

Protestants have generally been stronger on the covenantal tradition that searched for an ecological ethics, while Catholics have tended to stress the sacramental tradition. But, as shown in the preceding chapters of this volume, they are learning from, and building on, each other. My view is that these two traditions, covenantal and sacramental, are complementary. In fact, they are already in dialogue in scripture and church history. Usable ecological theology, spirituality, and ethics must interconnect these two traditions.

Each supplies elements which the other lacks. In the covenantal tradition we find the basis for a moral relation to nature and to one another that mandates patterns of right relation, enshrining these right relations in law as the final guarantee against abuse. In the sacramental tradition we find the heart, the ecstatic experience of I and Thou, of interpersonal communion, without which moral relationships grow heartless and spiritless.[5]

The Covenantal Tradition, Biblical and Modern

The notion that the Bible is anti-nature comes in part from the reading of the Bible popularized by German scholarship of the late nineteenth and early twentieth centuries. This scholarship read into the Bible its own sharp dualism of history against nature, setting the true God of history against the gods of nature. Although the biblical view of God expresses a transformation of the way God is seen as related to nature, there is also a lively sense of God's relation to and presence in nature that was overlooked in this stress on the God of history "against" nature.

Although God is seen as "creating" nature, rather than being an expression of it, the nature God creates is, nevertheless, alive and enters into lively relation to God. God delights in the creatures God creates, and the creatures return this rejoicing in joy and praise. Divine blessing inundates the earth as rain, and the mountains skip like a calf, the hills gird themselves with joy, the valleys deck themselves with grain; they shout and sing together for joy.

This language is typical of Hebrew scripture. There is no reason to write it off as "mere poetic metaphor," a judgment which reflects the modern loss of the experience of I-Thou relation to what we see around us. The experience of nature, of fields, mountains, streams, birds, and animals, in Hebrew sensibility, while not seen as "divine," is still very much animate, interacting as living beings with their Creator.

The modern nature-history split distorts the biblical view. In the biblical view, all things, whether they happen as human wars and struggles for liberation in and between cities or whether they happen as rain that brings abundant harvests or as drought that brings disaster to the fields upon which humans depend, are "events." In all such events, whether in cities or in fields, Hebrews saw the presence and work of God, as blessing or as judgment.

All such events have moral meaning. If enemies overwhelm the walls of the city or floods break down irrigation channels and destroy the fruits of human labor, God is acting in judgment upon human infidelity. When humans repent and return to fidelity to God, then justice and harmony will reign, not only in the city, but in the relations between humans and animals, the heavens and the earth. The heavens will rain sweet water, and the harvests will come up abundantly. Thus, what modern Western thought has split apart as "nature" and "history," Hebrew thought sees as one reality fraught with moral warning and promise.

There are problems in reading moral meaning and divine will into events in "nature." We would not wish to see in every flood, drought, volcanic eruption, and tornado the work of divine judgment. But when destructive floods rush down the Himalaya Mountains, carrying all before them into the Bay of Bengal, or drought sears African lands, we are right to recognize the consequences of human misuse of the land, stripping the forest cover that held back the torrential rains and overgrazing the semiarid African soils.

In these disasters today we have to recognize a consequence of human culpability and a call to rectify how we use the land and how we relate to the indigenous peoples who depend on these lands. As human power expands, colonizing more and more of the planet's natural processes, the line between what was traditionally called "natural evil," viewed as ethically neutral, and what should be called sin, that is, the culpable abuse of human freedom and power, also shifts. Hebrew moral sensibility takes on a new dimension of moral truth in which relation to God is the basis for both justice in society and prosperity in nature, while disobedience to God's commands of right relation brings both violence to society and disaster to nature.

Hebrew genius saw divine commands of right relation between human beings and the rest of creation enshrined in a body of law. Much of this law did not seem relevant to Christians, who believed that their new relation to God through Christ allowed them to discard a good deal of it. But some elements of this legal tradition take on new meaning today, particularly the tradition of sabbatical legislation. These are the laws that mandate periodic rest and restoration of relations between humans, animals, and land.

Hebrew theology of creation rejects the aristocratic split between a leisure-class divinity and a humanity that serves this divinity through slave labor that was typical of ancient Near Eastern mythology. In Genesis, God is described as both working and resting and thereby setting the pattern for all humans and their relations to land and animals in the covenant of creation. This pattern of work and rest is set through a series of concentric cycles, of seven days, seven years, and seven times seven years.

On the seventh day of each week, not only the farmer, but also his human laborers and his animal work force are to rest. "On the seventh day you shall rest, so that your ox and your donkey may have relief, and your homeborn slave and your resident alien shall be refreshed" (Exod. 23:12). In the seventh year attention is given to the rights of the poor and to wild animals, as well as to the renewal of the land itself. "For six years you shall sow your land and gather its yield; but the seventh year let it lie fallow, so the poor of your people may eat, and what they leave the wild animals may eat. You shall do the same with your vineyard and your olive orchard (Exod. 23:10–11). Slaves are to be set free and laborers to rest, as well.

Finally in the jubilee year, the fiftieth year, there is to be a great restoration of all relationships. Those who have lost their land through debt are to be restored to their former property. Debts are to be forgiven, and captives freed. The earth is to lie fallow, and animals and humans are to rest. All the accumulated inequities of the past seven times seven years, *between humans* through debt, loss of land, and enslavement, and *to nature* in overuse of land and animals, are to be rectified. All is to be restored to right balance.

This vision of periodic redemption and restoration of right relation underlies Jesus' language in the Lord's Prayer. It is a vision of redemption more compatible with finitude and human limits than the radical visions of the millennium and the once-for-all apocalyptic end of history through which recent biblical scholarship has read the meaning of the term "Kingdom of God." Modern revolutionary thinkers would have done better if they had taken the jubilee, rather than the millennium and the apocalyptic future, as their model of historical change. Periodic renewal and restoration of right relations is a more doable and less dangerous vision than final perfection.

Although Christians saw themselves as people of the new covenant—a covenant no longer limited to one people, the Jews, or to one land, but extended to all nations and to the whole earth—they also spiritualized and eschatologized these ideas in a way that lost the concreteness of Hebrew faith. Christians, in the early centuries, were city people, and the farmer ethic of sabbatical legislation was less meaningful to them. Believing in a Christ that had transcended the law, they saw themselves as mandated to ignore some good ideas, along with some bad ideas, in Hebrew legislation.

The Reformation, with its stress on historical, rather than allegorical, interpretation of scripture, brought new attention to Hebrew scripture. In the Reformed tradition there was a new stress on the idea of being a covenanted people, and this was identified with the social and political contracts binding local and national communities. Not all of this had positive results. There was a revival of tribal notions of being an elect People of God that fueled English and American religious and racial nationalisms.

But another aspect of the notion of covenant as the basis of political community gave birth to the idea of citizens who contract together to form civil society, who have mutual rights and obligations, and whose leaders are accountable to the citizens. These ideas have been the foundation of modern constitutional government. In the seventeenth and eighteenth centuries it was assumed that these citizens were limited to white propertied males, but gradually this concept of citizenship, and with it civil rights, was extended to all adult men, and eventually to adult women.

Slavery was incompatible with this idea of rights. It was gradually abolished, although more for economic than for humanitarian reasons. Although guaranteed by their relationship to particular political communities, these rights were seen in Enlightenment thought as "natural," grounded in the fundamental nature and dignity of the human person. The rights of those not able to be responsible citizens also received protection: children, the sick, the mentally ill or retarded, the imprisoned. Some nineteenth-century English liberals and progressive Evangelicals began to claim that rights should be extended to animals as well. Beating, torture, and painful ill-treatment of all kinds should be banned, whether toward humans in prisons, schools, armies, or hospitals, or toward animals in laboratories or farms.

Both environmentalists and animal rights activists today draw on this tradition of "natural rights." They seek to extend this concept to species and ecospheres and to sentient animals. Environmentalists argue that endangered species have the right to be protected against extinction, not simply because they are or might become useful to humans, but in their own right, as unique expressions of evolutionary life.[6]

The natural rights tradition is a necessary but insufficient resource for the ecological ethic we need today. As James Nash puts it in *Loving Nature*, "Rights are a way of conceptualizing the basic demands of justice" for humans and otherkind.[7] Attending to rights and responsibilities is a crucial step in translating love of nature into ecojustice. But protecting an animal or a plant because it is a member of an endangered species with a right to be is susceptible to an autarchic misinterpretation. Species are not endangered in isolation; they are endangered because the ecosystem of forest, prairie, or wetland in which they live is endangered. Ecological communities are the context in which particular animals or plants thrive or die.

It is, finally, all ecosystems, not just wild ones, but the ones in which humans must learn to share their lives with a great variety of animals and plants, that have to be protected. We need an ethic that encompasses the sustaining of ecological community, not simply the members of community in isolation from each other. The natural rights tradition is limited when it sees only the right of the individual in relation to the community; it needs to be developed to uphold the species group and the biotic community as the matrix in which the life of the individuals and species are sustained. What is needed is a new interconnection of the ethic of the individual and the ethic of the community, and the extension of this ethic beyond the human individual and group to the biosphere in which all living things cohere on the planet. Embodying such an ethic of eco-justice in policy and practice is a concrete way to redistribute power and show care for an earth community deformed by greed, domination, and unnecessary suffering.

The basic insight of the biblical covenantal tradition—that we must translate right relation into an ethic, which finds guarantees in law—is an essential element in building an ecological world order. The 1982 World Charter for Nature, signed by all members of the United Nations (except the United States), laid out the basic principles of such an ecological ethic. International treaties on climate change, protection of biodiversity and forests, and oceans and lakes are being negotiated to set limits to human abuse of the environment. A body of international law is beginning to emerge, although all too slowly and without adequate means of enforcement, that affirms the interdependency of the global human community with the earth community of air, water, animals, and plants.

The Sacramental Tradition

The sacramental tradition of Catholic Christianity complements the covenantal tradition that has been emphasized by Reformed Christianity and its secular heirs. It starts with the community as a living whole, not only the human community, but, first of all, the cosmic community. The human being not only mirrors cosmic community as micro- to macrocosm but also intercommunes with the whole cosmic body. God is seen not only as over against and "making" this cosmic body, but also as immanent within it. The visible universe is the emanational manifestation of God, God's sacramental body. God is incarnate in and as the cosmic body of the universe, although not reduced to it.

Hellenistic Judaism developed this vision of divine Wisdom as the secondary manifestation of God—God's agent in creating the cosmos, sustaining it, and bringing all things into harmonious unity with God.[8] Strikingly, Hebrew thought always saw this immanent manifestation of God as female:

Wisdom . . . pervades and permeates all things. . . . She rises from the power of God, the pure effluence of the glory of the Almighty. . . . She is the brightness that streams from everlasting light, the flawless mirror of the active power of God and the image of his goodness. She is one but can do all things, herself unchanging, she makes all things new; age after age she enters into holy souls and makes them God's friends and prophets. . . . She spans the world in power from end to end and orders all things benignly. (Wisdom of Solomon 8)

Contemporary ecofeminists are reclaiming this Wisdom tradition today as the underpinnings of a vision of a sacramental cosmology.

In the New Testament this cosmogonic Wisdom of God is identified with Christ. Jesus as the Christ not only embodies, in crucified form, the future king and redeemer, but also incarnates the cosmogonic principle through which the cosmos is created, sustained, redeemed, and reconciled with God. In this cosmological Christology, found in the preface to the Gospel of John, in the first chapter of Hebrews, and in some Pauline letters, Christ is the beginning and end of all things.

In the letter to the Colossians, the divine Logos which dwelt in Christ is the same Logos which founded and has sustained the cosmos from the beginning. "All things have been created through him . . . and in him all things hold together." This same Logos, through Christ and the Church, is now bringing the whole cosmos to union with God. "In him all the fullness of God was pleased to dwell and through him God is pleased to reconcile himself with all things, whether on earth or in heaven" (Col. 1:16–20).

New Testament and patristic cosmological Christology was a bold effort to overcome the threatened split between the God of Creation and the God of eschatological redemption, found in such gnostic systems as that of Marcion. This theology sought to synthesize cosmogony and eschatology and to bring together the Hebrew creational and the Greek emanational views of the relation of the divine to the cosmic body. Being and Becoming are dialectically interconnected. The Greek body-soul dualism was made more fluid, by seeing body as the sacramental bodying forth of soul and soul the life principle of the body.

Irenaeus, the second-century antignostic churchman, sought to spell out the cosmological Christology of the New Testament in a comprehensive vision of redemptive history. The visible cosmos is itself both the creation and the manifestation of the Word and Spirit of God. The Word and Spirit are the "two hands," by which God creates the world, and also the ground and principle of being of the cosmos.

Human freedom allows this connection to the divine source of being to be forgotten, and human relation to God and to each other becomes distorted. But God continually sends manifestations of the Word and Spirit that heal this relationship, culminating in Christ, whose work is now carried to fulfillment in the body of Christ, the Church. For Irenaeus, the Christian sacraments are the paradigmatic embodiments of this process of cosmic healing. The body itself, human and cosmic, is thereby regenerated, renewed, and filled with the divine presence, which is its ground of being. Irenaeus sees the entire cosmos becoming blessed and eventually immortalized by being ever more fully united with its divine source of being.

Later Latin patristic thought gradually dropped the lush prophetic visions of a redeemed earth that were part of early Christianity as being too dangerous to an empire that now claimed to be Christian. But medieval Latin thought, represented by thinkers such as Bonaventure, preserved elements of the idea of a cosmic presence of God through which we can be led upward in the "mind's road to God." Sacramental theologians of the Victorine School set their reflections on the sacraments of the Church in the context of the sacramentality of Creation.

This tradition was repressed by the dualists of mind against matter, Descartes and Newton and early modern European science. But the effort to bring mind and matter, God and creation, together in one unified vision lived on and was continually rediscovered in traditions of European philosophy, theology, poetry, and art. The Anglican Cambridge Platonists expressed this effort to bridge mind and matter, God and cosmos, in the seventeenth century; Fichte, Schelling and Hegel did so in the eighteenth and nineteenth. In poetry it was expressed in the English romantics, Coleridge and Wordsworth, and in theology in Tillich's view of God as ground of being. Ecological theologians of the late twentieth century, such as Thomas Berry, or Matthew Fox's rediscovery of the cosmological Christ, represent the new impetus to rediscover and reinterpret this tradition of sacramental cosmology.

Berry sees human-nature relations deeply threatened by Western technological exploitation. He calls for a deep metanoia that is necessary to bring about a new ecological consciousness. This metanoia must encompass many levels, including the technological, social, and cultural. For Berry, Western people are caught between the older stories of classical civilizations and the confident mechanistic scientism of modernity, both of which are under challenge today, and a new spirituality, rooted in the new universe story, that is waiting to be born. We need to create a new socioeconomic incarnation of the human species within its earth matrix. Although the technological aspects of this are necessary, the most important shift must be a renewed vision of our relation to the whole of the creation, a renewed way of telling the story of who we are.

Reclaiming the dynamic interaction of the covenantal and sacramental traditions is central to a renewed understanding of Christian redemptive hope as encompassing eco-justice. But this needs to be embodied much more deeply in our preaching, worship, and biblical study. We need to learn to reread these great traditions of covenantal ethics and sacramental spirituality in our biblical studies and teach it in our preaching.

This vision needs to become a visible part of how we design our churches and worship spaces. It needs to flow out in our stewardship of the land and church buildings, as well as through a community praxis of recycling and conservation of energy. It can be expressed in the transformation of our lands from wasteful overwatered lawns to natural grasses and permaculture gardens to help feed the poor. And it needs to be communicated through the public policy advocacy of church members and bodies seeking ecological health together with social justice. Only by embodying the vision of ecology and justice in its own teaching, worship, and praxis can the Church make itself a base for an environmentally responsible ministry to the larger community in which it stands. Eco-justice becomes central to the Church's mission only when it is understood as central to the Church's life. Anything less will lack credibility.

Notes

1. A major source of the condemnation of the Bible as the source of the Western culture of domination is Lynn White's essay, "The Historical Roots of Our Ecologic Crisis," *Science* 155 (10 March 1967): 1203–7.

2. Richard Austin's book was published by John Knox Press, Atlanta, Georgia, 1988. See the select bibliography in this volume for the other works mentioned in this paragraph.

3. Matthew Fox's book was published by Harper and Row, San Francisco, 1988, and Thomas Berry's book by Sierra Club Books, San Francisco, 1988.

4. See the select bibliography in this volume for works by the authors mentioned in this paragraph.

5. This summary of the covenantal and sacramental traditions is drawn from my book, *Gaia and God: An Ecofeminist Theology of Earth Healing* (San Francisco: HarperSanFrancisco, 1992), 205–53.

6. As an example of this approach, see Roderick F. Nash, *The Rights of Nature: A History of Environmental Ethics* (Madison: University of Wisconsin Press, 1989).

7. James A. Nash, *Loving Nature: Ecological Integrity and Christian Responsibility* (Nashville: Abingdon Press, 1991), 169.

8. For the culmination of the Hellenistic Jewish cosmological spirituality, see Erwin R. Goodenough, *By Light, Light: The Mystic Gospel of Hellenistic Judaism* (New Haven: Yale University Press, 1935).

Select Bibliography

PETER W. BAKKEN

Achtemeier, Elizabeth. *Nature, God and Pulpit*. Grand Rapids, Mich.: Eerdmans, 1992.

Adams, Carol J., ed. *Ecofeminism and the Sacred*. New York: Continuum, 1993.

Albanese, Catherine L. *Nature Religion in America: From the Algonkian Indians to the New Age*. Chicago: University of Chicago Press, 1990.

Anderson, Bernhard W., ed. *Creation in the Old Testament*. Philadelphia: Fortress Press, 1984.

———. *From Creation to New Creation: Old Testament Perspectives*. Edited by Walter Brueggemann. Minneapolis: Fortress Press, 1994.

Anglemeyer, Mary, Eleanor R. Seagraves, and Catherine C. LeMaistre, compilers. *A Search for Environmental Ethics: An Initial Bibliography*. Washington, D.C.: Smithsonian Institution Press, 1980.

Attfield, Robin. "Christian Attitudes to Nature." *Journal of the History of Ideas* 44 (1983): 369–86.

———. "Western Traditions and Environmental Ethics." In *Environmental Philosophy: A Collection of Readings,* edited by Robert Elliott and Arran Gare, 201–30. University Park: Pennsylvania State University Press, 1983.

Austin, Richard Cartwright. *Baptized into Wilderness: A Christian Perspective on John Muir*. Vol. 1 of *Environmental Theology*. Atlanta: John Knox Press, 1987.

———. *Beauty of the Lord: Awakening the Senses*. Vol. 2 of *Environmental Theology*. Atlanta: John Knox Press, 1988.

———. *Hope for the Land: Nature in the Bible*. Vol. 3 of *Environmental Theology*. Atlanta: John Knox Press, 1988.

————. *Reclaiming America: Restoring Nature to Culture.* Vol. 4 of *Environmental Theology.* Abingdon, Va.: Creekside Press, 1990.

Baer, Richard A., Jr. "Land Misuse: A Theological Concern." *Christian Century* 83 (12 October 1966): 1239–41.

Bailey, Liberty Hyde. *The Holy Earth.* New York: C. Scribner's Sons, 1915.

Baker-Fletcher, Karen. *Sisters of Dust, Sisters of Spirit: Womanist Wordings on God and Creation.* Minneapolis: Fortress Press, 1998.

Bakken, Peter W., Joan Gibb Engel, and J. Ronald Engel. *Ecology, Justice, and Christian Faith: A Critical Guide to the Literature.* With a foreword by Dieter T. Hessel. Bibliographies and Indexes in Religious Studies, no. 36. Westport, Conn.: Greenwood Press, 1995.

Ball, Ian, Margaret Goodall, Clare Palmer, and John Reader, eds. *The Earth Beneath: A Critical Guide to Green Theology.* London: SPCK, 1992.

Barad, Judith A. *Aquinas on the Nature and Treatment of Animals.* San Francisco: International Scholars Publications, 1995.

Barbour, Ian G. *Ethics in an Age of Technology.* San Francisco: HarperSanFrancisco, 1993.

————. *Religion and Science: Historical and Contemporary Issues.* San Francisco: HarperSanFrancisco, 1997. Revised and expanded edition of *Religion in an Age of Science,* 2 vols. (San Francisco: Harper and Row, 1990–91).

————, ed. *Earth Might Be Fair.* Englewood Cliffs, N.J.: Prentice-Hall, 1972.

Barnes, Michael, ed. *An Ecology of the Spirit: Religious Reflection and Environmental Consciousness.* Lanham, Md.: University Press of America and the College Theology Society, 1994.

Barth, Karl. "The Work of Creation." Chap. 9 in *The Doctrine of Creation,* translated by J. W. Edwards, O. Bussey, and Harold Knight, vol. 3, book 1 of *Church Dogmatics,* edited by G. W. Bromiley and T. F. Torrance. Edinburgh: T. and T. Clark, 1958.

Bauckham, Richard. "Jesus and the Wild Animals (Mark 1:13): A Christological Image for an Ecological Age." In *Jesus of Nazareth: Lord and Christ: Essays on the Historical Jesus and New Testament Christology,* edited by Joel B. Green and Max Turner, 3–21. Grand Rapids, Mich.: Eerdmans, 1994.

Beisner, E. Calvin. *Prospects for Growth: A Biblical View of Population, Resources, and the Future.* Westchester, Ill.: Crossway Books, 1990.

————. *Where Garden Meets Wilderness: Evangelical Entry into the Environmental Debate.* With an introduction by John Michael Beers. Grand Rapids, Mich.: Acton Institute for the Study of Religion and Liberty; Eerdmans, 1997.

Bergant, Dianne. *The Earth Is the Lord's: The Bible, Ecology, and Worship.* Collegeville, Minn.: Liturgical Press, 1998.

————. *Israel's Wisdom Literature: A Liberation-Critical Reading.* Minneapolis, Minn.: Fortress Press, 1997.

Berry, Thomas. *The Dream of the Earth.* San Francisco: Sierra Club Books, 1988.

Berry, Thomas, and Thomas Clarke. *Befriending the Earth: A Theology of Reconciliation between Humans and the Earth.* Edited by Stephen Dunn and Anne Lonergan. Mystic, Conn.: Twenty-Third Publications, 1991.

Berry, Wendell. "Christianity and the Survival of Creation." In *Sex, Economy, Freedom, and Community: Eight Essays,* 93–116. New York: Pantheon, 1993.

————. "The Gift of Good Land." In *The Gift of Good Land: Further Essays Cultural and Agricultural,* 267–81. San Francisco: North Point Press, 1981.

————. "God and Country." In *What Are People For?* 95–102. San Francisco: North Point Press, 1990.

————. "Two Economies." In *Home Economics: Fourteen Essays,* 54–75. San Francisco: North Point Press, 1987.

Bhagat, Shantilal P. *Creation in Crisis: Responding to God's Covenant.* Elgin, Ill.: Brethren Press, 1990.

Birch, Bruce C., and Larry Rasmussen. *The Predicament of the Prosperous.* Philadelphia: Westminster Press, 1978.

Birch, Charles. "Creation, Technology, and Human Survival: Called to Replenish the Earth." *Ecumenical Review* 28 (January 1976): 66–79.

————. *A Purpose for Everything: Religion in a Postmodern Worldview.* Mystic, Conn.: Twenty-Third Publications, 1990.

Birch, Charles, and John B. Cobb, Jr. *The Liberation of Life: From the Cell to the Community.* Cambridge: Cambridge University Press, 1981. Reprint, Denton, Tex.: Environmental Ethics Books, 1990.

Birch, Charles, William Eakin, and Jay B. McDaniel, eds. *Liberating Life: Contemporary Approaches to Ecological Theology.* Maryknoll, N.Y.: Orbis Books, 1990.

Birch, Charles, and Lukas Vischer. *Living with the Animals: The Community of God's Creatures.* Geneva: World Council of Churches, 1998.

Black, John. *The Dominion of Man: The Search for Ecological Responsibility.* Edinburgh: Edinburgh University Press, 1970.

Boff, Leonardo. *Cry of the Earth, Cry of the Poor.* Translated by Philip Berryman. Maryknoll, N.Y.: Orbis Books, 1997.

————. *Ecology and Liberation: A New Paradigm.* Translated by John Cumming. Maryknoll, N.Y.: Orbis Books, 1995.

Boff, Leonardo, and Virgil Elizondo, eds. *Ecology and Poverty: Cry of the Earth, Cry of the Poor.* Concilium. Maryknoll, N.Y.: Orbis Books, 1995.

Bonhoeffer, Dietrich. *Creation and Fall: A Theological Exposition of Genesis 1–3.* Edited by John W. de Gruchy. Translated by Douglas Stephen Bax. Vol. 3 of *Dietrich Bonhoeffer Works.* Minneapolis: Fortress Press, 1997.

Bonifazi, Conrad. *A Theology of Things: A Study of Man in His Physical Environment.* Philadelphia: Lippincott, 1967.

Bouma-Prediger, Steven. *The Greening of Theology: The Ecological Models of Rosemary Radford Ruether, Joseph Sittler, and Jürgen Moltmann.* Atlanta: Scholars Press, 1995.

———. "Why Care for Creation? From Prudence to Piety." *Christian Scholar's Review* 27 (spring 1998): 277–97.

Bradley, Ian. *God Is Green: Christianity and the Environment.* London: Darton, Longman and Todd, 1990.

Bratton, Susan Power. *Christianity, Wilderness, and Wildlife: The Original Desert Solitaire.* Scranton, Pa.: University of Scranton Press, 1993.

———. "Ecofeminism and the Problem of Divine Immanence/Transcendence in Christian Environmental Ethics." *Science and Christian Belief* 6 (1994): 21–46.

———. "Loving Nature: Eros or Agape?" *Environmental Ethics* 14 (spring 1992): 3–25.

———. *Six Billion and More: Human Population Regulation and Christian Ethics.* Louisville, Ky.: Westminster/John Knox Press, 1992.

Brueggemann, Walter. *The Land: Place as Gift, Promise, and Challenge in Biblical Faith.* Philadelphia: Fortress Press, 1977.

Bube, Paul Custodio. *Ethics in John Cobb's Process Theology.* Atlanta: Scholars Press, 1988.

Burrell, David B., and Elena Malits. *Original Peace: Restoring God's Creation.* New York: Paulist Press, 1997.

Callicott, J. Baird. *Earth's Insights: A Survey of Ecological Ethics from the Mediterranean Basin to the Australian Outback.* Berkeley and Los Angeles: University of California Press, 1994.

Carmody, John. *Ecology and Religion: Toward a New Christian Theology of Nature.* New York: Paulist Press, 1983.

Carroll, John E., and Albert LaChance, eds. *Embracing Earth: Catholic Approaches to Ecology.* Maryknoll, N.Y.: Orbis Books, 1994.

Carroll, John E., Paul Brockelman, and Mary Westfall, eds. *The Greening of Faith: God, the Environment, and the Good Life.* With a foreword by Bill McKibben. Hanover, N.H.: University Press of New England, 1997.

Catholic Bishops' Conference of the Philippines. "What Is Happening to Our Beautiful Land?" A Pastoral Letter on Ecology from the Catholic Bishops of the Philippines. *SEDOS* 4 (1988): 112–15.

Cherry, Conrad. *Nature and Religious Imagination: From Edwards to Bushnell.* Philadelphia: Fortress Press, 1980.

Chial, Douglas L. "The Ecological Crisis: A Survey of the WCC's Recent Responses." *Ecumenical Review* 48 (January 1996): 53–61.

Christiansen, Drew, and Walter Grazer, eds. *"And God Saw That It Was Good": Catholic Theology and the Environment.* Washington, D.C.: United States Catholic Conference, 1996.

Chung Hyun Kyung. "Welcome the Spirit; Hear Her Cries: The Holy Spirit, Creation, and the Culture of Life." *Christianity and Crisis* 51 (15 July 1991): 220–23.

Clark, J. Michael. *Beyond Our Ghettos: Gay Theology in Ecological Perspective.* Cleveland: Pilgrim Press, 1993.

Clark, Stephen R. L. *How to Think about the Earth: Philosophical and Theological Models for Ecology.* London: Mowbray, 1993.

Clinebell, Howard J. *Ecotherapy: Healing Ourselves, Healing the Earth.* Philadelphia: Fortress Press, 1996.

Clines, David J. A., ed. *The Bible and the Future of the Planet: An Ecology Reader.* The Biblical Seminar, no. 56. Sheffield, England: Sheffield Academic Press, 1998.

Coates, Peter. *Nature: Western Attitudes since Ancient Times.* Berkeley and Los Angeles: University of California Press, 1998.

Cobb, John B., Jr. *The Earthist Challenge to Economism: A Theological Critique of the World Bank.* New York: St. Martin's Press, 1999.

———. *Is It Too Late? A Theology of Ecology.* Rev. ed. Denton, Tex.: Environmental Ethics Books, 1995. Original edition, Beverly Hills, Calif.: Bruce Publishing, 1972.

———. "Sociological Theology or Ecological Theology?" In *Process Theology as Political Theology,* 111–34. Philadelphia: Westminster Press, 1982.

———. *Sustainability: Economics, Ecology, and Justice.* Maryknoll, N.Y.: Orbis Books, 1992.

———. *Sustaining the Common Good: A Christian Perspective on the Global Economy.* Cleveland: Pilgrim Press, 1995.

Cohen, Jeremy. *"Be Fertile, Fill the Earth and Master It": The Ancient and Medieval Career of a Biblical Text.* Ithaca, N.Y.: Cornell University Press, 1989. Reprint, Lanham, Md.: University Press of America, 1991.

Commission for Racial Justice, United Church of Christ. *Toxic Wastes and Race in the United States: A National Report on the Racial and Socioeconomic Characteristics of Communities with Hazardous Waste Sites.* New York: United Church of Christ, 1987.

Conradie, Ernst M. "Ecology and Christian Theology: An Introduction with a Comprehensive, Indexed Bibliography." *Scriptura* 47 (1993): 52–104.

———. "A Further Indexed Bibliography on Christian Theology and Ecology." *Scriptura* 52 (1995): 27–64.

Cuppitt, Don. "Nature and Culture." In *Humanity, Environment, and God,* edited by Neil Spurway, 33–45. Oxford: Blackwell Publishers, 1993.

Daly, Herman E., and John B. Cobb, Jr. *For the Common Good: Redirecting the Economy toward Community, the Environment, and a Sustainable Future.* 2d ed., updated and expanded. With contributions by Clifford W. Cobb. Boston: Beacon Press, 1994.

Daneel, M. L. "Earthkeeping in Missiological Perspective: An African Challenge." *Mission Studies* 13, no. 1-2 (1996): 130–88.

Dantine, Wilhelm. "Creation and Redemption: An Attempt at a Theological Understanding in Light of Contemporary Understanding of the World." *Scottish Journal of Theology* 18 (1965): 129–47.

Deane-Drummond, Celia. *Ecology in Jürgen Moltmann's Theology.* Texts and Studies in Religion, vol. 75. Lewiston, N.Y.: Edwin Mellen Press, 1997.

Deloria, Vine, Jr. *For This Land: Writings on Religion in America.* New York: Routledge, 1998.

———. *God Is Red.* New York: Delta, 1973.

Derr, Thomas Sieger. *Ecology and Human Need.* Philadelphia: Westminster Press, 1975. Originally published as *Ecology and Human Liberation: A Theological Critique of the Use and Abuse of Our Birthright* (Geneva: World Student Christian Federation, 1973).

———. "Religion's Responsibility for the Ecological Crisis: An Argument Run Amok." *Worldview* 18, no. 1 (January 1975): 39–45.

Derr, Thomas Sieger, James A. Nash, and Richard John Neuhaus. *Environmental Ethics and Christian Humanism.* With an introduction by Max Stackhouse. Nashville: Abingdon Press, 1996.

Dew, William H. "Religious Approach to Nature." *Church Quarterly Review* 150 (1950): 81–99.

DeWitt, Calvin B. *Caring for Creation: Responsible Stewardship of God's Handiwork.* Responses by Richard A. Baer, Jr., Thomas Sieger Derr, and Vernon J. Ehlers. Edited by James W. Skillen and Luis E. Lugo. Grand Rapids, Mich.: Baker Books, 1998.

———. *Earth-Wise: A Biblical Response to Environmental Issues.* Grand Rapids, Mich.: CRC Publications, 1994.

———, ed. *The Environment and the Christian: What Can We Learn from the New Testament?* Grand Rapids, Mich.: Baker Book House, 1991.

DeWitt, Calvin B., and Ghillean T. Prance, eds. *Missionary Earthkeeping.* With an introduction by J. Mark Thomas. Macon, Ga.: Mercer University Press, 1992.

Dimitrios, the Ecumenical Patriarch. *Orthodoxy and the Ecological Crisis.* Gland, Switzerland: World Wildlife Fund, 1990.

Doughty, R. "Environmental Theology: Trends and Prospects in Christian Thought." *Progress in Human Geography* 5 (1981): 234–48.

Dowd, Michael. *Earthspirit: A Handbook for Nurturing an Ecological Christianity.* Mystic, Conn.: Twenty-Third Publications, 1991.

Duchrow, Ulrich, and Gerhard Liedke. *Shalom: Biblical Perspectives on Creation, Justice, and Peace.* Geneva: WCC Publications, 1989.

Eco-Justice Working Group. *Environmental Justice Resources.* Elkhart, Ind.: National Council of Churches, 1998.

Edwards, Denis. *Jesus the Wisdom of God: An Ecological Theology.* Maryknoll, N.Y.: Orbis Books, 1995.

Elsdon, Ron. *Bent World: A Christian Response to the Environmental Crisis.* Downers Grove, Ill.: InterVarsity Press, 1981.

———. *Greenhouse Theology: Biblical Perspectives on Caring for Creation.* Tunbridge Wells, England: Monarch, 1992.

Engel, J. Ronald. "Ecology and Social Justice: The Search for a Public Environmental Ethic." In *Issues of Justice: Social Sources and Religious Meaning,* edited by Warren R. Copeland and Roger D. Hatch, 243–63. Macon, Ga.: Mercer University Press, 1988.

Engel, J. Ronald, and Joan Gibb Engel, eds. *Ethics of Environment and Development: Global Challenge, International Response.* Tucson: University of Arizona Press, 1990.

Evans, Bernard F., and G. D. Cusack, eds. *Theology of the Land.* Collegeville, Minn.: Liturgical Press, 1987.

Evdokimov, Paul. "Nature." *Scottish Journal of Theology* 18, no. 1 (1965): 1–22.

Everett, William W. "Land Ethics: Toward a Covenantal Model." In *American Society of Christian Ethics, Selected Papers, 1979,* 45–73. Newton Centre, Mass.: American Society of Christian Ethics, 1979.

Faith-Man-Nature Group. *Christians and the Good Earth: Addresses and Discussions at the Third National Conference of the Faith-Man-Nature Group.* F/M/N Papers, no. 1. Alexandria, Va.: Faith-Man-Nature Group, [1968?].

Faramelli, Norman J. "Ecological Responsibility and Economic Justice: The Perilous Links between Ecology and Poverty." *Andover Newton Quarterly* 11 (November 1970): 81–93.

———. "The Manipulative Mentality: We Do to Nature What We Do to People." In *Ecology: Crisis and New Vision,* edited by Richard E. Sherell, 59–76. Richmond, Va.: John Knox Press, 1971.

Faricy, Robert. *Wind and Sea Obey Him: New Approaches to a Theology of Nature.* London: SCM Press, 1982. Reprint, with a foreword by Mary Evelyn Jegen, Westminster, Md.: Christian Classics, 1988.

Ferré, Frederick. *Hellfire and Lightning Rods: Liberating Science, Technology, and Religion.* Maryknoll, N.Y.: Orbis Books, 1993.

———. *Shaping the Future: Resources for the Post-Modern World.* New York: Harper and Row, 1976.

Ferrell, John S. *Fruits of Creation: A Look at Global Sustainability as Seen through the Eyes of George Washington Carver.* Shakopee, Minn.: Macalester Park, 1995.

Finger, Thomas N. *Self, Earth, and Society.* Downers Grove, Ill.: InterVarsity Press, 1997.

———. "Trinity, Ecology, and Panentheism." *Christian Scholar's Review* 27 (1997): 74–98.

Finn, Daniel. "International Trade and Sustainable Community: Religious Values and Economic Arguments in Moral Debates." *Journal of Religious Ethics* 22 (fall 1994): 213–73.

Fowler, Robert Booth. *The Greening of Protestant Thought.* Chapel Hill: University of North Carolina Press, 1995.

Fox, Matthew. *The Coming of the Cosmic Christ: The Healing of Mother Earth and the Birth of a Global Renaissance.* San Francisco: Harper and Row, 1988.

———. *Original Blessing: A Primer in Creation Spirituality Presented in Four Paths, Twenty-Six Themes, and Two Questions.* Santa Fe: Bear and Company, 1983.

Fragomeni, Richard N., and John T. Pawlikowski, eds. *The Ecological Challenge: Ethical, Liturgical, and Spiritual Responses.* Collegeville, Minn.: Liturgical Press, 1994.

French, William C. "Ecological Concern and the Anti-foundationalist Debates: James Gustafson on Biospheric Constraints." *Annual of the Society of Christian Ethics,* 1989, 113–30.

———. "Subject-Centered and Creation-Centered Paradigms in Recent Catholic Thought." *Journal of Religion* 70 (January 1990): 48–72.

Fretheim, Terence E. "The Plagues as Ecological Signs of Historical Disaster." *Journal of Biblical Literature* 110 (1991): 385–96.

Freudenberger, C. Dean. *Food for Tomorrow?* Minneapolis: Augsburg, 1984.

———. *Global Dust Bowl: Can We Stop the Destruction of the Land Before It's Too Late?* Minneapolis: Augsburg, 1990.

Fritsch, Albert J. *Renew the Face of the Earth.* Chicago: Loyola University Press, 1987.

———. *A Theology of the Earth.* Washington, D.C.: CLB Publishers, Inc., 1972.

Galloway, Alan. *The Cosmic Christ.* New York: Harper and Brothers, 1951.

Geering, Lloyd George. *Tomorrow's God: How We Create Our Worlds.* Wellington, New Zealand: B. Williams Books, 1994.

Gibbs, John G. *Creation and Redemption: A Study in Pauline Theology.* Leiden, the Netherlands: E. J. Brill, 1971.

———. "Pauline Cosmic Christology and Ecological Crisis." *Journal of Biblical Literature* 90 (December 1971): 466–79.

Gibson, William E. "Confessing and Covenanting." In *Shalom Connections in Personal and Congregational Life,* edited by Dieter T. Hessel, 11–27. Ellenwood, Ga.: Alternatives, 1986.

———. "Ecojustice: Burning Word: Heilbroner and Jeremiah to the Church." *Foundations* 20 (October-December 1977): 318–28.

Gilkey, Langdon. *Maker of Heaven and Earth.* Garden City, N.Y.: Doubleday, 1965.

———. *Nature, Reality, and the Sacred: The Nexus of Science and Religion.* Minneapolis: Fortress Press, 1994.

Glacken, Clarence J. *Traces on the Rhodian Shore: Nature and Culture in Western Thought from Ancient Times to the End of the Eighteenth Century.* Berkeley and Los Angeles: University of California Press, 1967.

Goodenough, Ursula. *The Sacred Depths of Nature.* New York: Oxford University Press, 1998.

Goodman, Godfrey. *The Creatures Praysing God.* London: F. Kingston, 1622. Reprint, Norwood, N.J.: W. J. Johnson, 1979.

Gore, Al. *Earth in the Balance: Ecology and the Human Spirit.* Boston: Houghton Mifflin, 1992.

Gosling, David. *A New Earth: Covenanting for Justice, Peace, and the Integrity of Creation.* London: Council of Churches for Britain and Ireland, 1992.

Gottlieb, Roger S., ed. *This Sacred Earth: Religion, Nature, Environment.* New York: Routledge, 1996.

Gowan, Donald E. "'Highest of All Hills': The Transformation of Nature." In *Eschatology in the Old Testament,* 97–120. Philadelphia: Fortress Press, 1986.

Granberg-Michaelson, Wesley. *Redeeming the Creation: The Rio Earth Summit: Challenges for the Churches.* Geneva: WCC Publications, 1992.

———. *Tending the Garden: Essays on the Gospel and the Earth.* Grand Rapids, Mich.: Eerdmans, 1987.

———, ed. *Ecology and Life: Accepting Our Environmental Responsibility.* San Francisco: Harper and Row, 1988.

Gray, Elizabeth Dodson. *Green Paradise Lost.* Wellesley, Mass.: Roundtable Press, 1982. Originally published as *Why the Green Nigger? Remything Genesis* (Wellesley, Mass.: Roundtable Press, 1979).

Green, Elizabeth, and Mary Grey, eds. *Ecofeminism and Theology.* Kampen, the Netherlands: Kok Pharos, 1994.

Green, Ronald Michael. *Population Growth and Justice: An Examination of Moral Issues Raised by Rapid Population Growth*. Harvard Dissertations in Religion, no. 5. Missoula, Mont.: Scholars Press for Harvard Theological Review, 1976.

Gregorios, Paulos Mar. *The Human Presence: Ecological Spirituality and the Age of the Spirit*. New York: Amity, 1987. Originally published as *The Human Presence: An Orthodox View of Nature* (Geneva: World Council of Churches, 1978).

Gregory, Frederick. *Nature Lost? Natural Science and the German Theological Traditions of the Nineteenth Century*. Cambridge, Mass.: Harvard University Press, 1992.

Gunton, Colin E. *Christ and Creation*. Grand Rapids, Mich.: Eerdmans, 1992.

Gustafson, James M. *Ethics from a Theocentric Perspective*. 2 vols. Chicago: University of Chicago Press, 1981–84.

———. *A Sense of the Divine: The Natural Environment from a Theocentric Perspective*. Cleveland, Ohio: Pilgrim Press, 1994.

Habel, Norman C. *The Land is Mine: Six Biblical Land Ideologies*. With a foreword by Walter Brueggemann. Minneapolis: Fortress Press, 1995.

Hadsell, Heidi. "Creation Theology and the Doing of Ethics." *Horizons of Biblical Theology* 14 (December 1992): 93–111.

Halkes, Catharina J. M. *New Creation: Christian Feminism and the Renewal of the Earth*. Louisville, Ky.: Westminster/John Knox Press, 1991.

Hall, Douglas John. *Imaging God: Dominion as Stewardship*. Grand Rapids, Mich.: Eerdmans; New York: Friendship Press, 1986.

———. *Professing the Faith: Christian Theology in a North American Context*. Minneapolis: Fortress Press, 1993.

———. *The Steward: A Biblical Symbol Come of Age*. Rev. ed. Grand Rapids, Mich.: Eerdmans; New York: Friendship Press, 1990.

Hallman, David G. *Caring for Creation: The Environmental Crisis, A Canadian Call to Action*. Winfield, B.C.: Wood Lake Books, 1989.

———. *A Place in Creation: Ecological Visions in Science, Religion, and Economics*. Toronto: United Church of Canada Publishing House, 1992.

———, ed. *Ecotheology: Voices from South and North*. Geneva: WCC Publications; Maryknoll, N.Y.: Orbis Books, 1994.

Haney, Eleanor Humes. "Towards a White Feminist Ecological Ethic." *Journal of Feminist Studies in Religion* 9 (spring-fall 1993): 75–93.

Harakas, Stanley S. "The Integrity of Creation and Ethics." *St. Vladimir's Theological Quarterly* 32 (November 1988): 27–42.

Hargrove, Eugene C., ed. *Religion and the Environmental Crisis*. Athens, Ga.: University of Georgia Press, 1986.

Harris, Peter. *Under the Bright Wings*. London: Hodder and Stoughton, 1993.

Hart, John. *The Spirit of the Earth*. New York: Paulist Press, 1984.

Haught, John F. *The Cosmic Adventure: Science, Religion, and the Quest for Purpose*. New York: Paulist Press, 1984.

———. *The Promise of Nature: Ecology and Cosmic Purpose*. New York: Paulist Press, 1993.

Hefner, Philip. "Nature, God's Great Project." *Zygon* 27 (1992): 327–41.

Hendry, George S. *Theology of Nature*. Philadelphia: Westminster Press, 1980.

Hessel, Dieter T. "Ecumenical Ethics for Earth Community." *Theology and Public Policy* 8, no. 1-2 (summer-winter 1996): 17–29.

———. *Energy Ethics: A Christian Response*. New York: Friendship Press, 1979.

———. *For Creation's Sake: Preaching, Ecology, and Justice*. Philadelphia: Geneva Press, 1985.

———. "Spirited Earth Ethics: Cosmological and Covenantal Roots." *Church and Society,* July-August 1996, 16–36.

———. *Theology for Earth Community: A Field Guide*. Maryknoll, N.Y.: Orbis Books, 1996.

———. "Where Were/Are the Churches in the Environmental Movement?" *Theology and Public Policy* 7 (summer 1995): 20–31.

———, ed. *After Nature's Revolt: Eco-Justice and Theology*. Minneapolis: Fortress Press, 1992.

Hiebert, Theodore. "Re-imaging Nature: Shifts in Biblical Interpretation." *Interpretation,* January, 1996, 36–46.

———. *The Yahwist's Landscape: Nature and Religion in Early Israel*. New York: Oxford University Press, 1996.

Hill, Brennan R. *Christian Faith and the Environment: Making Vital Connections*. Ecology and Justice. Maryknoll, N.Y.: Orbis Books, 1998.

Hoogstraten, Hans-Dirk van. *Deep Economy: Caring for Ecology, Humanity, and Theology*. Atlantic Highlands, N.J.: Humanities Press, 1997.

Hough, Adrian Michael. *God Is Not 'Green': A Re-examination of Eco-Theology*. Harrisburg, Pa.: Morehouse, 1997.

Hughes, J. Donald. *Ecology in Ancient Civilizations*. Albuquerque: University of New Mexico Press, 1975.

Hutchinson, Roger. *Prophets, Pastors, and Public Choices: Canadian Churches and the Mackenzie Valley Pipeline Debate*. Waterloo, Ontario: Wilfrid Laurier University Press, 1992.

Irwin, Kevin. W., and Edmund D. Pellegrino, eds. *Preserving the Creation: Environmental Theology and Ethics*. Washington, D.C.: Georgetown University Press, 1994.

Jantzen, Grace. *God's World, God's Body*. Philadelphia: Westminster Press, 1984.

Jegen, Mary Evelyn, and Bruno V. Manno, eds. *The Earth Is the Lord's: Essays on Stewardship*. New York: Paulist Press, 1978.

John Paul II, Pope. "Peace with God the Creator—Peace with All of Creation." World Day of Peace Message, 1 January 1990. *Origins, CNS Documentary Service* 19 (14 December 1990): 465–68.

———. "Sollicitudo Rei Socialis." Encyclical Letter, "On Social Concern." *Origins, CNS Documentary Service* 17 (3 March 1987): 641, 643–60.

Johnson, Elizabeth A. *Women, Earth, and Creator Spirit*. New York: Paulist Press, 1993.

Johnston, Carol. *The Wealth or Health of Nations: Transforming Capitalism from Within*. Cleveland: Pilgrim Press, 1998.

Joranson, Philip N. "The Faith-Man-Nature Group and a Religious Environmental Ethic." *Zygon* 12 (1977): 175–79.

Joranson, Philip N., and Ken Butigan, eds. *Cry of the Environment: Rebuilding the Christian Creation Tradition*. With a foreword by Ian Barbour. Santa Fe: Bear and Company, 1984.

Jung, L. Shannon. *We Are Home: A Spirituality of the Environment*. New York: Paulist Press, 1993.

Kaufman, Gordon D. "Nature, History, and God: Toward an Integrated Conceptualization." *Zygon* 27 (December 1992): 379–401.

———. "A Problem for Theology: The Concept of Nature." *Harvard Theological Review* 65 (1972): 337–66.

———. *Theology for a Nuclear Age*. Philadelphia: Westminster Press, 1985.

Kay, Jeanne. "Concepts of Nature in the Hebrew Bible." *Environmental Ethics* 10 (1988): 309–27.

Kearns, Laurel. "Noah's Ark Goes to Washington: A Profile of Evangelical Environmentalism." *Social Compass* 44 (1997): 349–66.

———. "Saving the Creation: Christian Environmentalism in the United States." *Sociology of Religion* 57 (spring 1996): 55–70.

Keller, Catherine. *Apocalypse Now and Then: A Feminist Guide to the End of the World*. Boston: Beacon Press, 1996.

———. "The Lost Fragrance: Protestantism and the Nature of What Matters." *Journal of the American Academy of Religion* 65 (1997): 355–70.

King, Paul G., and David O. Woodyard. *Liberating Nature*. Cleveland: Pilgrim Press, 1999.

Kinsley, David R. *Ecology and Religion: Ecological Spirituality in Cross-Cultural Perspective*. Englewood Cliffs, N.J.: Prentice-Hall, 1995.

Kline, David. *Great Possessions: An Amish Farmer's Journal*. With a foreword by Wendell Berry. San Francisco: North Point Press, 1990.

Knierim, Rolf. "Cosmos and History in Israel's Theology." *Horizons in Biblical Theology* 3 (1981): 59–123.

Knitter, Paul F. *One Earth, Many Religions: Multifaith Dialogue and Global Responsibility*. Maryknoll, N.Y.: Orbis Books, 1995.

Kohák, Erezim. *The Embers and the Stars: A Philosophical Inquiry into the Moral Sense of Nature*. Chicago: University of Chicago Press, 1984.

Krueger, Frederick W., ed. *Christian Ecology: Building an Environmental Ethic for the Twenty-First Century*. North Webster, Ind.: North American Conference on Christianity and Ecology, 1987.

Kurien, C. T. "A Third World Perspective." In *Faith and Science in an Unjust World: Report of the World Council of Churches' Conference on Faith, Science, and the Future, Massachusetts Institute of Technology, Cambridge, U.S.A., 12–24 July 1979*, edited by Roger L. Shinn and Paul Abrecht, vol. 1, 220–25. Geneva: World Council of Churches, 1980.

Kwok Pui-lan. *Christology for an Ecological Age*. New York: Continuum, 1999.

Lampe, Geoffrey William Hugo. "The New Testament Doctrine of *Ktisis*." *Scottish Journal of Theology* 17, no. 4 (1964): 449–62.

Land, Richard D., and Louis A. Moore, eds. *The Earth Is the Lord's: Christians and the Environment*. Nashville: Broadman Press, 1992.

Lane, Belden C. *The Solace of Fierce Landscapes: Exploring Desert and Mountain Spirituality*. New York: Oxford University Press, 1998.

Leax, John. *Standing Ground: A Personal Story of Faith and Environmentalism*. Grand Rapids, Mich.: Zondervan Publishing House, 1991.

Lee, Charles. "The Integrity of Justice: Evidence of Environmental Racism." *Sojourners* 19 (February-March 1990): 20–25.

Lewis, C. S. "The Abolition of Man." In *The Abolition of Man*. New York: Macmillan, 1947.

Lilburne, Geoffrey R. *A Sense of Place: A Christian Theology of the Land*. Nashville: Abingdon Press, 1989.

Limouris, Gennadios, ed. *Justice, Peace, and the Integrity of Creation: Insights from Orthodoxy*. Geneva: WCC Publications, 1990.

Lindqvist, Martti. *Economic Growth and the Quality of Life: An Analysis of the Debate within the World Council of Churches 1966–1974*. Annals of the Finnish Society for Missiology and Ecumenics, no. 27. Helsinki: Finnish Society for Missiology and Ecumenics, 1975.

Linzey, Andrew. *Animal Theology*. Urbana: University of Illinois Press, 1995.

———. *Christianity and the Rights of Animals*. New York: Crossroad Press, 1987.

Linzey, Andrew, and Tom Regan, eds. *Animals and Christianity: A Book of Readings*. New York: Crossroad Press, 1988.

Linzey, Andrew, and Dorothy Yamamoto, eds. *Animals on the Agenda: Questions About Animals for Theology and Ethics.* Urbana: University of Illinois Press, 1998.

Lohfink, Norbert. *Theology of the Pentateuch: Themes of the Priestly Narrative and Deuteronomy.* Translated by Linda M. Manley. Minneapolis: Fortress Press, 1994.

Lonergan, Anne, and Carol Richards, eds. *Thomas Berry and the New Cosmology.* Mystic, Conn.: Twenty-Third Publications, 1987.

Longwood, Merle. "Common Good: An Ethical Framework for Evaluating Environmental Issues." *Theological Studies* 34 (September 1973): 468–80.

Lonning, Per. *Creation: An Ecumenical Challenge?* Macon, Ga.: Mercer University Press, 1989.

Lovejoy, Arthur O. *The Great Chain of Being: A Study of the History of an Idea.* Cambridge, Mass.: Harvard University Press, 1936.

Low, Mary. *Celtic Christianity and Nature: Early Irish and Hebridean Traditions.* Edinburgh: Edinburgh University Press, 1996.

Lowdermilk, W. C. "The Eleventh Commandment." *American Forests* 46 (January 1933): 12–15.

Lyons, James A. *The Cosmic Christ in Origen and Teilhard: A Comparative Study.* Oxford Theological Monographs. New York: Oxford University Press, 1982.

McCagney, Nancy. *Religion and Ecology.* Religion and Modernity. Malden, Mass.: Blackwell, 1999.

McDaniel, Jay B. *Earth, Sky, Gods, and Mortals: Developing an Ecological Spirituality.* Mystic, Conn.: Twenty-Third Publications, 1990.

———. *Of God and Pelicans: A Theology of Reverence for Life.* Louisville, Ky.: Westminster/John Knox Press, 1989.

———. *With Roots and Wings: Christianity in an Age of Ecology and Dialogue.* Maryknoll, N.Y.: Orbis Books, 1995.

McDonagh, Sean. *The Greening of the Church.* Maryknoll, N.Y.: Orbis Books, 1990.

———. *Passion for the Earth.* Maryknoll, N.Y.: Orbis Books, 1995.

———. *To Care for the Earth: A Call to a New Theology.* Santa Fe: Bear and Company, 1986.

McFague, Sallie. *The Body of God: An Ecological Theology.* Minneapolis: Fortress Press, 1993.

———. *Models of God: Theology for an Ecological, Nuclear Age.* Philadelphia: Fortress Press, 1987.

———. *Super, Natural Christians: How We Should Love Nature.* Minneapolis: Fortress Press, 1997.

McKibben, Bill. *The Comforting Whirlwind: God, Job, and the Scale of Creation.* Grand Rapids, Mich.: Eerdmans, 1994.

———. *The End of Nature.* New York: Random House, 1989.

MacKinnon, Mary Heather, and Moni McIntyre, eds. *Readings in Ecology and Feminist Theology.* Kansas City: Sheed and Ward, 1995.

McMichael, Ralph N., Jr. *Creation and Liturgy: Studies in Honor of H. Boone Porter.* Washington, D.C.: Pastoral Press, 1993.

McPherson, James. "Ecumenical Discussion of the Environment 1966–1987." *Modern Theology* 7 (July 1991): 363–71.

Maguire, Daniel C. *The Moral Core of Judaism and Christianity: Reclaiming the Revolution.* Minneapolis: Fortress Press, 1993.

Maguire, Daniel C., and Larry L. Rasmussen. *Ethics for a Small Planet: New Horizons on Population, Consumption, and Ecology.* With an introduction by Rosemary Radford Ruether. SUNY Series in Religious Studies. Albany: State University of New York Press, 1998.

Martin-Schramm, James B. "Population Growth, Poverty, and Environmental Degradation." *Theology and Public Policy* 4, no. 2 (summer 1992): 26–38.

———. *Population Perils and the Churches' Response.* Geneva: World Council of Churches, 1997.

Massey, Marshall. *Defense of the Peaceable Kingdom.* Religious Society of Friends, Oakland, California, Pacific Yearly Meeting, 1985.

Merchant, Carolyn. *The Death of Nature: Woman, Ecology, and the Scientific Revolution.* San Francisco: Harper and Row, 1980.

Meyer, Art, and Jocele Meyer. *Earthkeepers: Environmental Perspectives on Hunger, Poverty, and Injustice.* Scottdale, Pa.: Herald Press, 1991.

Mick, Lawrence E. *Liturgy and Ecology.* Collegeville, Minn.: Liturgical Press, 1997.

Moltmann, Jürgen. *The Coming of God: Christian Eschatology.* Translated by Margaret Kohl. Minneapolis: Fortress Press, 1996.

———. *God in Creation: A New Theology of Creation and the Spirit of God.* Translated by Margaret Kohl. San Francisco: Harper and Row, 1985.

———. *The Spirit of Life: A Universal Affirmation.* Translated by Margaret Kohl. Minneapolis: Fortress Press, 1992.

———. *The Way of Jesus Christ: Christology in Messianic Dimensions.* Translated by Margaret Kohl. San Francisco: HarperCollins, 1990.

Montefiore, Hugh, ed. *Man and Nature.* London: Collins, 1975.

Moule, C. F. D. *Man and Nature in the New Testament: Some Reflections on Biblical Ecology.* London: Athlone Press, 1964. Reprint, Philadelphia: Fortress Press, 1967.

Murphy, Charles M. *At Home on Earth: Foundations for a Catholic Ethic of the Environment.* New York: Crossroad Press, 1989.

Murray, Robert. *The Cosmic Covenant: Biblical Themes on Justice, Peace, and the Integrity of Creation.* Heythrop Monographs. London: Sheed and Ward, 1992.

Nacpil, Emerito P., and Douglas J. Elwood, eds. *The Human and the Holy: Asian Perspectives in Christian Theology*. Maryknoll, N.Y.: Orbis Books, 1978.

Nash, James A. "Biotic Rights and Human Ecological Responsibilities." *Annual of the Society of Christian Ethics* (1993): 137–62.

———. "Ethics and the Economics-Ecology Dilemma: Toward a Just, Sustainable, and Frugal Future." *Theology and Public Policy* 6 (summer 1994): 33–63.

———. *Loving Nature: Ecological Integrity and Christian Responsibility*. Nashville: Abingdon Press, 1991.

———. "Toward the Revival and Reform of the Subversive Virtue: Frugality." *Annual of the Society of Christian Ethics*, 1995, 137–60.

Nash, Roderick F. "The Greening of Religion." In *The Rights of Nature: A History of Environmental Ethics*, 87–120. Madison: University of Wisconsin Press, 1989.

Neuhaus, Richard John. *In Defense of People: Ecology and the Seduction of Radicalism*. New York: Macmillan, 1971.

Newsom, Carol A. "The Moral Sense of Nature: Ethics in the Light of God's Speech to Job." *Princeton Seminary Bulletin* 15, no. 1 (1994): 9–27.

Niebuhr, H. Richard. *Radical Monotheism and Western Culture: With Supplementary Essays*. New York: Harper and Brothers, 1960. Reprint, with an introduction by James M. Gustafson, Louisville, Ky.: Westminster/John Knox Press, 1993.

Niles, D. Preman, ed. *Between the Flood and the Rainbow: Interpreting the Conciliar Process of Mutual Commitment (Covenant) to Justice, Peace, and the Integrity of Creation*. Geneva: WCC Publications, 1992.

Noble, David F. *The Religion of Technology: The Divinity of Man and the Spirit of Invention*. New York: Alfred A. Knopf, 1997.

Northcott, Michael S. *The Environment and Christian Ethics*. Cambridge: Cambridge University Press, 1996.

Oelschlaeger, Max. *Caring for Creation: An Ecumenical Approach to the Environmental Crisis*. New Haven: Yale University Press, 1994.

Ogutu, Gilbert E. M., ed. *God, Humanity, and Mother Nature*. Papers from the First Regional God Conference of the New Ecumenical Research Association, Mara National Reserve, Kenya, May 1991. God: the Contemporary Discussion Series. Nairobi, Kenya: Masaki Publishers, 1992.

Oliver, Harold H. "The Neglect and Recovery of Nature in Twentieth-Century Protestant Thought." *Journal of the American Academy of Religion* 60 (fall 1992): 379–404.

Osborn, Lawrence. *Guardians of Creation: Nature in Theology and the Christian Life*. Leicester, England: Apollos, 1993.

Ovitt, George, Jr. *The Restoration of Perfection: Labor and Technology in Medieval Culture.* New Brunswick, N.J.: Rutgers University Press, 1987.

Owens, Owen D. "Becoming White: Steps toward Eco-Justice." *American Baptist Quarterly* 15 (March 1996): 60–71.

———. *Stones into Bread? What Does the Bible Say about Feeding the Hungry Today?* Valley Forge, Pa.: Judson Press, 1977.

Passmore, John. *Man's Responsibility for Nature: Ecological Problems and Western Traditions.* New York: Charles Scribner's Sons, 1974.

Pinches, Charles, and Jay B. McDaniel, eds. *Good News for Animals? Christian Approaches to Animal Well-Being.* Maryknoll, N.Y.: Orbis Books, 1993.

Pitcher, Alvin. *Listen to the Crying of the Earth: Cultivating Creation Communities.* Cleveland, Ohio: Pilgrim Press, 1993.

Pratt, Victoria L. "From Conquest to Communion within Creation: Toward an Intentional Theology of Restoration and Reconciliation." *American Baptist Quarterly* 15 (March 1996): 72–79.

Presbyterian Advisory Committee on Social Witness Policy. *Hope for a Global Future: Toward Just and Sustainable Human Development.* Louisville, Ky.: Office of the General Assembly, Presbyterian Church (USA), 1996.

Presbyterian Eco-Justice Task Force. *Keeping and Healing the Creation.* Principal Author, William E. Gibson. Louisville, Ky.: Presbyterian Church (USA), Committee on Social Witness Policy, 1989.

Preston, Ronald H. *The Future of Christian Ethics.* London: SCM Press, 1987.

Primavesi, Anne. *From Apocalypse to Genesis: Ecology, Feminism, and Christianity.* Minneapolis: Fortress Press, 1991.

Rae, Eleanor. *Women, the Earth, the Divine.* Maryknoll, N.Y.: Orbis Books, 1994.

Rasmussen, Larry L. *Earth Community, Earth Ethics.* Maryknoll, N.Y.: Orbis Books, 1996.

Redekop, Calvin. "Toward a Mennonite Theology and Ethic of Creation." *Mennonite Quarterly Review* 60 (1986): 387–403.

Regenstein, Lewis G. *Replenish the Earth: A History of Organized Religion's Treatment of Animals and Nature.* New York: Crossroad Press, 1991.

Reumann, John. *Stewardship and the Economy of God.* Grand Rapids, Mich.: Eerdmans, 1992.

Rhoads, David. "Reading the New Testament in the Environmental Age." *Currents in Theology and Mission* 24 (June 1997): 259–66.

Robb, Carol S., and Carl J. Casebolt, eds. *Covenant for a New Creation: Ethics, Religion, and Public Policy.* Maryknoll, N.Y.: Orbis Books, 1991.

Roberts, W. Dayton. *Patching God's Garment: Environment and Mission in the Twenty-First Century.* Monrovia, Calif.: MARC, World Vision International, 1994.

Rockefeller, Stephen C., and John C. Elder, eds. *Spirit and Nature: Why the Environment Is a Religious Issue: An Interfaith Dialogue.* Boston: Beacon Press, 1992.

Rolston, Holmes, III. "Does Nature Need to Be Redeemed?" *Horizons in Biblical Theology* 14, no. 1 (1992): 143–72.

―――. "Environmental Ethics: Some Challenges for Christians." *Annual of the Society of Christian Ethics,* 1993, 163–86.

Rosendale, George, Norman Habel, Shirley Wurst, Robert Bos, and the Rainbow Spirit Elders. *Rainbow Spirit Theology: Towards an Australian Aboriginal Theology.* Blackburn, Va.: HarperCollins, 1997.

Royal, Robert. *The Virgin and the Dynamo: The Use and Abuse of Religion in the Environmental Debate.* Grand Rapids, Mich.: Eerdmans, 1999.

Ruether, Rosemary Radford. *Gaia and God: An Ecofeminist Theology of Earth Healing.* San Francisco: HarperSanFrancisco, 1992.

―――. "Mother Earth and the Megamachine." In *Liberation Theology: Human Hope Confronts Christian History and American Power,* 115–26. New York: Paulist Press, 1972.

―――. "New Woman and New Earth: Women, Ecology, and Social Revolution." In *New Woman, New Earth: Sexist Ideologies and Human Liberation,* 186–214. New York: Seabury Press, 1975.

―――, ed. *Women Healing Earth: Third World Women on Ecology, Feminism, and Religion.* Maryknoll, N.Y.: Orbis Books, 1996.

Russell, Colin A. *The Earth, Humanity, and God: The Templeton Lectures, Cambridge, 1993.* London: UCL Press, 1994.

Rust, Eric C. *Nature and Man in Biblical Thought.* London: Lutterworth, 1953.

Ryan, Maura A., and Todd David Whitmore, eds. *The Challenge of Global Stewardship: Roman Catholic Responses.* Notre Dame, Ind.: University of Notre Dame Press, 1997.

Sagan, Carl. "Guest Comment: Preserving and Cherishing the Earth—An Appeal for Joint Commitment in Science and Religion." Letter signed by ten leading scientists. *American Journal of Physics* 58 (1990): 615.

Santmire, H. Paul. *Brother Earth: Nature, God, and Ecology in Time of Crisis.* New York: Thomas Nelson, 1970.

―――. "The Genesis Creation Narratives Revisited: Themes for a Global Age." *Interpretation* 45 (October 1991): 366–79.

―――. "The Struggle for an Ecological Theology: A Case in Point." *Christian Century* 87 (4 March 1970): 275–77.

————. *The Travail of Nature: The Ambiguous Ecological Promise of Christian Theology*. Philadelphia: Fortress Press, 1985.

Schaeffer, Francis A. *Pollution and the Death of Man: The Christian View of Ecology*. Wheaton, Ill.: Tyndale House, 1970. Reprint, with a concluding chapter by Udo Middelman, Westchester, Ill.: Crossway Books, 1992.

Scharper, Stephen B. *Redeeming the Time: A Political Theology of the Environment*. New York: Continuum, 1997.

Schreiner, Susan E. *The Theater of His Glory: Nature and the Natural Order in the Thought of John Calvin*. Durham, N.C.: Labyrinth Press, 1991. Reprint: Grand Rapids, Mich.: Baker Books, 1995.

Schwab, James. *Deeper Shades of Green: The Rise of Blue-Collar and Minority Environmentalism in America*. San Francisco: Sierra Club Books, 1994.

Schweitzer, Albert. *The Teaching of Reverence for Life*. Translated by Richard Winston and Clara Winston. New York: Holt, Rinehart and Winston, 1965.

Sheldon, Joseph K. *Rediscovery of Creation: A Bibliographical Study of the Church's Response to the Environmental Crisis*. Metuchen, N.J.: American Theological Library Association, Scarecrow Press, 1992.

Sherrard, Philip. *Human Image, World Image: The Death and Resurrection of Sacred Cosmology*. Ipswich, England: Golgonooza Press, 1992.

Shibley, Mark A., and Jonathan L. Wiggins. "The Greening of Mainline American Religion: A Sociological Analysis of the Environmental Ethics of the National Religious Partnership for the Environment." *Social Compass* 44 (1997): 333–48.

Shinn, Roger L. *Forced Options: Social Decisions for the Twenty-First Century*. 3d ed. Cleveland: Pilgrim Press, 1991.

Shinn, Roger L., and Paul Abrecht, eds. *Faith and Science in an Unjust World: Report of the World Council of Churches' Conference on Faith, Science, and the Future, Massachusetts Institute of Technology, Cambridge, U.S.A., 12–24 July 1979*. 2 vols. Geneva: World Council of Churches, 1980.

Simkins, Ronald A. *Creator and Creation: Nature in the Worldview of Ancient Israel*. Peabody, Mass.: Hendrickson Publications, 1994.

————. *Yahweh's Activity in History and Nature in the Book of Joel*. Lewiston, N.Y.: Edwin Mellen Press, 1995.

Sittler, Joseph. "Called to Unity." *Ecumenical Review* 14 (January 1962): 177–87.

————. "Ecological Commitment as Theological Responsibility." *Zygon* 5 (June 1970): 172–81.

————. *Essays in Nature and Grace*. Philadelphia: Fortress Press, 1972.

————. "A Theology for Earth." *Christian Scholar* 37 (September 1954): 367–74.

Skoglund, John E., ed. "Ecology and Justice." Special Issue. *Foundations* 17 (April-June 1974): 99–172.

Slattery, Patrick. *Caretakers of Creation: Farmers Reflect on Their Faith and Work*. Minneapolis: Augsburg, 1991.

Snyder, Howard A. *Liberating the Church: The Ecology of Church and Kingdom*. Downers Grove, Ill.: InterVarsity Press, 1983. Reprint, Eugene, Ore.: Wipf and Stock, 1996.

Soelle, Dorothee, and Shirley A. Cloyes. *To Work and to Love: A Theology of Creation*. Philadelphia: Fortress Press, 1984.

Sorrell, Roger D. *Francis of Assisi and Nature: Tradition and Innovation in Western Christian Attitudes toward the Environment*. New York: Oxford University Press, 1988.

Spencer, Daniel T. *Gay and Gaia: Ethics, Ecology, and the Erotic*. Cleveland: Pilgrim Press, 1996.

Spretnak, Charlene. *States of Grace: The Recovery of Meaning in the Postmodern Age*. San Francisco: HarperSanFrancisco, 1991.

Spring, David, and Eileen Spring, eds. *Religion and Ecology in History*. New York: Harper and Row, 1974.

Steck, Odil Hannes. *World and Environment*. Nashville: Abingdon Press, 1980.

Stewart, Claude Y. *Nature in Grace: A Study in the Theology of Nature*. National Association of Baptist Professors of Religion Dissertation Series, no. 3. Macon, Ga.: Mercer University Press, 1983.

Stivers, Robert L. "The Ancient Forests of the Pacific Northwest: The Moral Debate." *Theology and Public Policy* 5 (fall 1993): 27–48.

————. *Hunger, Technology, and Limits to Growth: Christian Responsibility for Three Ethical Issues*. Minneapolis: Augsburg Publishing House, 1984.

————. *The Sustainable Society: Ethics and Economic Growth*. With a foreword by Roger L. Shinn. Philadelphia: Westminster Press, 1976.

Stoll, Mark. *Protestantism, Capitalism, and Nature in America*. Albuquerque: University of New Mexico Press, 1997.

Stone, Glenn C., ed. *A New Ethic for a New Earth*. F/M/N Papers, no. 2. New York: Friendship Press, 1971.

Sturm, Douglas. *Solidarity and Suffering: Toward a Politics of Relationality*. Albany: State University of New York Press, 1998.

Styles, John. *The Animal Creation: Its Claims on Our Humanity Stated and Enforced*. London: T. Ward, 1839. Reprinted, with an introduction by Gary Comstock, Lewiston, N.Y.: E. Mellen Press, 1997.

Swimme, Brian, and Thomas Berry. *The Universe Story: From the Primordial Flaring Forth to the Ecozoic Era—A Celebration of the Unfolding of the Cosmos.* San Francisco: HarperSanFrancisco, 1992.

Taylor, Dorceta E. "Women of Color, Environmental Justice, and Ecofeminism." In *Ecofeminism: Women, Culture, Nature,* edited by Karen J. Warren. Bloomington: Indiana University Press, 1995.

Teilhard de Chardin, Pierre. *The Hymn of the Universe.* Translated by Simon Bartholomew. New York: Harper and Row, 1965.

———. *The Phenomenon of Man.* Translated by Bernard Wall. New York: Harper and Row, 1965.

Thomas, Keith. *Man and the Natural World: Changing Attitudes in England 1500–1800.* New York: Pantheon Books, 1983.

Tillich, Paul. "Man and Earth." In *The Eternal Now,* 66–78. New York: Charles Scribner's Sons, 1963.

———. "Nature, Also, Mourns for a Lost Good." In *The Shaking of the Foundations,* 76–86. New York: Charles Scribner's Sons, 1948.

———. "Nature and Sacrament." In *The Protestant Era,* translated by James Luther Adams, 94–112. Chicago: University of Chicago Press, Phoenix Books, 1957.

Tinker, George E. "The Integrity of Creation: Restoring Trinitarian Balance." *Ecumenical Review* 41 (October 1989): 527–36.

Torrance, Robert M. *Encompassing Nature: A Sourcebook.* Washington, D.C.: Counterpoint, 1998.

Traina, Cristina L. H. "Creating Global Discourse in a Pluralist World: Strategies from Environmental Ethics." In *Christian Ethics: Problems and Prospects,* edited by Lisa Sowle Cahill and James F. Childress, 250–64. Cleveland: Pilgrim Press, 1996.

Tucker, Gene M. "Rain on a Land Where No One Lives: The Hebrew Bible on the Environment." *Journal of Biblical Literature* 116 (1997): 3–17.

Tucker, Mary Evelyn, and John Grim, eds. *Worldviews and Ecology.* Maryknoll, N.Y.: Orbis Books, 1994.

U.S. Conference of Catholic Bishops. "Renewing the Earth." *Origins* 21 (12 December 1991): 425–32.

Van Dyke, Fred G., Raymond Brand, David Mahan, and Joseph Sheldon. *Redeeming Creation: The Biblical Basis for Environmental Stewardship.* Downers Grove, Ill.: InterVarsity Press, 1996.

Van Wensveen, Louke. *Dirty Virtues.* Atlantic Highlands, N.J.: Humanities Press, 1998.

Vorster, W. S., ed. *Are We Killing God's Earth?* Pretoria: University of South Africa, 1987.

Wallace, Mark I. *Fragments of the Spirit: Nature, Violence, and the Renewal of Creation.* New York: Continuum, 1996.

Wallace-Hadrill, D. S. *The Greek Patristic View of Nature*. New York: Barnes and Noble, 1968.

Ward, Barbara. "Justice in a Human Environment." *IDOC International/ North American Edition* 53 (May 1973): 25–36.

————. *A New Creation? Reflections on the Environmental Issues*. Vatican City: Pontifical Commission on Justice and Peace, 1973.

Webb, Stephen H. *On God and Dogs: A Christian Theology of Compassion for Animals*. With a foreword by Andrew Linzey. New York: Oxford University Press, 1998.

Weil, Simone. "Forms of the Implicit Love of God." In *Waiting for God*, translated by Emma Craufurd, with an introduction by Leslie A. Fiedler, 137–215. New York: Putnam's, 1951. Reprint, New York: Harper and Row, Colophon Books, 1973.

Welker, Michael. *Creation and Reality: Biblical and Theological Perspectives*. Minneapolis: Fortress Press, 1999.

Westermann, Claus. *Genesis 1–11: A Commentary*. Translated by John J. Scullion. Minneapolis: Augsburg, 1984.

Westhelle, Vitor. "Creation Motifs in Search for a Vital Space: A Latin American Perspective." In *Lift Every Voice: Constructing Christian Theologies from the Underside*, edited by Susan B. Thistlethwaite and Mary Potter Engel. New York: Harper and Row, 1990.

Whelan, Robert, Joseph Kirwan, and Paul Haffner. *The Cross and the Rain Forest: A Critique of Radical Green Spirituality*. Grand Rapids, Mich.: Eerdmans, 1996.

White, Lynn, Jr. "The Historical Roots of Our Ecologic Crisis." *Science* 155 (10 March 1967): 1203–7.

Whitney, Elspeth. "Ecotheology and History." *Environmental Ethics* 15 (summer 1993): 151–69.

Wildiers, N. Max. *The Theologian and His Universe: Theology and Cosmology from the Middle Ages to the Present*, trans. Paul Dunphy. New York: Seabury Press, 1982.

Wilkinson, Loren. "Christian Ecology of Death: Biblical Imagery and the Ecologic Crisis." *Christian Scholar's Review* 5 (1975): 319–38.

————. "The New Story of Creation: A Trinitarian Perspective." *ARC* 23 (1995): 137–52.

————, ed. *Earthkeeping in the Nineties: Stewardship of Creation*. Grand Rapids, Mich.: Eerdmans, 1991.

Williams, Daniel Day. "The Good Earth and the Good Society." In *God's Grace and Man's Hope*, 158–77. New York: Harper and Brothers, 1949.

Williams, George H. "Christian Attitudes toward Nature." Parts 1 and 2. *Christian Scholar's Review* 2, no. 1 (fall 1971): 3–35; no. 2 (spring 1972): 112–26.

————. *Wilderness and Paradise in Christian Thought.* New York: Harper and Brothers, 1962.

Williams, Terry Tempest, William B. Smart, and Gibbs M. Smith, eds. *New Genesis: A Mormon Reader on Land and Community.* Salt Lake City, Utah: G. Smith, 1998.

Wink, Walter. "Ecobible: The Bible and Ecojustice." *Theology Today* 49 (January 1993): 465–77.

Winter, Gibson. *Liberating Creation: Foundations of Religious Social Ethics.* New York: Crossroad Press, 1981.

World Council of Churches. "God in Nature and History." Principal Author, Hendrikus Berkhof. In *God, History, and Historians: Modern Christian Views of History.* Faith and Order Paper of the World Council of Churches, edited by C. T. MacIntire. New York: Oxford University Press, 1977. Report originally published in 1967.

————. *Now Is the Time: The Final Document and Other Texts from the World Convocation on Justice, Peace, and the Integrity of Creation, Seoul, Republic of Korea, 5–12 March 1990.* Geneva: World Council of Churches, 1990.

Worster, Donald. "John Muir and the Roots of American Environmentalism." In *The Wealth of Nature,* 184–202. New York: Oxford University Press, 1993.

Wright, Christopher J. H. *God's People in God's Land: Family, Land, and Property in the Old Testament.* Grand Rapids, Mich.: Eerdmans, 1990.

Wybrow, Cameron. *The Bible, Baconianism, and Mastery over Nature: The Old Testament and Its Modern Misreading.* American University Studies: Series 7, Theology and Religion, vol. 112. New York: Peter Lang, 1991.

Yasuda, Haruo. "Environmental Issues." In *Christianity in Japan, 1971– 1990,* edited by Yoshinobu Kumazawa and David L. Swimme, 114–29. Cincinnati: Friendship Press, 1991.

Young, Richard A. *Healing the Earth: A Theocentric Perspective on Environmental Problems and Their Solutions.* Nashville: Broadman and Holman, 1994.

————. *Is God a Vegetarian? Christianity, Vegetarianism, and Animal Rights.* With a foreword by Carol J. Adams. Chicago: Open Court, 1999.

Zizioulas, John. "Preserving God's Creation: Three Lectures on Theology and Ecology." Parts 1–3. *King's Theological Review* 12 (spring 1989): 1–5; 12 (autumn 1989): 41–45; 13 (spring 1990): 1–5.

Notes on Contributors

Peter W. Bakken is a Research Fellow at the Au Sable Institute of Environmental Studies. With J. Ronald and Joan Gibb Engel, he compiled *Ecology, Justice, and Christian Faith: A Critical Guide to the Literature* (Greenwood Press, 1995). He was on the task force that drafted the Evangelical Lutheran Church in America's statement "Caring for Creation: Vision, Justice, Hope" (1993). His Ph.D. dissertation (University of Chicago Divinity School, 1991) was entitled "The Ecology of Grace: Ultimacy and Environmental Ethics in Aldo Leopold and Joseph Sittler" and, with Steven Bouma-Prediger, he is editing a collection of Sittler's pioneering ecological writings (Eerdmans, forthcoming).

Ian G. Barbour has retired from Carleton College in Northfield, Minnesota, where he was Professor of Physics, Professor of Religion, and Bean Professor of Science, Technology, and Society. He received a Ph.D. in physics from the University of Chicago and a B.D. in theology from Yale University. Among his books are *Issues in Science and Religion* (Prentice Hall, 1966) and his Gifford Lectures, published in two volumes as *Religion in an Age of Science* (HarperSanFrancisco, 1990) and *Ethics in an Age of Technology* (HarperSanFrancisco, 1993). He was the recipient of the 1999 Templeton Prize for Progress in Religion.

Thomas Berry is a historian of cultures. He obtained his doctoral degree from the Catholic University of America with a dissertation entitled "The Historical Theory of Giambattista Vico." From 1966 until 1979 he directed the doctoral program in the history of religions at Fordham University. In these years he published his books *Buddhism* and *Religions of India*. From 1979 until 1995 he directed the Riverdale Center for Religious Research in

Riverdale, New York. His later writings include *The Dream of the Earth* (Sierra Club Books, 1988) and, with Brian Swimme, *The Universe Story* (HarperSanFrancisco, 1992).

Steven Bouma-Prediger is Associate Professor of Religion at Hope College, Holland, Michigan. He has a Ph.D. in religious studies from the University of Chicago. Recent publications include *The Greening of Theology: The Ecological Models of Rosemary Radford Ruether, Joseph Sittler, and Jürgen Moltmann* (Scholars Press, 1995) and, with Virginia Vroblesky, *Assessing the Ark: A Christian Perspective on Nonhuman Creatures and the Endangered Species Act* (Crossroad Press, 1997). He is a member of the Evangelical Environmental Network and the Christian Environmental Council.

Susan Power Bratton, Lindaman Chair of Science, Technology, and Culture at Whitworth College, is the author of *Six Billion and More: Human Population Regulation and Christian Ethics* (Westminster/John Knox Press, 1992) and *Christianity Wilderness and Wildlife: The Original Desert Solitaire* (University of Scranton Press, 1993). She has worked for the U.S. National Park Service as director of a field laboratory in the Great Smoky Mountains National Park and as coordinator of a research cooperative at the Institute of Ecology, University of Georgia. She has a Ph.D. in ecology from Cornell University and a Ph.D. in interdisciplinary arts and humanities from the University of Texas at Dallas.

Douglas Burton-Christie is Associate Professor of Christian spirituality at Loyola Marymount University, Los Angeles. He is the author of *The Word in the Desert: Scripture and the Quest for Holiness in Early Christian Monasticism* (Oxford, 1993) and is at work on a book entitled *The Texture of Spirit: Nature and the Poetics of Belief* (University of California Press, forthcoming).

John Chryssavgis was born in Australia. He received a degree in theology from the University of Athens and completed his doctoral studies at the University of Oxford. He was cofounder of St. Andrew's Theological College in Sydney, where he was Sub-Dean and taught patristics and church history. Since 1995, he has been Professor of Theology at Hellenic College and Holy Cross Greek Orthodox School of Theology in Boston. He is the author of many books and articles on the church fathers and Orthodox spirituality. His latest book is entitled *Beyond the Shattered Image: Orthodox Perspectives of the Environment* (Light and Life Publishing, 1999).

John B. Cobb, Jr., is Codirector of the Center for Process Studies and Professor Emeritus, Claremont School of Theology, where he taught for thirty-two years. He was born in Japan of Methodist missionary parents. His advanced education was at the University of Chicago. Among his books are *Is It Too Late? A Theology of Ecology* (Environmental Ethics Books, 1995); with Charles Birch, *The Liberation of Life* (Cambridge University Press, 1981); with Herman Daly, *For the Common Good* (Beacon Press, 1989); *Sustainability* (Orbis Books, 1992); *Sustaining the Common Good* (Pilgrim Press, 1994); and *The Earthist Challenge to Economism* (Macmillan, 1999).

Daniel Cowdin is Assistant Professor in the Religious Studies Department at Salve Regina University. In addition to undergraduate teaching, he participates in the Humanities Doctoral Program, which focuses on an interdisciplinary examination of technology. Prior to Salve Regina he was Assistant Professor of Social Ethics at Catholic University. He received his Ph.D. from Yale University and his M.A. from Colorado State University, where he focused on environmental ethics. He is a contributor to *Preserving the Creation: Environmental Theology and Ethics* (Georgetown University Press, 1994) and has published articles in *Christian Bioethics, Heythrop Journal,* and *Living Light.*

Marthinus L. Daneel, Professor of Missions, teaches part-time at Boston University. As founder of Fambidzano—the first AIC ecumenical movement in Zimbabwe—and of ZIRRCON, he has been engaged in a grassroots ministry among the Shona for more than three decades. He is recognized internationally as a leading interpreter of African Christianity and Traditional Religion. Of his twelve books and numerous journal articles, the best known are: *Old and New in Southern Shona Independent Churches* (Mouton, 1971); *God of the Matopo Hills* (Mouton, 1970); *Quest for Belonging* (Mambo Press, 1987); *Fambidzano* (Mambo Press, 1989); *Guerrilla Snuff* (Baobab Books, 1995); and *African Earthkeepers* (Unisa Press, 1999). He initiated the research for and coedits *African Initiatives in Christian Mission* (Unisa Press).

Calvin B. DeWitt is Professor of Environmental Studies at the University of Wisconsin, Madison, and Director of Au Sable Institute in Michigan, which serves eighty Christian colleges and universities in Canada and the United States with courses in ecology and environmental stewardship. He is a member of the University of Wisconsin graduate faculties of Land Resources, Conservation Biology and Sustainable Development, Water Resources Management, and Oceanography and Limnology, and a Fellow of the University of Wisconsin Teaching Academy. DeWitt also has been Chair of the Christian Environmental Council. His recent books are *Earth-Wise: A Biblical Response to Environmental Issues* (CRC Publications, 1994) and *Caring for Creation* (Baker Books, 1998).

Heather Eaton received an interdisciplinary doctorate in theology and ecology from the University of Toronto. Her special areas of concentration are religious responses to the ecological crisis, ecofeminism, cosmology, feminist theology, and social-ecological justice. She has published numerous works in these areas. She is currently teaching at the University of Ottawa. Prior to this she taught at St. Michael's College, the University of Toronto, and in the Faculty of Environmental Studies, York University.

William C. French is Associate Professor in the Theology Department at Loyola University of Chicago and is active in Loyola's peace studies and environmental studies programs. He received an M.Div. degree from Harvard University before completing his doctoral work in Christian ethics at the University of Chicago (1985). He has written widely on environmental issues and has had articles appear in numerous books and in such journals as the *Journal of Religion, Environmental Ethics, Peace Review, Theology and Public Policy, Soundings,* and *Second Opinion.*

Walter E. Grazer is Director of the Environmental Justice Program for the United States Catholic Conference. Formerly, he served as Deputy Director for the USCC's Migration and Refugee Services and as Policy Advisor for Food, Agriculture, and Rural Development. He is coeditor, with Drew Christiansen, of *"And God Saw That It Was Good": Catholic Theology and the Environment* (United States Catholic Conference, 1996). Grazer holds an M.A. in international relations, an M.S.W., and a B.A. in philosophy.

David G. Hallman has worked for over twenty years on energy and environmental issues on the national staff of the United Church of Canada and more recently as Climate Change Program Coordinator for the World Council of Churches. He is the author and editor of numerous articles and books on environmental issues, including *Ecotheology: Voices from South and North* (WCC Publications; Orbis Books, 1994) and *A Place in Creation: Ecological Visions in Science, Religion, and Economics* (United Church of Canada Publishing House, 1992). He is currently writing a book on spiritual values and ecology and another on climate change and global ethics.

Dieter T. Hessel, Ph.D. in theological and social ethics from San Francisco Theological Seminary, resides in Princeton, New Jersey, where he is a member of the Center of Theological Inquiry, Director of the ecumenical Program on Ecology, Justice, and Faith, and Codirector of Theological Education to Meet the Environmental Challenge. From 1965 to 1990, he was the Social Education Coordinator and Social Policy Director of the Presbyterian Church (USA). Recent books include *Theology for Earth Community: A Field Guide* (Orbis Books, 1996); *The Church's Public Role: Retrospect and*

Prospect (Eerdmans, 1993); *After Nature's Revolt: Eco-Justice and Theology* (Fortress Press, 1992); and *Social Ministry* (Westminster/John Knox Press, 1992).

Theodore Hiebert has a Ph.D. in Classical Hebrew and Hebrew Scriptures from Harvard University and is Professor of Old Testament at McCormick Theological Seminary in Chicago. He is the author of *The Yahwist's Landscape: Nature and Religion in Early Israel* (Oxford University Press, 1996) and has served as Director of the Chicago Theological Initiative in Eco-Justice Ministry.

Mary Ann Hinsdale is Associate Professor and Chair of the Religious Studies Department at the College of the Holy Cross, Worcester, Massachusetts. She received her Ph.D. from the University of St. Michael's College (Toronto). Her specialties are theological anthropology, ecclesiology, and women's studies. She is the author, with Helen Lewis and Maxine Waller, of *It Comes from the People: Community Development and Local Theology* (Temple University Press, 1995) and is coeditor, with Phyllis Kaminski, of *Women and Theology* (Orbis Books, 1995). Her article "Ecology, Feminism, and Theology" is widely used in women's studies courses.

Elizabeth A. Johnson, Ph.D. from Catholic University of America, is Distinguished Professor of Theology at Fordham University. Past president of the Catholic Theological Society of America, she serves on ecumenical and interreligious dialogues and on the editorial boards of the journals *Theological Studies, Horizons,* and *Concilium.* Her books include *Consider Jesus: Waves of Renewal in Christology* (Crossroad Press, 1990), *She Who Is: The Mystery of God in Feminist Theological Discourse* (Grawemeyer Award in Religion; Crossroad Press, 1992), *Women, Earth, and Creator Spirit* (Paulist Press, 1993), and *Friends of God and Prophets: A Feminist Theological Reading of the Communion of Saints* (Continuum, 1998).

Gordon D. Kaufman is Edward Mallinckrodt, Jr., Professor of Divinity, Emeritus, Harvard Divinity School. He received his Ph.D. from Yale University in 1955 and taught at Pomona College and at Vanderbilt Divinity School before coming to Harvard in 1963. He has published ten books and many articles. In *In Face of Mystery: A Constructive Theology* (Harvard University Press, 1993) he works out a biohistorical conception of humanity to deal with problems of religious and cultural pluralism and contemporary ecological understandings of our human situatedness in the world. His latest book, which also addresses these issues, is *God, Mystery, Diversity: Christian Theology in a Pluralistic World* (Fortress Press, 1996).

Catherine Keller, Professor of Constructive Theology in the Theological and Graduate Schools of Drew University, seeks to develop a critical spiritual discourse adequate to feminist, ecological, and social practices within a postmodern theological context. She is the author of *From a Broken Web: Separation, Sexism, and Self* (Beacon Press, 1987) and *Apocalypse Now and Then: A Feminist Guide to the End of the World* (Beacon Press, 1997). Currently she is writing *The Face of the Deep*, an inquiry into the tension between the biblical chaos of creation and the doctrine of *creatio ex nihilo*.

Heup Young Kim is Associate Professor of Systematic Theology at Kang Nam University, Kyonggi-do, Korea, and a 1997–98 Senior Fellow at the Center for the Study of World Religions. He received his M.Div. and Th.M. from Princeton Theological Seminary and his Ph.D. from the Graduate Theological Union. He has published *Wang Yang-ming and Karl Barth: A Confucian-Christian Dialogue* (University Press of America, 1996) and is currently working on two book projects: *Christo-tao: A Christology from an East Asian Perspective* and *Yi T'oegye and John Calvin: A Confucian-Christian Comparative Study*.

Paul F. Knitter, Professor of Theology at Xavier University, Cincinnati, received a Licentiate in theology from the Pontifical Gregorian University in Rome (1966) and a doctorate from the University of Marburg, Germany (1972). Among his publications are: *No Other Name? A Critical Survey of Christian Attitudes toward the World Religions* (Orbis Books, 1985); *One Earth, Many Religions: Multifaith Dialogue and Global Responsibility* (Orbis Books, 1995); and *Jesus and the Other Names: Christian Mission and Global Responsibility* (Orbis Books, 1996). He is also general editor of the Orbis Books series Faith Meets Faith.

Kwok Pui-lan is William F. Cole Professor of Christian Theology and Spirituality at the Episcopal Divinity School, Cambridge, Massachusetts. She has played an active role in the ecumenical discussions on ecological issues in the World Council of Churches, including addressing the assembly at Canberra in 1991. Her books include *Discovering the Bible in the Non-Biblical World* (Orbis Books, 1995) and *Introducing Asian Feminist Theology* (Sheffield Academic Press, forthcoming). Her essay "Ecology and Christology" appeared in *Feminist Theology* 15 (1997).

Peter K. H. Lee, born and raised in Hong Kong, received his higher education in the United States (Pomona College, Claremont School of Theology, Yale Divinity School, and Boston University). Ordained in the United Methodist Church, he served pastorates in California and Hawaii before returning to Hong Kong in 1966. For twenty years he directed the Christian Study Center on Chinese Religion and Culture and edited *Ching Feng,* a journal of cross-cultural theological studies. Since 1992 he has been Professor of Theology and Culture at the Lutheran Theological School, Hong Kong. Lee has been a visiting professor at various theological institutions, including Princeton Theological Seminary and Vancouver School of Theology.

Stan L. LeQuire is Director of Continuing Education at Eastern Seminary in Wynnewood, Pennsylvania. From 1994 to 1999 he was Director of the Evangelical Environmental Network. An ordained Baptist minister, he has served as pastor of churches in Massachusetts and Maine and has been a missionary in Africa, Asia, and Europe. LeQuire has served as editor of *Creation Care,* a magazine which encourages evangelical Christians to become active in environmental issues. He is also the editor of *The Best Preaching on Earth,* an anthology of sermons on creation care.

Sallie McFague is the E. Rhodes and Leona B. Carpenter Professor of Theology at Vanderbilt University. She received her B.A. in literature from Smith College and her B.D. and Ph.D. from Yale University. Her books relating to ecology and Christianity are *The Body of God: An Ecological Theology* (Fortress Press, 1993) and *Super, Natural Christians: How We Should Love Nature* (Fortress Press, 1997). She is working on a new book, tentatively titled "New House Rules: A Christian Theology for Planetary Living."

Daniel C. Maguire is Professor of Ethics at Marquette University. He has been the president of both the Society of Christian Ethics and the Religious Consultation on Population, Reproductive Health, and Ethics. Among his books are: *Death By Choice* (Doubleday, 1974); *A New American Justice: Ending the White Male Monopolies* (Doubleday, 1980); *The New Subversives: Anti-Americanism of the Religious Right* (Continuum, 1982); *The Moral Revolution: A Christian Humanist Vision* (Harper and Row, 1986); *The Moral Core of Judaism and Christianity* (Fortress Press, 1993); and, with Larry Rasmussen, *Ethics for a Small Planet* (State University of New York Press, 1998).

James B. Martin-Schramm teaches theological ethics at Luther College in Decorah, Iowa. The primary focus of his research has been in the field of Christian ethics and population policy. He was an NGO delegate to the 1994 United Nations Conference on Population and Development and has served as a member of the Population and Consumption Task Force of the President's Council on Sustainable Development. He is the author of *Population Perils and the Churches' Response* (World Council of Churches, 1997).

Vernice Miller-Travis is an urban planner with graduate and undergraduate degrees from Columbia University. She is a consultant to community groups and to the Environmental Protection Agency on environmental justice, Brownfields redevelopment, and sustainable urban revitalization. She was the principal research assistant for the report *Toxic Wastes and Race in the United States* (United Church of Christ, 1987). In 1988 she cofounded West Harlem Environmental Action and continues to cochair its board of directors. In the early 1990s she was the New York coordinator for the U.S. Citizens Network for the UN Conference on Environment and Development (the Earth Summit). From 1993 to 1998 she was the first director of the Environmental Justice Initiative of the Natural Resources Defence Council.

Patricia M. Mische is the cofounder and current president of Global Education Associates, a network of men and women in ninety countries working to advance global systems that can assure greater ecological integrity, peace, economic and social well-being, and human rights to all the world's peoples. She is Lloyd Professor of Peace Studies and World Law at Antioch College and also teaches ecology and peace courses at Columbia University Teachers College. She is the author of *Ecological Security and the United Nations System* (1998) and numerous other books and articles dealing with ecology, peace, and other global issues.

James A. Nash, Ph.D. from Boston University, served as Executive Director of the Churches' Center for Theology and Public Policy, an ecumenical research center in Washington, D.C., 1988–98, where he is now a senior scholar. During that decade he was editor of *Theology and Public Policy* and Lecturer in Social and Ecological Ethics at Wesley Theological Seminary. He served previously as Executive Director of the Massachusetts Council of Churches. He is a consultant on ethics and ecology for Millian Associates in Washington and Lecturer in Social and Ecological Ethics at Boston University School of Theology. Among his many writings is *Loving Nature: Ecological Integrity and Christian Responsibility* (Abingdon Press, 1991).

Eleanor Rae, a theologian with a Ph.D. in contemporary systematic theology from Fordham University, wrote a dissertation entitled "The Holy Spirit in Whiteheadian Process Theologians." She is the coauthor of *Created in Her Image: Models of the Feminine Divine* and the author of *Women, the Earth, the Divine* (Orbis Books, 1994). She serves as President Emerita of the North American Coalition for Christianity and Ecology and is the founder and president of the Center for Women, the Earth, the Divine in Ridgefield, Connecticut, an NGO in consultative status to the Economic and Social Council of the United Nations.

Larry Rasmussen has been Reinhold Niebuhr Professor of Social Ethics at Union Theological Seminary since 1986. His most recent books are: *Earth Community, Earth Ethics* (Grawemeyer Award in Religion; Orbis Books, 1996); *Moral Fragments and Moral Community* (Fortress Press, 1993); *Dietrich Bonhoeffer: His Significance for North Americans* (Fortress Press, 1990); and *Reinhold Niebuhr: Theologian of Public Life* (Fortress Press, 1991). He has also contributed to recent volumes in theology, ecology, and ethics, including *Theology for Earth Community: A Field Guide, Ecotheology: Voices from South and North,* and *Worldviews and Ecology.*

Martin Robra holds a Ph.D. in ecumenical social ethics from Bochum University. He is Executive Secretary of the World Council of Churches' Justice, Peace, Creation Team and minister of the Evangelical Church of Westfalia (Germany). Since 1994 he has been working with the World Council of Churches in the areas of theology of life, ecclesiology and ethics, and environmental ethics.

Barbara R. Rossing is Associate Professor of New Testament at the Lutheran School of Theology at Chicago. Her scholarly research focuses on the Book of Revelation's Babylon and New Jerusalem visions, with a book entitled *The Choice between Two Cities* (Trinity Press International, 1999). She also works on feminist, ecological, and liberation approaches to the Apocalypse and on the millennium. Previously, she served as chaplain to Harvard Divinity School, as pastor and teacher at the Holden Village retreat center, Chelan, Washington, and as ranger naturalist at Mesa Verde National Park, Colorado.

Rosemary Radford Ruether is a Catholic feminist theologian teaching at Garrett-Theological Seminary and a member of the Graduate Faculty of Northwestern University in Evanston, Illinois. She teaches courses on the interrelation of Christian theology and history to social justice issues. She holds a Ph.D. in classics and patristics (1965) from Claremont Graduate School in Claremont, California, and eleven honorary doctorates, the most recent from the University of Edinburgh, Scotland (1994). Ruether is the author or editor of thirty-two books, including *Gaia and God: An Ecofeminist Theology of Earth Healing* (HarperSanFrancisco, 1992), *Women Healing Earth: Third World Women on Ecology, Feminism, and Religion* (Orbis Books, 1996), and *Gender and Redemption: A Theological History* (Fortress Press, 1997).

William Somplatsky-Jarman is Associate for Environmental Justice for the Presbyterian Church (USA). He received his M.Div. degree from Yale

Divinity School. He has represented U.S. churches on the World Council of Churches delegation to the international climate changes negotiations in Berlin (1995), Kyoto (1997), and Buenos Aires (1998). In addition, Somplatsky-Jarman has coordinated the U.S. climate change petition campaign, represented the Presbyterian Church (USA) at the 1992 Earth Summit, and is currently Secretary of the Eco-Justice Working Group of the National Council of Churches.

Cristina L. H. Traina is Associate Professor in the Department of Religion at Northwestern University in Evanston, Illinois, where she teaches Christian theology and ethics. A graduate of the University of Chicago Divinity School, she has published articles and reviews on sexual and environmental ethics. Her book *Feminist Ethics and Natural Law: The End of Anathemas* (Georgetown University Press, 1999) addresses methodological questions common to natural law and feminist ethics, including moral implications of embodiment.

Louke van Wensveen is Associate Professor of Theological Ethics at Loyola Marymount University in Los Angeles. Educated at Leiden, Harvard-Radcliffe, and Princeton Theological Seminary, she publishes and teaches in the areas of business ethics, virtue ethics, and environmental ethics. Her book *Dirty Virtues: The Emergence of Ecological Virtue Ethics* (Humanity Books, 1999) traces the emergence of a rich ecological virtue ethic from the ranks of the environmental movement.

Mark I. Wallace is Associate Professor and Chair, Department of Religion, Swarthmore College. He is the author of *Fragments of the Spirit: Nature, Violence, and the Renewal of Creation* (Continuum, 1996) and *The Second Naïveté: Barth, Ricoeur, and the New Yale Theology* (Mercer University Press, 1990), editor of Paul Ricoeur's *Figuring the Sacred: Religion, Narrative, and Imagination* (Fortress Press, 1995), and coeditor of *Curing Violence: Religion and the Thought of René Girard* (Polebridge Press, 1994). He is an ordained Presbyterian minister, a member of the Colloquium on Violence and Religion, and active in the environmental justice movement in the Philadelphia area.

Preston N. Williams received an S.T.M. from Yale University and a Ph.D. from Harvard University. He is the Houghton Professor of Theology and Contemporary Ethics at the Harvard Divinity School. He teaches courses in Christian ethics and is particularly interested in issues of social and eco-nomic justice, human rights and nondiscrimination, environmental concerns, and African American religion.

Index

Preferential option for the poor,
sustainability and, 109–110
Prejudice, against creatures, 298–299
Premodernism, in radical ecology, 262
Presbyterian Church, 429–430
environmental evangelicals and, 589
Restoring Creation for Ecology and
Justice policy of, 573
President's Council on Sustainable
Development (PCSD), 442–445
Presumption, as vice, 175
Priestly images, 86
Priestly view of humanity, 136–138,
140–141, 143, 150
Priests
humankind as, 217
origin of Genesis story among early
Israelite, 136–138
Prima facie duties, 242
Prima vox, 322
Principles of Environmental Justice,
565–566
Privilege
as enjoyed by elite, 414–416
as sin, 106
Probabilistic chaos, 193
Process Christologies, 30, 32–33
Process ontology, 32
Process theology, 78–79
natural world and, 267
Procreation, restriction of, 408
Production. *See* Economic production
hidden ecological costs of, 475–476
Profligacy, as vice, 175, 177
Programme of Action (ICPD), 446–447,
448
Progress, conquest of nature in, 520
Project Global 2000, 599
Proletariat, Karl Marx on, 517–518
Property, ownership of, 416–417
Property rights, 416–417
Prophetic Christologies, 30–31, 32, 35–
36
God in, 38–39
Prophetic Christology, 45n, 48–49
Prophetic praxis. *See* Praxis

Prophetic religions, mystical religions
versus, 375–376
Prophetic tradition, natural world in, 5
Prophets, 309
covenants with Yahweh and, 340
cultural-change methods of, 419–420
deacons as, 433
of earthkeeping, 537–538
of Israel, 413, 414
military spending and, 418
teachings of, 49
Propriety, in Confucian tradition, 339
Prosperity, technology as fostering,
499–500
Prostitution, a metaphor of Roman
economy, 209–210
Protectionism, free trade and, 523–524
Protestantism, xliv. *See also*
Reformation
AICs and, 551n
covenantal ecotheology of, 605
in eco-justice organizations, 575
environmental defectiveness of,
xxxix–xl, 8–11, 12, 25
on natural law, 229, 247n
natural world in, 4
population growth issues and, 393
Puritanism in, 130
rising ecological awareness in
current, 11–12
science and, 458–459
and sustainability, 389
Taoism and, 359
virtue theory and, 156
work ethic of, 459–460
Prudence principle, 485
Psalm 104, creation narrative in, 141
Public health, siting of sewage
treatment plants and, 563
Public philosophy, "utilitarian
individualism" as, 371–372
Public policy
Catholic environmental agenda in,
585–586
Eco-Justice Working Group and, 577
education through, 480